THE
SACRED BRIDGE

The Interdependence of Liturgy and
Music in Synagogue and Church
during the First Millennium

ERIC WERNER

Professor of Liturgical Music
Hebrew Union College—Jewish Institute of Religion
New York—Cincinnati

LONDON: DENNIS DOBSON
NEW YORK: COLUMBIA UNIVERSITY PRESS
1959

Printed in Great Britain

TO ELIZABETH

Contents

Contents

Abbreviations

APB   *Authorized Prayer Book*, ed. Singer (London, 1924)

BLEW   F. E. Brightman, *Liturgies Eastern and Western* (Oxford, 1896, 1924)

CAF   *Constitutiones Apostolorum*, ed. Funk

Ch-P   W. Christ and M. Paranikas, *Anthologia graeca carminum christianorum* (Leipzig, 1871)

CSEL   *Corpus Scriptorum Ecclesiae Latinae* (Vienna, 1866–1939)

DACH   *Dictionnaire d'archéologie chrétienne*, ed. Leclercq and Cabrol

ELB   I. Elbogen, *Der Jüdische Gottesdienst*, 2nd ed. (Frankfurt, 1924)

GV   L. Zunz, *Gottesdienstliche Vorträge*, 2nd ed., 1892

HUCA   *Hebrew Union College Annual*, 1919–1951

IT   A. Z. Idelsohn, *Thesaurus of Hebrew Oriental Melodies* (Leipzig–New York, 1922–1932)

JBL   *Journal of Biblical Literature* (Philadelphia)

JE   *Jewish Encyclopedia* (New York, 1901–1906)

JM   A. Z. Idelsohn, *Jewish Music in its Historic Development* (New York, 1926 and 1929)

JQR   *Jewish Quarterly Review* (Philadelphia)

JTS   *Journal of Theological Studies* (Oxford)

LU   *Liber Usualis* (Tournay and Rome—Edition No. 780 of 1931)

MGWJ   *Monatsschrift für die Geschichte und Wissenschaft des Judentums* (Breslau, 1851–1938)

MLS   J. Jeannin, *Mélodies liturgiques syriennes et chaldéennes* (Paris, 1924–1926), 2 vols

MMB   *Monumenta Musicae Byzantinae* (Copenhagen)

MQ   *Musical Quarterly* (New York)

MAS   Hebrew Bible, Masoretic Text, ed. Kittel

NT   New Testament

OT   Old Testament

OC   *Oriens Christianus*, ed. A. Baumstark (Rome, 1901 ff)

PG   *Patrologia Graeca*, ed. Migne

PL   *Patrologia Latina*, ed. Migne

PO   *Patrologia Orientalis*, ed. R. Graffin and F. Nau (Paris, 1907 ff)

PR   *Pesiqta Rabbati*

REJ   *Revue des études juives* (Paris)

SIM   *Sammelbande der Internationalen Musikgesellschaft*

Str.-Bill.   Strack-Billerbeck, *Kommentar zum NT aus Talmud und Midrasch* (Munich, 1922–1928)

Tos   *Tosefta*, ed. Mandelkern

T & U   *Texte und Untersuchungen*, ed. Harnack

WGM   P. Wagner, *Einführung in die gregorianischen Melodien* (1911–1923)

W-S   Werner-Sonne, 'Theory and Philosophy of Music in Judaeo-Arabic Literature' in *HUCA*, XVI (1941) and XVII (1943)

ZFM   *Zeitschrift für Musikwissenschaft* (Berlin-Leipzig)

ZNTW   *Zeitschrift für die Neutestamentliche Wissenschaft* (Giessen, 1900–1939)

ZDMG   *Zeitschrift der Deutschen Morgenländischen Gesellschaft*, Leipzig

M before Hebrew syllable quotes the respective treatise of the *Mishna*

B or b before Hebrew syllable quotes the respective treatise of the *Babylonian Talmud* according to the pagination of the standard Vilna folio edition

Jer before Hebrew syllable quotes the respective passage from the *Jerusalemite Talmud*

R added to one of the names of biblical books refers to the respective *Midrash Rabba*, e.g. Gen.R. equals Genesis Rabba, Vilna edition. References are given according to the scriptural chapter and verse.

Old Testament chapter and verse references follow the numbering of the Masoretic text: New Testament references follow that of Nestle and Westcott.

LIST OF TALMUDIC ABBREVIATIONS

(Where not otherwise indicated, the reference is to the treatises of the *Babylonian Talmud*)

Ber.	Berakoth	Suk.	Sukka
Sanh.	Sanhedrin	Ar.	Arachin
Shab.	Shabbat	Tam.	Tamid
Ned.	Nedarim	Chag.	Chagiga
Yom.	Yoma	Sof.	Soferim
Ket.	Ketubot	Tos.	Tosefta
Sot.	Sota	Meg.	Megilla
		Pes.	Pesachim

Acknowledgments

IN presenting this book, the fruit of twenty years of study, I take delight in acknowledging my debts to many friends and colleagues:

To President Dr Nelson Glueck (Hebrew Union College—Jewish Institute of Religion), for his financial assistance, without which the book could not have been published.

To Prof. Salo Baron (Columbia University), who kindly sponsored the work and recommended it for publication.

To Mgr. Iginio Anglès, Prefect of the Pontifical Institute of Sacred Music, Rome, for a number of references and his friendly encouragement.

To Prof. Curt Sachs (New York University, Columbia University) for his never-failing moral and scientific support.

To Professor Julian Morgenstern (Hebrew Union College—Jewish Institute of Religion) for his active interest and wise counsel.

To Professors Abraham J. Heschel (Jewish Theological Seminary, New York), Simon Halkin (Hebrew University, Jerusalem), Egon Wellesz (Lincoln College, Oxford), and S. S. Cohon (Hebrew Union College, Cincinnati) for their kind and valuable advice.

To Mr Dennis Dobson (London), for his untiringly patient editorial help.

To Mr H. H. Wiggins (Columbia University Press), for his advice concerning the book's production.

To the Editors of the *Hebrew Union College Annual* (Cincinnati) for the release of two chapters, published previously under their Copyright.

To the memory of my martyred father, Prof. Julius Werner, of whose spiritual comfort I was mindful all through these years.

To my wife for her forbearance and lovingkindness.

Acknowledgment is also made to the following for quotations from works published by them: Aschendorff, Münster; Akademische Verlagsgesellschaft Athenaion, Potsdam; St Anthony Guild Press, Paterson, N.J.; Breitkopf und Härtel, Leipzig; British Academy, London; Byzantinische Zeitschrift; Clarendon Press, Oxford; Central Conference of American Rabbis, New York; Desclée et Cie,

Paris and Rome; Editions de Chevetogne, Paris; G. Fock, Leipzig; Hebrew University, Jerusalem; *Hebrew Union College Annual*, Cincinnati; Herder Verlag, Wien; F. Hirt, Breslau; H. Holt & Co. (Tudor Co.), New York; International Musicological Society, New York–Paris–Oxford; C. F. Kahnt, Nachfolger, Leipzig; Longmans, Green & Co., London; Levin and Munskgaard, Copenhagen; J. Marcus, Breslau; Monumenta Musicae Byzantinae, London–Copenhagen; W. W. Norton, New York; Oxford University Press, London–Oxford; Österreichische Akademie der Wissenschaften, Vienna; A. Picard et Fils, Paris; A. Probsthain, London; F. Pustet, Regensburg; *Revue du Chant Gregorien*, Paris–Solesmes; S. Schocken, Jerusalem.

The manuscript of the book was finished in 1950. Except in a few instances no reference could be made to books or publications of more recent date.

ERIC WERNER

Cincinnati, August, 1955

Since the final revision of the proofs, two works of eminent scholars have come to my attention. It is very much to my regret that I could neither incorporate their findings, where they were parallel to may own, nor take issue with them, where they were not. The two works alluded to are P. H. Schmidt's *Hebdomada Sancta* (Freiburg and Rome, 1954) and A. Baumstark's posthumous *Nocturna Laus* (Münster, 1957). This is to contradict Horace's advice:

Ne nonum prematur in annum!

E.W.

Foreword

JUDAISM AND CHRISTIANITY, with all their contrasts and antagonisms, share in a common heritage: in vital parts of Jewish ideology and ethics, Jewish holy books, and the Jewish soil as an unforgotten homeland. Only with the de-nationalization of this heritage, with its spreading to the Ephesians, Thessalonians, and the Corinthians, so many alien ideas changed the original kernel that an actual separation was inevitable. But however far the two religions drifted apart in their tenets, a sacred bridge still spans the abyss and allows for an exchange of views and moral concepts and, with them, of liturgical forms in which the dogmas and concepts find their way to the senses.

Images, it is true, do not cross the sacred bridge. They are not admitted to the Jewish (and for that matter to the neo-Platonic) side, where God and religion have been kept in a spiritual sphere beyond the anthropomorphic limitations of effigies. Rather, the possessions that have been carried from bank to bank belong in the realm of liturgical acts and facts, of words, and of melodies.

Almost half a century ago, the late Abraham Z. Idelsohn began to record an impressive amount of tunes sung in the archaic communities of the Middle East. Hidden among the thousands of sacred songs, he found in the liturgies of the Babylonian and Yemenite Hebrews melodic patterns so close to the Catholic chant that a connexion could not be disclaimed. Since the Babylonians and the Yemenites were separated from the Palestinian homeland at least two millenniums ago and never since had contact with one another or with Palestine, the conclusion cannot be avoided that these tunes still lived in the national centre when the Judaeo-Christian congregations began to build their liturgies with the help of Jewish cantors, but did not join the synagogal liturgy of the Dispersal.

Idelsohn's pioneering discoveries proved to be an epochal link between Antiquity and the Middle Ages. But his was a beginning, not completion. To his descendants he left a powerful stimulus and, with it, the duty of critical revision and of integration in the recent finds of ethno-musicology and theology, to give his scattered samples consistency, meaning, and breadth. As to religious history and comparative theology, the volumes written on these subjects fill our shelves to capacity. But we have been wanting in a critical comparison of the liturgical elements and expressions common to either religion.

It is our good fortune that Dr Eric Werner, Professor Idelsohn's learned successor at Hebrew Union College in Cincinnati, has the musical, linguistic, and theological equipment to be at home in all the fields of liturgy and to know exactly where to sink his spade in unearthing the buried piers of the sacred bridge.

CURT SACHS

New York University
Columbia University

Wer sich selbst und andre kennt
Wird auch hier erkennen
Orient und Okzident
Sind nicht mehr zu trennen.

GOETHE

Introduction

THE question of the interrelation between Church and Synagogue has often been put by laymen and scholars alike. While research in comparative theology, history of culture, and cognate subjects has created a great and richly informative literature, the practical applications which this interdependence has evoked have stirred few minds and fewer pens. Around the ceremonial acts which symbolize more or less faithfully the basic doctrines of each religion, a fabric has been woven, full of telling symbols and rich in beauty. These organized forms of common worship have evoked, both in Judaism and Christianity, the use of expressive arts, especially of those arts which are connected with the word, spoken or chanted: poetry and music.

Notwithstanding the individual efforts of some scholars during the last two or three centuries and their meritorious, but necessarily limited studies, *comparative liturgy* is a rather virginal field and has not been treated comprehensively as yet. This must be stated in view of the tremendous output dealing with the strictly theoretical side of our problem, especially the theology of Early Christianity and its relation to Rabbinic Judaism. A. Baumstark's attempt towards a *Liturgie comparée*, was a first approach, but fell considerably short of its aim, due to its limited scope and the author's lack of Jewish knowledge. This book has been written as the first comprehensive treatment of the subject; if it lays claim to being considered a pioneer effort in this field, its author is fully conscious of all the faults and pitfalls concomitant with such a venture.

No liturgical music is fully understood without profound appreciation of the liturgy itself, its structure and ideas. Every piece of liturgical music is to be interpreted in the light of its textual background, and its function in the framework of the service. The early literature that affords an insight into the development of fixed liturgies has to be carefully examined. Unfortunately, most of the historical sources are necessarily biased. This bias, as expressed by the mutual antagonism of the respective authorities, has resulted in the turbulent and often bloody history of that interrelation. Prejudice cannot be fully avoided, it being an intrinsic part of genuine religious conviction. The task of the historian calls for patient, detached, and critical interpretation of the source material. Whether, even in compliance with these postulates, it is possible to attain real objectivity remains still problematical.

Musical documents, of course, do not lend themselves to ideological slants, but their interpretation is beset with difficulties of their own. Apart from the problem of the proper transcription of ancient and primitive notations, reliable criteria are to be established by which the authenticity of written, and especially of oral, traditions can be gauged. To this end we have to resort to descriptive, homiletical, and in some cases theological sources.

Thus, the methods of the historian, the musicologist, and the theologian are essential for a comprehensive study of our problem. The author, therefore, feels obliged to render account of each method and its radius of application.

Historical Aspect

The historical method presents great difficulties. Although Palestine is claimed by all Christian Churches as the land of their birth, its real significance has, in the course of two millenia, dwindled to a vague historical memory, or to an eschatological image ('Heavenly Jerusalem').

In the development of organized liturgy, many regional, pre-Christian traditions were absorbed and assimilated. Frequently 'Pseudomorphoses' of this type distort the true picture. Examples of such complex and 'overlaid' structures are the liturgies of Byzantium and of the Syrian Churches.

All Christian liturgies of the Churches which originated during the first millennium have evolved around the same nuclei. Yet the differing languages, regional customs, and the specific folk-lores have wrought vast cleavages between them, both in form and content. Indeed, during the first seven or eight centuries the Churches were diverging ever more both in their doctrine and their liturgy.

To a lesser extent, the same situation prevailed in Judaism. This may come as a surprise to the reader, but it is none the less an undeniable fact. Although the Hebrew idiom has remained unalterably the language of all Jewish cults, many ancient liturgical forms have vanished, yielding to new ideas, for liturgy always reflects the tides of changing ideologies. Rabbinic Judaism, relying bravely on the strength of its ancient tradition, tried to stem the many disturbing currents by centralizing and unifying efforts. Yet at times these attempts were challenged, as we realize when we think of the various sectarian trends, such as the Essenes, the Karaites, or the apocalyptic visionaries.

Liturgical Aspect

In view of these facts we really must abandon the long cherished conception of a 'typically Christian' versus a 'typically Jewish' liturgy. There is but *one* principle that can truly be considered 'Christian' regardless of Church or denomination: the Eucharist. And likewise there is one nucleus around which all Jewish liturgies have evolved: the *Sh'ma'* (Deut. 5:6). All other parts of the services have undergone radical changes, in Judaism and Christianity alike. These changes were often the results of apologetic, or polemical attitudes, held by Church and Synagogue in their relation to each other. A detailed study of the practical consequences of such attitudes, most important for a proper understanding of ecclesiastical history and comparative religion, remains a desideratum. Excellent spade work has been accomplished in this field by Dr J. Parkes, the late Dr L. Ginzberg, Dom Gregory Dix, Dr L. Venetianer, Dr J. Mann, and others. While not losing sight of this problem altogether, we had to limit ourselves to the interpretation of such sources as afford us factual evidence of the *liturgical* interrelation of Church and Synagogue. The latent reasons for the liturgical analogies or divergences are not analysed here; we must content ourselves with the manifest ones. Otherwise the entire social, religious, and cultural history would have to encompass all the centres where Jews and Christians were living together for centuries (more or less peacefully). Such an attempt must be left to another generation of students.

For comparison and analysis of the liturgies themselves the *formgeschichtliche* method seems to us more conclusive in its results than the simple juxtaposition of individual texts or tunes. It also applies to our musical studies. It pays more attention to whole form types and structures than to occasional details, however interesting the latter might be. We preferred this method not only for the more cogent results it produces, but also on account of the relatively rich source material on the development of liturgical form types. This reason is especially weighty, where early sources of Jewish and Christian liturgy are concerned.

With regard to some of the conclusions resulting from the analyses of form types, it must be stated frankly: in many cases it was impossible to answer the basic question of 'who borrowed and who lent' in a definitive fashion. The growth of cultures does not obey Polonius's homely maxim; and every so often we shall encounter complex trends, instances of re-interpretation or resumption of ancient material, in a word: *constant borrowing and lending*. All kinds of influences, or rather *confluences* were at work in the development of the liturgies and their adjunct arts. To limit our studies to sectors where direct and obvious interrelations are evident would not only reduce the substance of the work, but also deprive the student of many vistas, hitherto unexplored. In the field of religious practice the relations are seldom clear-cut, never one-sided, and usually at the same time complex and subtle.

Some attention was paid to certain aesthetic questions in Church and Synagogue. The copious output of the Church Fathers dealing with the aesthetics and philosophy of music has also been considered, whenever their speculations exceeded the narrow path of dogmatic considerations. In this field the author is indebted to the fine studies of H. Abert, Th. Gérold, A. Baumstark, J. Jeannin, P. Wagner, P. Ferretti, E. Wellesz, and A. Gastoué.

Musical Aspect

Our musically notated sources originated a few centuries after the literary ones, and remain rare up to the ninth century. In most cases we may assume that they represent the residuum of centuries-old traditions, as the volumes of the *Paléographie musicale* have amply demonstrated. They often pose formidable problems of correct transcription; here the well-established results of the last fifty years of musicological research are accepted without detailed critique. A good deal of Roman, Byzantine, and even a little of ancient Armenian source material is now available in authentic transcriptions. Yet all this represents a mere fraction of the great treasury of liturgical music produced during the first millennium. Many sources are still undecipherable and will remain sealed books for the foreseeable future, perhaps for ever.

The long interval between the establishment of the oral tradition and its fixation in writing leaves wide margins for error. We may, however, rely upon our analyses and the resulting conclusions where at least one of the Jewish or Christian sources is based, directly or indirectly, upon a well-authenticated tradition. This authenticity has to be confirmed anew in each comparison of form types.

Where we are confronted with two sets of basically oral traditions, one Jewish, one Christian, the main criteria of age and genuineness are constituted by the diffusion of the melodies over vast regions, and their relative freedom from environmental influences. When, for instance, the Yemenite Jews, for many centuries almost without any contact with the rest of Jewry, and always remote from Christian influences, have preserved a musical substance which may be encountered, with little or no alteration, in either the Gregorian, Ambrosian, or the Occidental Jewish repertoire, we are obliged to accept their oral tradition as both authentic and of ancient origin.

This example touches directly upon a crucial problem of all musical comparisons. What may be compared and what should be compared? Individual tunes or entire musical structures? Melodic details or entire recurrent patterns?

In analogy with our treatment of liturgical texts, we are, in the musical sphere, firmly convinced that the analysis of whole melodic types will prove more effective for the proper evaluation of musical inter-relations than comparisons of individual tunes, however interesting they may appear. Indeed, we lack any exact knowledge of the 'case-history' of these tunes, their age, their provenance, their origin. To give but one example: it is sometimes possible to demonstrate certain conspicuous similarities between hymns sung by Jews of Spanish extraction, and Armenian church melodies, transcribed by monks during the eighteenth and nineteenth centuries. What conclusions might be drawn from such resemblances? The Hebrew hymns were not musically fixed before the nineteenth century in Germany and the ancient notation of Armenian hymns cannot be deciphered exactly. Whether the resemblance is the result of contact between the two groups in Asia Minor, where many Spanish Jews fled after 1492, or indicates an ancient common source, or is entirely accidental, cannot be decided in general. Any such thesis must needs rely on pure guesswork without sound foundation. Conversely, an ancient Armenian hymn type bears the superscription *Khosrovayin*, as a designation of a certain mode. Nerses Shnorhali, an Armenian Church Father of the twelfth century, links this mode and its name with the celebrated Rabbi Jehuda Halevi. It is obvious that the Armenian term is derived from Halevi's work *Kuzari*. In this case, we have at least a historical foundation upon which to start further detailed examination of the respective modes or form types.

Thus the history and development of entire musical structures can be traced with a much greater degree of accuracy. While our literary sources are usually deficient in musical details, they give often a fairly articulate description of liturgical rubrics or important texts. Such ancient sources are often paralleled by musical patterns bearing the landmarks of genuine antiquity. This holds true especially of old lectionaries with or without notation. None the less, even in such cases the superposition of later popular chants upon the old texts must not be left out of our consideration. All results of musical group-analysis are to be checked against the pertinent data culled from the field of ecclesiastical history. Only where historical, liturgical, and musical findings coincide may our conclusions be considered safe.

In accord with this approach, the book is organized in two parts: Part I, liturgical and historical studies; Part II, musical studies. Naturally, innumerable cross-references permeate and link the two parts, which in their arrangement parallel each other.

The history of ideas cannot boast Newton's proud dictum: 'Hypotheses non fingo'. While restricting pure guesswork to a minimum, the humanities must make use of well-founded working hypotheses, which seldom impair and often advance scientific thought. Even the rigid attitude of Newton's time had, in the natural sciences, to give way to a considerably more flexible philosophy. The noted biologist Lecomte de Nouy formulates this more recent concept in his *Road to Reason*: 'The man of science who cannot formulate a hypothesis is only an accountant of phenomena.' Similar ideas have been aired by Albert Einstein, R. Schroedinger, M. Planck, and other great scientists of our time. This book contains its share of verifiable data, but also a certain amount of necessarily hypothetical interpretation. May it be received benevolently as a first approximation to a wider vista for the understanding of two great religions and their cultural legacies.

Part I

Historic–Liturgical

CHAPTER ONE

The Jewish Liturgy at the Time of Primitive Christianity

THE INSTITUTION OF THE ANCIENT SYNAGOGUE

A KNOWLEDGE of Jewish worship in Palestine at the time of Jesus and the Apostles is indispensable if we would trace the roots of the later and more fully developed liturgies of Judaism and Christianity.

The Concept of Liturgy

The Greek term 'liturgy' would have meant little to Jesus and his disciples. For not always has the term 'liturgy' carried the exclusively theological significance attributed to it today. Originally it meant any public service or office. In this way it was used by Plato (*Leges* XII); and Aristotle expanded its compass to such an extent that even artists or jugglers fell into the category of 'liturgists'. A Berlin papyrus uses the term in a musical sense, referring to a particular manner of playing.[1]

Only after the spread of the Greek translation of the Old Testament (LXX—Septuagint) was the term liturgy narrowed to fit a strictly religious activity. The Hebrew words *'eved*, *'aboda* (servant, service), *kohen* (priest), *tziva*, *mitzva* (constitute, command, appoint, privilege), were usually translated by the Greek word 'liturgy' and its derivations. As in the English language of today, where the associations servant-service, office-official are still alive, so also Hebrew has preserved these ancient ideas. Gradually, however, the general term 'liturgy' has swallowed all of the finer nuances.

Of the ancient Christian authors it was chiefly the Apostle Paul, the 'Pharisee of the Pharisees', who still understood all of the various meanings of the Hebrew equivalents which lay hidden under the Greek word 'liturgy'. In his Epistles various activities, such as civil office, charity, missionary work, personal services of a friend (cf. Phil. 2:25) all easily differentiated by the three or four Hebrew words, were expressed by *liturgia* and its derivatives. Later on these various meanings faded away, until only the public worship and its order, preferably the Eucharistic service, remained.

Temple and Synagogue

During the life of Jesus these two ancient institutions coexisted, not without some rivalry, side by side. The institution of the Temple with its daily sacrifices and its minutely regulated cult was much older than the Synagogue, which was a layman's institution. And right at the outset it should be remembered that it was not the Temple but the Synagogue which set the pattern for the divine service of the primitive Christian community. The monopoly of the Temple, its festivals of pilgrimage, its minutely regulated sacrificial rituals were the jealously guarded prerogative of the aristocratic hierarchy of Priests and of the nationalistic Zealots. They represented the caste to whom the first Christians, consisting chiefly of *ammei-ha'aretz* or unlearned ones, felt decidedly antagonistic. It was in the synagogue that the people assembled for religious and secular occasions. Such was the case not only in the provinces, but even in the metropolis of Jerusalem. According to the Talmud,[2] there existed no less than 394 synagogues in Jerusalem at the time of the destruction of the Temple. In the synagogues devotional prayer took the place of the sacrificial ceremonies which remained exclusively a function of the Temple. Temple sacrifices ceased after the destruction of the Sanctuary in A.D. 70, and were replaced by devotional worship; and even prior to that time prayer was considered to be as God-pleasing as the sacrifice. It was in the synagogues that the immortal forms of Jewish and Christian liturgy came into being.[3]

The entire terminology of the Synagogue, whether referring to its dignitaries or to the conduct of the service, is familiarly understood in the New Testament; the original Hebrew terms were simply translated into Greek. While Early Christianity found its first articulate expression in the synagogues of Palestine, those of the Diaspora constituted the first debating forums for Judaeo-Christianity. In the Acts of the Apostles we read about these debates in the synagogues outside of the Holy Land;[4] and the most famous of the Diaspora synagogues, located in Alexandria, is described in detail in early rabbinic literature.[5]

Our knowledge of the Synagogue liturgy at the time of Jesus is very limited, since most of the descriptive sources originated in the following centuries. In spite of this, they may be considered primary documents, in as much as Jewish and Christian sources confirm and supplement each other.[6]

The Jewish liturgy of today is framed in traditionally circumscribed forms, some of which are regulated down to the smallest detail. Yet at the time of the primitive Church this liturgy was not as fully developed as it is today. For then many of its constituent elements were no more than nuclear cells, and others only vaguely delineated. In spite of the lack of comprehensive source material it is possible to trace all New Testament, and even most of the post-apostolic, traits back to the contemporary Jewish practice. To quote Oesterley:

> The influence of the Jewish liturgy on the early Church and its form of worship is nowhere so clearly to be discerned as in the prayers which have been preserved in early Christian literature and in the earliest forms of the Christian liturgy. Nobody, in reading the pre-Christian forms of prayer in the Jewish Liturgy and the prayers of the early Church, can fail to notice the similarity of atmosphere of each, or to recognize that both proceed from the same mould. Even when one perceives, as often happens, variety in the latter form, the *genus* is unmistakable.[7]

THE STRUCTURE OF ANCIENT JEWISH LITURGY
Hours of Prayer

The Synagogue knew of three daily services: one in the morning, one in the afternoon, and one in the evening. These times were usually based on Dan. 6:11 '. . . and he kneeled upon his knees three times a day, and prayed and gave thanks before his God . . .' and Ps. 55:18 '. . . At evening and morning and noon will I make my complaint and moan and He heareth my voice', and were considered as the legal and binding practice for all Jews about the year A.D. 100.[8]

It seems that, originally, the morning prayer was offered at early dawn, even before the morning sacrifice. By the first century A.D. the hours of daily prayer, as they are known to us today, had been definitely fixed; some time between seven and ten for the morning prayer, between three and four for the afternoon prayer (*mincha*), but with no exact time assigned to the evening prayer (*ma'ariv*). The Talmud[9] stresses dawn and dusk as the most suitable times for morning and evening prayer. In this connexion scriptural reference is made to Ps. 72:5 'They shall fear Thee while the sun shineth and so long as the moon beameth throughout all generations', and Ps. 32:6 'For this let

3

every one that is godly pray unto Thee in a time when Thou mayest be found'.

The New Testament mentioned the same times for prayer, as indicated in Acts 2:15; 10:3; 3:1. The 'normal' hours seem to have been 9 a.m., 12–1 p.m., and the late afternoon. While special evening prayers were strongly recommended to the Christians, there was no definite regulation for such a service.[10] The *Didache*[11] prescribed three daily services without indicating precise hours. Tertullian was the first to recommend a return to the old accepted hours of worship.[12] It is significant that he based his argument upon the scriptural passages mentioned above, which two centuries before had been considered normal by rabbis and Apostles alike. But in the monasteries of the fourth century one already encounters seven times of prayer distributed during the twenty-four hours of day and night. The authority for this innovation is based upon the reference to Ps. 119:164 'Seven times a day do I pray Thee because of Thy righteous ordinance'. These seven times of prayer later became the norm of Roman monastic life.[13]

Categories of Prayer

The contemporaries of Jesus knew various categories of prayer, which were established during the Tannaitic age (between 100 B.C. and A.D. 200). The Apostle Paul, having been a disciple of the great sage Rabban Gamaliel, was familiar with them,[14] though he did not mention all of them. Prayers of praise and exaltation were most esteemed, then expressions of thanksgiving; the individual petition or supplication was lowest in rank.

Besides these three categories, which were taken over by the Church, there were also doxological prayers, professions of faith, and another type, entirely *sui generis* in the realm of prayer, the *Beraka*.[15] Usually this term is translated 'benediction' or 'blessing'. The Greek translation has *eulogia*; yet neither of these paraphrases fully expresses the meaning of *beraka*. The word is a derivative of the Hebrew word for knee and implies first the act of genuflexion, then, in a wider sense, an acknowledgment, in a spirit of praise, of an act, or gift, of God. It must, according to the rabbinic rule, begin with three prescribed words which address God directly in the second person. One or two examples will clarify this principle: the prescribed form of words is indicated by the italics. '*Praised art Thou, Lord our God*, King of the universe, who hast not made me a bondman.' *'Praised art Thou, O Lord*, Giver of the Law.' The Apostolic literature knew and used the *beraka* formula in Greek: *'Eulogetos sy, Kyrie'*.

The Hebrew doxologies speak of God in the third person and invariably stress His eternity. The two most important doxologies are the *Kaddish* and the *Kedusha* (Thrice-Holy). (See also Chapter IX.)

The prayer of creed, called *Sh'ma'* after the first word, is actually a combination of three biblical passages:

Deut. 6:4–9, beginning 'Hear, O Israel, The Lord our God, The Lord is One . . .'; Deut. 11:13–21, beginning 'And if you will obey my commandments . . . to love the Lord your God . . .'; and Num. 15:37–41, beginning 'The Lord said to Moses: "Speak to the people of Israel. . . ." '

While there was much freedom in the service of the Synagogue at the time of Jesus (a rigidly fixed liturgy was frowned upon by the sages as engendering routine-praying), one set of prayers, the eighteen (really nineteen) *berakot* was already canonical and compulsory for every Jew. This set of prayers, called *'Amida* (stand), was pronounced standing, and certain passages were accompanied by genuflexion. Folding the hands, in submission to God's will, was likewise an old Jewish gesture,[16] as stepping back after the completion of prayer, 'as a subordinate takes leave from his superior'.[17]

The *'Amida* was usually recited silently and afterwards repeated aloud by the reader or precentor for those unable to read. The worshipper was permitted to insert private and spontaneous prayers or petitions in certain places, but only on workdays.[18]

A few passages, quoted from the *'Amida*, will best illustrate the character of this central prayer.

Beginning:

O Lord, open Thou my lips, and my mouth shall declare Thy praise.[19]

First beraka:

Praised art Thou, O Lord our God and God of our fathers, God of Abraham, God of Isaac, and God of Jacob, the great, mighty, and revered God, the most high God, who bestowest loving-kindness, and art Master of all things: who rememberest the pious deeds of the patriarchs, and in love will bring a redeemer to their children's children for Thy Name's sake. O King, Helper, Saviour and Shield. Praised art Thou, O Lord, The Shield of Abraham.

Fourth beraka:

Thou favourest man with knowledge and teachest mortals understanding. O favour us with knowledge, understanding, and reason from Thee. Praised art Thou, O Lord, gracious giver of knowledge.

Eighteenth beraka:[20]

. . . We will give thanks unto thee and declare thy praise for our lives which are committed unto thy hand, and for our souls which are in thy charge, and for thy miracles, which are daily with us, and for thy wonders and benefits which are wrought at all times, evening, morn and noon. . . . And everything that liveth shall give thanks unto thee for ever, and shall praise thy Name in truth, O God, our salvation and our help. . . .

Praised art thou, O Lord, whose Name is All-good, and unto whom it is becoming to give thanks.

Finally, the beginning of the *Kaddish* may be quoted:

Magnified and sanctified be His great name in the world which He has created according to His will. May He establish His Kingdom during your life and during your days, and during the life of all the house of Israel, even speedily and at a near time, and say ye, Amen.

(Response): Let His great name be praised for ever and to all eternity.

The similarity of the two first sentences of the *Kaddish* with the beginning of the so-called 'Lord's Prayer' is certainly no coincidence. We know that parts of the *Kaddish* were usually recited after a religious discourse, as a kind of pious dismissal.[21] For a further discussion of this and other similar prayers, see Chapter IX.

The Liturgy of the Weekday

1. *Morning.* After a ceremonial salutation[22] the service opened with a kind of exhortation to prayer, 'Praise ye the Lord who is to be praised', with the response 'Praised is the Lord; He is to be praised for ever and ever'. This corresponds roughly with the *invitatorium* of the Roman Church. Thereafter follows the praise of God the creator of all things, especially of light. This idea is elaborated upon with angelological overtones and climaxes in the first *Kedusha* (Thrice-holy). Two long-spun *berakot*—praise of God, the creator of light, and of Him, 'who had chosen Israel in love' lead to the *Sh'ma*. This was considered the core of the service, together with '*Amida*, and the rabbis watched keenly over the proper time and manner of its pronouncement.

It was answered by an affirmation of the *Sh'ma's* validity: 'It is meet and right', etc., ending in a *beraka* which addresses God as the Redeemer of Israel. Today's Hebrew prayer book contains the full quotation of the Song of the Sea (Exod. 15). While the Temple still stood, however, the chanting of this canticle was a prerogative of its priests.[23]

The *'Amida* was recited thereupon; it contained the second *Kedusha* of the morning service as well as a few spontaneous petitions of the worshippers. On certain occasions one of the penitential psalms, usually Ps. 6, was inserted and the service was concluded with the *Kaddish*. After the third century another prayer of the first rank, called the *'Alenu* after its first word, was introduced at the end of every service; it might be described as a strong affirmation of Jewish monotheism, couched in hymnic language. Its beginning reads as follows:

> It is for us to praise the Lord of all;
> His greatness to ascribe unto Him,
> Who formed the world in the beginning;
> Since he has not made us as other nations,
> Nor placed us like other families of the earth. . . .
> For we bend the knee and offer worship,
> We offer thanks before the King supreme,
> The King of Kings, the Holy One, praised be He, etc.

This prayer, in idea and form resembling the *Te Deum*, is ascribed to Rab of Babylonia, but probably some of its phrases are older and may even date back to the first or second century. In antiquity, the *'Alenu* was of great consequence, being the prayer characteristic of Neophytes and Proselytes, who, at the end of the conversion ritual, prostrated themselves before the Almighty, 'The King of Kings', thereby renouncing their previous allegiances.

2. *Afternoon.* The order of the afternoon service was very simple: after one or two psalms the *'Amida* and a doxological prayer were recited, and the service closed with the *Kaddish*, or in later times, with the *'Alenu*. It corresponded with the *Mincha* sacrifice of the Temple and bears that name.

3. *Evening.* After some psalm-verses the *'invitatorium'* was pronounced, to be followed by the counterparts of the two morning *berakot*—viz. the praise of God, the creator, of day and night, and of God 'who lovest thy people Israel'. Thereupon the *Sh'ma* was recited, followed by two ancient *berakot*—God, the Redeemer, and God, the

guardian of Israel. This last prayer is of extraordinary beauty and has in-fluenced many Christian evening prayers. To quote a few passages:

> Spread over us the tabernacle of thy peace;
> Direct us straight through thine own good counsel: . . .
> Remove from us enemy, pestilence, sword, famine and sorrow . . .
> O shelter us beneath the shadow of thy wings;
> For thou, O God, art our guardian and deliverer;
> Yea, thou, O God, art a gracious and merciful King:
> Guard our going out and our coming to life, and into peace, henceforth
> and for evermore.
> Praised art thou, O Lord, who guardest thy people Israel for ever.

In ancient times spontaneous prayers found place after this *beraka*; later, a group of psalms was inserted instead. The service closed with the '*Amida*, the *Kaddish*, and later, the '*Alenu*. It is to be noted that the evening service did not correspond to any Temple sacrifice, as did the morning and afternoon services. Hence some rabbis considered it as optional,[24] except for the recitation of the *Sh'ma'* and its *berakot*, which was—and still is—a matter of course.

The Liturgy of the Sabbath

Like all Jewish holydays the Sabbath began on the preceding eve. Probably the singing of psalms led to the solemn intoning of the sab-batical Psalm 92, followed by the *Sh'ma'* with its framework of *berakot* and by the '*Amida*, limited to seven *berakot*. This was read quietly by the congregation; then an excerpt of the '*Amida*, with some slight deviation, was rendered aloud by the cantor. The *Kaddish*, with its extended doxology, concluded the service. It is more than doubtful whether the solemn *beraka* over the wine, called *Kiddush*, which today is the climax of the Friday evening ritual, was a part of the public worship at the time of the Apostles. Probably it was reserved for the celebration of the Sabbath in the home.[25]

The morning service opened with psalms, especially Ps. 19, 34, 90, 91, 135, 136, 32, 92, 93, and the salutation of the congregation was expressed in the words of Ps. 84:5.[26] The Hallelujah Psalms (Ps. 146–150) and Miriam's Song (Exod. 15:1–19) served as the musical pre-amble to the ensuing *Sh'ma'* and '*Amida* prayers.

The nucleus of the Sabbath liturgy was then, as it is now, the public reading of the scripture. We shall give here only a brief summary of the many problems connected with the reading of the lessons; further discussion of this question must be left for a later chapter.

The lesson consists of two pericopes, one from the Pentateuch and one from the Prophetic literature. At the time of Jesus the threefold annual cycle of the Pentateuch and its division into the pericopes (Torah) was already well established; whether the same holds true for the Prophetic lesson (Haftara) is doubtful.[27] Both types of pericopes are mentioned in the famous passages Luke 4:16 f and Acts 13:15. (For the musical setting of the pericope, see Chapter III.)

The ritual of scripture reading was preceded and followed by several *berakot*. The *Kaddish* concluded it, followed by a second part of the liturgy which was reserved for the Sabbath and other holydays. This 'additional' part (*Mussaph* = addition) corresponded to the additional sacrifices offered at the Temple on Sabbath and other festivals. The *Mussaph* prayer consisted of the '*Amida* with six *berakot* and a special insertion for the Sabbath. It is of more recent origin than the other prayers. In the apostolic age the service was terminated by the Priestly Blessing, the Doxology (*Kaddish*) and possibly the '*Alenu* prayer.

The liturgy of the Sabbath afternoon was a kind of diminutive replica of the morning service. The Song of Songs and other psalm verses embellished the regular order of prayer. Sunset marked the conclusion of the Sabbath, and its services consisted of the chanting of psalms, the '*Amida*, and by a beautiful ceremony called *Habdala* (Separation). It symbolized the formal distinction between Sabbath (or festival) and workday and contained profound *berakot* over the kindling of light, over spices and again over wine.[28]

The Liturgy of the Three Festivals of Pilgrimage

These holydays were termed feasts of pilgrimage, for it was expected of every Israelite to attend one of them at least once a year at the Temple in Jerusalem.

The synagogue liturgies of the three festivals, Passover (Easter), *Shabuot* (Pentecost), and *Sukkot* (Tabernacles), had the same basic structure but differed from each other in those details which had a direct bearing upon the individual character of each festival.

Passover, the feast of *Matzoth*, of deliverance from Egypt, and the spring festival of ancient Israel, began on the eve of the first full moon in spring (14 Nisan) and lasted for seven days.

Shabuot was originally the festival of the firstlings; but, as the name indicates, its celebration took place on the fiftieth day after Passover. It was, obviously, a remnant of the ancient Pentecontade calendar of the Near East[29], which was of considerable import for numerous liturgies of Asia Minor and Palestine.

With the rise of Christianity the Jewish Pentecost gained a new significance as the anniversary of the revelation on Mount Sinai and the gift of the Torah. The rabbinic attempt to provide Pentecost (*Shabuot*) with a pseudo-historical significance may have had an apologetic and defensive purpose, namely, to establish a counterpart to the Christian Pentecost, which symbolized the outpouring of the Holy Ghost (Acts 2).

Sukkot, the feast of Tabernacles, a celebration of thanksgiving and a plea for fertility, was also a festive remembrance of the migration to the Holy Land. It continued for eight days, with its last day set aside as a feast of assembly. In pre-Christian and early Christian times, the rites of 'Drawing and Pouring Water' marked the climax of the *Sukkot* festivity at the Temple. Of this ceremony on the eve of the first day, it was said that 'whoever has not witnessed it has never seen a truly festive celebration'.[30] This custom fell into oblivion after the destruction of the Temple, since the Synagogue could not adopt sacrificial ceremonies which had been the exclusive prerogative of the Temple. We may, therefore, dispense here with a discussion of that most musical, and most popular of all Jewish feasts, in ancient times called simply *Hag* (the Feast).

The service of the eve of the three festivals corresponded, in general, to the liturgy of the Sabbath eve. But it contained an additional scriptural pronouncement on the meaning of the respective Holyday. The morning service consisted of the usual psalms, the modified '*Amida* and the other regular elements. The festival character was stressed by the solemn chanting of the *Hallel* (Great Praise: Ps. 113–118), which plays a decisive role in the Christian liturgy right up to the present day. (Since the *Hallel* displays a clearly musical structure, we shall discuss it further in the second (musical) part of the work.) After the *Hallel* followed the lesson, which was somewhat shorter than on the Sabbath.

Apart from the liturgical framework common to the three festivals, the following distinguishing features gave a special meaning to each of them.

(1) The home celebration on the eve of Passover, called *Seder* (Order). Though belonging to the domestic sphere, this ritual has been, rightly or wrongly, identified with Christ's Last Supper, and thereby assumed signal importance for the development of all Christian liturgies.[31] The ancient ritual of the *Seder* consisted, probably, of the following: (*a*) *berakot* over wine and unleavened breads; (*b*) narration of the Exodus from Egypt; (*c*) *berakot* over bitter herbs; (*d*) the *Hallel*, which was interrupted by the ritual meal; (*e*) grace after the meal; (*f*) conclusion of the *Hallel*. During the ceremony four cups of wine were blessed and drunk. The third cup was called the 'cup of salvation' in Judaism and became the archetype of the Eucharist in Christianity.[32]

(2) The prayers for dew and rain (at the beginning of summer and of winter respectively) were inserted in the liturgy of Passover and *Sukkot*, respectively. At the time of early Christianity, they existed only in their basic forms of brief petitions.[33]

(3) The solemn reading of the Decalogue took place on the day of Pentecost.

(4) The procession with the festive bouquet and the blessings over it during Tabernacles was accompanied by litanies. Most of these petitions grew out of the verse Ps. 118:25. This *Hosanna* (Save now!), originally a cry for help, became, in early Christianity, a kind of jubilation.[34] The liturgies of certain ancient fast days served as a pattern for certain rubrics of the service of the Eastern Churches.

The Liturgy of the High Holydays
(New Year and Day of Atonement)

It is remarkable how few traces the solemn liturgies of the High Holydays have left in Christian worship. Two important reasons may account for this strange fact: both holydays, the New Year as well as the Day of Atonement, were intrinsically connected with the Jewish eschatology, which, up to this day, has found unmistakable and unique expression in every prayer and ceremony of these holydays. Moreover, this sacred season emphatically stressed the concept of the God-given community of Israel, and its idea of collective responsibility was alien to Pauline Christianity with its emphasis on individual rather than collective salvation. God as the supreme Judge, His Kingdom and His Messianic message formed the ideological foundation for the liturgy of the High Holydays. Hence, very few elements of these services would find favour in the eyes of Christian authorities. None the less, a number of the prayers, and especially the lessons, of these holydays, have influenced the Christian liturgy.

The eve of the New Year (*Rosh Hashana*) had, in the first centuries of our era, the following liturgy.

Evening prayers as on week days; then the proclamation of the New Year with scriptural references, followed by the *Kaddish* and the '*Amida*, consisting of seven *berakot* (three plus one plus three) and petitions. The central *beraka* was called the Sanctification of the Day, glorifying the Kingdom of God. The last petition contained the plea that 'the faithful may be inscribed in the Book of Life'.[35] The *Kaddish*, with its great doxology, concluded the evening service.

Originally, the first part of the morning service was patterned after the Sabbath liturgy; the distinctive elements of the holyday's liturgy were the following:

(1) '*Abinu malkenu* (Our Father, our King), a long litany, allegedly composed by R. Akiba (second century) but probably originating in pre-Christian times.[36]

(2) After the reading of the holyday's pericope the sounding of the Shofar (ram's horn) created the specific atmosphere of the day.[37] Each blast of the Shofar was accompanied by a selection of psalm verses and other scriptural quotations.

The liturgy of the Day of Atonement (*Yom Kippur*), the holiest of all Jewish holydays, was characterized by two unique ideas: it provided for a collective as well as an individual atonement, according to the principle that (before God) 'All Jews are considered responsible for each other'. *Yom Kippur* was named 'Sabbath of Sabbaths', but, unlike the weekly Sabbath it was the most solemn fast day (from sunset to sunset). The concept of theocracy impressed its stamp upon each rubric of this holyday's liturgy.

From early morning until dusk, this day was filled with prayer and penitential worship.[38] The eve of *Yom Kippur* was celebrated like a Sabbath eve, with the following characteristic deviations: before the '*Amida* the scriptural command in Lev. 16:30 to celebrate the holyday was proclaimed. The '*Amida* itself contained the same six *berakot* as on the eve of the New Year plus one special benediction referring to the Day of Atonement. Afterwards the congregation recited aloud the common confession of sin.

The day's liturgy is today divided into four portions: Morning service; *Mussaph* (additional); *Mincha* (afternoon service); and *Ne'ila* (closing of the 'Gates of Heaven'). Whether this division was the actual usage during the existence of the Temple is a much debated question.

The morning service was the same as that of the New Year with one exception; the blast of the Shofar was omitted. In its place, the common confession, coupled with a fervent litany, closed the part before the lesson. There is no conclusive evidence for the existence of a special memorial service on the Day of Atonement. This was introduced centuries later.[39] Today the *'Aboda* ('Service' *par excellence*), a poetic and detailed description of the solemn sacrifices prescribed for the High Priest, recalls the Day of Atonement in the Temple. It is the high point of the *Mussaph* service.[40] All this became part of the Synagogue's liturgy only after the destruction of the Temple. The public confession, however, which followed, dates back to the earliest Christian times and belonged to the Synagogue as well.

The afternoon service concluded with the second lesson of the day, climaxed by the recitation of the book Jonah. *'Amida*, with public confession and *Kaddish* led to the fourth part of the liturgy, the *Ne'ila* portion. Psalm 145 prefaced a solemn *'Amida*, similar to that of the morning service. The confession and litany followed. The recitation of scriptural verses, of the *Kaddish* and a solemn repetition of the *Sh'ma'* finally closed the service.

Of other fast days or memorial days only the old festivals of *Hanukka* (Dedication of the Temple), *Purim* (the festival of Esther), and the 'Black Fast' of 9 Ab warrant mention here. *Hanukka* traditionally commemorated the Maccabean victory over the paganism of Antiochus Epiphanes and the revival of the Temple service, but this feast probably had a much longer history, dating back through many centuries. It was identified with the 'feast of lamps' (or candles) familiar in many cults of the ancient Near East.[41]

Purim was the gay, and perhaps resentful celebration of the deliverance of the Persian Jews from the murderous plotting of Haman. Again, the festival probably had a mythical background, as the juxtaposed names Esther (Ishtar) and Mordecai (Marduk) seem to indicate. It was celebrated in early spring.

The ninth day of Ab was dedicated to the tragic memory of the fall of both the First and Second Temple. It was, except for the Day of

Atonement, the most solemn of all fast-days, filled with a spirit of despair and hopelessness.

All three memorial days utilized the ordinary weekday liturgy, enriched and adorned by suitable passages from Scripture and (later) poetic insertions in the '*Amida*. On *Hanukka* a passage from the Maccabees was read, on *Purim* the lesson was the Book of Esther, and on 9 Ab the Lamentations were chanted.

Having outlined the regular order of service of the Synagogue in the early days of Christianity, we shall compare it and its later development with most of the corresponding components of Christian worship during the first millennium, confining ourselves chiefly to the chanted rubrics of the liturgy. This task will be approached first from the historical and philological, and then from the musical, points of view.

NOTES CHAPTER I

1. B 1125, 3, 23. For further references see the article 'Name und Inhalt der Liturgie bei den Alten', by Dr. P. Oppenheimer, O.S.B., in *Theologische Quartalschrift* (1932), pp. 35 ff.
2. *B. Ket.* 105a.
3. Also Philo, *De specialibus legibus*, I, 271 (ed. Cohn-Wendland).
4. Cf. *Tos. Sukka*, IV, 6; also Str.-Bill. IV, pt. I, p. 122, where all sources are given.
5. Concerning the Judaeo-Christian origin of the *Didache* see R. Harris, *The Teachings of the Apostles* (1887), p. 78; and A. Harnack, *Die Geschichte der altchristlichen Literatur*, II, p. 487.
6. Cf. A. Z. Idelsohn, *Jewish Liturgy*, p. xvii, n. 27.
7. W. Oesterley, *The Jewish Background of the Christian Liturgy* (1925), p. 125.
8. *B. Ber.* 27b. Cf. Str.-Bill., II, 696–8. Concerning parallels between New Testament and Jewish Liturgy, cf. Str.-Bill., IV, 1, Exkurs 7, 8, 10.
9. *Shab.* 118b.
10. Of the enormous literature only the most reliable standard works will be mentioned here: A. Z. Idelsohn, *Jewish Liturgy*; Kaufmann Kohler, *The Origins of Synagogue and Church*; Kaufmann Kohler, article 'Didache', *JE*, IV; Oesterley, *The Jewish Background of the Christian Liturgy*; Ismar Elbogen, *Der jüdische Gottesdienst in seiner geschichtlichen Entwicklung* (2nd rev. ed.).
11. 8:3.
12. *De Oratione*, XXV.
13. Cf. Idelsohn, *Jewish Liturgy*, p. 92. Cf. Ps. 106:30 and its interpretation in *B. Ber.* 26b.
14. Phil. 4:4; Col. 4:2; I Thess. 5:16.
15. Str.-Bill., II, 259–62; the custom is described as a Christian practice by Clement of Alexandria, *Paedagogus*, II.
16. *B. Shab.* 10a. J. A. Jungmann, in his *Missarum Sollemnia*, derives it from Germanic customs and ignores the ancient Hebrew tradition.
17. *B. Yoma* 53b. A. Baumstark, in his *Liturgie comparée*, pp. 69–71, knows only one type of fixed prayer, the *beraka*, and the accumulation of nineteen *berakot*, the '*Amida*. He is, however, mistaken in omitting the other categories of prayer; the petitional prayers he ascribes to Hellenistic influence without definite evidence.
18. *Ber.* 16, a, b. Str.-Bill., IV, pt. I, pp. 234 ff.
19. Ps. 51:17.
20. Cf. *GV*, pp. 380–2.

21. See Oesterley, op. cit., pp. 68 ff; Idelsohn, op. cit., p. 116; G. Dalman, *Die Worte Jesu*, p. 307; K. Kohler, op. cit., p. 101. The last-mentioned scholar attempts to trace the *Kaddish* to the first century B.C., but is not fully convincing.

22. The ancient Oriental formula: 'Peace be with you!', the *Salaam* of the Arabic, the *Shalom* of the Hebrew world, is more than just *Pax*. For the Semitic root $\sqrt{\overline{\text{šlm}}}$ stands not only for peace, but for fulfilment in the highest sense. Again Jungmann ignores the Jewish origin of the *Pax vobiscum* (op. cit. I, p. 450). Gregory Dix (*The Shape of the Liturgy*) is fully aware of this and of other Hebrew roots.

23. Whether Miriam's song belonged originally to the service of the Synagogue is doubtful. Certainly it was a part of the Temple's ritual, as some of the oldest Talmudic passages demonstrate (*B. Rosh Hashana* 31a). Cf. also Idelsohn, op. cit., p. 361, n. 16, and Jacob Mann in *HUCA*, II (1925), p. 282.

24. *Ber.* 27b.

25. Oesterley, op. cit., pp. 79, 170 ff; Idelsohn, op. cit., pp. 133 ff.

26. *B. Ber.* 32b.

27. Oesterley, op. cit., pp. 38 ff; ELB., pp. 155 ff; Idelsohn, op. cit., pp. 137 ff; Kohler, op. cit., pp. 92 ff; Str.-Bill., IV, pt. 1, pp. 154 ff; 'Readings from the Law', *JE*, pp. 647 ff.

28. Cf. the consecration of fire on Holy Saturday and its eulogy with the *berakot* of the *Habdala*. See also Seneca, *Epp. Mor.* IX, 5; Conybeare, *Rituale Armenorum*, p. 215; and Josephus, *Apology* II, 182.

29. Concerning the term Pentecontade see *infra* p. 97 n. 51.

30. *M. Suk.* V, 1. Extensive description of the ceremony at the time of Christ in Str.-Bill., II, 774–812. On the musical elements of the 'Water-Drawing' ritual see S. Krauss, *Talmudische Archaeologie*, III, pp. 83–84, and 277, n. 53–60.

31. Of the large literature on this subject only a few references will be given here, which are germane to our limited subject: Str.-Bill., IV, pt. 1, pp. 71–76; Oesterley, op. cit., pp. 156–200; J. Klausner, *Jesus of Nazareth*, pp. 328–9; P. Spitta, 'Die urchristlichen Traditionen über den Ursprung des Abendmahls' in *Geschichte und Literatur des Urchristentums* (1893); G. Bickell, *Messe und Pascha*, pp. 100 ff; D. A. Chwolson, *Das letzte Passamahl Christi und der Tag seines Todes*; *DACH*, pp. 525–33, article 'Messe'; Adrian Fortescue, *The Mass*, Chapters I–III.

32. J. Klausner (*Jesus of Nazareth*, p. 329) justly opposes E. Meyer's theory (*Ursprung und Anfänge des Christentums*, I, p. 177) that the *Hallel* was sung after each joyous celebration. In Jewish ritual this custom is unknown.

33. *M. Taanith* I, 1.

34. Cf. my extensive article 'The Hosanna in the Gospels', *JBL* (July, 1946).

35. Concerning this formula see Str.-Bill., II, pp. 169–76; also Dalman, op. cit., p. 171; *JE*, III, 312, article 'Book of Life'. Cf. also Chapter VII of this book, 'Excursus on the Antecedents of the *Dies irae*'.

36. *B. Taanith*, 25b; *B. Ber.*, 32b.

37. On the Shofar, too, many books and articles have been written. It is, by the way, not to be considered as a musical instrument proper. The best articles are: S. Finesinger, 'The Shofar', in *HUCA* VII and IX (1931–1932); S. Krauss, *Talmudische Archaeologie*, III, pp. 96 ff, and 282–3, nn. 129–38; C. Sachs, *The History of Musical Instruments*, pp. 110–12, where some statements are quite controversial; *JE*, XI, article 'Shofar'; Str.-Bill., I, pp. 959–61, II, pp. 481 ff. Otto Rank's psychoanalytical hypotheses, set forth in his study *Der Schophar*, are no more than idle dreams, marred by an abundance of factual errors.

A brief reminder may not be amiss, that the Shofar as 'Trumpet of the Day of Judgment' entered in all Christian liturgies or eschatologies. Cf. e.g. in the Sequence, 'Dies irae':

> *Tuba mirum spargens sonum*
> *Per sepulchra regionum*
> *Coget omnes ante thronum.*

Cf. also the alphabetical Midrash of the Rabbi Aqiba in A. Jellinek, *Beth Hamidrash*, III, 31, 28.

38. *B. Meg.*, 23a.

39. More about the service for the dead in Idelsohn, op. cit., pp. 230–1, and *JE*, VIII, 463, article 'Memorial Service'.

40. A poetic, exalted description of the Temple ritual on the Day of Atonement has come down to us in Chapter 50 of Ecclesiasticus.

41. About the antecedents of *Hanukka* cf. the profound study of J. Morgenstern, 'The Hanukkah Festival and the Calendar of Ancient Israel', *HUCA*, XX (1947).

CHAPTER TWO

The Liturgical and Musical Traits of the Earliest Christian Community

THE RESULTS OF EARLIER STUDIES

THE first Christians were Jews, both by faith and nationality; their ritual was the Jewish cult, their language Hebrew and Aramaic. While accepting the Jewish institutions of their time, they expanded and reinterpreted them under the influence of their new message of salvation. Before tracing the divergent courses of the unfolding Jewish and Christian cults, we must first establish the common basis of their liturgies. No matter how much they differed theologically, chronologically, nationally, and geographically, certain elements were common to all of their rites. Without exception, these basic concepts stemmed from Judaism. What were the Jewish cult institutions at the time that Christianity came into existence?

The three types of Jewish worship, well established in Jesus's lifetime, found their expression through three different media: in the sacrificial cult at the Temple in Jerusalem (the central sanctuary of the country); in the services of many local synagogues; and in private devotions. All of these are well known to us through Jewish and Christian literature. The question of which of those elements influenced the growing Church most was raised many centuries ago.[1] At first glance the problem may seem irrelevant to our study, but we shall, however, presently realize its importance. Since the Temple was destroyed in A.D. 70, at the very beginning of Christianity, any influence of its ritual upon the Church could only be second-hand and indirect. It was conveyed either through people who 'still could remember', or it was based entirely upon the testimony of written records—in this case, the Bible and perhaps Josephus. Yet the Bible describes only the First Temple, whose institutions were considerably different from those of the Second. If Christianity modelled part of its cult after the pattern of the Temple, it was a rather imaginary

Temple, ideally reconstructed according to the canonized documents. If this were the only link between Christian and Jewish liturgies we could easily dispose of it; the problem has, however, other aspects.

Some of the Church Fathers emphasized the Temple as the model institution to be imitated by the Church. Comparisons frequently stressed the type of hierarchy common to Church and Temple. Thus Jerome stated: 'What Aaron and his sons and the Levites were in the Temple, the same, Bishops Priests and Deacons are in the Church'.[2] Indeed, the Christian hierarchy is derived from the priestly organization of the Temple. We shall later see how this fact affected the transfer of musical and liturgical elements from Judaism to Christianity. In particular the Diaconus and Psalmista (*Anagnostes*) became instrumental in the development of musical liturgy.

Vitringa, the first scholar who dealt objectively with this question, admitted the similarity of Temple and Church, but considered the Synagogue, and especially the rural Synagogue, the strongest link between the Jewish and Christian liturgies. Early Christianity was a movement of the poor and the meek, its provenance the rural sections of Palestine. Jerusalem and its rabbis were opposed to the 'men from the country', or rather, they derided them because of their ignorance.[3] Small wonder, then, that the liturgical forms of the Metropolitan Temple were not well liked by the Judaeo-Christians. The hierarchic-theocratic aristocracy of the Temple was fiercely opposed to the gentle ideology of the poor and ignorant 'hillbillies', who adored and respected only the Kingdom of Heaven. The simple, plain, familiar synagogue of the rural communities was the most likely birthplace of Christian liturgy in Palestine.[4] But Vitringa paid little attention to these social and political circumstances, basing his theory of liturgical continuity from Synagogue to Church upon convincing authentic evidence from both sides. This theory was modified by Gustav Bickell, who endeavoured to prove that the section of the Christian liturgy preceding the Eucharist (or the entire Anaphora) is founded upon the Sabbath morning service of the Synagogue. In his opinion the Anaphora itself was decisively influenced by the ritual of the Paschal Supper, the *Seder*, as celebrated annually in Jewish homes on the eve of Passover.[5]

During the last four or five decades only a few scholars have seriously studied the relationship between the liturgies of Christianity and Judaism. The few Jewish studies on the subject will be discussed later

on; of the modern Christian scholars only three deserve mention:
W. Bousset, W. O. Oesterley, and A. Baumstark. While the first
two authors did not possess a fundamental knowledge of the primary
Hebrew sources (a deficiency painfully apparent in Bousset's writing),
Baumstark has this knowledge and also the sincere intention of coming
to grips with the ideology as well as the practice of the Synagogue. In
this sense his book *Liturgie comparée* (Monastère d'Amay, 1939) shows
a considerable advance beyond all earlier literature on the subject.
Many of his ideas display a valuable understanding of the development
of Jewish liturgy. None the less, even he is occasionally handicapped
by his lack of knowledge of the Daily Hebrew Prayerbook and the
actual practice of the Synagogue. Otherwise, he would not have believed that the ancient formulas 'In saecula saeculorum', etc., and
'Dignum et justum est' have 'completely disappeared' from the Hebrew
prayerbook. Actually, these formulas occur in the prayers of every
Hebrew weekday. Mistakes like these are not rare in Baumstark's
book; on the other hand, he shows a commendable familiarity with
post-biblical Hebrew sources and is fully aware of the close kinship
between Christian and Jewish liturgy. George Foot Moore's classic work
Judaism in the First Centuries of the Christian Era, which is of unique value
to the student of theology, does not compare Jewish and Christian
liturgies.

On the Jewish side the issue has not yet received the attention it
deserves. Only Ludwig Venetianer and Ismar Elbogen have discussed
the problem extensively, the former from the historical, the latter from
the literary angle. Both come to the same conclusion: the starting point
of early Christian liturgy was neither the Bible nor the cult of the
Temple, but the Synagogue. Yet, when we carefully scrutinize all of
our available sources, scant as they may be, we are bound to admit
that the predominance of the Synagogue is not quite as universal as
one might assume.

What, then, are the constituent elements in Christian cult common to
the liturgies of Synagogue and Temple?

1. *Liturgical Texts*. Most of the basic prayers originated in the Temple
but were adapted by the early Synagogue.

2. *Hierarchy*. The Hierarchy and its function was intrinsically connected with the Temple.

3. *Ceremonies and Ritual*. Ceremonies are frequently of synagogal

origin. Yet, certain elements, such as vestments, rites, *oblationes*, show the Temple as the birthplace of these institutions.

4. *Music*. The music of the Churches and its manner of performance can hardly date back to the Temple, since the time from 33–70 was too short for the foundation or imitation of a musical practice based upon the Temple ceremonial.

5. *Organization of the Ecclesiastical Year*. The Calendar, finally, is a mixture of many strata, comprising ancient Babylonian, Canaanite, pre-exilic Hebrew, and specific institutions of the Temple. Later, Greek and Roman pagan elements, often in skilful disguise, contributed to its eclectic character.

Since we are here concerned only with those parts of the liturgy which were usually chanted, we need not discuss the question of the Mass-Passa relationship at great length. Suffice it to state that the Eucharist, the Grace and the Blessing (the *Agape*) over bread and wine and the psalm-singing are ancient Jewish customs of the home ritual on the eve of Passover. Whether or not the supposition is correct that Jesus's Last Supper was really the Paschal *Seder* (as assumed by three Gospels and the vast majority of the Fathers), and if so whether that supposition can still be maintained today, is largely irrelevant to our purposes. It is evident that the principle of the Mass (Eucharist—Anaphora) is founded upon this assumption. But in order to decide whether the Temple or the Synagogue served as the model[6] for the liturgical institutions of the incipient Church, we must examine some additional material which has rarely been investigated hitherto.[7]

The term 'Synagogue' refers to Church in early Christian sources. It is thus used first in Jas. 2:2, 'for if there come unto your assembly (Greek: *Synagoge*) a man . . .'; and then frequently with the Fathers, e.g. Ignatius, Theophilus of Antioch, Firmilian of Caesarea. A church of the Marcionites on Mount Hermon actually had the word Synagogue inscribed on it. Since this church dates back as late as 318, we must conclude that Christianity used the term Synagogue indiscriminately until the fourth century.[8] Samuel Krauss offers the theory that to the Gentile Christians the expression Synagogue had a Jewish connotation.[9] While there is no doubt that Christianity in general preferred the term *ecclesia*, this was not a uniform rule. But by the end of the third century the antagonism between Judaism and Christianity had so deepened that even the most remotely Jewish nomenclature was banished by the ecclesiastical authorities.

LEANINGS TOWARD THE TEMPLE

The Temple (Gr. *hierón*) being the central authority of Judaism, was for that very reason antagonistic to all sectarianism, including early Christianity. Although early Christianity attempted to loosen these bonds of authority, we have at least one passage which shows adoration and even reverence for the Temple as the central sanctuary of both Jews and Christians. We find it in Clement of Rome, *To the Corinthians*, 41:

> Let each of you, brethren, in his own order give thanks unto God, maintaining a good conscience and not transgressing the appointed rule of his service, but acting with all seemliness. Not in every place, brethren, are the continual daily sacrifices offered, or the freewill offerings, or the sin offerings and the trespass offerings, but in Jerusalem alone. And even there the offering is not made in every place, but before the Sanctuary in the court of the altar; and this too through the high-priest and the aforesaid ministers. . . .

This passage is remarkable in more than one respect. Clement of Rome was probably the third Bishop of Rome. While it is assumed today that the Epistle from which we have just quoted was written between A.D. 95–100, it is not clear how its author, twenty-six years after the destruction of the Temple, could refer to this institution as a still existing authority, a problem which has been strangely evaded by many of the leading theologians.[10] Still, however early or late we set the date of the Epistle, we cannot fail to observe here a strong sentiment for the authority of the Temple in Jerusalem. This typically Jewish reverence alone ought to decide the question of Clement's Jewish extraction. In addition, he offers the first Christian prayer containing the Thrice-Holy (*Tersanctus*, the Jewish *Kedusha*), which was an established and important part of the worship in Temple and Synagogue and which we shall discuss later.[11] It cannot be denied, then, that the Temple influenced the development of Christian liturgy. We may summarize the respective influence of Temple and Synagogue upon Christian cult in the following way: during the existence of the Temple and for two generations after its fall, it was the Synagogue around which young Christianity centred, both for political reasons and out of a certain resentment against the Temple and its hierarchy. When all hope for its reconstruction had vanished and the Jewish hierarchy had disappeared, the idea of the Temple no longer represented a dangerous element to the leaders of the young Church. Thereafter, Christianity inclined toward the reconstruction of a wholly imaginary and idealized Temple. It is characteristic that at that time even the Hebrew term for 'Sanctuary' (*Heikhal*) was borrowed by the Byzantine Church.[12]

RELATION BETWEEN TEMPLE AND SYNAGOGUE

The principal and outstanding element of the Temple worship was, no doubt, the sacrificial cult, executed by a highly trained staff of professional priests who held their privileged position by dynastical birthright. The Synagogue, on the other hand, was the house of prayer, meditation and, most important, of study. In the Temple, priesthood prevailed in all its hierarchic splendour; in the Synagogue, it was the scholar and layman who moulded the service into a form which has lasted, essentially unchanged, up to the present day. Roughly simplified, we might say: the attitude of the Temple was theocratic and ritualistic, that of the Synagogue anthropocentric and democratic.

Despite all these basic divergences between the two main institutions, there was some common ground. The closest link was the Temple-Synagogue, that is the Synagogue established in the 'Hall of Stones' in the Temple (Solomon's Hall in the New Testament). We know of this remarkable place of worship through Jewish and New Testament sources.[13] It was identical with the 'Hall' in which Jesus debated with the rabbis (Luke 2:46), and the so-called 'Hall of Solomon' known from Acts 3:11; 5:12. This place of prayer was also used for meetings, readings of the Law and public discussions, but it served chiefly as the gathering place of the 'standing men' (*ma'amadot*).[14] These standing men, representatives from all parts of the country, were divided into twenty-four groups, and took turns in the performance of the ritual duties, and although laymen, had the privilege of standing by and witnessing the daily sacrifice in the Temple. Before the ceremony they met the officiating priest in the 'Hall of Stones' mentioned above, where they received the blessing in the presence of the people. After the sacrifice the standing men returned to the Hall where they attended a service of their own.[15] The participation of laymen from all parts of the country created an exceedingly strong link between the central sanctuary and the Synagogue. S. Krauss is quite right in calling the establishment of the Synagogue within the Temple a 'triumph of Rabbinism' (against the Sadducean hierarchical privileges). The same author draws our attention to another instance of interrelation between Temple and Synagogue, exemplified by the privilege granted the High Priest to read the Torah pericope on the Day of Atonement in the 'Hall of Stones', i.e. the Temple-Synagogue.[16] From the same source[17] we learn that the worship of the Temple-Synagogue was well organized; it had its own deacon (precentor, *hazan*) and synagogarch.

It stands to reason that certain features of the Temple ritual proper were transferred to the Temple-Synagogue, and since its service was regularly attended by the notables from the provinces, the ritual of the Temple did not vanish entirely with its destruction.[18] As a matter of fact, there are some indications in the Talmudic literature purporting to demonstrate that the continuity of tradition, particularly the liturgical continuity, was to be preserved by all possible means and devices.

Of the numerous details which bear out this continuity, we shall mention here only a few, belonging to different categories.

Ideological Continuity

The actual sacrifices were replaced either by the recitation of the divine statute and order of the respective offering, or by spontaneous or 'regulated' prayer. These noble substitutes for the sacrifices were emphasized and reinterpreted innumerably.[19] Long before the cessation of the sacrificial cult the psalms had expressed the substitution in poetic language:

> Sacrifice and offering Thou didst not desire—mine ears hast Thou opened.
> Burnt offering and sin offering hast Thou not required.
> Then said I, Lo, I come: in the volume of the book it is written of me
> I delight in Thy will, O God. . . .
> I have not hid Thy righteousness within my heart;
> I have declared faithfulness and Thy salvation,
> I have not concealed Thy loving-kindness and Thy truth from the great
>   congregation.[20]

Hosea's bold metaphor of 'Prayer as an offering of the lips' (14:3) has been paraphrased countless times throughout the entire Jewish and Christian literature. It was even transferred to the musical realm, where it became the postulate, 'Non voce, sed corde canere'! Krauss points to the identity of 'offering—*offertorium*'.[21] He might have added the Byzantine Anaphora and Prosphora. Similarly the Hebrew *'Aboda* (service at the sacrificial altar) in later times assumed the meaning of prayer, or rather of service; comparable to the *officium* of the Roman Church, or the *Amt* of the German Catholics, designating a solemn service. In its highest form, it must be considered a synthesis of the Greek *logike thysia* and the Hebrew 'offering of the lips'.

Continuity of Authority

The Academy of Jabne, founded by the great Rabbi Johanan ben Zakkai during the siege of Jerusalem, assumed some of the prerogatives of the Temple after its fall, e.g. the right of taxation and of the tithes; and the privilege of the shofar-signals by dynastic priests, i.e. members of the Temple's priestly caste. Moreover, it was the rule in Jabne that every *beraka* had to be answered with the full doxology 'Praised be His Name, Whose glorious Kingdom is for ever and ever', instead of the simple response 'Amen'. Though this fact may not seem important, it is, actually, of great significance. For the doxology quoted was permitted only in the Temple, whereas the 'Amen' was the typical response of the Synagogue.[22]

Continuity Through Personal Tradition

Of the several personalities who endeavoured to transfer the tradition of the central sanctuary to the country synagogue, none is as colourful and remarkable as R. Joshua ben Hananya, both as a traditionalist and as an adversary of Judaeo-Christianity.

He was a Levite priest, a member of the division of the singers,[23] who, together with his fellow-choristers, would go from the choir of the Temple to conduct the daily worship in the 'Hall of Stones', thus officiating at both services.[24] A personal disciple of Johanan ben Zakkai, he worked zealously for the preservation of the tradition of the Temple by transmitting it to the Synagogue. Many of his statements bear out this attitude. A man of the world, a statesman dealing with the Emperor Hadrian, a witty debater, and a wise and pious man, he tried his best to heal the breach existing between Temple and Synagogue, and at the same time to prevent an internecine schism in Judaism created by Judaeo-Christianity. He incessantly opposed the incipient split, which he considered disastrous and heretical. It speaks well for his wisdom and foresight that, on his death-bed, he gave comfort to his colleagues who were worried about the future of Judaism and the dangerous conception of Judaeo-Christianity, with the words: 'Be not afraid; even if you are bewildered and helpless, lacking defenders, the others are not much better off; for their wisdom has become rotten'.[25] He was not afraid of *Gentile* Christianity. All he lived for was the unity of Judaism proper, of its tradition, teachings, and religion, and we can take him as a trustworthy witness, emphasizing the close link between the Temple and its Synagogue, between Jerusalem and Jabne.

By now, we should be able to evaluate the degree to which the Temple and its tradition influenced the Synagogue, and we arrive at the following conclusions.

The Temple, holding national and central authority, had developed a type of liturgy which, with its hierarchy, its sacrificial cult, and its rigid organization, engendered a sharp distinction between the officers of the ritual and the community of the faithful, the latter being almost passive bystanders. The prayers offered in the Temple were collective, the psalms were rendered by a professional priestly choir and orchestra, and quite a few of its institutions were clearly directed *ad spectatores*. On the other hand, some of the customs and traditions survived the downfall of the central sanctuary and found a permanent place within the Synagogue, 'The Little Sanctuary', as it was sometimes called. Being an informal layman's institution, the Synagogue depended entirely upon the activity of its congregation, and stressed its private and lay character. In those early times, both the liturgy and the administration were in the hands of laymen. When the Temple ceased to exist, the Synagogue took over many of its functions, some of them by way of 'legal fiction', e.g. replacing the sacrifices by prayers and the reading of biblical passages referring to the offerings; here the individualistic, active, lay characteristics were always predominant. None the less, even here a decidedly professional element came into the life of the Synagogue, when the appointed *hazan* (cantor, psalmista, reader) took charge of many important parts of the liturgy. It is only natural that the introduction of the professional *hazan* brought back to the Synagogue some features originally reserved for the ritual of the Temple.

When considering the Church and its relation to Temple and Synagogue we must make another clear distinction between the Temple and

Synagogue, important at least for the first two centuries. The Judaeo-Christian Church recognized the Temple and its institutions, and most certainly borrowed some of the Temple customs, directly or indirectly, through the Palestinian Synagogue. The Gentile Church evolved in the Synagogue of the Diaspora and was little concerned with the actual Temple. Much later, when the individualistic character of early Christianity had faded away, and the collective ('Catholic') ritualistic tendencies grew ever stronger, the Church borrowed many elements from the Temple; not from the real one, however, but from its stylized image, existing only in the minds of Christian theologians.

THE CHIEF STRATA OF LITURGICAL MUSIC
IN CHURCH AND SYNAGOGUE

As we have seen before, there are some elements in the musical liturgy of Christianity and Judaism which stem from a common source. Their substance and contents are identical, as are frequently their forms and manner of performance.

The common elements are:

(1) The scriptural lesson, or reading, which in the course of time developed a highly organized system of pericopes, to be read or recited regularly and periodically. This public reading required a primitive musical intonation.

(2) The vast field of psalmody. In this work we understand by the term 'psalmody' not only the singing of psalms or psalm-verses, but the rendering of any scriptural or liturgical text, after the fashion in which psalms are chanted.

(3) The litany or the congregational prayers of supplication and intercession, especially on fast-days, which from time immemorial, have been used as important media of musical and religious expression.[26]

(4) The chanted prayer of the priest or precentor. This was a comparatively late and originally less important element of the liturgy that became predominant in the Synagogue and in some rituals of the Eastern Churches.

If we consider these four elements, we realize that they, or at least their rudiments, are common to the Temple as well as to the Synagogue and the Church. They constitute to this very day the main forms of liturgical music.

LANGUAGES OF PRAYER

This is the place to discuss the various languages of prayer used in the first centuries of Christianity. For our purpose this problem is more important than it appears on the surface, not only because the liturgical language exerts a powerful and vastly formative influence upon the music with which it is connected, but also because of the all-important role of the Book of Psalms, the book of prayer common to both the Jewish and the Christian Church. The bipartite structure of the verse in the poetic literature of the Old Testament demands an antiphonal rendering. Actually, these verse structures cannot exist in any other, non-parallelistic diction. It is important to note that all translations of the Psalter, from the Vetus Itala up to the most modern paraphrases, have taken pains to preserve the bipartite style of the original.

In general, one discerns three strata in the language of prayer through the centuries:

The Semitic period. (Hebrew, Aramaic, Syriac, etc.)

The 'ancient' liturgical languages (Greek, Latin, Old Syriac, Old Armenian, Old Slavonic). These languages exist today only as media of worship, and belong to the dead languages proper.[27]

The living vernacular (Arabic, Coptic, Georgian, Ruthenic, etc.). These languages are used for particular rites only, especially for originally schismatic groups that had returned to Rome. Since their reconversion happened in comparatively recent times, we need not further discuss them.[28]

A full understanding of the liturgico-musical interrelation between Synagogue and Church presupposes a critical study of the different strata within the liturgies, by comparing Hebrew-Aramaic, Greek, Syriac, and Latin texts. For our purposes, we may limit our investigation to the following points:

A. Literal Hebraisms. (Acclamations, proper names, interjections, etc., in Hebrew.)

B. Translated Hebraisms:

(a) Scriptural quotations from a translation ('Biblicisms').

(b) Post-biblical expressions, formulas, paraphrases, etc.

C. Hebraic-Aramaic structures of prayers and their transfusion with the body of ecclesiastical prayers. (To be discussed in Chapter VII.)

27

The last sixty or seventy years of theological and philological study have witnessed a remarkable change in hitherto unchallenged opinions. Today we know that not only three of the four canonic Gospels are based upon Aramaic sources (two of them, Matthew and Mark, perhaps being free translations from the Aramaic texts), but the entire attitude of the scholars has, in an increasing measure, turned toward an extensive critical and comparative study of rabbinic and other post-biblical sources.[29] In a way, this development parallels a similar change in the approach to the music of the Church. We need only think of Frédéric Auguste Gevaert's or Heinrich Bellermann's all-Hellenistic approach and, in contrast, of the findings of Peter Wagner, Dom Jeannin, Dom Mocquereau or Amédée Gastoué, to recognize their fundamentally new emphasis upon the Oriental sources of Gregorian Chant.[30]

In the centuries when Jewish and Christian liturgies were in their formative stage, the question of the proper language of prayer was frequently discussed. In the Jewish Church at least three idioms were considered: Hebrew, Aramaic, and Greek. Hebrew was then, in the second century A.D., all but a dead language. Its use was confined to religious and legal discussions, to scholarly expositions, and to prayer; and even there Aramaic had made considerable inroads, in spite of the opposition of the rabbis. One outstanding doctor, Rabbi Johanan bar Nappacha, opposed it strongly and consistently, yet without much success.[31] Thus, in the apostolic and post-apostolic centuries Aramaic prayers were at least used as often as were the Hebrew. This, however, does not hold true for all of Palestine; in Caesarea, for example, the language of the Synagogue was Greek. When a rabbi protested against the Greek recitation of the Sh'ma' (Deut. 6:4), the core of the Jewish liturgy, an outstanding teacher and rabbi declared that 'Whoever does not understand Hebrew may read the Sh'ma' in any language comprehensible to him, and he has done his duty perfectly'.[32] Finally, after a century-long struggle it was decreed that one may pray in any language familiar to the congregation.[33] In the entire Diaspora the language of the synagogues was Greek, as one may gather from the Pauline Epistles, which are chiefly addressed to the large Jewish Assemblies of the Diaspora. Even the public reading of Scripture during service must, at least occasionally, have been permissible in Greek, probably together with the original Hebrew text.[34] Moreover, we must not forget that there was a Greek synagogue in Jerusalem itself, where most of the prayers were recited in the *Koine* (Greek vernacular). These regional synagogues in Jerusalem contributed much to the uniformity of liturgical tradition throughout the Diaspora, since their authority was unquestionable.[35]

In no way different was the attitude of the early Church toward the language of prayer. The Apostles used all three languages according to their respective environments,[36] and if one interprets in a rationalistic manner I Cor. 14:16 ('. . . Wherefore let him that speaketh in an *unknown* tongue pray that he may interpret. . . .'), one may regard the entire passage as a plea for the unlimited use of the Greek vernacular in worship. This principle was generally accepted: the three languages of the Eastern Mediterranean region, namely Greek, Syriac-Aramaic and Latin, became the chief media of Christian worship. Yet some Hebraisms were preserved, or rather tolerated, as reminders of Christ's and the Scripture's native tongue.

Literal Hebraisms

Apart from the proper names, the liturgical rubrics of the Churches contain certain Hebrew words which have been borrowed for reasons of tradition or quotation. The most interesting group are the liturgical acclamations, like Amen, *Selah*, Hosanna, Hallelujah, *Maranatha* and others; these will be discussed extensively in Chapter VIII.

Other Hebraisms or rather Aramaisms have entered the liturgies as quotations from the New Testament where they occasionally occur.[37] They have had no influence on the development of the liturgy and have always remained unassimilated alien elements.

Translated Hebraisms

(1) To this category belong all the scriptural quotations from the Greek and Latin translations of the Bible, with which the liturgies are replete. When chanted, they fall into the classes of psalmody, responsorium, or doxology and will be treated under those headings. Their influence upon the form and the spirit of the liturgy cannot be overestimated; they add to the originally spontaneous, undefined texts wellestablished formal structures, mainly responses and refrain-psalms. These quotations ('Biblicisms') are familiar to every scholar and therefore do not warrant a special investigation.[38]

It is hard to understand that so accomplished a scholar as Baumstark

29

failed to recognize the biblical origin of phrases like 'In saecula saeculorum', or of the *berakot* (blessings, eulogies). He takes pains to demonstrate their *Talmudic* origin, overlooking such passages as Ps. 89:53; Ps. 72:18, 19; Ps. 135:21.[39] He even believes that these and corresponding passages have 'completely disappeared from the present Jewish Liturgy' and is therefore inclined to assume that the Christian sources offer more reliable testimony on Jewish worship than the Hebrew sources. *Actually, however, these passages can be found in every Jewish Prayer Book (e.g. A.P.B., pp. 33, 128, 136, etc.), and are said every day at least once.*

(2) Even more significant for the development of both text and music of the divine service are the many post-biblical Hebraisms. Originally integral parts of the Jewish worship, they were taken over by the early Christians, certainly not without active assistance on the part of the Judaeo-Christians. These passages bear the most eloquent testimony of the absorption of national Jewish elements by the Christian Church. Quotations from Scripture ('Biblicisms') do not indicate any direct connection with Judaism since many Gentiles knew the Greek text of the Bible or the Vetus Itala. But the above mentioned passages could have been borrowed only by Jews, well conversant with these texts and their liturgical functions in the service; nor were they accessible in translated form. Such Jews were the intermediaries between the liturgies of Church and Synagogue. In their mouths the very same words and tunes were alive which still resound in the Churches, demonstrating the Hebrew origin of some of the loftiest prayers of Christianity.

This state of transition is one of the most neglected corners in the field of comparative history of religion. Only a few scholars have seriously concerned themselves with that problem since Vitringa's *De Synagoga vetere* appeared in 1696. More recent authors, such as Bousset, in his once highly praised *Die Religion des Judentums zur Zeit Christi* (1903), have fallen very short of their goal due to their neglect of rabbinic lore and their ignorance of the details of Jewish worship.[40]

Jewish scholars, on the other hand, have only in relatively recent times begun to interest themselves in the development of Christian liturgies and their Hebraisms.[41] The Jewish scholars did not progress any further than the Christian New Testament scholars; as the latter were impeded through their lack of knowledge concerning rabbinical sources, so were the Jewish scholars impeded through their unfamiliarity with the maze of patristic material, especially that of Eastern provenance. Yet it must be clearly understood by both Christian and Jewish theologians and historians that the development of the Jewish *and* Christian worship is so closely interrelated and mutually involved, that the knowledge and the study of *both* liturgies is virtually indispensable to every serious student of either.

The following exposition is based mainly upon the present author's studies and research in this field. However, the discussion here is limited to such passages of the Christian liturgies which were, or are rendered musically, or have contributed to the development of the musical structure of the service. Since there is no one standard edition of Jewish prayers for all regional customs and tradition in existence, I have used the translations of the *Authorized Daily Prayer Book* (ed. Singer, London), and the *Union Prayer Book* I and II, edited by the Central Conference of American Rabbis, newly revised edition, Cincinnati, 1945. Where other Hebrew passages appear, there the respective sources are quoted in the text.

POST-BIBLICAL HEBRAISMS

Christian Texts	*Hebrew Texts*
1. O Thou holy God . . . who didst make man after Thine own image and didst endow him with Thy gifts, and didst teach him to seek wisdom and good understanding. . . .[42]	Thou favourest man with knowledge, and teachest mortals understanding. . . . O favour us with the spirit of knowledge, understanding, and discernment from Thee. . . .
2. Elect of God, O happy and blessed priest. Likened unto Aaron and the prophet Moses, who devised the vestments which Aaron always wore. . . . At the motion of the heels the earth resounded and the Tabernacle rejoiced. . . .[43]	He made excellent Aaron . . . he adorned him in glory . . . all of the vestments did He devise, and He girdled him with golden bells that resounded when he turned about. (Sirach 45, 7–10.) Ecclus. 45:7–10. Then the Tabernacle rejoiced. (*Midrash Tanchuma* III.)
3. It is meet and right. . . .[44]	It is meet and right. . . .[45]
4. Holy, holy, holy is the Lord of hosts; full of His glory is the heaven and the earth.[46]	Holy, holy, holy is the Lord of hosts; full of His glory is the earth.
5. We pray for heavenly peace, and God's benevolence, and for the salvation of our souls. We pray of the Lord, for the peace of the entire world, and the concord of God's churches.[47]	He who maketh peace in His heights, may He make peace for us. . . . May salvation from Heaven, with grace and peace be granted and this holy congregation be blessed, together with all other congregations.
6. Have mercy upon us, O God, ruler of all![48]	Our Father, our King, have mercy upon us!

7. May He implant in them the salutary fear of the Lord.[49]

And may He implant in them the fear of the Lord. . . .

8. Arise to God (through His Christ) bow to Him and praise Him.[50]

Arise and bless the Lord to whom praise is due.

9. Gather together Thy church from the corners of the earth into Thy Kingdom.[51]

Gather us from the four corners of the earth.

10. Praised be Thou for ever and ever, Shield of Abraham.[52]

Praised be Thou, Lord of the Universe Shield of Abraham.

11. Praised be Thou, King of the Universe, who (through Christ) hast created and who (through Him) hast ordered the chaotic.[53]

Praised be Thou, Lord, King of the Universe, who formest light and createst darkness, who makest peace and createst all things.

12. Thou hast abolished Death, Thou, who givest life to the dead (through Jesus, our hope).[54]

Faithful art Thou to quicken the dead. Praised art Thou, O Lord, who quickenest the dead.

13. And the host of angels, fiery and ardent, proclaim: 'One is holy, Phelmuni' and the Seraphim with the six-winged Cherubim sing to Thee incessantly the triumphal hymn 'Holy, holy, holy is the Lord of hosts; heaven and earth are full of His glory'.[55]

And one holy said to another unknown (Phelmoni) . . . (Dan. 8: 13) We shall revere and sanctify Thee according to the mystic utterances of the Seraphim, who always hallow Thy name in the Sanctuary . . . and they called one unto the other, saying: 'Holy, holy, holy is the Lord. . . .'

14. For Thou art the Father of wisdom. . . . The giver of law . . . wherefore adoration is due to Thee from every thinking and holy being.[56]

Thou favourest man with knowledge . . . Thou hast taught us and given us Thy Law. . . . Praised be Thou, O Lord, gracious Giver of knowledge.

15. For the Sabbath is rest from creation, the goal of the universe, the study of Law, thankful praise to God.[57]

For the Sabbath is rest from creation, . . . given to the study of Thy Law. (P.R. XXIII.)

16. . . . And Thou hast mercy upon Sion and rebuildest Jerusalem to erect in its midst the throne of David, Thy son.[58]

And to Jerusalem, Thy city, return in mercy . . . rebuild it soon in our days . . . and set up therein the throne of David.

17. We give thanks to Thee, O King, for everything. In the days of Esther and Mordecai . . . in the days of Judah Maccabi and of his brothers. . . .[59]

We give thanks unto Thee, for Thou art the Lord our God . . . (for *Hanukka* and *Purim* immediately following).

In the days of Mordecai and Esther. In the days of the Hasmonaean Matathias . . . and of his sons. . . .

18. Above all, we glorify and praise Thee (through Jesus) now and for evermore, Amen.[60]

For all that, Thy name, O our King, shall incessantly be blessed and exalted. . . .

19. Do not reject us unto the end, for the sake of Thy holy name; and do not break Thy covenants . . . for the sake of Abraham Thy friend, and Isaac Thy servant, and for Israel's sake, Thy Saint's.[61]

O Lord, let not wrath rule over us; save us for Thy name's sake. . . . We beseech Thee, give heed to the covenant with Abraham Thy friend, and let the binding (of Isaac) appear before Thee for Israel's welfare. (*APB* and *Mekilta* to pericope *b'shalach*.)

20. A whole lifetime and many centuries would not suffice for us to praise Thee as becomes Thy Dignity.[62]

Though our mouths were full of song as the sea, and our tongues full of exultation all our lives . . . we should still be unable to thank Thee and to praise Thy name.

21. God without beginning, without ending![163]

God without beginning, without ending!

22. . . . Gather him to the realm of the great ones, who rest with Abraham, Isaac and Jacob. . . .[64]

. . . Shelter him in the exalted places among the holy and pure, with Abraham, Isaac and Jacob. . . .

23. Save Thy people and bless Thine inheritance that Thou has assumed.[65]

Help Thy people, and bless Thy heritage . . . us.

24. Guard us under the protection of Thy wings, O our God; and keep away from us everything evil and hostile. Make our life peaceful, O Lord, have mercy upon us and upon Thy world, and save our souls, O Thou Good and Benevolent One! Praised be Thou, O God, who bearest good will, Praise be to Thee.[66]

Shelter me under the shadow of Thy wings; remove also the adversary from before us and from behind us. Grant abundant peace to Thy people Israel for ever; for Thou art the sovereign Lord of all peace everywhere. Praised be Thou, O Lord, who makest peace.

25. Praised be the Kingdom (of the Father, the Son, and the Holy Spirit) now and for evermore, into eternity without end. . . .[67]

Blessed be His name, whose glorious kingdome is for ever and ever. . . .

26. Sing a psalm to our Lord God . . . and spiritual songs in a sweet voice of melody. . . .
For unto Him belong psalms and blessings, Alleluias and spiritual songs. . . .[68]

For unto Thee, O Lord our God, . . . song and praise are becoming, hymn and psalm, blessings and thanksgiving. . . .

27. O living Being, Ruler, Lord, God Omnipotent Father, Adored One, it is worthy and true and just and meet in great seemliness of Thy holiness to praise Thee, to thank Thee, to glorify Thee, the one and only existing God. . . .[69]

O King, Lord our God, such is the duty of all creatures in Thy presence, to thank, praise, laud, glorify, extol . . . and adore Thee. Praised be Thy name for ever, . . . the great and holy God. . . .

28. O Lord, compassionate and merciful, long-suffering and plenteous in mercy, give ear to our prayer, and attend to the voice of our entreaty. . . . Thou art God alone, and there is none amongst the gods like unto Thee, O Lord; mighty in mercy, and excellent strength. . . .[70]

O God, who art slow to anger and full of mercy . . . hear our prayer and deliver us from all trouble.
. . . For there is none like unto Thee, O our Lord, living and everlasting God, mighty in strength, merciful to all Thy works. . . .

29. Bestow, O our Lord, in Thy lovingkindness . . . salvation to the oppressed, release to the prisoners, restoration to the tormented, healing to the sick. . . .[71]

As for our brethren, . . . such of them as are given over to trouble or captivity . . . may the All-Present have mercy upon them, release them, bring them to light.

30. O Compassionate, Merciful One, whose door is open to them that repent . . . open, our Lord and God the door of mercies to our prayers. . . .[72]

Open unto us, O God, the gates of mercy, before the closing of the gates. . . . Wide open are the gates of Thy mercy to all who truly seek to be reconciled with Thee.

31. The King of Kings, and Lord of Lords, who sitteth above the Cherubim. . . .[73]

The King of Kings, who sitteth above the Cherubim. . . .

33

32. Lord, we beseech Thee for the sick ones of Thy people, guard our priest . . . and . . . save alive the fruits of the earth, let them grow unharmed . . . protect our bodies and grant us peace.[74]

May it be Thy will, O Lord, speedily to send a perfect healing from heaven. Praised be Thou, O Lord, who healest the sick of Thy people Israel. . . . Bless this year unto us, O Lord, together with every kind of the produce thereof . . . give a blessing upon the face of the earth. . . . Grant abundant peace unto Thy people Israel.

33. We call upon Thee, Father of mercies and God of all comfort.[75]

May the Father of mercy have mercy upon a people that have been borne by Him. . . .

34. Father of mercies and God of all comfort, we make request. . .[76]

Father of mercies and God of comfort, we pray to Thee. . . .

35. For He is God, the Father of compassion, the merciful One, who willeth not that those whom He hath fashioned should perish, but repent and live.[77]

For as Thy name is mercy, so is Thy praiseworthy character . . . for Thou desirest not the death of a sinner, but that he return from his evil way, and live. . . .

36. Hear our prayer, O our Saviour, and return answer to our petition in Thy mercy. . . .[78]

Hear our voice, O our Lord; from Thy presence turn us not empty away; for Thou hearkenest in mercy to the prayer of Thy people Israel. . . .

37. In adoration of Thine almighty and victorious Lordship, every knee is bended, and by all shall be glorified Thy Kingship. . . . For Thou art God of peace . . . and hast made peace in heaven and earth. . . .[79]

It is our duty to adore the Lord of all things, to ascribe greatness to Him. . . . And we bend the knee and worship and glorify the supreme King of Kings. . . . He who maketh peace in His high places, may He make peace for us and for all of Israel. . . .

38. Strengthen and enlighten us, O Lord, to keep Thy commandments during this day and at all times. To the end that with enlightened minds we may ever do Thy pleasure. . . .[80]

Enlighten our eyes in Thy Law, and let our hearts cleave to Thy commandments . . . purify our hearts to serve Thee in truth. . . .

39. Father of mercies . . . who consolest us in all our troubles, hear even now the voice of our supplications, and prayers. Avert from us the wrathful punishment of our transgressions through thy loving-kindness. . . .[81]

Father of mercies . . . we beseech Thee, forgive our transgressions, O our Father . . . hear our prayer, O our King, and deliver us from all trouble and sorrow, . . . O living God . . . loving and good to all Thy works. . . .

40. Thou, Lord, by Thy mighty power, hast made sea and dry land and all that is therein. . . . Praised be Thou, O God, who takest good care of us, and hast clothed Thy servant with a garment of salvation. (Isa. 61 : 10.)[82]

Thou hast made the heavens and the earth, the sea and all that is therein. . . . Praised be Thou, O Lord, who hast chosen Thy people Israel in love.

41. Praised art Thou, O Lord God, creator of all creatures. . . .[83]

Praised art Thou, Lord, our God, King of the Universe, who hast created all. . . .

42. . . . Give us knowledge and faith and piety . . . unveil our eyes . . . so that we may seek and love Thee. . . .[84]

O put into our hearts understanding and discernment . . . enlighten our eyes in Thy Law . . . and unite our hearts to love and fear Thy name. . . .

43. . . . his soul and spirit, may it rest in green pastures, in the resting places together with Abraham, Isaac, and Jacob, and with all of Thy Saints.[85]

May God remember his soul . . . who has gone to his eternal rest . . . may his soul be bound up in the bonds of life with the souls of Abraham, Isaac and Jacob, and with the souls of other righteous who are in the paradise.

44. Lord . . . who art faithful to all of His creatures, just in all decisions, marvellous in strength and excellence. . . .[86]

Faithful art Thou, O Lord our God, and faithful are Thy words . . . righteous through all generations, O faithful God, who sayest and doest. . . .

45. Blessed Lord . . . who established the luminaries on high, and sendest forth light from heaven over all the world of mankind. . . .[87]

Be Thou blessed, O Lord our God, for the excellency of Thy handiwork, and for the bright luminaries which Thou hast made; they shall extol Thee for ever.

46. Enlighten our senses, O Lord, so that we may hearken and understand Thy life-giving commandments; and grant us through Thy grace and mercy that we may gather from them ground for our love and hope, and the salvation of our soul. . . .[88]

Enlighten our eyes in Thy Law, and let our hearts cleave to Thy commandments, be gracious unto us and teach us the statutes of life . . . put into our heart understanding and discernment . . . to do and to fulfil in loving-kindness all the words of Thy Law. . . . Because we have trusted in Thy holy name, . . . we shall rejoice and be glad in Thy salvation. . . .

47. Make me wise in Thy Law, O Lord, and enlighten our faculties with the knowledge of Thee; hallow our souls that we may be always obedient to Thy word and fulfill Thy commandments. . . .[89]

Teach me to understand Thy Law and enlighten our sense with Thy truth; hallow our souls so that we may always walk in Thy ways. . . .

48. Glorious art Thou who art to be worshipped in Thy Church in heaven by heavenly worshippers . . . by all intelligences and minds of beings of fire and spirit, who around the appointed place of the *Shekhina* of Thy greatness, in noiseless cries sing Holy and Hallelujah with mouths of fire. . . .[90]

Thou art holy and Thy name is holy, and holy beings worship Thee daily . . . all the hosts on high render praise unto Him, the Seraphim, the fiery Ophanim and the holy *Chayoth* ascribing glory and greatness . . . in tranquil joy of spirit, with pure speech and holy melody, they all exclaim with awe: 'Holy, Holy, Holy is the Lord of hosts'. . . . ('surrounding Thy *Shekhina*', in *Pirqe de R. Eliezer* IV).

49. For it is said: 'The likeness of what is above are the things which are below'.[91]

For as the realm of the earth below, so is also the realm of heaven above. (Also 34th ode of Solomo: 'The likeness of that which is below is that which is above'.) B. Ber. 58a. (Rabbis Sheshat and Shila.)

50. Maker of Creation, who hast set the seasons and times of the year out of His own power, bless Thou the cycle of this year of Thy bounty, O Lord![92]

Bless this year unto us, O Lord our God . . . give a blessing upon the face of the earth. . . . Praised art Thou, O Lord, who blessest the years.

51. O Lord, put custody on my mouth and a guard upon my lips, lest my heart fall into words of malice. . . .[93]

O God, keep my tongue from evil and my lips from speaking guile. . . .

35

52. Save Thy servants, O my Lord, who
hope in Thee
For the afflicted and those in captivity
Deliver them, God of Israel, from all
their tribulations
Send them, O Lord, help from Thy
holiness
And protect them from Sion.[94]

As for our brethren, the household of
Israel, save those who are given over to
affliction or captivity . . . may the All-
present have mercy upon them and bring
them forth from tribulation to enlarge-
ment, from darkness to light . . . may it
be the will of our Father in heaven to
establish the Temple, the house of life, in
Jerusalem, speedily, in our days.

Interpretation of Comparison

This list, which might easily be augmented, registers only early
liturgical texts, taken mainly from the Eucharistic services. The prayers
of the Offices (canonical hours) have only been touched on in this
comparison. Nor were the Roman Breviary or the Byzantine *Euchologion* actually considered. In spite of all these limitations, we have
before us a remarkable list of Christian analogies with post-biblical
Hebrew prayers. Nor can it be said that these Hebraic elements are
isolated phrases which were torn out of their context; in almost every
instance there is an unmistakable parallelism of structure and disposition
of the prayers of Christian and Jewish sources. Quite a number of
problems arise when we carefully examine these analogies. The first
question, where do we find most of the similarities, is easily answered.
No less than seventeen of the fifty-two quotations stem from the
Apostolic Constitutions.

This fact will not cause much surprise to the theologian. For the
past sixty years or so we have been aware of the intimate relation
between Jewish and Christian liturgies as expressed in the second,
seventh and eighth books of the *Apostolic Constitutions*, which also
contain the so-called Clementine liturgy. It was Kaufmann Kohler
who, in 1893, drew attention to the Judaistic elements in that great
ecclesiastical work.[95]

There are apparently only a few post-biblical Hebraisms to be
found in the Roman liturgy. Does this fact mean that the Roman
Church was influenced so little by Hebrew ideas and forms? Quite
to the contrary! Biblicisms are most frequent in this liturgy, and great
parts of the liturgical books, especially the Graduale and Antiphonale,
consist almost exclusively of translated scriptural passages.[96] Monsignor
Duchesne, the famous authority on liturgy, writes:

At Rome, at all events down to the ninth century, hymns were unknown;
chants, psalms, and other scriptural canticles alone being used. . . . The

offices . . . were entirely composed of psalms, antiphons and responds, and prayers. This primitive Roman usage agrees exactly with what was observed at Jerusalem in the time of Silvia. . . .[97]

It is evident that this remark does not refer to all liturgies in the Latin language, but to that of the city of Rome, which had its own tradition, and it is a well-known fact that the Roman liturgy was extremely conservative when it came to the introduction of non-scriptural passages for musically rendered texts. How is it possible, then, to reconcile the abundance of biblical Hebraisms, including names, phrases and acclamations, occurring in the Roman liturgy, with the lack of post-biblical Hebraisms therein? If there were no other evidence, one might assume that the Church severed all relations with Judaism soon after the first century; yet such a hypothesis is well-nigh untenable in view of the many midrashic elements in the writings of the Church Fathers up to Jerome and even later.[98] Moreover, the list of the Roman bishops shows a distinct influx of Judaeo-Christianity, of which Clement, apparently, was a staunch advocate. Paulinism and the doctrine of universal Gentile Christianity did not conquer Rome until a full century after Paul's death. Indeed, even in the third century Rome was still a subject of dispute between Gentile and Judaean Christianity, as demonstrated by the Pseudo-Clementines in almost every page of their writings.[99] Thus, there is ample evidence of continuous interrelation between Rome and Christian Jewry. Why, then, the strictly biblical (and anti-post-biblical) attitude of the Roman liturgy? The answer is that very few authentic Roman liturgical texts have come down to us. The first complete source, the *Sacramentarium Leonianum*, was probably written in the seventh century; until then we have only fragments, hints, quotations, etc.[100] In the three centuries which had elapsed since the redaction of the Pseudo-Clementines and the *Leonianum*, practice and spirit of the Roman liturgy, had, as everything else in Rome, undergone a fundamental change. Too much had happened during those 350 years that had shaken all of Europe and the Near East. Gentile Christianity had become the state religion. The cultural and military power was centred in East Rome (Constantinople) while Rome was relegated to a secondary provincial status. The final break with Judaism had been made in Nicaea in the year 325, and outlawed Judaeo-Christianity collapsed. Nor were the relations between the two Romes always friendly. The traffic lines had so changed that

37

West Rome lost many of its customers who now flocked to Constantinople. Small wonder, then, that everything Jewish was more or less taboo, except Scripture itself, which had, for all practical purposes, lost its Hebrew character; had lost it in fact for the next twelve centuries to come.

Much more surprising is the problem of the high ratio of the Old Armenian liturgy which is represented by twelve quotations. Did the Armenian Church maintain such close relations to post-biblical Judaism, or did it serve as a refuge for the Judaeo-Christians? If so, who transmitted the Jewish lore to that remote land? This problem is, if anything, even more puzzling than that of the Hebraisms in the Roman Church. Beyond the bare fact that the Armenian Church has many Jewish or Old Testament customs, not much can be found in ordinary reference works.[101] Once having discovered certain affinities, verified and confirmed by others, it is the inexorable duty of the scholar to trace back these connexions as far as possible. The problem with which we are confronted here is: Does the Armenian Church contain Jewish elements beyond the Hebraisms quoted above? If so, what is their origin?

Armenia was the first state where Christianity was adopted officially by the government and the dynasty as early as the fourth century (302–312). Yet, the Bible was translated into Armenian only a full century later, probably from the Old Syrian version.[102] Many typically Jewish customs were then and still are in usage in the ritual of the Armenian Church. We mention here only a few: (1) The sacrifice of animals, especially of the Paschal Lamb.[103] (2) On the day preceding the feast of the Transfiguration of Christ, the Church commemorates the Jewish festival of Tabernacles. On that day people sprinkle each other with water when they meet in the streets, obviously an ancient allusion to the Temple feast of drawing water during Tabernacles week.[104] (3) The Old Armenian lectionary is replete with Old Testament and other references to Judaism.[105] (4) Some mild dietary laws are still in force for the Armenian clergy. (5) There occur certain Hebrew terms for Armenian ceremonies, e.g.:

> kahana—priest (Hebr. kohen).
>
> karos—herald, crier (Hebr. kora). (Possibly a contamination of the Hebrew word, the Persian karoza and the Greek keryx.)

sabbat—sabbath (Hebr. *shabbat*).

bema—part of the altar—*bima*—Greek: *bema*.

abba—father—*abba*, etc.[106]

These facts of obvious Judaizing were known to the neighbouring sister-Church of Syria. In a series of official epistles exchanged between the Syrian patriarchs and their contemporary Armenian *Katholikoi* (*ca.* 1070–1136), the Syrian princes of the Church accused the Armenian Church of retaining Jewish ceremonies, while, at the same time, the Armenian *Katholikos* accused the Syrians of having relapsed into paganism. The chief arguments of the Syrians were that the Armenian Church used unleavened bread for the Eucharist; that it did not mix water into the wine of the Eucharist, just as the Jews did; that it sacrificed a lamb on the day of resurrection (i.e. Easter); and that it followed in other major matters the Jewish practice, e.g. in the hereditary succession of the Armenian patriarchate.

Whereupon the Armenians countered with the charge that the Syrians, contrary to the account of the Gospels, mix water into the wine of the Eucharist; that they used 'unclean food' such as oil into which insects or other animals had fallen, and were thus acting against 'the Law'. Finally, they objected strongly to the Syrian custom of adoring everything grown in the shape of a cross, calling such behaviour not much better than idolatry.[107]

All these facts point in one direction: the early Armenian Church must have been closely familiar with Jewish laws and doctrines. There are some historical facts which support this theory. We know that Tigranes, King of Armenia, invaded Southern Syria and Northern Palestine in the years 83–69 B.C., taking many Jews as prisoners to Armenia.[108] Moses of Chorene (fifth century A.D.) mentions seven cities where these Jews were settled; and Faustus of Byzantium, a good source for the time of A.D. 317–90, relates that King Shapur II of Persia removed about 200,000 Jews from Armenian cities to Persia into captivity; this must have meant the tragic end of Armenian Jewry.[109] It seems that in the four centuries of settlement the Jewish settlers had developed very satisfactorily; nor had they ever lost their contact with their people in Syria and Palestine. The Talmud tells us of some scholars who came from Armenia and mentions the flourishing Jewish Academy of Nisibis, on the Armenian border. We learn.

also, that the Jews of Antioch paid ransom for Jewish prisoners of war to Armenia in the second century.[110] Let us not forget that it was in Antioch, where, at that time, the conflict between Jews, Judaeo-Christians, and Gentile Christianity was carried on rather heatedly. When we furthermore recall that Armenia was closely linked to Syria; that Philo was one of the writers most popular with Armenian scholars;[111] that their customs remind us strongly of Jewish ceremonies; and that their liturgy contains a surprisingly high proportion of biblical and even post-biblical Hebraisms, we may safely assume that the tradition of the Armenian Church and its liturgy go back to the centuries when there was a well-established Jewish settlement, that is, between 100 and 380. This must have been the crucial period, since after that time and through the Persian invasions Jewry had disappeared in Armenia, and before that time the question of Christianity had no relevance.

THE 'JUDAIZING ARMENIAN CHURCH'

It was Conybeare who came closest to the problem of old Armenian Christianity. His edition of *The Key of the Truth*, an ancient document of the so-called Paulician Church, sheds light upon issues that were totally unexplored heretofore.

The origin of the term Paulician or Pauliani is controversial; so is also the anti-trinitarian doctrine of the sect. Some conservative Armenian scholars minimize the relevance of this group for the development of the independent (Orthodox) Armenian Church. Others, such as Arpee, and most recently, the Wardapet Abadjan (Vicar General of the Armenian Church in Jaffa) agree fully with Conybeare's assessment of the basic documents. The main difficulty which stands in the way of a unequivocal solution of the problem seems to be the question of documentary authenticity.

The chief document of this sect is *The Key of the Truth*. Its doctrine is virtually identical with the Judaeo-Christian Ebionites, of whom Hippolytus writes:

> They have Jewish customs, and claim that they are justified by the Law; and they claim that Jesus was justified and right in observing the Law.[112]

It was Paul of Samosata who was mainly responsible for spreading this Judaeo-Christian sect in Armenia. Even the modern Orthodox Church of Armenia has retained many of the customs of the old

Paulician sect. Here only a few of them which were adopted by the Orthodox Church are quoted:

(1) The Sunday begins on Saturday afternoon and ends on the eve of the next day, that is it lasts from sunset to sunset.

(2) The Armenians add 'Amen' to every prayer said by the priest.

(3) The Ave Maria and the devotion of the Rosary are unknown in the Armenian Church.[113]

(4) The Armenians have always spoken of Sunday simply as the first day of the week. The Greek word *Kyriake* (Lord's day) hardly occurs before John of Odsun (eighth century).

(5) The Old Armenians did not speak of churches, but of Synagogues, *Proseuchae*, and of shrines.[114]

For these 'judaizing' customs the non-orthodox Armenians were sharply vituperated. In one of these polemics we read:

> Nor do the Armenians keep the festival of Christ's birth. On the contrary, they are downcast in countenance and in tribulation on the very day of this holy feast, *just like the Jews*. . . .[115]

From the foregoing observations Conybeare's conclusions concerning the Adoptionist–Paulician Church are logical deductions. He writes (p. clxii): 'The Paulicians were probably the remnant of an old Judaeo-Christian Church, which had spread up through Edessa into Albania' (and other Armenian provinces).

A more recent author, Arpee, reaches a similar conclusion:

> The early Judaized Christianity of Armenia found entrance in that country from Antioch, where Unitarianism was always much in vogue. Not only was Paul of Samosata, the Unitarian leader, a Bishop of Antioch, but so was also his kindred spirit, Nestorius, native of Germanicia (Marash), before he became Bishop of Constantinople.[116]

In general, one may conclude: post-biblical Jewish tradition expanded in the Orient more after its separation from Christianity (Nicaea, 325) than before. Previously, Judaeo-Christians had thought their belief to be well compatible with Judaism, the faith of their fathers. It was only after the final separation that they realized there was no other choice left but that between Judaism and universal Gentile Christianity. This dates from about 250, when the serious struggle between the parent- and the daughter-religion had reached its height, to the year 380 which marked the end of the Jewish settlements in Armenia. We shall see later (in Chapter VII) that in the sphere of liturgical music, no less than in that of ceremonies, the Armenian tradition has preserved many ancient Jewish features.

For the present, our first task will be the quest for confirmation of our theories in those rubrics of liturgy which are always the most primal, the most essential, and the most informative of them all, namely the arrangements of lessons or pericopes throughout the year, the so-called lectionary. This rule is valid for all liturgies and traditions that have been discussed thus far. Hence, the next two chapters will be dedicated to the study of the scriptural lessons in Judaism and Christianity.

NOTES CHAPTER II

1. The entire problem is taken up and discussed *in extenso* in the once famous work of C. Vitringa, *De Synagoga Vetere* (Franequerae, 1696). Cf. in particular Ch. I and II. Also Oesterley, *Jewish Background of the Christian Liturgy*, pp. 95 ff.

2. St Jerome, ad Euagrium: Et ut sciamus traditiones Apostolicas sumptas de Vetere Testamento: quod Aaron et filii eius atque Levitae in Templo fuerunt, hoc sibi Episcopi et Presbyteri et Diaconi vindicent in Ecclesia. (Cf. Vitringa, op. cit., p. 9.)

3. The *ammei-ha'aretz* (country yokels) were either ridiculed or frowned upon by the scholars in Jerusalem. The New Testament term *nepios* (Matt. 11:25; 21:15, 16; Luke 10:21, etc.) comes next to the Hebrew expression. On the sharp, almost deadly enmity between the 'ignorant' and the 'learned' Jew, cf. Bousset, *Die Religion des Judentums im Neutestamentlichen Zeitalter*, pp. 216 ff.

4. Hence the enmity of the Oriental Churches towards instrumental music; this was a prerogative of the Temple, not of the Synagogue. For only the Temple employed a large priestly orchestra and a trained chorus. Even the Western Church continued its antagonism towards instrumental music until late into the twelfth century. Sidonius Apollinaris praises Theoderic, King of the Visigoths, for not using an organ even for secular occasions. (PL, LVIII, 449). In Byzantium, the organ was used at the imperial court to add pomp to all secular affairs exclusively. In the Pope's Sistine Chapel, no organ is permitted to the present day. Cf. Pope Pius X, *Motu Proprio*, 150: 'Although the music proper to the Church is purely vocal music, music with the accompaniment of the organ is also tolerated'.

5. Cf. G. Bickell, *Messe und Pascha*, pp. 100–22. Also W. F. Skene, *The Lord's Supper and the Paschal Ritual*. A middle position between the Church Fathers, Vitringa, and Bickell is held by W. Oesterley in his *The Jewish Background of the Christian Liturgy*. In this book he says (p. 87): 'However . . ., remembering that the synagogal liturgy was taken over from that of the Temple we agree with Prof. Bartlett that Christ was more associated with the synagogal type of worship than with that of the Temple. . . .'

6. Even among the so-called synagogal elements we find several instances where the Church has preserved the original and authentic practice of the Temple in contradistinction to Judaism which frequently renounced those elements, for the very reason that the Church had borrowed them. A good illustration of this relation is the Doxology, whose importance in the Synagogue steadily decreased, whereas it became all-important in the Church. See *infra* Chapter IX.

7. Almost the entire material is discussed in S. Krauss, *Synagogale Altertümer*, pp. 11–14. He maintains—not absolutely convincingly—that wherever Christian literature uses the term Synagogue for Church, it does so either in a derogatory mocking sense or in order to denote certain Judaistic inclinations within those churches. Cf. Harnack, *Die Mission und Ausbreitung des Christentums*, I, p. 429; C. Mommert, *Der Teich Bethesda bei Jerusalem*, p. 62;

against this theory A. Deissmann, *Die Urgeschichte des Christentums im Licht der Sprachforschung* (1910), p. 35, also Harnack in *Sitzungsberichte der Preuss. A. d. Wiss.* (1915), pp. 754 ff.

8. Against this, Schürer, *Geschichte d. jüd. Volkes z. Zt. Christi* (3rd ed.), II, p. 27, n. 48; pp. 361 ff. The Church Fathers mentioned above, viz. St Ignatius (*Ep. ad Polycarp.* IV), Theophilus of Antioch (*Ad Autolycum*, II, 14), Firmilian of Caesarea (*Ep. ad Cyprian.* in Cyprian's *Opera*, ep. 75) were all aware of the Jewish connotation of the term synagogue; only in the case of Epiphanius (*Adv. Haeres*, XXX, 18) do we meet an exception.

9. Krauss proves his point, following Schürer's argument, that in this case a church of the Ebionites or Nazarenes (Judaeo-Christians) is called Synagogue, in order to stress their Jewish leanings. In the Epistle to the Hebrews (10:25) the term synagogue may have been used in a neutral or syncretistic vein, but certainly not in Hermas, *Mandat*, XI, 9. (In Gebhardt and Harnack's ed. of the Apostolic Fathers.)

10. The text of Clement's Epistle is in every edition of the Apostolic Fathers. Of the relatively few scholars who tried to solve the chronological contradiction, G. Hoennicke (*Das Judenchristentum* [1911], p. 199) believes that 'Clement praises the Temple and the Ceremonial Law merely in order to stress the necessity of Law and Order'. While the author is convinced of Clement's Jewish extraction, there is no word about the apparent anachronism of our passage. The same attitude is represented by E. von Dobschütz in his profound study *Christian Life in the Primitive Church* (Engl. edition New York, 1904). He says (pp. 805–6): 'The O.T. legislation appears only as an analogy, as a proof that generally speaking there must be order. . . .' Similarly O. Pfleiderer, *Primitive Christianity* (IV Engl. ed. 1911), p. 343: 'The O.T. organization of priests and sacrifices may teach us that it is God's will that each member of the Church should abide in his own proper place and order. . . .'

No attempt is made to synchronize the passage in question. All things considered, we have only four alternatives:

(a) The Epistle of Clement was written at a time when the Temple was still in existence; so Wieseler and most of the older, mainly Catholic, authorities.

(b) Our passage or the entire Epistle is a work of much later origin and has been attributed to Clement by the actual writer in order to give it more authority. Thus J. H. Ropes, *The Apostolic Age* (N.Y., 1906), p. 319.

(c) The Epistle was written after the destruction of the Temple; but Clement wanted to set a pattern for the new institution of the Church, similar to that of the Temple. Therefore, he described the Temple as an actual existing reality. Thus T. Schermann, *Die allgemeine Kirchenordnung* (Paderborn, 1916), III, pp. 606–7; also Schürer, I, p. 653 and Krauss, op. cit., p. 89.

(d) The entire reference is made only for pastoral reasons in order to emphasize the importance of ecclesiastical discipline, as it had been exacted in the Temple. Thus the majority of recent scholars, as Pfleiderer, Harnack, and others.

A distinct reference to the chronological discrepancy is made in Herzog-Hauck, *Real Encyclopädie für protest. Theologie*, IV, 169: 'Chapters 40 and 41 do not prove that the Temple was still standing . . . for other authors who wrote undoubtedly after the Temple's destruction (Barnabas, Epistle to Diognetus, and the Talmudists) speak about the activities of the Temple in the present tense'.

This writer sees the problem the following way: Chapter I of the Barnabas Epistle is devoted to the destruction of the Temple. These are the pertaining passages: 'Moreover I will tell you likewise concerning the Temple, how these wretched men being led astray set their hope on the building, and not on their God that made them, as being a house of God. For like the Gentile almost they consecrated Him in the Temple, but what saith the Lord abolishing the Temple? Furthermore He saith again, "Behold, they that pulled down this Temple themselves shall build it." [Isa. 49:17.] So it comes to pass; for because they went to war it was pulled down by their enemies. Now also the very servants of their enemies shall build it up . . . but let us inquire whether there be any Temple of God. There is: in the place where He Himself undertakes to make and finish it. . . . Give heed then that the Temple of the Lord may be built gloriously. How? . . . by receiving the remission of our sins and hoping on the Name we became new, created afresh from the beginning. Wherefore God dwelleth truly in our habitation within us . . . this is a spiritual Temple built up to the Lord'. Thus far the Barnabas Epistle. Not only does he not speak of any real Temple in existence, he clearly hints at its destruction and is by no means concerned about it.

The Epistle to Diognetus is unmistakably an anti-Jewish propaganda document of Gentile Christianity. The anonymous author calls himself 'A Teacher of the Gentiles'. He refers to most of the Jewish laws as 'superstitions' and states for his purpose that the Jewish offerings were no better than those of the pagans. In his opinion, circumcision is ridiculous, and observance of festivals and fasts is a folly and a common silliness. His references to the Temple are made in a hostile and even vicious vein. They do not constitute any historic evidence either way. Concerning the Talmudists: their way of describing a past event is either in the form of a *praesens historicum*, or in the way of newspaper headings like 'Cleopatra Commits Suicide'. It has no bearing whatever on the actual time of the event described.

11. How highly venerated the Thrice-Holy was among the Jews may be seen from a Talmudic statement: 'Since the destruction of the Temple the World is sustained by the *Kedusha*' (*Sot. 49a*).

12. On Hebraisms in the Greek vernacular (*Koine*), cf. *Byzantinische Zeitschrift*, III, p. 155; IV, p. 185; XI, pp. 190, 599; XII, p. 442. See also *Zeitschrift fur Alttest. Wiss.*, XXII, pp. 83–113. On the recessive tendency of the Church towards the Temple, cf. K. Kohler, *The Origins of the Synagogue and Church*, p. 258.

13. *Yom.* 20, 2; *Ber.* 11, 2; *Suc.* 53, 1; *M. Sot.* VII, 8.

14. Cf. Krauss, op. cit., pp. 67–72.

15. *Jer. Ber.* 1, 7; *B. Tam.* 5, 1.

16. Cf. Krauss, loc. cit.

17. *M. Yom.* VII, 7.

18. The sacrificial cult did not stop immediately after the Temple's destruction; we hear occasionally of private sacrifices on the ruins of the Temple. Even some sects of the early Christian Church seemed to have offered animal sacrifices; cf. Conybeare: 'Les Sacrifices d'animaux dans les anciennes Églises chrétiennes', in *Actes du premier congrès internat. de l'histoire des religions* (Paris, 1900), II, pp. 44–50. Also Krauss, op. cit., pp. 88 ff.

19. Cf. Krauss, op. cit., pp. 96 ff; also F. Heiler, *Das Gebet*, pp. 221–2, with numerous further references.

20. Ps. 40 : 6–8, 10.

21. Cf. Krauss, op. cit., p. 97. It is interesting to note that the Karaites, a medieval Jewish sect, set the lesson, not the prayer, in the place of the sacrifice. Cf. J. Mann's article on 'Anan Liturgy' in the *Journal of Jewish Lore and Philosophy*, I (1919, Cincinnati).

22. Cf. *Ber.* IX. The Doxology of the Church originated in the Temple, not in the Synagogue, as Hoennicke, *Das Judenchristentum*, p. 258, erroneously believes. The entire question of the Doxology and its responses will be discussed extensively in Chapter IX. Here again, the Samaritans, the Sadducees, and even the Karaites have preserved the custom of the Temple and it does not appear improbable that the Church fashioned some of its liturgical ceremonies after the pattern of these sects which were always hostile to Pharisaism.

23. Cf. *Ar.* 11b.

24. *B. Suc.* 53a.

25. *B. Chag.* 5b. Cf. *JE*, article 'Joshua ben Chananya'. His word about the prophet Elijah (*Eduyot* VIII), seems to me a veiled expression of his hope for a reconciliation with the Judaeo-Christians. The sharp hostility against this sect was only a later development; we find even in the Talmud an anecdote about James, the brother of Jesus and head of the Judaeo-Christian group showing his great popularity among the Jews. ('*Aboda Sara* 16b; also *Koheleth R.* 1, 9.) In this story R. Eleazar suffers a misfortune and R. Akiba urges him to meditate, if he did not once commit a sin, for which he is now punished. And really R. Eleazar recalls that at a time long ago he had found pleasure in discussing the scriptural exegesis of a certain James. This report corroborates the quotation of Hegesippus, as given in Eusebius, *Hist. eccles.*, II, Chapter I, and with Josephus, *Antiquitates*, XX, 9, 1.

26. The liturgical acclamations of the various Christian rites are possibly the remnants

44

of ancient litanies, as e.g. *Kyrie eleison, Domine miserere,* etc., the so-called Diaconal Litanies. This name refers to a time when the deacon was still the liturgical protagonist. The *Kyrie eleison,* in particular, has reached far beyond the strictly liturgical sphere and has entered secular poetry as a general acclamation (in the medieval 'Leisen'). More about it in Chapter VIII, 'The Liturgical Acclamations'. In Judaism most of the litanies in use are recited before or during the season of the High Holydays, and an extensive and popular litany with the refrain *Hoshano* (Osanna) meaning 'Save us now!', is solemnly sung at Tabernacles.

27. The Gallican, Mozarabic, North African, etc., rites are extinct regional branches of the Roman rite; but the language used in these provincial liturgies was always Latin.

28. The use of living languages in the Roman Church is strictly limited since the Council of Trent (sess. XXII, c. 8). Mass, especially, must be celebrated in Latin.

29. The most important works on this question are: A. Schweitzer, *Geschichte der Leben-Jesu Forschung* (Tübingen, 1906); J. Weiss, *Das älteste Evangelium* (Göttingen, 1903); J. Wellhausen, *Einleitung in die ersten drei Evangelien* (Berlin, 1905); Strack-Billerbeck, *Kommentar zum NT aus rabbinischen und midraschischen Quellen* (4 vols., 1923–6); D. A. Chwolson, *Das letzte Passamahl Christi* (2nd ed., Leipzig, 1908); C. Torrey, *The Earliest Documents of the Primitive Church* (1940); S. Zeitlin, *The Crucifixion of Jesus* (New York, 1944–5).

30. In fairness to the older scholars it must be said that it was only in the last fifty years that Eastern sources (both literary and musical) have become available to the general scientific reader (*Patrologia Orientalis, Oriens Christianus,* etc.). Nor is it longer since Jewish scholars ventured into the field of comparing and studying the music of the Synagogue and the Church; yet their first attempts were rather primitive and naive, and have not progressed much beyond that stage. Not that Judaism was not at all times aware of its great original contribution to the song of the Church!

Manuello of Rome (a contemporary of Dante), a poet and satirist, expressed not only his personal opinions when he caustically remarks:

> 'What says musick to the Gentiles?
> Stolen was I, yea, stolen from the Hebrew land.' (Gen. 40 : 15)

This claim is very old in Judaism and usually coupled with the admonition, not to teach Christians traditional Jewish tunes.

31. *B. Sot.* 33a.

32. Rabbi Jose in *Jer. Sot.* III, 1; also *B. Sot.* 33.

33. Too much of Aramaic, however, was disliked by the rabbis, when it came to liturgical texts. The prayers compulsory in Hebrew are listed in *M. Sot.* VII, 2.

34. Cf. Justin, *Apol.,* I, 31; also Justin, *Dialog. contra Tryphonem,* c. 72.

35. Cf. Acts 6:9; 9:29.

36. Acts 21:40 and 22:2; also I Cor. 14:16 ff.

37. The literature about Aramaisms in the New Testament has grown so numerous in the last decades, that a special bibliography on this subject has become a strongly felt desideratum. The most extensive bibliographies in C. Torrey, *The Earliest Documents of the Primitive Church* (1940); also G. F. Moore, *Judaism,* II, and G. Kittel, *Die Probleme des Palästinensischen Spätjudentums und das Urchristentum.*

38. E.g. Pax vobiscum—et cum spiritu tuo; (*Const. Apost.,* VIII, ch. 13, 1). Repleatur os meum laude, ut cantem gloriam tuam tota die magnitudinem tuam. (Ps. 71:8.)

(Insertion) Patris; amen; et Filii, amen; et spiritus sancti, amen;
        Nunc et semper et in secula seculorum, amen.

Magnificate Dominum meum; et exaltemus nomen eius in idipsum (Ps. 34 : 3). This passage is taken from the Greek liturgy of St. James (Greek text in Hammond, *Liturgies Eastern and Western,* p. 36). Very interesting are the remarks of C. F. Burney, *The Aramaic Origin of the Fourth Gospel,* pp. 3 ff, wherein the author speculates about a probable influence of the Hellenistic Jews upon the style of the *Koine* as used in the New Testament and the apostolic writings.

39. Cf. A. Baumstark, *Liturgie comparée* (1939), p. 12.

40. Felix Perles's well-documented refutation of Bousset's work seems to have

impressed upon some of the New Testament scholars the value of rabbinical sources. G. Kittel speaks very much to the point, op. cit., pp. 5–20. Cf. G. F. Moore, 'Christian Writers on Judaism', in *Harvard Theol. Review*, XIV (1921).

41. For other comparisons see Oesterley, *The Jewish Background of the Christian Liturgy* (London, 1925), and P. Levertoff's fine study 'Synagogue Worship in the First Century' in *Liturgy and Worship*, ed. by W. K. L. Clarke and C. Harris, pp. 60–77. Also I. Elbogen, *Der jüdische Gottesdienst* (ELB).

42. *Liturgy of the Apost. Church of Armenia*, ed. Essaie Asdradzadouriantz (London, 1887); Missa Catechumenorum.

43. *Missal of the Armenian Church*, ed. Theodoros Isaac (Fresno, 1932), p. 27.

44. *Constitutiones Ecclesiae Aegyptiacae*, ed. X. Funk (together with the *Constitutiones Apostolorum*) (Paderborn, 1905), p. 99.

45. Cf. E. Werner, 'The Doxology in Synagogue and Church', *HUCA* (1945–6), p. 297. Cf. Baumstark, op. cit., pp. 87, 89. Here, with the scholar's instinct, he feels that this passage must be 'of the greatest antiquity', adding: 'Nevertheless, one does not find a Jewish Model of this passage'. In fact, this passage belongs to the few prayers of the old pre-Christian Synagogue.

46. *Sacrament. Serapionis*, ed. Funk, pp. 174–5.

47. Hammond, *Liturgies Eastern and Western* (London, 1878), p. 35. (Greek Liturgy of St James.)

48. BLEW, p. 53; Greek Liturgy of St James.

49. BLEW, p. 4; Clementine Liturgy.

50. BLEW, p. 8; Clementine Liturgy.

51. CAF, VII, ch. 25, pp. 410 f.

52. CAF, VII, ch. 33, pp. 426 ff.

53. CAF, VII, ch. 34, pp. 426 f.

54. CAF, pp. 428–9.

55. CAF, pp. 430–1.

56. CAF, pp. 432–3

57. CAF, pp. 434–5; also II, 36, 59; V, 20.

58. CAF, pp. 436–7.

59. CAF, pp. 438–9.

60. CAF, pp. 440–1.

61. Cf. A. Maltzew, *Die Liturgien der Orthodox-Katholischen Kirche des Morgenlandes* (Berlin, 1894); *None*; office of hours.

62. CAF, pp. 438–9.

63. CAF, p. 544.

64. CAF, p. 551.

65. CAF, p. 553 (after Ps. 28 : 9).

66. Hammond, op. cit., pp. 88–9; Liturgy of Constantinople.

67. BLEW, p. 362; Liturgy of Constantinople.

68. Cf. *Liturgy of the Apost. Church of Armenia*, ed. Essaie Asdradzadouriantz; during the Communion.

69. Hammond, op. cit., p. 106; Liturgy of Constantinople.

70. J. N. W. Robertson, *The Divine Liturgy of John Chrysostom and Basil the Great* (London, 1894), p. 11.

71. A. J. Maclean, *East Syrian Daily Offices* (London, 1894), p. 108.

72. Ibid., p. 103.

73. C. Wessely, *Fragments liturgiques et prières*, p. 430. (Papyrus Berlin 9794.)

74. Ibid., p. 439.

75. Ibid., pp. 442–3.

76. F. C. Conybeare, *Rituale Armenorum* (Oxford, 1905), p. 303.

77. Ibid., p. 304.

78. Ibid., p. 306.

79. Ibid., p. 451.

80. Ibid., pp. 459–60. It is remarkable that in the Armenian as well as in the early Greek liturgies the metaphorical interpretation of the word 'light' in the morning prayers

follows closely the Hebrew pattern, where immediately after the expression of gratitude for the light of the day thanksgiving is pronounced for the spiritual light of the Law and of the revelation.

81. Ibid., p. 472.

82. Ibid.

83. Ibid., p. 67. The typically Hebraic formula of the eulogy (*beraka*) has entered no Christian liturgy to such an extent as the Armenian; there we encounter frequently and at almost every occasion the ancient Hebrew formula. Only two examples will be quoted here in addition to the text:

'Praised art Thou, Lord our God, who through Thy law hast enjoined us to offer unto Thy Godhead fowls, turtle-doves, and young pigeons, which are a figure of the truth.' (Conybeare, op. cit., pp. 65-6.)

'Praised art Thou, Lord, God of Abraham, Isaac, and Jacob, who didst bless the offerings of the ancients by means of the preaching of the patriarchs.' (Ibid., p. 66.)

84. G. Wobbermin, 'Altchristliche liturgische Stücke', in *Texte und Untersuchungen*, XVII (New Series II, 3b), p. 18; Liturgy of Serapion.

85. Ibid., p. 14; also Conybeare, op. cit., p. 248, which is full of post-biblical Hebraisms. 'Many passages in the Church Fathers indicate that the prayers for the dead are Jewish in origin. . . .' (Salfeld, *Martyrologium* (1896-8.)

86. Clement of Rome, *Ep. I*, 59-60.

87. Conybeare, op. cit., p. 477.

88. Hammond, op. cit., p. 268; East-Syrian Liturgy.

89. Cf. Donald Attwater, *Eastern Catholic Worship* (New York, 1945), p. 189; Liturgy of Malabar—Thomas Syrian.

90. Maclean, *East Syrian Daily Offices*, p. 217.

91. Moses bar Kepha, *Two Commentaries on the Jacobite Liturgy*, ed. Connolly and Codrington (London, 1913), p. 35.

92. A. Maltzew, *Menologion der Orthodoxen Kirche* (Berlin, 1894); prayer for September 1st (13th) (New ecclesiastical year).

93. Roman Missal, before Praefatio; see also P. Battifol, *History of the Roman Breviary*, p. 115.

94. Roman Breviary (on weekdays); see Battifol, op. cit., p. 201, n. 2; also L. Duchesne, *Christian Worship: Its Origin and Evolution* (London, 1903), p. 233, and R. Stapper—D. Baier., *Catholic Liturgics* (Paterson, New Jersey, 1935), pp. 140-1.

95. Bousset, who twenty-two years later made the same original 'discovery', did not even bother to mention Kohler's really intuitive essay. Cf. K. Kohler, 'Ursprünge und Grundformen der synagogalen Liturgie', *MGWJ* (1893) and W. Bousset, *Eine jüdische Gebetssammlung in der Clementinischen Liturgie* (Göttingen, 1915-16).

96. Cf. P. Pietschmann, O.S.B., 'Die nicht dem Psalter entnommenen Messgesangstücke auf ihre Textgestalt untersucht' in *Jahrbücher für Liturgiewissenschaft*, 1932-3, pp. 87 ff; also F. Marbach, *Carmina Scripturarum* (Fribourg, 1907) and P. Dom Johner, *The Chants of the Vatican Graduale* (1940), pp. 4-10.

97. Cf. L. Duchesne, *Christian Worship: Its Origin and Evolution* (London, 1903), p. 452, n. 1.

98. Cf. W. Bacher, *Die Aggada der Tannaiten*, vol. I; S. Krauss, 'The Jews in the Works of the Church Fathers', *JQR*, V (1892), pp. 122-57, VI (1893), pp. 82-99, VI (1894), pp. 225-61; L. Ginzberg, *Die Aggada bei den Kirchenvätern* (Amsterdam-Berlin, 1898-1900); E. Werner, 'The Attitude of the Church Fathers to Hebrew Psalmody', *Review of Religion*, May, 1943; see also *infra* Chapter IX, on the Doxology in Church and Synagogue.

99. The best recent work on Judaeo-Christian sources is Carl Schmidt, 'Die Pseudo-Clementinen', in *Texte und Untersuchungen*, XLVI, 2, 1928, esp. pp. 242, 251, 287 ff, 313 ff, etc. Of older studies Hilgenfeldt's *Ketzergeschichte des Urchristentums* (Leipzig, 1889) is still a highly valuable source of information. Most recent is H. J. Schöps's *Theologie und Geschichte des Judenchristentums* (Tübingen, 1949), which contains valuable material. Since discovery of the 'Dead Sea Scrolls' the entire problem of Judaeo-Christianity has to be approached *de novo*.

100. Best expounded in A. Fortescue's splendid work *The Mass* (London–New York,

1922); cf. pp. 110–24. In passing it may be noted that in most Christian prayers concerned with death or burial or commemoration, one encounters post-biblical Hebraisms and can recognize the influence of midrashic elements; cf. D. Kaufmann, *Gesammelte Schriften* (Frankfurt, 1915), III, 517; also S. Krauss, op. cit. and L. Ginzberg op. cit.

101. Of the older reference works, the *Protestantische Real-Enzyklopädie* (P. Gelzer), contents itself by simply stating: 'A third important element is the specific Judaean character of the (Armenian) Church. The priests, especially the high clergy, resemble closely the dynastic institutions of the Jewish High-Priest cast'. No comment is given, no explanation is even suggested.

The first relevant source beyond this helpless registration of strange facts was given by Conybeare in his edition and translation of the ancient Armenian work *The Key of the Truth* (London, 1898). This important theological work conveys the doctrines of the so-called Adoptionist Church. Says Conybeare: 'The entire Christology of this Armenian sect . . . was Adoptionist, i.e. Christ was born a man by a virgin, who subsequently lost her virginity, and was chosen by God, when he had reached maturity, as His (adopted) Son. He never attained divinity, nor is the Trinity recognized by this sect. . . .' (*Key to the Truth*, pp. xxv ff.) Much later, a contemporary scholar has eventually taken pains to elaborate on the ecclesiastical history of the Armenian Church. Leon Arpee, in his *A History of Armenian Christianity* (New York, 1946), adds the following interesting remarks on the Adoptionist Church:

The heresy of Adoptionism, while well compatible with the synoptic Gospels (Harnack, *Lehrbuch der Dogmengeschichte*, 3rd ed., I, p. 652), was considered heretical by the Pope Zephyrinus (A.D. 190), and Theodotus, the Adoptionist leader, was anathematized in Rome. However, Paul of Samosata, another Adoptionist, flourished until 270. Under the name of Pauliani, his followers were excommunicated by the Council of Nicaea, 315–20. (p. 10.)

About the Judaistic leanings of that sect we quote from a notice in Ananias of Shivak (early seventh century) the following remarks: 'The Pauliani also keep the feast of Pascha on the same day as the Jews, and whatever be the day of the full moon, they call it *kyriake* (Day of the Lord), as the Jews call it Sabbath, even though it be not a Sabbath'. (*Byzantinische Zeitschrift*, 1897.) (*Key of the Truth*, p. clii.)

On the practice of Armenian animal sacrifices see Conybeare, *Rituale Armenorum*, pp. 54 ff, and p. 80, note (a). Another early medieval source states: 'Nor do they (the Armenians) keep the festival of Christ's birth. . . . On the contrary, they are downcast in countenance and in tribulation on the very day of this holy feast, just like the Jews. . . .' (Isaac Catholicos, *Invectiva in Armenios*, Ch. III, in *Key*, p. clix.) A detailed description of the Paulician doctrine is given in Arpee, op. cit., pp. 112 ff.

102. Thus Gelzer in the *Real-Enzyklopädie*, also Burkitt in *Encycloped. Bibl.*, IV; Hastings, *Encyclop. of Religion and Ethics*, and Ter Minassiantz, 'Die Armenische Kirche in ihren Beziehungen zu den syrischen Kirchen' in *Texte und Untersuchungen*, XXVI, 2, pp. 22 ff. Conybeare (in Hastings, *Dict. of Bible*) and S. Päonian, however, assume that 'the Armenians translated the Septuagint, supplementing it, however, and adjusting it to the Masoretic text. The only question remaining regards the medium through which they knew the *Massora*'. Conybeare believes that they knew it through the Hexapla text of Origen. Against this conception, very sharply, Ter Minassiantz, loc. cit. From the overall picture the first problem arises: How could Origen have known the Masoretic text? Does Conybeare understand under that term simply the Hebrew version?

103. Cf. Conybeare, *Rituale Armenorum*, pp. 54, 65, *et passim*.

104. Cf. Ter Mikelian, *Die Armenische Kirche*, pp. 36 ff.

105. Cf. Conybeare, op. cit., pp. 516–26.

106. Ter Minassiantz, op. cit., pp. 11, 12, etc., where he derives these words from the Syrian, not the Hebrew.

107. Ibid., pp. 112–17.

108. Cf. Josephus, *Antiquitates*, XIII, ch. 16, 4, 5. Also Faustus of Byzantium, ed. M. Lauer (Köln, 1879), pp. 101 f.

109. Cf. *Encyclopaedia Judaica*, article 'Armenien'; also Faustus of Byzantium, ed. Lauer, pp. 137–9.

110. *Jer. Gittin* VI, 48a; *B. Yebamoth*, 45a.

111. Cf. Gelzer in *Berichte der Königlich Sächsischen Gesellschaft der Wissenschaften*, May 4, 1895. Also A. Harnack, *Die Mission und Ausbreitung des Christentums* (3rd ed.), II, pp. 202–6: 'Here, too, Judaism must have prepared the ground, especially in the Armenian aristocracy'. Very elaborate, but not fully dependable is the Armenian Chronicle of Stephanos of Taron, in *Scriptores Sacri et Profani*, ed. Gelzer and A. Burckhardt (Leipzig, 1907); cf. there pp. 25 ff, 30 ff, where we read some details about the Jews after the period of King Tigranes Arsakuni.

112. *Philosophumena*, VII, ch. 34.

113. Malachia Ormanian, *The Church of Armenia* (London, 1913), pp. 175 ff.

114. Conybeare, *Key of the Truth*, pp. clxi ff.

115. Isaac Catholicos, *Invectiva in Armenios*, Chapter III; cf. Conybeare, op. cit., p. clix.

116. L. Arpee, op. cit., p. 14.

CHAPTER THREE

The Scriptural Lesson and its Liturgical Significance

THE HISTORICAL DEVELOPMENT OF THE LESSON

OF the many varied elements common to Jewish and Christian worship, the oldest and most venerable is the principle and practice of scriptural lessons. While the practice prevails to this day in almost all Oriental religions, it seems probable that the public reading of sacred writings was once a unique feature of the ancient Jewish ritual. Although we know of hieroglyphic and cuneiform versions of sacred texts, long before Mosaic Judaism stepped over the threshold of world history, there is no evidence that such writings were publicly and *regularly* read before a worshipping congregation. Even if we assume that the practice of reading sacred lessons was established before Judaism made it the core of its cult, it will be our duty to search for its origin and purpose. True, the Bible, with its laws for the public reciting of certain passages, apparently served a didactic, exhortative and legal purpose. But it would be taking too much for granted to assume the rational causes which were established in the last two millennia to be identical with the primeval motives of this ritualistic practice.

Let us consider for a moment the components and procedure of such a public reading in ancient times. Before a motley, ignorant and illiterate throng, scrolls or cuneiform tablets were ceremoniously exposed by a highly esoteric caste of priests, who read, or rather chanted, the sacred text in ancient modes. Then, as solemnly as they were unfolded, the scrolls or tablets were removed from the gaze of the congregations, and the ritual came to an end. It is certainly hard to believe that originally no more than didactic ends were pursued.

Small wonder, then, that historians and theologians have probed into deeper and darker recesses while searching for the original aims of this practice. Dr E. B. Löwensohn, today a forgotten scholar, first suggested the hypothesis that the principle of public reading was basically a theur-gic-magic practice.[1] Many students have followed his notion although we have no more evidence at our disposal today than we had about fifty years ago. And yet the probability that theurgy was the mainspring of cult readings has increased considerably.[2] This hypothesis has become more plausible through our knowledge of the significant fact that sacred texts were chanted everywhere according to certain rules. Fur-thermore, was not music in ancient times the 'magic art' *par excellence*? Was not the conjurer or medicine man the chanting and reading priest?

However, leaving the maze of conjecture and hypothesis behind us, and treading the comparatively firm path of documental history, we come face to face with the oldest sources in Deut. 31:10–12, Neh. 8: 7–8, Neh. 9:3, and 2 Kings 22:8–13, 23:1–3. If we accept these pas-sages, which are to a certain extent contradictory, we are confronted with the two chief traditions of public reading; Moses and Ezra are regarded as the men who introduced this custom in Judaism. Other sources of early rabbinic writings in Mishna, Gemara, and early Mid-rash concur with Josephus, ben Sirach and others in ascribing the authorship of the lessons to Moses, its regular institution in the worship of the Synagogue to Ezra.[3] Ismar Elbogen and Adolf Büchler[4] come to similar conclusions by different reasoning, viz. that the (weekly) *regular lesson* was well established between 444 and 250 B.C. While these facts are reasonably certain, we know very little about the texts, their divisions and the details of their rendering. That certain passages were read on the holydays and Sabbaths in the Temple is amply testi-fied by reliable sources. The Synagogue was, from the outset, more of a instructional than a ritualistic institution, so that the study of the Law and the prophets was more firmly established there than in the Temple.[5] The details of the regular reading, the times and occasions, the type of rendering, the texts to be read, their division into pericopes (lesson; *lectio*; *parasha*; *sedra*), the duration of the cycle, the codification and col-lection of the pericopes, come to us from sources as late as the third to the sixth century A.D., as far as Judaism is concerned. Nor is the situa-tion better in the Christian world; whereas Judaism had developed a more or less uniform system of scriptural lessons, the Church, or rather the Churches, follow in many cases purely local or regional traditions. Thus, we have to deal with at least six traditions of historic value: the Roman Catholic and its branches, Gallican and Mozarabic, the Greek

Orthodox, the Armenian, Jacobite, Syro-Palestinian and Nestorian. It is only through properly evaluating and comparing the traditions and customs of all these churches that we may reach conclusive results. An eminent authority on the lessons of early Christianity rightly stressed this point when he criticized a method which compared just *one* of these Church traditions (without regard even for its own different strata) with the sources and customs of the Synagogue.[6]

Christianity followed the Jewish example by instituting regular weekly (or in some Churches daily) lessons. Frequently we shall find in the Christian ritual that ancient Jewish traditions have survived all schisms and strifes, and date back to the period when Christianity was no more than one Jewish sect among others. Thus, if we want to understand fully the relation between Jewish and Christian worship, we must study the development of the scriptural lesson in both the mother and daughter religions.

The scriptural lesson was obligatory in the central sanctuary, the Temple, only on special occasions, as on the Day of Atonement (when the High Priest read the pericope), on the Day of Jubilees, or on the New Moons, etc.[7] Once a year, on the first day of Tabernacles, the King visited the Temple, exercising his privilege of reading the day's pericope, the so-called 'King's Parasha', remaining seated.[8] Probably the sacrifices, or at least some of them, were accompanied by the recitation of the pertinent laws of the Pentateuch. All in all, however, it seems that the Temple-cult contained few regular and no continuous lessons. Some scholars even reject the conception of the scriptural lesson as a regular feature of the Temple services at Jerusalem.[9] Where the basic facts concerning the actual lessons in the Temple are so doubtful and controversial, one cannot expect any accurate information about the manner of reading; we must admit that our knowledge on that subject is almost nil. The assumption that the priest recited or chanted the lesson prescribed for special occasions is, of course, reasonable; but nothing definite is known about the ritual accompanying the solemn quotations from the Law.[10]

Where the Synagogue is concerned we are on comparatively firm ground. There cannot be any doubt that in the ritual of the ancient Synagogue, which was more an institution of learning than of prayer, the regular and continuous lesson from Scripture played a most important part. Originally the lesson was a substitute for the sacrifice, the monopoly of the central sanctuary. Down to the present time, the Jewish ritual has provided for the reading of scriptural lessons and those passages prescribing the respective sacrifices on Sabbath and Holyday, instead of the actual sacrifice. This piece of 'legal fiction' was most strictly observed in the Synagogue of the Temple, to which we referred in Chapter II. Concomitant with the actual sacrifice in the Temple, the respective passages were solemnly recited in the 'Hall of Stones'.[11] It is only natural that this mainstay of synagogal life was surrounded by rigidly observed rules of etiquette. Even today it is customary for three men to 'stand by' the reading: the president of the synagogue (*archisynagogus, parnas*), the reader (*anagnostes*, lector, *baal kore*) and the man who has been 'called' to read. When the knowledge of the text and its language vanished more and more, the reader recited the entire lesson for the (three to seven) men called to the pulpit (Greek: *bema*, Hebrew: *bima*).[12] Until the fifth and sixth centuries A.D., the privilege to read from Scripture belonged in the first place to priests (*Aaronidae*), then to elders (the Presbyters of the Early Church), or scholars of merit.[13] The last remnant of this usage is the present custom of calling to the lectern first a 'Cohen' (*Aaronides*), then a Levite, and only after these a scholar, be he rabbi or layman.

In Luke 4:6 ff, the New Testament gives us a short description of scriptural reading in the ancient Synagogue. The president of the synagogue 'called him up', and, after pronouncing the prescribed eulogies, Jesus read from the Law; afterwards the book of Isaiah was 'given to him' and 'he found there' the chapter which he subsequently expounded in his homily. We shall return to this famous passage later on.

Who Read the Lesson?

In olden times and in Palestine, each man called upon to do so recited his portion of the lesson himself. When Hebrew was replaced by Aramaic or Greek an interpreter (*meturgeman*) was appointed to translate the original text, sentence for sentence, into the vernacular.[14] This practice of translating was not limited to the Synagogue. The Aquitanian pilgrim Aetheria Silvia, in her *Peregrinatio*,[15] relates an identical custom connected with the Church of Jerusalem of the fourth century. We find also a reader (*anagnostes*) employed both in the Synagogue and the Church;[16] in both cases he is considered a member of the lower clergy. The same holds true for the *hazan* (Greek:

hyperetes, precentor, psalmista, cantor, etc.) who often had to substitute for the regular reader, and in later centuries became the appointed cantor and minister of the congregation.

It is in this category that we shall have to search for the men who transmitted Jewish customs, texts, and chants to the growing Christian Church. We have selected two examples to demonstrate the historic development that connected the new Church with the Synagogue. The epitaph of an archdeacon of the fifth century reads as follows:

> Hic levitarum primus in ordine vivens
> Davitici cantor carminis iste fuit;

indicating that the deceased was of levitical descent and a fine singer of psalms; his name Deusdedit (Jonathan) adds further confirmation to his Jewish origin.[17] And of another Judaeo-Christian deacon it is said 'prophetam celebrans placido modulamine senem'.[18] This was obviously a reader or rather a *psalmista* of Scripture in the Church of the fifth century, as the expression 'prophetam celebrans placido modulamine' clearly indicates;[19] for David, the author of the Psalter, was considered a prophet by all Christian authorities.

When Were Lessons to be Read?

In the time of Ezra the lessons were read on special occasions and probably every Sabbath in the synagogues. Later, when in Jerusalem many houses of worship were erected beside the Metropolitan Temple, portions of the Pentateuch were read in these religious assemblies on the Sabbath, and Monday and Thursday, which were the market-days of the capital. The provincial and rural synagogues initiated this custom which has survived to the present day. Apart from these weekly regular lessons the holydays and fast-days as well as days of special significance had lessons of their own, a rather flexible custom, as we shall see presently.

What Texts were Read in the Synagogue?

Two types of lessons generated within the canon of the Old Testament: the regular weekly pericope was a *lectio continua* (continuous lesson), comprising the entire Torah (Pentateuch). Today it is arranged in an annual cycle beginning with the Sabbath after Tabernacles and ending on the last day of Tabernacles, the festival of 'Rejoicing of the

Law'. To every Sabbath and holyday another short lesson is assigned, called Haftara (dismissal, because it used to take place at the end of the service),[20] which is selected from the prophetic books. This is not a *lectio continua*, for the Haftara pericopes are theoretically supposed to be connected with the specific Torah lesson of the day, or to provide the scriptural basis for some of the holydays of the Jewish year. Hence, the prophetic lesson consists of isolated chapters selected for distinct purposes, and therefore do not require a continuous text. This is the so-called *eclogadic* type of lesson, which the Churches of today use more frequently than the older *lectio continua*. In the course of these studies it will be shown that the entire structure of lessons in both Church and Synagogue is a very complex labyrinthic edifice, full of bypaths and blind alleys, which are, in some way or other, subterraneously interconnected. The Torah lesson, of course, was always of primary importance, the prophetic pericope being of auxiliary character. This difference in rank was demonstrated even in the ceremonial prescribed for each lesson: the Torah pericope had to be read from the parchment scroll, where the text is written down without vocalization or punctuation; the prophetic lesson, on the other hand, was usually read from any present text, vocalized or accentuated. Hagiographic texts, if they were ever used for public readings, were for many centuries excluded from the lectionary of the Synagogue; they served chiefly for private study or devotion, although the Psalms, as prayers or chants, play a prominent part in the Jewish liturgy.

How was the Reading of the Lessons Performed?

The scroll was solemnly taken from the Ark, and with the singing of psalm verses was displayed to the assembled congregation. The reader chanted the pericope of the day in a manner determined by the rigid tradition prescribed by the ecphonetic accents of the Masoretic text of the Bible. This cantillation is called *trop* (Greek: *tropos*, mode, fashion) or *n'gina* (melody). The ecphonetic signs are called *ta'amim* in Hebrew. Theirs is a threefold purpose:

(1) To provide the scriptural text with a most elaborate punctuation, both syntactic and logical. Practically every word bears one of these punctuating signs.

(2) They indicate the cantillation, according to specific rules which determine the mode of the musical setting.

(3) They point out the syllable to be accentuated in accordance with the rules of Hebrew grammar as they were known to the Masoretes and grammarians from the fifth to the tenth century A.D.

The problems of cantillation and accentuation are of paramount importance for a full understanding of the musical liturgy of Christianity and Judaism.

The arrangement of the pericopes, their performance and notation, represent the oldest and most authentic common element of all liturgies.

THE SYNAGOGUE AND ITS LECTIONARY: SOURCES

The development of the lessons in the Synagogue was a long process progressing in two phases. The Torah lesson was arranged at least a century before Christ, while the prophetic pericopes required four more centuries until their final codification. There is an abundance of source material available, but it is far from homogeneous. Three different types of documents can easily be distinguished: (a) historical facts and data; (b) descriptive or regulative documents, homilies, commentaries; and (c) actual lectionaries or pericope books.

To the first category belong the biblical passages Deut. 31:10-12; II Kings 22:8-13, 23:1-3, Neh. 8:1 ff, Josephus, Luke and some Talmudic passages.[21] They confirm the existence of regular lessons but do not shed much light upon the division of the Torah for the weekly pericope. In particular, they give no information about the duration of the cycle. Although in these sources the ecclesiastical year appears as a well organized entity, the connexion of the lessons with the recurrent holydays cannot be clearly established.

The passage of Luke 4:16 reveals some interesting aspects of the customs in the rural communities of Palestine. According to A. Büchler (cf. n. 3), the correct interpretation of those verses rests upon the understanding of the word 'he found' (Luke 4:17) which indicates that the prophetic portion (Isa. 61) had previously been prepared and marked in the scroll by the archisynagogus or another official in such a way that Jesus could easily find the prescribed passage. Since lengthy unfolding of and searching in scrolls was not permitted on the Sabbath, Büchler concludes that the prophetic cycle was just then being established or at least *in statu nascendi*.[22]

The second category of sources gives either descriptions of the practice of the scriptural lesson or treats the matter *ex cathedra*, prescribing certain lessons for certain days. It is here that one finds more or less clear statements concerning the cycles, their division and duration. These sources stem almost exclusively from rabbinic literature and lend themselves occasionally to alternative interpretations. The following are their most significant data.

In Palestine the full cycle of lessons ran for three years, in Babylonia for one year. After the sixth or seventh century Palestine and the entire Diaspora accepted the annual Babylonian cycle.[23] The short cycle began after Tabernacles and contained the *lectio continua* for fifty Sabbaths; four 'special' Sabbaths had lessons of their own, handed down from olden times. The portions for the festivals, holydays, new moons and fast-days do not form part of the *lectio continua*, but are special sections. The three-year cycle started probably on the first or second Sabbath of the month Nisan, depending on the date of Passover (15 Nisan). It ended on the first Sabbath of Adar (the twelfth, and in a leap year the thirteenth month). Inserted between the end of the triennial cycle and its recommencement were the four 'special Sabbaths' mentioned above, whose portions were read annually.[24] The same practice applied to all annual festivals, holydays, etc., which interrupt the course of the regular lesson. These few facts may demonstrate the intricate and complicated connexion between pericope and the ecclesiastical year. So closely intertwined are regular lesson and holyday pericope, that in some cases, where the Talmudic injunctions are not fully articulate, we have to turn for better information to certain ancient homilies or *midrashim* which frequently follow the course of the *lectio continua*, yet indicate the 'isolated' lesson of the holydays. The oldest of these homilies is the *Pesiqta Rabbati* whose tradition extends into the time of early Christianity. We shall discuss these documents later.

The third group of sources are actual lectionaries or pericope books, which were used only for the preparation of the reader, since at least the Torah lesson had to be recited from a simple scroll without any marks of division or punctuation. These books are of relatively late origin (tenth–twelfth century) and do not say much about the development of the annual cycle of lessons. They indicate only the actual state and the finished codification of the scriptural portions; hence, they do not shed much light upon the motives that governed the evolution of the tradition preserved therein. They may be compared with the lectionaries of the Christian Churches of today, as for example the Roman or Greek Breviary, and are only of limited use for the present investigation.

THE CHURCHES AND THEIR LESSONS: SOURCES

More numerous, but less substantial, are the historical sources which relate to the practice of scriptural reading in the early Church. In the first two centuries at least three historians mentioned the lesson: Justin, Pseudo-Clement, and Irenaeus, to say nothing of Paul. Apart from Justin's account which contains only three lines, mere references to the existence of lessons are the only factual statements. Why this silence and this lack of detailed explanation in an age which, as a whole, was not averse to loquacious reports? Although the Jewish sources are a little more explanatory, they, too, are far from being verbose. The answer is that one does not discuss well-known matters of fact: the Old Testament pericope was firmly embedded in the liturgy of the Synagogue, which in turn served as the general pattern for the primitive Church. However, this situation changed completely when a new element was introduced into the Church, the lesson from the New Testament. This event, the regular New Testament pericope, must be dated well before the second half of the third century. From then on the sources are more abundant and explicit, reporting the radical deviation from the established Jewish practice.[25]

The second century witnessed the incipient separation of the Church from the Synagogue; but for many reasons the Old Testament lesson remained fully intact in the Christian services. Notwithstanding some outspoken anti-Judaistic writings of that period, the early Gentile Church denied the Old Testament to Jewry, proclaiming it the sole and legitimate property of the true Christians.[26] It stands to reason that Pauline and other didactic epistles were the first material used in the public reading of the Church. Justin reports that 'the writings of the Apostles and the Scriptures of the Prophets were read as much as time permits'.[27] Yet there is not the slightest indication that he was referring to a system of pericopes. Nor are the great Fathers, Irenaeus, Clement of Alexandria, and Tertullian much more enlightening in their references to the lesson.[28] The first document describing the lesson in detail is the *Apostolic Constitutions*, a great compilation of decrees, liturgies, ordinances, etc., which probably originated in the fourth century in Syria, but whose traditions date back at least one more century.[29] This dossier provides, in its second book, for two lessons from the Old Testament, for one from the Acts of Apostles, one from the Epistles, and one from the Gospels. Even more detailed instructions are given in the eighth book; there the lesson is divided into five pericopes, viz. from the Law, Prophets, Epistles, Acts, and Gospels.[30] Henceforth the number and the accuracy of our sources increase constantly. In addition to these descriptive accounts, there are a number of homilies which faithfully follow the course of the lessons, quite analogous to the Jewish homiletic sources mentioned above. They clearly indicate the substance of the lesson and, in some cases, the reason why a specific pericope was recited. The oldest homilies of this group are the sermons of Pope Leo I and Pope Gregory I.[31]

It is regrettable that the great scholar Jerome (d. 420) did not acknowledge his share in the order of the Roman lessons; although many students ascribe their arrangement to him, there is no historical evidence to bear out this theory. Yet, it cannot have been much later that the order of lessons was fixed; for Pope Gelasius (d. 496) most probably was the author of the Decretum Gratiani, which rules that almost the whole of the Bible should be read in the course of Divine Office (not during Mass) of one year. We have got an even more conclusive proof at our disposal since P. Alban Dold, O.S.B., discovered and published the oldest lectionary of the Western Church, which dates from the first half of the sixth century.[32] This venerable and highly interesting source will be discussed later; it may be mentioned in passing that in it the five pericopes were already reduced to three or four, viz. the Prophetia (any book of the Old Testament), the Epistle and the Gospel. The Roman and Greek Churches further reduced the number of lessons to two (for the Mass), while the Divine Office retained the threefold pericope, including the Old Testament lesson.[33] St Chrysostom still refers to the three-fold lesson, and some of the Eastern Churches of old have retained this type up to the present day, as the Nestorian, the Armenian and the Ambrosian rituals clearly indicate.[34] There are, however, certain exceptions from the rule, particularly evident on the so-called Ember Days of the Roman Church, in Quadragesima (Lent) and Holy Week in all Churches, when the number of lessons is greatly increased.

Originally, the arrangement of the pericopes implemented a *lectio continua*, as is amply demonstrated by the oldest known lectionaries, also by the succession of homilies mentioned above, and by some chroniclers of the early Church; foremost among them Cassian, who testifies that in his time the monks completed the reading of the New Testament in the course of one year.[35] Very early, the practice of the Cento (i.e. a motley combination of scriptural passages) entered the liturgy, unmindful of the rigid course of the *lectio continua*. It was the close relation between the complex ecclesiastical year and its pertinent pericopes which transformed the *lectio continua* of the Roman Church beyond recognition. The Eastern Churches have preserved a great deal more of the old type of continuous lessons to the present day. It was the task of these Christian and Jewish lectionaries to stress, within the framework of the *lectio continua*, the significance of the ecclesiastical calendar and its individual holydays. This double function naturally complicates every study of the lesson's evolution. In the Catholic Churches with their overlapping cycles of the *Proprium de Tempore*, which refers to the ecclesiastical year, and the *Proprium* and *Commune Sanctorum*, which refers to the secular year, the situation is even more complex than in the Synagogue with its leap years and 'special Sabbaths'.

It was the ancient *Proprium de Tempore* with its numerous lessons for the movable festivals, that time and again interrupted the otherwise set course of the *Proprium Sanctorum*.[36]

The Byzantine Church follows the old Jewish principle of naming the Sundays after the (evangelic) lesson read on these days; but, as Adrian Fortescue and S. Beissel, S.J., have pointed out, in the Roman rite the situation is much more complex. Fortescue says: 'We can find in our Missal hardly a trace of any system at all. The idea of continuous reading has become so overlain that there is nothing left of it.'[37] Although the great festivals are provided with lessons which bear out their significance, as for example Christmas with the narration of Christ's birth, or Epiphany with the story of the Magi, the choice of the lesson for ordinary Sundays, and even more for weekdays, seems often extremely arbitrary. Later, we shall attempt to approach this problem from an entirely new angle, namely the shift and partial retention of the Jewish year within the Christian calendar.

As in the Synagogue, psalm verses are chanted before and between the lessons. As in the Synagogue, the Gospel (and in Eastern Churches the Old Testament lesson) is chanted according to certain 'intonations', not simply read; and as in the Synagogue, a primitive notation was used for that chant. The Roman rite made a distinction between the reader of the Epistle, usually a subdeacon or a lector, and that of the Gospel, who must at least be a deacon. This distinction, which sets the rank of the Gospels above all other sacred writings, is of course lacking in the Jewish ritual. Yet, many traces of a former similar differentiation between Torah and prophetic lesson are still in evidence in the present-day ritual of the Synagogue.

In order to understand the development of the pericopes in the Christian Churches, it will be necessary to compare some of the oldest lectionaries of different rites with each other; to establish certain general principles of their genesis and to study the intricate relation between the lesson and the ecclesiastical calendar. Later they will be compared with the Jewish lectionary.

The oldest existing sources of the Western (Latin) Church are: The Gallican lectionary of the fifth-sixth century (WOLF);[38] the Gallican lectionary of Luxeuil (LUX);[39] the old Mozarabic missal of the ninth-tenth century (MOZ);[40] the Breviarum Romanum (ROM).[41] Sources of the Greek Church quoted hereafter are the Typikon and Pentecostarion (GREEK T and GREEK P), appearing in the Codex S. Simeonis at Treves and in four manuscripts in the Paris National Library.[42] The Armenian rite (ARM), including a description and texts of Johannes Ozniensis (Odsun), the Catholicos of Armenia in 718, who commented on the breviary then in use, appears in Conybeare, *Rituale Armenorum*.[43] Of the Aramaean lectionaries the following will be examined: the East Syrian lectionary (SYR);[44] the Nestorian lectionary of the 'Upper Convent' (NEST); the Jacobite lectionary (JAC);[45] a Syro-Palestinian lectionary (SYR-PAL).[46]

Since all these documents are heterogeneous in many respects, each of them will be described briefly before a systematic comparison will be undertaken. WOLF, LUX and MOZ belong to one family representing the ancient 'regional' rites of the Western Church, before their strict centralization under the uniform Roman order. As will be demonstrated later in detail, they display certain features which connect them with the Byzantine and Nestorian Churches. The causes of this East–West connexion are not yet sufficiently explored, and at present one can only state that some of the characteristic features are typical of the ancient Church in general. Concerning the lessons, all three sources show in principle the threefold pericope, viz. one Old Testament (*prophetia*) and two New Testament (Epistle and Gospel) readings. This, however, is no more than a general rule which is often violated by instances of four or even five pericopes. Usually, they contain a clear *lectio continua* which is interrupted only during the normal festival seasons by the *Proprium de Tempore*. WOLF alone shows an archaic type of ecclesiastical calendar, where the cycle of its lessons begins on the Vigil before Easter Sunday and ends with a series of pericopes on the morning of Holy Saturday.[47] This cycle was almost obsolete as early as the fifth century; moreover, it parallels in principle a likewise obsolete Jewish year of whose existence we know only through documents; Tertullian referred to this year as running from Easter to Easter, and so does Victorinus of Pettau (*ca.* 300); its most outspoken champion was Zeno of Verona (d. 380). St Ambrose was perhaps the last of the great Fathers to refer to it in a positive manner.[48] Thus, the most remarkable element of WOLF is its liturgical year.

The main sources of the Greek rite, GREEK T and GREEK P, likewise belong to one family, as Rahlfs has clearly proved. Here too, the original *lectio continua* is recognizable, though frequently overlaid by incidental insertions for different occasions, chiefly for special fast-days of the Byzantine and Egyptian calendar. The common element of these sources is that they provide Old Testament pericopes: (1) only for the vigils (eve) of certain feasts, (2) for the weekdays during the fasting season, including Lent, and (3) for some of the canonical hours on weekdays before Christmas, Epiphany and Easter. This fact suggests that the regular *lectio continua* of the Old Testament had been abandoned fairly early; its remnants are in evidence during Lent only. In contradistinction to the old Latin sources quoted above, GREEK T and GREEK P begin the lectionary with Christmas and follow up the *Proprium de Tempore* until Pentecost; thereafter they run the course of the *Proprium Sanctorum* according to the secular year.[49] But even in this family of sources the vigil of Easter Sunday (Holy Saturday) is generally recognized as the mainspring of the lectionary cycle from which all systems of pericopes are derived.[50] Another remarkable feature of both GREEK T and GREEK P is the unmistakable trace of an ancient pentecontade calendar.[51] For Easter was not preceded by a more or less strictly observed Lent period of forty days (Quadragesima), but by six plus one (the 'Great' or 'Holy') weeks—the seven weeks between Easter and Pentecost are common to Christianity and Judaism—and finally, it is possible to distinguish remnants of a pentecontade before Christmas, or rather, before Epiphany. We find an even more definite pentecontade calendar in the Nestorian Church. The interesting limitation of the Old Testament pericopes, as they appear in the Greek rite and its deviations, to the vigils of the feasts, and the weekdays of the fasting season cannot be explained by Christological or theological reasons only, as Rahlfs ventured to do. He says:

As the vigil of Easter in miniature, so is the entire fasting season regarded as a period during which the Christian, fasting and mourning, waits for the coming of the Lord and prepares himself for that joyful event.[52] Hence, the Old Testament lessons are most appropriate for the fast as well as for the Easter vigil.[53]

Actually, the roots of this matter are to be found in the ancient Jewish tradition which commenced the lectionary cycle two weeks before Passover, and that corresponds exactly with the time when the Greek Churches read Gen. 1:1. This thesis will be fully implemented later on.

Turning farther to the eastward, our attention is focused on the ritual of the Armenian Church. Some of its remarkable resemblances to the Jewish rite have been discussed previously. Conybeare, Rahlfs, and Baumstark concur in the conviction that the Old Armenian lectionary is so closely related to the Jerusalem rite at the time of Aetheria that one may declare these two traditions to be identical for all practical purposes.[54] Beyond that *terminus a quo*, however, ARM evidences some features which indicate an even greater age than either GREEK T or SYR-PAL. It provides Old Testament lessons (as far as our sources go) for all of the great feasts except Easter, which, for obvious reasons, kept strictly to the New Testament. In addition it contains numerous Old Testament pericopes in the *Proprium Sanctorum*, in particular for the days of patriarchs and prophets.[55]

In general, ARM shows no fully-fledged *lectio continua* of the Old Testament; actually no Old Testament lessons at all are assigned to ordinary Sundays. Baumstark presumes this deficiency to be caused by the old practice of Jerusalem which provided some kind of *lectio continua* now long forgotten, and where the choice of the individual lesson was left to the discretion of the officiating bishop.[56] A straight course of lessons is in evidence only during the Quadragesima and Holy Week, limited to Old Testament pericopes. They were read from Monday to Friday; yet ARM furnished pericopes only for Wednesday and Friday, except for the second week and Holy Week. These special weeks have a service and a lesson for each day.[57] There is a threefold Old Testament pericope discernible, consisting of Law, the Prophets and Hagiographa, in structure closely related to the Jewish custom. Moreover, the Wednesday lesson is not continued on Friday and vice versa, so that both Wednesdays and Fridays have their own *lectio continua*.[58] As in the Greek tradition, in ARM too, the Old Testament lessons of the *Proprium de Tempore* are in evidence only for the fasting season, the vigils and their feasts, whereby Easter Sunday again is excluded. In contrast to GREEK T and GREEK P, ARM has a large number of Old Testament pericopes in its *Proprium Sanctorum*. They are always assigned to anniversaries or special days of Old Testament figures or events. There are lessons for the 'Tabernacle of Kirjath ye'arim', on the days of Isaiah, Jeremiah, Eleazar the Maccabean, Elisha and Elijah, Jeremiah in Anathoth, the Deposition of Zechariah, etc.[59]

Of these memorial days the most interesting is the day of King David and James, the brother of Christ, which falls on December 26th. Only Baumstark comments on this truly astounding fact; he quotes a pilgrim of Piacenza (sixth century) who reports that on this day (December 26th) Jews and Christians assembled together in Hebron to celebrate the memory of King David.[60] Baumstark assumes this usage to reflect an old Jewish custom that was later on borrowed by the Palestinian Church. This hypothesis would also explain the numerous Old Testament memorial days of ARM as once regional customs of Palestine, the motherland and home of these heroes. The present writer proposes another explanation, which amounts to an expansion and a generalization of Baumstark's theory. In view of the pilgrim's report, it seems probable that December 25th, or its equivalent in the Jewish calendar, was a memorial day of King David. Now, we must bear in mind that both Jesus and his brother James *were 'sons of David'*, according to the genealogy in two Gospels! It is a well-known practice of Near Eastern mythology and religion to credit the son with some of his father's deeds, characteristics, and even exterior features.[61] More-over, the prophetic prediction which foresaw the coming of the Messiah out of David's seed was so familiar to every Jew, that in some respects David and Jesus were almost identified with each other as 'the Anointed', 'the King of Israel', 'the Good Shepherd', etc. What was more natural, then, than to celebrate David's anniversary at the same time as that of his most adored descendant? It was only after Christ's Divinity was proclaimed and recognized that He and King David were more and more dissociated from each other, and Christ's birth celebrated together with the Theophany and his Baptism on January 6th. This shift in the doctrinal as well as in the liturgical attitude of the Church was accomplished through the incessant pressure from jealous Gentile Christianity.[62] The original order was only partially reconstituted in the Western Church, when the Nativity was again separated from the Theophany and set back to December 25th. Still the Judaeo-Christians held out: according to their tenets Christ was the Messiah, the Son of Man, the King of Israel, the Son of David; his natural successor was his brother James, the first Bishop of Jerusalem and the head of the incipient Judaeo-Christian Church.[63] He, too, was a 'Son of David'; so the simultaneous commemoration of James and King David was a wise and natural step of a Church that had to pursue the narrow middle course between the fanaticism of Judaeo-Christianity and the anti-Jewish, gnostic Gentile Church.[64]

In passing, a few remarks should be made on the Old Armenian calendar. ARM starts its lessons on January 6th, the feast of Epiphany, but it seems that its New Year was celebrated in the fall. Conybeare states in a lengthy exposition that there are two calendars extant which frequently overlap and cannot be easily reconciled or related to each other.[65] On the other hand, the 'Dedication of the Church' (September 13th) was probably the last remnant of the ancient New Year's Day, since the ecclesiastical year of the Orthodox Church starts September 1st, according to the Julian calendar, which corresponds to September 13th of the Gregorian calendar. This was at the same time the 'Beginning of the Indictos' and took place fourteen plus one (twice seven plus one) Sundays before December 25th. It coincided with the last vestige of the ancient Jewish New Year, which usually falls between September 13th and 20th.[66] A similar pentecontadic tendency is evident in the Georgian *Kanonarion* which in all essential elements is closely akin to ARM.

Most obvious in this respect are NEST and SYR, here represented chiefly by the lectionary of the 'Upper Convent' of Mosul, and by Maclean's reproduction of the East Syrian order, published in the Syrian lectionary at Urmia in the year 1889.[67] Here we have to deal with an essentially pentecontadic calendar: the seven Sundays of resurrection after Easter are preceded by as many Sundays of fast and followed by three cycles of seven Sundays called 'of the Apostles', 'of the Summer' and 'of Elijah' respectively. Thereupon follow four or five Sundays 'of Moses' and four Sundays 'of Annunciation'. From December 25th to January 6th the two weeks of the birthday are intercalated, and after Epiphany seven Sundays mark the beginning of the fasting season. Thus, the scheme of the ecclesiastical year presents itself in the following table:

Epiphany plus (maximally) six Sundays
Seven Sundays of the Fast
Easter
Seven Sundays of Resurrection
Pentecost
Seven Sundays of the Apostles
Seven Sundays of the Summer
Seven Sundays of Elijah
Four Sundays of Moses
Four Sundays of Annunciation (Advent) plus
Two Sundays between December 25th and Epiphany

Altogether 52–54 weeks or Sundays.

If this in itself is not proof of a very ancient calendaric order, other features confirm even more convincingly the archaic character of the system. Exactly like the Synagogue, it provides a twofold pericope of the Old Testament, from Torah and the Prophets, whereby, in contrast to the other Eastern Churches, it adopts the Jewish terminology, dividing the biblical canon into Torah (Pentateuch), Prophets (former and latter, i.e. historical books and prophetic writings proper), and Hagiographs. The last mentioned category is, in accordance with the usage of the Synagogue, represented in the lessons only on special occasions, in addition to the regular chanting of the Psalter. The lessons from the New Testament are clearly patterned after the Jewish fashion, i.e. an epistolary pericope precedes the reading from the Gospel. This type of scriptural reading corresponds closely to the description given in the *Apostolic Constitutions*.[68]

Another archaic element of NEST and SYR is the prevalence of the *lectio continua* over eclogadic pericopes; where the latter are in evidence only for typically Christian feasts, the *lectio continua* undoubtedly emphasizes the resemblance to the ancient Jewish year. The more recent origin of the eclogadic pericopes lends probability to this assumption.[69] An old *lectio continua* runs straight through Genesis, Exodus and parts of Deuteronomy, a tradition unheard of in other Christian rites.

A careful study of the calendar of NEST and SYR and its connexion with the lectionary conveys the impression that the cycle of continuous lessons ends with the fourth Sunday of Moses (last half of October), to begin anew on the first Sunday of the fasting season, seven weeks before Easter. The intermediate Sundays show eclogadic Old Testament pericopes and *lectio continua* for the New Testament lessons of Advent only. It seems that Advent was considered as the beginning of the liturgical year, though the lectionary cycle suggests an older order. Again September 14th (Exaltation of the Cross) plays a curious part in the lectionary: its pericopes are patterned after the Good Friday lessons with the difference that instead of a Torah portion, a prophetic lesson is read, and that in place of the second Old Testament reading of Good Friday, taken from the prophets, we find a pericope from Acts, followed by a Pauline paragraph. It must be noted, that the *Old Testament pericope (Isa. 52) is identical on both days*. Without discussing further the details of the individual lessons it might be said in anticipation that the third Sunday of the 'Church's Dedication' contains the same Old Testament pericope as the Synagogue has on the feast of Hanukka, which of course, celebrates the Temple's Dedication.[70] This is the more remarkable as the respective calendar dates roughly coincide for most years. All these facts demonstrate the old age of NEST which is supposed to have originated around the year 350 or even earlier in or around Antioch, then the central place of teaching and administration of Eastern Christendom.

No other rite of the Eastern Churches has preserved such an abundance of documentary sources as the Jacobite wing of the Syrian Church. Of the many manuscripts at our disposal which are known and available to us, primarily due to the merits of Wright's catalogue and Baumstark's bibliography, we shall select three manuscripts of the Jacobite order upon which to base our examination, among them the so-called Athanasian lectionary, and the Syro-Palestinian order of the lessons, discovered and published by Mrs Agnes Smith Lewis.[71]

The normal scheme of JAC provides for two, sometimes three Old Testament pericopes with a frequently interrupted *lectio continua*. The earlier documents suggest Easter as both the ecclesiastical New Year and as the starting point of the lectionary cycle. The great lectionary of Athanasios, however, gives three Old Testament lessons and begins its cycle with the Sunday after Easter, 'Low Sunday' (Dominica in Albis). Baumstark is convinced that this Sunday was the most ancient date for the beginning of public reading.[72] Like many of the other systems discussed previously, JAC shows certain resemblances to the Jewish order, in particular by transferring the fast-day lessons of the Synagogue (Day of Atonement) to the great days of the Christian fasting season (as Good Friday or Holy Saturday). Baumstark was the first scholar to recognize and emphasize this fact, but even he was far from a full evaluation and understanding of the real state of affairs. The shifting of the two calendars, which must be considered as the mainspring of all these transfers and borrowings, completely escaped his attention. The individual analogies of the various orders within the Jewish system will be subject to further examination. Suffice it here to draw attention to the threefold pericopes of the Athanasian lectionary, where one lesson is drawn from the Torah and two from the prophets (in the Masoretic sense of the word, i.e. one from the earlier prophets—the historic books—and the other from prophetic literature proper).

The Syro-Palestinian order (SYR-PAL) is almost identical with the old Jerusalem system and consequently shows a close resemblance to ARM as well as to the so-called 'Jerusalemitic Typikon'.[73] It dates back to the early fifth century and contains many of the features already discussed in ARM; e.g. the day of David and James, this time December 26th, celebrated in a New Testament lesson from James 1; the Wednesdays and Fridays of Quadragesima as the only days with an Old Testament lesson; September 1st (or, according to the Gregorian calendar, September 13th) as the beginning date of the lectionary. On the other hand, SYR-PAL is more contaminated and generally is in a rather corrupt and confused condition. Remnants of a *lectio continua* are faintly discernible, yet they are overlaid with a double counting of Lent Sundays. (Old Testament pericopes are read only on holydays and during the fasting season, excepting, as usual, Easter, which was re-served for New Testament lessons exclusively.) Certain traits of SYR-PAL led Baumstark to believe that the document reflects the customs of the Egyptian Church of the ninth or tenth century, which would explain its fragmentary and confused state.[74]

A deep insight into the development of the Syriac lectionary system was afforded us through F. C. Burkitt's profound study 'The Early Syriac Lectionary System'.[75] Interpreting ancient manuscript sources of the British Museum, Burkitt gives a full lectionary for Holy Week, a partial lectionary for Lent, and a complete lectionary for Ascension Day, which in those times, according to the manuscript, 'fell fifty days after the Sunday of Resurrection', i.e. was identical with Pentecost.[76]

Of the many interesting features of this ancient lectionary a few must be stressed here, for their uniqueness or the emphasis they give to special pericopes on special days.

(1) Sunday–Monday of the first week in Quadragesima has the characteristic elements of Gen. 1 and Isa. 57–58, which in most of the lectionaries are read on Holy Saturday. In general, with the Fast there begins a more or less continual reading of the books Genesis, Proverbs and Job.[77]

(2) On Tuesday during Holy Week Joshua 5–6 is read, an archaic allusion to the Passover of Gilgal.

(3) On Thursday, the presumed day of Jesus's Passover meal, Gen. 37 with its reference to the betrayal of Joseph in Dothan is read, as well as Exod. 12:1–28 (Passover-law) and Num. 9:1–23, which again states the laws of the Passover celebration.

(4) The outstanding pericopes of Good Friday are:

Amos 8 and 9. (Wherein the privilege of the 'chosen people' is discussed and reinterpreted.)
Gen. 22. (The sacrifice of Isaac.)
Isa. 52–53. (The suffering servant.)
Jer. 38. (The prophet rescued from the pit.)
Ezek. 21. (Prophecy of the punishment of Israel.)

(5) Holy Saturday has most of its pericopes in common with other lectionaries, including occidental ones. The outstanding features are: the book of Jonah; Gen. 42 and 43 (Joseph and his brethren); II Sam. 1 (David's lament over Saul and Jonathan). II Kings 20 (Allusion to the

third day of Hezekiah's sickness). II Kings 2 (Elijah's ascension); Exod. 12–14 (The exodus from Egypt).

(6) The feast of Ascension falls, according to this old Syriac document, fifty days after Easter, and is, therefore, identical with Pentecost. Of its pericopes one is particularly striking, namely Deut. 5:6–6:9.

This lesson begins with the Ten Commandments and contains the complete prayer of *Sh'ma'* ('Hear, O Israel, The Lord, our God, is The One Eternal Being', etc.).

This feature itself would not be so astounding, were it not for the fact that the Jewish counterpart of Pentecost, the feast of *Shabuot*—also fifty days after Passover—was considered from very old times 'Feast of the Giving of the Torah on Mt Sinai' and emphasizes exactly the same pericope. Yet neither the idea of Christ's Ascension nor that of the Apostolic Pentecost, as described in early Christian literature, seems to engender any palpable connexion with the Jewish feast of the same season. We are led, therefore, to assume that this Ascension-Pentecost pericope was a remnant of the old Judaeo-Christian Church of Syria, which remained a powerful sect well into the third century.

Burkitt's explanatory remarks are chiefly of historical interest, but a few of them are pertinent to our subject: proceeding from our assumption that this lectionary contains traces of the Judaeo-Christian Church, we should be able to understand the following facts in their proper perspective:

(1) The lectionary has in its calendar no provision for the Virgin Mary nor for the typically Syrian 'Fast of the Ninevites'.

(2) The book of Leviticus is conspicuous by its absence; here Burkitt remarks 'perhaps it was thought unsuitable for Christian service'.

If we modify this observation to 'it was unsuitable for *Judaeo-Christian* Services', we might be nearer the truth. When this sect arose, the Second Temple with all its hierarchical institutions still stood. Even after its fall the Levites continued to live in a more or less splendid isolation—we know of cases in the fifth and sixth centuries where the descendants of the priestly caste prided themselves in their distinction.

The Judaeo-Christian sect, however, did not recognize such pedigrees, and was in general not too fond of the Temple's hierarchy. Moreover, their most influential wing, the Ebionites, were radical opponents of animal sacrifices.[78] The book Leviticus contains all the regulations of the sacrificial cult. The Ebionites considered these passages 'false pericopes, false statutes', not originating with God, and referred quite rightly to Ezek. 20:25–26: 'And I let them follow statutes that were not good and ordinances whereby they could not live. And I let them be defiled through their gifts (sacrifices), in that they caused to pass (through the fire) all that openeth the womb, in order that I might destroy them, to the end that they might know that I am the Lord'. Since the Judaeo-Christians were equally opposed to priestly hierarchy and animal sacrifices, they had to omit practically the entire book of Leviticus which contains the 'Priestly Code'.[79]

(3) One lesson of Easter Tuesday contains the 'Memoirs (*hypomnemata*) of Peter and Paul'. The references to Peter have been traced to the so-called Pseudo-Clementines, a major work of the Judaeo-Christian Church, and the memoirs of Paul contained a rather inflated story of Saint Thecla. Her story was often bound together with Ruth, Esther, Susanna, and Judith in the semi-canonical 'Book of Women'.[80]

(4) The oldest Syrian lectionaries avoid calling Palm Sunday by the later habitual name 'Sunday of the Hosannas'. Even this insignificant fact may be due to a Judaeo-Christian survival—namely the entirely misleading use of the Hebrew acclamation *Hoshano*.[81]

A glimpse back at the series of Christian sources that were discussed thus far will doubtless demonstrate that a systematic comparison of their Old Testament lessons with those of the Synagogue can lead to conclusive results only if a reasonable equation of the different calendars has been established beforehand. We have realized how intimately interwoven the system of the *lectio continua* is with the respective *Proprium de Tempore*, which in turn depends upon the ecclesiastical calendar. Here, then, the question will arise whether such a calendaric investigation lies within the scope and compass of this book; after all, there are many strata of liturgy and music that are more or less independent from the calendar. Thus, a detailed investigation does not seem warranted. However, in view of the fact that the lessons, their order and mode of performance (cantillation) certainly represent the most archaic and common strata of the Jewish and the Christian liturgy, and that the chant of certain psalms and prayers sometimes depends upon lesson and calendar, it seemed to this writer that a brief study of the old, almost forgotten and hardly recognizable calendars is indispensable to a full understanding of our subject.

THE ECCLESIASTICAL YEAR AND ITS CONNEXION
WITH THE PERICOPES

Considering the age of Christian and, even more, of Jewish tradition, one is always inclined to regard the customs of these institutions as a homogeneous organization, their ceremonies as preserved *in toto*, and their calendars as systems untouched by internal or external influences for many centuries. Yet, as Jacob Burckhardt states, 'History is change', and the student must always bear in mind that a religion is alive only so long as it develops organically, and that every development means change and transformation.

The historic sources of Judaism and Christianity, as well as the documents testifying to the practice of public reading, lend weight to the assumption of a series of specific and radical changes. Sometimes these changes concerned only one sect or one geographic region, as exemplified by festivals of local saints. Sometimes peripheric communities held on to ancient customs, while the central authorities had decided on a reformation or revision, due occasionally to political considerations. But more often dogmatic principles, familiar to every student of the Eastern Churches, were responsible for sudden changes. Thus, we shall be confronted with a maze of traditions of different eras, not unlike the various strata of an ancient site which have to be sifted and separated carefully by the archaeologist.

Certainly the outstanding, indeed the epoch-making change of calendar and custom came to pass because of the final separation of the Church from Judaism. How conscientiously aware the Church was even then of the calendaric implications is shown to us in the famous edict of Nicaea wherein the Easter term was so calculated that it could not possibly coincide with the first day of the Jewish Passover.[82] Unlike the Jewish festival, the Christian Easter is Janus-faced: it looks mournfully back to Christ's Passion, of which it is the end, and at the same time glorifies His Resurrection with all of its eschatological splendour. These Easter rejoicings would seem no longer to carry any memory of Passover, the Jewish festival of deliverance. Actually, it will be seen that almost all the Churches have retained some memory of Passa of one kind or another. The same holds true for *Shabuot* (Pentecost) and other occasions in the Jewish festival calendar. These facts are well known and have been analysed by numerous scholars.[83]

What is not known, and has hitherto been investigated only perfunctorily, is the fact that many of the ecclesiastic lessons, up to the present day, show traces of the gradual change from the Jewish to the Christian order. This situation has been complicated by the confluence of no less than four different calendars, namely (a) the official Talmudic Jewish year; (b) the old rural Jewish year, referred to in some biblical passages; (c) the early Christian order of the liturgical calendar; and the introduction of the Julian and Gregorian systems.

The following investigation has the purpose of establishing and demonstrating two theses:

(1) The year of the Eastern Churches, and partly that of the Roman Church too, is, in spite of its seeming 'newness', in fact a pseudomorphosis of the two old Jewish calendars.

(2) *The Christian order of the pericopes was the main instrument of that pseudomorphosis and not its consequence.*

Let us first consider the time at which the reading of the *lectio continua* starts. WOLF begins its course on the vigil before Easter and ends it on the morning of the same day, one year later. The same holds good for MOZ and was once valid for the Greek tradition, already modified by GREEK T and GREEK P. ARM begins its lectionary on Epiphany, January 6th; but it seems that the real ecclesiastical New Year was September 1st or, according to the Gregorian calendar, its equivalent, September 13th, the 'Beginning of the Indictos'.[84] NEST and SYR state as the initial day of the *lectio continua* the first Sunday of the seven-week fasting season before Easter. JAC has Low Sunday (Dominica in Albis), the first Sunday after Easter, and SYR-PAL September 1st (13th) as the commencement of the annual reading cycle. ROM stands out as the representative of the Latin year, which today runs from Advent to Advent, while the original course seems to have proceeded from Septuagesima to Pentecost, and from Advent to Septuagesima.[85]

This yields the following tabulation.

COMMENCEMENTS OF THE LECTIONARY CYCLE

Day of beginning	Lectionaries	Day of beginning	Lectionaries
Epiphany	ARM	Holy Saturday and Easter Sunday	WOLF, MOZ, GREEK T
Septuagesima	ROM		
First Sunday of Quadragesima	NEST, SYR	Low Sunday	JAC
		Pentecost	GREEK P
		September 1st (or 13th)	ARM, GREEK T, SYR-PAL

73

This tabulation suggests that the ancient pentecontade calendar played a significant part in the arrangement of the lectionary cycle. The old Jewish calendar shows similar traces:

ANCIENT JEWISH LECTIONARY CYCLE AND CALENDAR

7 Adar	End of old triennial cycle	
Veadar		} 1 Pentecontade
1 Nisan	Beginning of triennial cycle	
Passover (15 Nisan)		} 1 Pentecontade
Pentecost		
9 Ab		} 1 Pentecontade
New Year		
Yom Kippur (Ancient New Year)		
Last day of Tabernacles	Beginning (and end) of the new annual cycle	

Here, too, the first pentecontade is closely connected with the lectionary cycle. That will not come as a surprise to the biblical scholar, as it is known that many nations of the ancient Near East made use of the calendar of the pentecontadic year. In recent decades, two important studies have shed new light upon these obscure and enigmatic divisions of the year. Julius Lewy has traced back the origin and the mythological significance of the pentecontade to the Accadian and Northern Mesopotamian civilization,[86] thus demonstrating the age and wide compass of that tradition. Its relics in Scripture and apocryphal literature have been brought into sharp focus by Dr Julian Morgenstern's great study on the Jewish calendars.[87]

The oldest calendar of the Israelites was based upon the pentecontade. This system, however, being orientated to the theory of seven winds or seven seasons, was applicable only for relatively small regions. It was a farmer's calendar. When, under King Solomon, Israel expanded, a solar calendar became necessary; this system was practically identical with that of the Phoenicians. Later, a luni-solar calendar superseded the strictly solar one; it operated with lunar months and, in consequence, has had some system of intercalation, by which the lunar and solar years could be harmonized. The day now came quite naturally to be reckoned from sunset, and the day of the New or the Full Moon came to play an increasingly important role in the calendar. It was then, after the Babylonian Exile, that the Jewish year was organized in its present form, whereby Passover coincides with the first Full Moon of the vernal equinox.

This development was, however, not a consistent one. Time and again the more conservative-minded agricultural regions brought up the old pentecontadic idea, and some remnants of it did survive in both the Jewish and Christian calendars.

These discoveries led to a better understanding of the shifts in the Jewish calendar. There are two New Years, functioning as the pivotal points of the festival cycle, namely 1 Nisan (the Spring New Moon) and 1 Tishri, the New Moon of the fall: they are separated by six months. Into the first falls the Passover-Pentecost pentecontade, into the second the Veadar-1 Nisan pentecontade. Once, the lectionary cycle started on 1 Nisan; today this event takes place at the Sabbath after Tabernacles, which initiates a somewhat corrupted pentecontade leading to *Hanukka*. When the *triennial cycle* was still in use, 7 Adar served as the terminal date of the first pentecontade before the Nisan New Year.

With the rise and organization of Christianity, the old and almost obsolete pentecontades assumed new life and new significance. Easter-tide regained, on Christological grounds, its paramount importance as the time of Passion and Resurrection. The liturgical complexes of a New Year were transferred from 1 Nisan to the 14th and 15th of the same month, a process which had been in the making for centuries, during the gradual revisions of the Jewish calendar. At the same time, the liturgical element of the Jewish New Year with its prophetic connotation of penitence and atonement was, among Christians, shifted to the days immediately preceding Easter, the Christian time of mourning and preparation. Yet the ancient Jewish overtones of Passover, so deeply rooted in Synagogue and Early Church, could not vanish altogether. We shall see that the Christian lectionaries of Good Friday and Holy Saturday (particularly that of its eve, the old *Paraskeve* [Gr. = preparation for Passa]) in general retained the reference to the feast of Passover, the Exodus, the unleavened bread, etc. These ideas are overlaid with at least three strata of more recent origin: (a) the beginning of the reading cycle shifted away from 1 Nisan; (b) a number of Old Testament passages, integral parts and characteristics of the penitential season of New Year and the Day of Atonement (1 and 10 Tishri), were transferred to the fasting season of the Church; and (c) those portions of the New Testament that refer to the Passion and Resurrection of Christ were stressed. On the other hand, some of the Churches preserved certain features of the Jewish autumnal New Year on the days centring around September 1st (13th).

Having achieved this momentous transposition, the Church was confronted with an old Jewish and a new Christian problem: the setting of the Easter date. As was shown above (cf. Dr Morgenstern's paper), both 14 and 15 Nisan were feast days; and it took Judaism a long time to eliminate the 14th in preference to the 15th; up to the present day, the 14th is observed as a fasting day by the first-born, in commemoration of the slaying of the sons of Egypt and the deliverance of the Jews.[88] There is ample evidence in patristic literature that the Church had to cope with a similar dilemma. A whole sect, the Quartodecimans, arose against the choice made by the authorities, who chose the first Sunday following the Spring full moon. This sect, on the periphery of early Christendom and by no means influenced by Jewish environment, had its centre in Asia Minor. That their revolt against the central authorities started at the perimeter of the Christian orbit again confirms Morgenstern's thesis that regions, remote from the centre of activity frequently upheld and preserved older customs.[89] These tendencies are reflected in the patristic writings before and even shortly after the Council of Nicaea, which decided in favour of the final separation from the Jewish calendar.[90]

This decision had far reaching consequences for the calendar. Hitherto Easter had been set on a specific day of a specific month, 15 Nisan, which had to be the first day of the full moon according to Jewish calculation. Henceforth it was celebrated on the Sunday *after* the Spring full moon, to prevent the participation of Christians on the Jewish Passover, the most stubborn habit of the 'Judaizers'.[91] This new shift threw the old Christian pentecontade entirely out of gear. Its full significance could be preserved only in a homogeneous and uniform calendar, not in a system where the (liturgically) movable and the (secularly) fixed dates were constantly overlapping.

Thus far, little attention has been paid to the Western Church and its traditions. In the previous chapter, we saw that the Roman Church has kept itself relatively free from post-biblical Jewish texts in its Breviary. Certain other features of its liturgy, however, display most convincingly some ancient traces of the Jewish mother religion, in particular its lessons and its psalmodic tradition. The latter element, being the most important and most consequential, will be discussed elsewhere in this book, from the liturgical as well as from the musical point of view. The Western system of lessons, now under examination, cannot be considered as a one-way passage, as far as its relation to Judaism is concerned.

Actually, for at least six centuries, there had been enacted a subtle but rather bitter play and counterplay between Church and Synagogue. During this period both institutions borrowed from each other and reacted, patently or latently, to the opponent's move.

This relationship has been amply demonstrated in Ludwig Venetianer's study 'Ursprung und Bedeutung der Propheten-Lektion'.[92] According to Venetianer, a major part of the Jewish Haftara (prophetic) lectionary owes its arrangement to the anti-Christian endeavours of Jewish apologists during the first two or even three centuries of Christianity. While some of Venetianer's parallels are unconvincing, and others rather far-fetched,[93] a sufficient amount of established fact remains to bear out, at least in part, the author's basic hypothesis. It will not be amiss to examine in the following pages some of the most interesting results of his paper, and to comment on them. After a remarkable excursus on the significance of the psalm verses selected for the Gradual and Introit of the Mass, the author compares the lessons of the Eucharistic services of the Roman Church of today (ROM) with those of rabbinic Judaism, basing his investigations on the ancient collection of homilies called *Pesiqta Rabbati* (quoted below as PR). This source contains not only exegetic parphrases on many lessons of the year but uses as subsidiary texts many psalm quotations, seemingly selected at random. Venetianer juxtaposes the following 'Special Sabbaths' and Sundays and their lessons:

Sabbath *Shekalim*	First Sunday of Quadragesima
Torah: Exod. 30:12–20	Sunday: *Invocabit*. Ps. 91:15
Haftara: Ezek. 34:1–32	Old Testament lesson: Monday thereafter: Ezek. 34:11–16
	New Testament lesson: Saturday of the week: Matt. 17 (tithes)

The parallelism is not evident at first sight, but is definite none the less. The Sabbath *Shekalim* was in olden times the day when the population was requested to pay the Temple tax (*Shekel*). The New Testament lesson has preserved this significance. The Monday of that week had the same Old Testament prophetic lesson as the Sabbath; furthermore,

the Introit of the Sunday begins with the word 'Invocabit' (Ps. 91:15).
PR quotes Ezek. 34, comparing it with Ps. 91 in its extensive discussion
of Exod. 30:12–20.

Sabbath *Zakhor* (Remember)	Second Sunday of Quadragesima
Torah: Deut. 25:17–21. (Earlier probably also: Exod. 17:8–16.)	Introit of Sunday *Reminiscere:* Ps. 25:6
Haftara: I Sam. 15	Gradual of Saturday before Sunday (Ember Day of Quadragesima): Ps. 79:12
Psalm Quotation (*PR*): Ps. 79:12	
	New Testament: Matt. 17

The Torah lesson could not be retained by the Church, since it deals
with Amalek and its curse, a point to which early Christianity had
objected already. An obsolete lesson of Judaism, Exod. 17:8–16, containing the first references to Amalek (Moses with Joshua, Aaron and
Hur on the mountain) has left its traces in the New Testament lesson
(Matt. 17), i.e. the story of Jesus with Peter, James and John on the
mountain. The Sabbath is called *Zakhor* (Remember) which is the
first word of the lesson about Amalek. This is preserved, if by name
only, in the Church, where the analogous Sunday is called *Reminiscere*
after its Introit Ps. 25:6. Another psalm verse, Ps. 79:12, the Gradual of
the Saturday before, is quoted by *PR* in its exegesis.

Sabbath *Para* (Heifer)	Third Sunday of Quadragesima (*Oculi*)
Torah: Num. 19:1–22	Old Testament: Wednesday there-after: Ezek. 36:23–38
Haftara: Ezek. 36:18–32	Friday: Num. 20:2–13
Psalm Quotation (*PR*): Ps. 12:8	Friday before: *Communio:* Ps. 12:8

One may not always agree with Venetianer's conclusion that many of
the prophetic lessons of the Synagogue were selected as polemics and
apologetics against the Church's hostile interpretation of the Torah
portion of the Synagogue, but in many cases the facts speak for themselves, whatever the causes might be.

Passover. First day (15 Nisan)	Easter Eve (once the night before 15 Nisan)
Torah: Exod. 12:21–51 (twice also on Sabbath before)	Old Testament: Exod. 12:1–11 (also on Good Friday)
Haftara: Joshua 5 (today)	Ezek. 37:1–14
Ezek. 37 (formerly)	

This analogy is self-explanatory, after the above remarks on the shifting of the calendar.

Passover. Seventh day
    Torah: Exod. 13:17—15:26
    Haftara: II Sam. 22
    Psalm Quotation (PR): Ps. 35:17

Holy Saturday
    Exod. 14:24—15:3
    Ps. 35:17
    (also Introit of Palm Sunday)

Shabuot (Pentecost)
    Psalm Quotation (PR): Ps. 68:18

Pentecost
    Ps. 68 (Introit of Pentecost)

Rosh Hashana (New Year: 1 Tishri)
First day
    Torah: Num. 29:1–6
    Haftara: I Sam. 1
Second day
    Torah: Gen. 22 ⎫ (today)
    Haftara: Jer. 31 ⎭
    Psalm Quotations (PR): Ps. 47:6
    and 89:16 (formerly)

Various days
    December 28th
    Jer. 32
    Gen. 21 (in Brev.)
    Easter vigil
    Gen. 22
    Sunday after Christmas
    Ps. 47 (Alleluia)
    January 1st (Circumcision)
    Ps. 89 (Offertory of third Mass)

With the exception of the comparatively recent Jewish lesson Gen. 22 which in the Church is a lesson of the Easter vigil, all other passages point to the parallel between Christmas and the Jewish New Year. Venetianer concludes:

> This demonstrates nothing less than that the first Christian community celebrated the birth of Christ on the Jewish New Year. The transfer of Christmas to December 25th did not take place before the fourth century, but the fact that the Roman Church retained just those Psalms which are most characteristic of *Rosh Hashana* [Shofar references] . . . renders the best proof of our thesis.[94]

This hypothesis, at first sight not too convincing, receives an amazing confirmation, unknown to Venetianer, through NEST, which provides for the Sunday after Christmas Gen. 21 and I Sam. 1, the two old Jewish lessons of the New Year.[95]

Yom Kippur (10 Tishri, formerly
    1 Tishri)
Morning
    Torah: Lev. 16
           Num. 29:7–11
    Haftara: Isa. 57:14–58:14
Afternoon
    Torah: Lev. 18:1–30 (today)
           Lev. 23:26–32
          (formerly)

Fast-day lessons of the Church
    First Sunday of Quadragesima and
    Friday after Ash Wednesday
    Isa. 58:1–9a
    Easter vigil
    Jonah
    Gen. 1
    Ps. 27 (Gradual of Friday after
        Ash Wednesday)

Haftara:
Jonah
Deut. 6:4–7:11
Gen. 1:1[96]   (formerly
Deut. 7:12 ff   also)
Psalm Quotations (PR): Ps. 27

Sabbatum quatuor temporum Septembris
Lev. 23:26–32

With the exception of Lev. 16 and Num. 29, the most recent lessons of the Synagogue, the major part of Old Testament lessons occur in the Roman Church, either during the fasting pentecontade including its climax, the solemn eve of Easter, or on *Sabbatum quatuor temporum Septembris*, the Ember Day of September sometimes coinciding with *Yom Kippur*. Nor is this all: the full scope of this parallelism was unknown to Venetianer, who did not consult sources outside the Roman orbit. By comparing lectionaries of Eastern Christianity we shall understand the analogies in their full significance. We find Deut. 6:4–7, 11 and 7:12 ff in ARM, GREEK T, and the Georgian lectionary on the first Friday of the fast, this passage being *the first pericope of the lectio continua which runs straight to Holy Saturday*.[97] The second Torah portion of the Synagogue, Lev. 23 is conspicuous on the first Sunday of Quadragesima both in JAC and SYR-PAL. Isa. 58:1–12 is read in the Roman order not only during Lent, but also at its very beginning, namely the first Sunday of Quadragesima, NEST, LUX, WOLF and the Ambrosian rite. Thus we realize that the pericopes pertaining to *Yom Kippur* are read on the following days:

Date	Isa. 57:1–58	Lev. 23	Jonah	Deut. 6:4 ff	Gen. 1:1 ff
Beginning of Quadragesima	NEST, LUX, WOLF, AMBR	JAC, SYR-PAL		ARM, GEORG, GREEK T	NEST, ARM
Midfast	ROM				
Ember Day of Sept.		ROM		NEST (Sept. 14)	
Easter Vigil			ROM, JAC, SYR-PAL, NEST, WOLF, GREEK T		ARM, ROM, WOLF, LUX, JAC, SYR-PAL, GREEK T
Dec. 25 (or Jan. 6)					ARM, GEORG, SYR-PAL, GREEK T

According to this tabulation, most of the parallels to the lessons of *Yom Kippur* are to be found at the beginning of Quadragesima, in the Vigil of Easter and in the Christmas cycle. How must these facts be interpreted in the light of our theory? The *Pesiqta* makes the following interesting remark: 'The sons of Aaron died on 1 Nisan; why do we read about their death on *Yom Kippur*? To teach us that the death of the righteous atones in the same way as *Yom Kippur* atones.'[98]

This passage referring to a pericope which was read in Christian churches at the beginning of the Passion of Christ, has a suspiciously apologetic character, and Venetianer's hypothesis of a shifting of the Jewish order, for apologetic purposes, appears really plausible here. The fact that the Easter vigil adopted a good many traits of *Yom Kippur* is well known and confirms our theory. The Ember Day in September, on the other hand, shows in its liturgy probably the last traces of a transposition from the *Yom Kippur*, in spite of the radical change of the Christian calendar.[99] We have already mentioned the old custom of celebrating the birth of Christ on the birthday of the world; in Judaism the latter shifted from *Yom Kippur* to *Rosh Hashana*, but the older tradition was perpetuated in outlying Jewish communities at *Yom Kippur*. When the Church moved the birthday of Christ, it also transferred its typical lesson, so that we now discern two New Years of the Christian liturgical year, the Easter vigil and Easter, and Christmastide. Both have preserved certain elements of the two ancient Jewish New Years.

An analogous transposition of references may also be observed in Jewish sources. In its discussion of *Yom Kippur*, the *Pesiqta* quotes a great number of verses from Ps. 27, all of them alluding to Passover (Easter). Later it says, rather meekly: 'The rabbis understand this psalm as significant of *Yom Kippur* and *Rosh Hashana*'. Yet, without any clear motivation, the *Pesiqta* compares Ps. 27 with the Song of Moses, Exod. 15, verse for verse. This is read or chanted in the Greek and other Eastern Churches during the Easter vigil, stressing the identity with the Jewish Passover.

The Roman counterpart of the Jewish New Year, Atonement and Tabernacles cycle is Embertide; it has preserved some more of the Jewish pericopes:

Sabbath *Shuva* (Sabbath of Penitence between *Rosh Hashana* and *Yom Kippur*) Haftara:	*Quatuor Temporum Septembris* Friday Hos. 14:2–10 Saturday Mic. 7:14–20
Isa. 55:6–56:8 or Ezek. 17:21–18:32 } (today)	
Hos. 14:2–10 and Mic. 7:18–20 } (formerly)	

Satis superque! Here we break off our discussion and supplementation of Venetianer's paper, convinced that the parallels demonstrated by him can well speak for themselves.

It should be possible by now to formulate a general law about the preservation of ancient tradition in the realm of liturgy. Such a law has received a good, but somehow narrow formulation and interpretation in Baumstark's article 'Das Gesetz von der Erhaltung des Alten in liturgisch hochwertiger Zeit' ('The law of the preservation of ancient tradition in liturgically significant seasons').[100] Therein the author traces the ultra-conservative attitude of almost all Churches in questions of the liturgical or calendaric order and arrangement of the Easter and Christmas cycles; his paper is, however, limited to Christian liturgies and by this very fact inadequate for comparative use.

We must go one step further. Certain strata, common to both Christianity and Judaism, have been left untouched by all subsequent changes, and, though corrupted by pseudomorphosis, have survived up to the present day. It is only in the oldest layers that the original mould of tradition is discernible, as the connexion between New Year, Passover and the original pentecontadic calendar demonstrates. Thus, one may formulate the law of preservation as follows.

In Judaism and Christianity basic traditions are retained, even under changing circumstances, provided two conditions are fulfilled: (1) The traditions must have their roots in liturgically important seasons and must be traceable to their very beginning; (2) they must have grown in the mother soil of ancient custom, belonging to an older system of pre-Christian or pre-Jewish culture, in which they were originally rooted. The classic instance, of course, is the Nestorian calendar: though its pentecontades all have biblical or Christian names and functions, they stem directly from the old Babylonian-Accadian division of the year, which, in turn, had influenced the Jewish cycle of festivals.

How did the liturgical changes, so immensely important for the history of Western culture, come to pass? While this question with all its ramifications reaches far beyond the scope of this book, it may be answered here with regard to one very limited rubric, the lessons. It is our conviction that the order of lessons, far from being a *consequence* of the change, was one of its chief agents. In order to prove this thesis, we shall compare the most significant lessons of the various arrangements of the ecclesiastical year with regard to their status before and after their transformations during the development of ecclesiastical and synagogal liturgy. This will not only furnish the necessary proof of the thesis just stated, but will also guide us in our further study of the liturgico-musical interrelation between Church and Synagogue.

COMPARATIVE ANALYSIS OF THE LESSONS COMMON TO JUDAISM AND CHRISTIANITY

Having surveyed our sources but briefly, we have formulated our thesis and shall now proceed to the final examination of the material under the twofold aspect of the interrelation of calendar and pericope (the pericope being the variable element), and the interrelation of pericope and Church tradition, with the pericope here treated as the invariable element.

It might be useful first to recapitulate certain facts concerning the various Church histories which will furnish some fundamental information. The parent rites of Christianity stem from five ancient centres, viz. Rome, Antioch, Jerusalem, Edessa-Nisibis, and Alexandria. In the following comparison, the Alexandrian rite and its derivatives (Coptic, Ethiopian) are not included, since they came early under the dominant influence of the Greek rite and have since that time been entirely Byzantinized. The daughter-rites of Antioch and Jerusalem are JAC, GREEK T, SYR-PAL, and, to a certain extent, the old Gallican order, of which WOLF and LUX are the chief representatives. The derivatives of Edessa-Nisibis are NEST, SYR, and, to a major part, the Georgian rite. Between Antioch and Nisibis ARM holds an intermediate position.[101]

Of all these centres, the Roman and Antiochene rites have many common elements, whereas the East Syrian order of the liturgy is somewhat remote from the foci of events and decisions. It is just for that reason that NEST and SYR, perhaps also ARM, have preserved more ancient features than all of the other rites. After all, the origin of the Edessa liturgy dates back to the middle of the fourth century, and the Armenian and Georgian rites are hardly of more recent origin. The Monophysite (Jacobite) dispute, forming the background of JAC and SYR-PAL, arose in the fifth century and the final schism occurred in 527. The documents WOLF and LUX, both belonging to the Gallican rite, date back to the late fifth and the late seventh centuries respectively;

thus they were compiled before the final abolition of Gallicanism. GREEK T and GREEK P finally, though written relatively late (twelfth and thirteenth centuries), reflect faithfully the old Chrysostom liturgy of the early fifth century, the most important daughter-liturgy of Antioch.

We shall now compare the lessons as read at the oldest feasts of the *Proprium de Tempore* of the various Churches with the pericopes of the Synagogue (as recited on those days of the Jewish year) which, in our opinion, correspond to some of the ecclesiastical lessons. In all these tables the italicized lessons correspond to those of the Synagogue.

FIRST WEEK OF QUADRAGESIMA

Synagogue	ROM	WOLF, LUX, MOZ	JAC, SYR-PAL	ARM, GEORG	NEST, SYR	GREEK T and P
Combination of 1 Nisan and ancient *Yom Kippur* Lev. 23. Deut. 6:4. Gen. 1:1. Jonah, Isa 58.	*Invocabit* (Gradual) Ps. 91 (equals in Hebrew the word 'in-voice', call to payment)	Isa. 40 Isa. 58	*Lev. 23:23 Joel 2:12 Dan. 1*	Exod. 1, Jo. 1:14; *Deut. 6:4 Isa. 40:1*	*Gen. 1:1* (beginning of contin-uous les-son) *Isa. 58:1*	*Gen. 1:1* Isa. 1:1 Prov. 1:1
Sabbath *Shekalim* (Temple taxes) *Ezek.* 34:1–32	(Temple-tax) *Matt.* 17:24–27 *Ezek.* 34:11–46					

The idea of fasting dominates the lessons; hence the prevalence of those pericopes at the beginning of Quadragesima, which are read on *Yom Kippur*. More significant, however, is the equation with 1 Nisan, the initial date of the reading under the triennial cycle, as evidenced in the lessons of GREEK T, NEST, SYR, and, on the other hand, of the Sabbath *Shekalim* and ROM.

SECOND WEEK OF QUADRAGESIMA

Synagogue Sabbath *Zakhor* (Remember)	ROM	WOLF, LUX, MOZ	JAC, SYR-PAL	ARM, GEORG	NEST, SYR	GREEK T and P
Deut. 25:17–19 Deut. 26 I Sam. 15	*Reminiscere.* (Introit) Deut. 26: 12–19	Deut. 26 WOLF Deut. 25 LUX	Gen. 32:24–32 Jer. 36:21–31 Prov. 3:1–13 (JAC) Joel 2:12–20 (JAC)	Begin-ning of contin-uous les-son with I Kings 1; Prov. 1; Jer. 1	Continua-tion of lessons from Gen. 1, and Jos.	Continua-tion of lessons from Gen., Isa., and Prov.

Since the Synagogue offers no traditional counterpart for the second week of fasting, the Christian sources display a most heterogeneous mosaic of lessons. The only discernible traces of common background occur in Synagogue, ROM, LUX, and perhaps WOLF. The Eastern Churches show nothing common to all of them. We can expect real parallels again in Holy Week, where the Churches provide for *lectio continua* from the second week of Quadragesima up to Holy Week. The beginning takes place on Palm Sunday.

Synagogue: Sabbath *Haggadol* (the great) last Sabbath before Passover	ROM	WOLF, LUX, MOZ	JAC	SYR-PAL	ARM, GEORG	NEST, SYR, GREEK T and P
Exod. 12:1-20	Exod. 15:27-16:7		Gen. 49 Lev. 23:34	Num. 22:21-34		*Exod.* 12: 1-18
Ezek. 45:16-46	Matt. 21		(Tabernacles) Deut. 8	Judg. 5:1-11 (Deborah's		(NEST) Gen. 49
Mal. 3:4-24	Matt. 26-27	*Mal.* 3	Jos. 8 II Sam. 6 Prov. 1:20 Zach. 9:9 Dan. 8:1 Isa. 40	Song)	Zach. 9:9-12	Zach. 9

The most interesting of these lessons is JAC (Lev. 23:34), which contains the statutes of Tabernacles. It is a case in point of our contention that the selection of lessons was not a consequence but an instrument of the theological shifts and changes within the Churches. Palm Sunday is called in the Jacobite Church *ahad esh-sha-'anin*, the Sunday of the Hosannas; the remembrance of Christ's entrance into Jerusalem among the Hosannas of the throng being the distinguishing feature of the day. Hosanna, in Syriac, is also the word for the palm-branches; and these, in turn, are an integral part of the Jewish celebration of Tabernacles.[102] It is not known exactly at what time the Jerusalem-Syrian Church equated Palm Sunday with Hosanna- (Palm-branches) Sunday. It must have happened fairly early, since Aetheria already knew the custom and its name.[103] The juxtaposition of Matt. 21 and Lev. 23:34 in the Jacobite lectionary contributed to the institution of this custom. Under these circumstances we should not wonder that only the Aramean Churches emphasized this facet of Palm Sunday, for only there the Hosanna of Matt. 21 could linguistically be identified with the palm branches of Tabernacles.

Another interesting feature of Palm Sunday's lessons is WOLF's assignment of Mal. 3; this must date back to a very ancient tradition, since this chapter is not read in the course of a *lectio continua*; yet, it is not possible to recognize a direct connexion of that particular Sunday with the contents of the assigned passage. It seems that the tradition of the Synagogue simply was adopted and Palm Sunday (the last Sunday before Easter) was identified with the *Sabbath haggadol*, the last Sabbath before Passover.[104] This relation cannot have been one-sided, since the name *Sabbath haggadol* = Great Sabbath, itself displays the influence of the Greek Church which called Holy Saturday the *Sabbaton megalon* or *Sabbatum magnum*. It is hard to determine how close this interrelation was at one time or another.

The Torah portion concerning the old (Egyptian) Passover, Exod. 12, is read only in NEST and in the Synagogue; the Nestorian Church seems to have retained this lesson as a kind of memento of the approaching Passover-Easter. Time and again we shall encounter some of these Passover survivals in the lessons of the Easter vigil and those preceding them.

In all liturgies the lessons of Palm Sunday show almost exclusively eclogadic portions of Scripture, especially such as befitted best the significance of the day to Christianity: Zech. 9 (the Messiah on the white ass), Isa. 40 (the voice crying), Gen. 49 (Jacob's blessing), etc. One may say that the eclogadic lesson always interrupts the older *lectio continua*, whenever a new stratum of tradition is superimposed upon an older one.

Exceedingly conspicuous, yet, at the same time more complex are the interrelations and conflations characteristic of the lessons of Holy Saturday and the Easter vigil (see Table p. 87).

The lessons of Holy Saturday and the Easter vigil display many and variegated likenesses to Jewish lessons of Passover and *Yom Kippur*. The most ancient element seems to be Jonah, which is common to all Churches and to the Jewish Day of Atonement. To the same category belongs Gen. 1 which, in olden times, was read together with Jonah in the Synagogue. The idea behind the Genesis passage was the remembrance of the creation of the world, and dates back to a time when the Day of Atonement was celebrated on 1 Tishri, the autumnal New Year's day. But Jewish tradition knows of two 'birthdays of the world'. The older one was observed in the spring and later on abolished in preference to 1 Tishri.[105] In the writings of the Church Fathers some faint traces of that older tradition, the spring New Year, are still discernible.[106] But there is one important difference between the reading of Jonah and that of Gen. 1: while Jonah is especially well chosen for the Day of Atonement, its choice for Holy Saturday seems a little too

HOLY SATURDAY (EASTER VIGIL)

Synagogue	ROM	WOLF, LUX MOZ	'AC	SYR-PAL	ARM, GEORG	NEST, SYR	GREEK T GREEK P
Yom Kippur lectionary Lev. 16; Lev. 23; Num. 29; Lev. 18; Isa. 57–58; Jonah formerly Gen. 1:1 Deut. 6–7 Psalm quotation (PR): Ps. 27	*Jonah* Gen. 1:1 Ps. 27	*Jonah* Gen. 1:1 Hab. 2 Hab. 3 Dan. 3	*Num. 28–29* (Passover!) *Jonah*	*Jonah* Gen. 1–3 Isa. 60	*Jonah* Gen. 1–3 Isa. 60	*Jonah*	*Jonah* Gen. 1:1 Isa. 60–61 I Kings 17 II Kings 4
Passover—1st day lectionary Exod. 12 21ff Jos. 5	Exod. 12 1–20	Exod. 12	Gen. 40 Job. 27	Isa. 60	Exod. 12 Job. 38		Exod. 12 Isa. 63–67 Jos. 5
Sabbath of Passover Ezek. 37	Ezek. 37	Ezek. 37 Jos. 3 1–4			II Kings 2 Ezek. 37		Ezek. 37
Passover 7th day lectionary Exod. 13–15 II Sam. 22 Isa. 10–12 Psalm quotation (PR): Ps. 35	Exod. 14 2a–15 Ps. 35	Exod. 14–15 (MOZ)			Jos. 1 Jer. 38 Exod. 14–15 Dan. 3		Jer. 38 Exod. 13–15 Dan. 3
New Year lectionary Gen. 22 Num. 29 1–6 I Sam. 1	Gen. 22 Lament. 3, 22ff	Gen. 22	Num. 28–29	Gen. 22	Gen. 22	Gen. 22	Gen. 22

artificially contrived by the primitive Church, hence it is probably a Judaeo-Christian pseudomorphosis. After all, the idea of sincere penitence and its recognition by God is not too fitting for the eve of Christ's resurrection. On the other hand, Jesus referred to Jonah as to a symbol of his own destiny; cf. Matt. 12:40-42. We shall later on see that Jonah was, for doctrinal reasons, chosen for the Christmas cycle as well. Thus far the liturgical identity of Holy Saturday and *Yom Kippur* rests upon two conceptions; both are great days of mourning and fasting, both are memorials of the world's creation.[107]

The remainder of the Christian lessons reflects either directly Christ's death, or, more distinctively, the old Jewish Passover, with or without Christological overtones. Is it not surprising to find on the day, so burdened with sorrow, the exuberant passages of Exod. 14-15, or the consistent reminder of the Jewish Passover of Exod. 12:2?[108] A similar memory has survived in GREEK T's Josh. 5, the Passover in Gilgal, read in the Synagogue on the first day of Passover. To the same class belongs also JAC's Num. 28-29.

While these lessons follow the ancient Jewish practice, the situation is not so simple with regard to Ezek. 37, read in the Synagogue on the Sabbath of Passover and now an integral part of the Easter vigil in many Churches. Venetianer's assumption that Ezek. 37 was the original Judaeo-Christian lesson for Holy Saturday (prophecy of Resurrection), and that official Judaism had to adopt it for apologetic reasons, seems very plausible; for this passage really has no direct connexion with the ancient Passover.[109]

Similar is the case of Gen. 22 (Isaac's binding), read on the Jewish New Year's day and on the Easter vigil; here the Christological overtones prevail by far over the Jewish tradition, but the Isaac portion evidently dates back to ancient and genuine customs of the Synagogue.

Careful examination will reveal that the lessons of Quadragesima and Holy Week stem from three strata: (1) the oldest, which refers to Passover without a clear Christological interpretation; (2) the middle stratum, which shows pseudomorphoses of the Jewish High Holyday portions with distinct Christological overtones; (3) the third and most recent part which is made up of prophetic chapters of eclogadic character, like Dan. 3 or Isa. 60, which are chosen as direct predictions of the Messianic age.

The lessons of the Jewish High Holydays, on the other hand, when borrowed by the Church, were split into two parts by the successive calendaric shifts. One part was used for the eve of the liturgical New Year (Easter), the other for the concept of Christ's birth, as signifying the rise of a new era. The Judaeo-Christian celebration of Christ's birth on the day of *Rosh Hashana* induced the incipient Catholic Church to transfer the passages Gen. 1–3 from the autumnal cycle of the Synagogue to the new Christmas cycle. Thus, we shall find passages once characteristic of Theophany, birth of a prophet, creation of the world, etc., also in the early documents of the Christmas cycle. In later sources they gradually disappear.

The tabulation of Christmas lessons on p. 90 shows clearly the movement away from the autumnal New Year cycle of traditional Judaism toward the new Christmas and Epiphany season.[110] Historically and chronologically, Epiphany was the older festival and originally held the double significance of a feast of Theophany and of Christ's birth and adoration. In the Synagogue these ideas are entirely separate entities. The Jewish New Year constantly stresses the ideas of birth and moral rebirth. It is then that the passages Gen. 21 (Isaac's birth) and I Sam. 1–2 (Samuel's birth and Hannah's praise) are read. Moral rebirth is also the subject of Jer. 31, the Haftara for New Year, which contains the vision of a renewed covenant. Formerly, when *Yom Kippur* still had the function of the New Year, Gen. 1, the creation of the world, was recited. Since the abolition of the triennial and the introduction of the one-year cycle, this lesson has been shifted to the first Sabbath after Tabernacles, which still belongs to the autumnal cycle.[111]

True penitence and remorse, the keynote of *Yom Kippur*, finds its classic expression in Isa. 57–58 and Jonah; and it is astounding that these stern messages found their way into the jubilant atmosphere of the Christmas-Epiphany cycle. A part of the Isaiah pericope is read in WOLF, the oldest lectionary of the Latin Church. It is rather interesting to note its modifications; as its text did not coincide with the Jewish lesson, it probably started where the synagogal lesson ended.[112] As a result the idea of penitence is beautifully coupled with exultation and triumph.

> For our transgressions are multiplied before Thee
> And our sins testify against us:
> For our transgressions are with us;

Synagogue	ROM	WOLF, LUX, MOZ	JAC	SYR-PAL	ARM, GEORG	NEST, SYR	GREEK T, GREEK P
Lectionary of New Year, Sabbath (*Shuva*), Day of Atonement (*Yom Kippur*), and Tabernacles (*Sukkot*)							
Jer. 31	Jer. 31 (Dec. 28)		Jer. 31				Num. 24
Deut. 33 (Tab.)			Deut. 33 (Epiphany)				
Gen. 21 (New Year)						Gen. 21	
I Sam. 1₋₂ (New Year)			I Sam. 1$_{8-10}$			I Sam. 1-2	
Hos. 14 } Sabbath			Hos. 13$_6$-14$_3$	Mic. 5	Mic. 5	Mic. 4	Mic. 4; 5
Mic. 7 } *Shuva*			Mic. 7$_{1-20}$				
Isa. 57-58		Isa. 58-59		Prov. 1	Exod. 14	Exod. 2$_{1-10}$	Exod. 2; 14-16
Jonah				Jonah	Isa. 7; 40 ; 35	Isa. 7; 8; 9	Jos. 3
Lev. 16; Lev. 23 } *Yom Kippur*				Isa. 7; Isa. 8	Isa. 11; 9		Isa. 7; 8; 9; 11
Num. 29 formerly				Isa. 12			II Kings 2; 5
Gen. 1:1			Ezek. 34	Gen. 1-3	Gen. 1:1		Gen. 1
Deut. 6-7			Lev. 26				Dan. 2
Psalm quotations (PR): Ps. 27							Gen. 32
29:16	Ps. 29 Third mass. Christmas Ps. 85 (six times in Advent)						Judge s 6
85							
Gen. 1:1 } End of Tabernacles. Beginning of annual	Isa. 42 (MOZ)				Isa. 42	Isa. 42	Isa. 42
Isa. 42 } Jewish lectionary					Dan. 3		
Exod. 33 (Formerly in the week of Tabernacles)			Exod. 33-34 (Epiphany)				

And as for our iniquities, we know them. . . .[113]

As for Me, this is My covenant with them, saith the Lord,

My Spirit that is upon Thee, and My words

Which I have put in Thy mouth,

Shall not depart from out of Thy mouth,

Nor out of the mouth of Thy seed. . . .[114]

Arise, shine; for Thy light is come, and the glory of the Lord is risen upon Thee. . . .[115]

This is a clear indication that the arrangement of the lessons was instrumental in readjusting and shifting the ecclesiastical year away from the Jewish order, by reinterpreting certain Jewish traditions and charging them with Christological ideas.[116] The very same passages form an integral part of the Easter lessons of many of the Oriental Churches, implying a 'second shift' away from the autumnal cycle.

The book Jonah, typical in all other Churches of Holy Saturday, is read on the Vigil of Epiphany in SYR-PAL, again suggesting the transfer of Jewish customs to the Christian lectionary.[117] Obviously, this time the emphasis is not centred on Jonah, but on God's everlasting mercy, and the penitence and moral rebirth of the Ninevites. The same idea is stressed in the lesson Exod. 34 (SYR-PAL), the Theophany, which is read in the Synagogue on the so-called 'historic' fast-days. It prevails also in Hos. 14 and Mic. 7 (ROM, JAC), the prophetic portions of the 'Sabbath of Repentance' between New Year and the Day of Atonement. It is characteristic of the conservative attitude of ROM that these very portions are still read on the *Sabbatum Quatuor Temporum* of the autumnal season.

The element of Theophany, predominant at Epiphany, is by no means so important in the Jewish ritual; apart from the *lectio continua*, the pertinent passages, Exod. 33–34 and Deut. 33, occur as special lessons only on the feast of Tabernacles. Here, the connexion is just vaguely discernible: Deut. 33 appears as an Epiphany lesson in JAC only, and Exod. 33 as *lectio continua* for the Sunday after Epiphany in SYR-PAL. Both facts are singular and do not permit of any concrete conclusion. In Christianity the Old Testament elements of penitence, rebirth, and creation prevail by far over the idea of Theophany, which is hardly touched upon in its Old Testament pericopes. The New Testament lessons, of course, emphasize this main aspect of Epiphany.

Apart from the analogous pericopes which are directly connected with the system of the ecclesiastical year, there is abundant evidence of the preservation of individual pericopes, but lack of space allows us to cite only one here. Certain Pentateuch and prophetic lessons were juxtaposed in the early synagogal systems; we find them, in exactly the same combination, in Christian arrangements. Thus, Gen. 21 and I Sam. 1 are coupled in many Epiphany or Christmas lessons, just as they are juxtaposed in the liturgy of the Jewish New Year. It would be a highly meritorious task to analyse *all* lectionary systems of the Church and compare them with the order of the Synagogue.

One instance may demonstrate the extreme intricacy of some comparisons. We choose the analogous feasts of *Shabuot* and Pentecost.

Shabuot is the ancient festival of firstlings, but was later re-interpreted as the day on which the Revelation and Legislation took place on Mount Sinai. It follows Passover in an exact pentecontade, whereby each of the forty-nine days of *'Omer* was publicly and solemnly counted during the daily services. The *'Omer* was originally a wave-offering of sheaves of grain immediately after Passover (cf. Lev. 23: 10–14; *PR* XVIII; Lev. R. XXVIII, 5) and this sacrifice was accompanied by certain clearly pre-monotheistic rites. After the destruction of the Temple and the abolition of all sacrifices the *'Omer* was only retained as a symbolic counting of the days between Passover and *Shabuot*. With the rabbinic interpretation of *Shabuot* as the anniversary of the Revelation on Mount Sinai it obtained the following lessons: Torah: Deut. 16:9–12 and Exod. 19:1–20; 25. Haftara: First Day, Hab. 3; Second Day, Ezek. 1:1–28.

In the New Testament, it was on the day of *Shabuot* that the Holy Ghost manifested Himself, according to Acts 2, whereupon the Church was founded.

The lectionary of Pentecost and its octave in the Roman Church displays two basic motifs: the outpouring of the Holy Ghost which created the Church, and the remembrance of the *Manna* and the *'Omer*. Accordingly, the following passages are read or chanted:

References to the New Revelation	References to *Manna* and *'Omer*
Acts 2:1–11	Monday Introit: Ps. 81:17
John 14:23–31	Tuesday Offert.: Ps. 78:23–25
Acts 10:34; 42–48	
Acts 2:14–21 (quoting Joel)	
Joel 2:23–24; 26–27	

Ember Days after Pentecost

References to the New Revelation	References to *Manna* and *'Omer*
Joel 2:28–32	Lev. 23:9–11, 15–17, 21
Communion: John 3:8	Deut. 26:1–11

Under what circumstances did this selection of passages come into being? When Christianity arose, *Shabuot* was in Judaism not yet generally acclaimed as the feast of Revelation; rather, it was understood as the old agricultural festival of firstlings.

The incipient Jewish notion of *Shabuot* as memento of Revelation was countered by the Church with the interpretation of Pentecost as the festival of the New Revelation. The older, agricultural significance was not entirely forgotten, though, by the Church, but put into the background. (See in the lectionary Lev. 23, Deut. 26—firstlings, etc.) The Jewish sect of the Karaites has in its *Shabuot* lectionary the passage of Joel, which is first alluded to and then actually read in the Church; conversely, the *Shabuot* Haftara (Ezek. 1) forms a part of the Nestorian lectionary for Pentecost.[118]

Here we must terminate our investigation of the pericopes. The conclusions we have reached demonstrate that under certain conditions the synagogal traditions were preserved in most of the Churches. Christological, calendaric and dogmatic reasons were the chief causes of their changes, shifts and their deviations. Once the transposition of the calendar was accomplished, the chief points in the liturgical year carried on the old lessons, originally assigned to them in Judaism. In addition, even certain *calendaric* identities have escaped the subsequent rearrangements of the Christian ecclesiastical year. Thus, a few remnants of the pre-Christian calendar, together with their respective lessons, have survived to the present day. To sum up: the Latin, the Nestorian and Armenian Churches have preserved most faithfully the traditions of ancient Judaism. Geographically speaking they were all remote from the main ecclesiastical centres. One might have expected much closer parallelisms in the Jerusalemitic, Syro-Palestinian and strictly Jacobite rituals. In considering this apparently paradoxical situation, we are again reminded of Dr Morgenstern's theory that it is especially those regions which are remote from the central seat of authority and its constantly developing changes which tend to preserve and to cultivate older customs. Indeed, rather than Palestine, it was Rome, Armenia and East Syria which represented the outlying communities of the Jewish Hellenistic world. Nor was this relationship one-sided: there are numerous cases where the Jewish ritual was influenced, directly or indirectly, by Christian ideas and customs. This, however, began only in the eighth or ninth centuries, and we shall discuss the relative facts more extensively in Part II.

We have deliberately omitted from our examination one category of lessons which today holds a singular position but was once merely one pericope among others; the Lamentations. They form an integral and most remarkable part of the Roman liturgy of Holy Week; they are chanted in an ancient Hebrew mode, and the Hebrew initial letters of each are rendered musically. Their music is not a simple syllabic chant, but a clearly melismatic and archaic psalmody, precisely noted. While they, by virtue of their melismatic structure, constitute a singular feature of the Roman rite, many of the other lessons were once chanted in a similar fashion. The Greek, Armenian and Syrian Churches likewise have preserved this type of melismatic lesson. The Canticles especially were performed in this elaborately melismatic fashion by the Eastern Churches.[119]

The florid, but well regulated performance of certain lessons is another heritage of the Synagogue, as has been realized by many scholars. Even the simple readings are intended for ecphonetic performance, i.e. a kind of recitation at the borderland of psalmody and *Sprechgesang* (heightened, almost chanted speech). Its traditions and forms of notation are very old: some of them date back to the pre-Christian era of the Synagogue. In the next chapter we shall discuss these phenomena from the historical angle, whilst in Part II we shall undertake their paleographic and musical analysis.

NOTES CHAPTER III

1. E. B. Löwensohn, in *Jüdisches Literaturblatt*, 1894, pp. 127, 131, 133.
2. The studies in anthropology, folklore, psychology of primitive civilization and comparative religion, such as Frazer's *Golden Bough*, Freud's *Totem and Tabu*, Rank's *Essays* and others have contributed considerably to a deeper understanding of these phenomena, although the psychoanalytical articles in particular ought to be read with a good deal of caution.
3. The sources in M. Gaster, *The Biblical Lessons*, pp. 22 ff; ELB, pp. 156 ff; A. Büchler, 'The reading of the Law . . . in a triennial cycle', in *JQR*, V, pp. 420 ff; J. Hamburger, *Real-Encyklopädie*, article 'Vorlesen'.
4. ELB, pp. 157–9; Büchler, op. cit., p. 425.
5. Cf. E. Schürer, *Geschichte des jüdischen Volkes im Zeitalter Christi* (3rd ed., 1898), II, pp. 427–63; also S. Krauss, *Synagogale Altertümer*, pp. 170 ff.
6. A. Baumstark, 'Nichtevangelische syrische Perikopenordnungen des ersten Jahrtau-

sends' in *Liturgiegeschichtliche Quellen und Forschungen*, III (Münster, 1921) p. 184, writes: 'These correspondences [between Syriac and synagogal pericopes] teach us at least that one should approach the problems of the inter-relations between Jewish and Christian pericopes only with full consideration of the entire Christian material; the one-sided evaluation of one single Christian rite will almost necessarily result in wrong conclusions and perspectives.'

7. *M. Sota*, VII, 8; *M. Yoma*, VII, 1; *Jer. Yoma*, II, 8, 41a. Cf. Krauss, op. cit., pp. 172 ff, where also the entire literature on these questions is given.

8. *M. Sota*, VII, 8. The King read the passage Deut. 6:4; Deut. 11:13; 14:22; 26:12; 17:14; 27 and 28.

9. Krauss, op. cit., pp. 70–71. It is probable, however, that in the Onias Temple in Alexandria regular weekly lessons were the custom; (cf. M. Gaster, op. cit., p. 26). This is one of the first indications of intensive study of the Bible in the Diaspora.

10. Cf. Gaster, op. cit., p. 38. Gaster's assumption that, following the example of the Temple, the readers of the Church must have been ordained priests is erroneous; actually, the reader of the early Church was an *anagnostes*, or lector, a member of the lower clergy.

11. This peculiar substitution of the commandment for its actual fulfilment may be viewed as the last remnant of the ancient magic background of scriptural reading. Similar elements may be found in the old Armenian liturgy.

12. Most elaborate was the etiquette of the scriptural lesson in the Synagogue of the Temple on the Day of Atonement. An exact description is given in *M. Yoma*, VII, 1. A good translation and interpretation of this interesting passage is in Krauss, op. cit., pp. 172–3.

13. Cf. Eusebius–Philo, *Praeparatio Evangelica* viii, 7, 13.

14. ELB, op. cit., pp. 188 ff; *JE*, article 'Meturgeman'; also *GV*, p. 8.

15. *Peregrinatio Aetheriae*, ed. Heraeus, cap. 47. The same attitude is held by the Nestorian Church tradition; cf. A. Baumstark (Soghdische Texte, etc, in *OC*, V, p. 127).

16. Cf. Krauss, op. cit., p. 177, n. 2; (in an inscription of the Synagogue of Nicomedia).

17. Cf. G. B. de Rossi, *La Roma sotteranea cristiana*, III, 239, 242. See also *infra* p. 345, where we shall discuss the problem of the transmission of Jewish tradition extensively. The term *levita* for a *Christian* cleric is of considerably later origin.

18. Ibid.; also E. M. Kaufmann, *Handbuch der altchristlichen Epigraphik* (Freiburg i.B., 1917), pp. 272–3. Cf. E. Werner, 'The Common Ground', in *Atti del Congresso Intern. pro Mus. Cattolica*, Rome, 1950–51.

19. It is by no means astounding that the Church Father Epiphanius (Haer. XXX, 11) transliterated the Hebrew *hazan* into the Greek *hazanites*, which in turn he interprets as *hyperetes*, meaning caretaker.

20. *Haftara* = dismissal, means exactly the same as the Latin term *Missa* = mass; both words signify the completion of the public worship.

21. Cf. Josephus *Antiquities* XII. iii. 4. Josephus, *Contra Apionem* II. xvii. 175; and Luke 4 : 6. The *locus classicus* for the codification of the scriptural lesson is the great passage in the Babylonian Talmud, *Meg.* 31a, in which Rab (late third century) is credited with the final enactment. Cf. Büchler, op. cit., pp. 468 ff.

22. Büchler, *JQR*, VI, 11. So also Glaue, *Die Vorlesung heiliger Schriften im Gottesdienste*, p. 7; Vitringa, *De synagoga vetere*, III, pt. II, chapter 10, pp. 984, 1006, assumes that the regular prophetic lesson was introduced to demonstrate the Jewish belief in divine inspiration of the prophets against the Samaritans who recognized the Torah only. Such a reasoning would lead us into the pre-Maccabaean epoch. ELB, p. 175, follows this theory whereas L. Venetianer ('Ursprung und Bedeutung der Prophetenlektion', *ZDMG*, LXIII, 103 ff) puts forth the interesting theory that many prophetic lessons were institutions of Jewish apologies against the growing Judaeo-Christian Church, thus dating the codification of the prophetic lessons as late as the second or even the third century A.D. His theories will be discussed later. The recent sensational discoveries of prophetic scrolls in Palestine, dating from the first century B.C. shed entirely new light on this question, inasmuch as they contain certain marginal marks that in this writer's opinion indicate the beginning and end of the prophetic pericope. See *Bulletin of the American School for Oriental Research*, July 1948, October 1948, and January 1949.

23. Büchler, *JQR*, VI, 39–42. So also ELB, pp. 155–80; *GV*, pp. 6–8 and most scholars. Against this theory chiefly M. Gaster, op. cit., who is, however, not fully convincing.

24. Cf. the significant passage in the *Mekilta* to Exod. 16:35 as given in Büchler, loc cit.; 'R. Joshua says: . . . "The Israelites ate of the manna forty days after the death of Moses, for he died on 7 Adar, and the twenty-four days of Adar and the sixteen of Nisan (cf. Joshua 6:11) together make forty".' . . . It should be kept in mind that the portion referring to Moses' death (Deut. 34) was always read on 7 Adar, the anniversary of his death. These forty days mentioned before resemble strongly the forty days of penitence in the ecclesiastical year, the *Quadragesima*; moreover they end at the same time, the Feast of Easter—Passover. Yet, as we shall see, the original interval was not one of forty days, but one of seven weeks.

25. On the scriptural reading during the first two centuries, cf. Glaue, op. cit. (see note 22). While his assumptions are generally acceptable, his theory that the mention of the reader (*anagignoskon*) in Rev. 1:3 is a novelty, characteristic of Christendom, is entirely untenable. 'The person of the reader is an innovation which does not have a precedent in the ritual of the synagogue' (p. 33). Several synagogal readers of the period before the destruction of the Temple are known to us by name and location. An abundant list of all pertinent documents is given in Krauss, op. cit., pp. 131, 134 ff, where also all source material is quoted.

Likewise, Glaue's interpretation of Mark 13:14 and Matt. 24:15, 'The reader be mindful', is mistaken. Actually, the passage is a well-known Hebraism, meaning 'the intelligent (the reader) will understand', usually employed as a marginal note.

26. Cf. A. Harnack, *Die Mission und Ausbreitung des Christentums*, I, 204 ff.

27. *Apol.* 1, 67. Glaue, op. cit., pp. 64–65, interprets 'the writings of the apostles' in a very broad sense, comprising the gospels and all of the epistles extant at the time to which his investigations are limited. This seems a rather rash conclusion considering that John was probably not even written yet, and other parts of the New Testament not yet considered authoritative. That 'prophetic writings' includes all Hagiographa, as Glaue assumes, also goes too far. After all, Justin was, if not a Samaritan, at any rate born in Samaria, and hence completely familiar with the Jewish division of the Canon into Law, Prophets and Hagiographa. There is no reason to assume that Justin's terminology is different; the less so, since he refers to psalm-verses usually under the term 'hymn or psalm of David'.

28. Irenaeus, *Adv. haer.* IV. xxxiii. 8; Clement of Alexandria, *Stromata* vii. 7 (*PG*, IX, 46); Tertullian, *De praescript* xxxvi. (*PL*, II, 49–50.)

29. CAF, together with the *Didascalia* (Paderborn, 1905). The most important literature concerning the *Apostolic Constitutions* is given here: E. Brightman, *Liturgies, Eastern & Western*, pp. xlvi ff; F. X. Funk, *Die apostolischen Konstitutionen* (Rothenburg, 1891), pp. 96 ff; A. Harnack, *Die Lehre der zwölf Apostel* (Leipzig, 1884), pp. 241 ff; A. Baumstark, 'Die Apostolischen Konstitutionen', *Oriens Christianus* (1907), pp. 388 ff; K. Kohler, *The Origins of Synagogue and Church* (Cincinnati, 1926), pp. 250 ff, 295 f; K. Kohler, 'Ursprünge und Grundformen der synagogalen Liturgie', *MGWJ* (1893), pp. 491 f; K. Kohler, 'The Origin and Composition of the Eighteen Benedictions', *HUCA*, I, pp. 396 ff; E. Werner, 'The Doxology in Synagogue and Church', *HUCA*, XIX (1946), pp. 292 ff.

30. Cf. CAF, VIII, 5, 11.

31. Cf. S. Beissel, S.J., *Die Entstehung der Perikopen des Römischen Messbuches* (Freiburg, 1907), pp. 59–65.

32. P. Alban Dold, O.S.B., 'Das älteste Liturgiebuch der Lateinischen Kirche', in *Texte und Arbeiten* (Beuron, 1936), I pt., Fasc. 26–28.

33. Cf. *Liber Pontificalis*, ed. Duchesne, I, 230; also St Ambrose, *In Ps. 117*.

34. Cf. St John Chrysostom, *Homily 29 in Acts* (*PG*, LX, 218); also BLEW, p. 470; Conybeare and MacLean, *Rituale Armenorum*, pp. 387 ff; A. Baumstark, op. cit. (see note 6), pp. 14, 88, et passim; Alban Dold, op. cit., pp. civ ff.

35. Cf. Cassian, *PL*, XLIX, 844; and C. Callewaert, *De breviarii liturg.*, p. 121.

36. Cf. A. Fortescue, *The Mass* (N.Y., 1922), pp. 211–12: 'So the Proper of the Saints, once an occasional exception, now covers very nearly the whole year and the search for the Mass to be said has become a laborious process'.

37. Ibid., p. 259.

38. *Wolfenbüttel Palimpsest Cod. Weissenburgensis* 76, ed. P. Alban Dold. See note 32.

39. Cod. lat. 9427, ed. Mabillon. Paris Nat. Libr.

40. *Missale mixtum secundum regulam beati Isidori dictum Mozarabes*; also *Breviarium Gothicum*; ed. Ximenes in *PL*, LXXXV and LXXXVI; also H. Goussen, *Die christlicharabische Literatur der Mozaraber* (Leipzig, 1909).

41. Editio typica, 1914, and some of its older versions.

42. All these sources are described extensively in A. Rahlfs, 'Die alttestamentlichen Lektionen der Griechischen Kirche', in *Nachrichten der K. Gesellschaft der Wissenschaften von Göttingen* (Phil.-Hist. Klasse, 1915-16), also in *Mitteilungen des Septuaginta-Unternehmens* (1915), pp. 121 ff.

43. This excellent work (Oxford, 1905) was published together with a valuable study on the East Syrian Epiphany Rites by A. J. Maclean.

44. A. J. Maclean, *East Syrian Daily Offices* (London, 1894), pp. 264-81.

45. Jacobite Church MS, British Museum Add. 12134. This is extensively treated and analysed by Baumstark in his 'Nichtevangelische syrische Perikopenordnungen des ersten Jahrtausends', in *Liturgiegeschichtliche Quellen und Forschungen*, III (Münster, 1921). His thoroughness and exemplary methodology, however, do not always prevent him from extremely biased statements, whenever Roman Catholic dicta or dogmas are in question, or when Roman priority or authenticity in anything and everything under the sun is questioned. Occasionally I shall have to point out some of Baumstark's twisted arguments 'ad majorem curiae gloriam'.

46. Ed. Agnes Smith Lewis in *Studia Sinaitica*, VI (London, 1897, with supplement 1907). Also extensively discussed in Baumstark's work on the Syrian pericopes (see note 45), pp. 131 ff, and in Rahlfs, op. cit. (see n. 42).

47. Cf. A. Dold, op. cit., pp. xci-xciii.

48. Ibid., pp. xciii-xciv. Since Dold's work is not easily available here, I reproduce his quotations: Tertullian, *De ieiunio*, xiv; 'Victorinus of Pettau', in G. Mercati, *Varia Sacra*, Fasc. I in Matt. xxiv, p. 37 end; Zeno, *PL*, XI, 500-9 (tract. 45, 46, 47, 48, 49, 50, 51); Ambrose, *Ep.*, *xxiii* (*PL*, XVI, 1020) with the most interesting remark: 'Two things must be observed in the celebration of the Passa, the fourteenth day of the moon and the first month, called "of the new" ' (Exod. 23:15 and 34:18); later on: 'This month shall be to ye the beginning of all months, the first one shall it be in the months of the year' (Exod. 12:2) and 'Thou shalt prepare a Passa to the Lord Thy God (Deut. 16:1) on the fourteenth day of the first month' (Exod. 12:18 and Lev. 23:5).

49. Cf. Rahlfs, op. cit., pp. 125-6. His explanation of the reasons why the Old Testament lesson is restricted to the vigils and fasts is, however, untenable. We shall discuss this question later on.

50. Ibid. So also E. Schwarz, 'Osterbetrachtungen', *ZNTW*, VII (1906), p. 16.

51. By the term Pentecontade calendar is meant the division of the year into seven periods, each of seven weeks plus one day. The remainder of fourteen days is intercalated in different ways. See *infra*, pp. 382, 397.

52. Cf. Eusebius, *De solemnitate paschali*, iv.

53. Cf. Rahlfs, op. cit., p. 172.

54. Cf. Conybeare, op. cit., p. 512, *et passim*; also Baumstark, op. cit. (n. 45), pp. 138 ff, and Rahlfs, op. cit., pp. 153 ff.

55. Cf. Conybeare, op. cit., pp. 531-2; also Baumstark, op. cit., pp. 151 ff.

56. Cf. Baumstark, op. cit., p. 144.

57. Baumstark's hypothesis (*OC*, N.S. I (1911), p. 68) that the distinction of the second week stems from a time at which the fasting season lasted only six weeks, and where the second week was then the first week of Quadragesima, seems plausible enough. Yet, another interpretation is perhaps more appropriate. The sixth week before Passover coincided in the old Jewish calendar with 7 Adar, the end of the old triennial cycle (cf. p. 57) after which the eclogadic lessons of the 'special Sabbaths' interrupted the regular course; the beginning of the new cycle was probably to take place on the first Sabbath of Nisan. This would also explain, why ARM continues in its second week only on Wednesday and Friday the lessons of the first week. On Monday, Tuesday, and Thursday, however, there is an entirely new beginning of another continuous lesson which goes on until Holy Saturday. Moreover we shall see that the opening pericope, I Sam. 1 (Hannah's prayer) is today and was probably in olden times the prophetic lesson of the synagogal

New Year. We encounter here for the first time the extremely complex problem of the double Jewish calendar and its remnants in the ecclesiastical year. This highly important question will be discussed extensively later on.

58. It is well known that the choice of Wednesday and Friday as particular weekdays goes back to the Jewish custom of having scriptural reading on Monday and Thursday, the market days in Jerusalem, when the synagogues were open for prayer and lesson. The *Didache*, viii, already testifies as to the change from the old to the new choice of days. Cf. Epiphanius, *De Fide*, xxii; also Aetheria Silvia, *Peregrinatio*, xxvii. 5.

59. Conybeare, op. cit., pp. 516–32.

60. Baumstark, op. cit., p. 151, quoting P. Geyer, *Itinera Hierosolymitana*, p. 179; cf. also Aetheria Silvia's reference to the day and its significance in the Old Armenian and East Syrian Calendars. See especially Conybeare, *Rituale Armenorum*, p. 532, and the Calendary in Maclean's *East Syrian Daily Offices*.

61. Jesus is most frequently represented in paintings and mosaics as reddish-blond; this is due to his being 'a son of David' whose colour, likewise, was reddish, as we are told in I Sam. 16:12 and 17:42. This fact is certainly more than a mere coincidence.

62. Cf. my study 'The Hosanna in the Gospels' in *JBL*, July 1946, p. 120, where some of the Gentile 'anti-Davidic' sources are quoted.

63. Ibid., p. 115. It might be that the date of December 25th as Christ's Birthday was predetermined by an ancient, though hypothetical, Palestinian custom of celebrating King David on this day. Extensive bibliography on James the Just, in H. J. Schöps, *Theologie und Geschichte des Judenchristentums* (1949), pp. 487 ff.

64. In Spenglerian terminology such a borrowing and integrating is called pseudo-morphosis.

65. Conybeare, op. cit., pp. 509–13: 'That the calendar implied in the lectionary was already a conflation of at least two earlier ones, is certain; for the feast of the Innocents comes in it twice, on January 8th and May 18th, . . . herein we seem to trace two causes. Firstly, the conflation of the two systems of calendars, one of which placed Christmas on December 25th, the other on January 6th; and secondly, the circumstance that the same set of lessons as was used at Easter had to do duty for Epiphany as well' (p. 512). Conybeare's statement concerning the identity of lessons is only partially correct; only the Genesis pericope and elements of Exodus plus Dan. 3:1–90, which has to be considered a canticle that could be used at any solemn occasion, are really read on both occasions.

66. An analogous holiday of the Roman Church is the Embertide of September, which in its entire liturgy (*Sabbatum quatuor temporum*) reflects the spirit of the Jewish New Year. See further below. Cf. also Baumstark, op. cit., pp. 145 ff.

67. Baumstark, op. cit., pp. 14 ff; Maclean, *East Syrian Daily Offices*, pp. xxx and 264 ff.

68. Baumstark rightly points to some analogies of NEST with the synagogal rite, presuming that the geographical origin of this system was Antioch, probably also the cradle of the *Apostolic Constitutions;* cf. op. cit., pp. 16 and 174, also CAF, VIII, cap 5, no. 11, p. 476.

69. Baumstark, op. cit., pp. 31–2.

70. Cf. L. Venetianer, op. cit., p. 145; also ELB, p. 156.

71. A good description of the manuscript sources is given in Baumstark, op. cit., pp. 80–88. Our sources are: Brit. Mus. Add. 14438, cf. Wright, op. cit., p. 10; Brit. Mus. Add. 17103, cf. Wright, op. cit., pp. 32 ff; Paris Bibl. Nat., 27 (anc. fonds. 5); Brit. Mus. Add. 12139, cf. Wright, pp. 154–9 (Athanasius lectionary). The Syro-Palestinian lectionary was published in Mrs Lewis's *Studia Sinaitica*, VI (London, 1897, with a supplemental volume, 1907).

72. Baumstark, op. cit., p. 118.

73. Cf. Papadopoulos-Kerameus, *Typikon tes en Hierosolymois ekklesias* (St Petersburg, 1894); cf. also K. Krumbacher, *Geschichte der byzantinischen Literatur* (2nd ed. 1897), No. 137. It is to be understood that this 'Typikon' is not identical with the official Typikon of the Greek Orthodox Church. Concerning the Typikon see also A. Maltzew, *Die Liturgien der Orthodox-Katholischen Kirche des Morgenlandes* (Berlin, 1894), where a good discussion and translation is offered.

74. Baumstark, op. cit., p. 136.

75. *Proceedings of the British Academy*, XI (1923).

76. The chief source of Burkitt is Brit. Mus. Add. 14528. Even more surprising appears here a reference to the chronicle of Josua Stylites, who claims 'that Peter, bishop of Edessa [after 498] added to the festivals that of Palm Sunday' [Feast of Hosannas]. This seems to constitute a discrepancy with the report of Aetheria Silvia, who described the solemn celebration of Palm Sunday in Jerusalem shortly before 400. Dr August Bludau has, in his extensive interpretation of Aetheria's report, recognized this discrepancy and attempted a possible solution of the dilemma. Cf. Dr August Bludau, 'Die Pilgerreise der Aetheria', in *Studien zur Geschichte und Kultur des Altertums*, XV (Paderborn, 1927), p. 125 ff; see also my study 'The Hosanna in the Gospels', *JBL*, 1946.

77. Properly speaking, the Quadragesima lectionary does not begin before Monday of the sixth week before Palm Sunday. Cf. Baumstark, *Festbrevier der syrischen Jakobiten*, p. 206.

78. Cf. Jacob Lauterbach, 'The Pharisees and their Teachings', *HUCA*, VI (1929), where the author demonstrates that also the Pharisees were opposed to animal sacrifices, but were obliged to make considerable compromises in their attitude.

79. For a full discussion of this subject, see the valuable material in H. J. Schöps, *Theologie und Geschichte des Judenchristentums* (Tübingen, 1949), pp. 220–33.

80. Cf. also Wright, *Apocryphal Acts*, pp. 129 f.

81. These observations of mine amplify the findings of Burkitt.

82. Cf. Hefele-Leclercq, *Conciles* I, pp. 133–51, 450–88, 714 ff; also S. Reinach, *A Short History of Christianity* (London, 1922), p. 53; and J. Parkes, *The Conflict of the Church and Synagogue*, pp. 175 ff. Also, *Catholic Encyclopaedia*, art. 'Easter Controversy', and E. Schwartz, *Christl. und Jüd. Osterfesttafeln*, p. 138 ff. The best special study on the subject is J. Schmid, *Die Osterfestfrage auf d. ersten Concil von Nicea* (Vienna, 1905).

83. For instance: L. Venetianer, *Jüdisches im Christentum*; *JE*, article 'Pentecost', etc.

84. Cf. n. 66.

85. The Roman Church also pays some attention to the third week in September which coincides with the Embertide of autumn (*Sabbatum quatuor temporum*) whose lessons are patterned after those of the Jewish New Year and Day of Atonement. See *infra*.

86. Cf. Hildegarde and Julius Lewy, 'The Origin of the Week and the Oldest West Asiatic Calendar', *HUCA*, XVII (1942–43). Whether Quadragesima and Holy Week together make a pentecontade, or Quadragesima (forty weekdays plus their Saturdays and Sundays) in itself constitutes a pentecontade, cannot be decided easily. The scholars disagree sharply on this question. The problem is discussed extensively in Rahlfs, op. cit., pp. 190–3. It is highly significant, though, that a high Armenian clergyman of our times states: 'The system adopted in the Armenian Calendar for the celebration of Feasts is not based on the days of the week, but on those of the week. It thus constitutes a calendar which is peculiarly *Hebdomadal* in character.' Cf. A. J. Maclean, *East Syrian Daily Offices*, (London, 1894) Introd. xxiv: 'We notice also the division of the year into *shavu'i* or periods of about 7 weeks each. . . .'

Cf. Malachia Ormanian, *The Church of Armenia* (London, 1913), pp. 180 ff. We shall see later on (in Part II, Chapter II) that this calendaric system of pentecontades deeply affected the musical liturgy of the ancient Near East.

87. The most important studies in which Morgenstern has presented his theory: 'The Three Calendars of Ancient Israel', *HUCA*, I (1924), pp. 13–78. 'Supplementary Studies in the Calendars of Ancient Israel', *HUCA*, X (1935), pp. 1–148. 'The Hanukkah Festival and the Calendar of Ancient Israel', *HUCA*, XX (1948), pp. 1–136.

88. Cf. Morgenstern, 'Supplementary Studies in the Calendars of Ancient Israel', *HUCA*, X, pp. 23–24, 43–48; also 'The Calendar of Jubilees' in *Vetus Testamentum*, V (1955), pp. 35 ff.

89. Concerning the Quartodecimans see the articles in *Catholic Encyclopaedia*, *Protestantische Real-Enzyklopädie*, *Die Religion in Geschichte und Gegenwart* and *Hastings Encyclopaedia of Ethics*, where all sources are given.

90. Cf. Ambrose, *Ep. XXIII* (PL, XVI, 1020), see also n. 48. Also Augustine, *In Joh. 13:14* (PL, XXXV, 1500).

91. Since the eve of Passover should not coincide with a Sabbath, the Nicaean rule worked rather efficiently—in theory. Actually, we hear of complaints about 'Judaizers' who participated at the Jewish Passa meal until late in the tenth century.

92. Cf. *ZDMG*, LX, pp. 103 ff.

93. To quote but one instance of a mistake: The feast of the 'Sacred Heart of Jesus', to which Venetianer pays some attention, was instituted only by Pope Clement XIII in 1765 for special regions only and was given universal observation by Pius IX in 1856.

94. Venetianer, op. cit., p. 139.

95. Baumstark, op. cit., p. 36.

96. Gen. 1 was read in ancient times as the afternoon lesson on the Day of Atonement, when this feast was still celebrated on 1 Tishri and had the connotation of being the anniversary of the world's creation. Cf. Büchler, op. cit.

97. Cf. Baumstark, op. cit., p. 158.

98. Cf. Venetianer, op. cit., pp. 141–2.

99. Traces of this development may be seen in Tertullian's work *De ieiunio*, cap. 2, where he refers to a regular fast day at the beginning of autumn, observed by all Christians as a Divine institution. In this connexion he alludes also to the Jewish Day of Atonement.

100. *OC*, V.

101. Cf. Ter Minassiantz, op. cit., pp. 20 ff, and Ter Mikelian, *Die Armenische Kirche*, pp. 6, 61 *et passim*.

102. Cf. my article 'The Hosanna of the Gospels', *JBL*, July 1946, in which the entire literature is quoted and the root of the misunderstanding is discussed extensively.

103. Cf. Aetheria Silvia, *Peregrinatio* (ed. Heraeus), cap. 30–31.

104. On the name *Sabbath haggadol*, 'Great Sabbath', cf. the Kroner-Goldfahn controversy, in *Jüdisches Literaturblatt*, 1886, pp. 116, 156, 160, 165, 170. The individual pericopes of Holy Week are discussed in the following studies: 'Ein Georgisches Kanonarion', ed. K. Kekelidze, ed. Kluge in *OC*, second series, V and VI; G. F. Moore, 'Memra, Shekinah, Metatron', in *Harvard Theological Review*, Jan., 1922; F. C. Burkitt, 'The Early Syriac Lectionary System', *Proceedings of the British Academy*, XI (1923); F. C. Burkitt, 'The Old Lectionary of Jerusalem', *Journal of Theological Studies*, XXIV, pp. 450 ff, especially for the Lectionary of Holy Saturday. Cf. F. Danziger, *Ritus Orientalium*, II, pp. 552 ff.

105. Of the abundance of rabbinic references, only two may be mentioned here: R. Eleazar (championing 1 Tishri against R. Joshua (1 Nisan) in *Rosh Hashana* 11a; continuation of this controversy in *B. Rosh Hashana* 12a.

106. Cf. Ambrose, *Hexameron*, I, 4: 'Therefore in this beginning of the months created He the heavens and the earth, for there had to be a starting point of the world, and it was opportune to all that it should be the spring season'; also Gaudentius of Brescia, Sermon 1: 'for in the season of the spring did God create the world', and Leo the Great, 60th sermon: 'De Passione Domini IX', etc.

P. Alban Dold is certainly correct in surmising that 'The Jewish Passover according to Exod. 12 was the principal reason why all of the Fathers believed that the creation took place at the time of spring' (op. cit., p. xciv).

107. The last remnants of the old equation Holy Saturday = Day of Atonement occur in some of the most authoritative writings of the Church. Thus in the *Epistle of Barnabas*, cap. 7, ed. Funk, the sufferings of Jesus are interpreted as a fulfilment of the liturgy of *Yom Kippur*. Justin, likewise, maintains that the sacrifice of the Day of Atonement was definitely and for all times consummated by Christ's death (*Dialogus cum Tryphone*, cap. 40, 4 f). Still more outspoken is Tertullian, *De ieiunio*, cap. 2 (*CSEL*, XX, 275 f), where he correlates the Christian *Passa* and the Jewish Day of Atonement.

108. ROM, WOLF, LUX, MOZ, ARM, GREEK T, GREEK P.

109. Cf. Venetianer, op. cit., pp. 129–30. The explanation that Ezek. 37 is read on Passover, because the resurrection of the dead will take place in Nisan, is given—suspiciously late—by R. Hai Gaon during the ninth to tenth century.

The prayer before kindling the lamps on Holy Saturday in the Roman Church mentions some of the significant events of the day, in a kind of biblical review; the Exodus, the Burning Cloud in the Desert, Christ's Victory over the netherworld, and his resurrection. ('Vere dignum et justum est' in *LU*, p. 655.)

110. According to Dr Morgenstern's most recent study it is probable that Gentile Christianity adjusted Christmas (December 25th) to the ancient Syrian 'Festival of Lamps' which, in turn, is related to the Jewish *Hanukka* feast. (Cf. Morgenstern in *HUCA*, 1948. See n. 87.)

111. Of Christian lessons referring to the Birth day and New Year, Gen. 21 occurs in NEST and SYR; I Sam. 1 in JAC and NEST; Gen. 1 in SYR-PAL, ARM, GREEK T and GREEK P and Jer. 31 in ROM and JAC.

112. The text is not complete. It is a palimpsest and contains many lacunae. Cf. P. Alban Dold, op. cit., p. lviii.

113. Isa. 59:12.

114. Isa. 59:21.

115. Isa. 60:1.

116. The passage Isa. 60:1–10, while no longer a lesson of the Day of Atonement, forms still today an important and integral part of its prayers.

117. Cf. Rahlfs, op. cit., pp. 61–62.

118. On *'Omer*, cf. *JE* q.v., also article 'Pentecost', where the most important literature is cited. Concerning the Synagogue lesson, see *M Meg.* III, 5. The first allusion to *Shabuot* as festival of Revelation in the book of Jubilees VI, 21. This is the meaning of 'Panes legis primitivi' in *Missale Sarum*, ed. Dickinson, col. 437 (Feria quarta Pentec.).

119. Cf. Rahlfs, op. cit., p. 135. It should be understood that the Lamentations are the only section which the Roman lectionary has transferred from the greatest *historical* (in contrast to the religious-theological fast of *Yom Kippur*) fast-day of Judaism, 9 Ab. There the Lamentations create the wailing and hopeless atmosphere of the day and form the liturgical nucleus of the fast-day's ceremonial.

CHAPTER FOUR

The Musical Tradition of Lessons and Cognate Liturgical Forms

BASIC PROBLEMS OF SCRIPTURAL CHANT

AT the outset of the last chapter the hypothesis of a magic-theurgic origin of public scriptural reading was ventured. While this is only a more or less plausible conjecture, the situation is fundamentally different with regard to the function of music in worship. Here it is clear beyond any doubt that one of the three roots of music itself is magic craft. This has been amply demonstrated and it is not necessary to restate the facts.[1] Only one aspect of this subject warrants further elaboration: the philosophical-theological basis of musical practice for religious purposes.

The Ethos-Doctrine

The result of the sublimating process from magic to religious thought is the ethos-doctrine of music, the deeply rooted conviction of all ancient civilizations that music is capable of creating, as well as of expressing, certain clearly circumscribed emotions. Each type of music, every mode, has an 'ethos' of its own, an inherent character to which the listener will respond in a supposedly definite and invariable way.[2] One of the corollaries of the general doctrine of ethos is the belief that the 'effective' application of music for its various purposes, such as worship, therapeutics, warfare, etc., depends upon an appropriate and cosmologically ordained time, season and place. Thus, an 'effective' piece might fail to attain its purpose if rendered at a wrong season or hour, or at a not fully acceptable place. Innumerable references to this ideology, couched in outspoken or in esoteric terms, appear in ancient literature, and especially in the sacred writings of all Oriental religions, from the Bible to the Vedas, to Kung-fu-tse and the philosophers of the Far East.[3]

Where was the detailed application of these regulations more imperative than in the act of public reading or chanting of the Holy Scriptures? Accordingly, the rabbinic literature abounds with admonitions to *chant*, not simply to *read* Scripture in public. The earliest and most outspoken passage in this respect is probably the following: 'Whosoever reads Scripture without chant and the Mishna without intonation, to him the word of Scripture is applicable; "I gave them laws that were not beautiful".'[4] Here, too, as in so many other instances, the various Churches followed the Jewish tradition. Most of them have preserved modes of a *lectio solemnis*, i.e. systems that regulate the cantillation of the lessons. That this is not a recent institution is documented by numerous remarks, demands and criticisms of the Church Fathers which we will later discuss.

Thus far the state of affairs is clear and in no way particularly complex; yet our next question will unfold a series of intricate problems. The question arises: how are the regulations of scriptural chant, which stipulate the correct time, occasion, etc., musically implemented? The answer appears to be simple: through the individual modes of chanting, which vary according to the different texts, different seasons of the liturgical year, and other special occasions. Thus, the Haftara mode (for the prophetic lesson of the Synagogue) is different from the Torah chant; the latter, in turn, is varied for different seasons; the Torah cantillation of the High Holydays or other occasions differs from the ordinary sabbatical chant. The Roman Church knows a *lectio ordinaria* and a *lectio solemnis*, and the Syrian and Armenian Churches provide for similar differentiations. The term 'cantillation', however, covers a multitude of uncertainties. Does it stand for musically regulated chant, or for semimusical recitation, or merely oratorical rendering? Here again, one has to distinguish between the various rites, traditions, or geographic orbits, since the individual customs vary exceedingly.

There is abundant evidence that both the Synagogue and the Church demanded *musical* rendering; the existence of musical accents or neumes in the lectionaries seems to preclude any doubt on this point. None the less, the question concerning the primary function of these accents arose relatively early. Did they principally and originally indicate the course of the chant? When did they originate? Where and under what conditions?

Ecphonesis and Cantillation

A clear distinction between spoken recitation and musically rendered chant is a prerequisite for our study. The terminology of the various

Churches might help us to solve this problem. The rendering of the lesson is called in rabbinic literature: *ne'ima* (= tune), *trop* (Greek: *tropos*, kind, manner, type), *ta'am* (= style, taste), *k'ria* (= reading). In the Roman Church the terms are: *lectio, lectio solemnis, tonus* or *modus lectionis*; in the Greek Church: *ecphonesis* (= recitation); in the Armenian Church: *karos* (= reading, talking).[5] No more than three unequivocally *musical* terms are used among the eight cited! This seems to indicate that the musical element was referred to, but not predominantly, in the performance of the lessons.

It is generally understood that, in the ancient world, *to chant* meant to furnish the words and sentences with the most appropriate phonetic inflexion.[6] An original propensity toward a really musical rendering, toward an 'intonation', can hardly be doubted, in view of the numerous descriptions of chanted lessons. But it seems that in the course of time, in some sections of the Church, one of the mainstays of music faded away in daily use: the strictly ordered and definable pitch. Due to these aberrations we are confronted today with a threefold variety of one basic species. At the present time the three types are classified as plain Recitation (spoken), Ecphonesis (*Sprechgesang*, semi-musical recitative) and Cantillation (regular musical chant). Only the last two categories will be discussed here, because their practice follows certain rules indicated by the different systems of notation or accentuation. It is well-nigh impossible to define precisely the boundaries between these two types of performance. The acoustic regularity of the one type and its absence in the other constitute the only discernible difference, which, however, is all too often effaced. The 'primitive', acoustically unorganized rendering of Scripture is not easily accessible to musical evaluation and classification.

Ecphonetic Notations

The discrimination between, and exact interpretation of, these two systems is made more difficult through the various signs which the different Churches used for indicating the musical nature of the lessons. Many lectionaries contain symbols which are supposed to guide the reader in his performance. Yet it is not possible to state *a limine* that all these signs suggest a definitely *musical* performance. In most cases, particularly in the Eastern Churches, we may observe a gradual trend from so-called ecphonetic accents to a more exact musical notation. It will therefore be expedient to use a different terminology for the various phases of that development. Those signs which cannot be identified positively with exact musical phrases are called ecphonetic signs or accents; characters of complete musical phrases ought to be termed neumes, whether they are based on the earlier ecphonetic signs or not. Finally, those neumes, transliterated by scholars into modern notes, fall into the category of exact notation. The basic distinction between a neume and a note is that: the former usually stands not for a single note, but for a whole phrase, whereas modern notation has one sign for each individual note. Not all early neumes, and none of the ecphonetic systems can be transcribed in modern notation without the help of oral tradition.

According to this classification, the Jewish tradition employs ecphonetic signs, namely the accents of the Masoretic text of the Bible (MAS). These signs have been interpreted by various scholars in various ways, although the accents of MAS have not undergone any further development since their final codification about A.D. 850. The system of the Roman Church did have a similar beginning but developed into clearly defined neumes with diastematic lines. The Greek ritual too, began with ecphonetic signs similar to those of MAS. But these ecphonetic signs have, in the course of time, undergone several transformations, until they reached their final stage (after the thirteenth century) of stylization as neumes without lines but with diacritical (distinguishing) marks (BYZ). In the Armenian Church this evolution is still incomplete, for its signs hold the middle between ecphonetic accents and musical neumes (ARM NEUM). Although the Syrians cultivated an oral tradition of their lectionary accents, their exact meaning and significance has been forgotten since about the eleventh century (SYR ACC).[7] The chief documents of these various groups will be discussed in Part II. At present we are confronted with two problems: (1) What was the original function and significance of the ecphonetic signs, the parent system of all vocal musical notation? (2) Where and when did the ecphonetic accents originate?[8]

Surprisingly enough, it seems that the oldest and principal function of the ecphonetic accents was not the notation of the chant but the punctuation of the sentences. This holds true for all important systems of Judaism and Christianity, as demonstrated by O. Fleischer in his *Neumenstudien*.[9] And it is not only in Hebrew that the main accents are at the same time the most significant punctuation marks: our English comma, too, is derived from the neume *virga*, our dot from the final neume *punctus*. Considered logically, every punctuation aims at, and eventually determines, the syntactic accentuation of the sentence, upon which, in turn, depends the correct understanding of its meaning. Only at a later stage were the ecphonetic signs used to point out the flow of cantillation. *But cantillation itself is older than any notation.* In certain systems these accents have to serve a third purpose, namely to indicate the stressed syllable of each word. This additional function is typical of most of the Semitic languages.[10] It frequently happens that the tonal accent is not identical with the syntactic accentuation; it may even be antithetic to it. For such cases the Hebrew and Syriac languages employ a minutely graded hierarchy of accents; in MAS there can hardly ever be a doubt concerning the tonal or the syntactic accent.[11] This fact shows clearly that the indication of the chant was not the primary purpose of the MAS accents. For in primarily melodic chant, even when connected with words, the musical element predominates over the logical. In the (oratorical) ecphonesis, however, the intonation is determined by the structure of the sentence and its logical and syntactic relations; neither its music nor its notation are therefore in any way autonomous.[12] It is equally certain that the purely musical tradition of the cantillation antedates by far all attempts at notation.

Even where there is no clear musical cantillation, the coordination of tonal and syntactic accents in the ecphonesis frequently proves to be a powerful agent toward the rhythmization and inflexion of a language. Again, it was Fleischer who first stressed the importance of the accentuation for the innate rhythm of every language.[13] Thus, the Hebrew language in its classical diction, the prophetic style, has a tonal accent, placed usually on the last syllable of a word. Together with its indigenous poetic element, the *parallelismus membrorum*, it produces an inflexion that sounds (note the iambic-anapaestic character of Hebrew) somewhat like:

Tzaddík katamár yifrách; keérez bal'vanón yisgé.

> (The righteous flourishes like a palm-tree; like a cedar of Lebanon shall he grow high.)

The first half of this verse closes with a strongly emphasized accent that is considerably higher than the general pitch of the verse. The second half opens rather lower and again, just before the full stop, reaches its highest point in the final cadence. This type of ecphonesis, conditioned by the co-agency of tonal and syntactic accents, has been preserved in the psalmodic tradition of almost all Churches. Even where the tonal accent of the language was entirely different from the Hebrew rhythm, as for example in Latin, the original Hebrew scheme has been preserved and musically consolidated.[14] This occurred in the general process of crystallization toward such stereotyped musical formulas as the Psalm Tones of the Church or the prayer modes of the Synagogue, as will be shown later on.[15] Already in the early Middle Ages some writers were fully aware of the significance of syntactic accentuation for the inflexion of the verse-cadence. Byzantine writers obeyed the rule that the last thesis of a sentence must be preceded by at least two unaccented syllables.[16]

If the primary function of the ecphonetic signs actually was to fix the syntactic-logic accent, how could they later be applied to musical notations? What determined their external form, which, in many cases, looks very much like a shorthand musical script? In other words, what was the origin of these signs?

It is here that Fleischer's statements lose their general validity; this scholar derived all ecphonetic signs from the marks which a choir-leader or musician would draw in the air, while tracing the course of a melody. With a view to the old Syrian accents, consisting almost exclusively of dots, we shall modify Fleischer's theory by allowing that the ecphonetic signs in some cases developed from the marks by which a musician guided his subordinates in singing. Another influence, the grammatical, hardly of lesser importance, is unmistakable in a number of ecphonetic systems.

Cheironomy

The practice of drawing the course of a melody in the air is a very ancient one and well documented by old reports as well as by pictures and reliefs. It is called cheironomy and has played an important role in the development of musical notation. The Egyptians practised it, as we learn from numerous bas-reliefs upon which musicians are seen performing the hand movements, so typical of cheironomy; moreover, the hieroglyph for 'singing' is a hand.[17] The same holds true for the Babylonian-Accadian reliefs; among them the best known and most

5

instructive is that which represents the famous orchestra of King Asur-banipal and a scene of the King together with his wife and some musi-cians in a pergola.[18] Greek literature contains detailed documentation of cheironomy. One may even say that toward the end of antiquity cheironomy was considered an art *per se*, fully developed and generally known. Xenophon says: 'When I returned home, I did not dance, for I never had learned it; but I practised cheironomy, for this I had studied.'[19] Herodotus even speaks of a cheironomy of the feet [*sic*],[20] and Plutarch compares it with the Spartan sword-dance.[21] In the Roman world, too, numerous writers refer to it, among others Livy, with the words: 'Henceforth it became a usage with actors to sing their pieces according to hand-movements'.[22]

More numerous are the Jewish sources: the *locus classicus* is the passage Berakoth 62a. One should not use the right hand for unclean purposes, for it serves so sacred a function as the 'pointing out the *ta'amim* of Scripture'. Since at the time when this passage was written, regular accents had not yet been introduced into the biblical text, and since it was prohibited to use an accentuated or vocalized scroll for public reading, the term *ta'ame Torah* must mean here 'the cantillation of Scripture'. This is also Rashi's interpretation.[23] He reports that in his time (tenth century) Palestinian readers used to practise cheironomy when singing the scriptural lesson. Up to the late Middle Ages cheiro-nomy was well known among the Jews. R. Samuel Archevolti speaks of it with high praise, Petachyah of Regensburg reports it as a living custom of the Jews in Babylonia, and even the poet Heinrich Heine alludes to it satirically.[24] The *Dikduke ha-te'amim*, a grammatical He-brew source work of the tenth century, not only refers to it, but men-tions the fact that a certain scriptural accent (*shalshelet* = *n'gidah*) was indicated through a waving movement of the hand.[25]

This latest mention seems to confirm Fleischer's hypothesis concern-ing the genesis of the musical neumes, since the accent of the *shalshelet* is a waving line, fixing its movement. Yet the second question, as to the age and the geographic origin of the ecphonetic signs, must also be answered before we can proceed with the examination of the various systems of accents.

Here a distinction ought to be made between the most primitive signs of the ecphonesis, the so-called 'Ur-accents', and the later stages in the variegated developments of accentuation. Many nations and languages knew of the 'Ur-accents' (acute, circumflex, grave) and their function to indicate the inflexion of the voice: initium, colon, period. Fleischer has shown that these primitive accents were known to Greeks, Romans, Hindus, Armenians, Syrians, Jews, etc.[26] Whether they are derivatives from a common root is all but impossible to determine, in spite of Fleischer's insistence on such a hypothesis. At any rate, all ecphonetic signs, neumes, accents, and so on, should be considered as outgrowths of that primitive type of punctuation, for undoubtedly the original function of the 'Ur-accents' was to indicate the rise and fall of the voice in accord with the syntactic-logic accent.

Development of Ecphonetic Signs

The process of transformation from the 'Ur-accents' to exact musical notation was slow, complex, and often interrupted by linguistic vicissitudes, as for example, the introduction of a new script. A good many systems never have attained the status of real musical notation, others did not even reach the phase of elaborate ecphonetic signs.

Summing up, we might say that of the various ecphonetic traditions, only the Latin system has run the whole gamut to real musical notation, while the Syrian system stopped before reaching the phase of neumes. The Greek-Byzantine accents, on the other hand, went through a series of transformations and, eventually, attained a fully developed system of neumes, which only today can be deciphered with accuracy. The Armenian and the Hebrew systems surpass by far the accents of the Syrians, but still did not reach the stage of exact musical neumes.

The oldest document of these systems is of Syrian origin,[27] and owing to this fact many scholars assume Syria to be the cradle of ecphonetic accentuation.[28] It is in Syria, the country where Greek, Babylonian, Hebrew, and Egyptian civilizations met, where the European and Near Eastern cultures begat Christianity and its Churches, that we must look for the roots of the ecphonetic and neumatic systems. Later on, practically every Church created its own type of accentuation, always in close connexion with its liturgical language and its needs. Thus the Latin neumes have developed differently from the Greek, the Syriac accents are unlike the present Hebrew ones, and the Armenian signs are quite different from the Coptic ones. In every case, the individual language, its inherent rhythm and inflexion has determined the further development of its accentuation and ecphonesis.[29]

To prove assumptions concerning the geographical origin of ecphonetic notation, however, is a difficult undertaking. Only a detailed comparison of the various accent systems could accurately demonstrate the geographical and historical origin of the parent system. Such a comparison would have to investigate the syntactic function of each accent, its external shape, its traditional musical significance, and its name. An elementary example may illustrate this point: the origin of the term 'neume' itself is controversial. Some scholars derive it from the Greek *neuma* (= nod), others from *(p)neuma* (= breath), a theory which has proved to be untenable; others again from the Hebrew *ne'ima* (= tune, sweetness).[30] In spite of all learned investigations concerning this term and its etymology, no conclusive results have come forth in the last fifty years. Yet, in order to understand the oldest musical tradition, common to Church and Synagogue, the interrelation between their ecphonetic systems has to be examined carefully. For these insignificant looking signs were the bearers of the oldest musical tradition, after the classic Greek notation had fallen into oblivion. Some aspects of the accents will be studied later on (Part II, Chapter III).

JEWISH SOURCES CONCERNING CANTILLATION AND ACCENTS OF THE MASORETIC TRADITION

Literary Documents before the Ninth Century

As we observed previously, the Bible makes no positive mention of any cantillation. The passage Neh. 8:8, occasionally interpreted as an indication of chant, in no way refers to singing or even to a semi-musical rendering.[31] The first unequivocal statements about the chanting occur in the Talmudic literature, some of them in its oldest strata (first–second century A.D.). In view of the fact that these testimonies reflect practices and customs of at least two or three earlier centuries, we are on safe ground in concluding that regular cantillation of Scripture was a well established custom long before the Christian era.

This historic fact, however, *has nothing at all to do with the problem of the scriptural accents*, with which it is so frequently confused. The question of their age and origin is considerably more controversial. From the outset we ought to remind ourselves that we must not assume *a priori* a musical function of these accents, unless our sources say so explicitly.

(1). 'The right hand shall not touch filthy things . . . for one indicates with it the melodic formulas [*ta'ame*] of Scripture.'[32] Some scholars thought that this passage referred to the accents; indeed, the term used (*ta'am*) may designate either an accent or a modulation of the chant. Since Rashi (tenth century) the latter view has been accepted, and we have to consider our passage one of the first in Hebrew literature clearly referring to the practice of cheironomy.[33]

(2). '. . . and there in all of the sentences ye shall observe the division in the melodies [phrases—*pisuq ta'amim*].'[34] This indicates either the punctuating function of (supposedly written) accents (*ta'amim*) or the punctuating musical cadences of a (chanted) sentence. These two interpretations do not necessarily exclude each other. But if we accept the first one, it would have to be considered the oldest reference to the existence of accents, yet not necessarily to their musical function. The author of this statement was Rab, a famous rabbi of the third century. If he really alluded to written accents as the musical implementation of scriptural reading, it seems unintelligible that he did not mention the fact of cantillation at all. We shall postpone judgement on this passage until we have examined a very similar statement, viz.:

(3). 'Rab thought that any teaching of Scripture ought to be free of charge; but R. Yohanan said that [for instruction] in the proper division of the melodies [phrases—*pisuq ta'amim*] a compensation is permissible.'[35] If here the existence of punctuating accents is implied, the underlying premise is their connexion with chant; otherwise our first reference would lose all meaning. For the cheironomic indication of punctuation during the recitation does not make sense, unless it is implemented by its chanted performance. But there is no further evidence of correlation between the accents and the cantillation. This dilemma, however, can be solved. I proposed elsewhere that the existence of a few basic 'Ur-accents' would remove all contradictions.[36] These primary accents originally had a punctuating-syntactic function, and only in the course of subsequent centuries was the older scriptural cantillation adjusted to them. If one accepts this conjecture, (1) would refer to the melodic cadence only; (2) to the punctuating function of the 'Ur-accents'; and (3) to their simultaneously syntactic and musical significance.

All this is understandable only if we bear in mind that the scriptural scroll as used in the *liturgy* of the Synagogue (not for study) must not contain *any* sign of punctuation, accentuation, or of musical significance. Apparently the study of proper melodic divisions (3) or their public observance (2) was a matter of great concern to the rabbis, because the

absence of written punctuation in the liturgical scrolls made private preparation of the pericope (from marked study-scrolls) a necessity for the
reader. An unprepared reader might easily miss the correct division of
sentences, and misunderstandings, mistakes, even involuntary blasphe-
mies might be the result of his negligence. The foremost purpose of the
accents, therefore, was to make a clear demarcation between the sentences of Scripture. Then, owing to the parallelistic structure of biblical
diction, the next important task was the strict observance of the semi-
colon (*pausa*; Hebrew *'atnah*) within every verse.[37] These divisions or
punctuations need not necessarily be written symbols; many of them
were handed down by oral tradition from one generation to the next.
Here, the question arises: what are the first Jewish documents to speak
in unequivocal language of the existence of such punctuating signs
actually written?

(4). 'Thou wilt find that in the passage "Abraham, Abraham" [Gen.
22] there is a separating sign [*p'sik*] . . . but in the passage "Moses,
Moses" [Exod 3:4] there is no separating sign [*p'sik*].'[38]

Disregarding the evidence presented in (3) because of its vagueness,
this passage, then, is the first literary evidence that certain signs guided
the student of Scripture in his reading. The source itself is hardly
earlier than the fifth century A.D., although it might reflect older
traditions.

It is here that we must look for statements from early Christian
authors which might allude to these signs of punctuation. The earliest
author seems to be Clement of Alexandria (late second and early third
century). In his chief work, *Stromata*, III, iv, he writes:

(5). 'There are those who in loud [accented?] reading by their inflexion
distort Scripture to suit their own pleasure; and who by transposing
accents and dots, which are widely and usefully prescribed, satisfy their
desires. . . .'

Clement refers here to the Jews, since just before the beginning of
our passage he says 'that this nation has been chastised already'. The
implication of this statement would be absolutely clear if we but knew
whether Clement had in mind the Hebrew or the Greek text of the
Bible. Unfortunately this question cannot be answered, in spite of the
controversies about his knowledge of Hebrew. If he applied his remarks
to the accents in the text of the Septuagint it would have no bearing
upon our examination of Hebrew signs of punctuation and cantillation.

In Alexandria, the cradle of scientific Greek grammar, literary documents were provided with occasional punctuation even before Clement's time.[39] If, however, he alluded to a Hebrew manuscript, this would constitute the oldest and least ambiguous evidence for the existence of accents in biblical books.

More conclusive are some remarks of Jerome in his preface to his translation of the Bible (Vulgate). There he says:

(6). 'Everybody will notice either a horizontal line, or an obelos, or asterisks. And wherever he sees a preceding comma, [it is where] we have followed the Septuagint translation until the colon. But where he notices a sign like a star, he will know that we added [it?] from the Hebrew volumes up to the double colon . . .'

This and similar other remarks may refer to a primitive punctuation in the Hebrew Scriptures of his time. Again, we do not learn anything beyond the existence of *cola scriptus et commata*, i.e. the period (*punctus* =*sof pasuq*) and the semicolon (caesura, *pausa* = '*atnah*). In the second part we shall compare the punctuation of the early Greek and Latin translations with that of Jewish tradition, in order to ascertain in what way that tradition might have influenced the Christian translators.

The evidence presented thus far renders the existence of primitive punctuating signs most probable, at least since the fourth Christian century. But when and how were these signs expanded into an elaborate system and what is the evidence of this process?

The literary documents stating the adaptation of the 'Ur-accents' for *musical purposes* stem from a surprisingly late period; here, we shall quote only the most important source, the *terminus a quo*. Natronai Gaon (ninth century) says:

(7). 'While the scriptural accents with the melodies of cantillation were given to us on Mount Sinai. . . .'[40]

In this quotation the accents, for the first time, are officially considered to be a kind of musical notation to fix not only the punctuation, but also the cantillation of Scripture. The full development of the accents and their musical adaptation must have taken place during the period from the fifth to the ninth century. Thereafter, an uninterrupted flow of documents, descriptive and otherwise, gives us information about the further evolution and the interpretation of the 'accents of cantillation' as they were subsequently called.

We turn now to the examination of those Hebrew manuscript

sources, which antedate this last statement (7), in order to investigate the gap of four centuries which elapsed between the periods of testimonies (4) and (7).

Manuscript Sources before 900

Until *ca.* 1890 very few manuscripts of Scripture were known that would antedate our *terminus a quo* (7). Since Taylor's and Schechter's discovery of the ancient burial place of sacred writings near Cairo (henceforth referred to as Geniza), many manuscripts have come to light and have all but revolutionized our views on the subject of accents.

Heretofore the accepted facts were as follows. From the eighth to the tenth century two schools of Hebrew grammarians were at work, examining, vocalizing, accentuating, and critically editing the scriptural texts. These scholars, the Masoretes, worked in two academies, which were more or less independent of each other, the one in Babylonia, the other in Tiberias. The Babylonian school seems to have been the earlier one, but it was the later Tiberian system of accentuation and vocalization that was generally adopted by all Jewry.[41] A few of their known codices display the growth of accent signs from the 'Ur-accents' to a fully elaborated system. Before the late eighth century no biblical manuscript was known to contain accents or vowel signs.

With the discovery of the Geniza an abundance of older material has become available; some of these manuscripts, mostly scriptural fragments, but also liturgical poems, exegetic sketches, etc., present a *third* system of accents, the so-called Palestinian system.[42] Professor Kahle has devoted most of his scholarly work to the study of these sources, and has published his main results in two monumental works, *Masoreten des Ostens* (Babylonian school) and *Masoreten des Westens* (old Palestinian school). His latest publication on this subject is a comprehensive study *The Cairo Geniza*[43] where all pertinent problems are extensively discussed. In the following paragraphs we shall give a brief summary of his main conclusions, as far as they touch upon our subject.

The first manuscripts with accents date from the seventh century; yet it must be assumed that accentuated documents were in existence for at least 100–150 years earlier. That would lead us back to the sixth century. Our literary references (4) and (6), both come from the turning of the fifth century, and mention only primitive signs. Of the two categories of accents, the disjunctive (separating) and conjunctive (linking), the manuscripts of the Geniza, evidencing the old Palestinian system, show only the strongest accents of separation (*distinctivi*); these, however, are well developed. The connecting accents (*servi, coniunctivi*) are either missing altogether or were added later.

The signs used in these manuscripts consist chiefly of groups of dots and short lines; they bear a close resemblance to the Syriac ecphonetic accents. Dr Kahle assumes the origin of Jewish Masoretic activities to be in Syria (Nisibis) or Northern Palestine.[44] According to his theory, a Nestorian school of scribes and exegetes was the first to set up a system of ecphonetic signs applied to scriptural texts. He also suggests a direct interrelation between this Nestorian school and the contemporary rabbinic academy at Nisibis.[45]

Although the manuscripts do not say anything about the musical function of their accents, Kahle accepts this function almost without question. This view, in turn, is supported by some historic manuscripts of the Geniza, where occasionally marginal reference is made to the chanting of the accents as early as the eighth century.

Only a comparison of the oldest Nestorian ecphonetic lectionaries and the Geniza fragments would determine what elements are based on Jewish and which on Christian tradition. Such a comparison, to my knowledge, has not yet been undertaken; it remains one of the most difficult tasks awaiting students of the Semitic languages.

THE EARLY BYZANTINE, SYRIAN, AND SAMARITAN ECPHONETIC ACCENTS

The first scholar to direct wider attention to the accents of the Byzantine Church was the great Cardinal Jean Baptiste Pitra. He demanded a detailed scientific investigation of the fragments of Jacobite and Nestorian liturgies, with the object of recovering 'some of the oldest hymns and melodies of Israel'.[46] The musicological part of this examination was undertaken by Fétis and Coussemaker. They laid the groundwork for a more exact deciphering of the Byzantine neumes.[47] But it is only in our time that the study and knowledge of Byzantine notation has reached maturity.[48]

The interrelation between Byzantine and Hebrew accents in the lessons was the chief subject of studies by F. Praetorius and Carsten Høeg. These two scholars came to entirely different conclusions. Praetorius, who was by training more philologist than paleographer or musicologist, claimed that the Hebrew Masoretic system was borrowed from the early Byzantine ecphonetic lectionaries.[49] Høeg assumed a more intricate interrelation between Jews and Greeks, a theory substantially corroborated by my own investigations.[50]

The literary sources of the Eastern Churches say very little about the execution of the scriptural lessons; the terms employed are in no way indicative of a semi-musical manner. *Anagnosis, recitatio, lectio, kerygma* (solemn proclamation),[51] are the designations commonly used in the Greek and in the old Latin Churches. The Syrian Churches are no more explicit; the East-Syrian references show, if anything, less concern with the function of music in Christian worship than the West Aramean orbit. Discussing the homilies of Narsai, who was one of the princes of the Nestorian Church, Edmund Bishop makes this pertinent observation:

It is only necessary to read the early chapters of the first formal Western treatise on liturgy, the *De officiis ecclesiasticis* of St Isidore of Seville, to see how great is the contrast. The note of Church song is continually struck, and singing in one form or another is dwelt on by him again and again. It is hard to believe that, if singing had been any prominent feature in the celebration of the East Syrian Mass of Narsai's day, that rhetorical writer would have passed it over in silence. It seems much more probable that both he and Isidore spoke naturally and that each renders, the one by his reticence, the other by his abundance, the actual state of things around him.[52]

Such a statement, which is vindicated by the consistent silence of East Syrian liturgists when it comes to matters of liturgical music, should caution us against accepting hypotheses like those of E. Wellesz, who seeks the origin of ecphonetic musical notation in East Syria and even in Iran.[53] And yet, although his emphasis on Soghdian manuscripts has led nowhere to clear and tangible results, two arguments seem to support his persistent stress on potential Eastern sources. The first is the already mentioned Nestorian academy of scribes and exegetes in Nisibis, the second his assumption that a kind of 'lectionary script' existed in Babylonia long before the Christian era.

This second surmise has been verified during the last ten years to a degree which even Dr Wellesz did not expect. At least three, possibly four cuneiform 'lectionary scripts' have been excavated in Mesopotamia and Iraq, the last one dating back to the time immediately before

King Hamurapi (*ca.* 2000 B.C.). Still, we are unable to determine finally whether these enigmatic tablets had anything to do with musical or semi-musical performance. The inference, especially after the third discovery, seems to be that the series of apparently senseless syllables represents some kind of magic-musical formula, such as was used during the first six Christian centuries in Babylonia. However it is certain that the tablets do not contain an instrumental notation, as was at first assumed.[54] The so-called 'gnostic-musical alphabets', which were edited and interpreted by Charles E. Ruelle, Dom Leclercq, and A. Gastoué, show in general a remarkably low standard of melodic invention. If they were, in any sense, musical documents originating in the culture of Mesopotamia and Iraq, we must not expect to find anything of great significance from the music of the Middle East.[55] While the literary sources on the cantillation of Scripture are meagre in Christianity, there are other proofs of the semi-musical rendering of the lessons in ancient times. The numerous lectionaries with ecphonetic notation, most of them Byzantine, render eloquent testimony of scriptural chant. It is impossible to deal with these highly technical problems extensively, but a few remarks may elucidate their liturgical-historical significance.

The connexion between the Byzantine and the Syrian Churches was a very close one, as evidenced by literary and theological similarities and influences. Before the Monophysite schism (Jacobite Church), the Syrian and Byzantine Churches were liturgically and dogmatically one; the only difference consisted in the usage of their respective vernaculars for the liturgy. Even so, the Jerusalem worship of the fifth century was Greek and served as a model for the Byzantine observance. This fact should be verified by comparing the description given by Aetheria Silvia with contemporary Greek Fathers and lectionaries.[56] Thus, we should expect a close kinship of Byzantine and Syriac ecphonetic systems. Actually, however, these systems are widely divergent (*a*) in their external form, (*b*) in their function, (*c*) in the state of their present preservation. The Syriac system consists of a set of dots and simple lines; it resembles the signs of the old Palestinian Masora. Like these, the Syrian accents have a syntactic and grammatical function, which is not as prominent in the Greek system; moreover, their musical (oral) tradition has been lost at least since the eleventh century. Unfortunately, it was never laid down in didactic manuals such as the Byzantine *Papadikai*.[57]

This fact is clearly expressed by the great Syrian grammarian Gregory Bar Hebraeus (thirteenth century), who says:

> Since the accents symbolize a kind of musical modulation, it is impossible to examine or study them, except by constant hearing and by personal tradition as from teacher to student, from tongue to ear.

Afterwards he confesses that this musical tradition was already lost in his time.[58] Concerning the Syrian accents, neither written nor reliable oral tradition exists to inform us about the function and practical use of the signs which occur in some of their ancient lectionaries.

The Byzantine system has been extensively studied, and its relation to the Jewish accents will be examined later in Part II, Chapter III.

The Samaritans, too, use a cantillation of the Law, and have also developed a primitive system of signs. They are, in their shape and function, a contamination of Greek, Arabic, Syriac, and Masoretic accents, with Arab and Syrian influence prevailing. The same holds true for the mode of their cantillation. Their literary sources are not very old and always refer to the 'reading' of the Law, without any indication of accents or chant.[59] Arab customs and literature have pervaded the Samaritan tradition to such an extent that it should be approached with the utmost caution. We shall, therefore, pay no further attention to this remote aspect of our problem.

The Armenian Lesson; its History and Script

Since Joseph Strzygowsky's amazing discoveries of the Armenian origin of the Romanesque style, the last decades have given us ever more positive proof concerning the creative influence of Armenian civilization.

The outstanding literary source discussing the practice of scriptural reading is the commentary on the daily offices of the Armenian Church, written by John of Odsun (Otzeni) the Catholicos, A.D. 718. The Latin version from which we quote was written by John Baptist Amher, and bears the imprint of the Armenian Monastery of San Lazzaro, Venice, 1834.[60] Here, too, the terms employed for the public reading are not without ambiguity:

> The Holy Gospel is then extolled . . . and with elated voice we look again towards Him, who by the three-fold holiness has called upon us . . . and

in this sense retrospective, the Church reads the prophet Isaiah: whence through the glad enunciation the children of the Church were comforted, and sung a new song, nowadays of *meseti* which means in the Greek language 'singing praises' . . . that kind of song, the gradual, is used in the Church and generally brings forth the close attention of the listener. Thereupon follows the Alleluia . . . after the Holy Gospel has been proclaimed, we profess with raised voices the Holy Faith [the Nicene Creed].[61]

This is a description of the regular Sunday Mass. *Extollitur*, etc., seems to refer to the lesson of the catechumen's Mass; *ideoque elata voce*, etc., describes the *Trisagion* (not the *Tersanctus*) which apparently was sung aloud by all. *Ecclesia Isaiam legit*, etc., refers to an Old Testament lesson which has been retained for Holy Week and Advent; *canticum novum . . . Meseti . . . interpretatum 'Laudes cantare'*, etc., is a non-biblical Armenian hymn; this is followed by a gradual (*graduum cantus*), whereby the vague term *perlectus* is applied. The gradual is concluded by a solemn Alleluia before the chant or recitation (*elata voce profitemur*) of the Nicene Creed.

I was informed by P. Leonzio Dayan of the Armenian Monastery in San Lazzaro that the terms *legere, perlegere, voce elata*, etc., in the Armenian language correspond more or less with the Byzantine *ecphonesis*, indicating a semi-musical, and sometimes a strictly musical rendering, depending on the training of the individual priest. This assumption is confirmed by numerous 'accentuated' Armenian lectionaries.

Their scientific evaluation, however, has not developed beyond its initial stage. Scholars like E. Wellesz, C. Høeg, P. Aubry, K. Kevorkian and others began to compare the various neumes and to reconstruct the ancient scheme of Armenian ecphonetic notation.[62] Their main conclusion is that the Armenian system is in many respects closely akin to the Hebrew scheme, especially in the function of the accents for the pause and punctus (semi-colon and full stop). Sometimes the resemblance is obvious, as for instance in the hermeneutic connotation of some of the Armenian accents, which parallel certain Hebrew *ta'amim*. Even before the discovery of the ancient Palestinian system of accents, P. Wagner surmised that 'elements of synagogal cantillation and lesson practice have been retained in the Byzantine and Armenian tradition'.[63]

Indeed, this similarity is not at all surprising. The amazingly Judaistic character of the Armenian liturgical tradition,[64] as outlined above, will demand an even more detailed examination later on.

THE PERFORMANCE OF THE LECTIONARY IN THE LITURGY OF THE ROMAN CHURCH

The musical parts of the entire Roman liturgy were, in the Middle Ages, divided into the two principal groups of *Accentus* (Lesson, Oration, Prophecies, etc.) and of *Concentus* (the properly chanted Psalms, Antiphons, Responses, Introits, Hymns, Sequences, etc.). The terminology itself alludes to the varying degrees of note-word relations as determined by the principle of accentuation. It is not easy to trace back the history of the Roman lectionary notation to one origin: the first literary sources link it with the ancient Roman–Greek scheme of the accent: acute, grave, circumflex.[65] Even the first theorist of Roman musical practice, Aurelianus Reomensis (ninth century), always used the old Acute-Grave scheme as a yardstick for the proper measurement both of the rhythmic stress in the chant of the lesson, and for the indication of the proper inflexion of the reader's voice.[66] It was only in later times that the cadences and half-cadences of the lesson were connected with certain older psalmodic formulas, and that a 'tonus legendi' was established. The first clear indication of such a development comes from Bernard of Clairvaux (twelfth century), who demanded for the cadence of the lesson the same type of *differentiae* or *diffinitiones* which had long been established in the practice of psalmody.[67]

A slightly different picture, however, is presented by the paleographic evidence: it seems that the Latin Church really employed the classic system of acute and grave for its earliest codices. Later on, other ecphonetic signs made their appearance in Roman lectionaries and were transformed into a primitive musical punctuation which shows some similarity with the earliest Byzantine system. *Positurae* have little to do with the acute-grave scheme and indicate a melodic movement rather than a rhythmic measurement of syllables. P. Wagner sums up this development thus:

> The fathers of this type of lectionary notation selected out of the real (melodic) neumes a few and connected them with the earlier signs of punctuation, in order to fix certain typical melodic formulas of the liturgic lesson.[68]

These 'melodic formulas' of the lesson, on the other hand, show signs of a very ancient tradition and are in numerous instances identical with the cadences of Jewish and Armenian scriptural cantillation. Apparently, the practice of musically rendering the text of the Bible antedated by far the introduction of accents or primitive notation. These signs were adopted by the Masoretes in order to fix the traditional chant of the scriptural lesson.

The discrepancy between literary and paleographic sources concerning the accents of *lectio, oratio,* etc. (the group of rubrics termed *accentus*), has its analogy in the two musical traditions extant in the lectionary chant of the Roman Church. There is an obvious distinction between the *tonus communis* (of which the *tonus solemnis ad libitum* is but a slight expansion) and the more melismatic *tonus antiquus lectionis,* whose cadences already anticipate the *punctus* of the Psalm Tones. This development took place under pressure from the lectors and against the intentions of the Church; originally, lesson and psalmody were close neighbours, so to speak, but with strictly guarded boundaries. True, Eusebius praises the 'modest inflexion' of the cantor in rendering the psalms,[69] and the famous statement of St Augustine about St Athanasius goes still farther: 'He [Athanasius] made the lector render the psalms in so moderate an inflexion, that it came nearer recitation than singing'.[70] The passage shows, in contradistinction to Fleischer's interpretation, that this practice was not at all a common one. First, Athanasius *faciebat lectorem sonare,* i.e. he had to exert his episcopal authority to make the lector change his normal practice of real singing; second, Augustine refers to it expressly, speaking of it as a *praiseworthy but exceptional* practice. Even more outspoken is St Ambrose, who does not leave any doubt when he sets forth this distinction: 'One lector is more capable of a well articulated lesson, another better in psalm-singing'.[71] As A. von Harnack pointed out in his study on the lectorate, the lector had to function both as a reader and as a singer in the first two centuries; often, two lectors were in office, which explains fully Ambrose's observation. In later centuries the lectors gradually sought to arrogate the office and function of the cantor, the appointed psalm-singer. And the ecclesiastical authorities complained that the lectors cared too much for singing and paid too little attention to reading and reciting.[72] Even a Council had to concern itself with the problem: in Laodicea (*ca.* 361) it was decreed that in church nobody was permitted to sing as soloist, except the canonic cantors, who sing from an elevated place.[73] This 'elevated place' is, of course, identical with the *bima* (Greek: *bema*) of the Synagogue, from which the *hazan* (cantor) reads and sings.

In many respects the status and the function of the Jewish cantor parallels that of the Christian lector. He was the paid (not honorary) reader and singer of the Synagogue since the time of the seventh century; like the lector, he preferred to sing; very frequently, we find two *hazanim*, one for reading, one for singing, as was the case with the lectors; the *hazan*, too, was often at odds with his superiors. Even the complaints about the immodest life of the *hazanim* parallel those about the lectors: the *Constitutiones Apostolorum* warn the cantors and psalmists to lead a modest life, and admonish them not to indulge in throwing dice and other immoral pastimes.[74] There is hardly a medieval rabbinic book about synagogal liturgy that does not sharply inveigh against the liturgical and secular misconduct of the *hazanim*.[75]

EXCURSUS: THE FAST-DAY LESSONS IN CHURCH AND SYNAGOGUE

This subject, not immediately within the scope of our investigation, must be discussed now, because we observe here a rare example of terminology, lesson, typical oration, and psalmody of the Church taking their exact pattern from the model of the Synagogue.

(1) *Terminology*. The term *statio* (Greek: *station*) for the fasting on Wednesday and Friday in the Church is a direct translation of the Hebrew *ma'amad*, which in Talmudic literature means fast or supplication day.[76]

(2) *Lesson*. The scriptural Old Testament lessons of the Early Church on these days are unknown to us; but the Armenian lectionary has preserved the fast-day pericopes, Jer. 14, Isa. 56–57, Isa. 40, Joel 2, Jer. 8, Jer. 2, Isa. 1, all of which occur in the Jewish lectionaries for fast-days[77] (in the Synagogue between the fasts of 17 Tammuz and 9 Ab).

(3) *Oration*. The oldest description of Jewish fasting practice (*Taanith* II, 1) quotes this prayer:

Who has heard Abraham on Mount Moriah, He may hear you; He, that has heard our ancestors at the Red Sea, may hear you; He, that has heard Joshua in Gilgal . . . Samuel in Mizpah . . . Elijah on Mount Carmel. . . . He may hear you today.

The very same prayer is paraphrased in the epiclesis of the Mass, of both the Roman and the Eastern Churches.

While the practices of fasting and penitence are described in detail, very little is known about the lessons and prayers of a Christian fast-day during the first four centuries. It seems probable that the lessons were not very different from the Jewish fasting pericopes, as was suggested by the Catholic scholar J. Schümmer in his profound study on the practice of fasting in the Early Church.[78] The Old Armenian lectionary confirms this suggestion. The typical fast-day lessons of the Old Testament are Isa. 40; Lamentations; Gen. 22; Jonah; Isa. 58 and 60; chapters from Job and Proverbs.

Apart from these scriptural lessons the so-called Diaconal Litanies seem to have played a considerable part in the service of fast-days. They show, in spirit as well as in text, a close resemblance to early Jewish *Selihot*, penitential litanies during periods of calamity, like famine or drought. Ancient patriarchs, as Adam, Abel, Seth, Enoch, Noah, together with Abraham, Isaac, and Jacob are directly or indirectly invoked to act as intercessors. We encounter such litanies especially in the Nestorian and Armenian Churches.[79]

Even later, during the seventh and eighth centuries, Irish litanies show this style and trend quite unmistakably.[80]

Our comparisons of the various lectionaries as the oldest and most authentic parts of the liturgy in both Synagogue and Church lead us to expect similar results in the more highly organized forms of music as well. Of these, psalmody is by all standards the oldest, most authentic and most substantial element of the musical liturgy.

NOTES CHAPTER IV

1. The most relevant writings on the question are: Frazer, *The Golden Bough*; Frazer, *Folklore of the Old Testament*; R. Lachmann, *Die Musik des Orients*; C. Sachs, *Geist und Werden der Musikinstrumente*; C. Sachs, *History of Musical Instruments*; C. Sachs, *The Rise of Music in the Ancient World*; P. Quasten, *Die heidnischen Elemente im Vorgregorianischen Gesang*; T. Gérold, *Les Pères de l'Église et la musique*; A. Jeremias, *Das Alten Testament im Lichte der Kultur des alten Orients*. A survey of the ancient literature on this topic is given in Werner-Sonne, 'The Philosophy and Theory of Music in Judaeo-Arabic Literature', *HUCA*, 1941 and 1943.

2. This problem as it appears in Graeco-Roman, Judaeo-Arabic, and general medieval philosophy is discussed extensively in Werner-Sonne, op. cit.

3. Cf. Lachmann, op. cit., where a good bibliography can be found.

4. *B. Meg.* 32a. The scriptural quotation is Ezek. 20:25.

5. This is possibly another Hebraism of the Armenian Church: *qara* is in Hebrew the classical term for reading the Torah, and the Armenian term *karos* for the office of the reader is possibly derived from the Hebrew. Another etymology is *caroza* (Aramaic, occurring in Dan. 3:4) contaminated with the Greek *keryx* (= herald, announcer). Cf. also Komitas Kevorkian, 'Die Armenische Kirchenmusik', *SIM*, I, 55.

6. Cf. Strabo, *Geographia*, lib. I, p. 16 (ed. Basil., 1571); also the article 'Singen und Sagen', in Karl Lachmann, *Kleinere Schriften*; also Plato, *Republic* II and Plutarch, *De Pythiae oraculis*.

7. There is a highly specialized literature on these problems; a segment of its bibliography will be given in Part II, Chapters I, II and III, where the individual groups and their documents will be discussed. Concerning the decline of the Syriac tradition, cf. especially Bar Hebraeus, *Buch der Strahlen*, ed. Moberg, II, 127 ff.

8. On the other hand an instrumental notation, based upon the individual strings, holes, frets, etc., was developed by the ancient Greeks.

9. This fact, disputed for centuries, has been demonstrated beyond any doubt by Oscar Fleischer; his *Neumenstudien*, although written at the turn of the century, has remained a standard work of the first order. Its essential points have served as the basis of all later specialized investigation. His conclusions were generally confirmed in the most recent work on the subject: Carsten Høeg, *La notation ekphonétique*, *MMB*, subs., vol. 1.

10. A. Ackermann, *Das hermeneutische Element der biblischen Akzentuation* (Berlin, 1893), p. 88; also M. Japhet, *Die Akzente der Heiligen Schrift*, pp. 10 f, and Wickes, *The Accents of the So-called Prosaic Books of Scripture.*

11. Cf. E. Hommel, *Studien zur Phonetik und Lautlehre des Hebräischen*, where this question is fully discussed.

12. Conversely, about real music, Dionysius of Halicarnassus, *De compositione verborum* ed. Hanow, (Leipzig, 1868), p. 12: 'It is important to subordinate the words to the melody, but not the melodies to the words'.

13. O. Fleischer, op. cit., pp. 44 ff.

14. It is interesting to note that in the Armenian language, which has a similar rhythm to the Hebrew—iambic and anapaestic—the chant of plain psalmody often resembles some Hebrew traditions.

15. See *infra*, Part II, Chapter V, on psalmody.

16. This is W. Meyer's so-called *Satzschlussgesetz*. Cf. W. Meyer-Speyer, *Der Akzentuierte Satzschluss in der Griechischen Prosa* (Göttingen, 1891).

17. Cf. C. Sachs, 'Die Tonkunst der alten Ägypter', *Archiv f. Musikwissenschaft*, 1920, pp. 1 ff.

18. Cf. J. Finnegan, *Light from the Ancient Past* (N.Y., 1947), pp. 180–1, Fig. 81.

19. Xenophon, *Symposium* II, 19. These and many more sources of classical writers are quoted by Fleischer, op. cit., I, 28–30.

20. Herodotus, VI, 129, 'He "cheironomized" with his feet'.

21. Cf. Plutarch, *Moralia*. (ed. Dübner), p. 997 C.

22. Cf. Livy, VII, 2.

23. This passage has been commented upon by many eminent scholars, both Jewish and Christian, beginning with Rashi; see L. Cappelus, *Arcanum punctationis revelatum* (Leyden, 1624), p. 221; Buxtorf, *De antiqua punctatione*, p. 90; S. Baer-H. Strack, *Dikduke ha-te'amim* (Leipzig, 1876), p. 18; 'Manuel de lecteur', ed. Derenbourg, *Journal asiatique* (Paris, 1870–1), p. 416; E. Hommel, op. cit.; E. Werner, 'Preliminary Notes for a Comparative Study of Catholic and Jewish Musical Punctuation', *HUCA* (1940). Virtually all of them concur in the interpretation quoted in the text.

24. Cf. Samuel Archevolti, *Arugath habosem* (Worms), p. 7d; also the *Travelogue of Petachyah of Regensburg*, ed. Fürth (1884), p. 47. In a more satirical vein, Heinrich Heine, *Der Neue Apoll*.

25. Cf. Baer-Strack, op. cit., p. 18. Even more intimate are the connexions with other terms of Hebrew music; some of them have entered the musical terminology of Byzantine theorists. Cf. my article 'The Psalmodic Formula *Neannoe* and its Origin', *MQ* (January, 1942) XXVIII, pp. 93–99.

26. Cf. O. Fleischer, op. cit., pp. 49–68.

27. The Codex rescript. No. 9, fonds ant. in the National Library, Paris; (the so-called Codex Ephraemi Syri (fifth–sixth century).) C. Høeg, however, doubts that the ecphonetic notation contained in this manuscript is of the same age as the text itself. He is inclined to set the date of the ecphonetic marks considerably later. Cf. Høeg, op. cit., p. 107. Cf. *supra* n. 9.

28. Thus H. Besseler, *Die Musik des Mittelalters und der Renaissance*, p. 33; E. Wellesz, *Aufgaben und Probleme auf dem Gebiete der byz. und or. Kirchenmusik*, p. 70; F. Praetorius, *Ursprung der Masoretischen Akzente*, p. 11 ff; J. B. Thibaut, *Monuments de la notation*

ekphonétique, Chapter II; C. Høeg, op. cit., p. 142; E. Wellesz. *A History of Byzantine Music*, p. 216. In my study 'Prelim. Notes, etc.', *HUCA* (1940), pp. 339 ff, I have presented a highly differentiated point of view, to be discussed in Part II, Chapter III.

29. Here ethnic and linguistic particularism has blocked all centralizing efforts of the Church; for the Eastern Churches, while for at least four centuries members of the original Catholic Church, have persistently resisted all attempts aimed at the unification of their accentuation and chant.

30. This old controversy can hardly be decided one way or the other. Fleischer already realized this when he assumed that 'the Greek word *neuma* was borrowed by the Hebrews, then not understood in later times and identified by them with *ne'ima* (= sweetness, melody), retranslated again into Greek as *melos*, or *meligdupos* (= sweetsounding)'. Thus he presumes a two-fold borrowing and retranslating (op. cit., p. 32). See also the following authors on this question: H. Riemann, *Handbuch der Musikgeschichte*, I, 2, p. 82; WGM, II, p. 17; J. Wolf, *Notationskunde*, I, pp. 61–63; E. Werner, 'Prelim. Notes, etc.', *HUCA*, 1940, p. 337. At any rate, it is hardly probable that *neuma* was simply Greek or simply Hebrew. A cross-relation or contamination appears to have taken place. See also my study 'The Psalmodic Formula *Neannoe* and its origin', *MQ*, 1942, pp. 93 ff.

31. Fétis, in his *Histoire génerale de la musique*, I, pp. 443 ff, bases his theory of scriptura chant in the Second Temple upon the Nehemiah passage. In so doing, he follows the theories of some Protestant theologians of the eighteenth and nineteenth centuries, especially Gesenius, Ewald, and Hupfeld, which today can no longer be upheld.

32. *Ber.* 62a.

33. Cf. *supra*, n. 23.

34. *Ned.* 37b.

35. *Ned.* 37a.

36. Cf. E. Werner, 'Prelim. Notes . . .', *HUCA* (1940), p. 340.

37. Of the large grammatical literature which deals extensively with the accents, the best exposition of the evolution of accents is given in Bauer-Leander, *Historische Grammatik der Hebr. Sprache* (esp. P. Kahle's contribution); also A. Büchler, 'Untersuchungen zur Entstehung und Entwicklung der Hebr. Akzente', *Sitzungsberichte der K. Akademie der Wissenschaften* (Vienna, 1891), CXXIV, pp. 67 ff; P. Kahle, *Masoreten des Westens*, I, pp. 36–48.

38. Exod. Rabba c. 2. Of numerous parallel passages only two may be mentioned: Lev. Rabba c. 1, where the term *p'sik* seems to indicate a sign of punctuation, and later on in the same chapter, where the derivative term *hafsaqa* (disjunction, pausa) is used.

39. Cf. G. Maysen, *Die Grammatik der Griechischen Papyri aus der Ptolemäerzeit*, pp. 48–51; also M. Laum, *Das alexandrinische Akzentuationssystem* (Paderborn, 1928).

40. In *Machsor Vitry* (ed. Hurwitz), p. 91. Cf. S. D. Luzzatto, *Kerem Chemed*, III, 200. The best interpretation of this significant passage is given by A. Ackermann, in Winter and Wünsche, *Die jüdische Literatur*, III, 'Der Synagogale Gesang', p. 491.

41. For a brief description of these schools see Wickes, 'The so-called Prosaic Books', in *A Treatise on the Accents of Scripture*, I (Oxford, 1887); also Herzog-Hauck, *Encyclopedia*, article 'Bibeltext', and *JE*, article 'Masora'.

42. Traces of this oldest system were known before, but had been disregarded generally. Cf. S. Pinsker, *Einleitung in das babylonisch-hebräische Punktationssystem* (Vienna, 1863), pp. 9 ff.

43. British Academy (London, 1947).

44. Cf. Kahle, *Masoreten des Westens*, I, 24, 51. II, 42 ff; Note also the story in Barhad-bessaba 'Arbaia, *Eccl. Hist.* (PO, IX, 626).

45. Kahle's hypothesis is supported by Cassiodorus, *Institutiones*: '. . . just as near Alexandria an institute is supposed to have lasted for a long time, now also in the city of Nisibis in Syria it is rumoured that the Hebrews study assiduously. . . .' (*PL*, LXX, 1105.)

The founders of the Syrian School in Nisibis were Bar Soma and Narsai. Some of the statutes of that School are still extant: (a) statutes written by Husha, the Metropolitan of Nisibis, date 496, revised 587 and (b) rules and regulations edited by the Metropolitan Simeon about 590, newly revised by Ahad' Hvi, in 602. For excerpts of these rules cf. G. D. Malech, *History of the Syrian Nation* (Minneapolis, 1910); also A. Baumstark,

Geschichte der Syrischen Literatur, p. 128. These rules demonstrate a remarkable degree of organization and a high standard of scholarship. The shortest course of exegesis took three full years. Cf. also E. Sachau, 'Die Chronik von Arbela', *Sitz. d. Preuss. Ak., Hist.-Phil., Kl.*, 1915, pp. 91 ff; also F. Chabot, *Journal asiatique*, VIII (1896), 43 ff.

46. J.-B. Pitra, *L'Hymnographie de l'Église grecque* (Rome, 1867), pp. 33–34.

47. F. J. Fétis, 'Resumé philosophique de l'histoire de la Musique', in vol. I of *Biographie universelle des musiciens* (Paris, 1833); also H. E. de Coussemaker, *Scriptores medii aevi de musica*, I.

48. A good bibliography on this subject is given in G. Reese, op. cit., pp. 432–4, and E. Wellesz, *History of Byzantine Music* (Oxford, 1949).

49. Cf. F. Praetorius, op. cit. (see note 28). The first scholar who called attention to the resemblance between Byzantine ecphonetic signs and the masoretic accentuation before Praetorius was Dr E. B. Löwensohn (in *Jüd. Literaturblatt*, 1894, pp. 123, 127, 131), today a forgotten man. It is for the scientific record that his name is mentioned here. Löwensohn went so far as to equate certain ecphonetic signs with masoretic accents, and reached the conclusion that the question could be solved only 'by close examination of the oldest codes of the Eastern Church'.

50. Cf. E. Werner, 'Prelim. Notes, etc.', *HUCA* (1940), pp. 342 ff.

51. Cf. Pseudo-Dionysius the Areopagite, *De ecclesiatica hierarchia* III, 3, 5, 'After the older tradition [O.T.] the New Testament is read publicly'.

52. Cf. Dom R. H. Connolly and E. Bishop, 'The Liturgical Homilies of Narsai', in *Texts and Studies* (Cambridge, 1916), VIII, p. 117.

53. E. Wellesz, *Aufgaben und Probleme auf dem Gebiete der byz. und or. Kirchenmusik*, pp. 34–36. The same author in 'Die Lektionszeichen in den soghdischen Texten', *ZFM*, I (1919), pp. 505 ff.

54. Concerning the cuneiform tablets with hypothetical notation, see Canon Galpin, *Sumerian Music*; also C. Sachs, *Proceedings of the American Musicological Society* (1939), and in *MQ* (1941). The most recent discoveries seem to confirm Sachs's theory of the existence of primitive Babylonian notation; see especially the periodical *Iraq*, July 1946, where newly discovered tablets are photographed and discussed.

55. Cf. Ch. E. Ruelle, *Le Chant gnostico-magique des sept voyelles grecques* (Solesmes, 1901). Also: Dom H. Leclercq, 'Alphabet vocalique des gnostiques', in *DACH*; A. Gastoué, op. cit., pp. 26–30; E. Werner, 'The Conflict of Hellenism and Judaism in the Music of the Early Christian Church', *HUCA* (1947), p. 445.

56. The pertinent texts can be found in Rahlfs, op. cit., pp. 111–17; 100–2 *et passim*. See also Baumstark, op. cit., Chapters 1, 2.

57. Cf. Gregory Bar Hebraeus, *Le Livre des splendeurs*, and the German edition by Moberg (Lund and Leipzig, 1907, 1913). See also T. Weiss, 'Zur ostsyrischen Laut-und Akzentlehre' in Bonner, *Orientalistische Studien*, fasc. 5 (Stuttgart, 1933).

58. Bar Hebraeus, op. cit. (ed. Moberg), II, 108–11 and 126–8. There we read the following interesting passage: 'Mahp'kana: When I wanted to hear this accent from an eminent teacher in Melitene, he had to confess "I do not know it, nor did I learn it from my teachers. The holy one [Jacob of Edessa] learned it from the Greeks and he called it M'qarq'sana, perhaps on account of the manifold modulations of the sentences wherein it occurs. In our regions these accents are even unknown to the Greeks".'

59. Cf. A. Z. Idelsohn, 'Die Vortragszeichen der Samaritaner', *MGWJ*, LXI (1917), pp. 118–26. Also M. Heidenheim, 'Die Liturgie der Samaritaner', in *Bibliotheca Samaritana*, II, pp. 18, 22, *et passim*. Cf. A. E. Cowley, *Samaritans* (Oxford, 1915).

60. Cf. Conybeare, op. cit., pp. 488 ff.

61. Ibid., p. 501.

62. Cf. E. Wellesz, 'Die armenische Messe und ihre Musik', *Jahrbuch der Musikbibliothek Peters*, (1920), pp. xl ff. Also C. Høeg, op. cit., pp. 146 f; P. Aubry, 'Le Système musical de l'Église armenienne', *Tribune de Saint-Gervais*, 1901, 1902, and 1903; and K. Kevorkian, 'Das Interpunktionssystem der Armenier', *SIM*, I, pp. 54 ff.

63. Cf. *WGM*, I, p. 30.

64. Cf. *supra*, Chapter II.

65. Cf. *Paléographie musicale*, I, p. 100, where a curious sermon of a preacher of the fifth

or sixth century is quoted likening the apostles, doctors and masters of the Church to one great organ, upon which the Holy Spirit plays—*aptatum quibusdam accentibus, gravi, acuto et circumflexo.* . . .

66. Cf. Aurelianus Reomensis, *Musica disciplina* in Gerbert, *Scriptores de musica sacra*, I, 55.

67. Cf. St Bernard, *Opera*, I, 699 (ed. Mabillon, Paris, 1667).

68. Cf. WGM, II, p. 88.

69. Eusebius, *Hist. Eccl.*, II, 17.

70. St Augustine, *Confessiones*, IX, 33 (*PL*, XXXII, 800).

71. Cf. St Ambrose, *De Off.* I, 44.

72. Cf. Zonaras, *Ad Can. 22 Laodicensem*, in Gerbert, *De cantu et musica sacra*, I, 33.

73. Cf. Hefele-Leclercq, *Histoire des conciles* (1907-38) (Council of Laodicea, can. 17).

74. *CAF*, VIII, cap. 47. The old *hazan* before the seventh century was a kind of supervisor; reference has been made above to Epiphanius' use of the term *hazanites*. On the function and development of the *hazan* in the ancient synagogue, see the article 'Hazan' in the *Lewy-Festschrift*, pp. 176 ff. On the development of the Christian lectorate see Harnack, *Texte und Untersuchungen: Die Apostolische Kirchenordnung*, 'Das Lektorat in der Kirche' (Leipzig, 1886).

75. Of the abundant Hebrew literature on this subject, we quote only a few items accessible to the general reader: *JE*, VI, 284 ff (article 'Hazan'); *JM*, pp. 101, 505 ff; E. Birnbaum, *Liturgische Übungen* (Berlin, 1901, 1902).

76. See S. Bonsirven: 'Notre *statio* liturgique est-elle empruntée au culte iuif?', in *Recherches de science religieuse* (1925), pp. 258 ff.

77. Cf. Conybeare, op. cit., pp. 518-20.

78. Cf. J. Schümmer, *Die altchristliche Fastenpraxis* (Münster, 1933).

79. Conybeare, loc. cit.; also A. Maclean, op. cit., pp. 101-2, 252.

80. Cf. Irish *Liber Hymnorum*, ed. Bernard and Atkinson (London, 1898), II, pp. 14 ff; also *Missale Sarum*, ed. Dickinson, col. 888 (contra mortalitatem).

CHAPTER FIVE

The Psalmodic Forms and their Evolution

I f it is not easy for a person of our age to understand the atmosphere and the spiritual life of the Middle Ages as it developed in the West, even more obstacles stand in the way of comprehending the eastern Mediterranean culture, which was dominated by that supra-national entity called the Byzantine Empire. Also it is well-nigh impossible to set forth many features common to East and West.

The growing conflict between secular and ecclesiastical authorities is perhaps one common feature, but we would be deceiving ourselves were we to assume that the struggle arose under analogous circumstances and led to similar results in the East and the West.

Less obvious but more significant was another struggle, obscure but intense, that arose before the millennium had reached its end: the conflict between simple religious experience or pious devotion on the one hand and scholarly theology, the supposedly infallible interpretation of God's purposes, on the other. This antagonism arose in the seventh century and reached its peak in the Reformation eight centuries later. It was fought on two levels: within the society or the circumscribed group, and within the soul of the individual. At any level it is true that 'There is no clear border-line in the region of religious experience between the swamps and jungle of paganism and the sun-lit uplands of pure faith.'[1]

Working in an undeveloped, frequently semi-pagan society, the Church had to be careful not to discourage the 'meek in spirit', although at the same time its organization rested primarily upon an intellectual monasticism. In this dilemma it used to its best advantage the one book of the Old Testament that came to be the backbone of most liturgies, the Psalter.

It would be naive to assume that the psalms themselves were left untouched by their elevation to the one place which was equally holy to the devout simpleton and the monkish scholar. The transformations, selections, paraphrases to which the Psalter was subjected would warrant a very extensive study. From the magnificently illuminated 'Books of Hours' in the possession of the rich princes, down to the simply improvised *Laude* of Francis of Assisi's followers, one supreme path is followed —the great road of psalmody in all its varying forms. In these tunes alone the erudite cardinal as well as the illiterate peasant could pour out his soul in prayer—even if the latter could not pronounce the words. It is not possible to do full justice to the part played by psalmody in medieval civilization. Suffice it to be understood that whoever evaluates psalmody and its part in daily life approaches the spirit of the Middle Ages.

THE JEWISH ORIGIN OF PSALMODY

The term psalmody is understood to mean a type of musical setting which is governed by a coordination of syntactic and melodic accents. Not only do texts of the Psalter belong to this category but also any scriptural or liturgical passage, chanted in a manner whereby the structure of the sentence determines the length, the flow, and the phrasing of the syllabic melody. In general, the varying relationship between note and word is the essential factor in the chief forms of sacred music. Considering psalmody to be but a higher developed species of cantillation, this prime category of musical liturgy is characterized by the organic ties which link the syntactic structure of the scriptural text to its musical foundation. Here the individual word is of little relevance; it is the whole sentence with its caesura and cadence which represents a musical unit.

The *parallelismus membrorum*, that poetic dichotomy of biblical diction, has been carefully preserved in all translations; it is the foundation of psalmody. It was, moreover, the creative and distinctive element which, in the development of Jewish and Christian liturgy, caused such variegated forms of expression as the Response, the Antiphon, the Refrain-psalm, the Gradual, the Litany, and many others. Without that parallelism of diction our musical and liturgical expressions would be so much poorer, probably as monotonous as only constant hymn-singing could be. The abundance of varied forms, the scope of artistic imagery, all this is only understandable in the light of the fundamental concept of scriptural dichotomy.

The oldest element of the Christian liturgy was, as is generally known, the lesson and its framework of psalm-singing. We shall discuss this briefly because only a few of the ancient sources refer to the liturgy proper; the innumerable patristic remarks about private or monastic psalmody cannot be fully considered here. The oldest testimony about the connexion of lesson and psalmody was given by Tertullian, if we disregard Justin's somewhat vague observations.[2] The *Apostolic Constitutions* (fourth century) clearly indicate an already well-established order: 'After each two lessons, [someone other than the cantor] shall chant the hymns of David, and the people shall join in singing the last words of the verses.'[3] This rule presupposes the existence of four lessons; indeed, there were originally three or four readings from the Bible customary in early Christianity, as was shown in Chapter III. The first chant was inserted between the Epistle and the Gospel. Apart from the psalmody which accompanied the lessons, the liturgies displayed from the very outset an abundance of, and a strong preference for, this kind of sacred chant. These were often in opposition to other more recent forms, such as hymns.[4]

Of the regular two chants within the lesson, the first was always a response (*cantus responsorius*). We have this on the authority of Ambrose[5] and the old Mozarabic Missal.[6] The Nestorian liturgy shows the distinction between the two chants most clearly, using differentiating terms. The first chant (response) is called *Shuraya* (cf. the Hebrew *Shir* = hymn), the second is superscribed *Zumara* (cf. the Hebrew *Zamer* = sing).[7] This corresponds exactly with the tradition of the Roman and North African Churches, according to which the first chant is a more or less simple response, the second an elaborate Alleluia.

In the Mass, the first psalmody after the lesson is called the Gradual. This designation has an interesting history. The term Gradual alludes to the place where the cantor stood when chanting the psalms, called the ambo (steps in front of the altar, from Gr. *anabainein*, to mount stairs). We can trace this institution to the fourth century.[8] That 'elevated place' probably corresponds, as we saw before, to the synagogal *bima*. It aimed at an imitation of the revered Temple practice, where the Levites sang psalms while standing on the steps of the sanctuary. Curiously enough this fact has been consistently overlooked in the discussions of the term *gradual*. Yet, the Jewish origin of the ambo was well known to the medieval Church, as we learn from Amalarius:

> The lector and cantor ascend the steps according to ancient custom, concerning which it is written in the Book of Ezra; Ezra, the scribe, stood upon a wooden

stair, which he had made, to deliver his address. [Neh. 8; 4–5] And shortly after-wards: He stood out over all the people.[9]

Nor was this the only Jewish custom retained in psalmodic practice; text, chant, practice and details of psalmody in the Church are replete with minutely observed Jewish tradition. We quote here a few in-stances: in the Early Church one singer only chanted the psalmody, as is stated unanimously by the Church Fathers; later, usually two and three psalmists were employed. Isidore of Seville (seventh century) says:

Responses are these songs called, because a choir responds to the soloist; in former times one alone performed, now sometimes one, sometimes two or three, while the larger choir responds.[10]

The older synagogal practice provided for one precentor only, but already in the third and fourth centuries the rule was: 'The cantor must not chant the liturgy, unless at least two men stand by him'. This was to assure the proper responses or to correct his reading.[11]

Soloistic psalmody, without response, was also an old heritage of the Synagogue and probably of the Temple.[12] Levitic psalm-singing was, of course, one of the regular features of the Temple worship, as numer-ous scriptural passages indicate; but it was performed by a choir, not by a soloist. The custom of opening the regular worship with psalms, which we find in the ecclesiastic institution of the *invitatorium*, also dates back to the Jewish practice. The psalms of the *invitatorium* are Ps. 95 and 96; the very same pieces were sung by the Levites every evening.[13]

As for the psalms accompanying ecclesiastical lessons (the earliest and most common element in all Christian liturgies), we cannot find a syna-gogal parallel to this custom before the eighth century. The Talmud and Mishna are strangely silent, and only in the treatise *Soferim* (seventh–eighth century) is the psalmody during and after the lessons mentioned.[14] Nor do other post-biblical sources contain definite information about a regular lesson in the Temple, except for special days and the ever re-current *Sh'ma'*. This lack of evidence on the Jewish side admits only one of two alternative conclusions: (1) either the scriptural lessons did take place in the Temple and were accompanied by psalmodies or, (2) the psalmody between the lessons, as practised in the Synagogue of today, *was originally a Christian practice, as opposed to all previous assumptions,* and was borrowed by the Synagogue from the Church before the eighth century. It cannot be assumed that all rabbinic writings previous to the eighth century would make no remark about hymns or psalms which accompany the scriptural lesson, when the reading of the lesson itself is discussed so extensively. The single reference I was able to find mentions the singing of a psalm-verse (24:7) *after* the lesson.[15] This famous passage: 'Lift up your heads, O ye gates; . . .' (*Attolite portas* . . .) plays a significant part in the Roman liturgy; but it would be too far-fetched to derive the entire system of Gradual and Alleluia from this single Talmudic reference. Hence, it might be prudent to suspend judgement on this particular question.[16]

In general, however, the liturgical sphere of psalm-singing was perhaps the most important Jewish element in the development of sacred music in the Church. The Church Fathers as well as the rabbis were fully aware of this synagogal legacy. Pope Damasus, Pope Celestine, St Augustine, St Jerome, and many more spoke of the 'Davidic songs and their melodies', which the Church had saved and preserved.[17] Jerome, the great translator of the Bible, made St Paula, his contemporary, aware of the psalms, *ita ut psalmos hebraice caneret*.[18] For internal evidence we have the polemics against the Gnostic and anti-Judaic Marcionites because of their 'refusal to chant the Davidic Psalms'.[19] The monk Diodore of Tarsus *nolens volens* defended the Church's imitation of Jewish prayers and songs.[20]

The rabbis too were cognizant of this interrelation, and perhaps the most caustic remark comes from an Italian Jew of the thirteenth century, Manuello ha-Romi, a fine and learned poet:

> What says our music to the Christians?
> 'Stolen, yea stolen was I from the land of the Hebrews.'
> (Gen. 40:15)

Other Jewish sages of the Middle Ages held the same view.[21]

These statements were more or less sustained and confirmed by students of liturgics, but not as readily accepted by musicologists. During the latter half of the nineteenth century, Gevaert and his followers tried hard to disprove the existence of Jewish elements in the music of the Church, attributing a much greater influence to Hellenistic concepts. It was only during this century that such hypotheses became less and less tenable in view of accumulating evidence. Due to P. Wagner's and A. Gastoué's studies of the Gregorian tradition, and Idelsohn's examination of the Jewish tradition, these older views had to be abandoned.[22]

The respective theories of these scholars will be discussed in the musical part of this work.

PSALMODIC FORMS AND PRACTICES

The paramount importance of the Psalter for the evolution and structure of Christian as well as of Jewish liturgy is too well known to warrant special elaboration. Private devotions, monastic rituals, special religious occasions such a consecrations, dedications, exorcisms, etc., were no less replete with psalmody than the regular worship of Synagogue and Church.[23] Only such references to the psalms that have special or typical significance, can be discussed here.

Omitting consideration of the contents, we can distinguish four main formal schemes in the Psalter. They are: (1) The plain, direct psalm, in which strophic arrangement is not apparent. (2) The acrostic psalm, in which the verses or half-verses are arranged in alphabetic sequence (Ps. 119). (3) The refrain-psalm, in which each verse ends with the same refrain (Ps. 136). (4) The Hallelujah psalm, which either begins or closes with the jubilant acclamation (e.g. Ps. 145–150). Naturally, the different formal schemes were conducive to differentiated musical renderings.

Strophic psalms with refrain, such as Ps. 42 or 46, have but seldom influenced musical composition although they were the forerunners of the great literature of refrain-hymns.

Solo Psalmody

(Psalmus directaneus and responsorius)

This type, certainly the oldest in Synagogue and Church, was rendered by the precentor (psalmista, lector). Occasionally, if the congregation knew the psalm, it responded. P. Wagner's assumption that responsorial performance was practised even in the first centuries of the Gentile Church disregards one important factor, a prerequisite indispensable for responsorial usage: familiarity with the scriptural text which cannot be expected from a Gentile community without a standing tradition. Even in Judaism, the hazan chanted the psalms alone, and occasionally he was answered by responses. This category has survived in the Church in the psalmody of the Nocturns, the oldest element of daily worship. The

Nocturns and Lauds correspond exactly to the evening and morning service of the Synagogue. We shall see that in spite of all Christological interpretations even the selection of psalms was determined by ancient tradition.

The purely solo usage, however, was soon replaced by the *psalmus responsorius*. In all the Christian liturgies, this is the most common form of psalmody up to the present day. Not so in the Synagogue. While the responsive chant is one of the genuine forms of Jewish worship, the growing ignorance of the congregations in Hebrew matters and the arrogated monopolistic position of the *hazan* contributed, in the course of the centuries, to a regrettable deterioration of all liturgical forms. The *hazan* succeeded in usurping the performance of almost all psalms except the few of the *Hallel* (Ps. 113–118) and the verses which accompany the lessons and other ritual occasions. This development started in the ninth century and lasted up to the nineteenth, when the liberal reform of the liturgy strove to restore the former active participation of the congregation. Before the ninth century, however, the response was immensely popular in the Synagogue. The Hebrew term *'ana* (to answer, respond) is frequently used to describe this custom.[24] The acclamations, such as Amen, Selah, Hallelujah, Hosanna, etc., which will be discussed later on (Chapter VIII), played an important part in the responses.

The question arises here: who performed the responses, a trained choir or the congregation? That the congregation did so is not too plausible, since it would presuppose that it knew not only the tunes (which could easily be taught), but also the texts of many psalms by heart. On the other hand, our earliest sources do not mention a chorus, but constantly stress the ideal of *koinonia* (unison), *una voce dicentes, canentes*, etc.[25] We have a few short remarks by Augustine on this question. According to his report, the congregation joined in the psalm, if they knew it, *hypophonically* or *antiphonically*; if they did not know it, they listened and kept silent.[26]

Apparently there was some difference as to the status of psalmody in the Eastern and Western Churches. The *Apostolic Constitutions* assign a good deal of psalmody to the choir, thereby indicating the contemporary practice in Syria during the fourth century. Representing the Greek and the North African Roman Church, Chrysostom and Tertullian refer to psalmody as to a newer type of popular songs.[27] Ambrose, on the other hand, praises the wonderful psalmodic *unison* of the faithful.[28]

In the East, the population participated in many acclamations, in the Thrice-Holy, and probably in hymn-singing, but hardly in psalmodic singing proper. The famous travelogue of Aetheria Silvia (fourth century) may modify our conclusion. In her *Peregrinatio*, she refers frequently to the active psalm-singing of the population; but we must bear in mind that the community of which she speaks was not an ordinary one. She tells us herself that many of the faithful in Jerusalem had been instructed in the (Greek) language of the liturgy, and that in general, the educational standard of the community was exceptionally high.[29] According to her report, the people mostly sang hymns and canticles, not psalmody, which was more or less the prerogative of the monastic orders (*monazontes et parthenae*).

Indeed, the enormous growth of monastic life in the Orient caused the gradual deterioration of *popular* psalm-singing. None the less, wherever psalms were sung in the vernacular, rudiments of popular participation survived.

Not so in the West: by the time the *Ordinarium Missae* became popular, the texts and tunes of psalmodies had attained their first definite formulation in the Occidental *scholae cantorum* (fifth century). Naturally, the ordinary community felt happy to be relieved of the difficult task of psalm-singing in Latin, since such well qualified professional singers were available. The more the celebration of the Mass came into the foreground, the less other components of the worship were observed in lay congregations. It may safely be said that the form and text of the Latin Mass attained their overwhelming popularity only at the expense of all other forms of Catholic worship.

The situation in the Synagogue is somewhat similar to that of the Eastern Churches. In the first centuries after the fall of the Temple we hear a good deal about community praying and chanting, but we have no evidence of the existence of a choir until the ninth century. There is also no unanimity as to the method of rendering certain psalms, especially the *Hallel*. Some rabbis demanded a refrain-like performance, others a regular *responsorium*, and still others a repetition of each verse by the congregation. The definitive tradition seems to have been forgotten soon after the loss of the central sanctuary.[30] At any rate, the congregation together with its precentor took part in the performance of all prayers, spoken or chanted.

The chronicler Nathan ha-Babli (Nathan the Babylonian) renders the first account of a trained chorus. Since the passage is interesting and little known, we quote it here in full:

The *hazan* intones *baruk sheamar*, the choristers respond to each sentence with 'Praised be He'. When the *hazan* intones Ps. 92, the choristers respond by singing 'It is good to praise, etc.' [Ps. 92:2] whereupon the entire congregation recite the *p'suke de'zimra* [Laud-psalms] to the end. The *hazan* then intones *nishmat kol hay* [all living souls] and the young choristers answer by singing 'Shall bless thy name'. Thereafter the *hazan* recites one sentence and the singers respond with the next one and so forth up to the *Kedusha* [Thrice-Holy]. The congregation chants the *Kedusha* in a soft voice, and the choristers sing it aloud. Then the young men are silent and the *hazan* alone continues until 'Redeemer of Israel' at which all rise for the *'Amida* [18 benedictions]. In the loud repetition of *'Amida* and *Kedusha*, the choristers respond regularly until the end of the Sanctification 'Holy God' and thereupon the *hazan* ends.[31]

The report also speaks of the service connected with the solemn installation of the Exilarch in Babylonia. The choristers were the students of the Talmudic academy and were more or less trained boys and young men, comparable to monks.

Genuine responses are numerous: e.g. the response 'It is good to praise Thee', the answer 'Shall bless Thy name', etc.; the remark 'the singers respond with the next one'; and the 'regular' response of the *Kedusha* (expanded Thrice-Holy), continuing to the end of the Sanctification. The first 'Praised be He' is a typical acclamation, such as Amen, or 'Cum spiritu tuo', etc. The distinction between 'young choristers' and 'choristers', if made intentionally, would indicate an archaic form of antiphonal singing, as described by the *Apostolic Constitutions* and Aetheria Silvia.[32]

Nothing in Nathan's report stresses the trained chorus as a sensational novelty; apparently this institution was in existence for a considerable time. Nevertheless, if we assume that it started in the seventh century, we have a gap of six centuries after the cessation of the Levitical offices. Is it possible that the Christian practice and institution of trained, usually monastic, choruses served as a model? The report originated in Babylonia and reflects a period when Sassanid and Islamic rulers had oppressed the liturgical expansion of the Church for centuries. Until we know more about the Christian and Jewish communities of Babylonia during the eighth century, we shall be unable to come to a positive conclusion.

Acrostic Psalms

Since translations could hardly preserve the acrostic of the original psalms, the Western writers at first disregarded this type entirely. Not so the Syrians. Ephraem Syrus and later hymnodists of the Eastern Church used this scheme for some of their hymns or paraphrases.[33] The Fathers of the Western Church (Greek and Latin) understood the term acrostic as something quite different. Sozomen and other writers of his time call a short response-acclamation an acrostic; the *Apostolic Constitutions* are also of this opinion.[34] Only in Byzantine and Semitic poetry of the Church has the old alphabetic acrostic survived and, of course, in the liturgy of the medieval Synagogue. For the development of European poetry the acrostic was of minor relevance. It is, however, of considerable significance in the Synagogue where it was frequently used as a means of indicating the author's name.[35]

Refrain-Psalm

In all liturgies the refrain-psalm is of great importance. Apart from the patterns as given in Exod. 15 and similar scriptural poems, we have the report of Eusebius about the Jewish sects of Therapeutae in Alexandria (quoted from Philo, *De Vita Contemplativa*), where the practice of refrain singing is minutely described. Eusebius adds that the Christian psalmodic practice of his time corresponds exactly to the Alexandrian-Jewish custom.[36] Zunz mentions Augustine's refrain poems which the Saint called *Hypopsalma* (a refrain verse), comparing it with the medieval Hebrew term *pizmon*, which also seems to designate a refrain-verse or the whole refrain poem.[37]

The usual name of the refrain-poem was *acroteleution, hypopsalma* or *ephymnion*; Ps. 136 was performed as such. Still we hear relatively early that other psalms were rendered in a similar fashion. Thus, Chrysostom calls Ps. 42:2 an *acroteleution*, an indication that he quoted from a Greek text linking Pss. 42 and 43:5.[38] The Gnostics, too, composed free refrains for didactic-dogmatic purposes, as we learn from Sozomen and Ephraem.[39] Other examples of such periphrastic refrains occur in the apocryphal Acts of John and in some papyri of the first four centuries.[40] Both in the chants of the Western and the Eastern Churches these forms grew and developed into larger and more independent compositions, with the antiphon attaining the most widespread propagation. However, the Synagogue retained the original forms and did not develop them further; the response and the refrain psalm remained essentially unaltered.

The Hallelujah-Psalm or versus alleluiaticus

This warrants special consideration as the archetype of melismatic chant (see Chapter VI). A few remarks will suffice here: Jewish tradition as well as Christian exegesis invariably have understood the Hallelujah as a song performed by men and angels.[41] It is from this aspect that the Hallelujah, enhanced by its ecstatic musical rendering, assumed a distinctly mystical character in Judaism and in Christianity. As long as it remained within its original context (in the Psalter) it took no dominant part in the liturgy. But in Synagogue and Church it was separated from its original text and added to almost any other kind of poetry, as acclamation or 'pneumatic' (abstract spiritual) utterance. This development led to a certain disembodiment of the Hallelujah, which finally resulted in the omission of the word Hallelujah itself; only certain vowels were sung in its place: E U O U A E for sEcUlOrUm AmEn.[42] As such it became an optional close of the 'Little Doxology' (Gloria Patri), which concludes with the words Hallelujah, Amen, thus directly imitating the pattern of the Old Testament as given in Ps. 106:48, or I Chron. 16:36. The Jewish origin of the Alleluia-singing is attested by Augustine, Isidore and other Church Fathers. Most outspoken is Isidore: 'The lauds, that is Alleluia-singing, is a Hebrew kind of song'.[43]

The original liturgical function of the Hallelujah in ancient Judaism is not yet quite clear. While some scholars linked it with the pre-monotheistic worship of the New Moon,[44] there is certainly no trace of such a concept to be found in the Bible. According to the present writer's belief, the Hallelujah assumed quite early a distinctly liturgical function, closely connected with the doxology and the conception of theocracy. It was also one of the few acclamations in which the 'unlearned', those problem children of Jewish and Christian sages at the dawn of Christianity, could actively join in the worship of the Temple. Paul, the Apostolic Fathers, and the rabbis, all stress the response of certain liturgical formulas by congregational acclamations, such as Amen or Hallelujah. Its use in the doxologies of Synagogue and Church is extensively discussed in Chapter IX.

Thus far, actual psalm texts and their musical rendering have been the object of our examination. Yet, following our definition of the term psalmody, a great number of other musical forms fall into that category. Nor is the dividing line between psalmodic and melismatic forms always clearly discernible: on the contrary, the general course of musical development invariably shows a tendency from simple to more elaborate forms, *whenever professional musicians can use their free initiative*. This condition was prevalent from the sixth century on, in the Synagogue as well as in the Church. Mixed forms, such as certain Hebrew *piyyutim*, Syrian, Armenian, Byzantine poems, the Tract, Gradual-Responses, Antiphons and parts of the *Ordinarium Missae* of the Roman Church, belong to this somewhat elusive category. Most of these types will be the subject of our next chapter on mixed forms. In view of these facts the old classification into *accentus* and *concentus* seems untenable.

The questions of instrumental accompaniment, female or mixed choirs, extra-liturgical songs, etc., belong to the realm of moral theology and philosophy. They reflect the involved controversies of the theologians concerning the status and value of liturgical music, and will be discussed in Chapter X.

THE CANTICLES IN CHURCH AND SYNAGOGUE

While the canticles, in their liturgical function and their musical form, are closely related to the psalms, they bear certain characteristic features which secured for them a special lore in all liturgies.[45] The Synagogue of today uses in its liturgy only the following two canticles in chanted selections: Exod. 15 and Deut. 32. Read as lessons on great festivals or holydays are the prayer of Hannah (I Sam. 2), the song of Jonah (Jonah 2: 3) and the hymn of Habakkuk (Hab. 3). All Churches make use in their liturgies of fourteen canticles which are sung regularly:

1. The song of Moses and Miriam (Exod. 15)
2. The prayer of Moses (Deut. 32)
3. The prayer of Hannah (I Sam. 2)
4. The song of Habakkuk (Hab. 3)
5. Isa. 26
6. Jonah 2:3
7. The prayer of the three men (Dan. 3; Vulg. 52–90, apocryphal)
8. Azariah's prayer (Dan. 3; Vulg. 3, 26–49, apocryphal)

6

9. Hezekiah's prayer (Isa. 38)
10. The apocryphal hymn of Manasseh
11. The prayer of Zacharias (Luke 1:68–79)
12. The Magnificat (Luke 1:46–55)
13. The canticle of Simeon (Luke 2:29–32)
14. Gloria

Apart from the four last canticles, most are taken from the Old Testament. We should expect a wider use of them in the Synagogue than is actually the practice today. Indeed, almost all of the ten canticles were chanted or read in the older liturgies of the Synagogue. In his study (*supra*, pp. 77 ff) L. Venetianer demonstrated that the collection of homilies, the *Pesiqta*, alludes to nearly all of them as publicly rendered parts of the liturgy. Why did some of them disappear and others remain in the liturgy? What was the criterion of their selection? The answer is simple and obvious. The decisive criterion, of course, depended on the aptness of some of these canticles for a Christological interpretation. Those which could be easily interpreted in a Christian sense were rejected, the others retained.[46]

Thus, both canticles from Daniel were excluded since the Azariah prayer is apocryphal and was not accepted into the Jewish Canon. Isa. 26 likewise was eliminated, probably because the verses 17–19 were propitious to Christological interpretation and Isa. 38 has never been mentioned as a canticle in rabbinic literature. The Hebrew name for canticle is *shir* (Gr. *ode*, Lat., *canticum*, *hymnus*), and probably most of these terms that occur in earliest Christian literature designate the scriptural canticles.

On the other hand, the Church has incorporated in its hymn-book many apocryphal texts, some of which were composed before the organization of the biblical Canon. Certain passages of the books of Ecclesiasticus, Maccabees, Judith, Tobit, etc., were used in the same way as genuine canticles. Even as late a work as the fourth book of the pseudo-Ezra was accepted in parts and has provided the Church with some of its best known texts, such as the introit 'Requiem' and the introit 'Accipite iucunditatem'.[47]

Each of the two canticles regularly chanted in the Synagogue has two different musical versions. On weekdays or festivals they are chanted as psalmodies, whereas they are cantillated in a solemn mode once a year, namely on the occasion of their annual recurrence in the biblical lesson. The psalmodic version can scarcely be authentic since it was not regulated by ecphonetic accents; and, as in the case of the *Hallel*, there exists a Talmudic controversy concerning their proper (psalmodic) performance.[48] Thus, it is improbable that synagogal practice has influenced Christian liturgical usage of the canticles unless we assume that the Church has preserved the ancient traditions better than the Synagogue. This may be quite possible, but at best it is a conjecture.

In the Byzantine Church the canticles attained a special status because they were the models after which the so-called *kanones* were patterned. Each *kanon* contains eight or nine *odes* which correspond to the main canticles of the Old and New Testaments. While nothing definite is known about the origin of these *kanones* they reflect an ever recurrent principle of Near Eastern music, the idea of an archetypal repetition and paraphrase of a given textual or musical model motif.

E. Wellesz stresses this point when he writes:

> When the *odes* of the *kanones* took the place of the canticles, they were considered as earthly symbols of the heavenly hymns, in the same way as the singers symbolized the angels. Therefore . . . they had still to be variations of the old canticles. There was no question of a free individualistic handling of a theme. . . . The same is true of their music. . . .[49]

Wellesz then proposes the theory that the Byzantine hymns of the *kanones* were sung in imitation of the angelic choirs. This idea, however, originated not in Byzantium but in Israel. The rabbinic sources are full of legends and visions in which the heavenly host itself is stimulated to commence its own songs of exultation by the example of the Jewish community praising God in the *Kedusha* and Exod. 15.[50] The Greek Fathers were not unfamiliar with the Midrashic literature of Palestine, and probably transmitted their knowledge to their Church; they identified Christianity with an ideal Israel, a conception common to patristic literature since Clement of Alexandria.

If the chanting of canticles was not very conspicuous in the Synagogue, it was much more in evidence in the Temple. There, a rigid order prescribed that Deut. 32 should be divided into six parts, to be sung after the morning sacrifice, and Exod. 15 after the afternoon sacrifice. Likewise, the use of the psalms in the Temple was not left to arbitrary judgements. A certain selection was made, distributing most of the Psalter among the days of one week. A similar order exists in the Roman

Church, the so-called *cursus* which provides the order of the Divine Office (not the Mass) throughout the ecclesiastical year. This custom dates back to ancient times. We also find that the two main canticles of the Old Testament, Exod. 15 and Deut. 32 had a significant part in the liturgies of the Early Church. Their place was not in the Mass, but in Lauds, that rubric of the Christian liturgy which shows the closest resemblance to the morning service of the Synagogue.[51] In the following, we tabulate the liturgical use of Exod. 15 and Deut. 32:[52]

Temple	Greek Typikon	Mozarabic Ordo	Ambrosian	Roman	Armenian
Deut. 32 in 6 parts chanted after the morning sacrifice on Sabbath	Deut. 32:1–43 at Lauds on Sunday morning	Deut 32 on several Sundays	Deut. 32 instead of the 'Benedictus' Canticle on Sundays in Advent, Christmas and Epiphany	Deut. 32 at Lauds on one week-day, Easter and Pentecost vigil	Deut. 32 and Dan. 3 at Matins
Exod. 15 after the evening sacrifice	Exod. 15:1–19 at Lauds and in the Easter Vigil	Exod. 15 during Eastertide	Exod. 15 on several Sundays and in the Easter Vigil	Exod. 15 on Thursday, and four Sundays; also Easter and Pentecost Vigil	Exod. 15 on Holy Saturday

Paraphrases of the canticles were extremely popular. They assumed the character of hymns not only in the Byzantine Church, but in many other instances.

PLACE AND FUNCTION OF THE PSALMS IN THE VARIOUS LITURGIES
Terminology

In the literature of all liturgies we encounter a rich array of designations for psalms, psalm-verses, paraphrases, or for any kind of psalmodic poetry. For a deeper understanding of the close relationship between the ecclesiastical and the synagogal liturgy, it will be necessary to examine briefly the terms used for psalmodic forms together with their derivation.

Even a perfunctory glimpse shows us a threefold terminology: (1) alluding to literary and religious ideas, (2) referring to the various practices of performance, and (3) indicating liturgical-musical forms.

Rabbinic literature has, due to its rather simple types of performance, a richer vocabulary for categories (1) and (3). The expressions *shevach* (praise), *bakasha* (petition), *hallel* (laudation) belong to the first category. *Piyyut* (from Greek *poietes*), *pizmon* (Gr. *psalmos*), *alfabeta* (Gr. *alphabeta*) = acrostic, *kuklar* (Gr. *kyklarion*), *muvashach* (Arabic) = girdle-rhyme, are only a few which belong to the third category. The terms of (1) are derived from the ancient Hebrew vocabulary, whereas those of (3) are all borrowed, either from Greek or from the Arabs. Not very numerous are the terms indicating the manner of performance: *r'shut* (Hebrew: permission = preamble), *silluq* (Hebrew: finale), *hoshano* (Hebrew: save now, a litany), etc., again show no sign of foreign influence.

The Syrian (Monophysite) Church has many terms which are akin to the Hebrew names due to the close similarity of the two languages. Most of them, however, refer to categories (2) or (3), not to (1). Thus we find:

'Unita (Hebr. *'ana*) = Response
'Enyana (Hebr. *'ania'*) = Responsorial hymn
Riš-qolo = Model tune
Teshbuhta (Hebr. *shevah*) = Hymnic praise, often Canticle
Zumara (Hebr. *mizmor*) = Psalm
Shuraya (Hebr. *shir*) = Hymn
Sogitha (Aram. *Sugya*) = Dialogue Hymn
Madrasha (Hebr. *drasha*) = Homily Hymn (didactic)

Almost all of these terms allude either to the procedure of performance or to the literary type, as do didactic hymn, dialogue hymn, psalm, etc. Since the hymn was the greatest contribution of the Syrian Churches to the literature and music of Christianity, the preponderance of hymnic terms is not at all surprising. (See also Chapter VII.)

The terminology of the Byzantine Church, too, stresses the literary form and the practice of performance. Expressions like *kanon*, *hymnos*, *epihymnos*, *kontakion*, *kyklarion* (cycle of stanzas) *hirmos* (lit. tract, train), *antiphona*, etc., say very little about the poetic substance. As in the Syrian literature, the hymnic forms prevail here over genuine psalmodies. The turbulent history of the Armenian Church is reflected in some of the terms it used: Hebrew, Greek, and Syrian influences have left their traces in the liturgy (only a few are cited here):

Kahana (Hebr.) = priest
Sharakan (from Hebr.) = hymn-book
Shaddai (Hebr.) = God of might
Karos (from Hebr. and Greek) = reader, minister

Kav(f)aran (from Hebr. *Kippurim*) = expiation, atonement
Shbash (from Hebr. *Shamesh*) = acolyte
Mesedi (from Greek *mesodion*) = the psalm before the Epistle
Turgami (from Syriac *Turgama*) = interpreter
Bēm (from Greek *bēma*) = pulpit

These few quotations indicate that the Armenian designations cover all three categories of terminology; best represented is (1), which might suggest a more religious and ideological interest of the Armenian writers and liturgists.[53]

The Roman Church's emphasis on the spiritual contents of the psalms finds its expression in an abundance of terms like Jubilus, Lauds, Invitatorium, Penitential Psalm, Supplicatio, Alleluia, Miserere, etc. Many of the liturgical terms are derived from the practice of performance, such as: Responsorium, Antiphon, Gradual-Response, Psalmus directaneus, Responsorium prolixum, etc. Due to the systematic organization of the Roman liturgy, the third category is the strongest represented here; it comprises Introit, Gradual, Tract, Trope, Prose, etc., and all designations of psalms or psalm paraphrases which belong to the realm of hymnody.[54] In general, it might seem that the Jewish, Armenian and Roman terms express the contents of the liturgical function of psalmody rather than the manner of its performance.

In the Earliest Liturgies

In all primitive liturgies up to the fourth century the Psalter played an outstanding part. A distinction was made early between the eucharistic type of liturgy, Mass, and the regular offices, such as Vespers and Lauds.[55] The *Constitutiones Apostolorum*, reflecting an old tradition, rule that Psalms 63 and 140:1 shall be chanted at morning and vesper services respectively.[56] An even earlier document, Justin's address against Trypho, mentions Ps. 46 and 71 as hymns in praise of Christ, but fails to indicate the specific liturgical occasion of these psalms.[57]

For the *Agape* and the earliest Eucharistic liturgies Ps. 133 was very popular, according to Tertullian;[58] also Ps. 34, because of verse 9 with its Christological overtones, was widely used.[59] Before the Mass on Sunday, during Matins, Ps. 92, the Sabbath Psalm, was chanted indicating the Christian transposition to the Sunday.[60] Most of these psalms also form an integral part of the Synagogue ritual. This is best shown in a brief table:[61]

WEEKDAYS		SABBATH	SUNDAY
Synagogue	Church (before the great schism)	Synagogue	Church
		Morning service:	Eucharistic service:
Morning and evening	Lauds, Compline, etc.	Ps. 34; 90; 19; 91;	Ps. 34; 92; 93; 95;
Ps. 100; 145–50; 6	Ps. 100; 141:1; 63; 46; 71; 93	92; 93; 95; 135; 136; 33; 100	133; 136:1; 100; 63; 148–50
Evening: 91; 134; 3; 4:5	Compline: 91; 134; 4		

Not all of these psalms are documented before the seventh or eighth century in either Jewish or Christian sources. Even a perfunctory glance at this tabulation shows that the similarity in Sabbath-Sunday services is much closer than on weekday mornings, where only Ps. 100 is the common element. Compline and Jewish evening services, however, are all but identical in their psalm selection.

The reasons for the divergence on weekdays are not difficult to understand: the common element in the liturgy is, as Bickell has most clearly demonstrated, the Sabbath-Sunday identity.[62] The weekday liturgy of the Church was fixed much later and Judaistic elements hardly influenced it. An exception to this general rule is the *Completorium* (Compline) which, along with Vespers, follows the Jewish practice of psalm-singing before retiring. This was an early Christian custom which Clement of Alexandria had already praised.[63]

Whatever ancient description of psalmody we read, be it from the Gentile Christian, the Jewish, or even the pagan side, we cannot escape the thought that the invasion of psalmody into the ancient world must have been felt as an elemental, and often revolutionary force, that eventually broke all the conventions with which Hellas had surrounded her own musical tradition.

From the historic point of view, psalmody was the greatest legacy of the Synagogue to Jewish Christianity, and thence to the Gentile Church. This will explain the existence of certain, now forgotten, magic practices of psalmody in the Church; perhaps a remainder of some old Jewish conception. At any rate, it is a safe assumption that the continuity of musical tradition which the Synagogue itself could not uphold, was preserved by Judaeo-Christian cantors, as was demonstrated above. (pp. 53 ff).[64]

In spite of these identities and analogies, it would be rash to conclude that they simply indicate an indiscriminate or mechanical imitation of the Jewish practice of worship. Although some scholars have chosen this easy road, there are definite signs that the process of taking over synagogal customs was beset with many obstacles and resentments. Moreover, two facts should be mentioned, which, if seen in proper perspective, demonstrate the incipient divergencies of the Jewish and Christian points of view.

It has not often been noticed that immediately after the Apostolic period the element of psalmody is less mentioned than that of the spontaneous hymn. The entire Eastern Church in particular was partial to hymns from the time of Marcion onwards. He and his followers did not sing psalms, as we know from contemporary documents, and many of the Gnostics followed his example.[65] Bardesanes, Harmonius, Paul of Samosata, Isidore of Pelusium, all tried their hands at hymnic poetry and their disciples neglected the psalms. Even so orthodox a saint as Ephraem had to follow their example and decided to fight hymn with hymn, so that his creations might serve as effective counter propaganda for the orthodox Church.[66] This kind of Gnostic hymnody spread so dangerously that the Church had to take radical measures. The Council of Laodicea (360–81) strictly prohibited the singing of non-scriptural texts in Christian worship.[67] While this rule was not always followed and compromises were tolerated, at least the path was cleared for the psalms, and they were praised and commended over all other forms and texts.

The growing divergencies of Jewish and Christian liturgical forms show themselves also in the development of *choral* psalm-singing in the Church. This practice, under the powerful stimulus of monastic rule, finally resulted in the creation of a new form, the antiphon. To avoid a fairly common misunderstanding, it should be kept in mind that this term had a two-fold, or even three-fold meaning before the ninth century. As *antiphony* it designates the alternative singing of two choruses; this is an ancient Jewish practice, as we know from the Old Testament (II Chron. 20:19–21; Ps. 136; Neh. 12:31–42; etc.). During the third and fourth centuries this way of singing became very popular in the Church.[68] In Greek music theory it means 'to sing in octaves' indicating a mixed choir; yet the antiphon is an independent musical form which grew out of antiphonal singing.

The Synagogue did not expand its psalm-singing as the Church did, but it did not reduce it either. The monopolistic practices of the cantors had an effect exactly opposite to the stimulating choral singing of the monks. In many instances, especially during the late Middle Ages, it deteriorated to plain reading by the congregation, since the *hazan* would not or could not chant anything but brilliant coloratura pieces.

And yet there is sufficient historic evidence to show that, before the deterioration under the influence of the *hazan*, antiphonal psalmody was used in the Synagogue. It was especially the young people in the religious schools who cultivated this practice. The *Midrash Tehillim*, an early medieval commentary on the psalms, assigns antiphonal singing to the young.[69] Similar allusions occur in Talmudic and rabbinic literature.[70]

Most important here is Eusebius' famous excerpt from Philo's *De Vita Contemplativa*, the description of the Jewish sect of the Therapeutae in Egypt during the first century B.C.:

> They arise from both sides . . . forming two choirs, one of men, the other of women . . . then they sing hymns to God, in various metres and tunes, sometimes all together, sometimes alternately (*antiphonois harmoniais*) . . . later . . . they combine the two choirs to one chorus . . . like the Jewish people did when they went through the Red Sea. Of this kind of singing the choir of faithful men and women is reminiscent; and it is here, where in intoning and alternate repeating the lower sound of the male voices and the higher sound of the female in their combination create a lovely and truly musical *symphonia*.[71]

Wagner concludes that this testimony, coming from Eusebius, declaring the practice of his own times in accordance with the quoted description of Philo, proves the existence of antiphonal singing according to the Jewish manner, i.e. in octaves, as a custom of the early Church.[72]

Again and anew a question arises which can no longer be circumvented: why, and under what circumstances, was the concept of psalmody taken over from the Synagogue and introduced into the Church? The scholars differ considerably in their approach to this problem. Many such as P. Wagner, F. Probst, P. Dechevrens, A. Gastoué, G. Bickell, von der Goltz, *et al.*, assume a strict continuity leading from the Synagogue to the Church through the activities of proselyte Jewish cantors.[73] Others, including Ursprung, Achelis, Harnack, Quasten, *et al.*, tend to minimize that continuity, and stress the 'new spirit' in the old prayers.[74] L. Venetianer has come forth with a very original theory. Demonstrating that the Introits of the Roman Church use many psalm verses in reverse order, he linked this phenomenon with certain superstitious practices common to Jews and Christians in the first five or six centuries of Christianity.[75] Thence he concludes that much of the psalm-singing in the early Church was based upon Jewish sectarian conceptions which stressed the therapeutic power of the Psalter. This idea, at first glance apparently absurd, gains probability when we supplement it with patristic remarks about psalm-singing. In the following quotation from Diodore of Tarsus, who certainly was not fond of Judaism, the typical attitude of the Church Fathers is eloquently represented:

> . . . they [the psalms] calm carnal passions, . . . the evil inclinations, chase demons away, . . . they strengthen the pious fighters for the sufferance of terrible ordeals, . . . they heal the wounds that life has struck. . . .[76]

These remarks could easily be multiplied; nor is it surprising to encounter exactly the same attitude in rabbinic literature.[77] The magic papyri from Babylonia of the fourth to seventh centuries contained psalm verses, Hallelujahs and similar acclamations, and L. Blau's study of Jewish and syncretistic documents of magic character has confirmed the wide propagation of these practices and beliefs.[78]

Venetianer's significant analysis of the reverse order of the psalm verses in the Roman ritual does in no way explain the great popularity of the psalms in the Apostolic Age and after the Council of Nicaea. During the intervening centuries the forms we hear most about were hymns and canticles, not psalms. This was the period of the conflict between Judaeo-Christianity and the Jews.[79] After Nicaea the Jewish Christian Church declined rapidly, being crushed between the Synagogue and the Gentile Church.

The seemingly critical remarks of some of the Church Fathers were not made to antagonize the faithful against the psalms; quite the contrary in fact. (The psalms were held in great esteem, being sacred, and as *prophetia*, proper to be sung by all Christians.) The Jews were wrong in their music (instrumental accompaniment, Temple cult, etc.), as well as those who relapsed into 'the way of Jewish praying'.[80] These attacks against Judaism, however, should not be taken too literally; what these writers actually meant was not a Jew, but a Judaizer. This fact is well known among students of ecclesiastical history.[81]

In the Byzantine and Syrian Liturgies

It will be useful, when investigating those liturgies which originated between the fourth and ninth centuries, to distinguish between two different structures; that of the Office (canonical hours) and of the Mass, which in itself is divided into the Mass of the Catechumens and the Mass proper of the Faithful. From the historical point of view, the Offices represent an older phase of development and this fact will be borne out by the subsequent comparisons with the psalmodic elements in the liturgy of the Synagogue.

Psalmody in the Offices. At the very outset, the psalmodic terminology of the East Syrian (Nestorian) Church invites a comparison with Hebrew expressions. The *Quali d'Shahra* (voices of the morning) of that Church correspond, in many instances, to the arrangement of psalms in the Jewish *Shaharith*.[82] The division of the Psalter into twenty *Hullali* (cp. the Hebrew *Hallel*), each of which consists of two or more *Marm-'yathe* (elevations, standing; cp. the Talmudic *ramatha*) also suggests Synagogal influence.

This peculiar division of the 150 psalms plays a considerable part in the Eastern liturgies. The Byzantine order, as well as the Jacobite and Nestorian, knows this division and couples it with the distinction between psalms recited while standing (Syr., *marmitha*, Greek, *stasis*), and those recited in a sitting position (Syr., *motva*, Greek, *kathisma*).

No scholar, not even the profound and exact H. Schneider has troubled himself with tracing and investigating the historical and liturgical pre-conditions of this rather unusual division. Maclean has given us an exact account of the practice with a full tabulation of the division into the twenty *Hullali* plus their subdivision into *Motve* and *Marm-'yathe*.[83] Beyond this description of the actual practice we have nothing, except an interesting note in Pitra's *Juris Ecclesiastici Graecorum Historia*.[84] This note is a quotation from a chronicle of St John Moschus and St Sophronius, the latter Patriarch of Jerusalem (d. 638), and contains the Greek terms *stasis* (stand), in contrast to *kathisma* (seat). There, however, the Psalter is divided into *three* groups of fifty psalms each.[85]

The oldest sources seem to be: Cod. Psalter Vatic. Grec. 342 and Oxford, Auct. D. 4.1. In both of these codes the term *kathisma* is used in connexion with a group of twenty psalms; moreover, both sources state emphatically that this division was the usual practice of Jerusalem.[86]

Obviously, both the Byzantine and the Syrian Churches had borrowed this division about the end of the seventh century. For St Theodore of Studios (d. 826) knew both terms and divisions, and the same may be said of Nestorian patriarchs of the ninth century.

The *Hudra* (cycle) designates the book containing the proper section of the liturgy and of the Offices for Sundays, Feasts of Christ, and the principal Saint's Day and is, liturgically at least, identical with the Hebrew *Mahzor* (cycle), the prayer-book of the Festivals, High Holydays, and special Sabbaths.[87]

Whole psalms as well as individual psalm verses, or even centonized psalms, interwoven with Christological passages occur in the Offices of the three Churches under consideration (Byzantine, Jacobite, and Nestorian). Of these, the role of psalmody in the Nestorian liturgy comes closest to the Jewish ritual; especially the Sunday Offices, whose selection of psalms practically parallels that of the Sabbath morning liturgy of the Synagogue. Two interesting deviations from that general observation should be pointed out: Ps. 100, 117 and 118. In the old Ashkenazic ritual, Ps. 100 is omitted on the Sabbath, because it was considered tantamount to a thanksgiving offering for which the Temple had no provision on the Sabbath.[88] The oldest Jewish prayer book of the ninth century, however, does contain Ps. 100 for the Sabbath. Here the Nestorian Church has preserved the older Jewish tradition. Ps. 117 and 118, on the other hand, constitute an integral part of the *Hallel*, and as such were restricted to New Moons and Festivals. When we remember that the old Christian Sunday contained certain elements of the Passover ritual, we should understand the place of these two *Hallel* songs in the Nestorian liturgy, which, by the way, had its parallel in the Byzantine liturgy of Chrysostom.[89] The close parallelisms are best demonstrated in the following tabulation:[90]

THE PSALMS IN THE OFFICES

Sabbath morning in the Synagogue	Sunday Offices of the Nestorian Church	Sunday Offices of the Byzantine Church
Ps. 91; 100; 104 (several verses); 113:2–4; 93; 145; 146; 147; 148; 149; 150: 29; 92; 34; 90; 135; 136. Psalm verses (only those identical with the other rubrics are quoted): 79:8–9; 98:5; 84:5; 84:13; 85:5; 86:5; 33:1; 22:29; 34:4; 33:9–10.	Ps. 100; 91; 104; 113; 93; 147; 148; 149; 150; 117. Psalm verses: 79:8–9; 98:5; 84:5; 85:5; 86:5; 33:1–8; 22:29; 34:4; 33:9–10.	Ps. 90; 91; 100; 101; 17; 25; 51; 54; 55; 84; 85; 86. Psalm verses: 79:8–9; 33: 1–5; 22:29; 34:4; 33:9–10.

The psalmody of the Mass. Although the Byzantine Church, and probably the other Eastern Churches as well, officially frowned upon extended psalmody even as late as the eleventh century, the rituals as they have come down to us show little trace of such a limitation of psalmody.[91] It is true that the chanting of whole psalms does not occur very frequently in the Eastern Mass, but in its place we find all sorts of psalm paraphrases, centonizations, and especially insertions of psalm verses, torn out of their context, that give a Christological background to the Eucharistic service. There is an abundance of instances, and here we quote only three typical 'Christianizations' of psalms:

Rejoice and sing and give thanks. (Ps. 98:5) (insert) Thy Passover, O our Saviour, hath gladdened Creation. And brought to naught the altars of the heathen and set firm the Churches.

God is gone up in Glory, the Lord with the sound of the Trumpet. (Ps. 47:6) (insert) Blessed is the King who hath gone up, and by His ascension hath made glad. . . .[92]

This is a typical *Motva*-farcing of psalms as the Nestorian Church practises it.

When Israel went out of Egypt, the House of Jacob out of the barbarian people . . . (Ps. 114:1) (insert) through the dignity of Mother of God, save us, O Saviour.

Judah became His sanctuary, and Israel His dominion (Ps. 114:2) (insert) through the dignity of Mother of God, save us, O Saviour.

The sea beheld it, and fled; the Jordan was driven backward. (Ps. 114:3) (insert) through the dignity . . . etc.[93]

Here the opening of the Passover *Hallel* has received a positive Christian connotation. Even stronger is the Christological note emphasized in the following:

Rejoice in the Lord, O ye righteous (Ps. 33:1) (insert) with the smoke of spices be there a remembrance to the Virgin Mary, Mother of God.

Praise Him all ye peoples. (Ps. 117:1) (insert) with the smoke of spices be there a remembrance to the Holy Prophets, apostles and martyrs . . . etc.[94]

The last psalm verse also belongs to the *Hallel*, which, in one form or another, has been included in the Mass psalmodies of all Churches as a memorial of Christ's Passover. The connexion of the *Hallel* with the Passover Eve, the *Seder*, which is identified with the Last Supper, has played a significant part in the inclusion of verses from Ps. 113–118 in the psalmody of the Mass.

It is interesting to note that the Jewish ritual has carefully avoided (or eliminated?) those psalm verses that regularly accompany the Communion or its preparatory rubrics in the Christian liturgy. Particularly

Ps. 34:9, 'Taste (or, more literally translated, 'experience') and see how good is the Lord', which occurs in most liturgies during the partaking of the Communion is nowhere to be found as an isolated verse in the Jewish ritual but only as a regular passage of Ps. 34, which is, as a whole, recited on Sabbath morning.

In general, the psalms of the Mass reflect three different ideas and historical strata: Christianized references to the 'New Passa' and the Resurrection, certain transpositions from the Jewish Sabbath and Festival ritual, and a group of the so-called 'penitential' psalms, which occurs in the very same arrangement also in the Jewish ritual. The penitential grouping of these psalms must date back to an early rabbinic tradition. I have not been able, however, to trace this arrangement beyond the third century A.D., although it probably is considerably older.[95]

For these various conceptions and strata, the psalmody of the Mass differs not only from the Jewish Sabbath psalmody, but is considerably varied even within the Christian Churches. A short tabulation will clarify this statement:[96]

PSALMODY OF MASS

Synagogue Sabbath Morning and Friday Evening	Mass		
	Nestorian	Jacobite	Byzantine
Ps. 91; 100; 104; 113:2–4; 93; 145; 146–50; 29; 92; 34; 90; 135; 136	Ps. 82–101; 96–98	Ps. 93; 51; 23; 26; 29	Ps. 5; 26; 119–23; 124–8; 129–33
Psalm verses: 5:8; 55:15; 26:6–8; 96:1–9; 33:8–10; Ps. 145:1; 68:10; 35–36	Psalm verses: 145 : 1–7a; 144:15; 26:6–8; 68:33–36; 84:1–2; 33:8; 79:13; (106:48; 41:14; Doxologies)	Psalm verses: 145 : 1, 15, 16; 84:1–2; 116:12–14; 117:13, 14; 118:1; 118:26; 51:1, 17 Several verses from Ps. 135; 81; 36	Psalm verses: 92:1–5; 26:6–12; 114: 1–3, 5; 115:1–3, 5; 118:1–4, 26, 27; 51:1, 17 Several verses from Ps. 135 and 136

In the Armenian Church

This ritual deviates in some respects from that of the other Eastern Churches. Some of its features must be very old, for they seem to stem from pre-Christian Ages. With reference to psalmody, the Armenian Church has set aside certain psalm verses for Alleluias and Graduals accompanying the lessons. These pieces, mostly psalm verses or paraphrases, are the so-called *Jashou* psalms. Only a few Christological allusions occur therein, and they are generally considered the oldest psalmodic stratum of the Armenian liturgy.[97] Two instances, for Palm Sunday and Easter Sunday respectively, of these Christianized psalm verses are quoted here:

> The Lord God hath showed Himself unto us; make a joyful feast even unto the horns of the altar (Ps. 118:27).
> The Lord hath put on glorious apparel and hath girded Himself with strength (Ps. 93:1).
> Because He hath destroyed the sting of death by His holy cross. . . .[98]

Such cases, however, are not too frequent among *Jashou* psalms.

The Armenian Offices, in their selection of psalms and psalm verses, are reminiscent of the three Jewish services on the Sabbath: morning, afternoon, and evening. The following tabulation, while limited to those psalms or verses that are most typical of the Jewish or Armenian services, will demonstrate this:[99]

PSALMODY OF ARMENIAN OFFICES

Synagogue	Armenian Church
Sabbath morning, afternoon and evening	Matins: Ps. 119:12; 36:9; 148–50; 130:
Ps. 145–50; 90; 130 (only weekdays); 33;	1–8; 113
34; 91; 121–4 (in Sephardic or Levantine	Prime and Terce: Ps. 63; 64; 23; 143:8–
ritual); 51 (only on fastdays); 113–18	12; 51; 23
(only on Festivals or New Moons)	Sext and None: Ps. 51; 130; 91; 116; 117;
Afternoons and evenings: Ps. 119; 121;	118
123–34; 91; 144	Vespers and Compline: Ps. 86; 121; 91;
	123; 100; 34:1–7; 43; 29; 140–2

The Matins seem to correspond to the morning service of the Synagogue; Vespers and Compline roughly to Sabbath afternoon and evening. The usual element of the Christianized *Hallel* occurs in the Armenian ritual as well as in all other Christian sources, while the strong representation of penitential psalms is quite interesting. They almost identically parallel those psalm selections that form the so-called *Tahanun* (supplicatory part of the Jewish service).

In contrast to the other Eastern Churches, the Mass ritual of the Armenian Church has retained distinct phrases of its Judaeo-Christian antecedents. The most interesting part of the psalmody of the Mass is the so-called 'Great Entrance' which is accompanied by an abundance of psalm verses. When we bear in mind that the Armenian Church celebrates Mass on *Sundays only* (during Lent also on Saturdays) certain analogies with the Sabbath ritual become fairly obvious.[100] In the following, the scriptural verses of the 'Great Entrance' are cited: Isa. 6:3;

Ps. 19:5–6; Ps. 68:34; Isa. 62:10; Hab. 3:3; Ps. 24:7–10; Ps. 118:26; Ps. 26:6.[101]

The priest censes only the east and south walls of the church and re-cites: 'Cast up an highway for Him that rideth upon the Heaven of Heavens toward the East' (Ps. 68:34 and Isa. 62:10; facing the east) and: 'God shall come from the South and the Holy One from Mt Paran' (Hab. 3:3; facing south).

I am convinced that these two extraordinary quotations, nowhere duplicated in any other liturgy, emphasize the geographical location of Armenia with respect to Palestine; obviously the compilers of the early liturgy felt that God came from Jerusalem. This seems directly to con-firm the facts mentioned in Chapters II and III about the Judaistic charac-ter and origin of the Armenian Church.

Of the other Sabbatical psalm verses the Armenian Mass used Ps. 93:1–6; 29; 19:5–6; 24:7–10; 34; 148; 113:1–2.

While the question of rendering will be discussed extensively in the second part of this book, it might be anticipated here that Armenian psalmody still shows many traces of the original soloistic performance as customarily used in the Synagogue.

In the Roman Church

Not so much exposed to Gnostic or Christologic disputes as the Eastern Churches, the Latin liturgy, including the remnants of the provincial Gallican and Mozarabic rubrics, has preserved a straight and stable course characteristic in its consistent adherence to old-established principles. One of these principles is the undisputed predominance of the scriptural word. This in itself explains a good deal of the 'conservatism' of the Roman liturgy; for the authoritative preponderance of biblical elements entails naturally the demotion of other texts to secondary rank.

The Psalter has, both quantitatively and substantially, a most impor-tant share in the Roman liturgy. A glance at Mahrbach's computation of all biblical passages used in the Roman order of worship shows that no scriptural book contributes more to it than the Psalter.[102] Since this book limits itself to texts chanted in public worship, we can disregard here the regular and complete reading of all 150 psalms in the Breviary and in monastic liturgy, where all the canonical hours are observed, comprising the weekly reading of the complete Psalter.

The Synagogue has followed a similar course: as in ecclesiastical history, so in the evolution of Judaism, the Eastern area was beset by sectarianism (Samaritans, Karaites, Hasidim, etc.) and it took the concerted efforts of many sages to preserve the essential unity within the liturgy. As in the Churches, hymns and other free poetic forms threatened for a time (between A.D. 900 and 1600) to supersede scriptural texts and even the psalms. But this development stimulated by a super-emphasis upon rabbinic erudition and an inclination towards mysticism could not indefinitely hold the majority of the Jewish people under its spell. Thus, when the high tide of Midrashic-Cabbalistic hymns receded, the psalms regained their ancient position as Israel's foremost prayers.

With all these somewhat analogous developments, it would be a mistake to equate the role of chanted psalms in Church and Synagogue. Spiritually and liturgically, their function was and is different in many respects. In the early and medieval Church the spiritual significance of the psalms rested upon their authority as *prophetia*, their Christological reinterpretation as predictions of Christ. Moreover, when the spontaneous outpourings of glossolaly and prophetic-mystic hymns threatened to upset the unity of Christianity as well as the order of its worship, the psalms, with their ancient, well-established textual and musical tradition, served as regulators and teachers in the turbulent spiritual upheavals that preceded the fourth and fifth centuries. The last and most precious remnant of that period of spontaneity is probably the *Jubilus*, the musical, wordless-ecstatic hymn, the element of glossolaly converted to organized, melismatic psalmody.

The liturgical function of psalmody, apart from the Gradual, the Alleluia and the Gradual-response (the common forms of Synagogal and ecclesiastical song),[103] rested originally in the conception that the congregation should actively participate in the sacred proceedings. All Church Fathers praise the power of psalmody to stir the mass of the faithful to a unity of praise, 'una voce dicentes' as Augustine puts it. When the Latin language became extinct as a living vernacular, this function expired with it, except for the few acclamations which to this day are familiar to every Christian such as, Amen; et cum spiritu tuo; pax vobiscum, etc. These minute responses whose importance increased after the sixth and seventh centuries, will be discussed in a later chapter. Today, psalmody in the Church has the task of permeating the ecclesiastical year with scriptural words, of referring to the individual

Sundays and holydays, of implementing the respective lesson, and of beautifying lengthy and solemn ceremonies. This is in contradistinction to hymnic forms whose function is different.

In Judaism, the regular rendering of psalms served two functions: as a memorial of the Temple, demanded by the rabbis, and as a fulfilment of the Divine Commandment, 'Thou shalt love the Lord Thy God . . .' by daily praise and laudation. For let us not forget that the Hebrew term for the Psalter is *Sefer Tehillim*, 'The Book of Praises'. The latter function was, ever since Paul's demand,[104] most familiar to the Church; but its implementation was hindered by the retention of a sacral language, alien to the faithful. The following tabulation outlines the function of those psalms which are common to Jewish and Roman Catholic liturgy.

THE USE OF INDIVIDUAL PSALMS IN SYNAGOGUE AND CHURCH

Synagogue	Church
Ps. 6: First penitential psalm. Daily, except on Sabbaths, festivals and semi-festivals.	Idem. Offertory, Monday of Passion Week; at funerals.
Ps. 8: On the 'little Day of Atonement' (voluntary fast-day). Considered a psalm for the innocents.[105]	Office of the Angels; Office of Confessors, Martyrs, and Innocents.
Ps. 19: Sabbath morning (in the oldest Jewish prayer book)	Office of Christmas and Ascension; Sunday in Advent.
Ps. 23: Memorial service for the dead (late Middle Ages, possibly under Christian influence). According to Rashbam, to be said before eating bread.	Office of the dead. Before distributing the bread in the Communion of the Jacobite Church.[106]
Ps. 24: Sabbath morning before the lesson.	Holy Saturday, Ascension, funerals of children, Nativity.
Ps. 25: Second penitential psalm. On fast-days, especially Day of Atonement and in the Ten Days of Penitence between New Year and Atonement.	Good Friday, Holy Saturday, Office of dead.
Ps. 27: On the Ten Days of Penitence, in Oriental Jewry at funerals.	Good Friday, Holy Saturday, Office of dead.
Ps. 29: Friday eve, and Sabbath morning. New Year. Formerly at Pentecost and Tabernacles.[107]	Baptism, Epiphany, Pentecost.
Ps. 30: On *Hanukka* (because of its superscription).	Dedication of a church, Holy Saturday, Ascension, and Passion Week.
Ps. 33: Sabbath.morning, Day of Atonement.	Introit of All Saints Mass, also on the 17th Sunday after Pentecost.
Ps. 34: Sabbath morning, festivals.	Gradual of the Sacred Heart of Jesus; in the early Churches the psalm was sung regularly during Communion because of its v. 8.

INDIVIDUAL PSALMS IN SYNAGOGUE AND CHURCH

Synagogue	*Church*
Ps. 42–43: In Sephardic and Oriental Jewry on Tabernacles. The psalms are always read together just as in the Roman tradition where they constitute one psalm. Also on memorial services.	Offices of the dead. Holy Saturday, Passion Sunday.
Ps. 47: New Year after the sounding of shofar (cf. v. 5).	Epiphany, Ascension, Trinity Sunday.
Ps. 49: Mourner's service (salvation of the souls of the deceased).	Office of the dead (rescue from Hell).
Ps. 50: In the Temple after sacrifices. (A remark against its use in Judaeo-Christian Eucharist services in early rabbinic literature).[108]	Gradual of second Sunday of Advent. The psalm was used in the Early Church in the hope of speedy reappearance of Christ.
Ps. 51: Penitential psalm. On Day of Atonement and days of penitence.[109]	Lauds of Maundy Thursday, Good Friday, Holy Saturday, funeral services, Offices for dead and many Friday versicles and responses.
Ps. 65: On Day of Atonement and days of penitence.[109]	Introit to Mass for the dead (Requiem).
Ps. 67: Period between Passover and *Shabuot* (in mystic circles). Day of Atonement and days of penitence; end of Sabbath.	Offices of the dead. Introit of the Feast of the Cross, Holy Saturday.
Ps. 68: *Shabuot* (Pentecost).[110]	Gradual and Alleluia of Ascension, Communion of Ascension, Introit of Pentecost, Offertory of Pentecost (v. 29).
Ps. 76: Tabernacles, morning service.	Maundy Thursday, Holy Saturday.
Ps. 78: In the ancient liturgy on *Shabuot*.[111]	Introit of Pentecost-Monday; also offertory on Tuesday after Pentecost.
Ps. 79: Verse 10 in the prayer for martyrs and in memorial services.	V. 10 in tract of the Feast of Innocent Martyrs.
Ps. 80: Second day of New Year.	On the *Sabbatum Quatuor Temp.* (autumn Ember Days).
Ps. 81: New Year and Tabernacles.	Wednesday of autumn Ember Days.
Ps. 90: Sabbath, High Holydays, funerals.	Friday of autumn Ember Days and many Sundays, especially Sunday after Pentecost.
Ps. 91: Sabbath morning, and evening.	Compline of every Sunday; Lauds of Saturday; Holy Saturday.
Ps. 92: Friday eve, Sabbath morning; also in memory of sainted scholars and Rabbis (cf. v. 12).[112]	Holy Saturday; Septuagesima, especially v. 12 for masses of Popes, doctors, confessors, etc.
Ps. 94: On the 'Great Sabbath' (before Passover).	Good Friday.
Ps. 95: A preamble of services on Friday evening and Sabbath morning.	Invitatorium of many festivals and holydays, Matins of Christmas, Matins of Easter Sunday; Office of dead.
Ps. 96: Friday evening, New Moon.	Nocturn of Christmas.
Ps. 100: Every weekday and in older liturgies on Sabbath and festival mornings.	Every Sunday and festival morning service.
Ps. 103: Penitential psalm. Day of Atonement, days of penitence, every Monday and Thursday.	Compline of all Saturdays, Mass of Archangel Michael (Sept. 29th), Mass of the Angels, Ash Wednesday (Tract) and other fast-days.
Ps. 104: Fast-days; New Moon.	Vigil of Pentecost.[113]

157

Synagogue	Church
Ps. 107: Passover.[114]	Holy Saturday (after the Epistle); Tuesday after Easter; in litanies, and on the second Sunday of Quadragesima (Tract).
Ps. 111: End of Tabernacles; afternoon of Sabbath.	Vespers of Sunday.
Ps. 113: On all holydays and semi-holydays	Vespers of all Sundays.
Ps. 114: ,,	Vespers of all Sundays; Vespers of Epiphany, Easter and Pentecost.
Ps. 115: ,,	Office of dead.
Ps. 116: ,,	V. 12 and 13 at every Communion.
Ps. 117: ,,	Holy Saturday.
Ps. 118: ,,	On all Sundays (Prime), Maundy Thursday, Easter Sunday (Gradual of Mass), Easter Monday (Gradual of Mass), Easter Tuesday (Gradual of Mass), Easter Wednesday until Friday, Vesper of Easter Sunday, v. 25 and 26, form an integral part of every Mass. First Sunday after Easter (Low Sunday) at Matins and Prime.[115]

(Ps. 113–118 bracketed: **HALLEL**)

Synagogue	Church
Ps. 119: Afternoon service of Sabbath (partially).[116]	Friday of Advent, Ember Days; Friday after Ash Wednesday, every Sunday at Prime, Terce, Sext and None (parts), funerals of children.
Ps. 120: First psalm of pilgrimage (all psalms of pilgrimage in old ritual of late Sabbath afternoon) preceded by Ps. 104, the preamble, or 'Psalmos Prooemiacus' of the Byzantine Church. See note 113.	Maundy Thursday; Office of dead.
Ps. 121: Sephardic Sabbath morning; also on fast-days.	Office of dead.
Ps. 126: Grace after meals. Sabbath afternoon.	II Vespers of the Apostles, II Vespers of the Martyrs.
Ps. 130: Penitential psalm. Day of Atonement and days of penitence, on all ancient fast-days, also at funerals.[117]	At funerals, Office for dead (Vespers), 22nd, 23rd and 24th Sunday after Pentecost, as Introit or Gradual of the Mass.
Ps. 136: Every morning, especially Passover morning.	Opening verses on everyday Offices; second Sunday of Quadragesima (Tract).
Ps. 144: Sabbath late afternoon.	Every Saturday Vespers.
Ps. 145: Every day three times.	Every Saturday Vespers, Corpus Christi.[118]
Ps. 146: Every morning	Office of dead (Vespers).
Ps. 147: Every morning.	Maundy Thursday.[119]
Ps. 148: Every morning, verses from it after every lesson.	Good Friday, every morning (Lauds).
Ps. 149: Every morning.	Every morning (Lauds), all festivals and Sundays.
Ps. 150: Every morning, especially Passover and the New Year.	Every morning (Lauds), Holy Saturday, Office of dead (Lauds).

This systematic comparison of the liturgical use of the Psalter warrants a detailed analysis which, however, cannot be given here. Only a few conclusions which do not pretend to be definitive may be culled in the following:

Liturgical Identities. The most conspicuous identities belong to the services of Sabbath and Sunday. Practically all Synagogal Sabbath psalms have been distributed to either Saturday or Sunday (Ps. 91–93; 95; 100; 111; 119; 144; etc.) with two exceptions: Ps. 118, chanted every Sunday in Church, is in Jewish tradition reserved for festivals, holydays, and semi-holydays; and Ps. 145, an integral part of the daily morning services of the Synagogue has been transferred to Saturday Vespers. On the other hand, Ps. 150 is recited daily in the morning services of Church and Synagogue.

Remarkable are the identical functions of Ps. 91–93, which are part and parcel of the morning service of Saturday in Jewish as well as Christian ritual. Ps. 91, the Compline of Sunday and the Lauds of Saturday, are chanted in the Jewish service every Sabbath morning and evening. Ps. 111 serves at the Sunday Vespers as well as on the afternoon of the Sabbath. Ps. 144 belongs to Sabbath afternoon in Church and Synagogue alike.

No less interesting is the selection of psalms for fast-days, memorial or funeral services. Ps. 25; 27; 51; 65; 67; 103; 121; 130 are connected in Synagogue and Church with fasting, mourning, or penitence. Our tabulation shows an ancient, almost perfect, correspondence. Other psalms used for funerals, memorial Masses, Offices for the dead, etc., show equal distribution in the two rituals (Ps. 6; 8; 23; 24; 42; 43; 49; 79:10; 119). Ps. 8 is a prayer for innocents in Judaism as well as in Christianity; Ps. 23 is used in memorial services of the Synagogue, together with parts of Ps. 42 and 43. Ps. 49 is a rubric of the Jewish mourner's service, and Ps. 79:10 is the typical prayer for martyrs in the Synagogue as well as in the Church. More identities will be discovered after an extensive study of the tabulation.

Transpositions of the Liturgical Calendar

(1) Eastertide and Passover. Ps. 118 takes here the first place; it is both the Easter and the Passover psalm *par excellence* and was always so understood. It is sung during the entire week following Easter Sunday, being the last remnant of the seven-day long Jewish celebration of Passover.[120] Of the other *Hallel* psalms, Ps. 114 is sung on Easter Sunday and Ps. 117

on Holy Saturday. Of the typical Passover psalms, 107 and 94, the former is chanted on Holy Saturday and Tuesday after Easter, and the latter, Ps. 94, forms a part of the services of the 'Great Sabbath' that precedes Passover, and of Good Friday.[121]

(2) Pentecost-tide and *Shabuot*. The typical psalms of Pentecost are: 29; 68 and 78, all of which appear also on *Shabuot*.

(3) Holy Saturday and Day of Atonement. Attention was drawn above to the fact that the Eastertide of the Church has absorbed both Passover and *Yom Kippur* elements of the Synagogue and that in particular, the Holy Saturday corresponds in many respects, especially in the lessons, to the Day of Atonement. The distribution of psalms supports this observation. The following psalms are chanted on these days: 25; 51; 67; 92; 150; 135; 91; 148; and only one psalm, 103, a typical penitential poem, also forms a part of the Ash Wednesday service. Other psalms mentioned here belong also to the funeral or requiem services of the Church; for fasting and mourning services always are interrelated in the liturgies of Church and Synagogue.

Apart from these clearly defined liturgical aspects, the student will find a relationship between the Jewish New Year and Epiphany on the one hand, and the *Sabbatum quatuor temporum* (Ember Days of the autumn), on the other, which roughly coincide with the Jewish High Holydays. Finally, we emphasize again that only chanted psalms or versicles of psalms were considered here; many more resemblances than those pointed out here permeate the two liturgies.

Doxological Conclusion of Psalms. Almost all psalms or versicles chanted in the Church are concluded with the lesser doxology *Gloria Patri*. The liturgical and musical aspects of this doxology are discussed extensively in Chapter IX; yet a few explanatory remarks may be of value at this point.

The Trinitarian formulation of the lesser doxology, the affirmation of Christ's pre-existence, and the strict uniformity of the text in all but the schismatic Churches show clearly that the function of the lesser doxology was essentially dogmatic, apologetic, and hierarchic. The starting point was the same for Christianity and Judaism. The Church reached the pinnacle of *spontaneous* and quite free doxologies before the fourth century. Yet the Synagogue had developed other doxologies of dogmatic nature, while retaining the old ones (of the Psalter) only as memorials of the venerated Temple worship.

Later, the Church limited itself to but *one* lesser doxology for all services, returning to the strictly hierarchic function which these formulas had held in the Temple. The Synagogue with its freer and more flexible services developed greater variety in its doxologies. Their theocratic element lost its predominance and the dogmatic or liturgical aspects were emphasized. Thus, we behold here—*mirabile dictu*—the trend of the Synagogue away from the Temple, the trend of the Church back to it.

Why does the lesser doxology conclude all psalms and antiphons but not all hymns or sequences? The answer is simple: wherever the text originated in the Old Testament, the Church had to assure its Christological significance by adding the doxology, thereby proclaiming itself the *de jure* heir of both Temple and Synagogue of Israel.

Yet the Roman Church did not rest here, but, faithful to its principle of true catholicity, has been an inspiring agency to all nations that have embraced its doctrine. Thus were created, under the aegis of the Church, and to its glory, many new forms in all the arts, begotten by the respective genii of the many countries and languages of its flock. Since our investigation closes with the tenth century, we are chiefly concerned with those forms which arose out of plain psalmody, but exceeded in one way or another the boundaries of strictly syllabic composition. These semi-psalmodic forms will be discussed in our next chapter.

NOTES CHAPTER V

1. F. M. Powicke, *The Legacy of the Middle Ages* (Oxford, 1926), p. 39.
2. Tertullian, *De oratione*, XXVII (*PL*, I, 1301); also *De anima*, IX. See also Augustine, *Sermo clxxvi*, 1: 'This we learn from the apostolic lesson; thereafter we sang a psalm which was followed by the lesson of the Gospel'.
3. CAF, II, 57; also VIII, 5.
4. Mgr Duchesne writes in his *Origin of Christian Worship*, p. 168–9: 'I have already pointed out that the practice of chanting psalms between the lections of the Mass is as old as these lections themselves, and that both go back in direct line to the religious services of the Jewish synagogue. In the Christian liturgy these psalms constitute the most ancient and most solemn representation of the Davidic Psalter. We must take care not to put them on the same footing as the other chants, Introit, Offertory, and Communion which were introduced later, and then merely to occupy attention during long ceremonies. The gradual and similar chants had an intrinsic value, and during the time in which they were sung there was nothing else going on . . .' (cf. also *Paléographie musicale*, V, 30). Most recently, E. Werner 'The Origin of Psalmody', *HUCA*, XXV (1954), pp. 327 ff.
5. Cf. Ambrose, *Enarr. in Ps. 1*, Praef. n. 9.
6. *Missale Mixtum* (*PL*, LXXXV, 109 ff).
7. Cf. Conybeare, op. cit., p. 387.

8. Cf. *supra*, p. 58–59.

9. Cf. Amalarius, *(PL, CV, 1123)*.

10. Isidore, *De Offic. eccles.*, I, 9 *(PL, LXXXIII, 744)*; also Augustine in *PL, XXXVII, 1784.*

11. Cf. *Pirqe de R. Eliezer*, cap. 44. See also T. Gérold, *Les Pères de l'Église et la musique* (1931), p. 30, where the entire practice of Psalmody is derived from the Synagogue—though without any conclusive documentary evidence.

12. *B. Shab.*, 118b.

13. Cf. ELB, p. 82.

14. Ibid., p. 199. Cf. *Sof.* XIV, 9, 10.

15. *B. Shab.*, 30a.

16. Baumstark seems to be the only scholar who has given serious thought to this fact, which speaks against the entire Christian traditions. His conjecture that the Synagogue originally had the psalmody between the lessons, but later dropped it, seems rather unconvincing. Cf. Baumstark, *Liturgie comparée*, p. 49.

17. Cf. E. Werner, 'The Attitude of the Early Church Fathers to Hebrew Psalmody,' *Review of Religion* (May 1943).

18. In *Ep. XX ad Damasum* and in *Ep. 109*, *(PL, XXII, 902)*.

19. Cf. *T & U*, XLV; 'Marcion', pp. 144, 154, 175 ff.

20. *T & U*, Neue Folge, VI, p. 35.

21. Cf. E. Werner, 'The Oldest Sources of Synagogal Chant', *Proceedings of the American Academy for Jewish Research* (1947), p. 227, where other references are also given; also my paper on 'The Common Ground', etc., in the Congress book of the International Congress of Catholic Church Music, Rome, 1950.

22. A good bibliography in Reese, *Music of the Middle Ages*, pp. 431–4, 437–40. In addition, my recent studies: 'The Attitude of the Early Church Fathers to Hebrew Psalmody', *Review of Religion* (May 1943); 'The Doxology in Church and Synagogue', *HUCA* (1946); 'The Leading Motif in Gregorian and Synagogue Chant', in *Proceedings of the American Musicological Society*, (Detroit, 1946); 'The Conflict of Hellenism and Judaism in the Music of the Early Church', *HUCA* (1947); also E. F. Warren, *Liturgy of the Ante-Nicene Church*, pp. 180 ff.

23. One authoritative statement may suffice for many more: 'If the faithful keep vigil in the Church, David [i.e., the psalm] is first, middle, and last. If at dawn anyone wishes to sing hymns, David is first, middle and last. At funeral processions and burials, David is first, middle and last. In the holy monasteries . . . David is first, middle and last. In the Convent of Virgins . . . David is first, middle and last'. (Chrysostom, *Homily VI, De poenitentia*, quoted by Gerbert, *De Cantu et Musica Sacra*, I, 61.)

24. Scriptural references to '*Ana* are many, as any Hebrew Concordance will show.

25. See *infra*, Chapter X.

26. Cf. Augustine, *Enarr. in Ps. 44 (PL, XXXVI, 493)*; also *Enarr. in Ps. 46 (PL, XXXVI 525)*; and *Enarr. in Ps. 99 (PL, XXXVII, 1271)*.

27. Some of the main patristic statements in: Chrysostom, *Exp. in Ps. 114 (PG, LV, 464)*; Tertullian, *De ieiuniis*, cap. 13. See also *T & U*, VI, 4, 59 (Achelis, *Die Canones Hippolyti*). The entire question is discussed but not really answered in F. Leitner, *Der Volksgesang im jüd. und christl. Altertum*, Chapters V–VII.

28. Ambrose, *Enarr. in Ps. 1*, Praef. n. 9.

29. A. Silviae *Peregrinatio*, *(CSEL, XXXIX, 74)*.

30. Cf. *Jer. Shab.*, XVI, 1, 15c; also *B. Suc.* 38b; *B. Sot.* 20b. See also my study 'The Hosanna in the Gospels', *JBL* (July 1946).

31. Cf. 'Nathan ha-Babli' in Neubauer, *Medieval Jewish Chroniclers*, II, pp. 83–88.

32. CAF, VIII, 4; also *Peregrinatio*: 'Always the little ones are present and always respond to the singing'.

33. Cf. A. Geiger in *ZDMG*, LXX (1847), pp. 460 ff.

34. CAF, II, 57.

35. ELB, pp. 291, 207 ff, also *JE*, article 'Piyyut'. A famous piece of Latin acrostics is Augustine's *Psalmus contra partem Donati*, a didactic-polemic hymn against the sect of the Donatists *(PL, XLIII, 23 ff)*. Sometimes the dependence upon the Hebrew alphabet goes

so far, that Latin acrostics end with T, the last Hebrew letter. One example may be quoted:

> In epiphania ad nocturnam.
> A patre unigenitus, ad nos venit per virginem
> Baptisma cruce consecrans
> Cunctos fideles generans
> ....
> ....
> ....
> Sceptroque tuo inclito
> Tuum defende populum.

> (Wackernagel, *Das Katholische Kirchenlied*, I, p. 110.)

The Byzantine form of acrostic *par excellence* is the *Kontakion*. Its Semitic origin was clearly demonstrated by K. Krumbacher, 'Die Akrostichis in der griechischen Kirchenpoesie', in *Sitzungsberichte der phil.-hist. Klasse der K. Bayrischen Akad. der Wissensch.* (Munich, 1903), pp. 561–691.

36. Cf. Eusebius, *Hist. eccl.*, ed. Schwarz, II, 17.

37. Cf. Zunz, *Synagogale Poesie des Mittelalters*, p. 88. See *infra*, p. 256, n. 25.

38. For other instances see Leitner, op. cit., pp. 208–9.

39. Ibid., p. 209.

40. Cf. *Forschungen zur Religion und Literatur des Alten und Neuen Testaments* (Göttingen, 1921), pp. 110 ff, and Ch. Wessely in *Österreichische Monatsschrift für den Orient* (1884), 152.

41. Cf. H. Gunkel, *Einleitung in die Psalmen*, pp. 37 ff.

42. On the symbolic meaning of the Alleluia in the Catholic Church, see WGM, I, pp. 92–98.

43. *PL*, LXXXIII, 750.

44. Cf. Gesenius, *Hebrew Dictionary*, 'Hallel'; the literature on the problem in A. Jeremias, *Das Alten Testament im Lichte des alten Orients*, pp. 427, 556, 439, 429, 601 *et passim*. J. Wellhausen opposes the theory in his *Reste arabischen Heidentums*, p. 110.

45. On the difference between canticles and psalms, from the theological point of view, see Hilary of Poitiers, *Prologus in libr. Psalmorum*; Didymus, *Expos. in Ps.* 4 : 1 (*PG*, XXXIX, 1164); and Gregory of Nyssa, *In Ps. II*, cap. 3, (*PG*, XLIV, 494). The literature on these questions is given in W. Christ, *Beiträge zur kirchlichen Literatur der Byzantiner* (1870), pp. 24 ff. The definitive study on the liturgical use of the canticles was recently provided by H. Schneider, 'Die biblischen Oden im Christl. Altertum', *Biblica*, 1949.

46. A. Gastoué's remark that in Jewish Liturgy the canticles are not chanted (*L'Origine du chant rom.*, p. 4, n. 1) is a mistake of that otherwise excellent scholar.

47. The old African Church had a particular tradition about this apocryphal work of Pseudo-Ezra; cf. Dom Cabrol, *Le Livre de la prière antique* (Paris, 1900), p. 26.

48. *B. Sot.* 5, 4 (30b), and *B. Suc.* 38b.

49. Cf. E. Wellesz, 'Byzantine Music', *Proceedings of the Musical Association* (1932), pp. 1 ff.

50. Cf. the Targum to Ps. 148, also *Midrash Tehillim* to Ps. 104 and 145. See further below in the chapter on Doxology.

51. Lauds corresponds with the morning service, Vespers and Compline roughly with the evening services of the Synagogue. Cf. H. Schneider, op. cit. pp. 31–34.

52. Cf. also E. F. Warren, *The Liturgy of the Ante-Nicene Church*, p. 203.

53. It is deeply regrettable that no comprehensive work on Armenian liturgical music is available yet. While this writer has reached no definite conclusions about the puzzling and fascinating problems with which the oldest Christian liturgy confronts the scholar, he is in complete agreement with so reliable an authority as Prof. E. Wellesz, who writes: 'If one wants really to explore these matters . . . the necessary spade work would have to be done first by Orientalists, who are at the same time good musicologists and not by musicians proper. For only unceasing occupation with the subject will occasionally yield some tangible and fruitful results. The musicologist, on the other hand, can only after years

of preparatory studies attempt the tracing of Armenian music with all its inherent intricacies. . . .' (*Aufgaben und Probleme auf dem Gebiet der byznt. und oriental. Kirchenmusik* (Münster, 1923), pp. 94 ff.) The Armenian words are compared with Hebrew, Syriac and Greek terms according to Conybeare, *Rituale Armenorum* and Bedros of Constantinople, *Étude philologique et lexicographique* (London, 1945).

54. Some of the liturgical terms reflect the position of the celebrant or the congregation during the piece concerned, as in Hebrew, the '*Amida*—the standing prayer, in Latin the *Graduale*—psalm from the steps of the ambo; the Greek *Kathisma* and *Akathisma*—a hymn sung while the congregation is sitting or standing, the Nestorian *Motva*—an anthem sung while seated, etc.

55. Cf. Eusebius, *In Ps. 91* (PG, XXIII, 1172).

56. CAF, II, cap. 59.

57. Justin, *Contra Tryphonem*, Ch. 63, 14.

58. *Apol.*, cap. 39.

59. Ibid.

60. Eusebius, *In Ps. 91*, (PG, XXIII, 1172).

61. About the Byzantine selection of psalms for their canonic offices see next paragraph of this chapter. Cf. J. B. Pitra, *Juris eccles. graec. hist. et monum.*, II, pp. 220 ff, where also the *horologion* of the sixth century is transmitted.

62. Cf. G. Bickell, 'Die Kanonischen Gebetszeiten', *Katholik*, II (1873), pp. 417 ff. Also Bickell, *Messe und Pascha*, and C. Schmidt, *Gespräche Jesu mit seinen Jungern* (Leipzig, 1919), Excurs III.

63. Cf. Clement of Alexander, *Paedagogus*, II, 4.

64. As for the musical comparison between Jewish and Christian psalmody see Part II of this book, Chapters IV and V.

65. Cf. Harnack, 'Marcion', in *T&U*, XLV, pp. 144, 154, 175. Also Pamelius, *Commentary on Tertullian's De Carne*, cap. 20.

66. The original (Syriac) text in Assemani, *Biblioth. Orientalis*, I, 47 ff, where also the Syriac musical terminology is briefly discussed. Also Sozomen, *Hist. Eccl.*, III, 16.

67. Cf. Hefele-Leclercq, op. cit., 'I Laodicea, can. 59'.

68. The literature in Leitner, op. cit., pp. 220 ff, also WGM, I, p. 22.

69. Cf. *Midrash Tehillim*, ed. Buber, Chapter 14, n. 29.

70. Cf. *Jer. Sot.* V and *M.Er.* II:6. Saadya Gaon, (ninth to tenth century) still knew the antiphonem of the congregation according to tunes as taught in the School (cf. Harkavy, *T'shuvot ha-geonim*, Nr. 208).

71. Cf. Eusebius, *Hist eccl.*, II, 17, quoting Philo, *De Vita Contemplativa*, II, 83 (VI, 68: Cohn-Reiter). See also I. Heinemann, 'Über die Sektenfrömmigkeit der Therapeuten', *MGWJ*, November 1937.

72. WGM, I, p. 23.

73. E.g. WGM, I, p. 17.

74. Especially O. Ursprung, *Die katholische Kirchenmusik* (Potsdam, 1931—in Bücken's *Handbuch der Musikwissenschaft*), certainly not unbiased—perhaps for political reasons.

75. Cf. L. Venetianer, op. cit., *ZDMG*, LXIII, pp. 103 ff.

76. Cf. Harnack, *T&U* VI, N.F. VI, 4, 1901, p. 131 (Diodor von Tarsus).

77. Up to this day psalms are chanted by orthodox Jews if somebody is in peril or dangerously ill; they are supposed to chase away the Angel of Death.

78. Cf. L. Blau, *Das altjüdische Zauberwesen*, pp. 94, 102, 130; also A. Dieterich, *Abraxas*, p. 70.

79. Chrysostom, *Homil. in Ps. 150* (PG, LV, 497): 'All these instruments were permitted . . . by God only because of their [the Jews] imbecility, in order to spur their lethargic temper to more love . . . and their mind to more activity. . . .' Still sharper is Chrysostom in his *Homil. in Ps. 149*, 2 (PG, LV, 494): 'There are some who say that the tympanon signifies the mortality of our flesh, but the Psaltery reflects the glance upward to heaven, but I want to stress the fact that they [the Jews] ever played these instruments (in the wrong way) because of the clumsiness of their minds . . . thus God adjusted himself to their weakness. . . .' A modern scholar, Father J. Quasten, in a learned thesis (*Musik und Gesang in den Kulten der heidnischen Antike und christlichen Frühzeit* (Münster, 1930), p. 88)

calls these certainly biased patristic statements the 'real reasons of instrumental music in the Jewish cult', forgetting that at the time of these attacks, instrumental music was strictly prohibited in Judaism.

80. Cyril of Jerusalem, *Catechumenis Mystagogus*, V (*PG*, XXXIII, 1118 ff).

81. J. Parkes, *The Conflict of the Church and the Synagogue*, pp. 300 ff.

82. Cf. A. J. Maclean, *East Syrian Daily Offices* (London, 1894), p. 153.

83. Ibid., p. 259.

84. Rome, 1868, vol. II, p. 220.

85. Cf. also Cassian, *De institutis coenobiorum*, II, 2 (*PL*, XLIX, 77).

86. H. Schneider, op. cit., p. 254

87. Maclean, op. cit. pp. 86–95; also BLEW, pp. 578, article 'Hudhra'; 574, article 'Davidha'. Compare also the Nestorian *Zumara* (Alleluia Psalm) with the Hebrew *Psuqe de Zimra*, the Hallelujah Psalms of the morning service.

88. Cf. Idelsohn, *Jewish Liturgy*, p. 134, where also the sources are given and ELB, pp. 112–13, who gives a detailed account of the controversy centring on Ps. 100 for Sabbath.

89. BLEW, pp. 366, 368, 370.

90. The tabulation was computed from references in the following works: A. Maltzew, *Die Liturgien der Orthodox-Katholischen Kirche des Morgenlandes* (Berlin, 1894); M. Rajewsky, *Euchologion der Orthodoxen Kirche* (Vienna, 1861); J. N. W. Robertson, *The Divine Liturgy of John Chrysostom and Basil the Great* (London, 1894); R. F. Littledale, *Office from the Service-books of the Eastern Orthodox Church* (London, 1863); A. J. Maclean, *East Syrian Daily Offices* (London, 1894).

91. Cf. A. Baumstark, 'Denkmäler der Entstehungsgeschichte des Byz. Ritus', in *OC*, III Series, vol. 2, 1927, pp. 14–16.

92. Cf. Maclean, op. cit., p. 130.

93. BLEW, p. 364.

94. Ibid., p. 75.

95. The oldest source of penitential psalms seems to be *M. Taanith* II, where liturgies for fast-days are cited; the tradition probably antedates Christianity by one century, as we just recently learned in the newly discovered Sectarian Documents of Palestine. The influence of the penitential psalms and the earliest Hebrew *Selihot*, that originated out of these cycles, upon the earliest Christian liturgies has been demonstrated by Michel, *Gebet und Bild in Frühchristlicher Zeit*, pp. 44 ff.

96. Cf. BLEW, pp. 247 ff, also the corresponding passages in the Nestorian and Jacobite parts of the same work.

97. Ibid., p. 247; also pp. 358, 360 ff *et passim*.

98. Cf. Theodorus Isaac, *Missal of the Armenian Church* (Fresno, 1932), pp. 178–97.

99. Those psalms or psalm verses are considered typical by the author that occur at least twice in the Offices of one day; also that show distinctly transpositions from the Synagogal service. Cf. Th. Isaac, op. cit., Hymn for Maundy Thursday. The comparison of the Armenian Mass psalmody was based upon Conybeare, op. cit., pp. 447–88; also used were Essaie Asdradzadouriantz, *Liturgy of the Apostolic Church of Armenia* (London, 1887), and J. Issaverdentz, *The Sacred Rites of the Armenian Church* (Venice, 1888).

100. J. Issaverdentz, op. cit., pp. 33 ff.

101. After BLEW, pp. 431 ff.

102. Cf. Mahrbach, *Carmina Scripturarum*.

103. See *supra*, n. 4.

104. I Cor. 5:19; Col. 3:16, and especially Athanasius, *Ep. ad Marcellinum* (*PG*, XXVII, 42).

105. *Tosefta Sota* VI, 4.

106. F. Probst, *Liturgie der ersten 300 Jahre*, p. 314.

107. This psalm plays a significant part in the Jewish and Gnostic philosophy of music because in it seven times the voice of the Lord is mentioned. In rabbinic literature this is taken to allude to the seven or eight modes of music. See *infra*, Part II, Chapter II; also Werner-Sonne, 'The Philosophy and Theory of Music in Judaeo-Arabic Literature', *HUCA* (1941), p. 317. On the use of the psalm on *Shabuot* cf. *Soferim*, 18, 3; also E. Werner, 'The Origin of the Eight Modes', *HUCA* (1948), p. 221.

108. Cf. *Tosefta Menachot*, VII, 9, and *Sebachim*, II, 2.

109. Cf. *Tosefta Yom Kippur*, V, 15; cf. Ps. 51:5.

110. Rabbinic tradition connects the psalm with the giving of the Law on Mt Sinai; cf *Tosefta Erubin*, I, 10 and B. Pesach. 118b.

111. *Tosefta Succa*, III, 12, ed. Zuckermandl, p. 179.

112. *Tosefta Kidduschim*, VI, 10, ed. Zuckermandl, p. 343.

113. The Greek Church calls this psalm the 'prefatory psalm', 'Because with it Vespers, the Mass, and other prayers . . . start'; cf. Goar, *Euchologium Graecorum*, p. 23b.

114. Cf. *B. Pes.* 117a.

115. See my study on 'The Hosanna in the Gospels', *JBL* (July 1946); also *infra* Chapter IX.

116. For the musical significance of the eight alphabetic acrostics in Ps. 119, see E. Werner, 'The Origin of the Eight Modes', *HUCA* (1948), p. 221.

117. *M. Taanith* I, 2.

118. According to the Benedictine Rule, this psalm is to be sung every day before Lauds throughout the year as in the Jewish ritual.

119. Verse 12 of Ps. 146 is the origin and motto of the famous sequence for Corpus Christi, 'Lauda Sion Salvatorem', by Thomas Aquinas.

120. On the extremely important role of Ps. 118 in Early Christianity (Messianism and Eschatology) see my study 'The Hosanna in the Gospels', *JBL* (July 1946).

121. The question of the term 'Great Sabbath' was discussed on p. 86; and note 104 thereto (Chapter III).

CHAPTER SIX

Semi-psalmodic and Melismatic Forms in the Liturgies of Church and Synagogue

THE MAIN PROBLEM

IN all liturgical music the element of note-word relation plays a signal part. Two poles of this relationship are easily discernible. One lies in a strictly word-bound psalmodic structure where the setting is only the servant of the sentence and its syntactic accents. The other extreme is represented by the autonomous setting, which disregards the words altogether or treats them as a mere pretext for music. To this category belong the *Jubili*, the 'wordless hymns' of which St Augustine speaks so enthusiastically. Between these two poles, however, there is an infinite variety and nuance of the note-word relationship, resulting in a number of intermediate forms.

In order to understand these half-psalmodic, half-melismatic compositions it will be necessary to study the significance and function of the melismatic principle for the liturgy.

Robert Lach has examined the origin of melismatic music and the primitive forms of musical ornaments.[1] He has come to the conclusion that melismatic music originated as:

1. Infantile expression of sensual pleasure
2. Imitation of the singing of the birds
3. Primitive magic incantation
4. Imitation of musical instruments
5. Virtuosity of professional singers
6. Expression of religious ecstasy.

While all of these stimuli to expression may have been, at one time or another, apparent in the liturgy of Judaism and Christianity, only the four last mentioned have left definite traces.

In the Gnostic-magic papyri, the magic function of the Hallelujah singing, and of melismatic song in general, is manifest.[2] We are able to trace back these elements to very early times. The pre-Islamic Arabs knew the practice of musical incantations which often was connected with the trill *lilili*.[3] The close proximity of such cries to the Greek terms *alalazo, elelizo*, and to the ancient Semitic root *hallal*, from which the Hallelujah was later derived, indicates the long history of melismatic magic chants.

The imitation of instrumental music, too, has had its share in the long history of ornate chant. This is reflected in the often repeated admonitions of Byzantine theologians, forbidding the cathedral singers to appear in the theatre, to sing with accompaniment, or to make any instrumental-like music.[4] Conversely, many manuscripts of Hebrew music after the sixteenth century show a distinct tendency to imitate the effects of instrumental (especially string) music. As in Byzantium, so in the Synagogue of Europe it was the professional singer, the *hazan*, who craved for the forbidden instrumental accompaniment. He had to content himself with imitating the instruments in his chant whenever the words were unimportant enough or could be overlooked.

Another facet of the same condition was the desire of the professional singer to demonstrate his virtuosity to its best advantage. In the Roman and Greek Churches the members of the 'Schola Cantorum' were trained artists and it is quite plausible that certain melismatic forms owe their musical adornments to the desire of these men to exhibit their skill.[5]

In the Synagogue the *hazan*'s vanity and wish to let his voice resound in all its glory has become proverbial; but, on the other hand, this attitude has produced elaborate melismatic paraphrases of traditional motifs. These elaborations could take place only on those occasions when the words were familiar to everybody and a lack of proper diction would not be criticized too strongly.

In Church and Synagogue, extended melismatic chant was regarded as an ecstatic praise of God, 'sonus quidam est laetitiae sine verbis' as St Augustine puts it.[6] Such a conception places this type of singing in close proximity to the glossolaly of the Paulinian age (I Cor. 12:30; 14:5; Acts 10:46; 19:6). Augustine in another remark about *Jubilus*, seems to connect it with the early Christian practice of 'talking in tongues'.[7] Jerome, too, attempts an explanation of melismatic chant along the very same lines.[8] I venture to put forward my own conviction that the whole concept of the pure, wordless, melismatic jubilation should be considered the last, jealously guarded remnant of an organized musical form of glossolaly, if we permit ourselves a slight contradiction in terms.

The Jewish origin of the *Jubilus* is evident through its inseparable connexion with the Hebrew Hallelujah and the patristic statements that it represents 'mos ecclesiae orientalis'. Even the term *Jubilus* or *Jubilatio* itself tells something about its origin. Its etymology has, to my knowledge, been hitherto entirely overlooked. The word *Jubilus* displays an interesting fusion of Latin and Hebrew roots. The Hebrew *yobel* (ram, metonym. 'trumpet blast', thence jubilee year) together with the Latin *jubilare* (to call a person, to shout joyously as a rustic does: 'ut quivitare urbanorum, sic jubilare rusticorum' in Varro (116–27 B.C.) begot the hybrid term *jubilus* or *jubilatio*. The Vulgate version of the Bible melted these two entirely different words into one.[9]

What information concerning the background of melismatic chant can we gather from old Jewish sources? As in the early Church and in Byzantine tradition, it is considered the song of the angels and its human performance an imitation of the angelic hymns.[10] All available evidence points in one direction: the Hallelujah originally formed an integral part of the Jewish and early Christian doxologies, as is apparent from the doxologies of Ps. 106:48 or I Chron. 16:36. The euphonic and exultant Hallelujah would give, even to the primitive listeners, the opportunity to join in the proclamation of God's praise. All of this suggests that the liturgical function of the Hallelujah was, in early times, a priestly arrangement to organize popular participation in the cult of the Temple. The signal role which the Hallelujah has played in the liturgies of Church and Synagogue will therefore be discussed extensively in connexion with the doxology (Chapter IX).

All rabbinic sources agree that the singing of the *Hallel* psalms was either a simulation or an imitation of the angelic choir exactly as the Byzantines conceived it.[11] Even the rabbinic phraseology in describing it has been borrowed by the Church Fathers. To quote but one instance:

Talmud Yerushalmi, Pesach. 7 : 11, 35b	Jerome, *Epist.* 77 in *PL*, XXII, 697
Passover in the home and the sound of the *Hallel* makes the roof split.	Sonabant psalmi et aurata tecta templorum reboans in sublime quatiebat Alleluia.

Since the times of the Essenes, who allegedly preferred extended Hallelujahs in the morning service, the melismatic chant was considered indispensable to Jewish worship. At times, under the spell of mysticism, it became so preponderant that it threatened to obscure other, more essential parts of the liturgy. R. Solomon ben Adret (fourteenth century) had to issue a formal decree against the prevalence of melismatic chants (wordless hymns) at a time when Cabbalism had engulfed Western Jewry.[12] Four centuries later melismatic chants emerged again as a main element of the music of Hasidism, the mystic sect of the seventeenth and eighteenth centuries in Eastern Europe. There, forms like the *niggun* (wordless musical improvisation), the *shtil* (melismatic preamble or close of a psalmodic prayer) provided the Hasidic worship with its most characteristic features.

In ornate chant one must distinguish between autonomous and functional melismata. The first category comprises all songs or forms where entire parts are sung without words, or where the melismata hold absolute sovereignty over the words. All Alleluias, the *Jubili* of Gradual Responses and similar forms belong to this category in the Christian liturgy, as do the Hasidic *niggunim*, *shtils*, and certain hazanic renderings of parts of the *Tefilla* in the Synagogue. Apart from the pure melismatic style, we know of many forms where the melismata are merely functional, serving as punctuation (as in scriptural cantillation, or as the *flexa* and *punctus* of the psalm tones); or as an accentuating-rhetoric device of distinct phrases in tracts or antiphons. Sometimes the melismata have no other musical function than to lead up to the end of a melody. This type of ornament, the final melisma, is of paramount importance in all liturgical and even in secular music.

From the liturgical point of view, melismatic chant was always considered an embellishment of the worship in Church and Synagogue. Thus, in the hierarchy of the ecclesiastical year the greater or lesser amount of ornate chant stands in direct proportion to the degree of liturgical solemnity of the respective occasions. To exemplify: the chants of the weekdays are less adorned than those of the Sabbath or Sunday. And, as the antiphons of Easter or Pentecost or Epiphany are richer and more abundantly embellished than those of ordinary Sundays, so are the chants of the Jewish High Holydays more melismatic than those of the Sabbath. This principle applies also to the various stages of the individual feast-day; the songs of Vespers or of Lauds of a Sunday are not as ornate as the Mass of the forenoon (High Mass); nor can the prayers of the early Sabbath morning or of the afternoon be compared with the splendour of the chief prayers of the forenoon (*Mussaph*). This general rule of more melismata for greater solemnity leads to some specific questions: what liturgical forms are conducive to melismata? Is there a principle which, at least approximately, governs the liturgical use of melismatic chant? Is such a principle determined by the type of rendering, by the character of the text, or by the liturgical occasion?

Amédée Gastoué, one of the best authorities on early Christian music, has discovered the following interesting fact which might help us to solve the problem: Graduals whose verses are parts of the same psalm frequently belong to the same Church mode, use the same melismata and even the same melodic formulas. Moreover, these chants show a distinct similarity to Synagogal melodies.[13] Gastoué is convinced that both the Ambrosian (Milanese) and the Gregorian traditions are founded upon 'one and the same ornamental design, identical with that of the Synagogue, and that only certain minor retouchings have constituted the divergencies in the three musical liturgies of Milan, Rome and the Synagogue.'[14] Generalizing these analogies, we might expect to find melismatic elements in the following liturgical forms:

(a) In soloistic psalmody, or its cognate types.

(b) In laudatory and supplicatory prayers, less in proclamatory, dogmatic, didactic or narrative parts of the liturgy.

The practice as presented in (a) seems, indeed, to be a governing principle. In the Roman Church very few texts are sung by a soloist; however, outstanding among all of them is the Tract, a form richly embellished with melismata. P. Wagner has stated emphatically that this entire type is a direct remnant of the Synagogue worship.[15] The same holds true for the Offertory which developed melismata when the choir had relinquished its rendering to a soloist; certain soloistic Graduals followed the same rule. Moreover, many of these chants have formulas and melismata in common, according to Gastoué. The same principles are also applicable to the Syrian 'enyanas and Greek psalms and solo chants.

The statement (b) appears in a somewhat different light. Here, the use of melismatic style would be determined by the text and not by the manner of its rendering. In the Synagogue we find the ornate style chiefly in supplicatory, occasionally in laudatory prayers, but rarely in didactic or narrative passages. Yet there is one famous exception, the *Kol Nidre*. This legalistic formula, chanted on the eve of the Day of

Atonement, is rendered in a very ornate style, at least in Central and Eastern Europe. Apparently its chant was influenced by the general musical atmosphere of the Holyday, especially since it contains certain characteristic motifs which permeate the entire liturgy of the *Yom Kippur*. In the Church, melismatic chant expresses a mystic exultation and sacred enthusiasm, as we learned from Augustine's remark. Hence the main piece of ornate song, the Alleluia, is excluded from the service during Lent (*Alleluia clausum*), and from the Mass for the dead, and is replaced by the more moderate Tract as representative of melismatic chant.

There are, on the other hand, clearly supplicatory verses connected either with an Alleluia or, at least, with extensive melismata; thus Ps. 7:1 is a *versus alleluiaticus*; even a De Profundis, this most intense of all supplications, forms part of an Alleluia (on the 23rd Sunday after Pentecost). As in the Synagogue, there are not many narrative texts among the Alleluias of the Church. Thus, rule (b) seems, though to a minor extent, to be valid for Church and Synagogue alike. Finally, it is only fair to admit that these examinations are far from conclusive. The entire set of problems demands a detailed investigation to be undertaken by a liturgist who, at the same time, is conversant with musicology.

FORMS OF PSALMODIC STRUCTURE WITH INCIDENTAL MELISMATA

Litanies, Selihot, and Cognate Forms

The ancient liturgies of fast-days in Judaism and Christianity show many examples of primitive melismata in a prevalently psalmodic type of chant. The reason for this strange fact is the intrinsic connexion between fasting, penitence and the form of the litany, in Hebrew called *Seliha* (forgiveness). Following the pattern of ancient Babylonian rudimentary litanies, Judaism seems to have developed this type of prayer before the first century B.C. The reports of the so-called rain-fasting indicate the use of litany-like formulas, chanted by priests and responded to by the people.[16] The oldest litany of the prayer-book, however, is attributed to the great Rabbi Akiba, scholar, saint and martyr (*ca.* A.D. 100): 'Our father, our King! withhold the plague from thine inheritance!' etc. Here the refrain 'Our father, our King!' is sung by the congregation. In other old litanies of the Synagogue the response is at the end of a stanza (or after a set of verses). Yet, there is neither metre nor rhyme discernible in these pieces; occasionally we encounter alphabetic acrostics as the only indication of artistic endeavour.[17]

The litany was extremely popular in the Syrian Church, where it was called Ba'utha. In the East Syrian Church (Nisibis) it was called Shuhlaph Qāle (alternative songs). Both litanies are so similar to their Jewish counterparts that we are reminded of the close relation of the Nestorian and Jewish Masora, referred to above.[18]

In the Greek and Armenian Churches the so-called Diaconal Litany forms an integral part of the Mass of the Catechumens and comes closest to the ordinary Synagogue litanies.[19] The congregation joins in these petitions with the supplication Kyrie eleison. However, the place of the Kyrie in the Roman litany is not the same as in the Eastern Churches. Gregory the Great already noticed this discrepancy.[20]

In the Roman litany it occurs at the beginning and the end, and is said alternately by the precentor and the congregation. In the East it formed the people's response to the petitions in the Diaconal Litany.[21]

The Jewish liturgy knows both types of performance and either of them may occur in the morning service, that collection of prayers from which the Church borrowed some of its oldest liturgical pieces. In the following, we compare a Roman and a Greek litany with two Hebrew examples:

Jewish	Byzantine
. . . Listen to my prayer and supplication. . . . Save now!	It is lovely to me that the Lord heareth my voice, my supplications.
Thou givest faithfulness to Jacob, grace to Abraham. . . . Save now!	Save now, Son of God, those who sing to Thee Alleluia!
The nation . . . that approaches Death as a testimony to its fear of God. . . . Save now!	For He hath inclined His ear unto me; therefore through all my days will I call on Him.
Righteous is the Lord in all of His ways; and merciful in all of His deeds. . . . Save now![22]	Save now, Son of God, etc.
	The bands of death had compassed me, and the pangs of the nether world had overtaken me.
	Save now, Son of God, etc.
	Gracious is the Lord and righteous; and our God is merciful.
	Save now, Son of God, etc.
	(Ps. 116:1–3, 5)

Jewish	Roman
Cantor: O Lord, hear, O Lord forgive!	Precentor: Lamb of God that bearest the sins of the world, spare us, O Lord!
Cong.: O Lord, hearken and do, defer not; for thine own sake, because thy city, and thy people are called by thy name! . . .	Cong.: Lamb of God, that bearest the sins of the world, hearken unto us, O Lord!
Cantor: Have pity upon us, have mercy upon Thine inheritance!	Precentor: Lamb of God that bearest the sins of the world, have mercy upon us!
Cong.: O Lord, spare and be merciful.	Cong.: Christ, listen to us!
Cantor: Look, and answer us in time of trouble, for salvation is Thine, O Lord!	Precentor: Christ, hearken unto us!
	Precentor: Kyrie eleison.
Cong.: We beseech Thee, forgive, O good and forgiving God. . . .	Cong.: Christe eleison.
	Precentor: Kyrie eleison.[23]

In both cases the Christian litanies opened and closed with a *Kyrie eleison* or a similar cry of supplication; this nuclear cell of every litany, however, is not of Jewish origin. It is now certain that this well-known *votum suspirans* is a remnant of pagan rites, or more specifically, the transformation of an original Helios-Mithras hymn.[24] Like many other ancient prayers of Christianity, its actual origin has been overlaid by biblical paraphrases, especially Matt. 20:30 and Baruch 3:2.

The martyrological litanies of the Eastern Churches and some of the oldest Latin collects after the litany (*collectio post precem* as contained in the Missale Gothicum, the Stowe Missal and similar documents), bear a remarkable resemblance to the Aramaic prayers for the spiritual leaders, the congregation, etc., that appear immediately after the Torah lesson.[25] We observe this analogy only in passing, since these ancient litanies or collects are chanted neither in the Church nor the Synagogue of today. Similarly, the litanies of the *Stationes* (*statio* = *ma'amad*) echo the ancient customs of the Temple, as was recently pointed out by a Catholic scholar.[26] The practice of the Christian Church of chanting litanies on the eve of Pentecost parallels a similar Jewish custom on the eve of *Shabuot* (Jewish Pentecost). I was unable to trace the origin or development of these institutions. Probably most of these litanies or, at least, their basic forms and ideas, originated in an era when both Judaism and Christianity were suffering from persecutions by the secular powers. That would suggest the second and third centuries. Indeed, some of these litanies seem to have originated in that period, and it is quite possible that, once the scheme of the prayer became familiar to Judaeo-Christians, they conveyed it to the Gentile Church, whence it developed independently in the centuries to come.

Psalmodic-melismatic Form Types: the Antiphon

Some of the most important forms of the musical liturgy of all Churches belong to this category. The remarkable divergences between the various types, with respect to their literary and musical development, cannot be explained from the liturgical aspect alone. It was here that the genius of the respective population, its national and religious character, asserted itself. No less important was the genius of the various languages of the liturgies which created their own structures, their poetical as well as musical forms. In short, here, more than in any other sphere, the ethnic and regional forces determined the evolution of these psalmodic-melismatic types.

The oldest and best known specimen of this group is the antiphon. Originally, this term referred to a certain kind of rendering, viz. in alternating choirs or, using the terminology of ancient Greek musicians, in octave singing (chiefly between young people and adults, or men and women).[27]

Since both the practice of antiphony and the form of the antiphon are of outstanding importance for the history of liturgy and the history of music, we shall now briefly examine their origin.

From times of old, the Church exhibited great pride in the invention and institution of antiphony; yet, it is altogether impossible to attest to Christianity's claim of priority.

The first inkling of antiphony occurs in Hittite cuneiform texts, where we read:

The priests of conjuration play the little Istar-instrument, the man of the ivory-statue speaks . . . the *kitas* calls and chants. . . .

The ancient Babylonians, likewise, made use of antiphonal practice, as in the passage of the Gilgamesh-epic, where the women of Uruk call to the divine hero Gilgamesh:

'Who is fair among the men: who is marvellous among men?'
Answer: 'Gilgamesh is fair among men, Gilgamesh is marvellous among the men.'[28]

Apart from Babylonian hymns, which might or might not be interpreted as antiphonal, we find definite evidence of that practice in the Bible, namely in Neh. 12:31-42. Ps. 88 and 136. While the historical passages of Nehemiah need no further elucidation, the Psalms do. The superscription of Ps. 88 reads as follows: 'A song of the sons of Korach, to the choirmaster (?) on *Mahalat le'annot*, a *maskil* (?) of Heman the Ezrahite'. What does *mahalat le'annot* mean? The root *'ana* means 'to respond' (in a musical sense); *mahal* always indicates a choric arrangement, be it dance or some kind of group singing. Thus, perhaps, a free translation might render it as 'for antiphonal choir'. This is not so bold as it would appear, since some Greek translations have it as 'antiphonic ode'.[29] And our first historical source, the Church Father Socrates, in his ecclesiastical history, described the vision of St Ignatius of Antioch in the phraseology known to us from Isa. 6:3, the *Sanctus* or *Kedusha*. Polemicizing against heretical Arian hymns, Ignatius saw the angels in 'alternative [antiphonal] hymnody' praise the Holy Trinity.[30] Another tradition traces antiphony back to the monks Flavian and Diodore, who, under the reign of Bishop Leontius of Antioch (344–357) assembled clerics and laymen in alternating choirs during the nocturnal services. This report is documented by Theodoret of Cyrrhus[13] and somewhat modified by Theodore of Mopsuestia.[32] A further witness is St Basil of Neo-Caesarea who, in a letter to his clergy, defends and praises antiphony, thereby commending its practice, already established in the monasteries of Egypt, Libya, Palestine, Arabia, and West and East Syria.[33] The mutual corroboration of all these documents admits but one conclusion: the Church *developed* the practice of antiphony in Syria, especially in and around Antioch. Where did Syrian Christianity find this custom already established? The answer is simple: in the Jewish community of Antioch. We only have to be aware of the fact that in this town Jewry had all the privileges of citizenship since Seleucus Nicator (*ca.* 301 B.C.),[34] and that Antioch was the earliest and most important centre of missionary activity in the Apostolic and post-Apostolic age of Christianity.[35] Moreover, the descriptions of antiphony in patristic literature up to the fifth century show no appreciable difference from the report of Philo-Eusebius about the Therapeutae of four centuries previous, cited above (Chapter V).

The first signs of transition from that type of rendering, then called antiphony, toward the form of the antiphon appear in the fifth century. While *antiphonal practice* seems to have been a common heritage of Semitic lore, the form of the *antiphon* and its cognates in the various liturgies is an accomplishment of the Christian genius and perhaps the finest literary-musical creation of the synthesis of Orient and Occident, of which Christianity itself is the greatest monument.

The antiphon as an independent form had its origin in the repetition of one psalm verse as a refrain sung by the congregation, alternating with another verse by soloist or choir. This psalm-refrain-verse then was called *antiphona*. About the same time (end of the fourth century) a preamble to the psalm proper was sung by the choir, to be repeated after every psalm verse and at the very end. An example of this type, which has almost disappeared from the liturgies, is the Invitatory and Ps. 95 in the Matins of Easter Sunday. There the preamble reads: 'Surrexit Deus vere, Alleluia'. Then the Psalm 'Venite exultemus Domino', etc., is sung, always interrupted by the refrain 'Surrexit' which also closes the piece. A further development occurred in the monasteries, where antiphonal practice was familiar to everyone. 'Some monks felt that they ought to prolong the . . . psalms themselves by the melodies of antiphons and by adding certain melismata.'[36] The 'certain melismata', of course, refer to the Alleluia. But the tendency to extend the psalms by melodies of antiphons indicates that, at the time when this was written, the antiphon was already emancipating itself from the psalm. The next step was that the melody of the antiphon was intoned before the singing of the psalm, but was chanted in its entirety afterwards. Sometimes, the connexion with a psalm was completely abandoned; in such cases the antiphon is a psalmodic-melismatic piece *sui generis*, not necessarily antiphonally rendered and concluded with the Lesser Doxology *Gloria Patri*, etc. When congregational singing of psalmody gradually disappeared in the Roman Church and relinquished its place to professional singers or the singing clergy, the refrain was adorned with musical embellishments and fine melodic lines. Today this refrain alone is called the antiphon; frequently it is wholly autonomous. While the disappearance of popular psalmody on the one hand inactivated the congregation, at the same time it increased the artistic beauty of the liturgy by the magnificent expansion of the rudimentary forms.

The same process took place in the Eastern Churches, but with one interesting difference. The texts of the *Antiphonale Romanum* consist, almost without exception, of passages from the Bible, the *Acta Martyrum*, or the *Vitae Sanctorum* and similar books of the oldest Christian literature. None of them shows any distinct metrical structure, if we disregard the very controversial hypothesis of the metrical schemes of certain canticles and psalms. Consequently, the Roman antiphons do not show any metric influence either in their texts or in their music.[37]

This is different in the Churches of Byzantium and of Syria. The Greek counterpart of the antiphon is the *troparion*, the Syrian the *'enyana* (*'ana*, to answer). Both form types usually are couched in some kind of metre and, in contrast to the conservative Roman attitude, their texts were often creations of more recent poets, whose activities influenced the Eastern Churches up to the twelfth century.

Originally the *troparion* was a free poetic interpolation between the verses of a psalm or a canticle. Gradually the psalm verse (*stichos*) lost its dominant position and was superseded by the insertion. Thus, the *troparia* were expanded until they grew into independent poems called *stichera*, and usually had a strophic and metric form. Often the composer (*melodos*) and poet of a *troparion* or *sticheron* was one and the same person, a union frequently to be found in the entire Near East.

The *'enyane* are strophic antiphons, originally intercalations in psalms and canticles. Having gained almost entire independence from their biblical framework, they developed into refrain poems, and afterward abandoned even this last link to canonic literature.[38] It has been pointed out, however, that, unlike the genuine hymn forms of the Syrian Churches, the *'enyane* have preserved a greater freedom of metre and stanza, and so are frequently 'irregular' from the metrical point of view and therefore might be considered free poems.[39] These 'irregularities' can be grouped according to three principles: (1) unequal number of accents in each line; (2) unequal number of metric units and (3) introduction of foreign elements into an otherwise established scheme.

Seen from a wider angle, these irregularities are typical of certain poetic trends all over the Near East. While idea and principle of the antiphon originated in Catholic Christianity, it was again the dualistic character of the two continents, Orient and Occident, which designed the diverse liturgical-poetic forms. The East displayed a freer attitude, while a more conservative and rigid one is discernible in the Western orbit.

The Synagogue, too, inspired various types of singable poetry. Generally speaking, its literary creations correspond more to the poems of the Eastern Churches than to those of the Western. We saw the liturgical-poetic pattern of the antiphon evolve as a form common to all Christianity. None the less, not religious but ethnic forces shaped antiphonal forms of their own in the national Churches of the Orient. The liturgy of the Synagogue created forms accepted by Judaism all over the world. Again, in its two chief centres of the first millennium, in Palestine and in

Babylonia, these commonly accepted forms developed along different lines.

It was the liturgical function of the antiphon to express thoughts for meditation by those who recite the psalms. Amalarius calls the antiphon the soul and the psalm itself the body of sacred chant.[40] This would affirm the *associative* character of the antiphon. It might impress thoughts upon the faithful that are elaborated in the psalm; or it might remind them of the significance of that particular day, or of the present liturgical moment. Thus, the practices of insertion or refrain or repetition serve to intensify the leading idea of the antiphon.

Most of the various forms of the synagogal *piyyut* serve exactly the same purpose, be they intercalations between psalm verses or insertions between the ancient established prayers or separate memorials for festival occasions. Another function, the didactic-legalistic, was assumed by the *piyyutim* from the fifth to the seventh centuries when secular authorities prohibited instruction in and exegesis of scriptural and talmudic literature.[41] Since the *piyyutim* belong to the category of metrical hymns they will be discussed under that heading (Chapter VII).

Especially popular with the Jews were refrain poems; the Christian antiphon as well as the *troparion* and 'enyana belong to this type. Relatively early the Hebrew poet Ephodi praises the Hebrew forms for their aptitude in quoting biblical passages regularly and *in the original*. This probably may be a veiled criticism of the liturgical literature of Christianity which also quoted scripture in its refrain forms, but had to render it in translations.[42]

The refrain forms, antiphons and many early forms of liturgical poetry reflect the general tendency toward *centonization* of sacred texts, a tendency to which the Synagogue succumbed no less than the Churches. We have used the term *cento* before, and in the following we shall somewhat expand on its meaning. Almost all antiphons, 'enyane, and *piyyutim* are products of centonizations of sacred texts, yet their methods are as different as are their places in their respective liturgies. To combine an Old Testament verse with its Christological exposition, as is frequently the case in the Roman *Antiphonale*, is a course natural to the ideas of Christian liturgy. The Jewish centonization, at first content with stringing scriptural verses of similar thought together in a series (as in a *Seliha*), later blended midrashic, cabbalistic and legalistic passages, not contained in the biblical canon, together with scriptural verses or with mere allusions to them. Thus, a sort of pastiche style, highly characteristic of medieval Hebrew poetry, came into being. Its chief methods are centonization and allusion; its aim is multiple and emphatic association, constantly reminding the faithful of the specific liturgical occasion. This elaborate type of centonization has its counterpart in Byzantine and Syrian poems. To illustrate likeness and divergence in Jewish and Christian centonization, we shall give here a few examples. First, a simple biblical cento:

Jewish	*Christological*
Daily morning service	Gradual and Alleluia of Easter Monday
Let the glory of the Lord endure for ever; let the Lord rejoice in His works. (Ps. 104 : 31.)	Haec dies quam fecit Dominus: exsultemus et laetemur in ea. (Ps. 118:24.)
Let the name of the Lord be blessed from this time forth and for ever more. From the rising of the sun unto the going down thereof the Lord's name is to be praised. The Lord is high above all nations, and His glory above the heavens. (Ps. 113:2, 3, 4.) Thy name, O Lord, endureth for ever, Thy memorial, O Lord, throughout all generations, etc. (Ps. 135:13.)[43]	Dicat nunc Israel, quoniam bonus: quoniam in saeculum misericordia eius. (Ps. 118:2.) Angelus Domini descendit de caelo: et accedens revolvit lapidem, et sedebat super eum. (Matt. 28:2.)[44]
	English Translation
	This is the day which the Lord hath made: we will be glad and rejoice thereon. (Ps. 118:24.) Let Israel then say so; because to eternity endureth His kindness. (Ps. 118:2.) For the angel of the Lord descended from heaven, and came and rolled back the stone from the door, and sat upon it. (Matt. 28:2.)

The connective element of the Christian example is the idea of resurrection. In the Jewish example certain words are repeated over and over in different phrases, so as to establish a kind of 'progressive parallelism'[45] whereby the last word of a sentence forms the beginning of a new one. Unfortunately, this cannot be shown in the translation.

Another example of this peculiar style, florid with scriptural and legendary allusions, is compared with a Byzantine *troparion*:

Jewish	*Byzantine*
For Tabernacles	For Christmas
The Lord of his masters [Jacob] made haste, twice did He dwell in tabernacles, and Thou didst protect him against Aram [i.e. Laban] and Esau; hence his descendants went first to Sukkot [after the Exodus] and Thou hast covered them with a sevenfold, precious canopy.	Star, arisen out of Jacob [Jesus] Master, Thou hast filled with joy The wise star-gazers [Magi] who have learned the words Of Balaam, ancient seer, and they brought to Thee The first fruits of the Gentiles Manifest to whom Thou didst receive them, bringing welcome gifts.

Another example, also with Christological intent:

For Tabernacles	For Epiphany
(When beholding the ritual Citrus-fruit and the palm branches)	Once was the Jordan river, O Elisha, turned back by the mantle of Elijah, as he was received up, and the waters were parted hither and thither; and the watery way became a dry path, of a type indeed of Baptism, by which we cross the passage of the stream of Life. Christ hath appeared in Jordan, to hallow the waters.[47]
With the beautiful fruit I think of the wonderful sage [Abraham]	
With the Palm branches of the soul destined for sacrifice [Isaac]	
With the myrrh of the honest one, who won immortal life [Enoch]	
With the beautiful fruit I mean to atone for the thoughts of my heart	
With the palm-branches I atone for the insolent pride of my back	
With the myrrh I atone for the [moral] decay of eye and heart.[46]	

We give these illustrations in order to demonstrate how widely the results of a common practice (cento) may diverge if the guiding idea, the liturgical purpose, is different.

While biblical lore remained the common point of departure, the Jewish poets soon turned to poetic exegesis and to the Midrash, occasionally also to allegorical interpretation of a custom, as one may see in the last example. The Oriental Christian poet uses instead of rabbinic exegesis, Christological interpretation of the Old Testament, and frequently also metaphors and allegories for this purpose. Basically this difference spells the antagonism between Jewish Midrash and Old Testament Christology. Hence, the liturgical function of these pieces differs considerably. In the Jewish tradition, midrashic elements are emphasized to embellish the legalistic meaning of the feast; in the Christian, Old Testament elements are allegorized to link the new (Christian) feast with ideas of the Christian Canon.

Summing up, we might say that the basic form of antiphon, common to all Christianity, has neither literary nor musical correlates in the Synagogue, although both nuclei (antiphony and centonization) were concepts inherent to synagogal liturgy. Musically, only one direct, but independent parallel presents itself, namely the rule of R. Yehudai Gaon (ca. 720), prescribing that the two eulogies, which open and close any larger prayer, shall be chanted in the same mode. The chant of the prayer between, if sung at all, should be of a 'different, but not too different' mode.[48] The main reason why the form type of the antiphon did not attain the status and importance in Judaism that it commands in the

Churches lies in the monopolistic ambitions of the *hazan*, who, while emphasizing and expanding all soloistic forms, was inclined to suppress or to minimize all choir parts of the liturgy. Yet the creative freedom of liturgical poetry enjoyed by the Synagogue and the Eastern Churches, in contrast to the prevailing rigorism of the Roman Church, was conducive to the creation of poetic structures which are fairly common to Oriental Christianity and Judaism.[49] Some of them will be discussed in the next chapter.

Chanted Prayer

This category comprises most of the dogmatic hymnic prayers, provided they are chanted plainly. Some of the very oldest texts belong to this group, and much sweat and blood went into their redaction and acceptance. They are all chanted in free rhythm and no boastful artistry was allowed to compromise the dogmatic preciseness of these texts. They may be chanted by a soloist or by a choir.

Famous specimens of such prayers in the Synagogue are the *Sh'ma'* *Yisrael* ('Hear, O Israel') and its surrounding eulogies, the prayer of the *'Amida* (eighteen eulogies), of which the first three eulogies with the Thrice-Holy are especially outstanding prayers in Jewish worship, the *'Alenu* ('It is our duty'), and the *Kaddish* (Great Doxology).

In the Roman Church this category is represented by some parts of the *Ordinarium Missae*, excluding the *Kyrie; viz. Gloria, Credo, Sanctus,* and certain special items, such as the *Te Deum,* and the so-called Lesser Doxology, *Gloria Patri.* Only part of these texts is scriptural, like the analogous prayers of the Synagogue; most of them originated in the first four centuries of Christianity. They are without metre or rhyme and represent the basis and mainspring of the daily worship. The chant of the *Pater Noster* (Lord's Prayer)[50] displays a more primitive structure.

The Byzantine Mass has in its pre-Anaphora part the three ancient chants *Monogenes* (One-born), *Trisagion* (Holy God, Strong God, Immortal God, not to be confused with the Thrice-Holy or Tersanctus) and the Cherubic hymn, to which may be added the Nicene Creed (*Credo*), the Doxa (*Gloria*), and the Thrice-Holy.

The relatively recent Syriac-Jacobite Mass shows, in general, the same categories and rubrics as the Byzantine Church.[51] The Syrian-Nestorian rite, whose *ordo* is considerably older, dating back to Ishoyab

III (about 650), displays elements not to be found in the other Churches.[52] These are the so-called Canon which is chanted on special Sundays and some plainly chanted prayers of the *Hudra* (cycle), the great *Proprium* of the Nestorian rite.[53]

A somewhat intermediary position is held by the Armenian liturgy. Most of its chants correspond in text and function to the Byzantine order, but a few significant exceptions should be mentioned here:

(a) The *Jashou* psalms (Armenian *Saghmos Jashou*, 'psalms of dinner-time') are sung before the prophets' lesson, and are comparable to the Gradual or Tract of the Roman liturgy. They are frequently centonizations of three or four different psalms.

(b) The *Ktzord* (Arm. juncture) is the refrain of an antiphon; the latter itself is called *phokh* (alternation) which clearly indicates the original practice of alternating choirs.

Both types belong to the oldest, early Christian forms of musical liturgy; some of them may even date to pre-Christian times.[54]

Certain parallels present themselves rather conspicuously for textual or musical comparison. Liturgically, the following prayers show close kinship; a few typical instances may illustrate the point.

Te Deum—*Modim* ('We thank')
Sanctus—*Cherubikon* = *Kedusha* (Thrice-Holy)
Credo—*Symbolum Athanasianum*—'*Alenu* ('Upon us is the duty')

The *Te Deum* is one of the finest examples of centonized paraphrases of biblical verses.[55] The prayer *Modim* gives vent to a mood of praise and thanksgiving and shows a similarity in its execution, the genuflection.[56] The Byzantine *Euchologion* refers to it under the name of *Metanoia* and prescribes three genuflections where the Jewish liturgy knows but one. The Christian practice must have been very old, because the Mishna already forbids the repetition of the word *Modim* or of its genuflection, as a heretical Gnostic ceremony. Certain Judaeo-Christian interpolations still seem to have survived in the year 300 and had to be banished again.[57]

The *Sanctus* or the 'Triumphal Hymn', as well as the Byzantine *Cherubikon*, the Syriac *Qudasha* and the synagogal *Kedusha* are elaborations upon the verses Isa. 6:3 and Ezek. 3:12. Naturally, most of the

Churches, except the Roman liturgy, have added Christological traits to these Old Testament passages. All of the Christian liturgies combine Isa. 6:3 with Mark 11:10 and Ps. 118:25 and 26. Innumerable are the sacred poems which this angelological vision has evoked in pious poets of Christianity and Judaism. In liturgical music, too, the *Sanctus* together with its derivates has emerged as one of the most powerful and glorious praises. As one of the oldest parts of the Mass, if not *the* oldest, it warrants extensive examination, to be given in a later chapter.

The similarity between *Credo* and *'Alenu* is rather superficial; only the beginnings show a certain interdependence, emphasizing the belief in One God, the creator of all things. The rest of the prayers contain the doctrines of the two respective religions. The liturgical functions of these prayers stand out in sharp contrast to each other. In the liturgy of the Roman Church the *Credo* is the centre of the Mass, while the *'Alenu* stands at the very end of the service in the Jewish liturgy. Only on the High Holydays, for which it originally was composed (probably in the third or early fourth century), does it regain its prior majesty during the most exalted part of the worship.[58] Its introduction to the daily prayer book was no more than a matter of defensive and apologetic policy. It became a bitter necessity during the persecutions of the crusades, and we know of many an occasion when the Jewish martyrs died with the song of *'Alenu* upon their lips. Thus, it is not surprising that its solemn melody has survived up to the present day, and that the Roman Church took it over. (See Part II, Chapter VI.) As the *'Alenu* stresses the distinctive mission of Israel to carry the idea of pure monotheism, so does the *Credo* emphasize Christianity's distinctive doctrines. Hence it was and is called a *symbolum*, which originally meant 'a distinctive mark'.[59]

FORMS WITH EXTENDED MELISMATA
('ORNATE PSALMODY')

This category was probably the second phase of ecclesiastical or synagogal chant. To the first phase belong simple psalmody, cantillation of Scripture and chanted prayer together with pure melismatic forms. Hybrid types, in which the melismatic element prevailed, and hymnic-metrical forms constitute the second. Rhymed poetry, as sequences, tropes, etc., characterize the third phase which is contemporary to the development of primitive polyphony in Occidental music. In this book only the first two phases are considered, since after the tenth century the Church had completed the process of emancipation from the Synagogue.

Again, the relation between note and word serves as measure and criterion. As we shall encounter the most variegated attempts of blending psalmodic and melismatic expressions in the forms now under discussion, it will be impossible to establish very distinct categories.

IN THE SYNAGOGUE

Here the degree of melismatic tendency is determined neither by the poetic structure nor the subject-matter of the individual prayer. The decisive factor, at least in the first millennium, seems to have been the liturgical occasion or season. Thus, some reports praise the 'extended modulations' of the cantor during the holyday season, whereas the same prayer was rendered plainly on ordinary workdays or Sabbaths. We find the same tendency in those chants of the Church which form integral parts of daily worship. A simple tone of the Magnificat exists, but also the *Toni solemnes*, which, 'in great feasts of the first or second class may be used'.[60] Likewise, many prayers of the Synagogue undergo complete transformations of their musical performance when chanted on feastdays. Another, more negative, observation can be made. Only such prayer texts which are not in strict metre, or where the metre can be disposed of easily by the singer, lend themselves to melismatic embellishment. This point became relevant in the controversy which accompanied the introduction of strictly metrical poems, and consequently of strictly metrical tunes.[61]

Seen historically, the ascendancy of prevalently melismatic psalmodies accompanied the decline of congregational singing and the dominance of the musical liturgy by the *hazan*. This development was all but completed by the tenth or eleventh century. Significantly enough, the term chosen for these elaborate melismatic forms was *hižana*,[62] obviously derived from the word *hazan*. A Jewish convert to Islam, Samuel ben Yahya (twelfth century) used that term in such a connexion.[63]

In some of these *hazanic* forms certain typical phrases recur and give specific character to whole parts of the liturgy. Somewhat analogous structures occur in the Byzantine *Typikon*. Such resemblances touch, of course, only the surface of these prayers. We quote here two instances in juxtaposition:

Authorized Prayer Book, p. 73	*Typikon*
But Thou art holy, O Thou who dwellest amid the praises of Israel. And *one cried to another*, and said, Holy, holy, holy is the *Lord of hosts*; the *whole earth* is full of His glory. And they receive sanction *the one from the other*, and say, *Holy* in the *highest* heavens, the place of divine abode; *holy upon earth*, the work of His might; holy for ever and to all eternity is the *Lord of hosts*; *the whole earth is full of the radiance of His glory*. Then a wind lifted me up, and I heard behind me the voice of a great rushing: Blessed be the glory of the Lord from His place, etc.[64]	We sanctify Thee, who sittest above the Seraphim and Cherubim, and the multitudes of their host. And each one, covered with six wings, cries to the other: Holy, Holy, Holy is the Lord of hosts; heaven and earth are full of Thy glory. Hosánna in the highest. Blessed be He who cometh in the name of the Lord. Holy is He, who dwelleth in the highest of heavens . . . holy is the Lord of hosts here and all over the world, henceforth and for evermore![65]

Such recurrent phrases were also apt to become the vehicles for typical recurrent melodic formulas. And it was probably this correlation of repeated phrases in text and music that became responsible for the birth of the new musical technique of 'leitmotifs' in the Synagogue. Indeed this device is another remarkable facet of the generally associative method of the synagogal liturgy and pertains to texts as well as to their chant. Unfortunately, these literary associations are manifest only in Hebrew.

Most of the *hazanic* forms appeared after the seventh century and reached their peak during the eleventh and twelfth centuries. The oldest pieces are based literally or ideologically upon a scriptural verse or, frequently, on a midrash. This fact forms the *terminus a quo* for the introduction of recurrent melismata in originally psalmodic types. The process must have started in the seventh or eighth century and expanded gradually despite rabbinic opposition. Characteristic of their musical performance is the 'limited improvisation' by the cantor, along certain fixed modal lines, a practice familiar to all music of the Near East. Usually, the melismata embellish the beginning and the end of the piece, while its middle part is chanted in more or less plain psalmodic chant. The opening or strophic refrain remains the last element of responsive singing. However, there may have been considerable variations in the individual performances, due to standing local traditions.

IN THE BYZANTINE AND SYRIAN CHURCHES

Several scholars, among them Cardinal Pitra, Wellesz, Tillyard and others, have stressed the Semitic character of the Byzantine liturgy.[66]

The question in what forms this spirit finds its most adequate expression will be discussed briefly at this point.

In order to appreciate fully the parallels between the Greek and the synagogal forms, we must briefly analyse the cultural and liturgic background of both. In the Byzantine Empire monasticism attained the summit of theological and political power; practically all of the great theologians, writers, historians, etc., were monks. It was only natural that the liturgy, too, was subjected to their influence. Thus it happened that the monastic element, in no other way comparable with the status of the *hazan*, brought about the same results: the singer prevailed over the liturgical idea. In both Christianity and Judaism the theological superiors opposed this development and in both cases they were defeated. Only the collapse of the Byzantine Empire ended the monastic rule, exactly as the gradual decline of Jewish Orthodoxy terminated the dominant rule of the cantor by 1920.

A close examination of the practice of performance reveals more analogies. Up to the thirteenth century the *hazan* and the *paitan* (poet) were combined in one person, as were the *melodos* and poet in Byzantium up to the tenth century:[67] there, the professional soloist had a higher standing than in the Roman liturgy. This factor was conducive to a semi-improvisatory performance by the *hazan*. He was limited to certain basic modes and formulas, but free to elaborate upon them. With reference to the later [*sic*] form of the Kanon, Wellesz makes this observation:

> The composer did not have to compose an entirely different tune for a new Kanon; his task was rather that of a modest artisan who wished to add to an admired model something which seems permissible to him as an intensification . . . or a small variation. . . .[68]

This amounts to the principle of 'limited improvisation', for which certain pre-existing musical formulas (or *maqams*) are indispensable. Quoting Wellesz again from a recent article:

> I have found that Byzantine melodies are not composed in a mode as the Greek melodies are supposed to have been, but that the use of a certain group of formulas gives each melody its character, which is called *echos* or mode. The principle of the formulas was first discovered by Idelsohn in his study of the *maqams* in Arabic music, and for some time such groups were simply called *maqams*. My own investigations have shown that as a principle of melody construction the formulas are characteristic of the music of the Eastern Church.

They are also characteristic of the pre-Gregorian melodies in the West and of those groups of Gregorian melodies whose oriental origin is obvious. . . .[69]

The musical practice of 'limited improvisation' based upon the prevalence of standing or wandering melismata, has its poetic counterpart in the Byzantine and Hebrew forms of *Kontakion* and *Keroba* respectively.

The mottoes or intonations of the *Kontakia*, like those of the *Kerobas*, usually set the pattern for the whole poem. Hence it became a natural practice to borrow the tune of the motto or of the refrain from some older, more authoritative composition, in order to enhance the prestige of the new piece and make it, at the same time, tradition bound. Frequently, the familiar direction appears in the manuscripts—'to be sung to the melody of . . .'. This principle of contrafacts, called *hirmos* in Byzantine hymnody, is very old. It occurs far back, as certain superscriptions of the Psalter will refer to older tunes, e.g. Ps. 8, 9, 22, 45, etc. It was, of course, as familiar to the *hazanim* as it was to the Byzantine *melodoi*. The Hebrew term corresponding to the Byzantine *hirmos* and the Syrian *riš-qolo* is *ne'ima* while the Arabic term is *lahan*.[70]

It was Wellesz again who suggested that the incipits of the *Kontakia*, when paraphrasing a verse of the Psalter, might still preserve ancient Jewish or Syrian psalmodies in their music.[71] This hypothesis is sound and will be confirmed when analysed. (See Part II, Chapters VI and VII.)

It is not easy to define exactly the liturgical function and the spiritual substance of the *Kontakion* form. At best, we could approximate it by comparing it with a poetic homily, or, to be more exact, with a versified midrash.

Like its predecessor, the sermon of the early Church and the Synagogue, it had its place in the Office after the Lesson from the Gospel. When Romanus begins his *Kontakion* on the Ten Virgins, we are instantly reminded of the scene in the Synagogue of Nazareth described by Luke in 4 : 16–22, when Jesus, after having read the Haftara from Isa. 61, begins his sermon with the words: 'This day is this scripture fulfilled in your ears. . . .' We can see a clear development from the sermon in the Synagogue to the early Christian homily of Melito, from this to the homily in poetical prose of Basil of Seleucia and his contemporaries, and finally to the poetical homily of Romanus.[72]

This careful and valuable exposition disregards an important link, the element of the Hebrew midrash. Since Jesus's midrashic parables, this category of homilies has increased its popularity in the Eastern Churches. To render these homilies in poetic form was a small step, but of great consequence. They have become the texts of most melismatic psalmodies.

There is some other evidence that confirms the assumption of the midrashic-homiletic origin of the *Kontakion*: the angelological line in both the *Kontakia* and early *Kerobas*. How old this trend is can be seen from the various Jewish and early Christian elaborations on the Thrice Holy (Isa. 6:3) as we find them in ancient *Kedushas* and *Trisagia*. The famous *Cherubikon* of the Byzantine liturgy represents that type of Christological elaboration.[73] There are many more signs of the close interrelation between the early Greek Church and the Synagogue. Liturgical terms were borrowed by the Synagogue, such as the word *Kontakion* (Hebrew, *Kontak*), the term for the cyclic poem *Kyklarion* (Hebrew, *Kuklar*), and the very word liturgy was taken from the Byzantine vocabulary. The Byzantines, on their part, used Hebrew words, such as *Hekhal* (Sanctuary), *Levita* (Levite), etc. Moreover, the syllables of paradigms for the Byzantine *octoechos* (system of Psalm Tones), *neannoe*, *nanane*, etc., are of Hebrew origin, as I have demonstrated elsewhere.[74] We shall see later on that not only the paradigms but the entire modal system of the *octoechos* is of ancient Syro-Judaean extraction.

The use of musical instruments was forbidden in the Byzantine Church, as it was in the Synagogue. Chrysostom has no foundation whatsoever for his futile polemics and attacks on the Jews for their alleged use of instrumental music in the Temple, which, in his opinion, was only a divine concession to 'their weakness and stupidity'. He warned all Christians against imitating Jewish practices and customs.[75] Considering the close geographical neighbourhood, the many parallel trends in the two liturgies and the various transfusions which occurred, he must have had compelling reasons for such warnings. In this connexion, the legal formula of renunciation, which was obligatory for all converts from Judaism to the Byzantine Church, is of signal importance: 'I hereby renounce all customs, rites, legalisms, unleavened breads . . . Sabbaths, and superstitions, and *all hymns and chants* which are observed in the synagogues'.[76] This, indeed, epitomizes clearly the state of affairs between the Byzantine Church and the Synagogue.

The three rites of the Syrian Church, viz. the Jacobites (Monophysites), the Maronites and the Nestorians, two of which abandoned the old Church during the fifth century, their dogmatic and liturgical diversities notwithstanding, have developed but one type of sacred poetry and music, in which no specific group characteristics are manifest. The three principal categories of psalmody (cantillation), hymnody and melismatic chant are represented. From the literary point of view, the introduction of isosyllabic metre tended to efface the borderline between psalmody and hymnody, since it is visible but not audible, and therefore leaves music unaffected. From the musical point of view, pure melismatic forms are rare, since the principle of isosyllabism which prevails in the liturgical poetry of Syria is antagonistic to autonomous forms of music, such as extended coloraturas. Due to the lack of clear definitions, it is not easy to categorize the variegated and multiple forms of Syrian chanted poetry by one single criterion. Hence, it is not surprising to encounter, even in learned literature, a good deal of confusion and vagueness.[77]

If anything specific could be said about the Nestorian Church, further toward the East than the others and dangerously near to Iranian culture, it would be the fact that it displays a certain disinterest in all liturgical music. True, at the School of Nisibis, that famous academy of Nestorian theology, provision was made for a 'Reading Master' (*Maqreyana*) who also was in charge of the singing.[78] One of the teachers of Nisibis, Thomas (of Edessa?) wrote a book which bore the title *Dalevat Qale* (*Against the Tones*) and was a treatise against Church music.[79]

The liturgical poetry of all Syrian Churches has a rather flexible status in the ritual; a poem (*madrasha* or *'enyana*) may or may not be performed on special occasions or in certain places. Furthermore, different local traditions make for even more variety and confusion.

None the less, Syrian Christianity has made two outstanding contributions to musical liturgy: the new, isosyllabic metric hymn forms (to be discussed in the next chapter) and their liturgico-musical correlate, the *octoechos*.

Originally, the term *octoechos* was applied to a collection of hymns to be performed on eight successive Sundays. In later times this term was understood in a purely musical sense as the designation of the eight modes of a supposedly uniform system in all Syrian (and Byzantine) Churches. Its influence and dispersion cannot be overrated. Like the Syrian Church and its literature, whose historic function was that of an intermediator and propagator rather than of a creator, so the *octoechos*, itself not a Syrian creation, was of signal importance in building that Sacred Bridge from Syria to Europe and the Occident. The genesis and development of this system of modality will be examined in the second part of this book (Chapter II).

ORNATE PSALMODY IN THE ROMAN CHURCH

In historical perspective, the solo-psalmody of the primitive stage of Christianity was replaced by choral-psalmody and its various forms (antiphony, response, etc.). With the systematic training of ecclesiastic singers the soloist again claimed his right, with or without the collaboration of the choir. In the Roman Church, no less than in Byzantium and the medieval Synagogue, it was the 'professional' who extended and sometimes overdid the florid style. Yet he was held in check.

In the Roman liturgy, psalmodic and melismatic styles were welded into an organic synthesis in which the melismata, no longer modest functional embellishments, sometimes predominate. The main forms of this category are: the Introit, the Communion, the Gradual-Response of the Mass, the Offertory, and the Tract. The Gradual and the Tract belong to an older stratum than the other forms; they are simply elaborations of the psalmody of the Church's prime age (the Tract originally being a remnant of the Gradual).[80] The other forms are creations of the period between the fourth and the seventh centuries, at least in their present version. The soloist reigns supreme in the Tract and also dominates the Offertory; in other forms he is only an incidental, rather than an integral, factor.

Distribution of Psalm Verses

We encounter a magnificent expansion of the melismatic element wherever no strict limits were set to the art of the soloist, as in the Tract and the Offertory. Here the melismata constitute direct manners of expression. They are a proud array, not merely a functional part of the melody; they now set the melodic pattern and do not merely follow it, as in the simpler structures. Hence, they rightly may be considered 'open' forms in contradistinction to refrain or response types, the 'closed' ones, where the choir restricts the activity of the soloist. Apart from musical aspects, there exist genuine liturgical ties between the various texts of ornate Psalmody. A. Gastoué and, more convincingly, P. Wagner, have demonstrated that Introit, Gradual, Offertory and

Communion of all ancient feasts and the Pentecost season are inter-related by textual association. In some cases, as on the first Sunday in Quadragesima or on the first Sunday in Advent, the texts of all four forms are drawn from the very same Psalm.[81] The following example, the Proper for the first Sunday in Quadragesima, will illustrate this fact.[82]

Introit	Verse	Gradual	Verse	Tract	Offertory	Verse	Communion
Invocabit (Ps. 91:15)	Qui habitat (Ps. 91:1)	Angelis suis (Ps. 91:11)	In manibus (Ps. 91:12)	Qui habitat (Ps. 91:1) (entire psalm)	Scapulis suis (Ps. 91:4)	Scapulis suis (Ps. 91:4)	Scapulis suis (Ps. 91:4)

The Leitmotif

In the selection of the texts one recognizes instantly the principle of association, the forerunner of the 'leitmotif'. This is also, as we remember, one of the most effective devices of the Liturgy of the Synagogue. Here it has created an integration of the whole musical substance of which only faint traces are discernible in the Gregorian Chant. Evidently, the 'leitmotif' idea appealed to the musicians of Synagogue and Church equally. Perhaps it was due to the emancipation of the Gregorian Chant from the Orient (after the ninth century), that this device was not fully implemented in the Church.

The texts of the Tract and of the Gradual-Response are either excerpts from the Psalter or simple centonizations from other scriptural books. No Tract and only one Gradual shows metrical structure.[83] This fact alone would indicate the oldness of the two forms apart from other archaic features common to them. The name Tract (*Tractus*) itself betrays its origin from a time when the Byzantine influence was still a potent factor; it is actually a translation of the Greek term *hirmos* (train, tract).[84] This term indicated a typical melody pattern, which was placed at the beginning of a hymn and was applied to its stanzas. The Tract has preserved certain elements of that principle of construction, containing recurrent and pattern-like melismata, and was always restricted to two modes. Consequently, the rule of the *Ordo Romanus*, to sing tracts bilingually (in Latin and Greek) on Holy Saturday, that most archaic of all liturgical occasions, cannot surprise us.[85]

The Tract

As for its liturgical function, the Tract is substituted for the Alleluia on special days of penitence and mourning. It is, therefore, closely linked to the liturgical season between Septuagesima and Easter, the time of the *Alleluia clausum*. None the less, we encounter in the Tract texts like 'Jubilate Deo', 'Laudate Dominum', 'Benedicite', etc., which seem to contradict the spirit of the Lent season. Remarkable also is the Tract 'Attende coelum et loquar' (Deut. 32:1) for Holy Saturday; this is actually one of the fourteen canticles of the general Christian liturgy. On this day, however, a day of mourning and preparation, it is preceded by two other Tracts, Exod. 15 and Isa. 5:1–7, which are both canticles, and they are followed by two *Hallel* psalms (118, 117). All this before the lesson that proclaims the resurrection (Matt. 28). How can this selection be explained, not exegetically, but historically?

As pointed out before, the lessons of Holy Saturday combine elements of the Day of Atonement and of Passover.[86] The former corresponded to its status as the greatest Christian fast-day, the latter to its calendaric place, the Easter-Passover cycle. The same combination of Jewish and primitive Christian calendaric institutions can be seen in the succession of Tract and Psalms of Holy Saturday: Exod. 15 is the allusion to Passover, as the two *Hallel* Psalms (here named Tract) are remnants of the Jewish Easter liturgy. The two other Tracts (Isa. 5 and Deut. 32) belong to the ritual of the High Holydays, and, what is more important, to the Temple ritual.[87] Even the wording of the Latin text attests to the venerable age of this rubric, since Deut. 32 ('attende coelum', etc.) *is not quoted according to the Vulgate*, but according to the archaic Vetus Itala ('audite coeli, quae loquor'). Apparently, this version of the Tract was, at the time that the Vulgate was introduced, already well established and could not be replaced by the new version. All of these facts lead to one and the same conclusion: probably some of the Tracts of Holy Saturday are remnants, perhaps the only ones left, of the ancient Temple ritual. In this case, the preservation of so ancient a liturgical institution can only be the result of Judaeo-Christian efforts which, for sentimental reasons, strove to retain certain reminders of the greatest festival of their people.[88] At any rate, the combination of Passover and Atonement rubrics dates back to the primitive age of Christianity; and the melodies of the quoted Tracts, which without exception belong to one, viz. the eighth, Tone, and display archaic traits, support our hypothesis from the musical point of view. (See *infra* Part II, Chapter V.)

The performance of the Tract was strictly soloistic and must be considered a remnant of the cantorial chant of the ancient Synagogue.

The Gradual-Response

Not much different is the history and function of the Gradual-Response. Here the Graduals of Easter Week may serve as the starting point for our discussion. All of them are based upon Ps. 118, using different verses in connexion with the motto 'Haec est dies' (Ps. 118:24). Remembering that this psalm is Christianity's Messianic hymn *par excellence*, and at the same time the prescribed Passover Psalm of Judaism, the transposition and Christological interpretation of its passages must again be the concerted work of Judaeo-Christians.[89] Moreover, all these Graduals (and the antiphon upon the same text of Easter Sunday at Vespers) show exactly the same melody for both the preamble and the psalm verse. These uniformities, too, are indicative of the ancient tradition of the Easter Graduals. The chanting of the whole of Ps. 118 may have been customary in the early centuries of the Church. Today only fragments have survived, like vertebrae of a fossil from which the scientist has to reconstruct the anatomy of the whole organism. It is clear that all 'closed' forms with recurrent refrains were liable to be curtailed, since no 'cut' would affect the musical substance. The intonation of the psalm verse is always the same, no matter whether it is applied to a verse in the beginning or in the end. In 'open', especially in soloistic forms, abridgements do not occur frequently. One of the reasons was the soloist who did not want to be cut short and a Tract or an Offertory gave him the opportunity of singing vast portions of scriptural texts. Thus, the individual soloistic form always is more extended and less abridged than 'closed' or antiphonal structures, including such hymns of a somewhat later date which were built on a strophic pattern.

Abridgement of Psalm Texts

At the present time the Introit and the Gradual contain only one psalm verse. When and why were responsorial psalms reduced to single verses? Thus far this question has not been answered satisfactorily. Perhaps a comparison with the conditions in the Synagogue might suggest a hypothetical solution. Comparing a medieval report of a solemn service on the occasion of an exilarch's inauguration with other descriptions of ordinary services, we notice that the *hazan* cut short everything which was not of a melismatic nature, that is, he chanted the florid opening and closing of a prayer and recited the bulk of it either in a rapid psalmodic manner or only 'in an undertone'.[90] In the development of

Jewish liturgy, all forms originally of responsorial character, except those where the soloist himself chanted the refrain, were subject to curtailment and gradually were usurped by the soloist. This was especially true of the melismatic components. At present it is rare for a melismatic passage to be immediately repeated; yet repetition is the very essence of psalmodic style.

Thus, in the development of synagogal liturgy, the intrusion of melismatic structures in the beginning and ending of a psalm led to the curtailment of its proper psalmodic rendering. If we now, as a working hypothesis, assume that an analogous process took place in the Church, the following facts seem to confirm it.

The Germanus Parisiensis Codex, quoted in Duchesne, already uses the term 'a response is sung' (no longer a psalm) and the Ambrosian liturgy calls such a rendering a *psalmulus*, which means a little psalm.[91] Since Germanus died in 576, the abridged psalmodic rendering must by then have been a well-established practice, as corroborated by contemporary documents of the Mozarabic Church (Missale Gothicum). This reduction of psalmodic performance coincided with the triumphant rise of the melismatic style.

The *Apostolic Constitutions* already contain a passage that might be interpreted as an abridgement of the psalm text, a practice of the fourth century.[92] Since the melismatic style was always considered 'the custom of the Oriental Church' and the *Apostolic Constitutions* originated in Syria, we are inclined to consider the curtailment of the psalm text as contemporary with the earliest period of Christian melismatic songs, that is before 300.[93] The Gradual, an established rubric since Apostolic times, was then more and more confined to a few psalm verses surrounded by a rich melismatic framework.

The Introit and the Communion are of more recent date than the Gradual. The earliest passages which might be considered as references to these forms are found in the *Liber Pontificalis*. According to this not always reliable source, Pope Celestine I (d. 432) had ordered the 150 Davidic Psalms to be chanted antiphonally before the Eucharist.[94] The Introit and the Communion have been subjected to abridgement; in the Introit, the psalm has been reduced to one verse, in the Communion it has frequently disappeared entirely. This was partly due to a general limitation of all chants that were not considered indispensable parts of the sacred ritual, and partly to the fact that *choral* psalmodies heavily taxed (in earlier times) the memory of the singers, and hence had to be reduced to a modicum. This, too, accounts for a great many differences of style which can be encountered in the Gregorian Chant: soloistic forms expand up to a certain point and choral melismata tend to be cut short.[95]

The Texts of the Introits

Venetianer's study, *Ursprung und Bedeutung der Prophetenlektion*, has a preamble, quoted above, which demonstrates certain parallels between the Introits of Quadragesima and the lessons of the four 'Special Sabbaths' which, like Quadragesima, precede Easter-Passover. These parallels do not refer to scriptural texts or quotations, but to their rabbinical exegesis, especially to the ancient *Pesiqta Rabbati*. Although I do not follow Venetianer in every instance, but accept only his principles, his theories convince me that the similarities disclosed in the following juxtapositions are the results of historical interplay:[96]

Four Special Sabbaths	Four Sundays of Quadragesima
I. Exod. 30:12–20 Ezek. 34:1–32 *PR* quotes Ps. 91:5 and 15 in connexion with Ezek.	I. Introit: 'Invocabit' (Ps. 91:15) at the same
II. Sabbath *Zakhor* (Remember) (First word of Deut. 25:17)	II. Sunday Introit: 'Reminiscere' (Ps. 25:6)
III. Sabbath *Parah* (Heifer) Ezek. 36:16–38 *PR* quotes Ps. 25:15 in connexion with Ezek. 36:20	III. Sunday Introit: 'Oculi Mei' (Ps. 25:15)
IV. Sabbath *Rosh hodesh* (New Moon) Isa. 66:1–24, in which the Introit occurs. *PR* quotes Ps. 122 from which the psalm verses of Introit and Gradual are derived	IV. Sunday Introit: 'Laetare Jerusalem' (Isa. 66:10–11) Verse: Ps. 122:1 Gradual: Ps. 122:1 Verse: Ps. 122:7

It is irrelevant whether the prophetic texts themselves or their exegesis were selected for apologetic purposes directed against Judaeo-Christianity. It is equally possible that it was Judaeo-Christianity, familiar with rabbinic tradition, which tried to follow it. If this be the case, some of the Roman Introits may easily be remnants of the Judaeo-Christian phase of Christianity.

Communion and Offertory

Neither the Communion nor the Offertory has a counterpart in the Jewish ritual. This is only natural, as both of these forms are inseparably connected with the Eucharistic act. The oldest Communion in the

Oriental Churches was stereotyped: Ps. 34:9 'O taste and see that the Lord is good', a rather literal allusion to the Communion. The chant of the Offertory was introduced by Augustine himself, in the African Church.[97] Since it is basically the accompaniment of an offering, we might search for parallels in the liturgy of the Temple, of which we know but little. Still the prayer during or after the sacrifice has been preserved in the Eulogy XVII of the 'Amida, where it is termed 'Aboda (service; sacrificial prayer).[98] Its idea approximates to the Communion of the tenth Sunday after Pentecost: 'May the sacrifice of righteousness, the offerings and the burnt offerings be acceptable upon thy altar, O Lord', which is a rather free translation of Ps. 51:21. The Alleluia of the same Sunday is based upon the famous verse of Ps. 65:2: 'For Thee a hymn is waiting in Zion, and there the vows will be paid in Jerusalem' (Te decet hymnus Deus in Sion, et tibi reddetur votum in Jerusalem). 'Votum' stands for a vow of sacrifice. This verse is also an integral part of both the Introit and the Gradual of the Requiem Mass, which has retained some archaic features. Otherwise, the texts of the Offertories and of the Communions do not necessarily show an organic connexion with the liturgical act. Much closer to the Jewish ritual is the Dominical Blessing of Sacrifice in the Armenian Church; it is quoted here in excerpt and compared with ancient Hebrew texts.

Synagogue	*Armenian Church*
Reminders of Temple service	Canon of Animal Sacrifice; Dominical Blessing
On account of our sins we were exiled from our land, and removed far from our country; we are unable to go up in order to appear and prostrate ourselves before Thee . . . in Thy chosen house, that great and holy Temple which was called by Thy name. . . .	For although man fell away and was driven from the beautiful garden . . . and lost his glory and honour through the wiles and deep malice of the traducer, Thou hast restored him.
Accept, O Lord our God, Thy people Israel and their prayers; restore the service to the oracle of Thy house; receive in love and mercy both the fire offerings of Israel and their prayer. And may the service of Thy people Israel be ever acceptable to Thee.[99]	Now therefore, our beneficent God, we pray Thee and with humble supplications implore of Thee, accept in Thy mercy this offering at our hands for the propitiation of Thine almighty will.[100]

As we have seen, archaic elements, even of pre-Christian origin, such as the sacrifice of the paschal lamb, or that of a fowl, together with the appropriate Judaistic eulogies are not rare in Armenian worship.[101]

All Offertories of the Roman Church solemnize their proximity to the Eucharistic act by their melismatic chant, which is often performed by a soloist and provided with an Alleluia ending. In this respect they show a close affinity to the strictly Alleluiatic forms which will be discussed presently.

PURE MELISMATIC FORMS

There has been occasion to point out the strange silence maintained by the oldest Jewish sources about chants before and after the scriptural lesson.[102] Its oldest source, the tractate *Soferim*, originated not before the seventh century, whereas the ancient (and general) Christian tradition of Alleluia singing during or after the lesson is documented since the third century. It is puzzling that the Hebrew term Alleluia was retained in the face of strong anti-Jewish opposition. Is there any indication regarding the manner in which Alleluia singing after the lesson was transmitted to the Church? (The general problem of the liturgical function of the Alleluia is not touched upon here and will be discussed in Chapter IX.)

In the oldest Hebrew texts only one Alleluiatic verse is mentioned after the lesson, namely Ps. 148 : 13–14, ending with the Hallelujah which forms an integral part of these verses. At the time of Pope Damasus I the Alleluia was limited to Eastertide;[103] yet there is no evidence that in the liturgy it was sung as an acclamation, separated from its original scriptural context. Thus, in Cassian's time, the Egyptian monks responded the Alleluia only after the chant of an Alleluiatic psalm.[104] When did the use of the isolated acclamation Alleluia become a regular practice? Tertullian is our first source; he relates that many faithful used to add the Alleluia as an exclamation after all psalms in prayer.[105] Three documents, originating shortly thereafter, shed light upon this practice. The first one says:

A Hebrew word they [the monks of Antioch] would add to every verse as from one mouth, so that one could believe they were not a multitude of men, but a reasonable united being, uttering a wonderful sound. . . .[106]

And Cassian writes about the monks of Egypt:

Some of them believed they ought to sing twenty or thirty psalms [during the nocturnes] whereby they would lengthen their melodies by adding certain modulations. . . . [107]

Conversely, we have Jerome's testimony concerning the Jewish practice of his own time:

> Up to this day it is the custom of the Jews not to add an Alleluia to any psalm, unless it is prescribed as belonging to that very psalm. We, however, are accustomed to use Alleluias quite indifferently in the psalms, be they now of historical content, or sigh with penitent tears, or demand victory over the enemy, or pray for delivery from anxiety.[108]

The Free Alleluia added to a Scriptural Verse

While these testimonies of the separation of the Alleluia from its scriptural text give us a determining point near A.D. 350, Sozomen (fifth century) confirms the fact that in the Roman liturgy, especially the Mass, the Alleluia was still limited to the Easter cycle, and probably to genuinely Alleluiatic verses.[109] These sources seem to indicate a two-fold tradition: (a) the monastic tradition of the East, whereby the Alleluia was detached from its original source and added without discrimination to any text at any time, and (b) the Roman ecclesiastical practice that, at least up to Gregory I, provided Alleluiatic psalms for all Masses of the Easter cycle. If this theory is correct, we should find certain discrepancies in the oldest texts or references of the Alleluiatic verses. Indeed, such divergences are manifest in the oldest manuscripts. P. Wagner, who approached the problem from a different angle, reached the same conclusion, namely, that the Alleluiatic *verse* (any verse, followed by an Alleluia) is an institution of the time *after* Gregory I.[110] The Alleluia before this time was either a freely added acclamation, a *Jubilus* as Augustine terms it, or an integral part of an Alleluiatic *psalm*. Since all writers insist that the first mentioned practice, the 'wordless hymn', is a custom of the Oriental Church, the oldest form of genuine Alleluia singing in the Roman liturgy before the 'Eastern infiltration' parallels exactly the synagogal practice: it was simply the chant of a psalm which contained the Alleluia in the scriptural text.

In the synagogue such psalms belonged to the service before the scriptural lesson;[111] where was their place in the third or fourth century of the Western Church? As far as we know, in the *Missa catechumenorum*, the very beginning of the service; after the *Kyrie* and the Collect, the lessons were read with the Gradual and an Alleluiatic psalm (at least at Easter time). It would seem as if the freely added Alleluia had made its way from Lauds into the Mass itself, under the decidedly Eastern monastic influence.

Only in a few of the oldest melodies of the Alleluia can we find traces of synagogal tradition. From the liturgical point of view, the Alleluia was a new creation of Christianity and only in one respect does it continue its original function: in the Temple of old, and in the contemporary Synagogue, it served as an incentive to popular response to texts which the congregation hardly knew and probably did not always understand. Thus, the freely added Alleluia became immensely popular, though never easy to sing, and had the aura of sanctity about it. P. Wagner concludes, after a comparison of some of the oldest codices with regard to Alleluiatic verses:

> There must have been reasons to supply the (wordless) Alleluia-Jubili with new texts; these reasons must lie in the original length of the pre-Gregorian Alleluia-chants. . . . They must have appeared to their redactor so rich in melismata, that he felt it necessary to render these songs more liturgical by adding psalm verses, without curtailing the tunes themselves.[112]

Dom Ferretti, O.S.B., reaches somewhat different conclusions in his *Esthétique grégorienne* with regard to expansions of the *Jubili*.

Texts of Alleluia Verses

Concerning the texts of the Alleluiatic verses two observations can be made, which to my knowledge have been overlooked by the Gregorian scholars heretofore:

(a) Only in a few cases are the texts of the Alleluiatic verses taken from original Hallelujah psalms; and these exceptions take place in the *Sanctorale*, the immovable part of the ecclesiastical calendar which is of more recent origin than the *Temporale*.

(b) On certain days the Tract or Alleluia verses stem from *Hallel* psalms: 1. Saturday in Ember Week of Lent (as Tract, Ps. 117); 2. Holy Saturday (as Tract, Ps. 117); 3. Saturday in Easter Week (as Alleluia Ps. 118:24); 4. Saturday before Pentecost (as Tract, Ps. 117); 5. Saturday in Ember Week after Pentecost (as Tract, Ps. 117); 6. Saturday in Ember Week of September (as Tract, Ps. 117).[113] This interesting limitation indicates the following development:

A. Saturdays, especially the Saturdays of Ember Weeks, retained rudiments of the *Hallel* psalms as Alleluia verses or Tracts.

B. The psalm verses forming these Tracts and Alleluias are chanted, as in the Synagogue, by a soloist.

C. Ember Saturdays contain rather archaic elements in the calendar and liturgy of the Roman Church.

Considering these points, is it not possible that these *Sabbata quatuor temporum* were the original bearers of the Alleluia verses, before the separation between Judaism and Christianity took place, and that the general practice of singing psalm verses with 'isolated' Alleluias originated in those ancient days of prayer?

The solution of this problem must be left to a liturgist who has access to the oldest codices and lists of Alleluia verses. If the connexion between the *Sabbata quatuor temporum* and the *Hallel* psalms could be established historically, it would shed an entirely new light upon the institution of the Sunday liturgy in general and the end of Judaeo-Christian tendencies in particular.

When, in the course of centuries, the melismatic element became so predominant in the Alleluias that the melodies of the *Jubili* (the wordless parts) could no longer be kept in memory by the singers, these melismata were provided with new, non-scriptural texts, made to fit these tunes in syllabic order—the so-called sequences. This development started in the eighth and ninth centuries, when the syllabic-hymnic style had already conquered an important part of the songbook of the Church. Later, when these monastic creations, the sequences, tropes and proses, began to threaten the ancient character of the Roman liturgy, most of them were eliminated at the Council of Trent. The older hymns and cognate syllabic forms, however, were retained.

Surveying the results of this chapter, it becomes clear that more elaborate prayer forms, with the exception of the genuine hymn forms, correspond to more melismatic chants; this holds true for the Synagogue as well as for the Church.

On the other hand, the more the prayers deviate from pure scriptural texts, the more their structure and spirit diverge into the various liturgies of the ecclesiastical bodies. Still, a large number of common elements remain in these prayers, both of biblical and post-biblical origin. The Syrian *'enyane*, the Byzantine *troparia*, and the Roman litanies exhibit these Judaistic remnants very clearly.

Quite different is the situation with reference to metrical hymns and other sacred poetry. There we shall find ourselves at the crossroads, for the *genius loci*, the inherent characteristics of the respective languages, and many additional elements make for considerable differences.

To understand and appreciate fully the increasing divergences as they appear in hymnic literature, we shall, in the following chapter, examine the hymn forms of the various liturgies.

NOTES CHAPTER VI

1. Robert Lach, *Beiträge zur Entwicklungsgeschichte der ornamentalen Melopoiie* (Vienna, 1913), Part I, Chapter I; Part II, Chapters II and III.

2. Cf. Chas. Ruelle, 'Le Chant gnostico-magique des sept voyelles grecques', in Combarieu, *Congrès international d'histoire de la musique* (Solesmes, 1901). E. Poirée, 'Chant des sept voyelles', ibid. A. Gastoué, op. cit., pp. 29 ff. K. Wachsmann, *Untersuchungen zum vorgregorianischen Gesang*, pp. 24–34. J. A. Montgomery, *Aramaic Incantations* (Philadelphia, 1913), pp. 147 f, 201, pp. 223 ff.

3. Cf. E. Littmann, 'Der Beduinentriller *lilili*', in *Wellhausen Festschrift*.

4. E. Wellesz, 'Die byzantinische und orientalische Kirchenmusik', in Adler, *Handbuch der Musikwissenschaft*, I, pp. 128 ff.

5. WGM, I, p. 61.

6. Augustine, *In Ps. 99* (PL, XXXVII, 1272).

7. Augustine, *In Ps. 32:5* (PL, XXXVI, 283).

8. Jerome, *In Ps. 32* (PL, XXVI, 970).

9. Varro, *De Lingua Latina*, ed. Müller, 6, 6, 68, p. 99. Boissac (*Diction. etymolog. de la lang. grecque*), as well as White and Riddle (Latin-English Dictionary, s.v. *jubilaeus*) hold that the Hebrew and the Latin stems come from a common Sanskrit root.

10. For the literature on this matter see W.-S., *HUCA*, XVI, p. 290, n.128 and 132; also E. Werner, 'The Hosanna in the Gospels', *JBL* (July 1946).

11. Cf. E. Wellesz, 'Words and Music in Byzantine Liturgy', *MQ* (July 1947), 302. Also the same author's 'Byzantine Music', *Proceedings of the Musical Association*, 1932, pp. 1 f, where he says: 'These hymns in their turn imitated the divine canticles sung unceasingly by the angels in heaven'.

12. Responsum to the Jewish Community of Huesca; cf. G.A. 215.

13. Cf. A. Gastoué, op. cit., pp. 74 ff.

14. Ibid.

15. WGM, III, pp. 366 ff.

16. *B. Taanith* I, 6, 7; ibid. II, 1.

17. Concerning the literature and the development of the *Selicha* see L. Zunz, *Literaturgeschichte der synagogalen Poesie*, pp. 17 ff.

18. The literature on the Syrian forms in Baumstark, *Geschichte der Syrischen Literatur*, pp. 40–42.

19. BLEW, pp. 359, 368, 415–21; also Conybeare, *Rituale Armenorum*, pp. 123, 135, *et passim*.

20. Gregory I, *Ep. IX*, 12 (PL, LXXVII, 956), 'The *Kyrie eleison* we did not say nor do we say it as it is used by the Greeks, for in Greece all say it simultaneously, while with us it is pronounced by the clergyman and responded by the people; and hereabouts also the *Christe eleison* is said, which among the Greeks in no way is used.'

21. Cf. L. Duchesne, *Christian Worship: Its Origin and Evolution*, p. 165.

22. *APB* for Hoshana Rabba.

23. This and similar prayers in the old Praeconial litany: see Quasten, *Expositio ant. lit. gallicanae*, XVI (Münster, 1934).

24. This is generally acknowledged even by Catholic scholars. Cf. F. J. Doelger, *Sol Salutis* (Münster, 1930), pp. 5, 78, 79, *et passim*. The delicate subject is treated with the frankness that is no less admirable than its profundity.

25. Instances of these prayers in Duchesne, op. cit., pp. 198–201.

26. Cf. Johannes Schümmer, *Die altchristliche Fastenpraxis* (Münster, 1933), pp. 125 ff.

27. Cf. Pseudo-Aristotle, *Problems 19, 39a*, in C. v. Jan, *Mus. Scriptores Graec.*, p. 100.
28. In *Der alte Orient*, XXV, fasc. 1, p. 9; fasc. 2, p. 7. Ugaritic examples in M. Gaster, *Thespis*, pp. 231-51.
29. Symmachus' Bible Translation, in Ps. 88.
30. Socrates, *Hist. Eccles.*, VI, 8 (*PG*, LXVII, 692).
31. Theodoret, *Hist. Eccles.*, II, 19 (*PG*, LXXXII, 1060).
32. Quoted in a work of the thirteenth century (Nicetas Choniates, *Thesaurus Orthodox. Fidei*, 5, 30, in *PG*, CXXXIX, 1390). But this remark says no more than that either the practice, or certain texts, of antiphonal singing were translated from the Syriac into the Greek: 'And as Theodore of Mopsuestia writes, they translated from the Syriac into Greek that psalmodic species which we call antiphons. . . .' See also *Paléogr. musicale*, VI, pp. 20 ff, where this and other texts are given.
33. Basilius, *Ep. 207 ad cleros Neocaesar.* (*PG*, XXXII, 764).
34. Cf. Josephus, *Ant. Jud.* XII, 3.
35. Cf. Acts, 11:19-27; 13:1-14, *et passim*.
36. Cf. Cassian, *De inst. coen.* II, 2 (*PL*, XLIX, 77): 'Some of them chanted twenty or thirty songs, and thought that they should stretch them through melodies of antiphons and through the addition of certain modulations. . . .'
37. Cf. Gevaert,*La Mélopée antique dans le chant de l' Église latine* (Ghent, 1895), pp. 159 ff, where a chronology of the antiphons is attempted.
38. Cf. A. Baumstark, op. cit., pp. 244 f. See also H. Schneider, op. cit., pp. 264-5.
39. Cf. *MLS*, I, p. 77.
40. Cf. Amalarius, *De ordin. antiph.*, IV, 7.
41. See *infra*, Chapter VII, where the origin of the *piyyut* is discussed.
42. ELB, p. 294, quoting Ephodi, *ma'ase ephod*, Chapter VIII.
43. *APB*, p. 28.
44. *LU*, p. 697.
45. See also Chapter IX (Doxology), pp. 289 ff.
46. *Machzor for Tabernacles*, ed. Heidenheim-Bamberger (Frankfurt a. M., 1915), p. 51.
47. Neale-Littledale, *Hymns of the Eastern Church*, 2nd ed. (London, 1863).
48. *Geonica*, ed. Fuerst, Yehudai Gaon, 73 (Hebrew).
49. Again, it is not the different spirit of religiosity, nor the specific genius of the Indo-European languages versus the Semitic that is responsible for the difference between the Roman Church and Eastern Christianity; for there are elements in the Orient which adhere to Rome (Melkites, United Armenians, Maronites, etc.), but show exactly the same liturgical traits as their Orthodox brethren. The Byzantine Church bases its liturgy upon the Greek language; nevertheless, its spirit and the entire concept of its liturgical poetry and music is decidedly Near Eastern, quite unlike the Roman, which is systematic and legalistic. Apparently it was the ethnic and regional factor, not dogmatic divergences, which were the *results* of the ethnic and regional variances rather than their cause, that lies at the root of such divergencies.
50. WGM, III, pp. 57 ff; also G. Reese, op. cit., p. 182.
51. Cf. Baumstark, op. cit., pp. 328 ff.
52. Ibid., p. 198.
53. Ibid.; also Maclean, *East Syrian Daily Offices*, pp. 382-8.
54. Pierre Aubry, *L'Accent tonique dans la musique de l'Église*, pp. 41 ff, also BLEW, p. 579.
55. Cf. A. E. Burn, *Niceta of Remesiana, His Life and Works* (Cambridge, 1905), also Cagin, *Te Deum ou Illatio?* (Solesmes, 1906), and Patin, *Niceta und das Te Deum* (Munich, 1909).
56. *APB*, p. 7; about the origin of the formula 'May it be Thy will' see *Companion to APB*, p. xx and ELB, p. 89.
57. M. Gruenwald, *Über den Einfluss der Psalmen*, pp. 145 ff, also ELB, p. 57. The Talmudic passages: *M. Ber.*; *B. Ber.* 33b, *Sifre Deut.* 343.
58. Cf. *JE*, article 'Olenu', also ELB, pp. 80, 99.
59. Cf. St Cyprian, *Ep.* 69, n. 7. The daily *Credo* made its appearance, just as the daily *'Alenu*, as an apologetic and defensive rubric against heretic Arianism.
60. Cf. *LU*, p. 218.

8

61. For instance, in Yehuda Halevi's *Kuzari*, II, 71–72, where he opposes metrical poems as well as rhythmic tunes in worship.

62. ELB, pp. 283 ff; also J. Schreiner, 'On Samuel b. Yehuda', *MGWJ* (1898), pp. 123 ff.

63. Ibid. Actually Samuel identified *hižana* with the poetry of the *piyyutim*.

64. Concerning the codification of the Thrice-Holy in this 'sanctification of the Lesson', see Chapter IX, pp. 283 ff.

65. Cf. BLEW, pp. 323, 327, 385 ff.

66. Cf. E. Wellesz, *Aufgaben und Probleme auf den Gebiete der byz. und orient. Kirchenmusik*, pp. 49–59, where also a bibliography is given.

67. Cf. E. Bouvy, *Poètes et mélodies* (Nîmes, 1886).

68. E. Wellesz, 'Byzantine Music', *Proc. of Mus. Assoc.* (1932), pp. 10–13.

69. E. Wellesz, 'Words and Music in Byzantine Liturgy', *MQ* (1947), p. 306.

70. For a comparative terminology of musical theory (Hebrew, Arabic, Latin, Greek, English) see W.-S., *HUCA*, XVI (1941), pp. 305–11.

71. E. Wellesz, 'Stud. z. byz. M.', *ZFM*, XVI, p. 227: 'It will become necessary to search in *Kontakia* and other Byzantine hymns for initial verses, taken from the Psalter, and to compare these initial verses . . . with parallels in Jewish and Syrian psalmody'. In this connexion, the contrafact conception of the early tropes and sequences of the Roman Church is to be mentioned; P. Wagner attributes their origin to Byzantine influence and technique. The subject is discussed further in the next chapter.

72. E. Wellesz, 'Words and Music in Byzantine Literature', *MQ* (1947), pp. 299 ff.

73. For texts of such composition see Chapter IX, pp. 281 ff. For a general discussion of Jewish and early Christian angelology see the fine article on this subject in *JE*, I.

74. Cf. E. Werner, 'The Psalmodic Formula *Neannoe* and its Origin', *MQ* (January, 1942) XXVIII, pp. 93–99, where all sources are given.

75. Chrysostom, *Homily in Ps. 150*, (PG, LV, 497) and *In Ps. 149:2* (PG, LV, 494). More about Chrysostom's invectives against Judaism in J. Parkes, *The Conflict of the Church and the Synagogue*, p. 300, where he reaches the following conclusion: 'The only explanation of Chrysostom's bitterness . . . is the too close fellowship between Jews and Christians in Antioch. . . . It must be recognized that the ways of thinking of Jew and Christian were very similar . . . the Jews of the East were in a much more powerful position than their Western brethren for influencing their neighbours. . . .'

76. Cf. Assemani, *Cod. Lit.*, I, p. 105; an excerpt from it in Parkes, op. cit., p. 397.

77. To quote but one instance: the term *Shuhlaph Qale* is interpreted by Brockelmann, *Syrisches Lexicon*, as 'genus carminum, canticorum, antiphona': by Baumstark, op. cit., as 'alternative piece': by Assemani as 'cantus responsorius aut alternativus'. While realizing the common element—alternation—it is all but impossible to imagine its form or function, unless tangible examples are given, as in the studies of H. Grimme, D. Jeannin, and G. Hoelscher. Even then, contradictions are more the rule than the exception.

78. Cf. Baumstark, op. cit., p. 114.

79. Ibid., p. 122, n. 1.

80. WGM, III, pp. 100 ff.

81. Ibid., and pp. 322 ff; also Gastoué, op. cit., p. 239.

82. Codex Sangallensis 339. WGM, III, p. 326.

83. The Marian Gradual 'Benedicta et venerabilis'; cf. *LU*, p. 1092.

84. The recognition of this link between the Greek and Latin Church is a merit of P. Wagner; his elaboration has meanwhile been confirmed and expanded by Wellesz's *Eastern Elements in Western Chant*. pp. 62 ff.

85. Cf. *Ordo Romanus*, I, 40 (*PL*, LXXVIII, 955); also Wellesz's book mentioned in the last note.

86. Cf. *supra*, pp. 86–88.

87. ELB, p. 169, where most of the Talmudic sources are given. Even today Deut. 32 is the lesson for the Sabbath before or after the Day of Atonement.

88. This hypothesis is corroborated by the fact that Isa. 5 is read as lesson of the Holy Week in the ancient Jerusalemite lectionary (cf. Rahlfs, op. cit., p. 64), and Deut. 32 is sung in the Greek *Typikon* at the same season.

89. On the Messianic character of Ps. 118 and its role in Synagogue and Church, see my study 'The Hosanna in the Gospels', *JBL* (July 1946).

90. Cf. *supra*, pp. 136–7; and the frequent directions in more recent Hebrew prayer books.

91. Duchesne, op. cit., pp. 194 ff. The Rule of St Benedict still provided for five verses. Cf. Ferretti, op. cit., pp. 159 ff.

92. Cf. CAF, II, Chapter 57: 'Somebody shall [after the lesson] sing the hymns of David, and the congregation shall join the *akrostichia* [possibly here meaning a refrainverse]'. P. Wagner's attempt to establish a primary date in a sermon of Pope Leo the Great (440–61) wherein he says 'We sung the Davidic psalm not to our own elevation, but . . .' is not convincing. For the term 'canere psalmum' is used for the rendering of the whole psalm as well as of parts thereof.

93. Cf. Duchesne, op. cit., p. 168, where he says: 'I have already pointed out that the practice of chanting psalms between the lections of the Mass is as old as these lections themselves, and that both go back in direct line to the religious services of the Jewish synagogue. In the Christian liturgy these psalms constitute the most ancient and most solemn representation of the Davidic Psalter. We must take care not to put them on the same footing as the other chants, the Introit, Offertory, and Communion, which were introduced later, and then merely to occupy attention during long ceremonies.'

94. Cf. *Liber Pontificalis*, ed. Duchesne, I, 230.

95. It is a tempting thought to compare the texts of Introits with certain preambles (*R'shut*—prayer for the cantor to stand before God as the 'messenger of the congregation') of synagogal poems. Yet the differences far outweigh the similarities. After all, the Introit serves as an introduction to a short prayer, which is immediately followed by the *Kyrie*, the opening of the Ordinary of the Mass. Only if we were to stretch our comparison as far as to equating the '*Amida* with the Ordinary it might yield interesting results: but I do not think that such an equation is justified.

96. Cf. Chapter III, pp. 77–79.

97. Cf. Augustine, *Retractationes.*, II, 11 (*PL*, XXXII, 634).

98. The Talmudic passages in *M. Yoma* VII, 1; *M. Tamid* V, 1; *J. Ber.* II, 4; see also Elbogen in *Studien in Jüdischer Literatur* (Berlin, 1913), pp. 78 ff.

99. Cf. *APB*, pp. 234 ff; similar passages for every festival.

100. Cf. Conybeare, op. cit., pp. 55 ff.

101. Ibid., pp. 65 ff; we quote here the text of the eulogy: 'Blessed art Thou, Lord our God, who through Thy Law has enjoined us to offer unto Thy Godhead fowls, turtledoves, and young pigeons, which are a symbol of Thy truth'. Compare with this text the following ancient eulogy of the Hebrew ritual: 'Blessed art Thou, O Lord our God, King of the universe, who hast sanctified us by thy commandments and enjoined us to kindle the Sabbath lights'. It is not a very bold hypothesis to divine in the Armenian prayer a remnant of the eulogy used in the Temple for sacrificial purposes.

102. Cf. *supra*, pp. 131 ff.

103. Cf. Gregory, *Ep. 9:2* (*PL*, LXXVII, 956).

104. Cassian (*PL*, XLIX, 101).

105. Tertullian, *De oratione*, 27.

106. Cf. Cyprian, ed. Maurinorum (Venice, 1728), CCCX, quoted by Doelger, *Sol Salutis*, p. 132; compare with this and the following passages the conception as expressed in Numbers Rabba, Chapters 2, 24.

107. Cassian op. cit., (*PL*, XLIX, 77).

108. Jerome, *Comment. in Psalm.*, in Morin, *Anecd. Mor.*, III, 76.

109. Cf. Sozomen, *Hist. Eccles.*, VIII, 8, (*PG*, LXVII, 1536–1750). It seems even that originally the Alleluia was sung on Easter Day only, according to Sozomen, *Hist. Eccles.*, VII, 19.

110. WGM, I, pp. 93 ff.

111. Always with the exception of Ps. 148:13–14, which immediately followed the lesson. Is it possible to derive the practice of Alleluias, detached from the original context, from the synagogal practice of two ever-recurrent psalm verses after the lesson, which happen to contain the Hallelujah?

112. WGM, I, p. 94. Also Ferretti, *Esthétique grégorienne.*, pp. 176–91.

113. This statement is made with circumspection, after a thorough computation of the Alleluia verses in Gastoué, op. cit., p. 274, and WGM, III, pp. 397 ff, both of which base their tabulations upon the oldest Western Codices, mainly Cod. Monza and Cod. Sangallensis 339, while *Paléogr. music.*, I, III, also includes Cod. Montpellier (cf. Gastoué, op. cit., p. 296). Unfortunately there is no uniformity in the lists of Alleluia verses, and every idea of historical grouping remains problematical.

CHAPTER SEVEN

Hymns and Cognate Forms

DEFINITION AND GENERAL REMARKS

THE question which characteristic elements distinguish the hymn form from other poetic-musical types is not easy to answer. For the term 'hymn' is used to designate an ancient Babylonian adoration as well as, let us say, a modern religious song of the Unitarian Church. Yet, spiritually and formally, the differences are enormous. Therefore, a common ground and a common definition must be found, which can serve as an acceptable basis for a comparative examination of the hymn form. St Ambrose gives such a definition, and it might be worth while to test it. He writes:

A hymn is a song containing praise of God. If you praise God, but without song, you do not have a hymn. If you praise anything, which does not pertain to the glory of God, even if you sing it, you do not have a hymn. Hence, a hymn contains the three elements: *song* and *praise* of *God*.[1]

According to this definition, some of the psalms and most of the canticles fall into the category of hymns; indeed, Early Christianity frequently referred indiscriminately to all sung praises as hymns. In order to systematize our exploration, we shall further narrow St Ambrose's definition. In this chapter only such compositions will be studied which were intended for musical performance, and whose texture reveals some devices of poetic artistry, such as metre or rhyme, or at least an approximation to these patterns.

The hymn, as we understand it today, namely a religious poem composed in some kind of metre, was unknown to biblical Judaism and the Apostolic age alike. The few hymnic passages of the New Testament were considered canticles in the Early Church and will, therefore, remain outside our examination; they are generally recognized to be, in spirit as well as in form, a direct continuation of Old Testament poetry or apocryphal verses, such as Ecclesiasticus 51.[2] At which point, then, is it proper to speak of hymnody? Later fragments, such as the communion hymn of the *Didache* or the poetic part of the *Epistle to*

Diognetus (cap. 7) can here be mentioned only in passing, since they were, in all probability, not rendered musically.[3] At any rate, they were not considered part of the liturgy.

St Paul was the first to distinguish between canonical poems and free hymns.[4] Tertullian followed his example by singling out a song of praise. It accompanied the *Agape* and was chanted by persons stirred by spontaneous inspiration.[5] These were the famous songs of the charismatically gifted Christians. These hymns, creations of ecstatic improvisation, were not fixed in a literary sense. It is uncertain to what extent those hymnic songs became a part of the liturgy. The discoveries of the last decades, among which the Oxyrhynchos papyri and a number of heretical hymns are outstanding, seem to indicate that such songs did form an integral part of the Christian liturgy before the end of the second century.

The subject-matter of a hymn is variegated and extensive. Invocations of Divinity,[6] or apocalyptic visions of God's glory, such as dithyrambs attributed to celestial bodies (Ps. 19), or angelological praises, of which Isa. 6:3 has become the archetype, do not exhaust the compass of hymnology. Bold polemics against heretic sectarians,[7] and ritual dances with Christ in the centre,[8] also are legitimate representatives of hymnic expression. Indeed, there are few ideas in heaven and earth that have not been, at one time or another, the subject of a hymn, provided that it closed with the praise of God.

Ironically enough, the first Christian hymns show a distinctly heretical bent. At the same time, they employ more literary and musical artistry than the compositions of orthodox Christianity. One must bear in mind that the first three centuries were replete with internal strife as well as with polemics against Judaism, Paganism, and the political powers of the Roman Empire. They present a rather stormy picture, full of apocalyptic and Gnostic ideas.

The following examples originated all in the first three centuries; they were chosen to exemplify the most significant trends of early Christian hymnody and its formal, theological, and ethnic components.

One of the oldest and most interesting hymns of that period is the prayer of Jesus in the apocryphal Acts of John.

Now before he was taken by the lawless Jews . . . he [Jesus] gathered all of us together and said: Before I am delivered up unto them, let us sing a hymn to the Father, and so go forth to that which lieth before us. He bade us therefore make as it were a ring, holding one another's hands, and himself standing in the midst he said: Answer Amen unto me. He began, then, to sing a hymn and to say:

Glory be to Thee, Father; and we, going about in a ring, answered him: Amen.
Glory be to Thee, Lord: Glory be to thee, Grace. Amen.
Glory be to thee, Spirit: Glory be to thee, Holy One; Amen.
Glory be to thy Glory. Amen.
We praise Thee, O Father; we give thanks to thee,
   O Light, wherein darkness dwelleth not. Amen.
Now whereas we give thanks, I say:
  I would be saved, and I would save. Amen.
  I would be loosed, and I would loose. Amen.
  I would be wounded, and I would wound. Amen.
  I would be born, and I would bear. Amen.
  I would eat, and I would be eaten. Amen.
  I would hear, and I would be heard. Amen.
  I would be thought, being wholly thought. Amen.
  I would be washed, and I would wash. Amen.
Grace danceth. I would pipe; dance ye all. Amen.
  I would mourn; lament ye all. Amen.
The Eight [*Ogdoas*] singeth praise with us. Amen.
The Twelve [*Dodekas*] danceth on high. Amen.
The Whole on high hath part in our dancing. Amen.
Whoso danceth not, knoweth not what cometh to pass. Amen.[9]

This enigmatic text has come down to us in at least three versions; two are in Greek, one is in Latin, and was transmitted by St Augustine.[10] Originally, it epitomized the second part of the Acts of John, and was read before the members of the second Nicaean Council as a fragment of a 'Dialogue between a Jew and a Christian',[11] a typical piece of apologetic literature. The supposition upon which this part of the Acts of John rests has it that this was the hymn which Jesus sang with his disciples at the Last Supper. It thus refers by implication to Matt. 26:30. Today this passage is generally understood as the end of the ritual *Seder* service on the eve of Passover, and , in particular, the singing of the *Hallel* (Ps. 113–118). In spite of its anti-Jewish tendency ('lawless', later 'satanic Jews') the hymn is a fine illustration of Judaeo-Hellenistic synthesis.

In conformity to the rabbinic rule that every eulogy must be responded to by its listeners with Amen in order to make it legal, Jesus demands that his disciples follow that tradition.

On the other hand, the tenor of the hymn is Gnostic, as can be seen from the personification of Grace (Greek: *charis*), or from the bold references to the Gnostic constructions of the *Ogdoas* and *Dodekas*, which likewise are personified.[12] The conceptions of a dancing Grace or a singing *Ogdoas*, a fluttering Christ in the midst of the dancing Apostles belongs to the most amazing fantasies of Christian Gnosis, engendered both by apocalyptic Jewish and Hellenistic mystery ideas.

From the purely literary point of view, the hymn appears rather primitive, for the only artistic device applied is the principle of response, and a repeated antithesis of active and passive expressions, with no discernible trace of metre or organized rhythm.

On a higher literary level stands the famous hymn of Clement of Alexandria, called 'Praise of the Children':

> . . . Gather Thy simple Children
> To holy praises, faithful singing,
> Christ, the Children's leader!
> Thou King of Saints, Logos all-dominant,
> Who comest from the Most High,
> O Prince of Wisdom,
> Helper in grief, rejoicing in eternity. . . . etc.[13]

The Greek text shows a more or less free iambic-anapaestic metre in which the classic system is still vaguely recognizable. Judaistic elements are absent. Not much later than this hymn, the various poems were composed which today are contained in the Oxyrhynchos papyri. Chronologically and geographically in close proximity to Clement, they reveal, none the less, a more intricate trend in the Hellenistic-Jewish synthesis. Most interesting among them is the so-called Oxyrhynchos hymn, an exalted composition, written shortly before 300. This piece is of great importance, as it constitutes the oldest manuscript of Early Christianity containing musical notation together with the text, and thus is unique.[14] We quote here the fragment in translation:

> . . . all splendid creations of God . . . must not keep silent, nor shall the light-bearing stars remain behind. . . . All waves of thundering streams shall praise our Father and Son, and Holy Ghost, all powers shall join in: Amen, Amen! Rule and Praise (and Glory) to the sole Giver of all Good, Amen, Amen.

Here scriptural influence is undeniable. The allusions to Ps. 148:4,

Ps. 93:3–4 (the waters praising God), Ps. 19:1–2 (the heavens and stars) and other biblical passages seem obvious. Comparing this composition with the hymns of Clement of Alexandria or those of his successors, Synesius or Methodius, we find only one common element: the closing doxology with its invocation of the Trinity. In its substance, the Oxyrhynchos piece stands in close proximity to the well-known anonymous hymn of evening (the *hymnos hesperinos*), where, as in the Oxyrhynchos fragment, scriptural allusions are evident: 'to Thee belongs praise and hymn, and Glory . . . to the Father and the Son and the Holy Spirit, for aeons to come, Amen'.[15] This hymn, included in the *Apostolic Constitutions* (Book VII, Chapter 48), a source book known to embody many concepts of the Judaeo-Christian liturgy, reveals a noticeable propensity toward Hebrew style and substance.[16] Notwithstanding the Greek text, no trace of ancient Greek metre can be found in the hymn; again, the *Apostolic Constitutions* originated in Syria, and thence came an entirely new poetic style.

Its earliest representatives were the Syrian heretics, Bardesanes, his son Harmonius, and the excommunicated Bishop Paul of Samosata. Only when the heretic hymns had become a serious danger to the unity of the Church did there arise a poetic and religious genius who decided to fight heretic beauty with orthodox beauty, St Ephraem Syrus (306–373), the 'Kithara of the Holy Spirit' as he was called. Through his efforts, the hymn of the Eastern Church attained its first peak, and from his time on Syrian poetry exerted a decisive influence upon Byzantine and Armenian, and, to a lesser degree, upon Jewish hymnody. Rome, persistent in its conservatism, remained intransigent to the introduction of the metrical hymn for many decades to come.

In order to understand the style of Syrian hymnody, it is necessary to bear in mind the dogmatic-theological disputes in which a large stratum of the population took an active part, and which are rather difficult to comprehend in our time. As Ephraem's hymns served a distinct purpose, namely the preservation of the orthodox Church rather than the pure expression of religious exaltation, his poetic output in general is of a didactic, apologetic, and homiletic nature. He 'gathered the daughters of the covenant around him, and . . . like a father, thus he taught them to sing sweet responses'.[17] In a hymn, dedicated to Bardesanes, St Ephraem credits him with the introduction of metre and normative verse-feet (prosody).[18]

He [Bardesanes] created hymns,
He furnished them with chants,
He composed canticles
And he introduced metres [*mashkhato*].
In measures and in metre [*mitqalo*]
He divided the words.

There is no reason to doubt the truth of this statement; in view of the bitter ideological hostility as expressed by Ephraem against the heresies of Bardesanes and his followers, it was probably a generally known fact which Ephraem relates, for he had no particular reason to praise his adversary.

Concerning the problem of Syriac prosody, it is quite possible that Bardesanes was acquainted with classic Greek poetry and had merely modified older Greek literary patterns. This matter is rather controversial.[19] As for St Ephraem, he apparently borrowed Bardesanes' poetic and musical style as well as some Greek archetypes, as will be shown in Chapter I of the second part of the book.

What then are the distinguishing marks of that Eastern hymnody established by Ephraem and his followers? And what was its liturgical function? The question arises whether it was the liturgical desiderata or the genius of the language, that shaped those forms which subsequently proved to answer most adequately the specific needs. The close linguistic relation reminds us here of the fact that the style of the Hebrew language engendered its liturgical forms of response, antiphon and refrain-psalm. It is necessary to examine Syriac hymnody first, since, chronologically and geographically, Syria was the intermediary between Palestine and Byzantium.

FORMS AND TERMINOLOGY OF SYRIAC HYMNODY
Acrostic

In previous chapters reference was made to this characteristic form of Semitic poetry; in Scripture we already find examples of acrostics, such as in the eightfold alphabetic Ps. 119, or in Ps. 34, in which only one letter of the alphabet is missing. Although, strictly speaking, an acrostic cannot be *heard*, but only *seen*, it stands to reason that the device served two purposes: (1) to suggest an artistic continuity, and (2) to indicate clearly the beginning of a new verse or a new stanza. In post-biblical times, the acrostic served also to record the author's name, the names of patriarchs, saints, etc., and sometimes even whole doxologies.[20] Latin and Greek literature, too, made use of the acrostic arrangement well before the first century B.C. It is impossible to state with any amount of certainty whence the acrostic found its way into classical literature; but one may safely assume that its origin is Semitic.

Strophic Structure

The strophic structure of Syriac hymnody is not only a matter of literary import, but it has a direct bearing upon a musical practice common to the entire Near East: the principle of the *contrafact* (an old melody to which new words are applied) is closely linked to strophic structure. The Syrians call it *riš-qolo* ('head of song'), the Byzantines *hirmos*, the Arabs and arabized Jews *laḥan*, and the Jewish music theorists of the Middle Ages *ne'ima*. This design might be comprehended as a model strophe, the tune and rhythm of which sets the pattern for all the following stanzas.[21]

The importance of the *riš-qolo* for all hymn forms of the Eastern, and perhaps also of the Western Church, warrants a further study of its origin, be it from the musical or the literary point of view. Our preference for the musical approach is due to the fact that the device of the model strophe seems to be in use in some psalms, the superscriptions of which (e.g. 'Hind of the Morning', Ps. 22; 'On the Lilies', Ps. 45; 'On the Dove from Far Away', Ps. 56; etc.) indicate a contrafact tune (*laḥan*) familiar to the Psalmist's contemporaries. In some cases, strophic structure is also evident in the text of the Psalter. (Ps. 119, 107, etc.)

In the assemblies of Early Christianity, the faithful sang hymns individually or in groups. Since many of the attendants were illiterate, they learned their songs by heart, that means by *ear*. A model stanza can only be recognized as such when, after its ending, the melody begins anew. The practice of strophic singing must remain unintelligible to an illiterate group, unless it is implemented musically, namely by the repetition of the tune of the first stanzas.

The popular usage of breaking up a poem into musically identical structures by repeating its model tune may have originated the form type of the *riš-qolo*, which soon thereafter became the principal literary device of Syriac hymnody.

This basic form is defined by Gastoué in the following way. The *riš-qolo* is constituted by the pre-existence of a melody, or at least by a given rhythm that is characterized by an alternation of accented and unaccented syllables. The verse, or its equivalent, is based, not upon quantity (number or lengths of syllabic elements), but upon the number of its accents.[22]

By its very nature, every individual model of a *riš-qolo* could serve as a pattern for hundreds of poems moulded in the same melodic cast. And since the model stanza itself was flexible and left ample space for poetic licence of any kind, it is easy to understand why this form became exceedingly popular.

Thus, the terminology applied to some archetypes of sacred poetry clearly shows the interrelation between Syrians, Byzantines, Hebrews, and even Italians.

The Syriac term for stanza, or for a unit of two verses is *beitha* and means 'house'. The Hebrew counterpart is *bayith*, the Byzantine *oikos* (house), and the Italians have *stanza* (chamber). Obviously, a process of translation has taken place here, but it is not possible to state whether the Syrians or the Jews first used the term 'house'.[23] Easier to determine is the origin of the term *Kukulion*, a Byzantine designation for a prefacing, or intercalated stanza that deviates from the metre of the hymn proper. Its Aramean root is *kulklion* (enclave, cell, compartment) which occurs in Talmudic and probably also in Syriac literature.[24]

Another expression for a poetic preamble, *Prosomoion*, is of Byzantine origin, but has found its way into Syrian and Hebrew poetry, where it was corrupted to *Pizmon*, which, in the Middle Ages, designated a refrain hymn.[25]

Finally, the classic Hebrew term for any poetic hymn, *Piyyut* (from the Greek *poietes*—poet), shows distinctly the interdependence of Byzantium and Palestine during the first millennium.[26] To sum up: the Syrians adopted some Hebrew terms; the Hebrews adopted some Byzantine terms; and the Byzantines, in turn, borrowed both Syriac and Hebrew terms. All of them serve to indicate the strophic structure of sacred poetry.

Metre

This problem is no less intricate than the previous one. A satisfactory answer will be possible only when we know definitely whether parts of Scripture, e.g. psalms or certain hymnic passages of the Pentateuch, were understood or performed metrically. Unfortunately the biblical scholars are still far from any definite conclusion. G. Bickell, E. Sievers, D. H. Müller, and many others have carefully examined Scripture with respect to its possible metrical structure; but their results are vague, controversial, and by no means conclusive. Only the well-known facts of parallelism in various forms and degrees, and of an occasional strophic structure (e.g. Isa. 5, Jer. 32, Ezek. 37) can be considered as safely established principles.

None the less, there were quite a few famous historians, such as Josephus, Jerome and other Church Fathers, who insisted that certain passages of Scripture were written in a strictly metrical form, e.g. Exod. 15.[27] If some parts of Scripture are of genuinely metrical composition, their pulse is based upon a more or less fixed number of accents within each verse, a system called homotony. Certainly, there are neither traces of quantitative metre, nor of another system which counts the number of syllables (isosyllabism) discernible in the Bible.

This latter type of metre is characteristic of Syriac poetry; in the writings of St Ephraem the principle of an equal number of syllables for each verse is already fully established.[28] Neither the fragments of Melito of Sardis, nor those of Bardesanes, both forerunners of Ephraem, show the principle of isosyllabism. Whether Ephraem introduced it in the course of a liturgical reform, aiming at the exclusion of hymns which were in use until that time, but which no longer conformed to newer trends in dogmatic teaching, as E. Wellesz assumes;[29] or whether this new system was nothing but a far-reaching modification of Old Testament poetry, as A. Merx and G. Bickell believe, will probably remain conjectural.[30] P. Kahle states that:

Ephraem's verse with a fixed number of syllables is clearly influenced by the metre of the Greeks, and it seems that this kind of metre was introduced into Syriac poetry after Bardesanes' time, perhaps by Bardesanes' son Harmonius, who had studied in Athens. It was accepted by Ephraem and followed by all the later Syriac poets.[31]

In the earliest Hebrew *piyyutim* of the sixth century, the Syrian system of isosyllabism occasionally occurs, as I have demonstrated elsewhere. Apparently, the Hebrew poets experimented with all kinds of metric devices, and that of the Syrians, their next-door neighbours, was the closest at hand.[32] But the exact accentuation of either the Hebrew or the Syrian language customary in those centuries is not known to us. There remains a wide margin for error in all the theories. Ancient Hebrew hymnody (*piyyutim*) was arranged according to two different systems: (a) the supposedly indigenous principle of biblical poetry, where the number of stressed syllables are counted, regardless of the number of words or syllables (homotony), or, (b) in the Syrian fashion, where the number of syllables are counted, regardless of their accentuation (isosyllabism).[33]

It is well known that Byzantine hymnody adopted *in toto* the Syrian principles of isosyllabism; whether there are traces of this interrelation in Hebrew, Syriac, or Byzantine terminology referring to metre will be examined presently.

The Greek language had, of course, a rich vocabulary for all kinds of poetry, a heritage of its classic era. Although we shall encounter later on Byzantine translations of Hebrew or Syriac terms within the realm of *liturgy*, there are no Semitic traces discernible in the classic Greek terminology of prosody and metre. On the other hand, definite similarities exist between Hebrew and Syriac terms; but it will be the task of incisive chronological studies to determine who borrowed and who lent. The basic Syriac term for metre, *mitqalo*, is practically identical with the Hebrew *mishqol*, as is the Syriac *mushkhato* (measure) almost the same as the Hebrew *mesheh*. Beyond this basic etymological resemblance one knows very little about the literary thinking of either Syriac or Hebrew poetry of that early phase. It is only after the Arab conquest of the Near East that we hear more of the internal processes of development within Syriac and Hebrew hymnody.

Rhyme

The Syrian hymns of the classic period (*ca.* 350–750) show no signs of rhyme. But recently evidence has come forth which demonstrates that, in an earlier period (before 300), the Syrians knew at least the principle of close assonance, and even the so-called rhetorical rhyme (*Tiradenreim*). P. Kahle and E. Wellesz have drawn our attention to a rhymed homily by Melito of Sardis.[34] Apparently the Syrians did not pursue this style of poetry, since, from Ephraem's time on, rhyme became exceedingly rare in Syriac hymnody.

W. Meyer scrutinized this problem from the strictly linguistic point of view. After quoting Greek rhymed prose (in patristic passages, especially in the *Epistle to Diognetus*), he cautions against the assumption that the Greeks had adopted the rhyme from contemporary Latin literature.

By referring to canonical and apocryphal Hebrew as well as to early Syriac literature, he concludes that the Byzantines had taken over the device of rhymed prose, and perhaps of rhymed poetry, from the Semites, especially from the Syrians and the Jews.[35] Summing up, he writes:

> It is certain that, together with the principles of isosyllabic poetry and its constitutive elements, the rhyme, too, has migrated from the Semites to the Greeks and Latins. Thus, the origin of Latin and Greek rhythmic style is simple and followed a natural course. *Christianity* carried that style to the Occident and its essence remains *Christian.*[36]

The specimens of Syriac literature where a rhyme is used belong to the category of versified prose; their tenor is didactic, homiletic or dogmatic. They might, not unjustly, be compared to versified editorials or sermons. While Byzantine hymnody shares the indifferent Syrian attitude toward rhyme, Latin and Hebrew sacred poetry show a distinct preference for rhymed forms.

Up to the last thirty years, almost nothing of rhymed Hebrew poetry was known to us that antedates those *piyyutim* which betray the influence of Arabic poetry (*ca.* A.D. 900). Since some of the manuscripts of the Cairo Geniza have been evaluated, an abundance of Hebrew poetry has come to light which, in turn, antedates the Arabic sources by at least two centuries. This kind of poetry sometimes uses the suffix rhyme of the Arabic *Kasida*, sometimes approaches genuine poetic concatenation of thought and diction. It originated in Palestine during the sixth and seventh centuries under Byzantine rule.[37] Yet, while in Hebrew poetry the rhyme became a habitual feature, it was a rare element in Byzantine literature. Only the rhetoric ('political') rhyme played a part in it, and W. Christ's assumption that this type of rhyme was merely an extension of the Hebrew principle of parallelism has lost nothing of its plausibility.[38] Most of the few rhymed verses of Byzantine hymnody seemingly originated with Romanus, the great *melodos* of the Eastern Church. This poet, however, was of Jewish extraction and came to Constantinople from Syria. Apparently the rhymes which he introduced sprang from Semitic sources, and remained alien elements in Byzantine literature.[39]

Syrian influence on Hebrew poetry could have been only in metre, strophic structure and general form, not in rhyme. The rhyme cannot have come from Syria to Palestine. Either it was indigenous there, or, as W. Meyer suggests, it came from North African Semitic tribes.[40]

Form Types

The development of the Syrian hymn is so closely connected with the person of Ephraem, that it will not be amiss to quote the words of his biographer, Yaqub of Serug:

> Ephraem arose against the games and the dances of the young people, and he gathered the daughters of the covenant [virgins, pledged to chastity] and he taught them songs, both refrain-songs [?] and alternative songs [antiphons]. . . . And each time the daughters of the covenant gathered in the Churches on the Festivals and Sundays . . .; and he, like a father, stood in their midst, accompanying them with the kithara, teaching them the various kinds of song and the change [modulation?] of songs, until the entire city gathered about him, and the crowd of his opponents disbanded. . . .[41]

Surveying the main forms of Syriac hymnody, one may, applying sometimes formal, sometimes topical criteria, recognize the following types:

1. *Qala* (voice, sound, tone) is an exclusively liturgical poem in several stanzas, which, together with psalm verses, is rendered responsorially or antiphonally. In it, the model strophe, *riš-qolo*, prefaces the poem proper.

2. *Madrasha* (narration, treatise), one of the most popular forms of Syriac hymnody, can only 'under special conditions be equated with the hymn form', according to Baumstark.[42] Originally designating an apologetic or polemic poem, the term *madrasha* is applied to chanted hymns that lend themselves to responsorial performance, whereby the choir participates in singing an unvariable refrain-response ('Unitha, 'Unaya).

A special genus of the *madrasha* is the

3. *Sogitha* (dialogue), a dialogue hymn in simple metre, which became the pattern of the Byzantine *Kontakion*. It tends to antiphonal performance, and sometimes approaches the form of a ballad, interrupted by dialogue. In certain cases it resembles the occidental hymn. Baumstark considers it the germinal cell of religious drama, which unfortunately, never came into existence in the Eastern orbit.

4. *Memra* (saying), is a 'said', not a 'sung' poem of didactic or narrative content. Sometimes it is strophic, but, lacking musical rendering, it does not have a regular refrain. Its verses maintain strict isosyllabism.

5. *Ba'utha* (petition) comes next to the Occidental type of litany or

supplicatory prayer. It is usually rendered as a response, whereby the choir chants a refrain.

6. *Tešbochta* (praise) corresponds to the Greek type of ode, of which we read in the Pauline Epistles of the New Testament. The term *tešbochta* originally referred to scriptural poems outside the Psalter (canticles); later, it has become the name of a choric hymn of moderate length and simple structure.

7. *'Enyana* (Responsory) is the Syrian equivalent of the Latin Responsory; originally a series of stanzas linked together by a refrain, the *'enyane* later became an extremely popular form of chant in connexion with the paraphrased rendering of psalms and canticles. They are not hymns in the strict sense of the word.

8. *Maurebe* (Magnificats) are antiphonal insertions *between* the individual verses of the Magnificat. They belong to the category of poems without any *riš-qolo* like the form below:

9. *Tachšefto* (supplication), chants of supplication, arranged according to the system of the eight Church Tones (*Octoechos*).[43]

Sometimes a Syrian form type also lends itself to either recitation or chant. Such a genus, which can be chanted or read, is the *Ba'utha*; yet, the distinctive criterion established by D. Jeannin and H. Gaisser has it that the poems to be read rather than chanted usually display a stricter metric scheme than the genuine chants.[44] We shall encounter the very same principle in the literature of Hebrew *piyyutim*. The didactic-homiletic types of either Syriac or Hebrew poetry are stricter and more formalistic than the chanted hymns.

In contradistinction to the Western Church, many of the Syriac hymns are used liturgically as intercalations between the canonical prayers of the Mass or Office. This preference was fostered by the homiletic writings of the early Church Fathers; out of this ideological soil grew many of the Eastern hymns, again at variance with the practice of the Western Church. Both principles of intercalation and of doctrinal theology, implemented by the liturgical practice of Eastern hymnody, occur also in the poetry of the Synagogue, as we shall see presently.[45] Already I. Elbogen, though from a different angle, pointed out the similarity of certain pieces of Syriac with Hebrew hymnography.[46]

The two distinguishing components of Syriac hymnody, the dramatic and the homiletic elements, are clearly recognizable in the following

two examples. The first one is an ancient homily on the Passion, written
by Bishop Melito of Sardis in the middle of the second century:

> Thou wast commanding
> and He was crucified.
> Thou wast exalting
> and He was buried.
> Thou wast reclining on a soft bed
> and He was watching in a grave and in a coffin.
> O Israel, transgressor of the Law,
> Why didst thou commit this fresh crime
> by throwing the Lord into fresh sufferings;
> Thine own Lord,
> Him who formed thee,
> Him who made thee,
> Him who honoured thee,
> Him who named thee Israel.[47]

The other is a hymn response ('enyana) for Pentecost, replete with allusions to Acts 2.

> 1. The spirit who spoke through the prophets,
>   Who came and sheltered in the Apostles,
>   May He guard the Holy Church
>   Through His great and invisible strength!
> 2. The Holy Spirit, alive,
>   Equal in power to Father and Son,
>   Descended today from the 'Upper Chamber'
>   And gave strength to the Apostles . . . etc.[48]

Many Syrian hymns have been collected in the so-called Octoechos, a
corpus of troparia, songs, canticles, and hymns, composed or redacted
by Severus of Antioch and the Fathers Paul and Jacob of Edessa.[49]

The term Octoechos has a strong musical connotation, since it refers to
the eight modes (echoi) of the Eastern Churches. Indeed, the chant of all
Syrian hymns is, at least theoretically, regulated by the principle of
eight modes. (The origin and the musical evidence of the Syrian Octoechos will be discussed extensively in Part II, Chapter II.) Suffice it here
to state that the liturgical significance of the Octoechos is derived from
the custom of using the eight modes on eight successive Sundays, especially before Easter and after Pentecost.[50] The interrelation between Synagogue and Church often appears surprisingly close in some of the hymn

texts. A few examples may illustrate this fact. First the hymn of the *Hûllālā* (Hebrew, *Hallel*, Ps. 113-118):

We give praise and glory and exultation to the Proud and Heroic and Strong one, for the redemption and the victory of Thy people Israel, when Miriam sang responses with cymbals and drums to the Lord God [Exod. 15]. Praise ye, praise, praise Him, the tremendous *El* [Hebrew, God], who through his birth gave joy. Glorify, glorify, glorify, glorify Him, the tremendous *El*, who came to be born. Sing, sing, sing, sing ye to Him, the tremendous *El* . . . for to Him exultation and praise is due. . . .[51]

If this composition is a paraphrase of a biblical passage, and therefore archaic in style, there are other later hymns, which antedate and anticipate Hebrew *piyyutim* of the eighth century, as for instance:

The preamble before Lauds, a paraphrase of psalms (*Shabbehu*) (Ps. 63; 72:6-7; 143:6)	Prayer for dew and rain (Hebrew)
Pour, O Lord, the dew of Thy grace upon the thirsty soil of our souls, who in sin are dried up and fallow of good works; let as rain fall upon them the dew of Thy bounty and the drops of Thy mercy. For Thy dew cometh upon thirsty and weary soil, waiting for Thee, and Thy mercy is better than life itself, O our Lord and our God.[52]	May Thy grace be upon us as the dew upon arid soil; if because of a sin rain did not fall and a drought was decreed, may it be possible, by prayer and supplication, to cause Thee to stop the lack of rain. Our souls are thirsty as the soil for the dew [or rain] of Thy mercy, O Thou merciful King.[53]

Whenever such parallels are found, it will be seen that the Syrians as well as the Jews paraphrase biblical passages, quite different from the Roman hymn type, which is less intimately connected with Scripture. Only in the strictly didactic *Memre* or the apocalyptic *Madrashe* do the Syrians allow themselves free diction and extra-scriptural references. One such example will be found at the end of this chapter.

BYZANTINE HYMNODY
General Character and Development

When the great Cardinal Pitra first investigated and reconstructed the development of Byzantine hymnody, he demanded that:

One should profoundly study the hymnography of the Bible, the songs of old Israel, from which our old melodies took many a loan. Is it not thence, where the acrostics, the alphabetic stanzas, the refrains, the antiphonies, the parallelisms, yea, all those secrets of prosody of which we spoke, are derived? . . .[54]

Elsewhere this pioneering scholar conjectures that the principle of isosyllabism, which the Syrians used, had its origin in Judea and Syria.[55]

These postulates, made more than eighty years ago, have today renewed and unexpected meaning. While the decades after Pitra deviated in many respects from his ingenious leads, and attempted to minimize or even denounce his merits, many recent discoveries in the field of liturgies and musicology indicate that, after all, Pitra was on the right track.

Recent scholarship still discounts a direct connexion between Byzantine and Hebrew poetry as Pitra saw it. All evidence points to Syria as the intermediary between Palestine and Constantinople. And yet we shall see that in some cases a bridge connected the poetry of the Holy Land directly with Byzantium; this, however, was not the first phase of Greek hymnography. We may distinguish four periods of (Middle) Greek hymnody which often overlap each other.

The Gnostic-Hellenistic epoch was the earliest, rooted in the heresies of Asia Minor and Egypt. Of this stratum one example was given on p. 209. Another fragment of Gnostic character, the famous 'psalm of the Naassenes', is found in the *Philosophumena* of Pseudo-Origen.[56]

> The Law, the creator of the universe, was the first intelligence;
> But second was the First-born's light[57] poured forth.
> Third was the soul, that had left its shelter and had received the law,
> In watery form resting
> It labours, subject to death,
> Sometimes it rules, and beholds the Light,
> Sometimes dejected into misery it weeps.
> Now it weeps, and now rejoices;
> Sometimes it laments, sometimes it is judged;
> Sometimes it is judged, sometimes it dies.
> Sometimes it is born, and without an outlet, miserable of evil
> It entered the Labyrinth, wandering about, etc.[58]

In this typically Gnostic philosophy, not a trace of Judaistic or scriptural ideas is apparent. Even the following remark of Jesus is anti-biblical, ending with the words:

> The secrets of the holy (life)
> called *Gnosis*, shall I (reveal).

Quite different from these synchretistic compositions are the hymns of the second period, comprising the later third, fourth and the fifth centuries. There are a few hymns extant which, though not influenced by Syrian ideas and devices, reflect a Judaeo-Christian, biblicistic and scripture-quoting attitude. While the language is Greek, they present a Hebrew attitude and style. Unfortunately, we know very little about their authors and their doctrinal propensities. The first example of this kind is an anonymous hymn, translated by myself from Pitra's edition.

> Pascha, the holy day is renewed to us.
> Pascha, the new, the holy,
> Pascha, the mystic,
> Pascha, the all-venerable
> Pascha, Christ the Redeemer,
> Pascha, the great,
> Pascha, of the faithful,
> Pascha, that opens to us the entrance of the paradise,
> Pascha that sanctifies all faithful,
> [Save, O Christ, the Pope of Rome.][59]

One is reminded here of similar Jewish Passover hymns that glorify the Pascha in the same way. Comparable also are *Hanukka* poems, one of which opens every line with 'Light of Hanukka whose . . .'[60]

More interesting and more elaborate is a Christian hymn by Auxentius, a bishop of the early fifth century. I quote here in my own translation a part of it only and shall comment on some of its lines:

(Second stanza)

> The hosts in the heaven (a)
> Offer hymns,
> And we, men of the earth,
> The doxology:
> Holy, Holy, Holy is the Lord, (b)
> Full is the heaven
> And the earth of Thy glory.
> Creator of all (c)
> Thou spakest and we were born,
> Thou willest, and we were created.

(Sixth stanza)

> Who sittest above the Cherubim, (d)
> Who openest the heavens,
> Have mercy upon us and save us!
> Rejoice, ye righteous, in the Lord, (e)
> Praying for us,
> Glory to Thee, O Lord, (f)
> The God of the holy ones.[61]

(a) The paraphrase on Isa. 6:3 is obvious; in Hebrew hymnody the contrast between 'above' and 'on earth' is frequently stressed. (b) cf. Isa. 6:3; Hab. 3:3; and the Aramaic *Kedusha de Sidra.* (c) cf. Ps. 146:6; 148:5 and 33:9. (d) cf. Ps. 99:1; also prayer book for *Yom Kippur; piyyut*

P'sach lanu. (e) cf. Ps. 33:1. (f) cf. the regular eulogy of the *'Amida*: 'Praise to Thee, O Lord, the God of Holiness'.

T. Wehofer, who first drew attention to this poem and was also the first to analyse it, knew only of the *biblical* allusions of the composition; but that makes his conclusion no less valid:

In my 'Untersuchungen',[62] I was able to demonstrate the existence of a Judaeo–Christian literature, which . . . from the literary point of view does not belong to the Greek, but to Semitic literature.

Now we realize that during the fifth century, in the neighbourhood of Byzantium, in Chalcedon, the very same literary school emerged. . . . From the literary point of view, this hymn of Auxentius is of great importance, because it belongs to the few pieces that came down to us, surviving that tragic century of holocausts.[63]

None the less, the argument still might persist that the biblicisms of the poem do not necessarily indicate direct Hebraisms or Jewish influence, since the various Greek translations of the Bible were in the hands of every erudite Christian. To show a direct rabbinic (i.e. *post-biblical*) spirit and influence in Byzantine hymnography, in addition to the references made to the hymn quoted on p. 210, we quote here a hymn of Holy Saturday. Recently, this hymn was the object of minute examination by the renowned scholar of Byzantine hymnography, E. Wellesz. His analyses are convincing enough; yet, he failed to mention that these *Troparia* reflect directly, though with a sharp anti-Jewish twist, the rabbinic spirit and atmosphere. There are three versions of the text: the original Hebrew from the Midrash *Sifrê*, the Roman *Improperia*, and the Byzantine *Troparia*. Here they are juxtaposed, for the sake of convenience.

Hebrew	Roman	Byzantine
For had God brought us out of the house of oppression And not led us. . . . It would have sufficed. For had He led us in a pillar of fire and in a cloud and not fed us with manna . . . It would have sufficed. For had He fed us with Manna . . . It would have sufficed.	Ego te eduxi de Aegypto, demerso Pharaone in mare Rubrum. Et tu me tradidisti principibus sacerdotum Ego ante te praeivi in columna nubis; et tu me duxisti ad Praetorium Pilati. Ego te pavi manna per desertum: Et tu me cecidisti alapis et flagellis.	Before me, who delivered you from oppression? And now what return do you make to me? Evil for goodness. In return for a pillar of fire you have nailed me to a cross. In return for a cloud you have dug me a tomb. In return for the manna, you have offered me gall, in return for water, you have given me vinegar to drink. For the future, I will call the Gentiles, and they shall glorify me, with the Father, and the Holy Spirit.[64]

For two reasons it seems to me that the Latin version is older than the Greek. Its text is closer to the original Hebrew, and the Byzantine version ends in a strictly doxological formula, which reflects the handiwork of professional theologians. However that may be, both Christian versions display familiarity with the rabbinic text.

The third period of Byzantine hymnography shows unmistakable signs of Syrian influx and prevalence. With it the classic era commences. None the less, Judaeo-Christian traces still occur in this style, which is akin to certain passages of the *Constitutiones Apostolorum*, a compilation of the Syro-Palestinian Church. A few hymns, preserved in the Codex Alexandrinus, exhibit clearly the Judaeo-Christian nature of the *Constitutiones*. Two examples may illustrate this point.

> Daily shall I bless Thee, (a)
> And Thy name I shall praise for aeons,
> And for aeons of aeons.
> Let us this day pass without sin, living God!
> Praised be Thou, O Lord, God of our Fathers, (b)
> And Thy praiseworthy and glorious name
> Into the Aeons, Amen.

The hymn is predominantly Hebraic in language and mood; (a) is taken from Ps. 145:2 and (b) is the prescribed rabbinic form of eulogy with the orthodox response.

> Praised be Thou, Lord, teach me Thy judgements.
> Lord, our refuge wast Thou from generation to generation. (a)
> I said: Lord, have mercy upon me
> Heal Thou my soul, for I have sinned against Thee, (b)
> Lord, to Thee I take refuge. (c)
> Teach me to do Thy will,
> For Thou art my God,
> For with Thee is the fountain of life, (d)
> And in Thy light shall we see light.

With the exception of lines 1, 3, 6, and 7, all verses are almost literal quotations from Scripture; (a) is taken from Ps. 90:1; (b) is Ps. 6:3; (c) Daily morning service; (d) Ps. 36:10.[65]

Though well known in Byzantine Christianity, the last quoted hymns are in no way typical of its native hymnography. The classic style of its hymnody is bound up with the forms of the *Kontakion* and the *Kanon*. Prominent among the authors of these poems were the converted Jew

Romanus (from Beirut), Bishop Andrew of Crete (possibly of Jewish descent too),[66] Cosmas of Maiuma and Jerusalem, and John of Damascus (Johannes Damascenus). This golden age of Byzantine hymnody displays an abundance of genuine poetic expression, without neglecting homiletic-didactic concepts. It lasted from the early sixth to the ninth century, when the iconoclast conflict sounded the death knell to this greatest period of Byzantine literature.

The fourth phase, from the ninth to the fourteenth century, mirrors faithfully the gradual decline of the Byzantine Empire. This period is compilatory by nature, eclectic in style, and, above all, is apologetic and didactic. Writers like Photius, Zonaras, Theodoros Prodromos lent the splendour of their names to a few hymns. That does not mean, however, that the output of hymnic poetry declined; if anything, it surpassed in quantity that of past periods. Yet both style and ideological substance of these hymns are vastly inferior to that of the previous era, due to internal strife (iconoclasm) and the schism with Rome, which at that time flared up in unbridled violence.

Poetic Patterns and Main Forms

Like the Syrians, from whom they borrowed many of their poetic forms, the Byzantines cultivated Semitic patterns, such as acrostic, isosyllabism, refrains, etc.; they did not make much use of the rhyme.[67] Where it does occur, it is the so-called political or rhetoric rhyme (*Tiradenreim*), based merely on an assonant suffix. In the *Kontakia* of Romanus, the rhyme has the function of stressing certain words, and not that of a general poetic principle. An excellent example of that rhyme, quoted by W. Meyer from the *Epistle to Diognetus*, has to be dated as early as the third century. In it, there occur rhymes like these: pare*chousa* noun; phaner*ousa* mysteria; diang*ellousa* kairous, chair*ousa* epi pistois, etc.[68]

Soon after the sixth century the rhyme vanished completely from Byzantine hymnody while isosyllabism was further developed than it ever was in Syrian literature. Frequently, a model stanza of eight to twelve lines, each containing a different number of syllables, serves as *hirmos*. This intricate model stanza is faithfully imitated through all the following strophes.

The majority of Byzantine hymns falls into the three categories *Kontakion*, *Kanon* and *Sticherarion*. Of these, *Kontakion* and *Kanon* are the most interesting. A. Baumstark had suggested that the *Kontakion* (= little stick, *baculus*) was derived from the Syrian *Sogitha*, a kind of versified dialogue. Recently this theory has been refuted, and the Syrian *Memra* has been proclaimed the archetype of the *Kontakion*.[69] E. Wellesz suggests a stemma of the *Kontakion*, to which I added a Jewish branch, describing the earliest phases of Hebrew poetry, before it adopted Arabic patterns.[70]

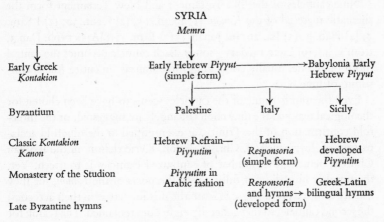

A *Kontakion* consists of a series of twenty to thirty stanzas, each repeating the metre and melody of the first one, called *hirmos*; a stanza is called a *troparion* or *oikos*. The *Kontakion* is usually preceded by one or two stanzas of different metre and structure, called a *Kukulion*. Sometimes this preamble is also termed *Proasma*. As the *Kukulion* has a Semitic root, thus, conversely, the Hebrew designation *Pizmon* (refrain poem) might have originated in the *Proasma* or the *Prosomoion* of the Byzantines.[71] The best specimens of the *Kontakion* are connected with the person and era of Romanus. Soon after his time, the form of the *Kontakion* became obsolete and was replaced by the *Kanon*.

The *Kanon*, which emerged as a seemingly new form, intends to attain, within the framework of liturgy, an ancient ideal: the psychological association which, in the mind of the faithful, would connect the sacred text with the specific season or occasion. The method, used by the poets of the *Kanon*, likewise employed two ancient principles that pervade the history of sacred poetry: the paraphrase or variation of

Sacred Writ, and the principle of free poetic intercalation between the scriptural passages. These are two concepts dominant in the hymnic literature and music of the Near East. Thus, extended variations and meditations on a scriptural text are built up in a series of stanzas, which surround or pervade the individual sentences of the biblical text. It is the literary device of many Hebrew *piyyutim* no less than of certain Syrian forms basically akin to the *Kanon*.

Nine canticles of the Old Testament and New Testament form the thematic material of the *Kanon*. (1) Exod. 15; (2) Deut. 32; (3) I Sam. 2; (4) Hab. 3; (5) Isa. 26; (6) Jonah 3; (7) Dan. 3; (8) Apocryph. Dan. 3, from v. 44; (9) Luke 1 (Mary's song). Each canticle becomes the central motif of an ode, usually containing three stanzas, an entire *Kanon* consisting of nine odes.

Even the number nine of the canticles seems to have been chosen for theological reasons: the nine choirs of angels are suggested, or the three-fold confirmation of the Trinity, as exemplified in the ninefold acclamation of 'Kyrie eleison, Christe eleison, Kyrie eleison' in the Roman Church; actually the number of canonized canticles is fourteen. Yet, the number nine did not fully satisfy the poets of the *Kanon*, for they usually omitted (as can be seen from the missing letters in their acrostics) the second canticle, so that generally eight odes remained. The reason for this omission is, according to Zonaras (twelfth to thirteenth century), the 'sad and unpleasant nature' of Deut. 32, where Moses chastized the impiety of the Children of Israel.[72] In my opinion, however, this is a *post factum* rationalization. The real reason will be found in the intention to conform everything in Byzantine hymnody to the principle of the *Octoechos*, the system of the eight modes.

A close parallel to the intercalated stanzas of the *Kanon* occurs in contemporary Hebrew poetry, where the *Shiba'ta* (seven-hymn) takes the place of the eight odes of the *Kanon*. It is a typical feature of all *Kanones* to interpret the Old Testament passages in an orthodox, sometimes artificially, Christological sense. Two examples may illustrate the ideology and the method of the *Kanon*. First a *Kanon* in honour of the Apostle Peter by Andrew of Crete, of which I quote Ode 3 (with reference to I Sam. 2):

> Not in wisdom, or in power or richness do we trust,   (a)
> But in Thee, the Father's embodied wisdom, O Christ.
> There is none holy but Thou, benefactor.[73]   (b)

Secondly, a *Kanon* on the Resurrection by John of Damascus of which I quote Ode 1 (with reference to Exod. 15):

> To Thee, Saviour God, who led through the Sea   (c)
> The people with dry feet,
> And who made Pharaoh drown with all his army,   (d)
> To Him alone let us sing, for He has fulfilled.
> Let all nations sing to Him   (e)
> Who is above the Cherubim,   (f)
> The Christ ascending
> To Glory, who seats over us   (g)
> On the right hand of the Father
> A hymn of triumph, for He has fulfilled.

These two stanzas present a perfect illustration of the method of variation and intercalation of Scripture: (a) Ps. 49:6; (b) I Sam. 2:2; (c) Exod. 15:19; (d) Exod. 15:21; (e) Ps. 117:1; (f) Ps. 99:1; the last allusion (g) is to Mark 16:19 and Luke 24:51.

We shall encounter exactly the same method of variation and allusion in Hebrew poetry; but there talmudic literature takes the place of the poetic passages of the New Testament.[74]

Terminology and Liturgical Function of the Byzantine Hymn

The Syrian influence on Byzantine hymnody is evident in a terminology which betrays its Semitic origin time and again. Whether by borrowed Syriac terms, such as *kukulion*, or by way of translated Syrian words, such as *oikos* = *beitha* (house = stanza), *kathisma* = *motva* (session-seated),[75] *ma'amad* = *stasis* (standing—stand),[76] *'unitha* = *hypakoe* (= response),[77] to mention only a few, the terminology of Byzantine hymns is replete with Syrian notions. In numerous cases, the Syriac term is the equivalent of a Hebrew word, as e.g. in *ma'amad* (Syriac and Hebrew = standing) = *'amida* (Hebrew) = *stasis* (Greek), or *'unitha* (Syr.) = *'aniath* (Hebrew) = response. While an extensive investigation of these relations remains the task of a special study, here two obscure Hebrew terms for poetic forms will be traced back to their Byzantine origin. For such is the intriguing relation of East and West: at first we witnessed Hebrew influence upon Syria; then the Syrian wave reached Byzantium, only to return to Palestine in a new form. The two Hebrew expressions to be investigated are *rahit* and *taidia*.

The term *rahit* designates a bolt or a beam; it symbolized scriptural passages serving as the framework in which the new paraphrases would be inserted. Sometimes, we find as a synonym of *rahit* the expression *dromos*, which is a Greek word, meaning runner, applied to a running refrain.[78]

The word *taidia* has been a subject of controversy for many years. Numerous etymologies have been suggested, thus far with no conclusive results.[79] *Ta ainea* is the Byzantine term for the early morning praises. Slightly corrupted (d for n) the word seems to have become part of the terminology of Hebrew poetry.[80]

The liturgical function of the Byzantine hymns is clearly reflected in the varying attitudes of the ecclesiastical authorities toward the introduction of new poetic texts.

Here a fundamental difference between the Eastern and Western Churches becomes obvious. From the beginning of Christianity, the question of hymns presented a veritable stumbling block to the authorities. The *psalmi idiotici*, those spontaneous outpourings beloved by heretics and despised by the orthodox, and the many heretical songs mentioned before made an authoritative and uniform policy essential for the ecclesiastical legislators.

Yet, in spite of several attempts to reach a general agreement, the various regional Churches followed much their own counsel, dictated by their different wishes and needs. The Eastern Churches cultivated the hymn to such an extent that by eclipsing the canonic text of the Mass, it sometimes became a danger to the integrity of the Eucharistic service. From time to time it was necessary to curb the liturgical use of the hymn.

The most radical measure was taken at the Council of Laodicea (360–381), whose canons 15 and 59 decree that only 'canonic' singers should be appointed, and be prohibited from singing any non-scriptural texts.[81] After a period of not quite a full century, during which one may detect signs of reluctant acceptance on the part of the Churches, the hymns returned victoriously to their former dominant position, at least in the Eastern Churches. Even shortly after Laodicea, the Syro-Palestinian Church must have been rather lenient in the matter of hymns, according to Aetheria Silvia's report.[82] The Western Church, while not absolutely impervious, still remained wary and critical of new forms and innovations. A dilemma, similar to that of the hymn form in Christianity, arose also in Judaism, when the sect of the Karaites insisted that only scriptural texts should be read and chanted during public worship. After a minor regional victory, the influence of the Karaitic purism abated, and the sect itself had no further share in the development of Jewish liturgy.[83]

Although the iconoclast conflict within the Greek Church again reduced the use of hymns, they made a comeback in the twelfth and thirteenth centuries. Today, the liturgy of the Eastern Churches is replete with hymns of all sorts that lend splendour and dramatic flavour to the service, creating for every holyday an atmosphere of its own. This holds true only partly for the Western Church, where the hymns have remained 'monoliths', as it were, i.e. occasional insertions in the otherwise homogeneous liturgy. The reason why the Western hymns are so clearly distinguishable from other parts of the service lies in their poetic and musical structure. It is strictly metrical and exact, in contrast to the other forms of Gregorian chant which are in free rhythm and a-metrical. Cardinal Pitra was right in saying:

More intelligent and generous than Plato, who would crown the poet only to guide him to the frontier of the country and to banish him, the Church opened its temples to him . . . and there he impressed his tunes upon the faithful, to (occupy) permeate, by day and by night, the long hours of the Oriental prayer. In no part of the Church has poetry been received with greater honour than in the fatherland of Homer. . . .[84]

We might add: and in the Fatherland of David, the royal poet. . . .

THE HYMNS OF THE ARMENIAN CHURCH

Armenia, converted to Christianity by Gregory the Illuminator (260–337), had developed a rich treasury of ecclesiastic literature. Its Judaistic elements, as they occurred in the diction of simple prayer, the lectionary and certain ritualistic terms, have been discussed before. It is more difficult to examine Armenian hymnography, since the sources are scarce and not easily accessible.

When the Armenian Church, in 536, separated from the Byzantine Church as a belated consequence of the Council of Chalcedon (451), which had ruled the Monophysite doctrine heretical, the Byzantine element had by then left distinct traces in the liturgy of Armenia. The country, situated between the great powers of Byzantium in the West, Persia in the East, and the Islamic-Arabic tribes in the South, had always been open to Syrian and Byzantine cultural influence, for these were its only Christian neighbours. Its cultural accomplishments, therefore, present a puzzling spectacle of rivalling Semitic and Greek forces, to which, later on, Slavonic and Turkish were added.

There are traces of Judaistic elements only in the oldest strata of Armenian literature. During the seventh century Armenian poetry suffered a setback from which it recovered only in the twelfth and thirteenth centuries. Nerses Shnorhali (The Gracious), the leading personality of that era, revised and increased the hymnal. It contains more than 1100 canonized hymns, most of them still in use today, and most of them composed after the twelfth century.

Unfortunately, the studies of European scholars on that subject are mostly outdated or not available; and authentic material, written in Armenian script and language, is not easily accessible.

The *Sharakan* is the great monument of Armenian hymnography. Its pieces range chronologically from the fifth to the fourteenth century. Stylistically, two parts are easily distinguishable by the different treatment of the verse. The oldest compositions have strophic structure, but show no concern for prosody or distinct metre. They are rhythmic stanzas, somewhat alike to scriptural strophes, with freely flowing verses.[85]

Of later date are metrical compositions, representing in their poetic systems a compromise between isosyllabism and homotony.[86] Old Testament reminiscences still play a major part in the hymns of the late twelfth century. One example may suffice to demonstrate this point:

> Thou who hast in Thy power created
> The superior world of the immaterial,
> And hast there established as masters
> The Great Lights,
> We bless Thy power, surpassing our understanding.

> Thou who in Thy royal abundance
> Hast created the Second World, which our senses can perceive,
> And in the Garden of Eden hast established as master
> The First Man,
> We bless Thy power, surpassing our understanding.

> Thou who hast set high
> Thine Church mysteriously,
> And hast there established as master
> The preacher of the Word of Truth,
> We bless Thy power, surpassing our understanding.[87]

This hymn resembles, in its exegetic substance as well as in its parallelistic and refrain style, some of the early Hebrew *piyyutim*; but it would hardly be possible to infer from this and similar instances a direct Jewish influence. More plausible is the assumption of a common source for both medieval Hebrew poets and Armenian writers, namely the contemporary Syrian hymnody. Most scholars have adopted this explanation.

One singularly late case of attested Jewish-Armenian interrelation should not remain unobserved. An Armenian scholar of the nineteenth century, P. Ingigian, maintains that Nerses Shnorhali borrowed an Arabic-Hebrew metre for his hymns, following the ideas and patterns suggested by Yehuda Halevi (1055?–1142?), the greatest post-biblical poet of Judaism, who had advanced them in his book *Kuzari*.

Ingigian bases his thesis upon the Armenian medieval chronicler Kiriakos Kantzagedzi (thirteenth century), whom he quotes after a manuscript in San Lazzaro:

> In our churches many hymns are [were?] sung in a manner called *Khozrovayin* [—of the Chazars—Kuzari], which Nerses had composed in the style suggested by the celebrated Rabbi Yehuda Halevi's poetry. These hymns are entirely different than the other hymns of our Armenian tradition. . . .

Padre Leonzio Dayan of the Armenian Mechitarist monastery of S. Lazzaro, Venice, to whom I am indebted for this information, was also kind enough to demonstrate a few of these *Khozrovayin* hymns for my benefit. Indeed, it was easy to see that in these hymns of Nerses the metre is closely observed and patterned after Halevi's *Hymns of Zion*. This adaptation has resulted in a metrical poetry most agreeable and flowing, which is not otherwise to be found in Armenian hymnody.[88]

The arrangement of the daily hymns in the Armenian Church seems to be patterned after the order of the Byzantine Kanon. There are usually eight hymns (lauds), which, together with the eight tones of the *Octoechos*, stress the significance of that number for music and hymnody in the entire Near East.[89]

The first hymn corresponds to the Song of Miriam (Exod. 15), and is but a poetic paraphrase of this canticle. The second hymn centres around the prayer of the Three Men in the Furnace (Dan. 3), the third is a close paraphrase of the Magnificat (Luke 1:46), the fourth quotes extensively Ps. 51, the fifth is based upon Ps. 148, the sixth upon Ps. 113, the seventh is again a composition paraphrasing a psalm, ending in the blessing after the meal, quite in Jewish style, and the eighth hymn (of the evening) is a poetic version of Ps. 121.[90] The selection of these hymns suggests an interesting comparison with the Jewish liturgy.

Armenian		Jewish	
Morning service	Exod. 15	Morning service	Exod. 15
	Dan. 3		
	Luke 1		
Hymns based upon	Ps. 51	(on fast-days)	Ps. 51
	Ps. 148		Ps. 148
	Ps. 113	(on New Moons)	Ps. 113
Grace after meals	Thanksgiving paraphrase	Midday	Thanksgiving psalm (usually Ps. 126)
Evening	Ps. 121	Sabbath evening	Ps. 121

With the exception of Ps. 113, which is a part of the *Hallel* and chanted on festivals and New Moons, the use of the Old Testament pieces in the Synagogue corresponds to their place in the Armenian liturgy. Once more our thesis is confirmed: of all Churches, the ritual of the Armenian Church comes closest to the practice of the ancient Oriental Synagogue.[91]

THE SYNAGOGUE AND ITS HYMNS UP TO THE ELEVENTH CENTURY

Historical Development and Function

An ever vital force in religious ideas, by virtue of its age-old experience, Judaism had cast a creative spell over most conceptions and expressions of the Holy. Yet there is one outstanding exception to that historic rule: in adopting the hymn form, Judaism followed an example instead of setting it. Indeed, the hymn form proper was originally alien to, and a latecomer in, the literature of the Synagogue. True, hymnic ideas and poesies were indigenous to the Children of Israel, as proved by canticles and psalms of the Old Testament; but, for the sake of clear distinction and style criticism, it is necessary to accept the principle of metre and rhyme as the criterion of hymnody proper, in Hebrew literature as well as elsewhere. Approximations to metrical forms already occur in the Midrash, the exegetic lore of Judaism. There, indeed, song-like types with or without refrains do exist; they are mostly brief, folkish stanzas. A short excerpt from these midrashic poems was quoted on p. 224. A number of sententious *gnomons* with rhyme-like assonance are also known from talmudic literature, but the true hymn form did not originate with Judaism, it was transplanted thereto.

The real origin of the *piyyutim* is not fully clear as yet. We do know, however, of at least two motivating causes for the rise of the Hebrew hymn. The first one was Justinian's *novella* 146, a law forbidding every kind of scriptural exegesis (*deuterosis*) or didactic talmudic instruction, hitherto offered in the Synagogue.[92] It became necessary to circumvent this prohibition, and new prayers were inserted in the century-old liturgy. They would not necessarily have to be hymns, but might have been prayers, couched intentionally in obscure language, in order to deceive the Byzantine oppressors. It is in this instance that Kahle did not visualize the entire picture.

But the Jews did not renounce these (forbidden) elements in their services, and found a compensation for them by introducing the forbidden elements into their liturgical poetry. They had to go to work cautiously. Only hints of these elements could be introduced into the poetry. That is one of the reasons why this poetry is sometimes so exceedingly difficult. Only experts in Talmud and Midrash were able to understand such hints. Nevertheless, by reciting, or singing and hearing this poetry in the services, they were convinced that they had fulfilled their obligations.[93]

Why was poetry required for these inserted prayers? And could even the best poetry replace irreplaceable passages, for which no substitute was permissible, such as the *Sh'ma'* or the *Tefilla*? Indeed, these prayers were never replaced nor put into the background of the liturgy, even after the introduction of the *piyyut*. Nor did their interpretation vanish.

Two other impulses, working within the body of the Jewish people, must not be overlooked, first the *Zeitgeist*: the stimulating, indeed, challenging example of Christian hymns and songs, by which not a few Jews had been so strongly attracted that they left their parental faith. We need only think of the two great *melodoi* of Byzantium, Romanus and Andrew, both of Jewish origin, in order to evaluate properly the attractions of Christian hymnody. Another aspect of the same picture was the increasing weariness of the Jews with the dry, dull setting of their worship, where music played a very insignificant part. By contrast, the radiant example of Christian church-music made them conscious of their own artistic poverty. After all, were they not the true descendants of the Psalmists? This line of reasoning helps us understand better the remarks of a later observer, a Jewish convert to Islam, Samuel ben Yahya. He refers here to the Babylonian Jews, ruled by Persia:

> When the Jews realized that the Persians enforced their prohibition of Jewish worship, they made prayers, in which they inserted the usual prayers, and called them *al-hižana* (songs). They composed for these many melodies and gathered often in order to sing and pray them. The difference between *hižana* and compulsory prayer is, that the latter is being read without melody; . . . yet, the *hižana* is sung eagerly and zestfully.[94]

The term *hižana* is, of course, the arabized version of the Hebrew *hazanut* (cantorate, cantorial chant); and it is revealing to hear that many of the poets (*paytanim*) called themselves 'singers' (*hazanim*). Recently, a corpus of Hebrew hymns was discovered in Sicily which bears the title *Hizzunim* (chants).[95]

Summing up, we might say that Justinian's and the Persian prohibition presented a pretext, and no more, for the introduction of the hitherto banished forms of synagogal hymns and songs. The Jews were eager to make their contribution to religious poetry and song as well as their neighbours, the Syrians and Byzantines. A further proof of this is the fact that after the deliverance of the Jews from religious persecution through the Arabic conquest in 636–50, they did not return to their simple prayers, eliminating the newly established forms. Quite to the contrary, they expanded their poetic output and adopted Arab forms and poetic devices.

Their first hymnic attempts were, like those of the Syrian and Greek Churches, simple centonizations of biblical passages. Many of these primitive hymns have become integral parts of the daily prayer book; they are most conspicuous in the morning service, the oldest part of the synagogal liturgy.

Artistic poetry in its opening phase did not limit itself to scriptural quotation. Since *deuterosis*, that is, *post-biblical* doctrine, was forbidden, it was *this* element that had to be strengthened. Consequently, the function of those scriptural references was not quotation but homiletic exegesis. Thus, the earliest poets (*paytanim*) such as Yannai, Jose ben Jose, Pin'has, Yehoshua, and Hedutha (sixth to seventh century), wrote mostly poems to be inserted in the *Tefilla* (the eighteen eulogies and petitions, of which mention was made in Chapter I). The *Tefilla*, part of which is certainly of pre-Christian age, contains a passage cursing sectarians and *Minim* (Judaeo-Christians);[96] it therefore was suspect and suppressed by the Byzantine authorities. Other passages, where poetic intercalations were customary, are the *Yotzer* benedictions of the morning prayer, especially the passages centring around the *Sh'ma'*. Only the second phase, chiefly represented by the Palestinian Kalir (eighth century) and the poets of the Sicilian school, extended the functional scope of their hymns. Even then, the intercalation in the *Tefilla*, called *Keroba* (probably derived from the root $\sqrt{\text{Krb}}$ > to approach, to offer, comparable to the Offertory), remained the most popular form, rivalled only by the *Yotzer* insertion.[97] Other, freer forms such as petitional prayers in the form of poetic allusions to Bible and Midrash sprang into being. Actually, some of the earlier *paytanim* expressly referred to the scriptural or midrashic passage around which they composed their poems.

Rabbinic Attitude to the Piyyut

As in all Churches, the introduction of new liturgical compositions of non-scriptural origin into the Synagogue at first met with stiff opposition from the ecclesiastical authorities, in this case, the rabbis. We cannot elaborate on the often highly technical and legalistic arguments brought forth by both sides pro and contra the *piyyut*. It may suffice to state that in Babylonia, where most of the Jewish authorities lived and taught, the introduction of new poetry, to be inserted into canonized prayers, was considered a danger to the integrity of the service. The same attitude was taken three centuries earlier at the Council of Laodicea. Especially strong was the rabbinic argument that the first three eulogies of the *Tefilla* must, under no circumstances, be interrupted, as did the new *Keroba*. A number of authorities, e.g. Yehuda ben Barsilai, demanded that now, under Arab rule, where Jewry had full freedom of worship, all insertions, hymns, etc., should be eliminated again. The accumulation of laudatory epithets of God, as they occur in many *piyyutim*, he termed, in accordance with the talmudic doctrine, a blasphemy, since even the attempt to enumerate God's attributes must lead to sacrilegious anthropomorphisms.[98]

In spite of all banishments and condemnations by the supreme authorities, the *piyyut* completely conquered the hearts of the Jewish masses. There were several reasons for the success of the new style of prayer. It rendered the service more flexible; it added variety. But most important was the fact that the *piyyut* as a new form was capable of reflecting the ideas of its author, the tendencies of the era, and that it was open to all important trends of its time. It was flexible, actual, and provided variety. Elbogen justly remarks:

> It was most meritorious that, through this new form, the religious ideas, the edifying legends, the comforting promises of the Midrash were transmitted to all circles of Jewry. How much devotion has the *piyyut* aroused, to how many faint-hearted has it given courage, to how many desperate souls new hope![99]

Inseparably connected with the *piyyut* were its tunes, which enlivened and gave new splendour to the congregations of the Diaspora. In the course of time, great poets arose, who could match the exultant language and the profound piety of the Psalmists. Our study does not extend to the twelfth and thirteenth centuries, when this summit of poetic accomplishment was reached, so memorable through the illustrious names of Yehuda Halevi and Solomo Gabirol.

Poetic Patterns and Form Types

Acrostic. This form type already appeared in the Bible, as we know from some Psalms and the Lamentations. In post-biblical literature, the Acrostic was used to indicate the strophic structure, or to convey the name of the author, or to perpetuate and glorify especially memorable passages from Scripture.[100] If the author's name was spelled out in the Acrostic, it was usual to add the epithet 'the meek' or 'the humble, small'. In Byzantine hymnody, we find the same practice, frequently in the poems of the converted Jew, Romanus, whose name-acrostic usually read 'Of Romanus, the humble one'.[101]

Metre. More controversial is the question of metre. Heretofore, two theories were presented. One has it that the earliest *paytanim*, previous to the adaptation of the Arabic system of metre, continued the biblical homotony, i.e. the principle by which the number of accented syllables of each *half-verse* varied between two and four. The other theory suggests that the number of stresses of every verse remains constant within a stanza. It is hard to prove the second theory, since the manuscripts do not show a poem written in individual lines, and so the end of a line is difficult to make out unless it is indicated by rhyme.

Elsewhere, I have proposed a third alternative. The earliest *paytanim* vacillated between biblical homotony and isosyllabism, the Syrian and Byzantine systems.[102] The examples quoted in my publication might, however, be considered incidental. This objection cannot be maintained any longer, as it is possible to show that biblical passages, quoted within a poem, were paraphrased in such a way as to fit into isosyllabism, and were left untouched, where the original text presented no obstacle to the isosyllabic scheme. Such an example is the following *Tokheha* (admonition) by Anatoli of Otranto (eleventh century). A part of the text is transliterated here to show the isosyllabic character of the poem; the scriptural passages are placed at the side, together with an English translation.

Anatoli	Scripture	English translation
El (e)lohim divrati	Edrosh el el (v)el elohim	I would have besought God,
Assim (v)tuv hegyoni	'Assim divrati. (Job 5:8)	and unto God would I have committed my cause.
Elav pi-karati	'Elav pe-karati (v)romam	Unto Him I cried with my
(V)romam tahat (l)shoni	tahat (l)shoni. (Ps. 66:17)	mouth, and a song of extolling was on my tongue.
Noda bigvurotav	(L)hodia' livnei ha-adam	To give praise to His majesty
Uvfilei nor'otav	(g)vurotav. (Ps. 145:12)	and to the wonders of His awe.
Nivra' im yoduhu	(V)'am nivra (y)hallel Yah. (Ps. 102:19)	The ones created by Him shall extol Him, for He
Ki yotzer hakol hu	Ki yotzer hakol hu. (Jer. 10:16)	hath made all.
Tahor hifli' 'etza	Hifli 'etza. (Isa. 28:29)	Pure and wonderful is He in
(V)davar mipi yatza	Mipi yetze. (Job 37:2)	counsel, and the word that goes out of His mouth.
Vayitzer adam (b)hokhma	Vayitzer adonai (e)lohim et ha-adam	And He made man in wisdom from the dust of the
'Afar min ha'-(a)dama, etc.[103]	'Afar min ha'-(a)dama. (Gen. 2:7)	ground. . . .

Lines 3, 4, 8 and 12 are literal quotations from Scripture; they occur only where the biblical text itself can easily be broken up into a system of six syllables, the metrical pattern of the poem. This fact demonstrates beyond any doubt that, even as late as the eleventh century, Hebrew poets experimented with the Syrian-Byzantine principle of isosyllabism. The first Hebrew poems implementing the isosyllabic pattern come from the sixth century, and seem to have originated in Palestine. The main poets of that period were Yannai and Pin'has.[104]

This Syrian system was abandoned by the Hebrew poets when they came in close contact with Arabic poetry. It is reported that Dunash ibn Librat formally introduced the Arabic system into Hebrew literature. Yet this novelty, while eventually victorious, did not remain unopposed.[105] Paradoxically enough, great poets, such as Yehuda Halevi and Al-Harizi,[106] who *habitually wrote poetry in Arabic metre*, objected to it as they would to a foreign intruder, but in their theoretical writings only.[107]

Rhyme. Rhyme occurs early in Hebrew literature, occasionally in the Bible, and might be considered connate to the language. The suffix rhyme, which in early post-biblical prayers functions as a rhetorical device, was already familiar to the earliest *paytanim*.[108] The genuine poetic rhyme, consisting of at least one syllable of the last word's root, seems to appear first in Yannai's poems (sixth century), before the Arab conquest of Palestine, and gained popularity rapidly. Together with the Arabic system of syllabic accented metre and strophic structure, it became a *sine qua non* in classic Hebrew poetry.[109]

The form types of synagogal hymns usually answered concrete liturgical needs and bear names to indicate their original functions. Sometimes their designations also have reference to their external shape, in which case foreign influences are easily discernible. Of these multifarious names and forms only a few are selected here for discussion.

Keroba, the great insertion in the *Tefilla*, has been explained before, as has been *Yotzer*. The *R'shut* (permission) or *P'ticha* (opening) are stanzas before the hymn proper; their metre is different from that of the poem which follows and makes them akin to the Byzantine *Kukulion*. The *Ofan* (way, tune, originally 'chariot-wheel' in Ezek. 1:14-17), the *Zulat* (close of stanza) and *Siluq* (finale) are strophic hymns, parts of the *Yotzer*-prayer and usually lead to the *Kedusha* (Isa. 6:3) which is the extended Tersanctus of the Jewish liturgy. The *Shiba'ta* (sevenfold) inserts seven stanzas in the *Tefilla*, which on Sabbaths consists of seven eulogies instead of eighteen. It might be compared with the Byzantine *Kanon* and its inserted eight stanzas. Byzantine influence also shows the *Kiklar* (Greek: *Kuklarion*), a cyclical refrain hymn. Of purely hymnic character is the *Shevach* (praise) of the Torah, especially of the Decalogue or Exod. 15, comparable, and etymologically identical, with the Syriac *Tešbohta*. In sharp contrast to this form stand the *Azharot* (splendour), didactic poems whose purpose it is to paraphrase and comment upon the 613 statutes contained in the Torah. The refrain-poem *Pizmon* has already been discussed, and in a class by themselves are the *Seliha* (litany), the *Qina* (lamentation), the *Hoshano* ('Save now'), and the *Ma'amad* ('Standing-prayer'; cf., n. 76, p. 259).

The last mentioned are all hymns for days of fast or penitence, and carry a litany-like refrain, such as 'Help us', 'Save now', 'Have mercy', etc. Due to the bloody persecutions during the Crusades and the rest of the Middle Ages, their number increased and multiplied until separate books of *Selihot*, *Qinot*, and *Hoshanot* had to be printed.

Not directly connected with the synagogal liturgy are the *Zemirot* (Songs), table-songs for Sabbaths and Festivals, frequently of a mystical character. Most of them originated after the thirteenth century.

Style and Rendering

The diction of the early hymns is still inseparably connected and replete with biblical, talmudic and midrashic passages and allusions. It is possible here to speak of literary leading-motifs that permeate entire compositions for a holyday. Often these allusions are couched in purposely obscure language, which for the average layman is hard to understand. In the course of time, certain differences developed between Palestinian, Babylonian, and Spanish hymnography. This distinction is well appreciated by Rapoport's dictum: 'In the Spanish *piyyutim* the soul addresses its Creator, in the Italian, German and French *piyyutim*, the Jewish nation entreats its God'.[110] Another paraphrase of the same idea is Delitzsch's word: 'The Spanish poetry paints with the brush of a Raphael, the Italian hews out its forms with the chisel of a Michelangelo'.

This distinction between a narrow didactic-legalistic and a free hymnic style is noticeable also in the hymns of the Syrian and Byzantine Churches, sometimes even within the poems of one and the same author. In Krumbacher's extensive *Miszellen* about Romanus, we read:

> With regard to the poetic presentation of Romanus, we can distinguish in his work two main categories of hymns: (1) a narrative; (2) an argumentative. Frequently, Romanus has applied both styles to one subject, by narrating the substance of his theme in one hymn, then, presuming familiarity with the subject, presenting his theological-dogmatic reasoning in another. . . .[111]

In the Spanish era (1050–1400), Judaism overcame the strictly allusive technique. Free from dogmatic boundaries and exegetic shackles, the Soul praises its Creator. This epoch, however, lies outside the scope of this book. The following three illustrations are given in order to exemplify the most frequent types and styles of earlier Hebrew hymnody.

Yet before citing examples, we shall attempt to characterize the *spirit* of Hebrew hymnody in a few words.

All poems of the Synagogue have one theme in common: they confront with the scriptural word the surrounding world, its events and changes. Scripture serves not as illustration of man's life, but just the opposite is intended: man's life is seen as metaphor, parable, or example of the only reality extant: the word of God in Scripture.

The constant allusions to scriptural words or ideas are hard to grasp for anybody not thoroughly familiar with the Hebrew text and they result in a kind of pastiche. This style is, as the reader must have noticed, quite familiar to the Eastern Churches as well. The difference between their hymnody and the Hebrew lies in the aims. The Christian uses the scriptural word almost exclusively as a tool for Christological purposes; the medieval Jew, thrifty with Hallelujahs and suffering in the knowledge of his God-ordained Exile, reminds himself scripturally of his present ordeal, but also of the Messianic promise. The former condition is earthbound and temporal; the latter divine and eternal.

Better than any scholar did Franz Rosenzweig, poet and theologian, interpret this fiery and trouble-torn spirit of Hebrew hymnody. His annotated translations of Yehuda Halevi give the profoundest interpretation of the world of *piyyutim*.

Our first piece is part of a *Keroba* for the eve of Atonement; the hymn originated in the eighth century and its author is unknown. The text of the regular *Tefilla*, between which the stanzas of the hymn are intercalated, is printed in capitals. The poem is a rhymed alphabetic acrostic with isosyllabic inclination. (Seven syllables for every first half of the verse.)

KING, HELPER, REDEMPTOR, AND SHIELD

Letter:	Aleph	I shall teach the paths of righteousness	
	Beth	The way ye shall walk in abundance	(a)
	Gimel	O people born upon eagle's wings	(b)
	Dalet	Accept ye the straight words	(c)
	He	Return ye to the fear of the Lord	
	Vav	And rend ye your hearts:	
	Zayin	This is the gate of righteousness, if ye return	(d)
	Chet	The acts of kindness of your ancestors I shall remember to strengthen you:	

PRAISED BE THOU, OUR LORD, SHIELD OF ABRAHAM

WHO IS UNTO THEE, LORD OF POWER . . . KING WHO
MAKEST DEAD AND ALIVE, LORD OF SALVATION:

	Tet	Foolish and perplexed are we in our deeds:	
	Jod	We fell into the trap, ashamed of our ire;	
	Khav	Humbly we call on Thee, answer us	
	Lamed	In Thy time of mercy (grace)	(e)
	Mem	Calm us in Thy forgiveness	

Nun   Let us hear: I have found atonement!   (f)
           Our wailing consider as a hymn
  Samekh Refuse us not, lead back out of the Netherworld   (g)
           The concealed ones, through revival by thy dew.   (h)

PRAISED BE THOU, OUR LORD WHO REVIVEST THE DEAD[112]

(a) Cf. Ps. 37:11; (b) Exod. 19:4; (c) Hos. 4:1; 14:2; (d) Ps. 118:19; (e) Ps. 143:1 and Targum thereto; (f) Job 33:24; (g) i.e. the dead, according to the Midrash; (h) dew has eschatological significance; cf. *B. Chagiga* 12b: '... and the dew, by which the Holy One, blessed be He, will revive the dead'.[113]

The following two hymns may indicate the trend of religious ideology, removed from the confines of strictly didactical needs. The first is the *'Adon 'Olam*, which reflects a high level of pure monotheistic thought. The second bears direct, even intended, reference to the iconoclast conflict within the Byzantine Church. It was only natural that the Jews took sides with the iconoclasts, sympathizing with their cause and hoping that their victory would result in a betterment of their own standing in the Byzantine government.

I

The Lord of all did reign supreme
Ere yet this world was made and formed;
When all was finished by His will
Then was His name as King proclaimed.

And should these forms no more exist,
He still will rule in majesty.
He was, He is, He shall remain,
His glory never shall decrease.

And one is He, and none there is
To be compared or joined to Him.
He ne'er began, and ne'er will end,
To Him belongs dominion's power.

He is my God, my living God;
To Him I flee when tried in grief;
My banner high, my refuge strong,
Who hears and answers when I call.

My spirit I commit to Him,
My body too, and all I prize;
Both when I sleep and when I wake,
He is with me, I shall not fear.[114]

II

All the world shall come to serve Thee
And bless Thy glorious name,
And Thy righteousness triumphant
The islands shall acclaim.

And the peoples shall go seeking
Who knew Thee not before,
And the ends of earth shall praise Thee,
And tell Thy greatness o'er.

They shall build for Thee their altars,
Their idols overthrown,
And their graven Gods shall shame them,
As they turn to Thee alone. . . .[115]

We are not too well informed about the rendering of synagogal hymnody. While an enormous number of *piyyut* tunes have come down to us, in both oral and written tradition, our knowledge of the musical performance itself is meagre. The ancient Jewish disinclination for prayers in a fixed form was overcome only after strenuous efforts by the rabbis. The lack of a clearly rhythmical element was not felt too strongly, for the preferred musical type of the Near East has always been the free, a-metrical and half improvised recitative. After the Islamic conquest of the Near East, many Arab tunes were borrowed by Jewish cantors and applauded by congregations. Yet, the originally strong Arabic influence wore off in the course of the centuries, and to-day only one type of Arabic metre is known to have left its imprint upon every melody with which it was connected: the so-called *Hazağ* metre: $\smallsmile\; \rule{0.3cm}{0.4pt}\; \rule{0.3cm}{0.4pt}\; \rule{0.3cm}{0.4pt}$ musically expressed ♪│ ♩ ♩. ♪│ ♩ ♩ . or ♩│ ♩ ♩ │ ♩ ♩│ ♩. In most other cases no relation between the metre of the text and the rhythm of the music is traceable.[116] Although the system of Arab metre paved the way for more measured tunes in the music of the Synagogue, it was not this element that enhanced the music of the higher developed *piyyutim*. The characteristic feature of these musical *piyyutim* was the principle of contrafacts. It became a general practice to transform attractive tunes of secular texts into religious hymns, whereby the Rabbis, anxious to prevent the singing of morally dubious words, usually provided the new text for the contrafact.[117]

In general, a threefold way of performance prevailed up to the fourteenth century:

(1) Simple response, whereby cantor and congregation alternate.

(2) Recitation of a piece by the congregation, to be concluded musically by the precentor.

(3) The congregation repeats the chant of the cantor and adds something of its own.

Wherever there was a trained choir, as e.g. in Babylon during the ninth and tenth centuries, the responsorial rendering would prevail; where no chorus was at the cantor's disposal, (2) and (3) were most popular.

The *hazan* (cantor) was called upon to provide appropriate tunes for the new metrical hymnody. The brevity of the weekday services did not give him time enough to introduce new melodies to good advantage. On Sabbaths or holydays, however, the congregation expected to hear new songs and waited eagerly for them. Like the English minstrel and the German minnesinger, the *hazan* embodied in his person poet and musician.[118] Idelsohn describes this state of affairs in the following words:

Gradually the traditional unrhythmical modes ceased to hold first place in the hearts of the people, who became interested mainly in singing (no longer in the homiletic niceties of the text), which now became synonymous with rhythmical song. . . . Yehuda Harizi, a Sephardic scholar and poet . . . leaves a satiric description of the 'art' of the *hazan*, of Mossul, counting all his grammatical mistakes in the prayers as well as in his poetry; relating how the *hazan*, self-satisfied with his artistic performance, exhausted himself and the congregation and wasted the time through his 'art', so that no time was left for the ritual proper. When Al-Harizi called the attention of the *hazan* and his adherents to the mischief, they declared that his poetry and his music were more important than the prayers themselves.[119]

Summing up, we observe that the chant of the old prayers, such as the *Tefilla* or the *Sh'ma'* were left untouched by the new metrical style of synagogal music. Thus, two strata coexisted side by side, that belonged to entirely different eras and styles. The old recitative disregarded more or less the new metres of the *piyyutim*, while, on the other hand, the cantors and the congregations, at least after the ninth century, preferred rhythmical tunes. They did not, however, replace the older chant, chiefly out of reverence for its sacred tradition, which associated the recitatives with the splendour of the Temple and the great rabbis.

This dualism in the musical style of synagogal hymnody has remained vivid up to the present day, and is very comparable to the two styles in Syrian and Roman church-music. There we shall also find two musical styles, depending upon the metrical or non-metrical character of the texts.

Concerning the interchange of ideas, it may be said that Syrian, Byzantine and Armenian hymnody unfolded from a nucleus of Hebrew style and conceptions; the Byzantine and Syrian hymns show even faint traces of early rabbinic ideas. But stylistically and poetically, the Synagogue learned more from the old Oriental Churches and their poetry, since Judaism admitted hymnody only at a time when it was already well developed in Christianity.

THE HYMNODY OF THE LATIN CHURCH

An extensive discussion of that well-explored subject would, by far, exceed the scope of this book. The present examination will deal with the hymnody of the Latin Church only in as much as it shows relations to Judaism or to Hebrew-Aramaic literature.

Deliberately the term 'Latin Church', and not 'Roman Church' has been chosen here. For the various centres of the Western Church were invested with far-reaching autonomies in liturgical details, and the use of the hymn is a point in case. The Council of Laodicea had prohibited all non-scriptural texts from public reading or singing in the Church, especially the *psalmi idiotici*. And hardly eighty years had passed when the Council of Vannes again had to rule: *Matutinis hymnis intersint.*[120] The Council of Braga (563) renewed the Laodicean injunction, but the subsequent Council of Tours (567) permitted the practice of hymnody. In Spain the authorities championed most energetically the cause of the hymn in the face of stiff opposition, and the fourth Council of Toledo (633) threatened the opponents of the liturgical hymns with excommunication. In Ireland, Gaul, Milan, Spain, and North Africa hymn singing was an integral part of the liturgy and popular with the congregations at a time when the Roman authorities had not as yet fully approved of it. The first millennium ended before the Roman Office-books made any mention of hymns.[121] It was Ambrose, Bishop of Milan, whose authority backed the hymn to such an extent that, in spite of Rome's reluctance, the sacred poetry of the Church had become a distinct component of the liturgy, expanding into a treasury of hymns.

Poetic Patterns and Form Types

Most of the external adornments of poetry, such as acrostics, rhymes, strophes, etc., came into Latin hymnody via Byzantium or North Africa. The Syrian or Byzantine models of these patterns make it quite plain that none of these elements originally were indigenous to Latin literature. W. Meyer convincingly demonstrated the Semitic origin of these forms and there is no need to repeat his conclusions here.[122] The rhyme begins very modestly with the so-called *Tiraden* assonance, an arrangement in which groups of verses end with the same vowel. Similar beginnings are evident in old Hebrew and Syriac literature. Only toward the end of the tenth century did the genuine rhyme conquer the Latin hymnody, never to vanish again.

Of a different nature is the subject of stanzas. St Hilary of Poitiers (fourth century) composed a hymn 'Lucis largitor splendide' in eight stanzas, and other pieces where strophes were indicated by alphabetical acrostics.[123] It is doubtful if the number eight was just chosen at random, in view of the origin and the significance of the widespread principle of the *Octoechos*; this doubt is greatly strengthened by the fact that eight is the regular number of stanzas in most of the Ambrosian hymns.

It is only in *metre* that a transfusion and combination of Eastern and Western elements took place. In the Middle Ages, metrical, non-metrical, quantitative and accentuating systems existed peacefully side by side. It is true that the Venerable Bede wrote: 'Rhythm is the euphonious, non-metrical, but isosyllabic . . . composition of words, as it is usual in popular poems',[124] which obviously favours the accentuating and negates the quantitative principle of metre. But some half century after Bede, Theodulph of Orleans (d. 821) still wrote such an impeccably classic distich as this, strictly based upon quantitative metre:

> Gloria, laus, et honor, tibi sit Rex Christe Redemptor:
> Cui puerile decus prompsit Hosanna pium.[125]

The occidental forerunner of the new accentuating metre was the old popular *Versus Saturnius*, which existed as early as the third century B.C. Its scheme is ∪ ⏊ ∪ ⏊ ∪ ⏊ ∪ ‖ ⏊ ∪ ⏊ ∪ ⏊ or ∟ ∟ ∟ − ‖ ∟ ∟ ∟ (quantitative system). To the first half-verse usually one syllable was added, and thus the exceedingly popular verse of many hymns came into being:

Veni creator spiritus
Mentes tuorum visita, etc.

or

Jesu redemptor omnium
Quem lucis ante originem, etc.

or

A solis ortus cardine
Ad usque terrae limitem, etc.

wherein little attention is paid to the quantity of the syllables.[126] Thus, the four-foot iambic dimeter, a mixture of old Latin quantity metre and of the more recent Semitic accentuating system, became the favourite pulse-beat of Latin hymnody. Like the *Hazağ* metre in Hebrew poetry, the four-foot dimeter resulted in this musical rhythm:[127]

A so - lis or - tus car - di - ne

Substance and Style

The 'classic' Latin hymn-type, such as constitutes the majority of the hymns in the *Liber Usualis*, does not thrive on biblical quotations or allusions, as do its Syrian, Byzantine or Hebrew counterparts. Nor is it often didactic or polemic in character; it expresses genuine *Praise*. Only before the tenth century do we find dogmatic compositions or poems based on the Bible, such as Augustine's Psalm against the Donatists, or Commodian's didactic poems.

An interesting exception can be found in some old Irish hymns which overflow with scriptural references. Two fragments may illustrate this point:

Irish-Latin

Prayer of Abel, son of Adam, of Elijah, of Enoch, come to help us!
Noah and Abraham, Isaac, the admirable youth,
May they come to succour against the illness,
May starvation not reach us!
We pray to the father of the three quaternities and Joseph the prophet.   (a)
May Moses the good leader protect us, the man who protected his people when it crossed the Red Sea! etc.

Jewish litany in time of drought and famine

The first benediction closes with the words:
He who answered Abraham on Mount Moriah may answer you and hear the voice of your crying this day; blessed art Thou who redeemest Israel.
2nd: He who answered our ancestors on the Red Sea may answer you, etc.
3rd: He who answered Joshua in Gilgal may answer you . . . etc.
4th: He who answered Samuel in Mizpah, may answer you . . . etc.
5th: He who answered Elijah on Mt Carmel, may answer you . . . etc.
6th: He who answered Jonah in the belly of the fish, may answer you.
7th: He who answered David and Solomon his son, in Jerusalem, may answer you . . . etc.

(a) is a midrashic reference to Isaac (or Jacob?), who became the ancestor of the twelve patriarchs.

> Deliver me, O Lord, my body and my soul, from all
> existing evil, that envelops the earth,
> Deliver me, O Lord of gatherings, as Thou hast delivered
> Elijah with Enoch, from the world!
> Deliver me, O Lord, from all evil upon earth, as thou
> hast delivered Noah, son of Lamech, from the flood!
> Deliver me, O Lord, King of pure light, as Thou hast
> delivered Isaac from the hands of his father Abraham! etc.[128]

Most of the Jewish litanies followed this pattern.

Of these two hymns the former is a prayer to protect Ireland against the plague that raged there in 661 and 662, while the latter is a litany of the ninth century, part of a martyrology. Both pieces are strongly reminiscent of fast-day prayers, as given in *Mishna Ta'anith*.

Yet these compositions are exceptions, and scriptural references rarely occur in Latin hymnody. Why this lack of biblical poems here, whereas Syrian, Greek, Armenian, and Nestorian hymns are replete with scriptural allusions?

The answer is simple: it rests with the use of literal quotations from Scripture, as they appear in the respective liturgies. In the East, the scriptural passages rarely appear in undiluted form; they serve most frequently as the solid framework into which the poets build their hymns. With the exception of signal passages in the Mass, isolated biblicisms are read rather than chanted. In general, the Eastern Churches thrive more on paraphrases or elaboration of Scripture than on its pure word.

Compared with this type of liturgy, the musical ritual of the Roman Church consists, to an overwhelming degree, of psalmodic, antiphonal, or responsorial forms, all of which contain some scriptural quotation or other. This rigid attitude of the Roman Church in the face of persistent demands to give more freedom to contemporary poetic expression is evidenced by its reluctance to comply with these desires. When the authorities eventually yielded to the spirit of the times, they set aside the hymnic forms to be included in the authentic books of the Church as a distinct liturgical category. They were mostly non-biblical; they displayed a simple, easily recognizable metre, and they were, without a single exception, strictly Christological in their substance. In spite of all of these safeguards, a time came when hymns, proses, and sequences so flooded the liturgy that its core, the *Ordinarium Missae*, was all but obliterated. The Council of Trent (1545–63) eventually limited the number of hymns, and banished all sequences with the exception of five. This radical measure saved the integrity and homogeneity of the Roman liturgy.

The Christological praise of the Creator, or of Mary, or of a saint, finds appropriate expression in these free poetic outpourings, of which one may be quoted as an illustration. This is the famous invocation of the Holy Spirit, by Hrabanus Maurus (ninth century).

Translation (by John Dryden)

Veni Creator Spiritus,
Mentes tuorum visita:
Imple superna gratia
Quae tu creasti pectora.

Qui diceris Paraclitus,
Altissimi donum Dei,
Fons vivus, ignis, caritas,
Et spiritalis unctio. . . .

Accende lumen sensibus,
Infunde amorem cordibus,
Infirma nostri corporis
Virtute firmans perpeti. . . . etc.

Creator Spirit, by whose aid
The world's foundations first were laid,
Come, visit every pious mind;
Come, pour Thy joys on human kind;
From sin and sorrow set us free,
And make Thy temples worthy Thee.

O Source of uncreated light,
The Father's promised Paraclete,
Thrice holy Fount, thrice holy Fire,
Our hearts with heavenly love inspire;
Come, and Thy sacred unction bring,
To sanctify us while we sing.

Refine and purge our earthly parts;
But, oh, inflame and fire our hearts,
Our frailties help, our vice control,
Submit the senses to the soul;
And when rebellious they are grown,
Then lay Thy hand. and hold them down.

This superb invocation is sung on Pentecost, the Feast of the Holy Spirit. No didactic, apologetic, or homiletic element mars the beauty of the deeply religious poem. Hebrew poetry attained a similar freedom from the restraints of the didactic or biblically allusive style only during the twelfth and thirteenth centuries, in the great poems of the Spanish School.

Liturgical Function

All hymns were, originally, spontaneous outbursts of religious emotions. Their liturgical function has, in the course of time, and under different spiritual climates, undergone many and decisive changes. In the Eastern Churches they were gradually integrated in, and connected with, the daily liturgy, the feasts, and the memorial days of Saints. The method by which this integration took place was one of psychological association through intercalation between parts of prayers, designated for the various occasions. In addition, the Eastern Churches do not strictly distinguish between hymns and psalmodic forms, antiphons, canons, etc. While most of their hymns are preserved in special books, so are the psalmodies of every month, as e.g. in the Byzantine Church; but the Eastern authorities show no preference for any of the archetypes of liturgical chant.

In contrast to this integration of hymnody in the body of the liturgy, the function of the Latin hymn is more flexible. The daily morning service contains no hymns, except the canonical hours, where a single 'Ambrosian' hymn, the last remnant of a richer ritual, speaks of vanished splendour.[129] The poetic poverty of this ritual was felt during the Middle Ages, and it is hardly a coincidence that the followers of St Francis of Assisi endeavoured to enrich the liturgy by composing *laude*, supplementing the liturgical Lauds.[130]

Throughout the Roman liturgy, the hymn is connected with a particular *day* of its calendar, not with a particular *prayer*. There is no intercalation of a hymn between stanzas of another prayer, as in Syrian, Byzantine, or in the Jewish liturgy. Indeed, the *Ordinarium Missae* knows of no insertion or intercalation whatsoever. The hymn is the ornament of Sundays, or Feastdays, or days of Saints, or of the *Proprium Missae*.

Their poetical strain tends to intensify, in the hearts of the faithful, feelings which correspond to the particular Festival. . . . In other parts of the Divine Office, however, in which a canticle of the New Testament constitutes a climax, the hymn is inserted near this song of thanks, for it is only then that the highest point in the development of religious emotions is reached.[131]

Certain hymns are assigned to entire seasons; thus the famous 'Alma redemptoris mater' is sung during the Advent and Christmas season, glorifying the Virgin. The 'Salve Regina' closes the service of the Virgin from the end of the Easter season to Advent. Again, in contrast to the Eastern Churches, yet parallel with the custom of the Synagogue, the Roman Church clearly distinguishes between psalmodic or responsorial chants, based upon Scripture, and the more recent hymns. Finally, another difference between the Roman hymns and all others is the practice of repeating in each stanza the tune of the initial strophe. While this principle obtains for many Greek and Syrian *hirmoi*, there are numerous hymns in the Eastern Churches where each stanza has a different melodic version of the model strophe.

The sequences are the only exceptions from this rule in the Roman liturgy. Today, only five sequences are admitted to the regular service. Their origin is not quite clear; they seem to be outgrowths of the alleluiatic *jubili*. Words were fitted to the 'wordless hymns', usually producing pairs of parallel lines.[132] At any rate, either new words were applied to old melodies or new melodies were composed with entirely new words. It is possible that the entire sequence-form was engendered by Byzantine examples. Lately, E. Wellesz has brought forward very weighty arguments for the Byzantine origin of the sequence, which might result in the reversal of the hitherto accepted theories.[133]

Of the five sequences, one ignores the principle prevalent in Roman liturgy, not to make use of the device of intercalation within the prescribed course of the service. This is the famous sequence for the dead, 'Dies irae, dies illa', a poem, that has in turn become the antecedent of other great poetic compositions.[134]

This poem of beauty, blood and tears, is attributed to Thomas of Celano (*ca.* 1190–1260), a Franciscan monk, who allegedly wrote it during the fearful days of the 'black death'.[135] Already Mone has drawn attention to earlier versions of the text, antedating Thomas of Celano. It is a reasonable assumption that the Latin poem originated about 1000, when occidental Christianity was expecting the coming of the Millennium. Thomas of Celano probably was only its last, though masterful, redactor.[136]

The following Excursus on the antecedents of the 'Dies irae' pursues two purposes: first, to contribute additional material to the theory of the Byzantine origin of the sequence form; second, to show the Jewish, post-biblical origin of this truly tremendous poem.

EXCURSUS ON THE HEBREW AND BYZANTINE ANTECEDENTS OF THE 'DIES IRAE'

In the Jewish Prayerbook for the New Year and the Day of Atonement, a *piyyut* is placed in the centre of the service. This prayer, called *Unethane toqef*, portrays the terrors of the day of judgement; for the New Year is considered the 'day of writing' (the judgement), and the Day of Atonement the 'day of sealing it'. It is, therefore, most appropriate to chant a prayer describing the eschatological events of such a day, both in heaven and on earth. Hitherto, the poem was attributed to a

Rabbi Amnon of Mayence (end of the eleventh century) who, according to the legend, pronounced it in the Synagogue before his death, after cruel torture by the Bishop of Mayence.

As early as 1906, Dr A. Kaminka directed attention to the similarity of literary motifs that occur both in the 'Dies irae' and the *Unethane toqef*.[137] He then suggested a common source, perhaps an Aramean or Syriac penitential poem, and quoted a few, which approximate the ideas of the 'Dies irae' and the Hebrew prayer.

When studying Byzantine hymnology, my attention was arrested by a poem of Romanus on the re-appearance (*Parousia*) of Christ, which contains all the literary motifs of the *Unethane toqef*. In the profound study by Paul Maas on the chronology of Romanus' hymns, the author quotes evidence, beyond any possibility of a doubt, which proves the fact of Romanus' Jewish extraction.[138] He writes:

It appears from these two stanzas [of a poem quoted before] that Romanus was born a Jew and that he held a high office at the imperial court. . . . Concerning the Jewish descent of Romanus, one will probably see a confirmation of this fact in the absence of almost all anti-Jewish polemics in his hymns. . . . Shall we read the reason of his conversion between the lines of his hymn?

> Often from fear of the now ruling laws
> Hast Thou come to baptism, and hast become, what thou became
> Hating the new (faith).[139]

I then proceeded with my investigation, asking my colleague, Dr M. Zulay, of the Hebrew University of Jerusalem, for corroboration from his side. This I promptly received. Dr Zulay wrote to me:

There is no doubt whatsoever that the *Unethane toqef* originated in Palestine during the Byzantine rule. The German legend does not state that R. Amnon *composed* the poem, but that he *recited* it before his death.

Dr Zulay also kindly sent me a copy from a Geniza manuscript, at present at the British Museum, that probably dates back to the late eighth century.[140] The text of this Geniza version differs considerably from the now accepted recension of the current prayer books. It is impossible to outline here the *variae lectiones* and to discuss their significance; that must be left to a special study. Here we have to content ourselves with a comparative tabulation of the literary motifs, their order of succession, and formulation, as they occur in the *Unethane toqef*, the hymn of Romanus, and the 'Dies irae'. A few notes and comments will be added.

Unethane toqef (Geniza version)	Theological motifs of the Hymn of Romanus upon Christ's Reappearance[141]	Comparable parts of the Sequence 'Dies irae'
The angels shudder, fear and trembling seize them.	Everything trembles, The books are opened	What a tremble will there be
Thou dost open the books of record; Thou dost call to mind all things long forgotten.	The hidden things are made public. [Follows a description of the coming of the Antichrist. Then:]	The book will be opened All hidden things will appear.
The angels shudder: they say it is the day of judgement, for in justice, not even they are found faultless before Thee.	The angels are dragged before the throne. They cry: 'Glory to Thee most just judge!'	The awesome trumpet will sound over all the graves. Whom shall I ask for protection, when even the just ones are not safe?
The great trumpet is sounded.	Upon the sound of the trumpet. . . .[142]	Counting the sheep, grant me space among the lambs, segregate me from the goats.
They are not pure before Thee.	Nobody is pure before Thee. . . .	My prayers are not worthy, but Thou, Good One, be gracious unto me.
As the shepherd mustereth his flock, so dost Thou cause to pass, number . . . every living soul. . . .	Like a shepherd he will save. They all will bow before Thee.	
But penitence, prayer, and charity can avert the evil decree.	Therefore: Penitence and prayer will save you!	
Even unto the day of his death Thou waitest for the sinner, and if he repent, dost immediately receive him.	The injury of the sin we may heal through the remedy of remorse.	

The resemblance is obvious. While some of the motifs go back to Dan. 7, the motifs exposed in the above tabulation demonstrate the Jewish-apocalyptic source of both Romanus' hymn and the 'Dies irae'.

I shall sketch here additional evidence of Byzantine elements in the shape of the *piyyut* (apart from a Byzantine word actually occurring in the Hebrew text). Thus far it has been overlooked that the Hebrew version observes the principle of Byzantine metre, viz. the law of isosyllabism. After a poetic preamble of different metre, comparable to the Byzantine *Kukulion* and the Syrian *Prūmyon*, the Hebrew text is arranged in lines of eight, sometimes seven syllables. The only exception to that scheme is the refrain: 'But penitence, prayer, and charity may avert the evil decree', a practice that again conforms with the Byzantine habit of setting the refrain in a metre different from the body of the hymn.

The conclusions that result from this example are truly remarkable. The contents and the substance of the Hebrew composition are drawn from post-biblical Jewish literature and ideology; but the external form of the Jewish hymn betrays unmistakable Byzantine traces. The

Byzantine and the Latin poems show the same Jewish conceptions, but are couched respectively in typically Byzantine and Middle-Latin styles; the Latin stanzas with three rhyming lines no longer show Byzantine influence. This problem will be investigated in detail elsewhere.

Here one statement representative of the whole field of hymnody may suffice: the basic conceptions originate in the Near East. Through the medium of the Church they were being transformed in Europe, and, in this transformed state, returned to the Near East, where, under the spell of ethnically variegated folklore, they formed new strata of liturgical art, superimposed upon the old ones. Hence a consequence of the literary and musical development of the ancient liturgies must be clearly perceived: the more complex and artistic the liturgical forms became, the more they were monopolized by professional artists, be they poets or singers, *paytanim*, *hazanim*, or monks. As a negative corollary of this evolution, the active participation of the lay congregation shrank excessively; and in order to evaluate the people's activity in the 'professionalized' worship of those centuries, we shall have to go back to certain irreducible nuclei of popular prayer, in our case to the acclamations that accompany the public service.

NOTES CHAPTER VII

1. Gerbert, *De cantu et musica sacra*, I, 14.

2. An excellent analysis of the Hebraistic elements of these hymnic passages in Strack-Billerbeck, *Kommentar zum N.T. aus Talmud und Midrash*.

3. These hymnic attempts, however, are important milestones on the road to the literary-musical hymn; the *Didache* piece is a genuine liturgical eulogy (*beraka*) in strict Jewish style, the passage from the *Epistle to Diognetus* an early attempt at rhythmic poetry.

4. Col. 3:16.

5. Cf. *Apology*, Chapter 39.

6. For instance; El Shaddai, El Elyon (God in the highest, supreme God, Choregos). Cf. Th. Zahn, *Acta Johannis* (Erlangen, 1882), p. 220.

7. Cf. Irenaeus, *Adv. haer.*, I, Chapter 15, 6.

8. Cf. Th. Zahn, *Acta Johannis*, pp. 220 ff.

9. Best edition of the text in *Handbuch der N.T. Apocryphen* (Tübingen, 1909–3), pp. 425 ff, and *Acta Apostolorum Apocrypha*, II, 2, ed. Bonnet (1903), pp. xxxvi ff. The English translation after M. R. James, *The Apocryphal New Testament*, pp. 253 ff. The allusion: 'Grace danceth. I would pipe; dance ye all, I would mourn; lament ye all' refers to Matt. 11 : 16–17; Luke 7 : 32.

10. Augustine, *Epist. 237 ad Ceretium* (PL, XXXIII, 1034 ff.).

11. According to *Concilia*, ed. Hardouin (Paris, 1715), IV, p. 298. The analysis of the hymn as given by T. Gérold in his *Les Pères de l'Église et la musique* (p. 195) is unconvincing, for he cannot actually prove that the corresponding melody was syllabic. A similar reasoning may be encountered many centuries before, in Yehuda Halevi's *Kuzari*, II, 71–74, where the result is equally inconclusive; however, Gérold is right in doubting that extended and

complicated hymns have ever been popular. The history of synagogal and ecclesiastical hymnody shows clearly that only relatively simple and short hymns have survived in popular usage; it is different with professional soloists, be they Jewish or Christian.

12. The placing of Jesus in the midst of the twelve circling disciples has a suggestion of ancient astral myths (*Zodiac*). In particular the term *Ogdoas* affords special attention, for it is a musical-calendaric-religious symbol. It is discussed further in Part II, Chapter II. At the time of the Acts of John, the *Ogdoas* represented the 'Root and substance of all things' (*Irenaeus Contra Haer.* in *Ante-Nicene Fathers*, I, p. 316).

13. Cf. Ch.-P., pp. 37–38. In the introduction of the work, p. xix, Christ directs the reader's attention to the fact that in certain parts of the hymn the number of eight syllables is consistently prevalent.

14. Editions: (1) Grenfell and Hunt, *The Oxyrhynchus Papyri*, XV, 22. (2) Th. Reinach, 'Un Ancêtre de la musique de l'Église', *Revue Musicale* (July 1922), p. 24. (3) R. Wagner, 'Der Oxyrhynchos Notenpapyrus', *Philologus*, LXXIX (1924), pp. 201–21. (4) H. Abert, 'Ein neuentdeckter frühchristlicher Hymnus mit antiken Musiknoten', *ZFM*, IV (1921–22), pp. 527 ff. (5) E. Wellesz, 'The Earliest Example of Christian Hymnody', *Classical Quarterly*, XXXIX (Oxford, 1945), pp. 34–45. (Most careful critical edition.)

15. Cf. Ps. 65:1, whose Latin version, 'Te decet hymnus Deus in Sion', etc., forms one of the most frequently sung versicles of the Roman liturgy. Concerning the *hymnos hesperinos*, cf. Ch.-P., pp. xxii and 39–40.

16. Cf. Kaufmann Kohler, *The Origins of Synagogue and Church* (1929), pp. 250–9; Idem, 'The Origin and Composition of the Eighteen Benedictions', *HUCA*, I, pp. 387 ff; W. Bousset, *Eine jüdische Gebetssammlung in den Apost. Constit.* (Göttingen, 1916–17); W. Oesterley, *The Jewish Background of the Christian Liturgy* (Oxford, 1925), pp. 125 ff; L. Finkelstein, 'The Development of the '*Amida*', *JQR*, N.S. XVI (1932), pp. 23 ff. See also Chapter IX *infra*.

17. Cf. Lamy, *Opera Ephraemi Syri*, III, 6; also Yaqub of Serug in Assemani, *Bibl. Or.*, II, 1, p. 61.

18. Cf. Jeannin, *Mélodies liturgiques syriennes*, I, p. 66. On the strophic structure of Ephraem's hymns, see H. Grimme, *Der Strophenbau in den Gedichten Ephrems* (Freiburg, 1893).

19. For a good survey of Bardesanes' position see P. Kahle, *The Cairo Geniza* (Schweich Lectures of the British Academy, 1941. London, 1947), pp. 192–4.

20. According to the *Pesiqta Rabbati*, fol. 73a, the first verse of Ps. 92 spells, as acrostic, the name of Moses. It seems that the earliest traces of acrostics in the Bible date back to the sixth century B.C. Cf. *JE*, article 'Acrostics'; K. Krumbacher, *Geschichte der Byzantin. Literatur*, pp. 667 ff; L. Zunz, *Gottesdienstliche Vorträge* (2nd ed.), pp. 391 ff; W. Meyer, *Gesammelte Abhandlungen zur mittellateinischen Rhythmik*, II, pp. 108–11; Th. M. Wehofer, 'Untersuchungen zum Lied des Romanos, etc.', *Sitzber. der Philos.-Histor. Klasse der Akad. der Wissensch.*, CLIV (Vienna, 1907), pp. 3–6.

21. The difficult and involved literary-musical terminology of the hymnology and music of the Eastern Churches warrants a special investigation from the liturgical as well as from the musical point of view. In the limited framework of this book only the basic sources can be given: G. Reese, *Music of the Middle Ages*; W.-S., 'Theory and Philosophy of Music in Judaeo-Arabic Literature', *HUCA* (1941, 1943); H. G. Farmer, *History of Arabic Music*; E. Werner, 'The Origin of the Eight Modes', *HUCA* (1948); Dom Jeannin, *Mélodies liturgiques syriennes*; T. Schaeder, 'Bardesanes von Edessa', *Zeitschr. für Kirchengeschichte*, LI (1932); F. Feldmann, *Syrische Wechsellieder von Narses* (Leipzig, 1896); P. Kahle, 'Die Samaritanischen Marka-Hymnen', *OC*, III (1932), pp. 7 ff.

22. Cf. Gastoué, op. cit., p. 61.

23. Cf. Ch.-P., p. lxvii; Dunash ibn Librat, *Literatur-Blatt des Orient*, IV, 232.

24. See Jastrow, *Dictionary of Talmudic and Rabbinic Literature*, article '*Kulklion*'. Also, Payne-Smith, *Lexicon Syr.*, II, 3559, and S. Krauss, *Lehn-& Fremdwörter im Talmud*, p. 518. Baumstark's etymological attempt is not convincing; there can be no doubt that the origin of the word is Aramaic, not Greek. Cf. Baumstark, *Festbrevier der Jakobiten*, p. 102, n. 2.

25. Cf. Ch.-P., p. lxvii; also lx. The medieval term *pizmon* was hitherto derived from the old French *pseaume* or the Greek *psalmos*. Cf. ELB, p. 208, and, for the etymology of

the word, H. Brody and K. Albrecht, *Die neuhebr. Dichterschule der Spanisch-Arabischen Epoche*, p. 17; also L. Zunz, *Synagogale Poesie*, pp. 88, 367, and *JE*, article 'Pizmon'.

26. On the exact etymology of *piyyut*, see Zunz, *Gottesdienstliche Vorträge*, p. 393, and S. Krauss, op. cit., II, p. 443 (see *supra*, n. 24).

27. Cf. Josephus, *Antiquities*, II, 16, 4; also *Stilistik*, ed. Koenig, p. 341, where patristic testimonies are collected. Further references in Josephus, *Antiqu.*, IV, 8, 44; VII, 12, 3.

28. This does not mean that Ephraem always and invariably made use of this device, but undoubtedly he knew it and implemented it. Baumstark, the best authority on Ephraem, writes: 'Indispensable for the *Memra* is a structure of verses which have the same number of syllables; apart from the metre of seven syllables which Ephraem used exclusively, chiefly the five and twelve syllabic metre merit consideration.' (*Geschichte der syrischen Literatur* (1922), p. 40.) It is necessary to bear this statement in mind against Jeannin's rather vague classification of metres.

29. Cf. E. Wellesz, 'Melito's Homily on the Passion', *JTS*, XLIV (1943), pp. 41–52.

30. Cf. A. Merx, *Hiob*, pp. lxxxiii ff, and G. Bickell, *Ephrem, Carmina Nisibena*, pp. 32–39; also *ZDMG*, XXXV (1881), pp. 416, 418, 419. As for criticism, see W. Meyer, 'Anfang und Ursprung der lateinischen und griechischen rhythmischen Dichtung', in *Gesammelte Abhandlungen über mittellateinische Rhythmik*, II, pp. 67, 107, 110, 112. Also Jeannin, op. cit., I, pp. 61 ff.

31. P. Kahle, *The Cairo Geniza*, *supra*, n. 19, also p. 193. The difference between Bardesanes' and Ephraem's poetic styles is already described in Sozomen, *Hist. Eccl.*, III, 16. I had, independent of Kahle, reached similar conclusions in my study 'The Conflict between Hellenism and Judaism in the Music of Early Christianity', *HUCA* (1947). See Chapter I of Part II of this book.

32. *Infra*, pp. 238–9.

33. With due respect to the elaborate studies of Kahle and M. Zulay, who observed Syrian influence in Hebrew poetry, it should not be forgotten that more than a hundred years ago a great Jewish scholar had ventured the very same conjecture. When everybody ascribed the metrical system of Hebrew poetry to Arabic influence, S. D. Luzzatto, in his *Betulat Beth Yehuda*, p. 13, suggested that Palestinian as well as Babylonian Jews had learned the devices of metrical poetry from the Syrians, not from the Arabs.

34. See *supra*, n. 29, also Kahle, op. cit., p. 30. Cf. C. Bonner, in *Studies and Documents*, ed. K. & S. Lake, XII, 1940.

35. Cf. W. Meyer, op. cit., pp. 116–18.

36. *Ibid.*

37. P. Kahle, op. cit., pp. 29–30, and more profoundly, S. Spiegel in *The Jews: their History, Culture and Religion*, ed. L. Finkelstein (New York, 1949), I.

38. Cf. Ch.-P., p. cvii; 'Yet this resemblance of verse structure seems to stem not so much from a Greek pattern, as from the parallelism of Hebrew canticles'.

39. Cf. P. Maas on Romanus in *Byzant. Zeitschrift*, XIV (1905), p. 645, and the same author in XV (1906), pp. 30–32.

40. For an extensive presentation of the subject, see G. Hoelscher, *Syrische Verkunst*; also Jeannin, op. cit., I, Chapter V. Also J. Schirmann, in *Publications of the Schocken Institute* (Jerusalem, 1953–4).

41. Cf. Yaqub of Serug in Bedjan, *Acta Martyrum et Sanctorum*, III, 665 ff; also A. Hahn, in *Kirchenhistorisches Archiv*, fasc. III, p. 63.

42. Cf. Baumstark, op. cit., p. 39.

43. An extensive bibliography on the forms of Syriac poetry is given in Hoelscher, op. cit., and in Baumstark, op. cit., pp. 39, 40, 47, 48, 51, 52, 72, 244. For examples of these forms, see Jeannin, op. cit., I, 72 ff.

44. Jeannin, op. cit., p. 70.

45. Cf. S. Salaville, *Liturgies orientales* (Paris, 1932), p. 82.

46. ELB, p. 277; also M. Sachs, *Die religiöse Poesie der Juden des Mittelalters*, pp. 177 ff.

47. Cf. P. Kahle, 'Was Melito's Homily Originally Written in Syriac?', *JTS*, XLIV (1943), p. 53.

48. Cf. *Breviarium iuxta ritum ecclesiae Antiochenae Syrorum* (Mossul), VI, 227.

49. Cf. Baumstark, *Das Festbrevier der Syrischen Jakobiten*, p. 45; also E. W. Brooks, 'The Octoechos', in *Patrologia Orientalis*, VII, preface, and Salaville, op. cit., pp. 186–7.

50. Baumstark, op. cit., pp. 267 ff.

51. There are many prayers in the Synagogue which show distinct resemblance to the Syriac hymn, especially the paraphrases of the morning psalms in the extended services of the High Holydays. The Syriac piece is quoted after Baumstark, op. cit., pp. 116–7, n. 2. The author adds: 'This piece must be very old. For its entire sound and style, the references to the Exodus, and the Hebrew name of God reminds of Synagogal worship'.

52. Ibid., p. 122, n. 3. It is understandable that Baumstark wrote, p. 129: 'A comparative examination of the complete Synagogal rite with the old Syrian service is an urgent desideratum'. This book strives to answer, at least in part, that need.

53. The translation of the Hebrew from the services of the eighth day of Tabernacles and the first day of Passover.

54. J. B. F. Pitra, *L'Hymnographie de l'Église grecque* (Rome, 1867), pp. 33 ff.

55. Idem, *Analecta Sacra*, I, pp. liii ff.

56. Ps.-Origen, *Philosophumena*, V, Chapter I. Actually, the work was written by Hippolytus; text after E. Miller, *Origenis Philosophumena* (Oxford, 1851).

57. Reading *phaos* instead of the corrupt *chaos*.

58. Translated by E.W. after the text in Ch.-P., p. 32. Also E. Miller, *Origenis Philosophumena* (Oxford, 1851), p. 122. The text is frequently corrupt. The edition in *Monumenta Ecclesiae Liturgica*, I, 2, n. 5165, is almost unusable. See also Legge's translation in Hippolytus, *Philosophumena* (London, 1921), I, p. 145.

59. The Greek text in Pitra, *Hymnographie*, p. 37. The last line seems to me an added marginal note of a scribe, since it fits in no way into the archaic attitude and style of the hymn.

60. Cf. Menachem Zulay, 'Eine Hanukka-Qeroba von Pinhas hak-kohen', *Mitteilungen des Forschungs-Instituts für Hebräische Dichtung*, I (Berlin, 1933), pp. 164–5.

61. The text in T. Wehofer's study 'Untersuchungen zum Lied des Romanos auf die Wiederkunft des Herrn', *Sitzungsber. u. Abhandl. der Philos.-Hist. Kl. d. Kais. Akad. d. Wissensch.*, CLIV (Vienna, 1907), 11–19. This remarkable study will be quoted extensively later on.

62. T. Wehofer, 'Untersuchungen zur altchristlichen Epistolographie', in *Sitzungsber. u. Abhandl. der Philos.-Hist. Kl. d. Kais. Akad. d. Wissensch.*, CXLIII (Vienna, 1901).

63. T. Wehofer, op. cit. (*supra*, n. 61), pp. 17–19. Compare with his conclusions the statements of Ch.-P., p. xix: 'Since for these reasons nothing of these poems [Psalms, Odes and Spiritual Songs, cf. Paul, Eph. 5:19] has been related, nor as a whole been saved, I suppose that all three names refer to those sacred poems which the Christians adopted from the Synagogue, together with their musical modes. . . . Thus it is apparent that the Christians in their gatherings used almost the same chants and hymns which the Jews had in their synagogues, well until the fifth century, from which time the Codex Alexandrinus stems, as all paleographic evidence clearly shows.' I reach similar conclusions in Chapter IX on the Doxology.

64. The Latin and the translated Byzantine text are taken from E. Wellesz, *Eastern Elements in Western Chant* (London, 1947), pp. 23–25. See also my remarks reviewing Wellesz's book in *MQ* (July 1948).

65. See Chapter IX, where the form of eulogies of the Early Church is discussed extensively. The text of the hymn quoted here is found in Bunsen, *Analecta Antenicaena*, III, 88.

66. Cf. A. Landshuth, *Limmude ha-'avoda*, p. 46.

67. Cf. W. Meyer, op. cit., pp. 92 ff; also P. Kahle, *The Cairo Geniza*, pp. 28–32, where he concludes: 'We find rhymed sentences in the Greek text also, and it may be that rhyme was developed after that time [end of the second century] in Syriac literature. But it is very difficult to say anything definite here, as nothing of the older type of Syriac poetry is preserved.'

68. Cf. W. Meyer, op. cit., p. 116.

69. Cf. Campbell Bonner, 'The Homily on the Passion by Melito, Bishop of Sardis', *Studies and Documents*, ed. Kirsopp and Silva Lake, XII (1940).

70. Cf. E. Wellesz, *Eastern Elements in Western Chants*, pp. 48–49.

71. See *supra*, n. 25. Cf. also the extended controversy in *Literaturblatt des Orients*, IV, pp. 90, 486, 519, 605, and V, p. 719.

72. Cf. Ch.-P., pp. lxiv ff: 'Zonaras seems to see the cause of this fact [the omission of the second canticle, Deut. 32] in the sad character of the second canticle, where Moses impugns the impiety of the Israelites and their imbecility.' Cf. also E. Wellesz, *MQ* (1947), pp. 301 ff. See also H. Schneider, op. cit. pp. 254 ff.

73. Text in Ch.-P., pp. 158 and 226.

74. In spite of all theological and linguistic differences, sometimes the scriptural basis of a poem prevails over all divergences of culture and languages. In the following, one example is quoted for many. The Byzantine version is a '*Kanon* of the bodyless', by St Joseph the Hymnographer (d. 883), quoted from *Hymns of the Eastern Church*, ed. J. M. Neale (London, 1876), No. 6. Compared with it is a famous poem of Yehuda Halevi, Divan No. 45 (Spain, twelfth century):

Greek	Hebrew
Stars of the morning, so gloriously bright,	Stars of the morning in perpetual dances,
Filled with celestial resplendence and light.	To Thee they owe their bright resplendence;
These, that, where night never followeth day,	
Raise the Trisagion ever and aye.	Sons of the heavens are ever on guard,
These are Thy counsellors: these dost Thou own,	They, in eternal day, braid Thy wreath of glory,
Lord God of Sabaoth, nearest Thy throne.	They are Thy ministers, counsellors, yea!

Both poems spring from the same scriptural motif, viz. Job 38:7.

75. The Nestorian term *motva* means session and corresponds exactly with the Greek *kathisma*. Cf. Ch.-P., p. lxii; also Maclean, *East Syrian Daily Offices*.

76. The expression *ma'amad* has, in its Latin translation *statio*, permeated the terminology of the Roman Church. There it is used, according to its Talmudic significance, as the designation of fasting and petition services (M. *Taanith* 4, 2, and *Gemara* thereto). Cf. S. Bonsirven, 'Notre statio liturgique est-elle empruntée au culte juif?' in *Recherches de science religieuse* (1925), pp. 285 ff. Cf. also Tertullian, *De jejunio*, cap. 16, *CSEL*, XX, p. 296; and John Chrysostom, in E. Preuschen, 'Die Apostelgeschichte', in *Handbuch zum NT*, IV, I, p. 101. The question is extensively treated in Johannes Schümmer, *Die altchristliche Fastenpraxis* (Münster, 1933). The term *ma'amad* is also used as a form of chanted prayer, exactly as the *akathisma* or *stasis*, in the letters of Ben Baboi (*ca.* 780), in *Geniza Studies*, II, pp. 551 ff (in Hebrew). Also P. Kahle, op. cit., p. 26.

77. *Hypakoe* is often equated with *hypopsalma* (*Const. Apost.*, II, No. 57) or *epihymnion* (Ch.-P., pp. xvi and lxix).

78. Cf. L. Zunz, *Synagogale Poesie*, p. 79; Brody-Albrecht, op. cit., p. 19.

79. Cf. J. Perles, in *Byz. Zeitschrift*, p. 63; also S. Krauss, op. cit., II, 443, 262; also Zunz, *Synagogale Poesie*, pp. 88, 367; most recently Ben Yehuda, *Thesaurus*, p. 1868, verb. t-j-d.

80. Cf. M. Steinschneider, 'Jüdische Literatur', in Ersch-Gruber, *Enzyklopädie*, p. 424, notes 45 and 51; also *Literaturblatt des Orients*, IV, pp. 687, 540; and W.-S., op. cit., *HUCA* (1941), where a comparative terminology is given.

81. J. Hefele, *Conziliengeschichte*, I, pp. 746, 793 ff; about the interpretation of the canon, see Nisard, *L'Archéologie musicale et le vrai chant grégorien*, p. 9; also T. Gérold, *Les Pères de l'Église et la musique*, pp. 34 ff. In this connexion attention should be directed to Ps. 151 of some of the Septuagint versions, an early *psalmus idioticus*, exalting David's victory over Goliath.

82. Aetheria Silvia, *Peregrinatio*, ed. Heraeus, cap. 24, 1, 2, 4, *et passim*. The Fourth Synod of Toledo (633) had already expressly praised St Hilary of Poitiers as an excellent author of hymns. Cf. Hardouin, op. cit., III, pp. 583 ff.

83. ELB, pp. 358 ff; also J. Mann, 'Anan's Liturgy', *Journal of Jewish Lore and Philosophy*, I, p. 343.

84. Cf. J. B. F. Pitra, *L'Hymnographie de l'Église grecque*, p. 23.

85. Cf. Félix Neve, *L'Arménie chrétienne et sa littérature* (Paris, 1886); also P. Aubry, *Le*

Rhythme tonique dans la poésie liturgique et dans le chant des Églises chrétiennes (Paris, 1903), pp. 70–80. The name *Sharakan* itself might be a derivative from the Hebrew *Shir* (song, hymn, poem). According to the sources quoted in N. Ter Mikelian, *Das armenische Hymnarium* (p. 88), the Fathers St Isaac (d. 440), and St Mesrob were the first poets of the Armenian Church.

86. Cf. Nerses Ter Mikelian, op. cit., which contains a list of authors together with an interesting analysis of the structure of Armenian hymns.

87. Text (in Armenian) in *Charakan* (Constantinople, 1828); quoted here from P. Aubry's French translation, op. cit., p. 72.

88. Cf. P. Aubry, op. cit., p. 76; also L. Petit, article 'Arménie', in *Dictionnaire de théologie catholique*, I, col. 1963–5. He concludes his explanations as follows: 'It is true that the Greek system of metre proved to be an imitation of the Syrian pattern, and it is difficult, at the present state of science, to state whether the Armenians are the immediate tributaries of the Greeks or of the Syrian. . . .' About the *Khozrovayin* hymns, cf. P. Ingigian, *Archeology of Armenia* (1835), III, 42–6. (In Armenian.)

89. For an extensive examination of the sources of the *Octoechos*, see Chapter II of Part II. Ter Mikelian, op. cit., p. 4, however, emphasizes that 'a complete *Kanon* of the Lord's feasts must contain seven, not eight, hymns'.

90. Cf. Dulamier, 'Etude sur la liturgie arménienne', *Journal asiatique*, Vth series, vol. 16, p. 277; also F. Neve, 'L'Hymnologie arménienne', *Le Muséon*, IV (1885), pp. 359–68.

91. ELB, p. 125. The author quotes from *B. Taanith* 28b, where we read that the great liturgical authority of the third century, Rab, came from Palestine to Babylonia and found there the custom of reciting the *Hallel* on New Moons. Being under the impression that the custom was old and genuine, he approved of it.

92. The best translation and interpretation of that law is given in P. Kahle, op. cit., pp. 33 ff, and 24. There also the meaning of the crucial term *deuterosis* is discussed, but the author's explanations are not fully convincing.

93. Ibid., pp. 26–27. See also S. Spiegel, op. cit., pp. 536 ff.

94. The quotation after Schreiner's translation in *MGWJ*, XLII (1898), pp. 123 ff; see also J. Mann, 'Changes in the Divine Service of the Synagogue Due to Religious Persecution', *HUCA* (1927), pp. 241 ff; also Chapter IX of this book where this question is discussed in connexion with the doxology.

95. Cf. Jefim Schirmann, 'Hebräische Poesie in Apulien & Sizilien', *Mitteilungen des Forschungs-Instit. für Hebr. Dichtung*, I (Berlin, 1933), p. 132.

96. Of the vast literature on this subject only the best and most recent studies are listed here: ELB, pp. 254–68, also 41–67; K. Kohler, 'The Origin and Composition of the Eighteen Benedictions', *HUCA*, I, pp. 387 ff; L. Finkelstein, 'The Development of the '*Amida*', *JQR*, N.S. XVI, pp. 1 ff, 127 ff; J. Mann, 'Changes in the Divine Service of the Synagogue Due to Religious Persecution', *HUCA*, IV (1927); J. Mann, 'Genizah Fragments of the Palestinian Order of Service', *HUCA*, II (1925); E. Werner, 'The Doxology in Synagogue and Church', *HUCA*, XIX (1946); S. Schechter, *Studies*, pp. 97 ff; *JE*, article 'Didache'.

97. Cf. *GV*, p. 379, note d; also M. Sachs, *Religiöse Poesie der Juden*, p. 178 and Zunz, *Synagogale Poesie*, p. 65 ff.

98. On the opposition against the *piyyut*, see ELB, pp. 301–3; J. Mann, op. cit., *supra*, n. 94; L. Ginzberg, 'Epistles de Ben Baboi', *REJ*, LXX, p. 130; foremost L. Ginzberg in *Ginze Schechter*, II, pp. 508 ff (written in Hebrew).

99. ELB, p. 290.

100. For example see ELB, p. 291.

101. About the epithet 'the humble' see Steinschneider, 'Jüdische Literatur', in Ersch-Gruber, p. 428, n. 24; also *Literaturblatt des Orients*, VI, pp. 131, 245, note.

102. See Chapter I of Part II of this book. A few examples of pre-metrical poetry in M. Black, *An Aramaic Approach to the Gospels* (2nd ed., Oxford, 1954), pp. 293 ff.

103. The vocalized text is quoted after Jefim Schirmann, op. cit., p. 121.

104. *Supra*, n. 102. For the literature, see S. Spiegel, op. cit.

105. Cf. *JE*, article 'Dunash ibn Librat'; also Al-Harizi, *Tachkemoni*, XVIII, ed. Kaminka (Warsaw, 1899), and ELB, p. 295.

106. It is probably no coincidence that R. Ephodi praised the value of Hebrew for sacred poetry: 'For unlike Christian hymns, which use a translation of the Bible, the Hebrew poet is free to use the original, whenever it suits him.' Cf. *Ma'asse Ephod*, cap. VIII.

107. See Yehuda Halevi, *Kuzari* (Cassel), II, 70, 72, 78; also H. Brody, *Studien über die hebr. Dichter der spanischen Periode*, pp. 17 ff.

108. It is not necessary to search, as Kahle does, op. cit., pp. 26–28, for foreign patterns of rhymed poetry. They probably evolved from the chain-figures of biblical diction (concatenation).

109. On the subject of rhyme, cf. M. Zulay, *Studies of the Research Institute for Hebrew Poetry*, II (Berlin, 1936); also A. Kober, 'Zum Machsor Jannai', *Jahrbuch der jüd. Literar. Gesellschaft* (Frankfurt, 1929).

110. Rapoport, *Bikure ha-Itim*, VIII, p. 184 (in Hebrew).

111. Cf. K. Krumbacher, 'Miszellen zu Romanos', *Abhandl. d. Bayr. Akad. der Wissensch., Phil.-Hist. Kl.*, XXIV (Munich, 1909), p. 89.

112. For parallels, cf. Ch.-P., p. 95.

113. The Hebrew text and all biblical references are quoted from the fine study of Rafael Edelman, *Zur Frühgeschichte des Machzor* (Stuttgart, 1934), p. 31. Translation by E. W. The best modern study is S. Spiegel, op. cit.

114. Translation after the Union Prayer Book, newly revised, vol. I, p. 98.

115. Translation by Israel Zangwill. On the Jewish attitude to iconoclasm, cf. N. H. Baynes, 'The Icons before Iconoclasm', *Harvard Theol. Rev.*, 1951, pp. 93 f.

116. Cf. *JM*, pp. 116 ff.

117. Cf. Simon Duran, *Magen Avot* (Livorno, 1785), p. 55 (in Hebrew); also M. Lonzano, *Shete Yadot* (Venice, 1617), fol. 140 (in Hebrew).

118. See *supra*, pp. 236 ff. Also S. Spiegel, op. cit., p. 548.

119. Cf. *JM*, p. 125; Al-Harizi's report in *Tachkemoni*, XXIV, pp. 220, 227 (in Hebrew).

120. Canon No. 14 of the Council of Vannes in Hefele, op. cit., I.

121. WGM, I, p. 166; also Walafrid Strabo, *De rebus ecclesiasticis*, cap. 25, (PL, CXIV, 256).

122. W. Meyer, op. cit., II, pp. 18–25.

123. The text of this hymn in A. Daniel, *Thesaurus Hymnologicus*, IV, p. 127; also G. Dreves, *Analecta Hymnica*, I, p. 148.

124. In *PL*, X, 173.

125. Text in *LU*, ed. 1931, p. 525; see also WGM, I, pp. 164–5.

126. Cf. WGM, I, p. 168.

127. Ibid., III, p. 463.

128. The translation of the text, inaccessible to me in the original, in *DACH*, VI, col. 2914–15. A similar spirit prevails in early proses. Similar pieces in the Sarum Missal.

129. As evidenced in the rule of St Benedict; cf. also the words of Ambrose's biographer, Paulinus; 'His famous devotion did not only enter into the daily services of his own Church [Milan], but also spread throughout almost all Occidental provinces.' (PL, XIV, 31, cap. 13.) The daily hymn shows the same character as authentic hymns of Ambrose. Thus, Lauds of Tuesday and Thursday contain hymns by Aurelius Prudentius, an imitator of the Ambrosian style.

130. Cf. G. Reese, op. cit., p. 237; also J. Handschin, 'Über die Laude', *Acta Musicologica*, X (1938), p. 14; and F. Liuzzi, 'Ballata e Lauda', in *Annuario dell'Accademia di S Cecilia* (1930–31). The *Laude* are free hymns of praise, in the Italian language.

131. Cf. R. Stapper–D. Baier, *Catholic Liturgics* (Paterson, New Jersey, 1935), p. 136.

132. This is W. Meyer's contention; cf. op. cit., II, p. 96; later withdrawn. Even more convincingly WGM, I, pp. 253, 255.

133. Cf. E. Wellesz, *Eastern Elements in Western Chant*, Part IV, Chapter 1, 'The Origin of Sequences and Tropes'. So also Baumstark, *Liturgie comparée*, p. 113.

134. E.g. its poetic use in Goethe's *Faust*; see also G. Rietschel, *Lehrbuch der Liturgik*, p. 469.

135. WGM, I, pp. 274 ff.

136. Cf. Mone, *Lateinische Hymnen des Mittelalters*, I; qu. 'Dies Irae'; also G. Dreves,

Die Kirche der Lateiner in ihren Liedern (1908), p. 89; also *Les questions liturgiques et paroissiales* (Louvain, 1931), pp. 260 ff. Recently, Jungmann, *Miss. Sol.*, I, pp. 541 ff.

137. Cf. Armand Kaminka, 'Das *Unessane tokef* und das Dies Irae', in *Freie Jüdische Lehrerstimme* (Vienna, 1906), p. 63.

138. P. Maas, 'Die Chronologie der Hymnen des Romanos', in *Byzant. Zeitsch.*, XV (1906–7), pp. 1–44.

139. Ibid., p. 32.

140. MS British Museum, G 5557 or., fol. 67b–68b.

141. Text and some notes concerning Romanus' hymn are quoted from T. Wehofer's profound study, 'Untersuchungen zum Lied des Romanos auf die Wiederkunft des Herrn', in *Sitzungsber. d. Akad. d. Wiss.; Phil.-Hist. Klasse* (Vienna, 1907), vol. CLIV, fifth study.

142. The idea of a trumpet signal for the beginning of the Day of Judgement occurs in Old Testament biblical and apocryphal literature; in the *Tefilla* of the eighteen benedictions the prayer for the blowing of the trumpet as a signal for the Messianic age is repeated three times daily. Here God is viewed to sound the shofar. The recently discovered Dead Sea Scroll on the war between the Children of Light and the Children of Darkness stresses the motif of the 'trumpet of judgment' very fully.

CHAPTER EIGHT

The Liturgical Acclamations

THE LITURGICAL FUNCTION OF THE ACCLAMATION

LITURGY is a premise of organized worship. As such, it cannot be the monopolistic activity of a priestly class alone, the less so in the democratic stage of a religion. The people and the community of the faithful must have a share in the liturgical acts, even if only by adding a weighty word. Many factors in the development of Judaism, Christianity, Islam, and even Buddhism demand the participation of the community. There is an abundance of antecedents even in the pagan cults. One need only think of the short invocations, as they occur in Homer,[1] in Babylonian-Accadian rituals with repeated responses[2] such as, 'O Shamash, Lord of Judgement, O Adad, Lord of Divination'[3] to comprehend fully the liturgical importance of the short formula of acclamation. Similar calls or exclamations of liturgical character occur even in primitive civilizations, where they remain an unorganized mass cry.[4]

Even the well-developed liturgies have preserved remnants of this rudimentary stage; and it is mainly due to these more primitive elements that liturgy itself might be considered a no-man's-land between the realms of folklore and of art. These primitive nuclei might be termed stylized folklore, to which were later added artistic or theological compositions. Instances of this process are conspicuous in the literature and liturgy of Judaism, Catholicism, and Protestantism. Thus, the ancient popular refrain from Num. 10:35:

> Rise up, O Lord, and let Thine enemies be scattered;
> And let them that hate Thee flee before Thee

was taken over and shaped in a more artistic form in Ps. 68:2. Similar primitive refrains, retained in the liturgy, are the *stichoi* of Ps. 136:1–3:

> O give thanks unto the Lord for He is good;
> For His loving kindness endureth for ever.
> O give thanks to the God of Gods,
> For His loving kindness endureth for ever.
> O give thanks to the Lord of Lords,
> For His loving kindness endureth for ever.

that once were so popular that a prophet quoted them as outbursts of national joy (Jer. 33:11). Ps. 118 with its opening and closing refrain is a further example, particularly significant as a part of the *Hallel* that, in ancient times, was already considered a popular response.[5] Its outstanding verse, the *Hosanna*, is quoted as the welcome of the multitude when Jesus entered Jerusalem (Matt. 21:9). All of these acclamations, while originally spontaneous and naive expressions of religious emotion, have remained unchanged in the liturgies, or have become the nuclei of more artistic compositions based upon them.[6]

The same principle holds true for the musical element. Gevaert has shown convincingly that many of the early antiphons can be reduced to simple melodic and popular clauses,[7] and P. Wagner demonstrated the same practice as applied to the Tract.[8]

In the same way, if to a lesser degree, suppressions of popular songs, or calls, occur in the established liturgies. The reason, usually dogmatically expressed, is that the gradual purification of monotheism demanded such suppressions, and we find it so in Judaism no less than in Christianity and Islam. Thus, the so-called Thirteen Attributes of God (Exod. 34:6–7) are recited on all festivals, but the last verse is sharply curtailed. Pagan acclamations, suppressed by Islam, are also known to us.[9] In Christianity, both pagan and orthodox Jewish acclamations had to be eliminated, or, at least, reinterpreted in Christological fashion. A case in point is the *Hosanna*, of which we shall speak later. Another is the transformation of Greek pagan acclamations, such as *chaire* (be of good cheer), or of corybantic outbursts, with which Athanasius constantly had to cope in Miletus.[10]

Special attention must be paid to the centuries of transition from one religion to the other. During that period the popular acclamations were still naive expressions of belief untainted by theological arguments; the primitive Christian community had not yet established an organized worship. Its spontaneous acclamations represented the active part that the congregations played during the first two centuries, when no more than the core of the liturgy was in existence. From still another point of view the acclamations represent an intermediate stage in the transition; while they were sung, their place is between the literary and the musical forms of worship, constituting a natural transition from the spoken to the chanted stage of liturgy.[11] For this reason they and their extensions into the dogmatic realm, the doxologies, have been placed at the end of the historical and literary part of this book.

Half-spoken, half-sung, spontaneous, unorganized but zestful, no longer bound to the strict Synagogue liturgy but not yet Christian in the full sense of the word: thus we have to imagine the popular acclamations of primitive Christianity.

The acclamations were refrains or simple, closing exclamations; for more cannot be expected from a new, untrained, and heterogeneous community. Yet they were often sung, as we know from numerous sources.[12] Considered a spontaneous expression of the *vox populi*, the formula 'let all the people answer' was equally familiar to the spiritual leaders of Jerusalem, Byzantium, Antioch and Rome. Thus, Jerome praised the 'thunderlike Amen' that resounded in Roman basilicas.[13] This is the ideal of the acclamation by the *koinonia*, the religious unison of the faithful community.[14] The acclamation, a truly important aspect of the *koinonia*, served three functions:

(a) Of demonstrating the active participation of the community.

(b) Of loud confirmation and profession of their faith (Amen).

(c) Of outlets for spontaneous sparks of religious emotion (Hallelujah, Selah, Hosanna, *Maranatha*, etc.).

THE ACCLAMATIONS OF THE SYNAGOGUE AND EARLY CHURCH

Amen

The ritual meaning of *Amen* is 'affirmation, is oath, is acceptance'.[15] It is by far the most important acclamation. As oath, it is prescribed in the legalistic passage Deut. 27:15. It serves as a usual affirmation after eulogies or praises, prescribed unanimously by all rabbinic authors.[16] In the Bible it appears chiefly as the expression of acceptance, e.g. I Chron. 16:36; Ps. 72:19; 106:48; etc., usually placed at the end of a doxology. In Judaism the *Amen* was considered imperative for the close of certain prayers. In Alexandria the congregation was requested to respond the *Amen* by a signal with a white flag.[17] In the Synagogue the precentor must not continue upon a *beraka* before the congregation has responded the *Amen*.

This manifold function was taken over by the Church, which followed the example of the Apostles, who, being Jews and familiar with the rules of Jewish worship, took the *Amen* as a matter of course. (I Cor. 14:16; Rom. 9:5; etc.) The *Amen* holds a special significance in the Apocalyptic literature, as can be seen in Rev. 5:14; 19:4; 1:6; 7:12;

etc. Here it always concludes a formal doxology, built strictly after the Jewish pattern. In conformity with rabbinical law, the passages of Revelation conclude every *beraka* with the prescribed *Amen*, e.g.:

> Grace be unto you, and peace . . . from Jesus Christ
> To Him be Glory and dominion for ever and ever. Amen.
> (Rev. 1:4-6)

In the same Judaeo-Christian book the word *Amen* is even personified. 'These things saith the Amen, the faithful and true witness, the beginning of the creation of God' (Rev. 3:14). This conception is entirely in accordance with the Midrashic significance of the *Amen*. In liturgical use, however, the Church understands it only as a strong affirmation of the foregoing prayer.

Concerning its musical rendering, a slight difference between Synagogue and Church is noticeable. Christianity established early trained choirs, consisting of monks or of men of the lower clergy, who tended to stretch the musical performance of the responsorial amen. It sometimes fell into the category of melismatic songs or formulas, and while never extended to unliturgical length, it served occasionally as a substitute for the Alleluia.[18] This development was caused by constant repetition of the acclamation, as we notice it even in modern music, like the Amen at the end of the Credo in Beethoven's 'Missa Solemnis'.

In Judaism trained choirs were usually not available, at least not before the ninth century; therefore, the *Amen* remained what it originally was, a simple congregational response, not to be stretched or extended.

Hallelujah (as a Simple Exclamation)

Usually the Hallelujah is found at the end of a doxology or of an Alleluiatic psalm verse. In the former function it will be discussed in the next chapter. As the end of, or as addition to psalm verses, it was already known to Tertullian.[19] In the Eucharistic service it seems to be of a later date. As an integral part of the worship we encounter it first in the fourth century in Palestine where its Christian usage originated.[20] Pope Damasus introduced it in the Roman Mass[21] and its further development has been discussed before in Chapter VI. It may be added here that the Eastern Churches cultivated it even more than the Western Church; in spite of its radical Christianization, it was always understood to be a 'mos ecclesiae orientalis', a typical custom of the Oriental Church, borrowed from the Synagogue, as Cassiodorus and others knew.[22]

Hosanna (Save Now)

From the viewpoint of religious history, the Hosanna constitutes by far the most interesting case of transformation and modification. In Judaism it originally held a twofold significance: that of an appeal to the King, tantamount to an acclamation of homage; and that of a cry for salvation. Both meanings are well substantiated in Old Testament literature.[23] In Christianity, the original meaning (Matt. 21:9; Mark 11:9-10) was exactly the same: appeal and homage to royalty, and plea for salvation. This last meaning, obscured by a too literal translation from the Hebrew, was lost early in Christianity, and in the *Didache* (second century) the Hosanna had already entirely shed its supplicatory character. The other implication of the Hosanna, the appeal to royalty, was gradually sublimated, until it attained the significance of an exultant cry, equivalent with the Hallelujah. The various phases of this development are still clearly discernible.[24]

In Judaism, on the other hand, the Messianic-royal notion of the Hosanna was discarded as soon as it became a watchword of incipient Christianity.[25] Its supplicatory note was emphasized and deepened the longer oppression and persecution of the Jewish people lasted. Thus, special penitential and supplicatory cycles of litanies were written in the Middle Ages, whose regular refrain was Hosanna; therefore, they were called *Hoshanot*.[26] During the period when the Hosanna had become the exultant exclamation of the triumphant Church, the Jewish *Hoshana* in its literal meaning 'Save now!' truly represented the despondent and martyrlike feelings of the Jewish communities who were burned in their own Synagogues or outlawed by Christian princes.

Liturgically, the Hosanna has become an integral part of the daily Christian Mass of every denomination, and is closely connected with the Thrice-Holy.[27] On Palm Sunday and in the time after Easter, it approximates the liturgical and musical role of the Hallelujah, as a memorial of the Hosanna cries which accompanied Jesus's entrance into Jerusalem.

In the Synagogue, the Hosanna is just one verse among others in the *Hallel* (Ps. 118 : 25) and, as such, chanted on all festivals. Only during the season of Tabernacles, when the *Hoshanot* are chanted as a kind of processional, does the Hosanna stand out as a distinct and emphasized rubric of the service. It is always rendered responsorially, according to an old talmudic interpretation and rule.[28]

Selah

The meaning of this word is obscure; the Septuagint translates it by *diapsalma*, that is, an instrumental interlude.[29] It occurs almost exclusively in the Psalter and has been taken over by Christianity without any change. Frequently it stands for an *Amen* or some similar affirmation.

Many suggestions have been made concerning its liturgical or musical function in the Temple; whatever it might have been, the word has lost its meaning in the Church as well as in the Synagogue. It is sung or recited at the end of a passage and is understood as something like 'So be it'. No further attention is paid to this once important acclamation.[30]

Non-Hebrew Acclamations

While the foregoing acclamations are genuine Hebrew words, and were embodied as such in Christian liturgies, there are others, also of Hebrew origin, which have been translated into the various ecclesiastical languages, especially into Syriac, Latin and Greek. Examples of these follow: *Kyrie eleison* (Greek, for 'Lord save or deliver us!'). Although Scripture contains numerous similar expressions, such as 'Deliver us', 'Have mercy upon us', etc., no literal antecedent of the *Kyrie* occurs in the Greek Bible.[31] A. Fortescue, an outstanding liturgical authority, writes:

> The surprising thing about the *Kyrie eleison* is that it is not mentioned earlier. The Apostolic Fathers and Apologists do not quote it, nor the Fathers of the fourth century before St John Chrysostom. Nor is there any hint of its use in the early Latin Fathers. It began to be said apparently at Antioch (and Jerusalem), as the answer to the litany form of prayer, that was first a speciality of the Antiochene rite that spread throughout the Church from that centre. . . .[32]

Indeed, the *Kyrie* occurs in Aetheria's well-known travelogue as a custom of the Syro-Palestinian Church;[33] but most recently it has come to be considered, even by Catholic scholars, as a Christianized hymn to Helios-Mithras, of a period that indulged in various syncretistic experiments.[34] Thus, we may view it as a half-biblical, half-pagan acclamation that, through its constant liturgical usage—which it originally did not have—became thoroughly Christian in character. This hypothesis might explain the long silence of the Church Fathers concerning the *Kyrie*.

The *Kyrie* opens the Ordinary of the Mass of the Roman Church today, the Mass of the Catechumens in the Byzantine Church since the fourth century, but plays only an insignificant part in the other Eastern Churches.

Its rendering is always responsorial, and alternates with the call *Christe eleison*. Since the Roman Mass has it nine times (three *Kyrie* plus three *Christe* plus three *Kyrie*) it was often farced or provided with a Trope, i.e. to its melismata new hymnic words were applied. The melody was melismatically adorned, while the original words of the *Kyrie* were subjected to long stretched poetic paraphrases.[35]

> *Dominus vobiscum (The Lord be with you)*
> *Pax vobiscum (Peace be with you)*
> *Et cum spiritu tuo (And with thy spirit)*

These are standing greetings, common to all Christian liturgies. The *Dominus vobiscum* occurs in the Old Testament (Ruth 2:4; Judges 6:23; etc.) as well as the *Pax vobiscum* which, in its older version *Pax vobis*, was an all too literal translation from the Hebrew as we know it from the Bible.[36] Its liturgical use is spread throughout Christianity; its liturgical function is usually to indicate the end of one rubric, or the beginning of the next, or simply a solemn salutation.[37] The response to it, 'Et cum spiritu tuo' is, as Fortescue rightly remarks, likewise 'a Semiticism founded on biblical use and means simply "and with you"'.[38]

Maranatha (Lord, come ye)

This now obsolete acclamation occurs only in the writings of the Early Church, especially in Paul's Epistles and in the *Didache*. The word is West Aramaic and seems to have been the expression of the faithful, who were eagerly waiting for Christ's reappearance during the first three centuries.

In Paul's Epistles as well as in the *Didache* it is usually linked to the closing doxology. Nothing is known about its musical rendering, if there ever was any.

Of these acclamations, only the Amen, the Hallelujah, and the *Kyrie* have risen to paramount liturgical significance in Christianity and Judaism respectively. The reason for the fact that *Selah* or *Dominus vobiscum* did not attain the same rank probably lies with linguistic changes. The *Selah* or *Maranatha* were no longer understood by the congregations, and habitual salutations, such as the *Dominus* or *Pax vobiscum* lacked that aura of sacredness that is a prerequisite of outstanding liturgical components. It is true, they were elevated from their vernacular usage into the sacred sphere, but here the development ended; for they did not command a dogmatic, nor a strongly emotional meaning.[39] In Judaism similar salutations entered the liturgy, especially before the eulogies over wine or as a preamble to the saying of grace after the meal. For the same reasons as their kinsmen in Christian liturgy, they never reached the rank of an acclamation that might be called typical of the one liturgy or the other. They are almost interchangeable, in sharp contrast to the doxologies, to which they are closely related. The doxologies play so important a part in the development of musical liturgies, so often have they become the expression of doctrine and dogma, and so vitally did they influence the musical structure of the worship, that we shall devote the next chapter to them.

NOTES CHAPTER VIII

1. Iliad, i, 37, 451; also xvi, 233.

2. Thureau-Dangin, *Rituels accadiens*, pp. 20–22, 35, 41; also Reisner, *Sumerisch-babylonische Hymnen*, and S. Langdon, 'Calendars of Liturgies and Prayers', *American Journal of Semitic Languages*, XLII (1915–16), pp. 112 ff.

3. Cf. E. Bezold, *Ninive und Babylon*, p. 101; also F. Craig, 'Assyrian and Babylonian Religious Texts', in Delitzsch & Haupt, *Assyriologische Bibl.*, XIII, pp. 5 ff.

4. Cf. Zimmel, 'Psychologische und ethnologische Studien über Musik', *Zeitschrift für Völkerpsychologie*, XII (1881), pp. 264 ff. Cf. the profound observation in J. Huizinga, *Homo Ludens* (New York, 1950), pp. 18 ff.

5. See *infra* the remarks on the Hosanna.

6. On the other hand, many such popular refrains, known to us from ancient literature, never attained any liturgical significance, e.g. the well-song of the children of Israel (Num. 21:17) or the refrains of the Deborah-song (Judges 5 ff). In the latter instance, the responses are limited to simple terms or words, such as:

> . . . Praise the Lord! (2)
> . . . I shall sing to the Lord, the God of Israel (3)
> . . . From the Lord, the God of Israel (5)
> . . . with Israel (7)
> . . . Praise the Lord! (9)
> . . . The people of the Lord (11)

After verse 11 no such popular acclamation occurs in the text. It is remarkable that only alternative verses end with a refrain that might have been used in responsorial chant. Is it an indication of such performance?

7. Cf. E. Gevaert, *La Mélopée antique dans le chant de l'Église latine*, pp. 83 ff.

8. WGM, III, pp. 352 ff.

9. J. Wellhausen, *Reste arabischen Heidentums*, p. 108.

10. Theodoret, *Haeret. fabul.*, IV, 7 (PG, LXXXIII, 426).

11. According to E. Peterson, 'Epigraphische und formgeschichtliche Untersuchungen', in *Forschungen zur Literatur des Alten und NT*, ed. Bultmann & Gunkel, N.F. 24, p. 192, the conceptual idea behind the expression 'Out of one mouth' is of something just between exultant crying and hymnic singing.

12. Rev. 1:6; 5:14; Rom. 1:25; 11:36; Eph. 5:19, etc.

13. Cf. ELB, pp. 495 f; *DACH*, I, 240 ff; Jerome (*PL*, XXVI, 355).

14. Cf. F. Leitner, op. cit., p. 233, where the literature is quoted; also Ignatius, *Ad Ephesos*, cap. 4. 'Una voce dicentes, una voce cantantes' (in *Ascensio Isaiae*, VII, 14). This is an old Jewish principle, cf. Canticum Rabba to 8: 11, 12.

15. *B. Ber.* 45a; cf. I Kings, 1:36; see also G. Dalman, *Die Worte Jesu*, pp. 185 f.

16. *M. Ber.*, IX, 5; parallel passages: *Tosefta Ber.*, VII, 4; *Tosefta Ta'anith*, I, 11; *Jer. Ber.*, 14c.

17. *B. Suc.*, 10b.

18. A. Fortescue, *The Mass*, p. 337; also Gerbert, *De cantu*, etc., I, p. 440; also *Canones Hippolyti*, cap. 19, 146–7.

19. Cf. Tertullian, *De oratione*, cap. 27.

20. First in Hippolytus of Rome, in *Traditio Apost.*, in Hennecke, *Neutestam. Apokryphen*, pp. 581 ff.

21. St Gregory the Great, *Epist.* IX, 12. 'In order that the Alleluia might be said in the Roman Church, it has supposedly been transmitted from the Church of Jerusalem of St Jerome's tradition at the time of St Damasus [366–384].' (*PL*, LXXVII, 956.)

22. Cf. Augustine, *Enarratio in Ps.* 99, in *PL*, XXXVII, 1272, also *PL*, XXXVI, 283. See also Aurelianus Reomensis' statements about the Jewish origin of the Alleluia in Gerbert, *Scriptores*, I, 'Musica disciplina', cap, 20. Wellesz's study in *Annales musicologiques*, II (Paris, 1954) is valuable.

23. See my study 'The Hosanna in the Gospels', *JBL* (July, 1946), where the entire literature is quoted and analysed.

24. Ibid. The expression 'Salvation to our God' of Rev. 7:10 still corresponds with the Messianic appeal of the Hosanna; probably the Greek word *sotheria* is just a translation of the Hebrew *Y'hoshua*, from which the word Hosanna is derived.

25. Cf. E. Werner, op. cit. (*supra*, n. 23), pp. 119 f.

26. ELB, pp. 219 ff; also pp. 138 f and 323.

27. It had not yet changed its meaning in the text of the Gospels, as A. Fortescue suggests, op. cit., p. 322. It is true, however, that the idea of homage, one of the meanings of Hosanna, is fully borne out in those Christian liturgies that connect it with the Thrice-Holy, the supreme homage.

28. Cf. my study on the Hosanna, *supra*, n. 23, pp. 114–18.

29. So also Origen, *In psalmos* (*PG*, XII, 1060).

30. G. Vincent, *Notices et extracts des MSS de la Bibliothèque du roi*, XVI, 291, n. 2, makes this observation: 'Concerning the literal meaning of *Selah*, it is probably one of the frequent abbreviations which one encounters so often in Talmudic and rabbinic literature'. See also H. Gunkel, *Einleitung in die Psalmen*, article 'Selah'.

31. E.g., Septuagint, Ps. 4:2; 9:14; 25:11; Isa. 33:2; Baruch 3; etc. In the New Testament, Matt. 9:27; 15:22; Mark 10:47; etc.

32. Cf. A. Fortescue, op. cit., pp. 231 ff. See also E. Bishop, 'Kyrie eleison', *Downside Review*, XVIII (1899), pp. 249 ff, and XIX (1900), pp. 44 ff.

33. In *Peregrinatio Aetheriae* 24, 5 (*CSEL* XXXIX, 72, ed. Geyer).

34. Cf. F. J. Doelger, *Sol Salutis* (Münster, 1930), pp. 5, 65, 78–79, *et passim*.

35. Examples of such 'troped' Kyries in every Roman Kyriale; also Fortescue, op. cit., p. 238. Sources in Cardinal Bona, *Rerum Liturgicarum* II, cap. 4, pp. 335–7. The Jewish liturgy knows of similar customs; thus, certain prayers, e.g. the *Barku*, are chanted in long sustained phrases, during which the congregation recited, in an undertone, the poetic paraphrases of the canonical text.

36. Cf. the first Roman Ordo 'Pax vobis' with the second 'Pax vobiscum' in *PL*, LXXVIII, 942, and ibid., 971.

37. Cf. BLEW, pp. 35, 36, 115, 117, 392, 426, *et passim*.

38. Cf. A. Fortescue, op. cit., p. 246.

39. A special case is the papal acclamation, 'Christus vincit; Christus regnat; Christus imperat', which today serves as the solemn salutation of the Pope. It seems to have originated during the eighth (or late seventh) century, and has an exact Jewish counterpart in 'The Lord hath reigned; the Lord does reign; The Lord will reign for ever and ever'. This doxology occurs first in the treatise *Soferim*, which was redacted during the seventh century. Whether there is a genuine relationship between these two acclamations remains a matter of further research.

CHAPTER NINE

The Doxology in Synagogue and Church

THROUGH the magnificent variety of the world of Christian prayer, so manifold in all its forms and churches, there runs, like the proverbial red thread, the rigid formula of the Lesser Doxology. It recurs so often in each service, so majestically does it conclude the individual prayer, that this formula is familiar to every Christian, no matter in which ecclesiastic doctrine he is brought up and to what liturgical usage he may be accustomed. Since the doxology emphatically affirms the principle of Trinity, it appears to the Jew as a typically Christian element of the Divine Service. This inference, however, is not correct. It will be the purpose of this chapter to demonstrate what layman, theologian, and musicologist are likely to overlook, namely, that the doxology is no homogeneous entity, but is the end result of an extremely complex historical development. As are many other parts of the liturgy, the doxology, in both its liturgical and musical aspects, is of distinctly Jewish origin. Then, from the second century up to the fifth it became a no man's land between Judaism and Christianity; later, the shibboleth dividing the numerous sects of the Eastern Church on one side and the Roman Church on the other. Yet, during these formative struggles, the doxology was the soil out of which grew some of the formal principles which determine the shape of ecclesiastical and synagogal liturgies to this very day: the response, the closing hymn and the cento of psalms. All of these structures have greatly enhanced the inspirational and aesthetic powers of the Divine Service in both Church and Synagogue.

CONCEPTION AND IDEA OF DOXOLOGY

Our examination is confronted at its very outset with uncertainty and ambiguity concerning the term 'doxology'. Of the more than thirty definitions given in encyclopedias, dictionaries, commentaries, etc., none are in complete agreement. In most cases a doxology was explained as a praise of God in solemn, if rigid, form, usually at the end of a prayer; sometimes it was considered synonymous with the eulogy, sometimes not. But a clear and general definition has not been attained, even in the most recent literature. Doxology (*Legein ten doxan*) means 'to proclaim glory'. Yet, the word glory, as near as it comes to *doxa*, does not contain all of the nuances and connotations of the Greek term. It has been demonstrated by Caspary,[1] more extensively by Morgenstern,[2] and lately by G. Kittel,[3] that *doxa* assumed in the Septuagint the full meaning and significance of the Hebrew root $\sqrt{Kbd}$ (glory, honour, light, aura, shining glory), and was imposed upon the originally unpretentious *doxa*. The liturgies of Christianity, following faithfully the vocabulary of the New Testament, use *doxa* almost exclusively in the sense of praise and glory. Yet not every passage where there is an affirmation of God's glory can be termed a doxology. Conversely, the passage I Tim. 6:16:

> The Lord of Lords, who only hath immortality, dwelling in Light unapproachable; whom no man hath seen, nor can see; to whom be honour and power eternal. Amen.

while not containing the word *doxa*, represents a true doxology.[4] Paradoxical as it sounds, we must exclude the term *doxa* as the necessary criterion of the doxology. We may deduce that only two elements form the criteria necessary for the doxology: the proclamation of God's praise (in the third person) coupled with an affirmation of His infinity in time. The usual Greek formulas for eternity are: 'Into the aeons of aeons' (for ever), also 'From generation to generation'[5] and in the early third century: 'Glory . . . now and for ever, and into the aeons of aeons'.[6] Although the term *eulogia* or *eulogetos* occurs not infrequently in the doxologies, it is not an integral part of them. The doxology of the Church is, consequently, not merely benediction, but a praise into infinity. The term *doxologia*, in this sense, seems to be generally accepted as early as the late second century, chiefly among the apologists;[7] certainly in the third century, where Origen uses the word in our sense,[8] and in the liturgy of the *Apostolic Constitutions* we find the term *doxologia* next to *doxa* in the very body of a doxology.[9] Up to the fourth century, the texts of the doxologies range widely from a genuine prayer to a short formula at the end of an epistle, or from a real liturgical preamble to an interjected, informal confirmation of faith.[10] When the centuries of the far-flung missionary activity of Christianity drew to a close and its expansion had almost reached its height, the internal struggles within the body of the Church occupied more and more of its literature.

This phase, common to every new religion, might be termed the intro-spective, and in this period was created the major part of the dogmatic literature, of which liturgy is always a faithful expression.

The originally spontaneous and flexible prayers crystallized more and more into a fixed and well balanced set of liturgical forms. It was at this juncture that the Christian doxology attained its final form and word-ing. The details and the reasons for this decisive development will be analysed below. Here it shall only be pointed out that, under the pres-sure of Arianism and other Gnostic sects, the Western Church formed two doxological prayers, called today the Greater and the Lesser Doxo-logy. The Greater Doxology is already well established in the *Apostolic Constitutions* and is a poetic paraphrase of Luke 2:14, usually known as the Gloria in Excelsis, upon which the Great Doxology proper fol-lows.[11] It became in time an integral part of the Mass. This chapter is concerned with the Lesser Doxology only, which has the following text:

Glory to the Father and to the Son and to the Holy Spirit, now and always and for ever.[12]	A. Gloria Patri et filio et spiritui sancto
	B. (sicut erat in principio) et nunc et semper in saecula saeculorum. (Alleluia) (Amen).[13]

The emphasis lies obviously upon two elements: (a) the Trinity, (b) its pre-existence from the beginning of time. The anti-heretic implications are apparent and we need not discuss them here. However, there are some problems embedded in our formula that are not so obvious and hence warrant a closer examination. In the Latin version, the doxology is usually followed by an Alleluia and concluded by Amen. This struc-ture, however, presupposed a responsory rendering of the text. Why?

We recall that the practice of doxological conclusions goes back to ancient Jewish custom. The five books of the Psalter end always with primitive doxologies requiring responses; sometimes, as in Ps. 106:48 the response is indicated in the text:

> And blessed be His glorious name for ever;
> And let the whole earth be filled with His glory.
> Amen, and Amen. (Ps. 72:19)
>
> Blessed be the Lord, the God of Israel,
> From everlasting and to everlasting.
> Amen, and Amen. (Ps. 41:14)

Blessed be the Lord for evermore
Amen, and Amen. (Ps. 89:53)

Blessed be the Lord, the God of Israel,
From everlasting even to everlasting.
And let all the people say: 'Amen'.
Hallelujah. (Ps. 106:48)

Blessed be the Lord, the God of Israel,
From everlasting even to everlasting.
And all the people said: 'Amen' and praised the Lord.
(I Chron. 16:36)

Let everything that hath breath praise the Lord.
Hallelujah. (Ps. 150:6)

But we will bless the Lord
From this time forth and for ever,
Hallelujah. (Ps. 115:18)[14]

If we compare the ecclesiastical form with the scriptural versions just quoted, we are immediately confronted with an essential discrepancy. The Christian form starts with *Gloria* or, in Greek, with *doxa*; its wording fixed and uniform since the Council of Vaison (529). In the liturgy of the Temple and the Synagogue and in the Scriptures, we find various doxological forms. Frequently, but certainly not always, they are introduced by *baruk*, thereby assuming the type of the *beraka*. The forms most cognate to the Christian doxology are (a) eulogy, (b) *invitatorium* and (c) benediction. A eulogy is almost identical with the Jewish *beraka*; the *invitatorium* is a psalm-verse, containing a call to worship, usually Ps. 95:1–4 at the beginning of the service. The benediction, however, is a privilege of the ordained priest and has no direct part in general Church liturgy.[15] Yet the borderline between doxology and eulogy seems frequently to be effaced.[16]

Much more complex is the situation on the Jewish side. Here the structure of a doxology is more fluid and not bound up with certain unchangeable terms, like *Gloria Patri*, etc. Of the manifold Hebrew passages with doxological implications we quote here only a few which are today still in liturgical use.

Hear O Israel, the Lord our God, the Lord is One
Praised be His name whose glorious kingdom is for ever and ever.

Praised be His glorious name unto all eternity.

Praise ye the Lord to whom all praise is due
Praised be the Lord to whom all praise is due for ever and ever.

The Lord will reign for ever, thy God, O Zion
From generation to generation, Hallelujah

Blessed be the Lord for evermore; Amen and Amen
And blessed be His glorious name for ever;
And let the whole earth be filled with His glory
Amen, and Amen.[17]

All formulas, except the fourth, contain the verb $\sqrt{Brk}$ (to bless). Thus we may infer that, in the Jewish custom, a doxology approximates a *beraka* of God's infinity in time; yet it is neither a eulogy among other eulogies, nor, as in the Church, a prayer *sui generis*. We shall arrive later at a more exact definition. While the Christian doxology is an all-important part of the service, repeated many times in each liturgy, the Hebrew doxologies occupy comparatively few passages in the service of the Synagogue. True, these passages are nuclear parts, as the *Sh'ma'* or the *Kaddish*; true, in all our instances just quoted, the responsory rendering is apparent and called for. But we do not encounter a doxology at the end of each synagogal prayer.

The passage 'from generation to generation' in the fourth example is the Hebrew original of the Greek *apo geneas* quoted above, as is 'for ever and ever' in the first and third or 'from everlasting and to everlasting' for *in saecula saeculorum* or *eis tous aionas* (for ever and ever). The last one is interesting as it comes as near as possible to the Greek idea of *doxa*. Here again, *kabod* is the corresponding Hebrew term.

THE OUTSTANDING DOXOLOGIES IN JEWISH LITURGY

In the liturgy of rabbinic Judaism we frequently encounter doxological formulas, but of outstanding relevance for the spirit of our prayer are only four real doxologies.

1. Praised be His name whose glorious kingdom is for ever and ever.
2. Praised be the Lord to whom all praise is due for ever and ever.
3. The responses of the *Kedusha*.
4. Praised be His Glorious name unto all eternity. (The Sanctification response of the *Kaddish*.)[18]

It will be noted that these formulas have a number of elements in common: (a) They are all genuine responses, as we shall see presently. (b) They all contain the idea of God's infinity in time. (c) They are frequently mentioned together as one family of prayers, sometimes even considered together.[19] (d) They have replaced the old Temple doxologies, taken from the end of the five books of psalms, as is indicated in

M. Ber. IX, 5.[20] (e) They all have been, at one time or another, subjects of controversy between Judaism and Christianity. (f) They belong to the oldest parts of Jewish liturgy. It is not the aim of this examination to give a full historical account of the genesis of these formulas or of their influence upon the general spirit of the Divine Service. This chapter limits itself to investigations of the form and the rendering of these doxologies. In addition, where the subject under discussion warrants it, certain essential comparisons between Christian and Jewish liturgy will be attempted.

Praised be His Name whose Glorious Kingdom is For Ever and Ever

The Mishnaic passages, in which this doxology is referred to, indicate quite clearly that it was at all times a genuine responsory.[21] Moreover, this formula belonged originally to the service of the Temple, later to be taken by the Synagogue. However, this Mishnaic reference to the *barukh shem* (Praised be His name) is rather enigmatic, since it starts out with the 'Corruption of the Sadducees' (in *Talmud Jerushalmi*; here, 'of the *Minim*').[22]

Mishna: At the close of every benediction in the Temple they used to say 'For everlasting'; but after the Sadducees (the heretics) had taught corruptly and said that there is but one world, it was ordained that they should say 'From everlasting even to everlasting'.

Gemara: Why is this so? Because one does not respond 'Amen' in the sanctuary; and how do we know that one does not respond 'Amen' in the Sanctuary? As it is written 'Stand up and bless the Lord, your God, from everlasting even to everlasting' and let them say 'Blessed be Thy glorious name that is exalted above all blessing and praise'. Is it possible that all the blessings had only one praise? Scripture teaches us that (they) exalted for each blessing and praise, etc.

Assuming that the term *Minim* stands for Judaeo-Christians, it is interesting to note that the conclusion, 'from everlasting to everlasting', used in the Temple, and the Amen permitted exclusively in the Synagogue, were combined in the standing formulas of the Church: 'For the whole aeon as it is now and for all aeons, Amen'[23]; 'For aeons of aeons, Amen'[24]; 'From generation to generation, Amen'[25]; For generations of generations and for aeons of aeons, Amen'.[26]

The formula 'Praised be His name whose glorious kingdom is for ever and ever', used in the Temple as response upon every *beraka*, has been a controversial subject within the synagogal service, because it interrupts the *Sh'ma'*. Although it is a genuine response, and has always been understood as such, the real cause for debate was not its text but its rendering. And this, in turn, was a reaction against the 'carping of the *Minim*'.[27] Should it be said aloud or in a whisper? Since every doxology originally had a responsorial function, we ought to assume that the normal rendering would be aloud. And thus it was in the Temple and perhaps in the first decades of our era. But in order to differentiate between the importance and the authority of the *Sh'ma'* (Hear, O Israel) and of the *barukh shem k'vod* (Praised be His name whose glorious kingdom is for ever and ever), the rabbis ordered that one should say the latter in a whisper.[28] Yet the same passage tells us that R. Abbahu said: 'It was ordered that men should say it in a loud voice because of the carping of the *Minim*; but in Nehardea, where there are no *Minim*, they say it even to this day in a whisper'.

Two main questions arise: Why has the *barukh shem* been taken over from the Temple into the Synagogue? And: In the worship of the Synagogue, whose function was it to pronounce the formula, whether aloud or in a whisper? It is evident that, following the destruction of the central sanctuary, the ancient Synagogue attempted to come as near as permissible to the cult of the Temple. Thus the idea of answering the enunciation of the Tetragrammaton by a doxological response and confirmation, as once practised in the Temple, seems a most natural procedure, especially after the proclamation of the *Sh'ma'*.[29] Yet this would, to this writer's knowledge, represent the only case in which a genuine response is to be uttered 'in a whisper', even though respect for the *Sh'ma'* be the reason. Elbogen proposes just this theory. Indeed, the Talmud implicitly recommends the whispering, as we have seen.[30] Nevertheless, there are valid reasons for believing that this was not the original practice. As Aptowitzer rightly remarks: 'In public worship there cannot be a whispered response; there is in the literature not one example of a whispered response or eulogy'.[31] Was R. Abbahu's report of the loud recitation of the 'Praised be His name whose glorious kingdom is for ever and ever'—against the 'carping *Minim*'—not rather a *restitutio in integrum*? Finally, why would the *Minim* find the *Sh'ma'* a vulnerable point for their carping and what was their own attitude to the *barukh shem*? Originally the *Sh'ma'* was no bone of contention between Judaeo-Christians and Jews. Thus, in the Pseudo-Clementine *Homilies*, which show a distinctly Jewish influence, we read that Peter exclaims against the idolators: 'Hear, O Israel, thy [*sic*] God, the Lord is one'. Later on, with the Trinitarian doctrine prevailing, the situation changed fundamentally.[32] Rabbinic literature knows of many instances in which the *Minim* attempted to prove the existence of the Trinity by quoting scriptural verses which mention the name of God three times.[33] On this, Aptowitzer adds the following comment:

> They (the Christians) could find their proof even in Deut. 6:4, The Lord our God the Lord is one . . . the 'one' would not disturb them, it was even wind in their sails: one in three persons. In order to refute this interpretation, the *barukh shem* was added in a loud voice: Blessed be the name of His glorious kingdom, etc. This means, as R. Simlai (Jer. Ber. IX. 1, 12) explains: all three terms designate one and the same being, one Name, one idea; His kingdom.[34]

This reasoning presupposes that the Christians themselves did not make use of the *barukh shem*. Obviously, if it was to be an anti-Christian demonstration, it would lose its sense entirely if the Christians used it themselves. Yet just this fact is the one overlooked both by Aptowitzer and by Elbogen. We read in the liturgy of James:

> Priest: Thy Kingdom lasteth through the aeons of aeons.
> Praised be the Name of the Lord, our God for ever and ever.[35]

Shortly afterwards, ibidem:

> Priest: Be the Name of the Lord blessed for ever and ever.
> Blessed be the Name of Thy Kingdom for ever and ever.

Not the literal text, but a majestic paraphrase and augmentation of our formula is to be found in the *Sacramentary* of Serapion:

> For thou art the Most High of all the beginning, of power and strength and dominion and of the whole Name, to be pronounced not only in this aeon but also in the one to come, the hereafter.[36]

With the exception of the last instance, all the quoted examples are real responses in the Christian liturgy; which shows that the *Minim* were using formulas very similar to the *barukh shem*. These facts may caution us against accepting uncritically certain statements about the *Minim*; resentment on both sides has greatly impaired the reliability of our sources.

What, then, remains as a plausible interpretation of the changing rendition of the *barukh shem*? It is well known that the *Ma'amadot*, after having attended the sacrificial service at the Temple proper, went to the 'Hall of Stones' within the Temple, where they had a service of their own, in the style of a Synagogue, and were joined by some of the priests.[37] (Cf. Chapter II.)

Now, when the Temple fell, it was a natural reaction to remember its glory with a sorrowful whisper of its existence. The murmured rendering of the *barukh shem* may well have been an expression of mourning which was abandoned when the *Minim* began to carp at the praying Jews because of that very silence following the *Sh'ma'*.[38] Only then, and for a comparatively short time was the *barukh shem* recited aloud.

Praised be the Lord to whom all Praise is Due For Ever and Ever

If the *barukh shem* is an insertion into an otherwise closed and well-rounded liturgical form, the recitation of 'Praised be the Lord to whom all praise is due for ever and ever' represents a spontaneous response answering a call to worship. The present formula is the response to the '*invitatorium*'—'Praise ye the Lord to whom all praise is due'. Although it seems to be a paraphrase of Neh. 9:5—'Stand up and bless the Lord your God from everlasting to everlasting'—the omission of 'your God from everlasting to everlasting', and the addition of 'the Blessed One (to whom all praise is due)' are more than coincidental.[39]

The *Barku* (*Invitatorium*) and its subsequent response constitute one of the most important doxologies, since it is recited twice daily in the course of the morning and evening prayer. Furthermore, it is the initial formula before grace after each meal and before each public scriptural reading. Here the sharp distinction between the different functions of the doxology in Church and Synagogue becomes obvious. In the Church the doxology is almost invariably the opening or closing formula, in Judaism it is interwoven in the entire texture of the liturgy. We come upon it as an '*invitatorium*', like the *Barku*, as an intermediate exclamation in the *barukh shem k'vod*, as a hymnic prayer in the *Kedusha*, and as an inserted laudation in the *Kaddish*.

Christian worship contains a rubric which, in many respects, is comparable to the call to worship exemplified by the *Barku*. This is the *invitatorium* which, in a technical sense, consists of verses of Ps. 95:1-6, or paraphrases thereof.[40] Its function is almost identical with that of the *Barku*. The daily Matins always starts with that call to worship; but it is also used in other parts of the Church service.

The Early Church, however, used other invitatorial formulas, chiefly before the Mass of the Faithful. All of them are genuine *responsoria* and some of them clearly resemble the *Barku* and its responses.[41]

Some of them might be quoted here in order to present a comparison between the liturgical forms as employed and expanded by Synagogue and Church.

Turn ye to God through His Christ, bow your heads and pray! (Clementine Liturgy.)[42]

Come ye, let us praise the Lord and sing about our salvation. (Syriac Liturgy.)[43]

Praised be Thou, our God, always, now and for ever into the aeons of aeons. Amen. (Liturgy of Constantinople.)[44]

Ye children, praise the Lord, sing praise of the name of the Lord! (*Apostolic Constitutions*.)[45]

The importance of the form and rendering of the *Barku* and its response is greatly enhanced by the fact that it serves as a calling together to public worship, and is worded in so-called progressive parallelisms.

This technique is characteristic of the so-called 'open' forms of poetry, for it develops steadily from one phase to the next with continual allusion to preceding words or passages. This type of poetry has greatly influenced the music with which it is connected, favouring the retention of, and the elaboration upon, certain characteristic musical phrases.[46] The classic example of this type of parallelism is the *Kedusha*.

The Kedusha

An extensive study of the development and the significance of the *Kedusha* would fill an entire book; and the literature on this subject is so vastly expanded and specialized that it cannot be our task here to deal with it *ab ovo*. We have to limit the scope of our investigation to the following points: (a) misconceptions in the recent studies on the history of the *Kedusha*; (b) the *Kedusha* and the Church; (c) the formal structure of the *Kedusha*; (d) the responsorial doxologies in the *Kedusha* and the tradition of their performance.

In the liturgy of the Synagogue the *Kedusha* appears in three main types: (1) the *Kedusha* of the early morning service (so-called *Yotzer*); (2) the *Kedusha* as an integral part of the '*Amida*; and (3) the *Kedusha* at the end of the weekday's morning service (called *Kedusha de Sidra*). The text of (1) and (3) follows here, that of (2) later.

KEDUSHA OF YOTZER

The Name of the Divine King, the great, mighty and dreaded One, holy is He; and they [the angels] all take upon themselves the yoke of the Kingdom of Heaven one from the other, and give leave one unto the other to declare the holiness of their creator; in tranquil joy of spirit, with pure speech and holy melody they all respond in unison, and exclaim with awe:

Holy, Holy, Holy is the Lord of Hosts: the whole earth is full of His glory. [Isa. 6:3]

And the Ophanim [class of angels] and the holy beings with a noise of great rushing, upraising themselves towards the Seraphim, thus over against them offer praise and say: Blessed be the glory of the Lord from His place. [Ezek. 3:12]

KEDUSHA DE SIDRA

Hebrew: And one cried unto another, and said: Holy, Holy, Holy is the Lord of hosts; the whole earth is full of His glory.

Aramaic: And they receive sanction from each other, and say: Holy in the highest heavens, the place of His divine abode; holy upon earth, the work of His might; holy for ever and to all eternity is the Lord of hosts; the whole earth is full of the radiance of His glory.

Hebrew: Then a wind lifted me up, and I heard behind me the voice of a great rushing—[saying] Blessed be the glory of the Lord from His place. . . . The Lord shall reign for ever and ever. [Exod. 15:18]

Since the *Kedusha* doxology constitutes a most ancient part of the Jewish liturgy, it is but natural that the scholars began relatively early to study its history and development. Only in the last eighty years has the question been examined with the historic-philological methods of modern scholarship. No complete unanimity was reached even among the Jewish students, of whom K. Kohler, I. Elbogen, L. Finkelstein, A. Marmorstein, L. Ginzberg, J. Mann, and V. Aptowitzer have treated the subject most extensively. Among the Christian scholars, important and original contributions came from A. Baumstark, P. Drews, Dugmore, A. Fortescue, and W. O. Oesterley. W. Bousset's observations on the subject were not cited, since they are mainly based upon a previous study by K. Kohler, to which, however, Bousset gave no credit.

The chief question which concerned all of the Jewish scholars was the respective age of the three *Kedushas*. Various theories were expounded about the oldest of the three forms. Kohler believed that the *Kedusha* of *Yotzer* is the oldest, having been introduced under the influence of the Essenes, who are known to have stressed the visions of the heavenly throne or chariot, to which the characteristic passages of Isa. 6:3 and

Ezek. 3:12 refer.[47] L. Ginzberg agrees in many respects with Kohler's theory.[48] Elbogen views the *Kedusha de Sidra* as the oldest and attempts to refute the hypothesis of Kohler and Ginzberg.[49] L. Finkelstein suggests that the *Kedusha* of the *'Amida* was introduced into the Synagogue by the rabbis at the time of Hadrian, since the priests of the Temple were too conservative to permit any innovations in the Temple cult.[50] A. Marmorstein, however, defends Rashi's statement that this *Kedusha* is a post-Talmudic composition.[51] He does, however, overlook the passage Enoch 39:12, which contains part of the *Kedusha*, and the early Christian documents which will be presented in the following pages. These documents leave little doubt as to the pre-Christian origin of the *Kedusha* itself.[52]

The oldest Christian source of the *Kedusha* is Clement of Rome; his version of Isa. 6:3: 'Holy, Holy, Holy is the Lord Sabaoth, full is the whole creation of His glory', is not completely identical with the Septuagint, which has 'earth' instead of 'creation'.[53] From here to the next recension, the so-called 'Serapion liturgy', a most important change occurs. This version reads: 'Holy, Holy, Holy is the Lord Sabaoth, full are *heaven and earth* of Thy glory; full is the heaven, full is also the earth of Thy magnificent glory.'[54]

This becomes then the authoritative version, as we see in Athanasius,[55] Cyril of Jerusalem,[56] and all outstanding Church Fathers. A solemn Christian version of the *Kedusha* is to be found in the *Constitutiones Apostolorum*, where we have the following recension:

> And the glowing host of angels, and the penetrating spirits say: 'One is holy, Phelmuni'[57] and the Seraphim . . . proclaim the triumphal hymn in unceasing voices: 'Holy, Holy, Holy, is the Lord Sabaoth, full are the heaven and the earth of Thy glory'.[58] And the others of the multitude of ranks, the archangels, the thrones, the dominions, proclaim: 'Blessed be the glory of the Lord out of His Place'.[59] But Israel . . . chants: 'The chariot of God is ten-thousandfold thousand extolling thee; the Lord is among His people in Sinai, in the Sanctuary'.[60]

The deviation of this version of the *Kedusha*, particularly of Isa. 6:3, from the original text has, to my knowledge, been discussed only by three scholars, A. Baumstark, J. Mann and J. A. Jungmann, S.J. Dr Mann rightly ascribes the change to a Trinitarian interpretation of the *Sanctus* in which the 'all' (Gr. *pasa*) is omitted and for it 'heaven' is added, symbolizing Jesus sitting in heaven at the right hand of God.[61] And he adds: 'It was at a time, when Christianity was not yet triumphant in the Roman Empire, so that "the whole earth" could not yet be full of Jesus's glory, that in the Christian liturgy this sentence was remodelled in a general way to denote "heaven and earth are full of thy glory" '. Yet Dr Mann overlooks two important facts. First, several older versions of the *Sanctus* do have the 'whole creation' or 'earth', as seen in the case of Clement of Rome above and Cyril of Jerusalem, both older than the *Apostolic Constitutions*. Second, while he well knows that the Targumic version of Isa. 6:3, introduced in the daily liturgy as part of the *Kedusha de Sidra*, contains the paraphrase 'heaven and earth', as suggested in the Christian liturgies, he neglects the far more relevant source of Exodus Rabba: 'The upper ones [angels] and the lower ones [mortals] are the courtyard of God as it is said, "The whole earth is full of His glory . . . they told him it is written—Do I not fill the Heaven and earth?" '[62] This passage is significant in more than one respect. The story is an incident of the journey of the Rabbis Gamaliel, Joshua, Eleazar b. Azariah, and Akiba to Rome. There, a *Min* (Judaeo-Christian) approached them and asked them why God does not observe the Sabbath.[63] Their answer was that any man is allowed to move about in his dwelling on Sabbath. What, then, is God's dwelling? At this point, they quote Isa. 6:3 and Jer. 23:24. What was the real purpose of the *Min's* mockery? In this writer's opinion, the sectary intended to vindicate, through Scripture, what Jesus said in Matt. 12:6–8 and Luke 6:5, 'The Son of Man is Lord also of the Sabbath'. If he could demonstrate that God was 'Lord of the Sabbath', he would, at the same time, identify Jesus with God and thereby justify his statement.

Dr Baumstark contents himself with the conclusion: '. . . There can absolutely be no doubt about the original Hebrew Tersanctus being an integral part of the Eucharistic prayer', but stresses the nationalistic narrowness of the *Kedusha*.

Wholly one-sided, and partly biased, are the comments of J. A. Jungmann, S.J., about the relation *Sanctus-Kedusha*. He almost completely ignores the contemporary Judaistic literature on the subject. Moreover he commits a number of serious errors. Two of them will be mentioned:

(1) Jungmann claims that only in the Christian liturgy does the *Sanctus* contain the words 'coeli et terra'. He derives from this assumption a whole catholic theology, adducing further proof of this supranational

theology by quoting a passage from the Egyptian St Mark Anaphora. Every one of these alleged 'Christian deviations' from what he deems the classic Jewish text can be found in the oldest Hebrew prayer books as well as in the most recent. The 'coeli et terra' passage occurs already in the Aramaic *Kedusha de Sidra* (quoted above), the additional quotations from the Egyptian Anaphora are copies of the passage in the *Authorized Prayer Book*, p. 127, and belong, according to Elbogen, to the oldest strata of the *Kedusha*.

(2) The same Catholic scholar maintains that the *Kedusha* simply refers to 'hosts of angels' without any distinction, while the Christian liturgies identify them by names. Again he is mistaken, as witness the quotation above under the heading *Kedusha* of *Yotzer*.

All of Jungmann's theological conclusions, based upon these erroneous premises, collapse with them.

Quite recently C. W. Dugmore undertook the meritorious task of comparing the early Christian liturgies with ancient synagogal worship.[64] In his refutation of Oesterley, Dugmore remarks concerning the *Kedusha* that, in contradistinction to other prayers, 'the third benediction, was a new thing, and it is impossible to maintain that it, too, is imbedded in the prayer of Clement of Rome I'. This scholar maintains that the reference to Isa. 6:3 was not given in a really *liturgical* sense. But how can this opinion prevail in the face of the statement of Clement following immediately upon the Tersanctus; 'Yea, and let us ourselves then, being *gathered together in concord with intentness of heart*, cry unto Him as *from one mouth* earnestly, that we may be partakers of His great and glorious promises'.[65] What else but a common worship does Clement mean when he speaks of a gathering in concord, whereby many cry out as from one mouth? Moreover, Dugmore entirely overlooks the clear statement of Clement of Alexandria that 'we ever give thanks to God, as do the creatures who praise Him with hymns of whom Isaiah speaks in an allegory'.[66] Dugmore also completely neglects the *Sanctus* of the Egyptian Papyrus *Der Balyzeh* of the early third century.[67]

Returning to the chief question, the age of the *Kedusha*, it is certainly not easy to find one's way through this maze of contradictions and conflicting opinions. However, the following facts stand out as indisputable.

(1) The Early Church knew the *Kedusha*, at least the juxtaposition of Isa. 6:3 and Ezek. 3:12.

(2) The change from the whole earth—the whole creation—heaven

and earth must have occurred between the time of Clement of Rome (*ca.* 80–95) and Serapion of Thmuis (d. *ca.* 360–80).

(3) The Targum, too, has the paraphrase 'heaven and earth'. Even more clearly does it appear in the Midrash, Exod. Rab., quoted above, where it is ascribed to four outstanding *Tannaim* in their refutation of a sectary.

(4) The *Kedusha de Sidra* incorporated the Targumic interpretation.

(5) If the *Kedusha* had been introduced into the liturgy after the time of the first *Tannaim*, it would have stirred considerable discussion in the Talmud, but of this there is hardly a trace.

(6) The oldest document of the characteristic juxtaposition of Isa. 6:3 and Ezek. 3:12 is given in *Tos. Ber.* 1, 9 under the name of R. Judah. These facts seem to indicate that the 'The Lord will reign' (Ps. 146:10) is a later addition; neither the *Kedusha* of *Yotzer*, nor the *Kedusha de Sidra* has it, and it is likewise absent from the *Trisagion* of the Church. The *Kedusha de Sidra*, however, has besides the Hebrew, the Aramaic text with the interpretation, 'heaven and earth' and, as concluding passage, Exod. 15:18, which suggests a slightly later origin. Therefore, it appears most probably that the *Yotzer* is the oldest *Kedusha* and was introduced in the first century of our era. This conclusion concurs with the view of K. Kohler and L. Ginzberg on this subject, although these scholars employed an entirely different approach.[68]

Thus far our discussion has touched only upon the mere nucleus of the *Kedusha*; yet its most characteristic features are the later elaborations. But it is beyond the scope of this chapter to examine these in detail. We must limit ourselves to some brief remarks and to a general survey of the poetic structure of this glorious prayer, having in mind its actual utilization in the service. The so-called 'Great *Kedusha*' of the Ashkenazic rite has the following text:

(A) *Reader*

We will reverence and sanctify [variant: sanctify and reverence] Thee according to the mystic utterance of the holy Seraphim, who sanctify Thy Name in holiness, as it is written by the hand of Thy prophet, And they called one unto the other and said,

(B) *Congregation*

Holy, Holy, Holy is the Lord of Hosts: The whole earth is full of His glory.

(C) *Reader*

His glory filleth the universe: His ministering angels ask one another, Where is the place of His glory? Those over against them say, Blessed——

(D) *Congregation*

Blessed be the glory of the Lord from His place.

(E) *Reader*

From this place may He turn in mercy and be gracious unto a people who, evening and morning, twice every day, proclaim with constancy the unity of His Name, saying in love, Hear——

(F) *Congregation*

Hear, O Israel: The Lord is our God, the Lord is One.

(G) *Reader*

One is our God; He is our Father; He is our King; He is our Saviour; and He of His mercy will let us hear a second time, in the presence of all living (his promise): 'To be to you for a God'.

(H) *Congregation*

'I am the Lord your God.'

(I) *Reader*

And in the Holy Words it is written, saying,

(J) *Congregation*

The Lord shall reign for ever, thy God, O Zion, unto all generations. Hallelujah!

(K) *Reader*

Unto all generations we will declare Thy greatness, and to all eternity we will proclaim Thy holiness, and Thy praise, O our God, shall not depart from our mouth for ever, for Thou art a great and holy God and King. Blessed art Thou, O Lord, the holy God.

According to Elbogen, all of these insertions originated toward the end of the first millennium, and were influenced by the literary technique of contemporary *Piyyutim*. Most of them are—in spirit, if not in form—anticipated in *Pirqe de R. Eliezer*, IV end.[69] (A) in particular is already given in *Soferim* XVI, 12. The variant with the inverted preamble is an allusion to Isa. 29:23. We find in the so-called Egyptian order of the Church a preamble of a doxology which strikingly resembles the introductory formula of the *Kedusha*. Because of its similarity to the phraseology of several Hebrew prayers, I quote the entire passage:

288

We will give praise to Thee, O Lord (through Thy Son Jesus Christ, our Lord). . . . We sanctify Thee and glorify Thee (through Thine only-begotten Son, our Lord, Jesus Christ;) (through Him) be glory and power, and honour to Thee (and Him) (and to the Holy Spirit,) now and for ever into the eons of eons, and everybody say: Amen.[70]

The *Kedusha* concludes with a doxology, 'The Lord will Reign' (J) and the closing *beraka* 'From generation to generation . . . the God of Holiness' (K). As befits a solemn, extended prayer such as the *Kedusha*, the real doxology is placed at its end; the principle of eternity is stressed three times: 'The Lord will reign'; 'From generation to generation'; 'From generation to generation . . . and Thy praise, O Lord, shall not disappear from our lips for ever and ever'. Here, the Hallelujah of the doxology is part of the scriptural quotation, but we know many other cases where it has been freely or spontaneously added. It is especially impressive in this place, for with it the congregation ends the *Kedusha* proper in a glorious fashion.[71]

The poetic structure of the 'Great *Kedusha*' deserves our special attention because of its chain technique which always links the last words of the *hazan* with the first words of the congregational responses. Evidently this is a style highly suitable for musical composition. Indeed, few poems of our prayer-book have inspired the liturgical composers to such achievements as has the *Kedusha*. This 'chain-figure', a kind of climactic parallelism, as employed in the *Kedusha* responses, is a most ancient form of Semitic praying. We find traces of this technique already in Babylonian texts.[72] It seems that this archaic style has conquered, through Judaism, some of the older parts of the Church liturgy. Thus we have passages like these:

(A) *Congregation:* It is meet and right. . . . (Heb.: 'It is true and right.')
   Minister: It is meet as well as true and just. . . .
(B) *Congregation:* Holy, Holy, Holy is the Lord Sabaoth. . . .
   Minister: Holy art Thou, as it is true, and all-holy. . . .
(C) *Deacon:* Lord, bless us. . . .
   Minister: The Lord will bless, and He will honour. . . .
(D) *Minister:* Blessed be the name of the Lord our God into the aeons. (Ps. 113:2)
   Deacon: In the fear of God, and in faith, and in love precede ye. . . .
   Congregation: Blessed be he who comes in the name of the Lord. . . .
      (Ps. 118:26)
   Deacon: Lord, bless us. . . .
   Minister: O God, save Thy people, and bless Thine inheritance. (Ps. 28:9)[73]

The Jewish liturgy, of course, is full of such instances, and in most cases they indicate responsorial rendering.[74] In the *Kedusha* this technique is carried out so consistently that we cannot but assume that the intention existed to link the responses by musical motifs corresponding to the words to be repeated. We shall see later, in the musical part of this study, that indeed the practice of *tones fixées* is frequent in the doxologies of both the Ambrosian and the Gregorian tradition, and in the musical tradition of the *Kedusha* for the High Holydays.

In view of the frequent and familiar instances of chain technique, the theory of Aptowitzer that 'there is no instance in the liturgy in which the reader repeats anything which was previously enunciated by the congregation'[75] cannot be seriously maintained. How elaborate and well developed the responsorial style actually was, we learn from the description given in the *Sefer Yuhasin*, describing the installation of the Exilarch during a divine service and quoted in Chapter V, p. 136. This is, to the writer's knowledge, the earliest account depicting the performance of a choir in addition to that of a professional *hazan* and the traditional responses of a congregation. According to that primary source, the event took place in the ninth century in Babylonia.

About a century before, we encounter there, scrutinizing the few extant sources, the name of a great scholarly and liturgical authority, R. Yehudai Gaon.[76] These sources bring out two facts quite clearly: first, Yehudai Gaon was a traditionalist, but of a conciliatory nature, and, second, he was a person of commanding authority.[77]

E. Birnbaum had already stated—long before the newly discovered sources of the Geniza were known—that it was Yehudai Gaon who favoured the early *hazanim* with the support of his authority. This great leader possessed the stature that was necessary for the firm establishment and a further development of the musical tradition of the Synagogue.[78] Thus we read in the *Sefer ha-eshkol*:

Rav Tzemach wrote: Close to us are the *hazanim* . . . and the first *hazanim* received the tradition from the Master Rab Yehudai and it is said that the tradition was in their hands [from other *hazanim*] and he had it from his teacher [as far back as] Raba [third century] until the first four *hazanim* received the tradition from the Master Rab Yehudai (who had received it from his teacher). . . .[79]

This confluence of two streams ('*from other hazanim*') of tradition in the person of Yehudai Gaon indicates the broad basis upon which he was able to establish a genuine, regulated tradition of synagogal chant.[80] It is even possible that this great rabbi was himself a *hazan* or was, at least, keenly interested in the lot of *hazanim*, for it was he, the blind sage, who decided that blindness should not bar the appointment of a *hazan* who was otherwise qualified for that office.[81]

It seems hardly too bold, in view of these supporting facts and sources, to state that *the authentic tradition of synagogal music goes back to R. Yehudai Gaon and that he is to be considered as the guiding spirit in the development of Hazanut.*

The Kaddish

In order to give the *Kedusha* its proper structure, it was necessary *to add to it* the doxology. Of the *Kaddish*, on the other hand, the doxology is the original cell. It was around this cell that the *Kaddish* was built; for this prayer as a whole is a doxology *par excellence*. The oldest rabbinic sources indicate clearly that the doxological passage—'Praised be His glorious name unto all eternity'—was the nucleus of the *Kaddish* prayer.[82] This formula seems to represent an ancient Semitic custom born out of the spirit of the language. Already the Palmyra inscriptions show similar compositions; the best known of them is perhaps the Eulogy for an Unnamed God, or to 'the unknown God': 'to bless his name for a long eternity'.[83]

In the *Kaddish*, the 'Praised be His glorious name unto all eternity' was from the very first understood as a doxological response. To pronounce it at the proper time and on the proper occasion was considered so important that any Jew present had to interrupt his activities, even his own prayer, in order to pronounce this response.[84] This response was so generally known that we even read of a dream in which that response was made and of a subsequent discussion of it.[85] In former times, both the *Kaddish* and the *Barku* were much more often repeated than they are today, even in the orthodox liturgy. They were used as a doxology which closed or opened every important moment of the synagogal rite. Indeed, we know hardly another prayer so perfectly fitted to serve as a frame for all the greater segments of our worship. We do not refer here to the famous contents of the prayer but to its formal aspects. Is it not remarkable that the main doxology—'Praised be His glorious name unto all eternity'—*opens* with Amen, thus linking the sanctification of the reader with that of the congregation? The fundamental idea of doxological praise is stressed to the utmost: the adoration, exaltation, and glorification of the Almighty in the *infinity of time and space* being sole substance of the prayer. All of its supplicatorial elements have been recognized as later insertions when the *Kaddish*, contrary to its original purpose, became the memorial prayer for the deceased. Once again we see that, like every genuine doxology, the *Kaddish* is a series of responses. Following the nuclear passage—'Praised be His glorious name unto all eternity'—only the shortest possible forms are chosen for the responding congregation: 'Blessed be He', and 'Amen'. Everything else is left to the reader. That is the reason why this prayer, more than any other, has become so popular with the cantor, and why the musical tradition of the Synagogue knows of so many renderings of that doxology. All of them use the principle of 'leading motifs' reflecting the musical atmosphere of the particular festival or of that liturgical unit of which the *Kaddish* forms a part.[86] We shall discuss more exclusively, in Part II of this study, this most interesting occurrence of 'leading motifs' in ancient synagogal music.

Since the text of the *Kaddish* was considered very important, the reader was confronted with two tasks in connexion with its musical rendering. First, he had to chant a melody which in each case was to reflect the different ideas of the occasion or season. Secondly, he had to prolong his performance beyond the time of simple recitation, in order to give the worshippers sufficient time to meditate over the text. These demands, when fulfilled, created a great variety of moods and tunes in which one and the same text was musically rendered throughout the ecclesiastical year. Such a development does not signify a lack of understanding of the basic text but, quite to the contrary, a rich association of ideas and emotions connected with the *Kaddish*.

This prayer reached its loftiest height in a hymn by Yehuda Halevi. He uses the opening verse of the *Kaddish* as refrain after five stanzas. The tone of the hymn is mystical. To the creature crying for salvation and help, the heavens open—he is overwhelmed and cannot but stammer the familiar words of the *Kaddish*:

(Last two stanzas. Trans. E. W.)
Whom I desire,
To whom I aspire,
My tower and shield
And only guard:

All a-glowing,
Light a-flowing,
Unconcealed,
   Unveiled, revealed:

MAY HE BE PRAISED
AND BE EXTOLLED
AND BE ADORED   (Opening verse of
AND SANCTIFIED.   *Kaddish*.)

The similarity of the so-called Lord's Prayer to the text of the *Kaddish* is well known and has frequently been discussed. It is not necessary to review here the results of that comparison.[87] Yet the interesting question has not been posed whether and how the Church reacted to the *Kaddish* proper. For that the Church knew of the *Kaddish* cannot be doubted.

Outside of the Gospels, we do not find any allusion to the *Kaddish* as such in patristic literature. Although there are numerous Christian prayers with strong allusions to the text of the *Kaddish*, it is not possible to speak of an influence either through or upon the *Kaddish*.[88] More frequent than these inklings, however, are the stern warnings and the admonitions addressed to faithful Christians, not to relapse into *modum Judaeorum precandi*. Occasionally hints of the kind of these Jewish prayers are given, for instance:

'Hallowed be Thy name' [Matt. 6:9]. Holy is, by its very nature, God's name, whether we say it or not. Yet by those sinners it is sometimes profaned. As Scripture says: '*Because of you* my name is continually blasphemed before the Gentiles' [Isa. 52:5.][89] [The *Kaddish* begins with 'Hallowed . . . be His great Name'.]

This seems to be a veiled allusion to the *Kaddish* linked with an anti-Jewish pronouncement. Our conclusion then is that the Church Fathers made no specific mention of the *Kaddish* because of its very similarity to the Lord's Prayer. More important than the text of the *Kaddish* itself is the fact that it was considered the perfect prayer corresponding to the demands postulated in the Talmud: 'It is possible that a man might ask that his needs be fulfilled and afterwards pray. It has already been explained by Solomon when he said: "To listen to song and prayer". Song is prayer and prayer is pleading (for necessities).'[90] Dr G. Klein has demonstrated convincingly that the Lord's Prayer, too, answers all of the requirements demanded by Jewish tradition. It consists of three parts: (a) the glorification of God (praise); (b) the individual prayer (pleading, prayer); and (c) the closing doxology (thanksgiving).[91] Furthermore, the right kind of prayer must contain both the remembrance of God and remembrance of His kingdom. We find all of these elements in the *Kaddish* as well as in the Lord's Prayer. These requirements were, of course, familiar to Early Christianity, as we can learn from Paul, the Apostle to the Gentiles.[92]

In view of the abundance of beautiful prayers, born of devotion and faith, it was certainly a wise principle to have every important prayer contain the ancient, yet simple formula of the *beraka*, lest this *embarras de richesse* become a chaotic effusion of subjective emotions and thoughts. Thus the Jewish liturgy, through its typical forms of *beraka* and doxology, preserved its essential integrity. Yet there are scholars who decry this uniformity of Jewish prayer. The most unjust of them is Dr Baumstark who, in a discussion of Hebrew liturgy, concludes: 'It is undoubtedly in connexion with its anti-Christian attitude that we have to understand the obvious one-sidedness, by which the so-called *beraka*, in its typical form, dominates the development of synagogal prayer.'[93] This scholar overlooks two important facts: (1) the form of the *beraka* was already well developed before the rise of Christianity, since it appears frequently in the Psalter and other pre-Christian literature; (2) the stereotyped formula of the *beraka* is actually analogous to the Christian Lesser Doxology, *Gloria Patri*. This doxology is required at the end of every antiphon, every longer prayer, and every psalm-responsory. It is, exactly as the *beraka*, a fixed and mandatory formula which reflects the century-long struggles and the controversies involving certain dogmatic issues, such as the Trinity, the pre-existence of Christ, and the like.

This identity of *beraka* and ecclesiastic doxology can be seen in a drastic example, where, on the Jewish side, a prayer, based upon a scriptural passage, is concluded by a *beraka*, while the Christian prayer (of the same scriptural passage) ends with the Lesser Doxology:

Latin	*Hebrew (Translated—Auth. P.B., p. 127)*
Te decet laus	For unto thee, O Lord our God . . . song and
Te decet hymnus	praise are becoming, hymns and psalm, . . .
Tibi gloria	blessings and thanksgivings from henceforth
Deo Patri et Filio	for ever. Praised art thou, O Lord, God and
Cum Sancto Spiritu	King, great in praises, . . . who makest choice
In saecula saeculorum.[94]	of song and psalm, O King and God, the life
	throughout the world-ages.

These endings could easily be exchanged with each other.

The Small Doxologies

These short verses, like 'Blessed be God, the King of Israel', or 'Blessed be God for ever, Amen and Amen', formed an important function in the ancient prayers of Judaism. Each book of the Psalter closes with such a doxology. But, what was the origin of these doxologies and how were they applied in the liturgy? What religious conceptions did they embody?

In contradistinction to the usual *beraka* these short formulas do not address God directly. They must rather be considered concluding and solemn statements of God's power and greatness. Nor is it a coincidence that they do not use the personal pronoun *Atta* (you), but speak of the Lord in the third person. Moreover, as indicated both by the text and by ancient custom, these doxological statements were to be answered by a congregational 'Amen'.[95] It may therefore be assumed that all of these closing doxologies had, from the very beginning, a liturgical function in public service, namely, that of arousing the congregation to a loud affirmation, declaring, through the Amen, their adoration of God's majesty in space and time.

These short doxologies have even today their legitimate function in the daily and sabbatical liturgies. Again Baumstark is badly mistaken, when he states: 'In the rite of the later Synagogue, the doxological formula has almost disappeared, while it has become a dominant element in Christianity.'[96] A glance into any Jewish standard prayer book would have taught him better.

While the popular response seems to be the immediate liturgical purpose of these doxologies—the declaration of God's greatness affirmed by a general Amen—it does not fully explain the original idea, the *principium essendi* behind these doxologies. Perhaps we shall come nearer a solution of the problem if we examine and classify the texts of those passages.

We find that emphasis is laid upon:

(a) The glory of God's name (Ps. 72:19, and *baruk shem*).

(b) God as Israel's Lord (Ps. 41:14; 106:48; I Chron. 16:36; etc.).

(c) God as King of Israel and the Universe (Ps. 146:10; Exod. 15:18; etc.).

(d) God's praise in eternity (Ps. 89:53; Ps. 115:18; etc.).

Of these forms, (d) is the simplest and shortest. While the other types show a decidedly theocratic tendency, (d) originated in a period when theocracy was not the dominating ideology, perhaps during the reign of the later Kings. After the Babylonian Exile, theocracy was at least theoretically understood as Israel's constitutional law. Moreover, the great majority of our doxologies are versed from Levitic psalms, or phrased after I Chron. 16:7-36. What, then, would be more natural than a strongly theocratic declaration? Several times in this study we had occasion to refer to the fact that the doxologies were typical of the liturgy of the Temple rather than of the Synagogue. Considering, finally, that the *Tetragrammaton* could be pronounced in the Temple only, we conclude that *the basic idea of the doxology was a reaffirmation of theocracy in the mouth of the priestly caste. Such reaffirmation was considered a priestly prerogative inherent in the constitution and tradition of the Temple cult.*

If this be so, we should expect that, in the centuries after the destruction of the Temple, the role of the small doxologies would decline, since the priestly caste had lost its chief function. Indeed, such a development seems to have taken place. The doxology, 'Blessed be God from this time forth and for evermore', which was required in the Temple, was replaced by the simple Amen in the Synagogue. The small doxologies were eventually connected with the 'sentences of praise' in order to preserve as many reminiscences of the Temple as possible. Only one new doxology of significance originated in the Diaspora, the 'God reigns, God has reigned, God will reign for ever and ever', and this formula was not placed, as one would expect, at the end of a prayer.

Thus we realize that the small doxologies of the Temple lost their original function to a great degree and were retained in the Synagogue as mere reminders of ancient glories. The responsorial rendering, so typical of genuine doxologies, was reserved more and more for *Barku*, *Sh'ma'*, *Kedusha*, and *Kaddish*. Yet there are certain liturgies in which the Temple doxologies flourished long after the destruction of the Sanctuary. If our interpretation of the background of the doxologies is correct, it was the Sadducees who made them essential part of the Temple cult. The spiritual heirs of the Sadducees were the Samaritans, and, later on, the Karaites.[97] Thus we should perhaps be able to discover the last traces of the Sadducean practice of the doxology in the liturgy of the Samaritans and the Karaites. And, indeed, a close examination of these liturgies fully verifies the aforementioned connexion between the two sects. Most of the Samaritan prayers conclude with a short doxology like 'For ever', or 'God for ever, Amen' or similar abbreviations of the psalm doxologies.[98] In some cases the text indicates even a responsorial rendering of these closing words. We remember that the Samaritans possess to this very day remnants of the Temple cult and of a priestly family. They use short doxologies very frequently and they adhere to several other tenets of the Sadducees. Sometimes we even find greatly expanded passages of doxological character in the body of their prayers. In spite of the obvious parallelism between such doxologies and psalm verses, we must use caution against overrating the authenticity of these Samaritan sources. Not unwarrantably does J. Freudenthal stress the syncretistic tendencies of the Samaritans:

> They dedicate their Temple to *Zeus Xenios* (II Macc. 6:2; Joseph, *Ant.* XII, 5, 5) they adore the One God of Israel, they were the soil in which that Simon Magus and his followers grew, the men who mixed pagan, Jewish and Christian doctrines into an amorphous hodge-podge.[99]

We are considerably better informed about the liturgy of the Karaites. The last five decades have brought to light much material hitherto unknown. That the Karaites professed many of the principles to which both Samaritans and Sadducees adhered, we are well aware.[100] As we know from a profound study by the late Dr Mann, this affinity frequently affected the very details of their liturgy. Thus, these short doxologies are more numerous in the liturgy of the Karaites than in that of the Samaritans, where they were, by no means, scarce. Anan ruled that the prayers must consist solely of psalms or of verses from the psalms. Consequently the doxologies at the end of the five books of the Psalter were in constant use. The doxology, Ps. 106:48, was read four times daily during the seventy days of fasting.[101] After the 'stand up and bless' (Neh. 9:5 instead of the post-biblical 'bless') the reader adds the doxologies at the end of the first four books of the Psalter. Likewise at the end of Ps. 113, 114, 116, 117, 118 the congregation performs 'Bending of the knees'.[102] Three of these psalms close with Hallelujah. Most frequently we encounter the doxologies Ps. 72:19, and the formula 'From this time forth and for ever' at the end of a prayer.[103] Dr Mann concludes his learned investigation with the remark:

> It is evident . . . that Anan endeavoured to reinstate the service of the Temple, as he conceived it, modified, of course, by the alterations in consequence of the cessation of sacrifices. The services were limited by the number and the times of the sacrifices for the day. . . . The priest had to do the reading just as if he offered up the *Korban* (sacrifice) in the Temple. The Levite was to

recite the psalm of the day just as his ancestor chanted it in the Sanctuary at Jerusalem. . . .[104]

In view of all of these documents there is no room for doubt that the small doxologies were inseparably connected with the idea of a Temple cult, with a hierarchy and, in the last analysis, with the principles of theocracy. As daily reminders of these aspects they have retained their place in the Prayer Book. It was perhaps the revival of a hierarchy, modelled after the pattern of the Temple, that ultimately determined the favourable attitude of the Church toward Doxology; and this development was, in some respect, a curious pendant of the Jewish picture.

DOXOLOGIES OF THE EARLY CHURCH

When Origen stated that each proper prayer should end in a doxology, he was, as it often happens, merely registering the contemporary and traditional practice of the Church.[105] Actually we find doxologies throughout the New Testament. Yet one fact must be stressed again and again, for it has been neglected or not completely understood thus far: the fact that in the *canonical Gospels* we encounter only one doxology— at the end of the Lord's Prayer—and moreover, the authenticity of this passage is doubtful and heavily disputed.[106] The usual explanation that the Gospels do not include liturgies is, of course, correct, but it replaces one problem with another. Even if we consider the Gospels as literature of religious propaganda (in the best sense of that misused word) even then, the almost complete absence of liturgical passages is remarkable. There are several instances of individual prayers, but they represent the most sacred spirit of individualism, in fact, they are in spirit and expression anti-liturgical.[107] It should not be forgotten that Early Christianity was a movement of the poor and the meek; its roots lay in the rural section of Galilee. Jerusalem, the priests, and many of the rabbis were opposed to the 'men from the country' (*'amme ha' arez*), or rather, they despised them because of their ignorance.

The small local synagogues with their unceremonious, almost intimate, attitude toward prayer and God were the birthplaces of Christian liturgy. There was no room in those communal houses of worship for rigid and solemn formulas, such as the Temple doxologies of the hierarchical cult of Jerusalem. This explains the almost complete absence of all liturgical material in the Gospels.[108] The Pauline literature, however, is replete with doxologies; indeed, for the organization of a new *ecclesia*, a modicum of liturgical order is indispensable. In this stage, the doxologies usually are direct translations or paraphrases of the familar Hebrew formula, as Rom. 11:36; II Cor. 11:31; Phil. 4:20; I Tim. 1:17, etc. The references to Christ take the form of an added 'through (or for) Jesus Christ' or, infrequently, 'for His sake'. Jesus is considered the High Priest of the new community. The earliest instance of a doxology to Christ himself is found in Polycarp's prayer where we read:

> Thee I praise, Thee I bless, Thee I glorify through the everlasting and heavenly High Priest Jesus Christ . . . through whom there be glory to Thee and Him and the Holy Spirit, now and always into the coming aeons, Amen.

Yet the direct addressing of the Lord classifies this piece more as a hymnic prayer than a doxology.[109]

Even here Jesus is considered the 'heavenly High Priest'; and we may safely say that all these forms are Hebraic in style and spirit. Only in the third century does the Trinitarian type of doxology become dominant in the liturgical literature of the Church. This development coincided— being far more than a coincidence—with the gradual return to hierarchical institutions in the Church. Liturgy, ministry, and ritual crystallized in those centuries, and with them the doxology assumed its regular and dominant position at the end of every important prayer.[110] Yet it took one more century before the clearly Trinitarian type was standardized. This was a necessary development, since it became urgent to stress the perfect equality of the three Divine Persons. When the Arian heresy threatened the unity of the Church, denying the eternity of the Son, and speaking of a time when 'the Son was not', the Catholic Church accentuated all the stronger the pre-existence of Christ and formulated the final text of the doxology: 'Gloria Patri et Filio et Spiritui Sancto, sicut erat [sc. Jesus] in principio et nunc et semper et in saecula saeculorum, [Alleluia], Amen.[111] With this passage every psalm or antiphon is to be concluded, as we hear from Cassian around A.D. 400.[112] Finally, in 529, the second Synod of Vaison decreed it a required part of the liturgy of the Western Church. However, it is significant for the stronghold the Arians had in the East that, because of the objection of the Byzantine Church, the first part, 'As He was from the beginning', has not been fully accepted even to this day.[113] The final text of the doxology became so all-important that it almost displaced the older small doxologies. Today they form only a secondary place in the Catholic liturgy and are rarely chanted, whereas the 'official' form is often chanted antiphonally and has grown, when coupled with Alleluia, into little 'ecclesiastical symphonies'.

Beraka and Doxology

Let us now compare briefly the development of the doxology in Church and Synagogue. The Church, beginning with the small doxologies of the psalms, reached the pinnacle of spontaneity and richness of doxological expression in the fourth century. Then, for dogmatic reasons, it returned to a rigid yet elaborate formula uniform throughout the entire service. Judaism added new forms, but retained four or five individual doxologies as pious mementoes of the Temple. Thus we see again that hierarchic constitutions (as in the Church) favour strict, uniform, small doxologies; the freer conditions with the Synagogue permitted greater variety and greater length. Moreover, it is possible to say that the eulogy (*beraka*) still had an important function in the early Church, but the stronger the function of the doxology, the less significant became the eulogy. While we still find at the end of the second century perfect *berakot* modelled after the best Hebrew pattern, such as: 'Blessed art Thou, Lord Jesus Christ, Son of God, who hast deigned even me, the sinner, worthy of Thy lot', this archetype gradually fades out of the liturgy and literature of the Church, and in the sixth century hardly any traces of eulogies remain.[114] Conversely, the Synagogue preferred the direct address of the *beraka* to the more impersonal, formal, praying type of doxology.

Now we are perhaps better equipped to draw a distinction between *beraka* and doxology. The *beraka* does not necessarily have a ritual function; all daily activities are to be sanctified by the *beraka*, with its direct address to God, the King of the Universe. The *beraka* may be pronounced by one individual without response except Amen. The doxology, however, is essentially a ritual act, and where and whenever a doxology was properly, that is responsively, performed, the presence of ten male Jews was originally required. Whereas the form of the *beraka* is but a frame into which the different contents have to be fitted with reference to each occasion, the form of the doxology has but one content, the objective, exultant, absolutely impersonal praise of God's glory in infinity. That explains why, according to rabbinic doctrine, the faithful set the pattern for the heavenly hosts when intoning the *Kedusha*, for here, as in any doxology, we reach beyond human prayer, avoiding any personal complaint, petition, or even reference to ourselves.

The Greek liturgy of St James, which did not adopt the Western standard doxology *Gloria Patri*, shows the Jacobite dislike of the impersonal style of doxology and has retained a direct *beraka*-like address to God, connected with a genuine eulogy at the end: '. . . to the grace and the mercies and the benevolence of the only begotten Son of Thee, through whom Thou be blessed into the aeons of aeons, Amen.'[115]

These forms occur rather frequently in the liturgies of the Eastern Churches and show unmistakable remnants of Jewish spirit, viz. the form of the *beraka* which has been all but abolished by the Western Church. There, the few examples of genuine *berakot* still extant are either relegated to insignificant places within the public liturgy, or—evidencing the fine feeling of those who organized the Roman breviary —they are limited to private devotion, such as the grace after meals. What does this usage signify, which veers away from the individualistic eulogy toward a uniform and often repeated doxology? In this writer's opinion, it reflects the trend from the unceremonious, private devotion of the Early Church to collective worship; from spontaneity to systematization, from religious individualism to religious collectivism.

THE HALLELUJAH IN THE DOXOLOGY

A full-fledged discussion of the Hallelujah and its liturgical and musical history would easily fill a large book; so colourful and rich is its history that Cardinal Pitra, the great liturgist, could say 'the story of the Hallelujah is a poem itself'.[116] Here we shall deal only with the Hallelujah as part of the doxology, or as an isolated doxological call.

Although the word itself does not have a musical connotation, the Hallelujah has always been connected with song and praise. Jewish tradition, as well as Christian exegesis, has invariably understood the Hallelujah as a song performed by men or angels. This interpretation goes through the entire rabbinic and patristic literature, as we shall see below. The recitation of the *Hallel* is concluded by a *beraka* or song, preceded by a semi-doxological passage:

(a) For it is good to praise Thee and to sing Thy beautiful name, for from this time forth and for ever Thou art God;
(b) Blessed art Thou O Lord our God, O King great in praises. God of Praise, God of wonder who chooses songs of praise. King, O God, who lives for ever.

The *Nishmat* prayer, which closes with this eulogistic passage (b), also contains doxological psalm-verses. These constitute good illustrations of prayers which are just at the border line between *beraka* and doxology. Both of the above-mentioned prayers are referred to in the Talmud and reflect an old and venerable attitude identifying the *doxa* idea with hymnic song.[117] Consequently, Gunkel's theory that the congregational Hallelujah was the germinal cell of all hymn-singing is not so bold as he imagines.[118]

The original liturgical function of the Hallelujah is not yet quite clear. Some scholars have linked it to the pre-monotheistic adoration of the new moon.[119] In the psalms, however, no trace of such origin is extant. An entirely different approach seems to promise more enlightenment. Some of the Hallelujah psalms, e.g. 135:21; 118:2-4; 106:48; 113:1; 146:1; 148:1; 149:1; 150:1-6 demand either responsorial or antiphonal rendering. Sometimes even the text states this kind of performance as in Ps. 106:48, or I Chron. 16:36. In both of these cases the Hallelujah forms the end of a doxology. Such a passage always signifies a confirmation of faith in the deity. The euphonic and exultant Hallelujah would give even the uninitiated primitive listeners the opportunity to join the proclamations of God's praise. Therefore it stands in the beginning or at the end of a psalm, the former a signal and invitation, the latter a closing call of primitive and sacred joy. This suggests that the liturgical function of the Hallelujah was, in primitive times, a priestly device to organize popular participation in the divine service. Various sources tell us that the Hallelujah was a regular rubric in the liturgy of the Temple, especially on Passover and *Sukkot*. This fact is a stumbling block for Grätz's theory that the Hallelujah was not used in the Temple but was the *invitatorium* of the minister in the Synagogue.[120] Yet Grätz is right, in so far as, long before the fall of the Sanctuary, some of the psalms were introduced in the Synagogue, and the Hallelujah was separated from its context and used whenever an exultant ending was indicated.

The Talmud says that the Hallelujah was even used as a salutation at the end of the service.[121] The doxological Hallelujah is usually juxtaposed to Amen, as we saw in Ps. 106:48; I Chron. 16:36, and Rev. 19:1-8. The latter follows, in every respect, the Jewish tradition with reference to the occasion upon which the Hallelujah is recited; as a triumphal song of the heavenly hosts over the fall of the arch-enemy

Babylon (i.e. Rome). It is remarkable that the Midrashic sources also unanimously associate the Hallelujah with the destruction of the wicked, exactly as the passage in Revelation. We read in *Midrash Tehillim* to Ps. 104:35:

> Rabbi Simon bar Abba said: From the beginning of the book [the Psalter] up to this point there are 103 psalms and none of them contains the Hallelujah; yet when it comes to the destruction of the wicked, as it is said . . . 'Let sinners cease out of the earth and let the wicked be no more' . . . then we say, 'praise, my soul, praise the Lord, Hallelujah'. And why? Because it is said: 'And when the wicked perish, there is joy. . . .' (Prov. 11:10.)[122]

Not unlike the *Kedusha*, with which it is often compared, the Hallelujah is considered a song of human beings and angels. It is from this aspect that the Hallelujah assumed both in Hellenistic Judaism and in the Early Church a distinctly mystic-esoteric character, greatly enhanced through its ecstatic musical explanations, poems, prayers, throughout Judaism and Christianity. The Targum of Ps. 148, discussing the Hallelujah, is full of angelological associations of the same type as Rev. 19:1–6, or the Midrash quoted above. The *Zohar* links—quite naturally—the song of the Hallelujah to the harmony of the spheres, an idea which had already been proposed by Philo.[123] In general, it may be said that the Hallelujah in both its function and philosophical aspect is very similar to the primitive *Kedusha*. In a few cases, these two prayers have been combined, as for instance in the Apocalypse of Moses: 'Hallelujah, Holy, Holy, Lord of Hosts, Glory to God Almighty, for ever and ever'.[124] Here we have a Hallelujah connected with a *Kedusha*-like, genuine doxology.

In this atmosphere of esoteric exaltation grew the Hallelujah of the Early Church. Paul and his disciples, introducing the pneumatic ideology in their teachings, make the famous distinction between 'psalms, hymns, and spiritual songs' (Eph. 5:19; Col. 3:16), a still disputed passage.[125]

The separation of the Hallelujah from its original contexts, its use as spontaneous acclamation, together with its 'pneumatic' colour, led to a certain disembodiment, to a spiritualization of the Hallelujah, which finally resulted in the omission of the word Hallelujah itself, so that only certain vowels of it were sung—AEOUIA.[126]

When the Hallelujah was finally established in the Latin doxology, its vowels were often changed to EUOUAE = sEcUlOrUm, AmEn. In this form, the *Jubilus* became the great wordless hymn of the Church which Augustine praised in such eloquent terms.[127] The melismatic rendering of the *Jubilus*, with its drawn-out coloraturas, added to the doxology an element of splendour and warmth, greatly enhancing its solemnity.

We find a revival of these wordless prayer-songs, the ecstatic *Niggun*, in the world of Hasidism, a world which in many respects was strangely similar to that of Christianity before the fourth century. This use of 'songs without words' must have been popular also in the medieval Synagogue for a long time, since Solomon ben Adret (fourteenth century) sharply opposed this kind of performance.[128]

The position of the Hallelujah at the very end of the ecclesiastical doxology and its gradual expansion into independent and elaborate musical compositions of considerable length engendered, in the course of time, the emancipation and, to a certain extent, the secularization of the hymnic acclamation. Thus it became occasionally a magical formula,[129] a war-cry,[130] a signal,[131] a joyous call,[132] and even a song of boatmen.[133]

Since, in Jewish liturgical usage, the doxology does not necessarily close a prayer, and since the small doxologies in general do not play a great part, the Hallelujah of the Synagogue has—since the fall of the Temple and its priestly chorus—decreased somewhat in significance. It is only in the *Hallel* that its old glory renews itself, and even then not always with the proper responsorial rendering. The liturgical and musical tradition of the Hallelujah disappeared when the rabbis frowned upon the triumphal songs of the Temple; while they waited for the 'destruction of the wicked', the Hallelujah itself faded from their lips. Yet we shall see, in the second part of our study, that it did not entirely perish; re-interpreted by the Church, it became one of the most important musical heritages of all Christian worship.

MASORETIC EVIDENCE OF THE RESPONSORIAL RENDERING OF THE HALLELUJAH

In the Masoretic text the Hallelujah occurs twenty-two times, both at the beginning or at the end of a psalm and once in the middle of Ps. 135:3. It is remarkable that the Masoretes were extremely consistent in their accentuation of this acclamation. The initial Hallelujah always bears the *Legarmeh* accent and there is only one exception to that rule, Ps. 146; even here it is doubtful whether this Hallelujah really opened the psalm. (Neither the Masoretes nor the Church Fathers came to a clear decision, due to the equivocal writing of the Hallelujah between two psalms, so that it could be considered as beginning or end. The practice of the Vulgate is to set a Hallelujah at the opening of every psalm which closes with Hallelujah, but not necessarily to add a Hallelujah at the end of a psalm which opens with Hallelujah.[134]) Since the second strongest *distinctive accent regularly* precedes the final Hallelujah, it stands to reason that this procedure indicates a caesura in the rendering, i.e. the break in the responsory, where the soloist ends and the chorus begins. Interestingly enough, R. Yehuda Hayyug referred in his *Sefer Hanikud* (Book of Punctuation) to three kinds of accents for the three poetical books (Job, Proverbs, and Psalms) of Scripture, 'standing types, elevation types, knowledge types'.[135] As Dukes has already noted, this division considers chiefly the musical function of the accents. 'Knowledge' in our context seems to indicate hermeneutics; 'standing', the static, resting; 'elevation', the ascent, the lifting of the voice (*vox elevata*). According to Ibn-Bal'aam, the *'ilui* (ascent) seems to stand for an extended melody in the higher tones of the scale (preceding the close). This evidence indicates that the final Hallelujah was rendered in a descending phrase of the congregation, since it closed the psalm. The Hallelujah was preceded by a sustained note higher in the scale and this is still the practice in Gregorian and Jewish psalmody. The Gregorian *Jubili*, however, contain only scant remnants of their oriental provenance; the decisive form-elements of these chants are of Western origin, probably connected with the rise of Sequence and Prose. Closer than the Gregorian Hallelujahs to the Jewish tradition are the Byzantine Alleluias, as we shall see later on in Part II.

NOTES CHAPTER IX

1. W. Caspary, *Die Bedeutung der Wortsippe* Kabod *im Hebräischen* (Leipzig, 1908).

2. J. Morgenstern, 'Biblical Theophanies', *Zeitschrift für Assyriologie*, 1911, pp. 139–73, and 1913, pp. 15–60.

3. G. Kittel, in *Forschungen und Fortschritte*, VII, No. 35–36, p. 457.

4. It is well known that a paraphrase of I Chron. 29:11 forms the closing sentence in the Lord's Prayer, Matt. 6:13. The version in the Gospel is a real doxology. Recently, however, the passage has been considered spurious by several scholars.

5. Cf. *Martyrium Polycarpi*, Chapter 21 end, in *The Apostolic Fathers*, ed. Lightfoot (London, 1891), p. 197.

6. Cf. Ps. Athanasius, *De Virginitate* (PG, XXVIII, 265 ff.).

7. Cf. Justin Martyr, *Dial. cum Tryphone*, XXIX, 1.

8. Cf. Origen, *De Oratione* 9 (PG, XI, 557). Text in my 'Doxology', *HUCA*, XIX, p. 278.

9. Cf. CAF, VIII, Chapter 13, v. 10.

10. This development is clearly reflected in the gradual expansion of the introductory prayers, which gradually absorbed most of the 'Mass of the Catechumens'. See also *infra* pp. 281 ff.

11. Cf. CAF, VII, 47, 1.

12. Cf. Hammond, *Liturgies Eastern and Western*, p. 53.

13. My translation: Glory be to the Father and the Son, and to the Holy Spirit, as He was in the beginning, and now and always unto endless ages. Amen.

14. This doxology is the end of a hymnic prayer of priests and perhaps of professional musicians.

15. The blessing of water, of incense, etc., while belonging to the liturgy, precedes the actual service.

16. E.g., in the formal grace of the Roman Church: 'Benedictus deus in donis suis et sanctus in omnibus operibus suis, qui vivit et regnat in saecula saeculorum'. See also in CAF, VII, Chapter 49 (*Didascalia*): 'Benedictus es, Domine, qui nutris me a pueritia mea. . . .'

17. On these and the following passages in general, see the Authorized Prayer Book, annotated edition by Singer and J. Abrahams. On Hebrew doxologies cf. L. Blau in *REJ*, XXXI and LV; also A. Büchler, *Die Priester und der Cultus*, pp. 175 ff; ELB, pp. 26, 495 ff.

18. See Aptowitzer in *MGWJ*, LXXIII (1929), pp. 93 ff and L. Finkelstein, 'The Development of the '*Amida*', *JQR*, N.S. XVI.

19. Cf. *Soferim*, ed. Müller, Chapter 16, last *Halakah*; also ibid. 225 ff. See also J. Mann, 'Anan's Liturgy' in *Journal of Jewish Lore and Philosophy*, I, p. 345.

20. Also: *Tos. Ber.* VII, 4; *Tos Ta'an.* I, 11; *Ta'an.* 16b. The real birthplace of the doxologies was the Temple, not the Synagogue, as Hoennicke assumes (*Das Judenchristentum*, p. 258). Concerning the New Testament doxologies, see *infra*.

21. *M. Yoma* III, 8, IV, 1, VI, 2. *Ber.* IX, B, *Ber.* 63a. The entire history of the formula has been discussed in ELB, pp. 494 ff, and more extensively by V. Aptowitzer, loc. cit., pp. 93 ff. Aptowitzer's interesting hypothesis suffers somewhat from his persistence in attributing political reasons to any change of the liturgy. Finkelstein in his article on the benedictions of the *Sh'ma'* (*REJ*, 1932, p. 23) and ELB, p. 496, state that the 'Praised be His name', etc., involves an antiphonal rendering. That is extremely improbable, since it would imply that the *Sh'ma'* was read by a group of men instead of the cantor. However, I assume that both scholars really mean a responsory, not an antiphon.

22. Cf. *Jer. Ber.* IX, 5, 14c.

23. Cf. Jude 25.

24. Cf. CAF, regularly at the end of each prayer in the seventh book.

25. Cf. *Martyrium Polycarpi*, 14.

26. Cf. Clement of Rome, *Ep. I*, Chapter 61, 3. Beyond these well-known Hebraisms it is worth noting that the practice of the concluding Amen is strictly in accord with the established Jewish usage, viz. that it is to be said by the worshipping congregation in answer to the prayer or the eulogy of the precentor. Consequently we look in vain for such an Amen in the Gospels, because no congregation is presupposed. There the Amen, usually at the beginning of a sentence, means 'verily, truly'. Paul, however, takes a very strong and traditional attitude in I Cor. 14:15–17, where he asks: 'What is it then? I will pray with the spirit, . . . and I will sing with the understanding also. Else when thou shalt bless with the spirit, how shall he that occupieth the room of the unlearned say Amen at thy giving of thanks, seeing he understandeth not what thou sayest? For thou verily givest thanks well, but the other is not edified'. In my opinion, this passage is an indirect reproach levelled at Philo because of his enthusiastic description of the silent worship of the Therapeutae.

27. *B. Pes.* 56a.

28. Ibid.

29. Similar cases of doxologies, borrowed from the Temple, are quoted in *Soferim*, ed. Müller, p. 252. Cf. also Midr. *Tehillim* 104 and the references *infra* in the discussion of the small doxologies.

30. Cf. *B. Pes.* 56a.

31. Cf. Aptowitzer, op. cit., p. 110.

32. Cf. Ps.-Clement., *Homilies*, III, 57 (PG, II, 147). Compare with this distinctly Judaeo-Christian attitude, refuting the Gnostic arguments against monotheism, the passage Deut. R. II, 33, 104c. The sentence quoted is only a part of the long and extensive religious disputation between Peter and Simon Magus, the representative of Parsistic Dualism and Pre-Marcionitic Gnosis. It is regrettable that the Pseudo-Clementines, a most interesting document of Judaeo-Christianity, in particular of Ebionism, have thus far obtained little attention from Jewish scholars. To this writer's knowledge, the only recent study of it from a Jewish point of view is J. Bergmann's article in *REJ*, XLVI (1903), pp. 86 ff. O. Bardenhewer, *Geschichte der Altkirchlichen Literatur*, II, 618, the best authority, writes on that subject: 'In diesem Zusammenhang genuegt es festzustellen, dass die Schrift im wesentlichen die Anschauungen der alten Judaisten, Ebioniten oder Elkesaiten, vertritt. . . . Die Theorie von der Identität des Christentums mit dem Judentum ist mit umso grösserem Nachdruck in den Vordergrund gerückt'. Only very recently the desideratum has been provided by H. J. Schöp's book, *Theologie und Geschichte des Judenchristentums* (Tübingen, 1950).

33. Cf. Travers Herford, *Christianity in Talmud and Midrash*, pp. 307-12, 255-66 *et passim*.

34. Cf. Aptowitzer, op. cit., p. 113.

35. Cf. Hammond, op. cit., pp. 51 ff.

36. Cf. *Sacramentarium Serapionis*, in *CAF*, XII, i. It is worth noting that this passage is a literal quotation from Paul's Epistle to the Ephesians (1:21); but Paul refers to Christ, while Serapion praises God the Father. The Roman Church uses here Dan. 3:52 (not included in the Jewish canon) and Ps. 72:19.

Resp. (a) Benedictum nomen gloriae tuae sanctum, et laudabile, et superexaltatum in saecula. (Ad laudes in festo Nominis Jesu.)

Resp. (b) Benedictus Dominus Deus Israel, qui facit mirabilia magna *solus*: et benedictum nomen majestatis eius in aeternum. *Vers.* Replebitur majestate eius omnis terra; fiat, fiat, et benedictum nomen. (In festo S Trinitatis.)

Since the very passage which was to emphasize the exclusively Jewish monotheism against the concept of Trinity was used in the Church on the festival of the Trinity, we must conclude that either the theory of the anti-Christian use of the prayer was wrong or else that its polemical tendency was an absolutely empty gesture.

37. Cf. *Jer. Ber.* I, 7; *Tamid* V, 1; also Krauss, *Synagogale Altertümer*, pp. 67-72. We know of this remarkable synagogue within the Temple from both Jewish and New Testament sources. It is identical with the 'Hall of Stones', where Jesus argued with the Rabbis (Luke 2:46). It is the assembly place mentioned in Acts 3:11; 5:12.

38. Not because of the *Sh'ma'* itself and certainly not because of the *barukh shem* which they used in some variants. It was the silence or the murmuring after the watchword of Judaism that provoked the embarrassing questions of the *Minim*.

39. The Karaite liturgy used the Nehemiah passage literally; as for Karaite doxologies, see *infra*, pp. 296-8.

40. The custom of singing Ps. 95 on the eve of the Sabbath is comparatively recent and owes its origin to the mystics of Safed in the sixteenth century.

41. Cf. Origen, *De Oratione* 9 (PG, XI, 557); see *supra*, p. 305, n. 8. The Roman Church uses Ps. 95:6 (94:6) and Tob. 13:10 as *invitatorium*.

42. Cf. Hammond, op. cit., p. 7. If 'through Christ' is omitted, the passage is identical with *Kumu barku*, etc. (Neh. 9:5.)

43. Cf. Hammond, op. cit., p. 59. At the end of the Mass of the Catechumens, being the preamble to the Mass of the Faithful (Ps. 95:1).

44. Ibid., p. 82. At the beginning of the Mass of the Catechumens.

45. Cf. CAF, VII, 48, i, p. 456; cf. Ps. 113:1.

46. See *infra*, Part II, pp. 347, 528

47. Cf. K. Kohler, 'Ursprünge und Grundformen der synagogalen Liturgie', *MGWJ* (1893), pp. 491 ff, and the same author's 'The Origin and the Composition of the Eighteen Benedictions', *HUCA*, I, pp. 396 ff.

48. Cf. L. Ginzberg, 'Notes sur la Kedouscha et les bénédictions du Chema', *REJ* (1934), p. 77; see also *Geonica*, I, p. 124.

49. Cf. ELB, pp. 520 ff.

50. Cf. L. Finkelstein, 'Les Bénédictions du Chema', *REJ*, XCIII (1932), p. 3.

51. A. Marmorstein, 'L'Age de la Kedouscha de l'Amida', *REJ*, XCVII, pp. 35 ff.

52. More recently, A. Baumstark has expressed a theory not unlike those of Kohler and Ginzberg, concerning the influence of the *Yotzer* prayer upon the early Christian liturgies. Cf. his study 'Das eucharistische Hochgebet und die Literatur des nachexilischen Judentums', in *Theologie und Glaube*, II.

53. Clement of Rome, *I Cor. 34:6*, in *The Apostolic Fathers*, ed. Lightfoot, p. 23.

54. Cf. E. von der Goltz, *Das Gebet in der ältesten Christenheit*, p. 337.

55. Cf. Athanasius, *De Trinitate et Spiritu*, 16 (*PG*, XXVI, 1208).

56. Cf. Cyril of Jerusalem, *Catech.*, V, 6 (*PG*, XXXIII, 1113).

57. Dan. 8:13. The Hebrew *Phelmuni* is retained in CAF.

58. Isa. 6:3.

59. Ezek. 3:12.

60. Ps. 68:18. In *CAF*, VII, 35, 3–4, p. 430.

61. J. Mann, 'Changes in the Divine Service of the Synagogue due to Religious Persecutions', *HUCA*, IV, pp. 264 ff.

62. Jer. 23:24; Exod. R. XXX, 6, 44a.

63. This seems to have been a Hellenistic idea; cf. Philo, *De Allegoria* 1, 3: 'For never ceases the creating Lord, but as natural as it is to the fire to glow, or to the snow to cool, thus it is for God to create. . . .' Another midrashic version sets Ps. 133:4, 'throughout the heavens is His glory', in opposition to 'the whole earth is full of His glory' (Isa. 6:3) and comes, likewise, to the conclusion that heaven and earth are full of His power. Cf. Midr. *Hechalot*, in Jellinek's *Beth Hamidrash*, I, pp. 40–47 (3rd section, end). Cf. A. Baumstark, 'Trishagion und Queduscha', *Jahrb. für Liturgiewissenschaft*, III (1923), pp. 18–32. Also J. A. Jungmann, S.J., *Missarum Sollemnia* (2nd ed., 1949), II, pp. 161 ff.

64. C. W. Dugmore, *The Influence of the Synagogue upon the Divine Office* (London, 1944), pp. 76 ff and 108 f.

65. Clement of Rome, *Ep. I*, 34, in *The Apostolic Fathers*, ed. Lightfoot, pp. 23 and 71. As to the authoritative Christian interpretation, see *Handbuch zum NT*, ed. H. Lietzmann, Ergaenzungsband, *Die Apostolischen Väter* (Tübingen, 1923). The commentator of Clement, Dr Knopf, offers proof (pp. 102 ff), in various ways convincing, that the pertinent passage in Clement is an integral part of a liturgy. 'Clement presupposes in this, as in all other liturgies, the *Trisagion* pronounced by the congregation or at least repeated by it. The *Trisagion* is certainly one of the very oldest parts of our liturgy.'

66. Clement of Alexandria, *Stromata*, VII, 12 (*PG*, IX, 512). Cf. also Paul Drews, *Untersuchungen über die Clementinische Liturgie*, II, p. 21. Dugmore erroneously identifies the third benediction of the '*Amida* with the *Kedusha* itself and takes the fact that the Palestinian version of the '*Amida* does not contain the full *Kedusha* as proof that the *Kedusha* did not yet exist at that time. Moreover, he disregards entirely the juxtaposition of Isa. 6:3 and Ezek. 3:12, as evidenced both by the *Apostolic Constitutions* and by the different recensions of the *Kedusha*. Yet this juxtaposition of the two prophetic passages is a definite proof of a direct inter-relationship between the Jewish and the Christian liturgies and can never be dismissed as mere coincidence.

67. Cf. T. Schermann, 'Der liturgische Papyrus *Der Balyzeh*' in *T & U*, XXXVI, 1b. Also C. Wessely, 'Les plus anciens monuments du Christianisme écrits sur papyrus', II, *Patrologia Orientalis*, XVIII, pp. 425–9, and Roberts and Capelle, *An Early Eucholoium* (Louvain, 1949).

68. See *supra*, n. 47. In the James Liturgy, one of the oldest of extant liturgical texts, the *Trisagion* occurs twice, once immediately after the praise of God as creator and light-giver (as in the *Yotzer*), and the second time in the Anaphora after the response 'It is meet and right'. It is followed by 'Holy art Thou, King of the Universe'. Cf. Hammond, op. cit., p. 40. All these facts suggest that the *Kedusha* of *Yotzer* is the oldest.

69. ELB, pp. 62–64.

70. Cf. T. Schermann, *Die Allgemeine Kirchenordnung, Frühchristliche Liturgien und Kirchliche Überlieferung*, I, p. 85 (Kirchenordnung II, 50a–50b). Translation: 'We thank Thee, O God, through Thy Son Jesus Christ, our Lord, that Thou hast enlightened us,

making manifest Thine immortal light. Having completed the fullness of the day and drawn near the beginning of the night, we are filled with the light of day which Thou hast created for our joy; nor are we wanting, through Thy grace, the light of eventide. We sanctify and glorify Thee through Thine only-begotten Son, our Lord Jesus Christ, through whom there shall be, for Thee and for Him, together with the Holy Spirit, glory and power and honour now and for evermore. And all shall say: Amen.'

71. The Hallelujah as the end of a doxology demands a special and thorough investigation which cannot be given here. J. A. Jungmann, op. cit., I, p. 525 relegates the *Hallel* to a footnote.

72. Cf. P. Jensen, 'Texte zur assyrisch-babylonischen Religion', in *Keilschriftliche Bibliothek*, ed. E. Schrader, VI, 2, pp. 112–42 *passim*. For this reference I am indebted to Prof. J. Lewy.

73. Hammond, op. cit.: (A), p. 12; (B), p. 16; (C), p. 50; (D), p. 51.

74. This has been realized, at least for the *Kedusha*, by K. Kohler in 'The Origin and the Development of the Eighteen Benedictions', *HUCA*, I, p. 396.

75. Cf. V. Aptowitzer, 'Praised be the Name . . . etc'. 'Geschichte einer liturgischen Formel', *MGWJ*, LXXIII (1929), p. 105.

76. Cf. J. Mann, 'Les Chapitres de Ben Baboi', *REJ*, LXX (1920), pp. 113 ff; L. Ginzberg, *Geonica*, II, pp. 52 ff; J. Mann, 'Changes in the Divine Service', *HUCA*, IV, pp. 252 ff; I. Elbogen, *Studien zur Geschichte des Judischen Gottesdienstes*, p. 23; ELB, pp. 520 ff; L. Ginzberg, *Ginse Schechter*, II, pp. 550 ff (Hebrew).

77. Cf. L. Ginzberg, *Geonica*, II, 52 ff. Cf. J. Mann, 'Les Chapitres de Ben Baboi', *REJ*, LXX, p. 115: 'This Gaon [Yehudai] was outstanding among the leaders of the Babylonian academies. His authority commanded such a respect that later generations accepted his decisions as binding, in spite of all the arguments which might have been held against them'. More about Yehudai Gaon's merits on behalf of tradition in Mann's article just quoted, pp. 131, 135, 142; also in the same author's article on 'Changes in the Divine Service', *HUCA*, IV, pp. 252 ff.

78. Cf. E. Birnbaum, 'Über die Verdienste der Gaonen um die jüdische Liturgie und den Synagogengesang', *Israelitische Wochenschift*, 1903, No. 4.

79. Cf. *Sefer ha-eshkol*, I, Chapter 25, ed. Auerbach (Halberstadt, 1867), p. 55 (Hebrew).

80. L. Zunz, *Die Synagogale Poesie*, 2nd ed., pp. 113 ff, quoting as source Ben Asher's work on the scriptural accents and Petachyah's travelogue, and Ephodi's grammar (end of preface, 8).

81. In *Or Zarua*, I, 116 (Hebrew). Even more interesting is the recently discovered text which shows that it was Yehudai Gaon who introduced the *Kol Nidre* sung by the *hazan* in Sura. See L. Ginzberg, *Ginse Schechter*, II, p. 120. All of these sources make it evident that Yehudai was instrumental both in the foundation and in the preservation of Jewish musical tradition.

82. *Sifre Deut*. 306; *Ber*. 3a, 21b; *Sot*. 49a. The literature is given in ELB, pp. 92 ff and 527 ff.

83. Cf. M. Sobernheim, 'Palmyrenische Inschriften', *Mitteilungen der Vorderasiatischen Gesellschaft*, 1905, p. 9; also Franz Rosenthal, 'Die Sprache der Palmyrenischen Inschriften', *Mitteilungen der Vorderasiatisch-Ägyptischen Gesellschaft*, XLI, p. 85, n. 2.

84. Cf. *Ber*. 21b.

85. Cf. *Ber*. 57a.

86. Cf. Maharil, *Rosh Ha-shana*, ed. Warsaw, f 38b (Hebrew).

87. Cf. G. Chase, 'The Lord's Prayer in the Early Church', in *Texts and Studies* (1891), I, 3. This is the most complete investigation of the matter and contains also the older literature on the *Kaddish*. More recent is A. Baumstark's interesting but strongly biased study, 'Wege zum Judentum des Neutestamentlichen Zeitalters', *Bonner Zeitschrift für Theologie und Seelsorge*, IV (1927). Allusions to the text and spirit of the *Kaddish* are not infrequent, especially in the Apocrypha; cf. e.g. Tob. 8:9; II Macc. 7:39; Psalm of Solomon 2:37 and 10:7–8. The Catholic Mass for the dead makes use of a passage from Macc. See also K. Kohler, 'Ursprünge und Grundformen der synagogalen Liturgie', *MGWJ* (1893), pp. 490 ff. Literature in ELB, pp. 527 ff.

88. Cf. *Acta Pilati*, ed. Tischendorf (1876), A, cap. XVI, end, p. 285 (Greek), 'Praised be

the Lord, who hath taught rest and peace to His people Israel in all His words'; (Hebrew), 'Praised be God who maketh peace to His people in all His words'. And further: (Greek), 'And then the Lord shall be established upon all the earth; on that day the Lord shall be One, and His Name shall be One' (Zech. 14:9).

89. Cyril of Jerusalem, *Catechesis Mystagogica*, V (*PG*, XXXIII, 1118 ff.)

90. Cf. *Ber.* 31a, also 33a; and *Debarim* R. II.

91. Bibliography in Dr G. Klein, *Der Älteste Christliche Katechismus und die Jüdische Propaganda-Literatur* (Berlin, 1909), pp. 257 ff.

92. I. Tim. 2:1; Phil. 4:6; I Thess. 5:17 f, etc. Cf. Friedrichsen, *Theol. lit. Zeitung* (1918), 3109.

93. Cf. A. Baumstark, 'Wege zum Judentum des Neutestamentlichen Zeitalters', in *Bonner Zeitschrift für Theologie und Seelsorge*, IV (1927), p. 32.

94. The same passage in the Byzantine liturgy; cf. *Horologion Mega*, ed. Romana, p. 58.

95. See *supra*, pp. 277-8.

96. Cf. A. Baumstark, *Liturgie comparée*, p. 73.

97. Cf. *Sanh.* 90b; *Sifre* to Num. 112; also *JE*, article 'Sadducees', col. 632.

98. Cf. M. Heidenheim, 'Die Liturgie der Samaritaner', in *Bibliotheca Samaritana*, II, pp. 18, 22, 56, 136 ff *et passim*.

99. Cf. J. Freudenthal, *Hellenistische Studien*, I, 2 (1875), p. 95.

100. On the connexion between Sadducees, Samaritans, and Karaites, see K. Kohler, 'Dositheus, the Samaritan Heresiarch', *American Journal of Theology*, XV (1911), No. 3.

101. Cf. J. Mann, 'Anan's Liturgy', *Journal of Jewish Lore and Philosophy*, I, p. 343.

102. Ibid., p. 345.

103. Cf. Harkavy, *Studien und Mitteilungen*, II, pp. 19, 20, 38.

104. Cf. J. Mann, 'Anan's Liturgy', *Journal of Jewish Lore and Philosophy*, I, p. 345.

105. Origen, *De oratione*, c. 33 (*PG*, XI, 557).

106. Cf. G. Chase, op. cit., pp. 168-76.

107. Cf. Matt. 6:5-8.

108. Most of the doxologies express, explicitly or implicitly, the theocratic ideal; and in spite of his somewhat biased generalizations, Dr Baumstark is not entirely wrong when he makes the bold statement: 'The idea of God as supreme ruler (Königtum Gottes) is alien to the Christian concept of prayer'. ('Vom geschichtlichen Werden der Liturgie', *Jahrbücher für Liturgiewissenschaft*, V, 21.) Yet this statement is valid only for the immediate disciples of Jesus; already in the apostolic literature we frequently find God addressed as *despota* (lord); *Pantokrator* (ruler of all); *basileus* (king); and the like. This was the natural consequence of Christianity's organization as a Church whose ideal High Priest was Jesus. Later on, after the reconciliation between the Church and the Roman Empire, the Church regressed to the establishment of a replica of the old Temple hierarchy, quite contrary to the ideology of its founders and fathers. In the period between the third and the sixth century, the old hierarchic theocracy was re-established, a fact to which the mere title of Augustine's work *De Civitate Dei* bears eloquent testimony.

109. Cf. *Martyrium Polycarpi*, XIV, in *The Apostolic Fathers*, ed. Lightfoot, p. 195.

110. Cf. Dr F. Gavin's excellent study *The Jewish Antecedents of the Christian Sacraments* (London, 1928), p. 105, where he states: 'With the gradual disappearance of the "charismatic" and the supremacy of the resident ministry in the second century, a unique position was granted the bishops, and the so-called monarchical episcopate became the normal constituent characteristic of the Church hierarchy'.

111. Many Christian scholars believe erroneously that the custom of the closing doxology originated in the ancient Synagogue, and even assume that every *beraka* is a doxology. The learned Fortescue (in *Catholic Encyclopedia*, V, article 'Doxology') goes so far as to derive the doxology from the apocryphal Prayer of Manasseh: 'Tibi est gloria in saecula saeculorum, Amen'. Yet this prayer was never used either in the Synagogue or in the Temple, as far as we know. After the conclusion of this book, Dr L. Wallach kindly directed my attention to an article of the late Dr A. Spanier, in which this scholar discussed a similar problem. ('Stilkritisches zum Jüdischen Gebet', *MGWJ* (1936), pp. 339 ff.) Unfortunately, Spanier reaches no conclusive result at all, since he fails to distinguish between eulogy and doxology. Hence, he had to suggest certain different types of eulogies (transitional, final,

etc.), and he was not aware that the respective attitudes of Synagogue and Church toward the doxology are consistently antagonistic to each other. This was a consequence of the opposite philosophies of Christianity and Judaism with regard to the principle of hierarchy. Dr Spanier did notice, however, the continuity of certain formulas in the liturgies of the Sadducees, Samaritans, and Karaites.

112. Cassian, *De Inst. Coen.*, II, 8 (*PL*, XLIX, 94).

113. Cf. Walafrid Strabo, *De Rebus Ecclesiasticis*, Chapter 25. It is well known that the Arian philosophy was, in many respects, close to the tenets of Judaism. Accordingly Athanasius called the Arians 'New Jews'.

114. Marty. Carpi, Papyli Agathonices; cf. *T & U*, III (1888), pp. 440 ff. The ecclesiastical form of the *benedictio* is an essentially different thing and pursues purposes quite different from those of the *beraka*. The clerical blessings are the accompanying formulas of a ritual act, viz. of a *sacramentale* which covers three fields: (1) the rite itself, e.g. consecration of water, of a church, of an organ, and the like; (2) apotropaic acts, e.g. defence against evil spirits, but not exorcism; (3) the well-being of the faithful, 'from the consecration of private homes to the blessing of radishes, also all exorcisms, from the healing of the insane to exorcising rats'. Cf. Adolf Franz, *Die kirchlichen Benediktionen des Mittelalters*, I, pp. 14 ff.

115. Cf. E. Hammond, op. cit., pp. 28, 31, 26 *et passim*.

116. J. B. F. Pitra, *L'Hymnographie de l'Église grecque*, p. 35.

117. Cf. *PR* 117, ibid., 118b, and *Ber.* 59b. According to the medieval Jewish legend, St Peter was the author of the *Nishmat* prayer; cf. Jellinek, *Beth Hamidrash* V, VI (Introduction).

118. Cf. Gunkel, *Einleitung in die Psalmen*, pp. 37 ff, and Guedemann, *Geschichte der jüd. Kultur in Italien*, pp. 44 ff.

119. Cf. Gesenius, *Dictionary*, 'Hallel'; the literature on the problem in A. Jeremias, *Das AT im Lichte des alten Orients*, pp. 427, 556, 439, 429, 601 *et passim*. Wellhausen opposes the theory in his *Reste arabischen Heidentums*, p. 110. Considering the Greek onomatopoeic calls *elelizo, alalazo*, the Bedouins' trill *lilili* (E. Littmann), the old *ululare*, the *Hailly* cry of ancient Mexico (cf. Heiler, *Das Gebet*, p. 47), additional reasons do not seem necessary, when the onomatopoeic element which, according to Aristotle, is a potent creator of words, is so obvious.

120. Cf. H. Grätz, *Kritischer Kommentar zu den Psalmen*, pp. 91 ff.

121. Cf. *B. Yoma* 53b.

122. The same remark under the name of R. Yehuda b. Simon b. Pazi, in *Ber.* 9b; similar references in *Pirqe de R. Eliezer*, ed. Friedlaender, Chapter XVIII, to Ps. 92:8 and Ps. 104:35; also Lev. R. Par. IV, perhaps a corruption of the analogous passage in *Berakot*.

123. Cf. *Zohar*, ed. Vilna, I, fol. 231a (to Gen. 49:24; also to Job 38:7, and Ps. 148). See also W.-S., *HUCA*, XVI, p. 290, nn. 128 and 132.

124. Cf. Conybeare, 'Apocalypse of Moses', *JQR* (1894), p. 235.

125. Cf. E. Werner, 'The Attitude of the Early Church Fathers to Hebrew Psalmody', *Review of Religion* (May, 1943), p. 343, n. 18.

126. It seems that many magic practices were involved in the metamorphosis of the Hallelujah. Since Amen, Selah, and Hallelujah were all used as magical incantations throughout the Near East in a completely syncretistic fashion, and the AEOUIA was familiar to many as an efficient formula, it seems probable that the Hallelujah lost its consonants and thrived by its vowels as a result of magic ideologies. Cf. L. Blau, *Das Altjüdische Zauberwesen*, pp. 94, 102, 130; see also C. Wessely, *Neue Griechische Zauberpapyri*, p. 29, line 279; and A. Dieterich, *Abraxas*, p. 70.

127. Cf. Augustine, *Enarratio in Ps. 99* (*PL*, XXXVII, 1272, also *PL*, XXXVI, 283). The ecstatic rendering of the *Hallel* was familiar to the rabbis, as we see in *Jer. Pes.* 7:11, 35b: 'Passover in the house and the *Hallel* shatters the roof!' This passage was probably the model of Jerome's statement: 'Sonabant psalmi et aurata tecta templorum reboans in sublime quatiebat Alleluia' (*Epist. 77*, in *PL*, XXII, 697).

128. In a *responsum* to the Jewish Community of Huesca; cf. G.A. 215.

129. Cf. J. A. Montgomery, *Aramaic Incantations* (Philadelphia, 1913), pp. 147 ff, 201, 205, 223 ff, etc. See *supra*, n. 126.

130. Bede (*PL*, XCV, 49–50).

131. Cf. Jerome (*PL*, XXII, 896). Elsewhere he writes: 'Quocumque te verteris, arator stivam tenens Alleluia decantat' (*PL*, XXII, 491).

132. Sometimes secular folk-songs contain small doxologies, as e.g. 'Glory! glory, hallelujah!' in the Battle Hymn of the Republic.

133. Sidonius Apollinaris (*PL*, LVIII, 488). Not without a smile do we read the observation of Gregory I: 'Behold the Brittanic tongue which heretofore had known nothing but to make a barbaric noise! Already it has begun to sound the Alleluia in divine Hebrew praises' (*PL*, LXXVI, 411).

134. Cf. Augustine, *Enarr. in Ps. 105 (106)* (*PL*, XXXVI). Graetz opposes this concept: (Cf. H. Graetz, *Kritischer Kommentar zu den Psalmen*, pp. 91 ff.)

135. Cf. Ewald-Dukes, *Beiträge zur Geschichte d. ältesten Auslegung des Alten Testaments* (Stuttgart, 1844), Pt. III, p. 197. Also Ibn Bal'aam, *Liber de Accentibus*, ed. Mercer (Paris, 1565–6), sign. D IV, recto (in Hebrew).

CHAPTER TEN

The Aesthetic and Ethical Evaluation of Music in Synagogue and Church

THE AESTHETICS OF RELIGION

'SPIRITUALLY we are all Semites.' This famous dictum of Pope Pius XI was, at the time of its proclamation, a bold statement from the political point of view. Nowhere is it applicable with more justification than with regard to the aesthetic and ethical attitude towards sacred music, as held by the authorities of Judaism and Christianity. It is well known that the terms 'aesthetic' and 'ethical', when referred to matters religious, have a curious quality of evasiveness. Moreover, our modern conceptions of the beautiful and the moral are by no means identical with the early Greek, Gnostic, Jewish, and Christian ideas bearing the same names, notwithstanding the fact that Socrates, Plato, Moses, Amos, and Jesus were the godfathers of these very concepts.

To biblical literature the idea that music is beautiful is evidently alien; music had its place in the ritual of the Temple, or it served as a spontaneous expression of an individual or a group, but it did not have any direct connexion with the 'aesthetically beautiful'. That conception is linked to visual sensations only, as the Song of Songs and similar poems seem to indicate. Even so late a book as Ecclesiasticus, which describes in the most glowing terms the cult of the Temple, used the word beautiful only where a visual sensation was involved.[1]

Otherwise, the epithet 'beautiful', when employed in Scripture, is always on the borderline between the aesthetic and the ethical. A few examples will demonstrate the point: 'For it is a *pleasant* thing [the Hebrew word *na'im* indicates the pleasant, the agreeable, and the morally good simultaneously], if thou keep them [the words of the wise] within thee' (Prov. 22:18) or: 'Behold how good and how pleasant (*na'im*) it is, when brethren dwell together in unity' (Ps. 133:1). Here the Hebrew terms are *tob* (morally good) and *na'im* (pleasant, agreeable). A similar combination is found in the following verse: 'The Lord is good (*tob*);

sing praises to His name; for it is lovely (*na'im*)' (Ps. 135:3). The juxta-position of the 'good Lord' and the fitting praises that are 'lovely' is perfect.

In the entire lengthy description of the first Temple (I Kings, Ch. 5–8), the word 'beautiful' does not occur; it does occur, however, in Prov. 31:30, where it has a derogatory sense: 'Favour is deceitful, and beauty (*yofi*, sensual prettiness) is vain'.

The acoustical beauty of a voice or of an instrument is usually des-cribed as 'sweet', 'agreeable', 'strong'. Hence, the purely aesthetic ele-ment in matters musical is not fully represented in Old Testament and early rabbinic literature; they either stress the social point ('agreeable'), or the sensual ('sweet'), or the majestic one. This type of description is found in Sirach and Josephus, perhaps under the influence of Hellenism.

Quite unlike the classic Greek aestheticism with its sharp distinction—beautiful or ugly—Judaism poses another antithesis: holy—profane. Two characteristic passages may clarify this. In the beautiful Ps. 23, the Psalmist concludes:

> Thou anointest my head with oil;
> My cup runneth over.
> Surely, goodness and mercy
> Shall follow me all the days of my life;
> And I will dwell
> In the house of the Lord for ever.

To the Jewish singer, the last promise of the psalm means happiness, bliss, and beauty altogether. Similarly, with sharper emphasis: 'And they [my priests] shall teach my people the difference between the Holy and the Common and cause them to discern between the unclean and the clean' (Ezek. 44:23).

From this passage the standard prayer has been derived which is re-cited at the end of every Sabbath: 'Praised be Thou, O Lord our God, King of the Universe, who makest a distinction between the Holy and the Profane, as between light and darkness . . .'

In one respect, however, Jewish and Greek conceptions of the aesthe-tically valuable are very much akin; as in platonic philosophy the truly Good is also the truly Beautiful, so in Judaism, the genuinely Holy is also the Beautiful and the Good. Thus a resemblance to the concept of Plato's *kalokagathia* (the beautiful *and* good) is in evidence in Jewish thinking. This is fully borne out, when we compare Plato's remarks about Socrates' ugliness with the Talmudic anecdote of R. Joshua ben Hananya and the king's daughter:

> R. Joshua ben Hananya was an ugly hunchback. Once a king's daughter ridiculed him on account of his ugliness and marvelled, rather dubiously, that a treasury of wisdom should be sheltered in so unattractive an abode. Whereupon R. Joshua asked her in what kind of vessels they preserve their best wines: in silver, gold, or clay. She informed him that the best wines are kept in containers of simple clay. Then he asked her why she was so astounded that beauty of learning and wisdom was sheltered in his—physically unattractive—person.

The core of the comparison of Socrates and R. Joshua may be expressed in the following statement: mere external pleasantness is, on the highest level of Greek and Jewish philosophy, spurned in preference to a 'beautiful soul'. In Scripture the identity of beauty and holiness is best expressed in Ps. 29:2; 96:9 ('beauty of holiness').

From the foregoing pages it will be understood that a purely aesthetical evaluation was unheard of in primitive Christianity, before Hellenistic ideas infiltrated it. Even then, the authorities watched the merely beautiful in the Church with an ever wary eye.

Quite in conformity with the ideologies of the entire Near East, music is not so much a thing of beauty as an ethical force. The various formulations of the so-called 'Ethos-doctrine of music' in the different civilizations of the Near East merit a special study. Here only an outline of the basic idea and its application in Judaism and Christianity can be presented.

In the Near East a special mood is attributed to each melody-type; conversely, each of these modes is capable of evoking in the listeners its specific ethos. R. Lachmann, one of the greatest authorities of Oriental music, describes the theory of ethos in these words:

> The mood or character [of these melody-types] is, what the Greeks term *ethos*; it encompasses both the expression and the effect of the modes. The melody-types are courageous or in love, sad or merry, thoughtful-meditative or ecstatic, and they are capable of transmitting all of these emotional conditions to the listeners.[2]

The musical ethos frequently depends, for its 'effectiveness', upon the right hour or the right season, or the right place.

> Only at its indigenous time can a melody-type unfold its full emotional power. . . . In the Near East it is customary to run the whole gamut of the classic *maqams* during one feast day; there the order of succession of the musical

pieces is set according to their respective connexions with the various times of the day.[3]

Very early, cosmological systems were linked with the model types and their ethical qualities. In classic Arabic literature, a mode is usually representative of a character, a planet, a season, colour, taste-quality (bitter, salty, sweet, sour), temperature, etc.[4] Let us bear in mind that the conception of the ethos of melody-types is very ancient and was extremely popular in antiquity and during the early Middle Ages.[5] Yet it would be naive to construct a specific ethos purely from its musical or cosmological connotations. Dr Sachs rightly remarks that 'no single feature makes up an ethos, neither modal structure nor astrological connotation'.[6]

In view of the fundamentally religious function of music, we cannot be surprised that the ethos-doctrine found its staunchest champions, as well as its most consistent implementation, in the realm of liturgical music, be it pagan, Christian, or Jewish. Long before Aristotle, the Pythagorean philosophers stressed and utilized the conception of musical ethos in their cults, and the great Stagirite does no more than describe a well known fact, when he says: 'Some persons fall into a religious frenzy whom we see restored by the use of sacred melodies, as if they had found healing and purgation'.[7] There ensues a lengthy discussion of the merits and demerits of the respective modes of Greek music which, theoretically, it is easy to understand. But only a charlatan will claim that he can identify the ethos of every piece of ancient Greek music by merely listening to it. At any rate, the strong ethical connotation that music has had in all ancient civilizations must be kept in mind as we proceed to examine the attitudes of Synagogue and Church to their respective chants.

THE ETHOS OF VOCAL VERSUS INSTRUMENTAL MUSIC

In Judaism, as well as in early Christianity, the primacy of vocal over instrumental performance seems so firmly established, so much of an *a priori* attitude, that it may sound preposterous to debate this matter anew. But it needs renewed examination, since, being presented as a 'foregone conclusion', it has consistently confused every freer view and every unorthodox opinion, until it has become something of a dogma, blindly accepted by all students of ancient Church music.[8]

In the first chapter of the second part of this book there is offered a theory suggesting why, at certain times, both Judaism and Christianity have frowned upon any instrumental performance of music; but this negative attitude was by no means permanent nor at any one time generally recognized or accepted. There is no doubt, however, that the leaders, not the common adherents, of early Christianity condemned instrumental music, while praising the singing of psalms.

This seems inconsistent with the practice of the psalmists and priests, glorified in the Old Testament. Yet the reasons for this reversal are subtle and complex. The following quotation from Pseudo-Cyprian represents only one aspect of the opposition to instrumental music; actually, a variety of reasons (shall we say rationalizations?) was mustered to banish any non-vocal performance by Christians.

> The fact that David danced before God, is no excuse for those Christians who sit in the Theatre . . . for then harps, cymbals, flutes, tympana, and others sounded for the glory of God, not of idols. Through the scheme of the devil, holy instruments have become illicit. . . .[9]

The frequent participation of instrumental music in the mystery cults of Asia Minor and Greece constituted another reason for resentment on the Christian side; this will be discussed in the following chapter. Even the danger of becoming 'Judaized' must have seemed imminent in the minds of several Church Fathers, such as John Chrysostom,[10] or Theodoret of Cyrrhus.[11] Still, in the Middle Ages, this argument had a staunch champion in Thomas Aquinas, who opposed the organ, because it 'might Judaize the Church'.[12] Another cause against instrumental music was seen in the Christian doctrine of 'Spiritual sacrifice' (*logike thysia*) that disapproved of every element of sacrificial cult. Since, in Judaism at least, instrumental music was linked with the sacrifices of the Temple, the Christian reasoning quite consistently condemned all liturgical forms accessorial to sacrifice, and especially rejected instrumental performances.[13]

Notwithstanding all these arguments and quotations, it would be a bold inference if we were to assume that there was no instrumental music in the liturgy of the Early Church. Quite to the contrary! Why all these outbursts, why all this frenzied searching for all kinds of reasons to justify the prohibition of instrumental music, if there was actually no violation of these injunctions? This thought alone should make the student cautious. Moreover, there are numerous utterances in favour of instrumental music that cannot easily be discounted as heretical or irrelevant. The passages in Rev. 5:8–13; 14:3; etc., envision a heavenly celebration that gives the impression of the author having imagined and described a very earthly pattern.[14] Here the music of kitharas is taken for granted. Another document referring to the kithara is the epistle of St Ignatius to the Ephesians 4:1.[15] Similar remarks are not rare in the works of Clement of Alexandria,[16] and Cyril of Alexandria in his Lexicon states: '*Psalmos* means a musical utterance for which the instrument is played rhythmically according to harmonic notes'.[17] In a bitter attack against certain vigil-celebrations St Augustine complained against the frequent use of kitharas at such occasions.[18] These Christian festivities in honour of martyrs seem to have been quite gay affairs, and were by no means sanctimonious; otherwise Jerome would not have advised virgins: 'Budge ye not a span of a finger from your mother's elbow at these vigils'.[19]

Let us now summarize the early Christian attitude towards instrumental music. The authorities were more or less afraid of it since it carried too many reminiscences of pagan cults or of the ritual of the Jewish Temple. When Neo-Platonic trends made inroads into the ideologies of the Church their ascetic conceptions were, to a great degree, absorbed by the ecclesiastical authorities; hence, the only music they aspired to was the inaudible *musica mundana*, the harmony of the celestial spheres.[20]

The Synagogue had banished all instrumental music without exception as a symbol of mourning over the destruction of the Temple; this fact shows that the alleged Christian fear 'lest the Church become Judaized' was not the real reason after all. Nor, for that matter, does the Jewish sentimental motivation of the prohibition of instrumental music fully explain the radical measures the rabbis deemed necessary. The actual reasons that lie at the bottom of both the Jewish and Christian antagonism against instrumental music were of a defensive and apologetic nature. They will be discussed in the next chapter.

PSALMODY VERSUS HYMNODY IN CHURCH AND SYNAGOGUE

The Greeks considered tragedy the highest of all poetical forms; in occidental civilization there have been periods when the opera, the symphony, the oratorio, or the musical Mass, respectively, were considered the acme of musical expression. Hence it is not surprising to find considerable debate about the respective merits of the poetic or musical forms of the liturgy, such as psalms, canticles, or hymns. Especially from the fourth century on, when the various forms were well established and clearly distinct from each other, the discussion of the value of sacred poetry and its respective music became a carefully camouflaged platform for the airing of certain dogmatic and theological opinions.

Thus, Didymus attempted to draw a firm line between psalms and hymns, declaring: 'The man of practical life prefers psalmody; the man of theoretical life prefers hymns'.[21] Augustine, however, termed this distinction a 'vainly established one'.[22] In the background of this dispute lies probably the remembrance of Didymus' thundering attacks against the Manichaeans, of which sect Augustine had been a member before becoming a Christian. Chrysostom states that the 'high powers' (angels) prefer the hymn to the psalm.[23] Why does he stress this point? He insists that the common man should sing psalms every day, on his travels, in his shop, in his home, 'and no artificial accompaniment nor musical study is necessary'.[24] Hymns were higher in his esteem, as one may learn from his comments on the miraculous escape of the Apostles Paul and Silas (Acts 16:25 ff), that he attributes to their hymn-singing:

Behold the famous and efficient powers of hymns! . . . Not only did the Apostles not suffer any detriment, but more splendid they escaped, than they had been heretofore. . . . Everybody of their fellow captives was deeply impressed and reformed. . . . Do you now recognize the power of hymns, sung to God?[25]

Thus, saints and angels sing hymns or canticles, such as the Thrice-Holy; the common man is well off with chanting psalms every day. It seems to me that the ascetic trend of the Church stressed the virtue of the Psalter, for it contained a number of penitential songs. This idea is prevalent in St Ambrose's dictum: 'God is pleased not only by being praised, but by being reconciled'.[26] The penitential character of the Psalter is also emphasized by St Niceta, who remarks: 'The Psalter does not despise the sinners, but brings them healing through tearful penitence'.[27]

Apparently hymns and canticles were not considered conducive to penitence and humility, as were the psalms; and this observation might explain the theological discrimination between the types of sacred chant, as well as account for the opposing factions of the Church in the fourth and fifth centuries. Usually heretics composed new hymns, spurning the traditional Psalter. Hence heresy was often eager to replace the psalms by new hymns. The Marcionites and some of the Syrian poets were especially notorious for their heretic hymns. Thus the chronicle observes 'the heretics have replaced St Peter by Marcion as prince of the Apostles; and instead of psalms they wrote their own hymns' (*Madrashe*).[28] Under the spell of monasticism, the reverence for ascetic life had grown very strongly, especially in Egypt and in Byzantium. The penitential Psalter suits a monk better than glorious and splendid hymns; and we recall here the anecdote of the abbot Sylvanus of the Sinai monastery, who sternly disapproved of *troparia*, *hymns*, and the *Octoechos*.

Similar discussions occur in rabbinic literature, with the modification that genuine hymns (*piyyutim*) were not considered at all, for simple chronological reasons, since the *piyyut* did not originate before the sixth century. The only alternative left is between the psalms and the canticles, other prayers not being of scriptural origin. The educational and cathartic quality of the psalms is acknowledged in Judaism no less enthusiastically than in the Church. As for the canticles, they were considered the songs by which the angelic hosts incessantly praise the Lord.[29] This idea, in Christian literature first suggested in the 'Hosanna in the Highest' of Matt. 21:9 and Mark 11:9, is an old rabbinic principle, formulated 'as it happens above, so may it happen beneath' (upon earth). The classic expression of this thought occurs in the *Kaddish*, the great doxology of the Synagogue, where we read: 'He that maketh peace in His heights, may He also make peace for us . . .'[30]

The position of psalmody within Judaism after the destruction of the Temple was apparently well stabilized. It was engraved in the eternal prayer book of the Jewish people as with a stylus of bronze. The following points will elucidate the Synagogue's attitude toward psalmody:

(1) The daily psalm-singing in the morning service, a remnant of the Temple, was always considered obligatory and taken as a matter of course.[31]

(2) Psalmody was simple and uniform in its rendering up to the end of the Talmudic era (about 680). The entire congregation was able to sing it or, at least, to respond to it. This is evident from a number of rabbinical statements.[32]

(3) Careful distinction was made between the various types of psalmodic rendering, such as response, solo psalmody, or refrain-psalm. The discussion of this subject as recorded in *B. Sota* 30b actually concerns

itself with the rendering of a canticle, Exod. 15. In other passages the *Hallel* is similarly analysed, and also various types of vocal rendering are mentioned.[33]

(4) The concept of congregational unity, identical with the New Testament and Early Christian idea of *koinonia* was well established in rabbinic literature, and the Christian postulate 'una voce dicentes' is anticipated in Talmudic lore: 'They sing the *Sh'ma'* with one mouth, one voice, in one melody'.[34]

If we compare this passage with the Christian utterances which stress in the same way the unison of the faithful, the Jewish priority cannot be doubted. It is, therefore, hard to understand why some fine Catholic scholars search in every direction but the Jewish for the origin of this simple notion. Pythagoreans, Hellenists, and all kinds of Church Fathers are quoted, where a simple reference book of rabbinics would have yielded many pertinent quotations.[35]

THE ATTITUDE OF THE CHURCH FATHERS TO JEWISH TRADITION

At a time when the Christian Church had to fight both secular oppression and the internecine strife of anti-Jewish heretics, such as Marcion and his followers, it was politic to pursue a middle course that did not make too many concessions to its Jewish factions on one hand, nor to the anti-Jewish extremists on the other. The result of this statesman-like policy was the preservation of a united Catholic Church, even though, after only four centuries, it fell prey to sectarian schisms. Still, up to the present day, and in spite of the exceedingly vast regional differences, the elements that are common to all Catholic churches outweigh the differences or dissensions.

This cautiously shifting attitude of the Church is evident in the representative statements concerning the Psalter and the liturgical use of psalmody. It is not suggested here that in those early centuries, when Christianity lacked a centralized authority, an 'inner circle' decided upon matters of dogma and religious practice. What is meant here is the historic interpretation that the Church sanctioned and gave its full blessing *post factum* only to those writers who did keep to a middle line, disputing uncompromisingly the Jewish as well as the extremist Gentile faction. Often enough these writers attacked both wings of the Church; and while their writings contained unfair, demagogic, and sometimes false statements, in the end it was these Fathers who succeeded in guarding the Church from falling into disastrous extremes: *Medium tenuere beati*. . . .

Eusebius lauds, in a famous passage borrowed from Philo, the canticles of the Jewish Therepeutae as 'suitable' for the Christian practice of his own time.[36] Two centuries before, Justin Martyr had traced the origin of Christian song back to a declaration by Jesus himself,[37] and the Popes Damasus and Celestine seem to compare the chants of the Church with the tradition of the Synagogue.[38] But the anti-Jewish opposition did not remain silent; Diodore of Tarsus had some difficulty in explaining why Hebrew terms and customs were retained by the Church. He also had to defend—rather lamely—the use of Jewish chants in the Church; this for the benefit of his anti-Jewish friends.[39] A part of this passage may be quoted:

Question: If it is a fact that the infidels seduce men by singing certain songs, and if it is true that the Jews were permitted to sing them only because of the stubbornness of their minds, why does the Church sing them?
Answer: Not the singing itself is condemnable, as suitable only for simple minded ones, but the singing with the accompaniment of heartless instruments, dance, and the rattling of the krotala [a kind of castanets].

On the other hand, Jerome advised St Paula, his contemporary, to come to Palestine, if she wanted to chant the psalms in Hebrew. This she accomplished, attaining full mastery of the Hebrew language, 'so that she was able to chant the psalms in Hebrew'.[40]

If the Church had to assume a more or less apologetic attitude whenever the Jewish origin of the Psalter was under attack, some of its greatest spokesmen did not hesitate to turn this very fact skilfully against the Jews themselves. Here only two representative remarks will be quoted which may stand for many more. They are chosen from the Latin Fathers who are, in general, less hostile toward the Jews than their Eastern colleagues. The first is from St Ambrose, the second from St Augustine.

The hymns, the canticles, and the psalms should be to us manifestations of God. Thus the Lord's Testament is called a canticle, because we sing the remission of all sinners, and the just acts of the Lord in the Gospels, in sweet exaltation of our heart. The Lord Himself did not disdain to say: 'We have sung unto you, and you have not danced' (Matt. 11:16–17). He sang for us in the Gospel forgiveness of sins: the Jews should have applied themselves to it, not in histrionic gestures of the body, but spiritually. They failed to do so, hence they are to be reprehended.[41]

From the theological point of view it should be noted that this last statement is in open contradiction to Paul, Rom. 11:1, 2. Yet let us not forget the relevant fact that Paul was of Jewish descent, while Ambrose and Augustine were not.

Ten strings are known of the psaltery, and ten commandments of the Law. To sing and to chant (*psallere*) is usually an occupation of loving men. For the old man is in fear, the new one in love. Thus do we discern two Testaments, the Old and the New. . . . Love, then, sings the new song . . . even the old man could have a psaltery of ten strings, for to the Jews in the flesh the Law of the Ten Commandments was given: but he who lives in the Law cannot sing the new song. For he stands under the Law and yet cannot fulfil it. He possesses the organ, but does not use it. . . .[42]

These are mild words compared with Chrysostom's thundering against the vile, stubborn, treacherous and despicable Jewish people; and yet even they can be understood by a fair-minded person, if he takes into account the pent-up emotions which the incessant conflict of Synagogue and Church had engendered throughout the centuries.

THE PARTICIPATION OF WOMEN IN THE LITURGICAL CHANT

Paul's rule, 'The women shall be silent in the assemblies' (I Cor. 14:34), was in strict conformity with the dicta of the rabbis and the practice of the contemporary Synagogue. Yet the Apostolic rule was not unanimously accepted in the Church. As late an authority as Ambrose championed the psalm-singing of women in the services. Since he links his remarks to Paul's injunction, mentioned afore, his remarks merit at least partial quotation. He says:

The Apostle commands the women to be silent in Church; yet they sing well the psalms. For the psalm is sweet and appropriate to every age and either sex: here the old ones abolish the sternness of their age, the sorry elderly men (*veterani*) respond it joyfully, the young men may sing it without the objection of licentiousness . . . and even tender girls chant the psalm without detriment to their female modesty, and the virgins can sing the hymn to God . . . sweetly, but in all respectability. . . . How laboriously do we endeavour to maintain silence and order in church, when the lessons are being read? If one talks, all silence him; but if a psalm is chanted, everyone implements the silence, for all recite it and nobody silences them. . . . What a great chain of unity is this working towards one great chorus of all the people![43]

An older contemporary of his, Ephraem, had taught choruses of virgins to sing his hymns, as mentioned in Chapter VII. This practice may have initiated the choir singing of nuns in the Church, for which we have abundant documentation,[44] and must not be confused with the singing of choirs that mix the sexes. This kind of singing was, after a century-long debate, altogether forbidden by the Church, as it is still forbidden in Orthodox Judaism.

The reasons were, by and large, identical with those of the rabbinic prohibition: 'The voice of woman leads to licentiousness'.[45] The heretics have unscrupulously used female choirs as a means of popular attraction. Yet, in all antiquity, female singers and musicians were in ill repute, as we know from many sources.[46]

Compromises between the extremes were sought and occasionally attempted during the first eight centuries of Christianity. A case in point is evidenced in the Syrian *Testament of the Lord* (fifth century), which would tolerate a female response, if the psalm itself was intoned by a male singer.[47] There is an analogous utterance by a Babylonian rabbi, who was inclined to be lenient to responses by women, but sharply condemned their *leading* activities in singing.[48] The fourth and fifth centuries of Christianity witnessed the same attitude of the Church in general, as Aetheria Silvia's travelogue demonstrates.[49] The general rule seems to be that in those countries where licentious ceremonies had not been very popular heretofore the authorities were considerably sterner against female singing; while in those provinces where female participation in folk-festivals and ceremonies had been an age-old custom they were more liberal.

Surveying now the parallel as well as the contrary trends of Synagogue and Church with regard to the evaluation of song and music, it is obvious that the purist element of the Orient, in the face of its customary licentiousness, has prevailed over the more lenient attitude of the Western civilizations. Notwithstanding the many limitations in the development of musical performance caused by this orthodox attitude, we are bound to consider them, historically at least, controlling aspects of the ethos doctrine of music. To have preserved this ancient legacy of the Near East is certainly a great merit of Judaism as well as of Christianity.

NOTES CHAPTER X

1. Eccles. Chapters 48–50.
2. Cf. R. Lachmann, *Musik des Orients* (Breslau, 1929), p. 62.
3. Ibid.
4. W.-S., *HUCA* (1941), pp. 276 ff; also H. G. Farmer, *Sadya Gaon and Music* (London, 1943), pp. 8, 9, 13.
5. See *infra*, Part II, Chapter II.
6. Curt Sachs, *The Rise of Music in the Ancient World*, p. 250; also E. Moritz von Hornbostel, 'Tonart und Ethos' in *Festschrift für Johannes Wolf* (Berlin, 1929) pp. 73–78.
7. Aristotle, *Politics*, VIII (V), Chapter 7.
8. Cf. e.g. Stapper-Baier, *Catholic Liturgics* (Paterson, 1935), p. 50: 'Instrumental music is permitted for the sole purpose of sustaining and accentuating the liturgical chant. It has no independent character . . . the one musical instrument which is specifically ecclesiastical is the organ.' All these statements are true today and have been so for some time, but are not representative of the whole history of the Church and may mislead a naive reader.
9. Ps.-Cyprian, *De spectaculis*, cap. 3 (*CSEL*, III, append. 5).
10. Chrysostom, *Homily on Ps.* 150 (*PG*, LV, 497).
11. Theodoret, *In Ps.* 150 (*PG*, LXXX, 1996); also *De sacrificiis*, 16, and Eusebius, *In Ps.* 91 (*PG*, XXIII, 1172).
12. Thomas Aquinas, *Summa*, II, qu. 91, 2: 'Our Church does not admit musical instruments, such as kitharas or psalteries, in the divine worship, lest it seem to Judaize.' His argument coming almost a thousand years after the prohibition of all instrumental music in Judaism seems absurd and betrays a complete ignorance of contemporary Jewish customs.
13. Cf. O. Casel, *Die Liturgie als Mysterienfeier* (1923), pp. 105 ff.
14. So also F. J. Doelger, *Sol Salutis*, p. 128.
15. Cf. W. Bousset, *Kyrios Christos* (1913), p. 287.
16. Cf. Clement of Alexandria, *Paedagogus*, II, cap. 4: 'If you sing or chant psalms with the accompaniments of kithara or lyre, you cannot be blamed. In that case you imitate David, the righteous King of the Hebrews, who pleased God.'
17. Cf. Payne, *Instrumental Music is Scriptural*, p. 46.
18. Cf. Augustine, *Enarr. II, in Ps.* 32:5 (*PL*, XXXVI, 279).
19. Jerome, *Epistola 107*, 9, 2 (*CSEL*, LV, p. 300).
20. Cf. W.-S., pp. 288 ff; also *infra*, Part II, Chapter I.
21. Didymus of Alexandria, *Expositio in Ps.* 4:1 (*PG*, XXXIX, 1166).
22. Augustine, *Enarr. in Ps.* 67:1 (*PL*, XXXVI, 813).
23. Chrysostom, *In Epist. ad Colossenses*, III, 9, 2 (*PG*, LXII, 363).
24. Chrysostom, *In Ps.* 41:2 (*PG*, LV, 158).
25. Chrysostom, *Sermo X in Ps.* 38. Now considered spurious.
26. Ambrose, *Praefatio in Ps. I, No.* 5 (*PL* XIV, 923).
27. Nicetius, *De Psalmodiae Bono*, cap. 1, in Gerbert, *De cantu, &c.* Now the treatise has been published under the name of Niceta, by Turner, *JTS* (1923), pp. 225 ff.
28. Cf. O. Braun, Maruta von Maitherkat, *De sancta Nicaena synodo* in *Kirchengeschichtliche Studien* (Münster, 1898), IV, 3, p. 47.
29. Cf. *Hullin* 91b, and throughout rabbinic literature. Cf. Longfellow's *Sandalphon*:

> The angels of wind and fire
> Chant only one hymn, and expire
> With the song's irresistible stress.

See also *supra*, p. 303.
30. Cf. my 'Hosanna in the Gospels', *JBL* (July 1946), p. 119.
31. Cf. *B. Soferim*, ed. Higger, 1937, Chapters 17–20; ed. Müller, Chapters 18–20; also *B. Sukka*, 38b, and *B. Pesahim*, 117a–118.
32. E.g. *B. Sota* 30b; *Soferim*, cap. 18, 2; or Nathan ha-Babli's report on the congregational singing quoted in Chapter V, p. 136 of this book.

33. Called *haqriya* or *hiqra* (emphatic reading, proclaiming in elevated voice), in *Soferim*, ed. Müller, III, 10.

34. Cf. Cantic. Rabba to Cant. Cant. 8, 12. Compare with this the passage of *Ascensio Isaiae*, IX, 28 (124 ed. Charles). See *supra*, Chapter VIII, n. 14; so also the Judaeo-Christian Clement of Rome (*I Cor. 34:7*): 'And we, gathered in concord, of one mind, shall call to Him as from one mouth: Holy, Holy, Holy. . . .'

35. Cf. e.g. O. Casel, *Das Gedächtnis des Herrn in der altchristlichen Liturgie* (Freiburg, 1922), p. 31; or J. Quasten, *Musik und Gesang in den Kulten der heidnischen Antike und christlichen Frühzeit*, (Münster, 1930), Chapter 4.

36. Eusebius, *Hist. Eccl.*, II, 17; Philo, *De vita contemplativa*, ed. Mangey, II, 471–86; also Wendland, 'Die Therapeuten und die philonische Schrift vom Beschaulichen Leben', in XXII supplement of *Jahrbuch für Klass. Philologie* (1896), pp. 695–772; and I. Heinemann, *Die Sektenfrömmigkeit der Therapeuten* (Breslau, 1935).

37. Justin Martyr, *Contra Tryphonem*, c. 106.

38. Cf. E. Werner, 'The Attitude of the Early Church Fathers to Hebrew Psalmody', *Review of Religion* (May, 1943).

39. *T & U*, NS, VI, 35. The text there is rightly attributed to Diodore; the entire work, *Quaestiones et Responsiones ad Orthodoxos*, in PG, VI.

40. Jerome, *Ep. 108* (PL, XXII, 902).

41. Ambrose, *In Ps. 118*.

42. Augustine, *Sermo 33*.

43. Ambrose, *In Ps. 1* (PL, XIV, 925).

44. Cf. O. Braun, op. cit. (*supra*, n. 28), p. 87; also *Peregrinatio Aetheriae*, XXIV, 1 *et passim*; and F. Chabot, *Synodicon orientale ou recueil des synodes nestoriens* (Paris, 1902), p. 486.

45. *B. Ber.*, 24a.

46. E.g. Horace, *Satires*, 1, 2; Lucian, *Dialogi meretricii*, 12, 1, 311, *et passim*.

47. Cf. J. Quasten, op. cit., p. 119.

48. *B. Sota*, 48a.

49. *Peregrinatio Aetheriae*, XXIV, 1–4.

Part II

Musical Comparisons and Studies

NOTE TO PART II

All chant is dependent upon the rhythm of its text. Therefore basically identical tunes are bound to differ in musical detail, determined as they are by the flow of their words. Consequently the author has been obliged in a number of cases to modify melodies for comparison so as to demonstrate their common elements. He wishes to stress, however, that in emphasizing the melodic archetypes common to a number of variants, he follows a principle already stated in his Introduction.

CHAPTER ONE

The Conflict between Hellenism and Judaism in the Music of the Early Christian Church

THE problem with which we shall deal in the following pages is an old one. Since musical history was first written, it has been a subject of inquiry. In the Middle Ages that history was narrowly regarded as an ecclesiastical matter and was viewed from a theological basis. Only in the Renaissance, when Ornithoparchus, Glareanus, and Tinctoris ventured a more secular treatment of musical history, do we encounter the beginnings of a systematic search for the primary sources of ancient music. During the nineteenth century the historical-philological method was applied to these sources, combined with profound musicological analysis by scholars such as Bellermann, von Jan, Gevaert, and others. Their efforts led to concrete and significant results, although they overemphasized the Greek-Hellenistic stratum in the music of the Early Church. The theological writers of the early Middle Ages were all but neglected, however, and many valuable clues in their writings were therefore overlooked. The new trend of cultural and religious history has rectified that one-sidedness and a more balanced portrait of the problem can now be drawn.

The 'territorialistic' approach of scholars like Rostovzteff, Strzygowsky, and Herzfeld has produced many fine results and has taught us a series of lessons which are now in some respects in direct opposition to the concepts and methods of former schools. Their main principles are:

(1) Hellenism cannot be separated from the culture of the Near East;

(2) But the historic development of Asia Minor during the seven or eight centuries of Hellenism must be understood as a continuation of previous millennia, not as an entirely new era.[1]

(3) The ancient traditions of the Near East have often been transformed into, and disguised as, Hellenistic 'pseudomorphoses' (Spengler).

(4) The all-important religious tendencies of the time should not be evaluated in ecclesiastical or systematic terms exclusively, as was done by Schürer; for the ancient, indigenous traditions were stubborn and capable of deceptive adjustments to new ideas and forms.

A complete musicological study ought, then, to investigate our problem on the basis of the three different levels on which the musical contest between Hellenism and Judaism took place, namely: the practice of performance; melodic tradition and structure; philosophical and theological attitudes. The key to the solution of the entire question would be a comprehensive analysis of the ethnic and local musical traditions of the peoples in the Hellenistic sphere and epoch. Unfortunately our knowledge of their music is quite insufficient, since almost all of our sources spring from the philosophical-theological realm, whose authors showed little interest in an unbiased representation of the lore of the *dii minorum gentium*.

In spite of this handicap we shall endeavour to utilize Syrian-Aramaean sources, in so far as they are accessible to us; musicologists have heretofore examined them too little. This writer is firmly convinced that the Syrian and north-west Mesopotamian countries played a far greater role in the development of Church music than is generally recognized.

It is true that the Syrians were not a very creative people, and that their function was mainly that of translator and go-between. Just because of this we must carefully trace that function, for it is our only opportunity to appraise the relative shares of Judaism and Hellenism in the music of the Syrian Church.

In general it seems amiss to search for every detailed indication of some single 'influence' or other. Asiatic culture grew not in years or decades, but in centuries and millennia. We cannot and should not evaluate the whole fabric from individual wefts or threads. Consequently, this chapter does not presume to be more than a preamble of the far greater complex of liturgico-musical interrelations between Church and Synagogue.

THE SOURCES
Hellenistic Sources

What we know about the Hellenistic music of the Near East comes to us through three channels of information, viz. Greek, Jewish, and

Christian, none of which even pretended to be objective. The authors of our historic sources were:[2]

(a) The Greek intellectuals, who spoke with condescension and occasionally with contempt of all music which did not strictly follow the 'pure and straight' path of classic Greek music.[3] It was their ever-repeated lament that the standard of Hellenistic music had fallen far below the level of a serious art. This indictment is even today echoed by modern scholars such as Riemann and Reinach, although our conceptions of the 'purity' of classic Greek music have undergone considerable modification.[4] For the mixture of Hellenic and Near East lore, the ancient authors show little regard, and we have to interpret their remarks with a good deal of caution.

(b) The Jewish intellectuals, our second category of sources, viewed with enmity and with great fear the ever-broadening inroads of Hellenism in Jewish life. If the bias of the Greek authors rested upon aesthetic-philosophic reasons, the sharp prejudice of the rabbis, on the other hand, was caused by a burning desire to erect a protective 'fence around the Law', which prevented them from attaining any objective attitude. Considering the vast number of Greek terms even in the Talmudic language, it must be admitted that their fears were not altogether groundless.

(c) The authors of the Christian Church during the four centuries of unfolding Christianity displayed a slowly changing attitude. At the outset their conception of the spiritual value of Hellenistic culture was all but identical with the orthodox Jewish, but gradually they came to terms with it, and finally—just before the final collapse of the Roman Empire—they began to appreciate its nobler implications. This generalization reckons with many exceptions, but the victory of the Gentile-Hellenistic Church over the Judaeo-Christian sects at Nicaea in 325 clearly demonstrates the spiritual trend of the times. We shall see, later on, that the Church even absorbed some Hellenistic tunes and musical ideas, incorporating them in its older Judaeo-Syrian stratum.

In general our sources pay more attention to instrumental music than to songs. We must not assume, however, that this instrumental music was independent of vocal music. On the contrary, vocal music is taken as a matter of course, since the ancient nations could hardly conceive of any music whose chief element was not song. The instrument is merely the variable element. It is in this sense that we hear of the various types of music which accompanied the religious ceremonies. The chanted words formed the liturgy, the instruments added the specific colour.

Music in the Hellenistic cults—of secular music we know next to nothing—had manifold functions. The most characteristic were: accompaniment of sacrificial worship; apotropaic protection from evil gods; epiclese; katharsis before, and initiation into, the mysteries; funeral; magic and sorcery.

The most frequent sacrifices were solemn libations. Plutarch relates that these libations were accompanied and dignified by a sacred paean.[5] On another occasion he offers a rationalistic explanation when he assumes that music was played during the sacrifices to cover up the groaning of the beasts or, in the Carthaginian sacrifices to Saturn, the crying of the children.[6] Actually, the function of music in all these cases was apotropaic—a principle which holds true even of some of the Temple music of Jerusalem. The *sistra* of the Egyptians to drive away the evil Typhon, the bells of the Phrygians to chase away hostile shadows and demons, even the *paamonim* on the garment of the High Priest, when he entered the Holy of Holies[7] and hundreds of other illustrations demonstrate, beyond any doubt, the basically magic and apotropaic power of music.[8] The efficacy of music for the purpose of epiclese was a strongly implemented belief of all polytheistic religions. Music invokes the gods to render help and assistance to the praying person. In the cult of Rhea Kybele, one of the most popular religions of Asia Minor, cymbals and bells played a significant, clearly epicletic part.[9] The theory has been proposed that the shofar and the trumpets in the older strata of the Bible had exactly the same purpose.[10] The Christian Arnobius ridicules this type of music, asking the pagans whether they want to awaken their sleeping gods.[11] The analogy of this polemic with the famous passage, I Kings 18:27, where Elijah mocks the priests of Baal and asks whether their god is travelling or asleep, is obvious.

The cathartic power of music was one of the chief tenets of Pythagoreanism; and this idea is one of the few conceptions of musical ethos which has survived up to the present day (e.g. in the fire and water ordeal in *The Magic Flute* by Mozart). The martyrium of St Theodotus relates that at the holy baths and baptisms, which formed an important part of the cult of Artemis and the Magna Mater (Kybele) in Asia Minor, flutes and tympana, or hand-drums were played.[12] So worldly an author as Ovid tells us that, on such occasions, the Phrygians 'howl and the flute is played furiously, while soft hands [of the priestesses] beat the bull's hide [drums]'.[13]

Flutes and cymbals were also in evidence at funerals in all the cults of Asia Minor and even in Palestine. In general, there is an abundance of documents testifying to the use of these instruments in all the mysteries and synchretistic religions of the Near East.[14]

Only in the last sixty or seventy years have documents of musical sorcery been uncovered; most of them stem from Egypt and Hellenistic Babylonia.[15] As we know through Blau's penetrating studies, Jewry did not keep itself free from these superstitious practices.[16] Most probably the recitation of these texts was accompanied by music, since in many of them the Gnostic alphabet appears as well as musically arranged vowels, and they are often concluded by Hallelujahs. We know today that these arrangements had a musical connotation which the Jews had learned from the Babylonian Gnostics and Manichaeans of the third to seventh centuries.[17]

We have, in the previous pages, attempted to give a brief synopsis of the descriptive sources of Hellenistic music, written in Greek and Latin. Unfortunately, nothing of Aramaean literature has come down to us which might shed some light upon our problem. Hence, we can match the Gentile sources only with the reports given by Jewish and Christian authors. They are, however, hardly ever descriptive in the true sense of the word, in as much as both pursue decidedly theological ends and are strongly biased against anything that does not conform to their cere- monial and theological concepts.

Jewish Sources

Instrumental music in general, and Greek music in particular, is des- cribed as euphonious (*qaliphonon* = *kalliphonon* = *euphonious*) in con- temporary rabbinic writings.[18] The rabbis even considered the Greek language the one most fitted for song.[19] Numerous musical terms, borrowed from the Greek language, demonstrate clearly how deeply the culture of Hellenism had penetrated the daily life of Palestine. Only a few illustrations need be quoted:

qathros = *kithara* = lyre
nimin = *nema* = strings
psanterin = *psalterion* = string instrument

pandura = *pandura* = instrument with three strings
sumponia = *symphonia* = consonance, ensemble, perhaps bagpipe[21]
hadrolis = *hydraulis* = water organ
karbelin = *choraulai* = a choir of flute players; perhaps organ[22]
eyros = 'airos' = gong made of bronze[23]

It is characteristic that Greek musical terms are used almost exclusively for instruments, their parts, their tuning, etc. The Hebrew vocabulary was perfectly sufficient to express all of the nuances of *vocal* music. Indeed, the Hebrew language has an abundance of terms for describing vocal forms, melodies, range, volume, etc.

Surrounded by so many Greek elements, it is understandable that the spiritual leaders of Judaism considered Hellenic music a medium of temptation to abandon Israel's faith. Most significant in this respect is the Talmudic statement: the apostasy of R. Elisha ben Abuya was due to the Greek melodies (or to the Greek instruments which were always in his house).[24] The prohibition against attending, on the eve of Passover, an *epikomon*, a festal procession with flutes and cymbals and probably Greek songs, may also stem from the fear of assimilation of Hellenistic customs. In the Talmudic treatise *Sukka* 50b, we read occasionally about the musical instruments significant of the cult of Asia Minor.

After the destruction of the Temple, instrumental music was banished in Judaism, an expression of mourning over that disaster. The rabbis usually based this injunction upon Isa. 24:9 and Hos. 9:1; yet it is clear that the two reasons for the rabbinic opposition to instrumental music were of a quite different nature. Philo and the Sibylline oracles display both contempt for any musical instrument well before the fall of Temple and land. In both cases spiritual worship is regarded as more exalted than any other sensuous ceremonial.[25] Philo, in particular, emphasized the value of spiritual hymns and praises[26] even when they are not actually pronounced by 'tongue or mouth', prayers which only the Deity can hear.[27] In much stronger terms the Sibyl turns against the pagan type of music:

> They [the faithful] do not pour blood of sacrifices upon the altar; no *tympanon* is sounded, nor cymbals, nor the *aulos* with its many holes, instruments full of frenzied tones, not the whistling of a pan's pipe is heard, imitating the serpent, nor the trumpet calling to war in wild tones.[28]

This passage reveals much better than all the rabbinic explanations the actual situation. It is a remarkable fact that the three instruments mentioned were considered unsuitable for the Temple service: the *aulos* (*halil*), the *tympanon* (*tof*) and the cymbals (*tzeltzelim*). These played a considerable part in the Psalter; yet the rabbis had a low estimate of them. Hugo Gressmann was the first to realize this strange fact, without offering any concrete explanation.[29] The later antagonism toward these instruments probably had the following reason: all three instruments were sacred attributes of Kybele. The Greek and Latin sources are full of allusions to these instruments as the originally Asiatic accessories of the orgiastic cults of the *Magna Mater*. If such applications made the instruments suspicious to the Jewish authorities, it must have been their use in the Jewish syncretistic ceremonies of Zeus Sabazios. There the serpent, together with the flute and the cymbals, held central significance. This explains the allusions of the Sibyl who, like the rabbis, felt horror and contempt for these renegade Jews and their customs.[30]

Gradually other instruments—originally very popular and used frequently in the Temple—were considered suspicious and unclean through their use in synchretistic religions; hence the rabbis frowned upon most of them, even upon their noblest representative, the *kinnor*.[31]

Vocal music, however, if of a sacred nature, was exempt from these strictures. Since its texts were exclusively in the Hebrew or Aramaean idiom, derived from Scripture, the songs were not likely to become a medium of syncretism.

Christian Sources

Up to the third century, the Christian sources reflect almost the same attitude toward Hellenistic music as contemporary Judaism. The very same distrust of instrumental accompaniment in religious ceremonies, the same horror of flute, *tympanon*, and cymbal, the accessories of the orgiastic mysteries, are here in evidence. Clement of Alexandria may be quoted first, since he was in many respects a Hellenist, and certainly not a Judaeo-Christian. He wrote:

One makes noise with cymbals and *tympana*, one rages and rants with instruments of frenzy; . . . The flute belongs to those superstitious men who run to idolatry. But we will banish these instruments even from our sober decent meals.[32]

Arnobius, likewise a Gentile Christian, follows the same trend, as does

335

Gregory of Nazianzus, always referring to the 'sounding bronze' (aeris tinnitus—cymbals) and the 'sounds of the flute' (tibiarum soni).[33]

Some of the Church Fathers, especially Clement of Alexandria, and occasionally Chrysostom, used Philo's allegory, where he likens the human tongue to the God-praising lyre.[34]

That vocal music is more pleasing to God and more suitable for Christians was assumed by all the Church Fathers without exception. In one instance, however, they had to be even more circumspect than the rabbis. Their vernacular consisted of the ancient languages, and the danger of the infiltration of Greek or Latin pagan influences was much more imminent to them than to the rabbis. They tried, therefore, to restrict the texts of their songs to biblical passages, chiefly from the Psalter, as did the contemporary rabbis.

In the course of time, Hellenistic and Aramaic-Asiatic forces made gradual but significant inroads into the liturgy of the Church and wrought a profound change upon its attitude toward syncretism. We know that the Kyrie eleison of the Mass is a transformation of an original Helios-Mithra hymn.[35] As we shall see later on, a piece of Hellenistic composition, the Nemesis hymn of Mesomedes, was later incorporated in a Kyrie.[36] Recognizing the pagan origin of both text and melody (sun hymn; Nemesis hymn) we may readily conclude that the Church gave up its once intransigent puritanism. Another indication of this strategic retreat are the numerous paintings, mosaics, etc., in which Christ is identified with Orpheus or sometimes with Orpheus and David.[37]

On the other hand, the musical terminology and structure of the Armenian and Nestorian songs show a considerable amount of Semitic and Hellenistic traits superimposed upon the native lore. Here we need only refer to the studies of the late Komitas Kevorkian, in which this gifted scholar offered the first scientific accounts of Armenian Church music.[38] It appears that the Armenian Church, in particular, has preserved an astonishing amount of ancient tradition, both in its liturgy and music. We intend to deal extensively with this highly intriguing problem elsewhere.

One of the most important questions concerns the synthesis of Oriental, Hellenistic, and European chant under the aegis of the Church. As in Rome itself the pagan Pantheon was re-dedicated to the memory of All Martyrs, and as in Byzantium St Sophia took the place of the goddess Minerva, as Neo-Platonism assumed a Christian mantle, so were the chants of Syria and Palestine recast by the enthusiastic leaders of the new religion.[39]

Early monasticism played a great part in this period of change and transplantation. The great monastic society, assimilating all nations of the Mediterranean basin, formed a spiritual bridge between Orient and Occident. The recently discovered 'Dead Sea Scrolls' shed surprising new light on the part which certain Jewish sects had in the ideological origin of Christian monasticism.[40]

From the pagan side came the great contributions of Hellenistic music theorists. The three greatest, Philodemus of Gadara (*ca.* 110–40 B.C.), Nicomachus of Gerasa (*ca.* A.D. 100), and Aristides Quintilianus (third–fourth century A.D.), were all hellenized Syrians or Palestinians.[41]

Christianity, after some hesitation, accepted their theories and digested them in a great synthesis of Orient and Occident, of which the erudite Boethius and the saintly Cassiodorus were the first and most influential champions in so far as their books touched on music. Only after this synthesis was it possible that the ancient oriental heritage of both the liturgy and the music of the Church could be forgotten, until modern science rediscovered the deepest and most genuine strata of Early Christianity.

Since Hellenistic ideas reached deep into East Syria and Persia, it would be a mistake to leave these regions outside the scope of our investigation. Indeed, there is increasing evidence that the early hymns of the Syrian Church reflect to a considerable degree the musico-literary technique and structure of Hellenistic patterns. Thanks to Parisot's and Jeannin's works on the hymns of the Syrian Churches, we possess a better understanding of the actual precepts which effectuated the synthesis of the Aramaean and the Greek spirit in the Christian sphere.[42]

Musical Sources

Among the few authentic documents at our disposal, we must distinguish between primary sources, such as have been transmitted to us in musical notation, and secondary ones, which are either insecurely established or based on modern reconstruction. We shall give only the musical text; analysis and comparative treatment will be given in the following chapter. This musical source material has been selected as representative of the different melodic styles and of the various types of performance.

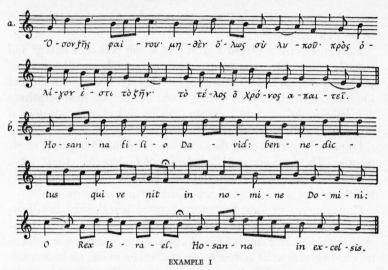

EXAMPLE 1

a. *Skolion* of Seikilos, of Tralles in Asia Minor. (1st–2nd cent. A.D.) (Notated)
b. Antiphon *Hosanna filio David*, of the Roman Church. (Notated)[43]

EXAMPLE 2

a. Helios hymn of Mesomedes. (Greek-Syrian composer, *ca.* A.D. 130.) (Notated)[44]
b. Antiphon *Accipiens Simeon* of the Roman Church. (Notated)[45] (Transposed)

338

EXAMPLE 3

a. Nemesis hymn of Mesomedes. (Notated)[46]
b. Kyrie Tone VII. (Notated)[47]

EXAMPLE 4

Christian hymn from Oxyrhynchos in Egypt. (Third century) (Notated)[48]

EXAMPLE 5

Toni Psalmorum of the Roman Church, compared with Hebrew Psalmodies.[49]

    a, b, c. Hebrew Psalmodies
    d. Tone VIII of the Roman Church
    e. Tone VI of the Roman Church
    f. Tone IV of the Roman Church (ancient form)

EXAMPLE 6

Ancient version of the 'Aboda of Yom Kippur. (Oral Tradition)[50]

EXAMPLE 7

The *Tropos Spondeiakos* after Clement of Alexandria and Plutarch, compared with Jewish and Christian chants. (Reconstruction by E. W.)[51]

EXAMPLE 8

a. *Te Deum*, after the Ambrosian version. (Notated)[52]
b. *Sh'ma'* of the Yemenite Jews. (Oral Tradition)[53]

EXAMPLE 9

a. Nestorian Psalmody (Oral)[54]
b. Psalmody of Yemenite Jews. (Oral)[55]
c. Mode of lamentations of the Roman Church.[56]

a. *sāg-di-nan mār l'a-lla-hu-tah, val-nā-šu-tah dlā pu-lā-gā.*

b. *Lu-cis Cre-a-tor op-ti-me Lu-cem di-e-rum pro fe-rens.*

c. *qa-diš qa-diš-at, qa-diš bkul é-dōn, a-lo-ho mšab-ho mqa das lqá-dị-še*

d. *sah-dē hray-tun ta-ga-rē va-si-mạt hun baš-maya.*

zvan tu naḥ I-mar-ganyā-ta bad-mā d'ar div ša-vray-hun.

e. *Shir ha-shi-rim a-sher lish-lo mo-*

yi-sho-ke-ni min shi-kot pi-hu.

EXAMPLE 10

a. Nestorian Hymn. (Oral)
b. Gregorian Hymn. (Notated)
c. Maronite *Kedusha.* (Oral)
d. East Syrian Psalmody. (Oral)[57]
e. Song of Songs; cantillation of the Persian Jews. (Oral)[58] (Transposed)

343

THE LEVELS

The Practice of Musical Performance

Before we examine these musical sources in detail, we should acquaint ourselves with the manner in which music was actually performed in the era of the disintegrating culture of antiquity. In the synopsis of Hellenistic music given above, its role in the mystery cults has been emphasized, but these were by no means the only occasions when music played a significant part. At the symposia, in the theatre, at secular processions and parades, and in real concerts and recitals, vocal and instrumental music was very much in evidence. Ascetic tendencies independent of Christianity, on the other hand, repudiated music completely. It is an historic irony that the Neo-Pythagoreans, the followers of the idolized inventor of music, led the battle for a 'disembodied' music (the harmony of the spheres), such as could not be heard by human senses at all.

Between these extremes the young Church had to find its way. The third century marked the turning point in the Church's attitude towards instrumental music; it was being tolerated, while suspected. A canonical book, Revelation, had visualized the host of elders prostrate before the Lamb playing, with harps, the 'new song';[59] Clement of Alexandria defended the playing of the lyre by quoting the great example of King David.[60] As in most cases, he patterned his ideas on Philo, who excepted the lyre from the accusation of sensuality.[61] But stern animadversion and censure of instrumental music appeared in the *Canones* of St Basil, which were written towards the end of the fourth century.[62]

Two questions with regard to musical performance arise. Who sang the prayers and hymns in Church and how were they rendered? As to the first question, the ideal of the Early Church was, according to the apostolic literature, the *Koinonia*, i.e. the congregation singing in unison with one or more men functioning as precentors. This community singing was led by psalmists, *anagnostes*, lectors, deacons and other clergymen. Our most reliable testimonies come from the *Apostolic Constitutions*,[63] Cyril of Jerusalem,[64] and the pilgriming woman, Aetheria Silvia.[65] Judging from this evidence, the lectors' and psalmists' function was well-nigh identical with that of the messenger of the congregation in rabbinic literature. In fact it has long been surmised that the Early Church recruited its cantors from among Jewish proselytes.[66]

We have, in Chapter III of Part I, adduced two epitaphs of Judaeo-Christian *psalmistae*, Deusdedit and Redemptus, whom Pope Damasus I brought with him to Rome.[67] These rare testimonies will probably be augmented by the recent systematic examinations of sectarian Jewish tombs in Israel and Jordan. The new discoveries have cast fresh light on the genesis and development of the lectorate and cantorate.[68]

These and other investigations leave no doubt on the continuity of musical tradition linking sectarian Judaism with Early Christianity. The men, who conceived the tradition were lectors, cantors, or *psalmistae*, and some of them were praised for their *placidum modulamen*.

The 'pleasing cantillation' would justify Athanasius's characterization of recitation of Scripture as 'melodious';[69] the *tonus lectionis* of today is, on the other hand, no more than an emphatic speaking with semi-musical cadences. Leitner is evidently right when he links the Athanasius passage to the Hebrew-Syrian type of melodic cantillation.[70]

Two other types of musical rendering in the Church, the responsory and the antiphon, were likewise of Jewish origin. There is no need to cite the numerous ecclesiastical authors who claim the invention of both forms for Christianity: the passages II Chron. 20:19-21, Neh. 12:31-42 and Ps. 136 make it perfectly clear that both the responsory and the antiphon were details of a well-established Jewish heritage which the Church adopted.[71]

The participation of women in the congregational singing of Synagogue and Church warrants special consideration. Marcion had formed a female choir, and Paul of Samosata, also a heretic, composed psalms for women singers.[72] Significantly, the antagonism toward the female voice became violent only in the Gnostic crisis of the Church. J. Quasten's hypothesis, that the practice of the Gnostics was the decisive reason for the complete prohibition of female activity in the common liturgy, is quite unconvincing.[73] After all, the Pauline rule, 'let the women be silent in the holy assembly', in I Cor. 14:34 was written long before Gnosticism came on the Christian scene. When finally the *Didascalia* of the 318 Fathers gave the apostolic rule a legal formulation, there were still voices raised in defence of female choirs.[74]

The underlying reason was of a different nature. It becomes obvious when we compare the background of the defenders of women singers with that of their opponents in the fourth and fifth centuries. In the opposition were: Tertullian (North Africa), Jerome (Rome, Palestine),

Cyril of Jerusalem (Greece, Jerusalem), and Isidore of Pelusium (Greece).[75] The defenders were: Marcion (Black Sea), Ephraem Syrus (Nisibis), Bardesanes and his son Harmonius (Edessa). This tabulation seems to indicate that the Western regions were more puritanic than the Syrians. To be sure, Gnostics had no monopoly in female singing, as is shown by the example of Ephraem, who instituted women's choirs. This practice spread all over Asia Minor. The Arabic *Canones of the Apostles* even admits female lectors and deacons.[76] A kind of compromise attitude is found in the Syrian *Testament of the Lord* (fifth century), which permits a female response to the psalm intoned by a male precentor.[77] This is quite analogous to the statement of a Babylonian *Amora*, R. Joseph, who accepted responses by women but not their leading the songs.[78] The very same practice is described by Aetheria Silvia as a usage of the Church at Jerusalem in the fourth century.[79]

The main centre of liturgical development during the third century was Syria, where the new Christian hymns were introduced.

The invention of a new metrical system by the Syrian poets is of great consequence for our study. It is inseparably linked with the development of Church music and, as it seems to this writer, also with that of the Synagogue. For it was due to the new metrical scheme of the Syrians that the corresponding music also was forced into metric structure. This conception of music is much closer akin to Hellenistic than to original Jewish theory and practice. The superabundance of metrical hymns in the Aramaean Churches demanded strongly rhythmic tunes which had been known to the Greeks for centuries, but entered synagogal music only in the ninth century, when the *piyyut* conquered the liturgy. The question remains, however, whether the Syrians were really the inventors of the new poetic style. Since W. Meyer has demonstrated their priority, we must at least assume it. We shall discuss this matter later from a broader viewpoint.

Another peculiarity of the Aramaean pieces deserves a brief description: their preference for half-choirs, when responses or antiphons were sung. We have already mentioned the biblical origin of these forms, but it seems that they were organized and cultivated in Syria before they became wholly integrated in the Roman or Byzantine plainsong. This conclusion is not only based upon the ever-repeated patristic statements that the Graeco-Syrian monks Flavian and Diodore (of Antioch and Tarsus) invented and fostered the antiphonic practice[80] but also upon new and fully convincing evidence which has been produced by P. Odilo Heiming. This scholar has demonstrated that many of the Syriac hymn manuscripts were actually arranged for half-choruses. Further, he investigated the leading stanzas and compared them with Byzantine patterns. The result displays an intricate interrelation between Syria and Byzantium, where the Eastern wave met the Western wave.[81]

Melos and Rhythm

(I) The three archetypes of early Church music can be defined according to one single criterion: the relation between note and word. Considering psalmody but an elaborate form of cantillation or *ecphonesis*, that old and venerable category is characterized by the organic links which bind the syntactic structure of the scriptural text to its musical formulation. The individual word is of no relevance; only the whole sentence with its caesura and cadence makes a musical unit. The parallelism of Scripture which has been carefully preserved in all translations created the dichotomic structure of musical psalmody.

If we compare Ex. 5 (p. 340) with either 2b or 3b (pp. 338–9) the difference is plain and fundamental. In psalmody we find melodic movement only at special significant places of the sentence: at the beginning, at the pause (*'atnah*), and in the final cadence. The rest of the sentence is recited upon the *tenor* without any melos. There is no discernible *tenor* in the other two examples, however, nor any clear dichotomy, nor its characteristic attributes, the punctuating or final melismata. The melody, while closely bound to the words, if not to single syllables, flows more freely and is more autonomous. Now psalmody is a direct Jewish legacy to the Church. This is also true of the *lectio solemnis*, the cantillation of Scripture. Not only are these two elements, the core of the ancient musical liturgy, common to both Synagogue and Church, they also are by far the best preserved and most authentic features. For the first attempts at musical notation in Judaism and Christianity concerned themselves with the fixation of these two forms. The musical organization of the Jewish raw material, however, remained the task of the different Churches and varied considerably with the individual ethnic traditions. Even here we find occasionally Hellenistically inspired fragments; our Ex. 2a and 2b give such instances. Parts of the Helios hymn of Mesomedes were integrated in the antiphon 'Accipiens Simeon' for the feast of Purification.

347

(II) Much more complex is the genesis of the second archetype, the hymnic syllabic composition. This form is linked to the syllable or the word rather than to the sentence. No *tenor* of recitation, hardly a *pausa*, and seldom a final melisma in the cadence, occur in hymnic forms. But its music is a faithful expression of the metrical poem, since it obeys in all details the accents of the text. If we desire to understand its history, our first task must be the study of the hymn metres. But we meet with serious difficulties. Hellenistic poetry was based upon the system of quantity, but the earliest Aramaean and Greek-Christian hymns do not observe this scheme. Let us compare Ex. 4, the earliest musical document of Christianity, the Oxyrhynchos Hymn, with Ex. 10a, b, and c (a Nestorian and a Gregorian hymn and a Syrian *Kedusha*), with regard to their texts:

Ex. 4. Oxyrhynchos Hymn[82]

. . . Of the assembly shall be silent . . . nor shall the lightbringing stars be left behind. All of the roaring rivers shall sing hymns to [with clear reference to verses 3–4 of Septuagint Ps. 92, Hebr. 93] Our Father, and the Son, and the Holy Spirit. All the (heavenly) powers (host) shall respond: 'Amen, Amen'. Power and praise to the (sole) giver of all good gifts. . . . Amen, Amen.

Ex. 10a.[83] (Octosyllabic metre: probably $\smile — \smile — \smile — \smile —$)

sagdinan mar l'allahutāh	We pray, O Lord, to Your Godliness
valnatzhutah dla pulāgā	And to Your glory undivided.

Ex. 10b.[84] (Octosyllabic metre: scheme $\smile — \smile — \smile — \smile \smile$)

Lucis creator optime,
Lucem dierum proferens,
Primordiis lucis novae
Mundi parans originem:

Qui mane junctum vesperi
Diem vocari praecipis:
Illabitur tetrum chaos,
Audi preces cum fletibus. etc.

Ex. 10c.[85] (Pentasyllabic metre: perhaps $\smile — — \smile —$)

qadiš qadišat	O Holy of Holiness,
qadiš b'kul 'edon	Holy throughout the ages,
aloho m'šabho	The praiseworthy God.
m'qadaš l'qadiše	Holy to His Holy ones,
d'men srofe d'nuro	He who by the Seraphim of fire
bromo metqadaš	In the heights is sanctified,
v'men krubē d'hilē	And by the Cherubs of His Host
b'hedro metbarah	Is praised in awe.

The first text is at least partially based upon the old principle of quantity, while the following three hymns show hardly any quantity. There might be some doubt concerning the Syrian text, since we do not know its original correct accentuation, but in the Latin hymn, the accentuation is evident. The Syrian and Latin texts have, however, one principle in common: their verses always contain the same number of syllables. This scheme finally replaced the classic conception of metre both in the Roman and in the Greek Churches.

It is generally assumed that the Syrian practice of numbering syllables was of no influence upon the Hebrew poetry, which counted accents rather than syllables. This writer has found, however, that some of the oldest *piyyutim* followed the Syrian scheme. One more example may be added to those given in Chapter IX.

Strict heptasyllabus. (*Ephraem's metre:*
‿ ᷓ ‿ ᷓ __ ‿ ᷓ [86])

Mital mashkim b'hazilo	From the early dew that He maketh flow,
Umituv heled b'higodlo	And from the best time of his life that He maketh grow,
Yaakov yarash b'hevlo	Jacob inherited in his portion
Matan adam yarhiv lo.	A man's gift that maketh room for him.
(Yannai)	

There probably existed older sources of the same literary type before the era of the *piyyutim* quoted above (seventh century). It is only through the findings in the Geniza that we know the *Mahzor Yannai* at all. None the less, the priority of the Syrians in using the syllabic type can hardly be doubted.[87]

Again, there are indications which point to Hellenism as the agent under whose aegis the Syrians evolved their system. The historian, Sozomen, in his biography of Ephraem Syrus, writes:

Harmonius, the son of Bardesanes, having been well instructed in Grecian literature, was the first who subjected his native language to metres and musical laws, and adapted it to choirs of singers, as the Syrians now commonly chant; not indeed using the writings of Harmonius, but his tunes.[88]

This passage would suggest the Syrian hymnodists as heirs of the Greek tradition. Indeed, when we consider that Judaism kept itself free from such metric conceptions until the sixth or even the seventh century, while living all of the time in close contact with Aramaean Christianity, there is perhaps some reason to doubt the originality of Syrian hymnody. This suspicion becomes even stronger when we contemplate the rapidity with which the Syrian type swept all over the Western and Eastern Church. To be sure, the contemporaries of Ephraem and the champions of the new form in the Roman orbit, such as Ambrose, did not immediately abandon the traditional quantity system, but neither Augustine nor Gregory I heeded quantity much longer.[89] Had the new system been entirely alien to Romans and Greeks, it would have encountered much more opposition than it actually did.

Another factor must be considered: the type of melody. When we compare the oldest Latin hymn melodies with those of the Syrians, we find some surprising analogies in their flow and structure.[90]

Their rhythmic identity, dependent upon the octosyllabic scheme of the Syriac and of the Roman hymn, needs no further elaboration. If we search for the Greek models of the Syriac metres, the closest likeness appears in an anacreontic scheme with Ephraem's heptasyllabic metre. The following example is taken from August Hahn's work, who first ventured the conjecture that Harmonius borrowed this metre from Anacreon:[91]

He ḡē meláina pinéi	The black earth does drink,
Pinei de dendre' autēn	It drinks the plant itself.

or:

Mythinai d'eni nēso	They continue to relate fables
Megiste diepousin	In the largest island.[92]

These Greek rhythms (*Acatalectic Pherecrateus; logaoedic Tripody*) were used for popular processions. It seems that the women sang them at the mystery cults, often in strophic responses.[93] Let us, in this connexion, remember that Ephraem, after whom that very metre is named in Syria, taught it to women in responsorial style.[94]

Contemporary Jewish literature offers neither isosyllabic poems nor strophes nor even descriptions of such types of hymns before the sixth or seventh century. This fact admits of one conclusion only: the hymn form is originally alien to Judaism and is a Graeco-Syrian element in the music of the Church.

(III) In the third archetype, the melismatic style, the melos has no immediate relation to the word. This is the oldest form of 'absolute' music, entirely emancipated from metre, syllable, word, or sentence. What is its origin? After all, singing without words was not such a common practice in antiquity; even today, coloratura singing is a rather extraordinary thing. In the Church it is invariably connected with the jubilant rendering of the Alleluia; which fact alone suggests Jewish origin. The acclamation *Hallelujah* may have had, as I have suggested previously, a definite liturgical function, to give the uninitiated, primitive listeners the opportunity of joining the proclamation of God's praise.[95] Gradually it loosened itself from its original context and, used as spontaneous acclamation, together with its pneumatic colour, led to a certain disembodiment, to a spiritualization of the watchword. The last step was the omission of the word *Hallelujah* itself, in whose place only its vowels were sung—AEOUIA, to be changed later to EUOUAE.

The Hallelujah grew as an expansion of a verse or of an entire psalmody. Cassian's statement confirms this conception: 'Some of them [monks] felt that they ought to prolong the . . . psalms themselves by melodies of antiphons and by *adding certain melismata*'.[96] In other words: *the melismatic, wordless Jubili are mere expansions of final melismata in the psalmody*. This theory can be further confirmed by comparing certain final melismata of the oldest Jewish strata with similar extended Alleluias of the Church.

EXAMPLE 11[97]

In our four illustrations the history of the *Jubilus* is clearly reflected: (a) is a very common Jewish psalmody formula, familiar in the occidental as well as in the oriental Synagogue; (b) and (c) are two final melismata of the Gregorian chant, miniature expansions of the original mode; (d) gives a splendidly extended version of a *versus alleluiaticus*.

The technique of the melismatic ecstatic singing was imitated in syncretistic circles, where it was used for magical purposes. The imitation, however, was poor and inorganic, and presents a bizarre picture. Compare the fragment of a Gnostic-magic incantation with a Gregorian passage:

EXAMPLE 12[98]

The utter monotony of both these examples is obvious. It might be due to the idea that certain intervals or tonal figures, if repeated over and over again, can exert a strong magic appeal, even more than stubbornly reiterated words or vowels, which were also the common stock-in-trade of magic papyri. The Gregorian example is perhaps a lost wave of that syncretistic practice which somehow crept into the authentic songs of the Church. Dom Leclercq describes the curious passages of the incantations as 'remnants of hymns, in which one can recognize a mixture of elements, Jewish, pagan, and Christian'. But, he goes on to declare, 'we will not be too bold if we imagine in them (*pressentir*) translations or pasticcios of Bardesanes' Syriac hymns'.[99] This conjecture seems hardly convincing, since the analysis of Syrian hymns indicates their strongly metrical character. The magical pieces show no discernible rhythm nor metre, and convey, in general, a rather amorphous, not to say chaotic, impression.

From the very outset the *melismatic* type was identified with religious ecstasy. Created by spontaneous emotion, it was frequently rendered as improvisation, both in Synagogue and Church. When the Western Church attempted to systematize its songs according to the misunderstood teachings of Greek theorists, it was the melismatic type which suffered most.[100] Forced into the Procrustean bed of the eight Church Tones, it was modified and mutilated. Still, we must consider this a cheap price for its essential preservation: without the occidental arrangement it would have disappeared altogether.

Thus we realize, as in the case of psalmody, a Jewish heritage preserved in the Church by means of Greek theories and systems.

(IV) We have sketched in the previous pages the origin and the structure of the three archetypes which constituted the backbone of the Church's musical liturgy: psalmody, hymn, and melismatic song. In addition to these types we encounter, at a fairly early stage, certain mixed forms which blended psalmodic elements with melismatic or syllabic hymnic features. They are common to the oldest strata of the Roman, Greek, Syrian, Nestorian, and Armenian chant, but developed independently according to the customs and requirements of their specific liturgies. An ancient Jewish instance is Ex. 6 (p. 340).

In the Roman plainsong we find many of these hybrid structures, the most interesting of which are the tunes of the *Ordinarium Missae*, the Tract, the Gradual-Response, the later Antiphons, and the Lamentations, a special version of the *Lectio Solemnis*. In most of these compositions Jewish and Hellenistic elements were merged in various degrees, generally blended to a perfect unity. In contradistinction to the Eastern Churches, Rome was quite conservative when it came to changes in, or modifications of, its liturgical traditions. As far as we can see today, there were few, if any, other formative forces besides the Hebrew and the Greek which constitute the nucleus of the Roman chant. Only in the eighth and ninth centuries did West European notions (Gallic, Germanic, Irish) begin to make inroads into the rigid body of Roman tradition.

(a) The tunes of the *Ordinarium Missae* (the nuclear prayers of the Mass). Here a rare opportunity of comparing Hellenistic with Jewish impulses presents itself; Ex. 3a and 3b juxtaposed the Nemesis hymn of Mesomedes, a Hellenistic piece of the second Christian century, with the *Kyrie* VI of the Gregorian tradition. In the Greek composition the relation between note and word is strictly syllabic—one note to each syllable; but the Christian version of the same melody uses punctuating and final melismata. In short, it adjusts the Hellenistic passage to the more Hebraic melismatic character of the *Kyrie*.

Quite the reverse development is discernible in the assimilation of an original Hebrew motif to another *Kyrie* piece. Idelsohn was the first to compare the two compositions, but without much elaboration. The Jewish cantillation contains certain initial and final melismata. While its melody has been essentially left untouched by the Church, it has been well-nigh divested of its flourishes by the syllabic distribution of the new Latin words to the ancient Hebrew tune.[101]

EXAMPLE 13

In both cases the Church has balanced Hellenistic against Jewish elements by adding or effacing the typically oriental melismata.

(b) The process was not always as smooth as here, nor the result as well composed. This is especially obvious in some of the antiphons, where the rigidly parallelistic structure of the scriptural verses often disturbed the flow of Hellenistic melody. Classic examples of this forced adaptation are Ex. 1a and 1b.

The easy-going drinking song of Seikilos was pressed into the distich:

Hosanna filio David; benedictus qui venit in nomine Domini.

Rex Israel: Hosanna in excelsis.

Here, a good deal of the Hellenistic melody has been absorbed, but the Christian arrangers, as was their custom, insisted upon emphasizing the *pausa* in each verse. Thus they had to add a pausal melisma for the words 'David' and 'Israel'.[102] The adaptation tried, moreover, to stress the two-fold *Hosanna* of the first and second verse by the identical musical phrase, thereby cramping the flow of the Greek cadence.

(c) Another archaic form of the plainsong, the Tract, reveals prevailing Hebrew elements. Its style is very florid, like that of *Hazanut* and it is indeed performed by a soloist during the Mass. It probably antedates all other music of the Mass, except the Alleluia.[103] P. Wagner has pointed out that the roots of the Tract lie deeply in the solo psalmody of the Synagogue, especially in the punctuating melismata of cantillation. Two arguments put forth by this illustrious scholar make his thesis most plausible: the fact that the Tract texts (with few late exceptions) are exclusively biblical, and the identity of some of their melodies with chants of the Yemenite Jews. We shall return to this archaic form type in Chapter IV.

(d) The punctuating melismata which play so great a part in cantillation and psalmody were a driving force of aggressive power. The old singers of the Church were so accustomed to them that these little flourishes were dragged by them into originally Hellenistic melodies of clearly syllabic character. The famous hymn of Oxyrhynchos, so controversial it may appear otherwise, is a case in point. A comparison of Ex. 4 with a classical Greek composition like Ex. 2a evidences certain fundamental divergencies. The text of the hymn proper ends with 'Amen, Amen' followed by a small doxology beginning with *kratos ainos* and ending with *panton agathon, amen amen*. In all these endings, we encounter the typical final melismata of Jewish psalmody although, in melody and structure, the piece is distinctly Hellenistic, even written in the Greek letter notation. We quote here from Ex. 4 (p. 339) the characteristic passages.

EXAMPLE 14

The question then arises: how did the Egyptian Christians come to be acquainted with Jewish psalmody and its practice? Fortunately, this question can now be answered satisfactorily. Clement of Alexandria, writing shortly before the time of the Oxyrhynchos hymn, wrote:

> Further, among the ancient Greeks, in their banquets over the brimming cups, a song was sung called a *skolion* after the manner of the Hebrew psalms, altogether raising the paean with the voice [indicating his knowledge of Hebrew psalmody].

Later on, Clement gives some hints about that mode of psalmody, and this writer essayed, by comparing Clement's statements with those of Plutarch, Aristides Quintilianus, and others, to reconstruct the *Tropos Spondeiakos*, the mode alluded to. Ex. 7 shows the occurrence of that melodic type in Hebrew as well as in Roman and Syrian psalmody. In most of the corresponding examples,[104] the final melismata are outstanding and colour the cadence much in the same way as in the Hymn of Oxyrhynchos. (Cf. *supra*, p. 341.)

(e) Perhaps the most interesting instance of the Roman policy of balancing Hellenistic and Jewish features against each other is the case of the Lamentations. Liturgically, they belong to one of the oldest strata of Christian worship. Musically, the tradition is variegated, heterogeneous, and not always authentic. Of the numerous versions we select two, both of which occur also in Jewish cantillation:

EXAMPLE 15[105]

Originally, the cantillation of the Yemenite Jews (Ex. 9b) was full of the little melismata demanded by the disjunctive accents of Scripture and has been preserved in that form. While the Church has adopted the characteristic mode, it rigidly simplified it and retained only the punctuating melismata of *pausa* and *punctus* (*'Atnah—Sof Pasuq*). (Cf. *supra*, p. 342.)

Again we behold the Jewish gem in a Greek setting, as often before. Notwithstanding the obvious melodic identities, the deeper reasons for the Christian modifications must not be overlooked. But it is not possible within the scope of this study to examine the manifold causes which, in the course of centuries, engendered a kind of stylistic unity within the traditional music of the Churches as well as that of the Synagogue. Here only a theory can be offered without full implementation. That organic unity was forged on the two levels of practical music and theological speculation.

In the realm of practical music (*musica humana*), the two main causes which made for homogeneity of style were (a) the associative power of certain melodic types and (b) the organization of musical notation. In the oldest layers of Church music, we find what amount to primitive leading-motifs which set the pattern for later compositions. While this development is especially visible in the Gradual-Responses of the Gregorian chant, an analogous principle prevails also in the music of the Synagogue. The origin of this technique is probably purely musical; it is but natural to imitate older tunes, particularly when they are surrounded by an aura of holiness. Once this practice was established, a further element was added, which lent a new significance to the leading-motifs: they were used to serve as *hermeneutic expressions* of the various texts to which they were applied.[106] Venturing a drastic anachronism, one might say that the leading-motifs functioned as 'cross references' in the extended liturgies of the Churches and the Synagogue.

In Judaism, the leading-motifs have become so familiar to every worshipper that he automatically associates certain tunes with entire holydays whose liturgy they permeate. The *Missinai* tunes were among the factors which helped to create the unique atmosphere of the Jewish holyday service. While the plainsong never reached this unity of style, there is evidence enough that it was aspired to and in certain forms also achieved, notably in the Roman Gradual-Responses, the Greek *hirmoi*, and the Syrian *'enyane* and *riš-qole*.[107] The influx of the various ethnic groups and of their tunes prevented the Gregorian chant from becoming completely homogeneous; but it obviated also a potential monotony. The more nationalistically-minded Byzantine and Syrian Churches did not fully escape that monotony. Judaism, on the other hand, avoided such sameness of style due to its migrations and its various regional *minhagim* (customs of worship).

The other factor contributive to the unification of musical style was undoubtedly the notation. We meet here with a situation not at all unique in the centuries of slowly disintegrating antiquity. While the Greeks had developed an exact system of musical notation, it had been so completely forgotten that in the seventh century St Isidore of Seville could write: 'Unless tunes are preserved by memory, they perish, since they cannot be written'.[108] Yet the Oxyrhynchos hymn was written in the Greek notation as late as the third century. As in other fields of culture, most of the accomplishments of Greek music were thrown overboard by zealous religious, and perhaps ethnic, fanatics who had arisen in and with Christianity. To be sure, a new notation had to be organized; but it did not begin where the Greeks had left off. Its oldest documents can be traced to the seventh century, and there were probably earlier attempts.[109] Still, there remains a lacuna of almost three centuries, which we are unable to bridge.

It is not surprising that the new system was vastly different from the Greek conception, for it had to serve another purpose. The Greek notation had to define each tone, since its music was syllabic-rhythmic, and its phrases not melismatic. The Church required a method by which the most venerable elements of liturgical music could be fixed, namely the cantillation of the scriptural lesson and psalmody. The Greek system, with its minute description of every tone, would have proved very cumbersome had it been applied to the new task. *Phrases* or *syntactic units* had to be provided with notation, not individual syllables. Hence the ecphonetic origin of the Greek and Roman neumes. Indeed, the primitive neumes, which stood for entire phrases of both text and music, were much more practical for their purpose than any other system.

It was O. Fleischer who, in his *Neumenstudien*, proved indisputably the common origin of the Hebrew, Armenian, Hindu, Greek, and Roman systems of accentuation. F. Praetorius investigated the origin of the Hebrew *te'amim*, claiming that the Masoretes borrowed the ecphonetic system from Greek lectionaries. He offered no real proof for this contention.[110] From Kahle's penetrating studies (*Masoreten des Ostens* and *Masoreten des Westens*) we know that the relations were by no means that simple and one-sided. According to his theory, a Nestorian school of scribes and exegetes was the first to set up a system of ecphonetic signs applied to scriptural texts. He also suggests an interrelation between the Nestorians and the rabbinic academy at Nisibis.[111] That there existed an intimate connexion between the Syrian and the earliest Hebrew accents cannot be doubted, since their similarity is evident. Unfortunately the musical tradition of the Syriac accents had been lost for many centuries, as we learn from Bar Hebraeus.[112]

In my study on 'Musical Punctuation', the theory was presented that the earliest Masoretic accents were a combination of signs borrowed from the contemporaneous Syriac system and the older Hebrew cheironomic tradition. Be that as it may, Syriac and Hebrew elements must have played a decisive role in the genesis of the new ecphonetic system which became the starting point of our modern musical notation.

Once again, the course of events followed the general pattern: pure Greek culture was abolished, and the new conceptions, on which the entire development of Church music depended, came from Aramaean-Hebrew sources. And again we realize how the Asiatic raw material was polished and rearranged by the application of Greek methods. They systematized but also mutilated the originally syntactic function of the Semitic notation, yielding to the ever increasing demands for exactitude and precision. The decisive break with the principle of ecphonetic notation occurred with the introduction of the first horizontal staff, in order to define an exact musical pitch, a *note fixée* for the early neumes. This happened in Western Europe some time in the ninth century.[113] Neither the Byzantine nor the Syriac nor the Hebrew systems followed Rome in this ingenious adventure: their neumes retained their primitive phrasing character almost to this day. Had it not been for the didactic manuals for the choristers (*papadikai*), the Byzantian neumes would today be as undecipherable as the Syriac system, whose signs lost all meaning once the oral tradition had disappeared. A somewhat better knowledge is preserved of the Old Armenian system, which, in numerous points, resembles the early Masoretic accents.

The individual systems of notation—Hebrew, Byzantine, Syriac, Roman, etc.—contributed much, by isolating their music from that of other Churches, to a crystallization of the style, of which they are a part. It is perhaps not an idle speculation to contemplate the course of musical history, if there had not been ten systems but only one system of notation. It is a safe guess that, in such a case, the oriental forces would be much more in evidence than they are today. For, during the first millennium of Christianity, wave after wave came from Asia, throwing men, ideas, and traditions on the shores of Europe. We can appreciate such a hypothetical case in the history of art where no barrier of language or notation isolated the East from the West. The Basilica, the Romanesque style, the Mosaics of Ravenna, the Christian manuscript illustrations of the first seven centuries—all these came from Asia and were transformed in the Mediterranean orbit, not always to their advantage.[114] The policy which governed these transformations and pseudo-morphoses, however, was determined on the highest level, the dogmatic-religious.

The Attitude of the Authorities in Academy, Synagogue, and Church

In the intellectual world of declining antiquity, there was considerable controversy about the nature and the true purpose of music. These discussions took place in the sphere of a philosophy which considered music in terms of either a science or a moral power. We know of only a few deviations from this general path, and these originated chiefly in Syria and Palestine; Philodemus of Gadara and the Syrian Iamblichus do not quite fit into the musical philosophy of the Hellenistic era. To the men of the Academy as well as to the Neo-Pythagoreans and the Neo-Platonists, music was an abstract *episteme* which, if applied wisely and correctly, could lead the adept into the highest spheres of metaphysical knowledge. Hence music was considered by these thinkers a cathartic force.[115] Few of these men knew anything of Jewish doctrines and customs; and it is characteristic that even Plutarch likened the God of the Jews to Dionysos, seriously believing that the 'feast of drawing water' during *Sukkot* was a kind of Bacchanalia.[116] Jewish music, too, seemed to him bacchic and orgiastic, and consequently unacceptable from the philosophical or ethical point of view. Nor was he the only writer of the time who felt so; it would be easy to duplicate his remarks by quotations from many lesser authors.

In general, the attitude of the Hellenistic philosophers showed a Janus-Head. One side viewed music as a science, like any other, to be taught by rational methods. It had certain links with the order of the universe and with its microcosmic reflection, the human soul. This is the Pythagorean conception. The other side emphasized the more elemental, emotional forces of music in connexion with its supposed magical powers. This is the Orphic-Dionysiac ideology. At the very end of the Hellenistic era, a great philosopher attempted a synthesis of both concepts. Plotinus wrote:

> The tune of an incantation, a significant cry, . . . these have . . . power over the soul drawing it with the force of . . . tragic sounds, for it is the reasonless soul, not the will or wisdom, that is beguiled by music, a form of sorcery which raises no question, whose enchantment, indeed, is welcomed. . . . Similarly with regard to prayers: the powers that answer to incantations do not act by will. . . . The prayer is answered by the mere fact that part and other part (of the cosmos) are wrought to one tone like a musical string which, plucked at one end, vibrates at the other also.[117]

The entire history of music could be represented as an incessant struggle between these two conceptions, the Orphic-tragic (Romanticism) and the Pythagorean (Medievalism, Classicism). In the music of the Church, these two conceptions are frequently at odds. Still, it is not possible simply to identify the Orphic-Dionysic style with the Orient, the scientific Pythagorean with the West; for both come from Asia and both have been assimilated by the Occident. For example: the inclusion of musical science in the Seven Liberal Arts did not, as generally assumed, originate in Europe, but in Nisibis, as T. Hermann has demonstrated.[118]

The rabbis were not influenced by these speculations to a very great extent. To them music was either a *melaha*, an occupation, or a *hochma*, a science.[119] As an art it had only one legitimate function: to praise God. As a science it was part of the propedeutics, analogous to the Western *quadrivium educationis*, together with mechanics, astronomy, optics, and mathematics.

Concerning the music of Hellenism, the rabbinic position was unequivocal: they viewed it with the greatest suspicion, rightly connecting it with the orgiastic cults of Asia Minor. The statement that Greek tunes had caused the apostasy of a famous rabbi, quoted above, speaks for itself.

The Early Church held, at least in the first two centuries, exactly the same principles as normative Judaism. But under the impact of Eastern Gnosticism and philosophic Hellenism it had to modify its rigid position. Yet it was a well-planned, strategic retreat, and sight of the ultimate goals was never lost.

The first weakening of these principles concerned instrumental music. In Byzantium, where the Emperor was *de facto* the head of the Church, kithara-playing survived, and later on the organ conquered the court, if not the liturgy. In fact, the organ was considered the secular instrument *par excellence*. The clergy, however, opposed its use in church and consequently no documents of instrumental music have survived in Byzantium.

Another instance of the flexible policy of the authorities is the case of non-scriptural hymns. Although the Council of Laodicea had banned them, they had a strong revival, and eventually became the greatest contribution of the Eastern Churches to Christian liturgy.

A characteristic aspect of that complex evolution is reflected in the varying viewpoints of the ecclesiastic authorities with regard to Jewish forms of prayer and song.

The great Eastern authors all seemed to fear the spell of Judaism. In all of their apologetic writings, warnings against just such temptations were sounded. During the incessant schisms within Eastern

Christianity, no terms of abuse were so common as 'Judaizer' or simply 'Jew'.[120]

This apprehension is absent in the leading circles of the Western Church. The Popes Damasus and Celestine championed the psalmodic forms, especially the responses and antiphons, borrowed from Jewish tradition.[121]

Apparently the Western authorities did not feel the need of impugning the survival of Jewish traditional forms in the liturgy of the Church. This more tolerant attitude was due to two causes of entirely diverse nature.

In the first place, the Roman Church was much more conservative than the Eastern sects. This fact is reflected in its whole tradition and is well known to every student of comparative liturgy. Since the oldest forms are all of Jewish origin, they have survived in the Latin Church by virtue of its consistent traditionalism. The intonations of the Hebrew letters *Aleph, Beth*, etc., at the beginning of the verses of Lamentations, or the correct (non-Latin) accentuation of Hebrew proper names in Gregorian chant are proofs of that inheritance. In the second place, a danger was absent in the Western orbit which beset many of the Asiatic Churches: the close proximity of great Jewish centres, whose eruditional and numerical powers were feared as inducements to Judaizing. Dr James Parkes sums up this antagonism in the following words:

The only explanation of his [Chrysostom's] bitterness . . . is the too close fellowship between Jews and Christians in Antioch. . . . It must be recognized that the ways of thinking of Jew and Christian were very similar. . . . The Jews of the East were in a much more powerful position than their Western brethren for influencing their neighbours. Europe at this period contained no great intellectual Jewish centre. Jewish scholars were largely concentrated in Palestine and Babylon.[122]

Certainly the Roman Fathers were in no way more tolerant than their Eastern colleagues when it came to *actions* against the Jews. But they were more conservative in matters of liturgical tradition and less perturbed by the threat of Jewish influence. Besides, the Eastern Christian population was more familiar with, and therefore more positively opposed to, Jewish customs and institutions.

THE FORCES
Static Forces

While this disquisition deals mainly with music of religious character, it would be a mistake to neglect the force of age-old ethnic ideas, which have, at times, in ecclesiastical garb, modified liturgical styles. It is, to quote just one instance, quite impossible for a student not to recognize the difference between Eastern and Western theologians. Although they belonged to one Church before the schism, their ways of thinking were vastly disparate. Thus, the dialectics of a Syrian Church Father resemble much more the Midrashic or Talmudic style of reasoning than the more factual Latin argumentation, notwithstanding his violent contempt for everything Jewish.

We shall now seek to show these static forces at work. They were sometimes of ethnic or local character, sometimes reflecting the usual conservatism of religious authorities.

These tendencies were strongest in the Roman and Armenian Churches. This is evident in the preservation of the oldest musical strata side by side with more recent features. The Roman conservatism was a result of the statesmanlike policy of the Church, which held the ethnic forces in balance. Only during a period of transition did regional traditions reign, such as the Gallican, Mozarabic, or German, in the fields of liturgy or musical notation. Finally they all were superseded by the centralizing policy of the Roman hierarchy.

Here a basic fact should be observed, important for the understanding of musical history: the Roman Church created in its liturgy the monumental framework which subsequent centuries filled with an abundance of artistic forms. As soon as the level of art-music was reached, the different styles of it reflected the varying tendencies of the periods. Gothic, Renaissance, Baroque, Classicism, and even Romanticism could evolve and express themselves in Church music. Even the secular music of Europe was fed by the Gregorian chant well into the seventeenth century. Yet its foundation remained unchanged.

No such development is noticeable in the Eastern Churches. There the level remained more or less static in the folk-song stage, and no art-music enriched the liturgy. Nor is it possible to discern definite stylistic changes or evolutions. This cannot be due to the divergent organization or theology of the Churches, since none of them, not even the Roman enclave in the Near East, has ever created or performed any art-music comparable to the European accomplishments. The conclusion is inevitable that not religious or dogmatic principles, but *ethnic* forces determined the stagnation in the East, the evolution in the West.

The very same partition goes through Jewish liturgical music. The

13

musical style of the oriental and Levantine Jews remained stationary and only in exceptional cases rose above the level of folk-lore. European, and especially Ashkenazic, Jewry accomplished its great artistic creations in the *Missinai* tunes of the late Middle Ages.[123] Subsequently, the liturgical music of European Jewry reflected in its course most of the tendencies and stylistic changes of the Christian church music.

Returning to the Eastern Churches, we find in the music of the Armenian Church a decidedly folkloristic character, quite unlike the Gregorian chant, where every folk-song was subjected to consistent stylization. The terminology, notation, and rendering of Armenian psalmody are akin to Hebrew cantillation in its earliest stages. Other phases of Armenian sacred music reflect the manifold features of its turbulent national history. Byzantine, Syrian, Turkish, and Russian elements were moulded into a not too homogeneous popular style.

The West Syrian Churches consistently resisted the sway of their Arab environment, at least in their musical traditions. Their chants represent a decidedly older and differently organized style than those of their Arab neighbours. Again the Church was the preserving power, in this case supported by the ancient cultural bonds with Byzantium and Palestine.

The nature and history of the Nestorian liturgy and its music is quite different. Its oldest sources, above all its calendar and its lectionary, show traces of very ancient and authentic tradition.[124] The musical influences, as far as they can be determined, seem to be more secular than ecclesiastic in origin. It is Iranian culture, whose superior creative power slowly squeezed out of East Syrian Christianity the more systematic but weaker Byzantine forces, and this in spite of the great tradition of the Nisibis academy. Here local perseverance prevailed over the infiltration from the West. True, Nestorian doctrine and liturgical forms are Christian; but, under the surface, old Iranian ideas were at work for many centuries.

While the Persians had a musical culture of their own, it was neither highly developed before the Arabian epoch nor was it supported by the Iranian Mazda religion. The Persian kings had to import music and musicians; even the crown-prince Bahrām Ghūr (*ca.* 430) was sent by Yezdegerd I to the Arabian Lakmid court, in Al-Hī ra, to be educated in music.[125] Later on, the young prince colonized ten thousand singers and

dancers 'from Hindustan all over the country'.[126] Thus Persian civilization does not seem to have created as much music as sculpture or archi-
tecture. This lack becomes conspicuous in Christian worship where the
Syrian liturgy is celebrated by and for a semi-Persian population. We
have already mentioned the great academy at Nisibis where Scripture
and its interpretation were scientifically studied.[127] Its founders were
Bar Saoumâ and Narsai, both Syrians.[128] Narsai's liturgy and homilies
lack almost all references to singing, excepting the cantillation of Scripture. Even the Sanctus is, in his liturgy, a curt answer of the people.[129]
    The cause of that silent type of worship, in which the koinonia
apparently did not play a great part, is probably Mazdaism and its
individualistic-esoteric liturgy. All this was anti-Hellenic and anti-Jewish,
propagated by the Sassanids.[130]
    The Nestorian Church was surrounded by adversaries. Considered
heretic by the Syrian and Byzantine Church, it felt the hard rule of the
Sassanid dynasty which attempted to impose Mazdaism upon it, and
in its turn, it looked upon the Jews of Mesopotamia as its enemies, theologically and nationally. Cantillation of Scripture, the oldest musical
tradition, was preserved, while new elements, due to constant internal
and external pressure, could not survive.[131] The theology was under the
spell of the West, its liturgical forms under the influence of the East,
chiefly Iran. This antinomy of forces, theological doctrine versus folk
custom, resulted in a stalemate and ultimately in the century-long
stagnation of Nestorianism.

Dynamic Forces

    After the collapse of the West Roman Empire, only one great state
was capable of carrying the banner of Christianity through the ruins of
the old Commonwealth, namely, Byzantium. The Roman Church
limited its activities in Europe to missionary tasks until the tenth century, while Byzantium expanded northward and its Church conquered
Russia. Byzantine liturgy and music became the pattern of the Russian
Orthodox Church.
    Its music displays, besides old Slavonic features, both Hellenistic and
Jewish traits. The bulk of the Známmeny Raspéw (orthodox song) is
syllabic, like Hellenistic and early Byzantine music, but final melismata,
borrowed from psalmody, occur regularly. The modality corresponds

to Byzantine and to Western Oriental systems.[132] This also holds true for other Slavonic church music, in particular for Macedonian and Bulgarian chant. There we encounter even the Hellenic-Jewish *Tropos Spondeiakos* alluded to by Clement of Alexandria.[133]

There is still another element common to the music of Byzantium, of the Arabs, Turks, South-east Russians, and of the Eastern Jews: the Phrygian Mode with augmented second. The Arabic *maqamat Hedjaz* and *Husseini* contain this characteristic interval, and it is equally familiar in Turkish folk-songs, Byzantine, and Russian chants. The Eastern Jews believe—erroneously—that this mode, called *Ahaba Rabba*, originated in Palestine in pre-Christian times. We do not know the actual source of that expressive mode, but there are many indications that it is not very old, possibly not older than the invasion of the Turks in the twelfth century.

Under the cloak of Hellenistic scholarship, Byzantium succeeded in transmitting a good deal of its musical practice to the Western Church. Today some scholars are convinced that also the Western system of the eight Church Tones evolved in Byzantium, before it was transmitted to, and transformed in, Italy and France. If the Western structure of Church Tones came via Byzantium, it certainly did not originate there; no Middle-Greek treatises on music prior to the eleventh century are extant. The little we do know of their musical theories has reached us through Syriac, occasionally through Arabic, sources. The main feature of that system, the eight Church Tones, occurs first in Syriac sources, where it had an originally liturgical connotation.[134] Farmer has investigated some of these sources, and has reached the conclusion that Syrians, Jews, and pre-Islamic Arabs shared the theory of modality and stimulated its systematization.[135]

This writer came to the same conclusion when he found that some of the most important terms of Byzantine musical theory, the *enechemata*, were borrowed from the Hebrew. They were paradigms, used for the different modes of final or punctuating melismata, mostly words derived from the Hebrew *Nin'ua'*. In Hebrew also, the word has a musical significance.[136]

Here we are confronted with one of the thorniest problems of musicology: namely the genesis of the *Octoechos*, or the principle of the eight modes of the Church. An extensive research of this question would warrant a voluminous study and reach far beyond the scope of this chapter. None the less, the problem is of such great consequence that a brief excursus is obligatory.

In modern musicology, there are three principle trends of thinking with regard to this subject. (1) The older view, as represented by Gevaert, Reinach, Jeannin, and most of the French scholars. These consider the Syro-Byzantine conception of the eight modes a natural derivation from the classic Greek system of the *harmoniai*. (2) In sharp contradistinction thereto, R. Lachmann, A. Baumstark, K. Wachsmann, and H. G. Farmer emphasize the liturgic-cultic origin of the Syrian *Octoechos* and doubt, at least as regards the first five centuries, a decisive Greek influence upon the modality of pre-Gregorian chant which, in their opinion, was almost wholly oriental in form and substance. (3) A mediating position is held by scholars like Curt Sachs, Peter Wagner, E. Wellesz, G. Reese, U. Bomm and others, who assume that the systems of all modes were the results of constant repetition of certain melodic formulas. These passages of sacred folk-lore crystallized in the course of centuries to fixed phrases, the nuclear cells of the modes. These were then superimposed upon recurrent liturgical rubrics and connected (erroneously) with the Greek *harmoniai*.[137]

With due respect for the fine work of these scholars, I venture to say that some of the most important aspects of the problem have been overlooked. Since the matter is of great consequence, we shall treat it in the next chapter.

NOTES CHAPTER I

1. Cf. Strzygowsky, *Asiens Bildende Kunst*, p. 596.

2. Dealing with a symbiosis of several nations during a period of seven or eight centuries, it was necessary to simplify the manifold sources into a few main categories. Since most of the really relevant sources will be discussed in detail later on, the danger of oversimplification is not too imminent.

3. Cf. Plutarch, *De Musica*, Chapter 17, quoting Plato.

4. Cf. H. Riemann, *Handbuch der Musikgeschichte*, I, 1, pp. 163 ff, also Th. Reinach, article 'Musica' in Daremberg-Saglio, *Dictionnaire des antiquités grecques et romaines*, 2, pp. 2074–88. A far more positive attitude toward the music of Hellenism in W. Vetter's article on 'Music' in Pauly-Wissowa, *Realenzyklopädie des klassischen Altertums*.

5. Plutarch, *Quaest. conviv.* 7, 7, 4, 712. About origin and conception of the paean, see F. Schwenn, 'Gebet und Opfer' in *Religionswissenschaftliche Bibliothek*, ed. W. Streitberg (Heidelberg, 1927), pp. 18 f.

6. Plutarch, *De superstitione* 13, 171. The question is fully discussed in J. Quasten, *Musik und Gesang in den Kulten der heidnischen Antike und der christlichen Fruehzeit*, pp. 36 ff.

7. Exod. 28:35. The best interpretations of that mysterious passage in H. Gressmann, *Musik und Musikinstrumente im Alten Testament*, pp. 6 ff, where also the older literature is given. Of recent scholars Curt Sachs, *History of Musical Instruments*, and Solomon Finesinger, 'The Musical Instruments of the Bible' in *HUCA* (1926), follow in principle Gressmann's explanation.

8. See also B. Ugolinus, *Thesaurus Antiquitatum Sacrarum*, XXXII, 1057 f.
9. Ibid.
10. Cf. Gressmann, op. cit., p. 9.
11. Cf. Arnobius, *Adversus nationes* (*CSEL*, IV, 265 ff.)
12. *Martyrium Theodoti* (*Studi e Testi*, ed. de Cavalieri, VI, 70).
13. *Fasti* 4: Exululant comites, furiosaque tibia flatur
    Et feriunt molles taurea terga manus.
14. By far the best accumulation of ancient sources about the use of percussion instruments in antiquity is still the extensive treatise of Friedrich Adolph Lämpe in Ugolinus, op. cit., XXXII, col. 867–1092, where hundreds of quotations are given.
15. The original Greek text in M. Berthelot and C. Ruelle, *Collection des anciens alchimistes grecs* II, pp. 219, 434. Also C. Wessely, 'Neue Zauberpapyri', *Kais. Akademie der Wissenschaften* (Vienna, 1893); C. Høeg, 'La Théorie de la musique byzantine', in *Revue des études grecques* (1922), pp. 321–34, and, most extensively, Klaus Wachsmann, *Untersuchungen zum vorgregorianischen Gesang* (Regensburg, 1935), pp. 50–77. It cannot be said that our present knowledge permits an exact evaluation of these magic manuscripts in terms of music. Not even knowing whether or not Zosimos of Panopolis, our main source, was a Christian, we should be most cautious in our hypothesis, especially since patristic literature shows not the slightest trace of any influence of such alchemistic-magic sects.
16. Cf. L. Blau. *Alt-Jüdisches Zauberwesen* (Strasbourg, 1898).
17. This is the contention of A. Gastoué, which today cannot seriously be disputed. Cf. A. Gastoué, *Les Origines du chant romain*, pp. 27–33; also Dom Leclercq, article 'Alphabeth vocalique' in *DACH*.
18. Cf. S. Krauss, *Talmudische Archaeologie*, III, p. 276, n. 43.
19. Cf. *Jer. Sota*, 7, 2, 21.
20. Cf. Krauss, op. cit., III, p. 85.
21. Ibid., pp. 86–88.
22. Ibid., p. 91.
23. Ibid., p. 93.
24. B. *Chagiga*, 15b.
25. Cf. Philo, *De spec. leg.*, II, No. 193 (V 114, Cohn-Wendland); Idem., *De spec. leg.*, I, No. 28; Idem., *De plantatione*, No. 148.
26. Idem., *De vita Mosis*, II, No. 239.
27. Idem., *De spec. leg.*, I, No. 271. Paul turns against this conception in I Cor. 14:14–19; Rom. 10:9–11. Without mentioning Philo's name, it is obvious that Paul considers Philo's ideal of silent prayer insufficient.
28. *Oracula Sibyllina*, ed. Geffcken, 8, 113, p. 147.
29. Cf. Gressmann, op. cit., p. 29. He writes: 'Die Flöte, die in älterer Zeit auch bei religiösen Gelegenheiten wie Wallfahrten und Festreigen Verwendung fand, wurde später infolge religiöser Scheu aus dem Kultus entfernt. In der Chronik fehlt sie ganz, nach dem Talmud spielt sie beim Gottesdienst nur eine beschränkte Rolle . . . Das später fixierte Gesetz hat die Flöten ebenso wie den Reigen um den Altar . . . mit Stillschweigen übergangen'.
30. About this sect see Gressmann, *Die orientalischen Religionen im hellenistisch-römischen Zeitalter*, pp. 110–24; also P. Reitzenstein, *Die hellenistischen Mysterienreligionen*, pp. 105–8; and F. Cumont, *Acad. des Inscript. Comptes rendus*, 1906, p. 63. The best epigraphic sources in Ramsay's comprehensive work, *The Cities and Bishoprics of Phrygia*, I, pp. 639–53. Two of the arch-priestesses of Zeus Sabazios were the Jewesses Julia Severa and Servenia Cornuta.
31. Like the *kinnor* upon which frivolous persons play in B. *Sanhedrin* 101a.
32. Clement of Alexandria, *Paedagogus*, II, 4.
33. Arnobius, *Adversus Nationes*, (*CSEL*, IV, 270); also Gregory of Nazianzus, *Oratio* V, 25, (*PG*, XXXV, 708–9).
34. Clement of Alexandria, *Paedagogus* II, 4; Eusebius, *In Ps. 91* (*PG*, XXIII, 1172); Chrysostom, *In Ps. 149* (*PG*, LV, 494).
35. Cf. F. J. Doelger, *Sol Salutis* (Münster, 1930), pp. 5, 78–79, *et passim*. The Catholic scholar treats the delicate subject with a frankness which is as admirable as his profundity.
36. Cf. *Kyriale Vaticanum*, No. VI, 'Kyrie rex genitor'.

37. Cf. R. Eisler, *Orphisch-Dionysische Mysteriengedanken*, pp. 15, 46, 353, 395, *et passim*; also O. Ursprung, *Die katholische Kirchenmusik*, p. 9.

38. In *Sammelbände der Internationalen Musikgesellschaft*, I (1899-1900), pp. 54 ff; also the same author's *Musique populaire arménienne* (Paris, 1925); see also E. Wellesz, 'Die armenische Messe und ihre Musik', *Jahrbuch d. Musikbibliothek Peters* (Leipzig, 1920).

39. Cf. *Paléographie musicale*, I, pp. 19 ff.

40. Of the vast literature on the Dead Sea Scrolls we cite only: *Israel Explor. Journal*, 1950-55; *JBL*, 1949-52; *Theol. Rundschau*, XIX (1951), pp. 97-154.

41. Cf. H. Abert, *Die Musikanschauung des Mittelalters* (Halle, 1905).

42. Dom J. Parisot, *Rapport sur une mission scientifique*, etc. (Paris, 1899); Jeannin, *Mélodies liturgiques syriennes et chaldéennes* (1924-28); also *OC*, N.S. III (1913), 3. In broad historical aspects the problem is treated by E. Wellesz, *Aufgaben und Probleme auf dem Gebiete der byzantinischen und orientalischen Kirchenmusik* (1923), pp. 95 ff, and A. Baumstark, *Die christlichen Literaturen des Orients*, p. 119. The ancient ethnic traditions of East Syria and Iran underwent a decisive transformation under the hands of Graeco-Syrian monks. It is with this thought in mind that we shall later on attempt to analyse the structure of some of the Aramaean hymns. While no ancient or even medieval documents of these melodies are extant, it may be assumed that they belong essentially to a fairly old stratum. Their occasional resemblances to Gregorian formulas seem to confirm such an assumption. See our examples 9a, b, 10a, b; *infra*, p. 343.

43. Quoted after A. Gastoué, *Les Origines du chant romain*, pp. 40-41, who gives the best transcription.

44. Quoted by C. Sachs, *Die Musik der Antike* (Potsdam, 1928—in Bücken's *Handbuch der Musikwissenschaft*), p. 16.

45. *LU*, p. 1253.

46. Cf. C. Sachs, op. cit., p. 13.

47. *LU*, p. 29; cf. *supra*, n. 36.

48. Quoted by H. Besseler, *Die Musik des Mittelalters und der Renaissance* (Potsdam, 1931—in Bücken's *Handbuch der Musikwissenschaft*), pp. 45 ff.

49. Quoted from *Graduale Romanum* and E. Werner, 'Preliminary Notes for a Comparative Study of Catholic and Jewish Musical Punctuation', *HUCA*, XV (1940). (a) IT, I, p. 71, No. 27; (b) IT, II, p. 115, No. 103; (c) IT, II, p. 46, No. 1.

50. Quoted by Idelsohn, *Manual of Musical Illustrations* (from MS 4E, No. 81, in the Library of the Hebrew Union College).

51. Tabulation of the *Tropos Spondeiakos*, quoted in excerpt from E. Werner, 'The Doxology in Synagogue and Church', *HUCA*, XIX (1946), pp. 333 ff, where all sources are given. See also my article 'The Attitude of the Church Fathers Towards Hebrew Psalmody', *Review of Religion* (May 1943).

52. Antiphonale Ambrosianum, or *LU*, p. 1541, in slightly different version.

53. Cf. IT, I (Yemenites), p. 71.

54. Cf. Dom Parisot, op. cit., No. 321.

55. Cf. *JM*, p. 63, No. 9.

56. Cf. Oscar Fleischer, *Neumenstudien*, II, 22-23.

57. Cf. Parisot, op. cit., Nos. 350, 62, 316; *LU*, p. 261.

58. Cf. *JM*, p. 52, No. 2.

59. Rev. 5:8. Cf. also the famous passage of the Acts of Thomas where the female Hebrew flute-player enchants the Apostle into prophetic ecstasy. See H. Gressmann, *Die Musikinstrumente des AT*, p. 16.

60. Clement of Alexandria, *Paedagogus*, II, 4.

61. Philo, *Legum Allegoriae*, I, 5, 14; (I, 64 ed. Cohn). Later on, he likens the lyre to the universe and the microcosm of the human soul.

62. Cf. F. Leitner, *Der Volksgesang im jüdischen und christlichen Altertum*, p. 261, who quotes W. Riedel, *Die Kirchenrechtsquellen des Patriarchats Alexandrien* (1900).

63. CAF, III, II, I; VIII, 10, 10: II, 28, 5; VI, 17, 2; VII, 45, 2, *et passim*.

64. *PG*, XXXIII, 804.

65. *Peregrinatio Silviae*, ed. Heraeus, cap. 34, 73.

66. Cf. WGM, I, pp. 17 ff.

67. Cf. *supra*, p. 54.

68. Cf. E. M. Kaufmann, *Handbuch der altchristlichen Epigraphik*, p. 272.

69. Cf. Athanasius, *Ep. ad Marcellum* 12 (*PG*, XXVII, 24).

70. E. F. Leitner, op. cit., p. 196.

71. We refer here to the basic forms, not to their later elaborations in the Occident. On European transformations, see *infra*, pp. 511 ff.

72. Leitner, op. cit., p. 263.

73. Cf. P. Quasten, op. cit., pp. 123 ff.

74. Ibid., p. 124.

75. Isidore's reasons against female singing are almost literally identical with the Talmudic formulation. A woman's voice is a sexual incitement (*B. Ber.* 24a): 'urged into the excitement of the passions through the sweetness of melody. . . .'; quoted by P. Quasten, op. cit., p. 121.

76. Ibid., p. 120.   77. Ibid., p. 119.   78. *B. Sota*, 48a.

79. Cf. *Peregrinatio Silviae*, 24, I: '. . . descendere omnes monazontes et parthenae, et non solum hii, sed et laici praeter viri et mulieres . . . dicuntur hymni et psalmi responduntur. . . .'

80. Cf. Sozomen, *Hist. Eccl.* III, 20, (*PG*, LXVII, 1100); also Theodore of Mopsuestia (*PG*, CXXXIX, 1390). The first Christian author to claim the Syrian origin of the antiphon is Socrates, *Hist. Eccl.*, VI, Chapter 8 (*PG*, LXVII, 692). It should not be forgotten that, at the time referred to (*ca.* 270), Jewry was predominant in Antioch and probably had introduced there the old familiar antiphonal practice.

81. Cf. P. Odilo Heiming, *Syrische Enjane und Griechische Kanones* (Münster, 1932), pp. 40 ff.

82. Cf. H. Abert, 'Ein neuentdeckter frühchristlicher Hymnus', *ZFM*, IV (1922), pp. 524 ff. Also O. Ursprung, 'Der Hymnus aus Oxyrynchus', *Theologie und Glaube*, XVIII (1926), pp. 387 ff. The original text in facsimile in *The Oxyrynchus Papyri* XV, ed. B. Grenfell and A. S. Hunt (London, 1922), No. 1786, pp. 21 ff.

83. Cf. Dom Parisot, op. cit., No. 62, p. 67; No. 350, p. 240.

84. *LU*, p. 261.

85. Cf. Dom Parisot, loc. cit.

86. Cf. *Studies of the Research Institute for Hebrew Poetry* (Jerusalem, 1936), II, p. 227.

87. G. Reese, in his splendid work, *Music in the Middle Ages*, p. 68, gives a definition of Syriac meters which can easily lead to misunderstandings. He writes: '. . . correspondence between lines being obtained through equality not in the total number of syllables in each but in the number of tonic accents'. This point is not at all certain. W. Meyer, op. cit., p. 115, writes: 'Durch jenes semitische Vorbild wurden diese Völker angeregt, die Quantität der Silben nicht mehr zu beachten, . . . dagegen auf die Silbenzahl zu achten. . . .' and p. 108: 'Dennoch ist nicht der Wortakzent an die Stelle der Versakzente getreten; . . . dagegen wird die Silbenzahl der Zeilen berechnet und mit einigen Schwankungen eine bestimmte Zahl festgehalten'. The whole theory needs still further elucidation; it is based upon Pitra's erroneous conjecture that the Syriac and Byzantine hymns with acrostics and isosyllabic verses are a legacy of the Synagogue. The more recent literature on the problem after Hoelscher's *Syrische Verkunst* was not accessible to me. See also E. Wellesz, op. cit., pp. 48–60.

88. Cf. Sozomen, *Life of Ephraem*, III, Chapter 16.

89. Cf. W. Meyer, op. cit., p. 119. Note the psalmodic type of the *Te Deum*, Ex. 8a (*supra*, p. 342).

90. Cf. No. 10a and 10b (p. 343): they follow the same pattern.

91. Cf. Augustus Hahn, *Chrestomathia Syriaca, sive S. Ephraemi carmina selecta* (Leipzig, 1825); see also H. Burgess, *Select hymns and homilies by Ephraem Syrus* (London, 1853), p. xlvii.

92. A. Rossbach and R. Westphal, *Griechische Metrik*, III, p. 493.

93. Ibid., III, pp. 494–6. The poem, by Yannai, quoted *supra*, p. 349, is likewise a heptasyllabus, and its metre a logaoedic tripody.

94. Yet Assemani already doubts the originality of Ephraem's heptasyllabus; he writes: 'Errant quoque, qui unum dumtaxat carminum genus, videlicet septem syllabarum,

Ephraemo tribuunt. . . .' (I, p. 61). And: 'Hallucinantur enim, qui Ephraemum asserunt excogitasse versus heptasyllabos, Narsetem hexasyllabos, Balaeum pentasyllabos . . ., nam longe ante hos auctores iam Syri carminibus huiusmodi utebantur ut Bardesanes et Harmonius.' (Ibid.)

95. For a full discussion of the Hallelujah see my study 'The Doxology in Church and Synagogue', *HUCA* (1946), pp. 323 ff.

96. Cf. Cassian (*PL*, LIX, 77): 'Quidam enim vicenos seu tricenos psalmos, et hos ipsos antiphonarum protelatos melodiis et adiunctione quarundam modulationun debere singulis noctibus censuerunt.'

97 (a) IT, VII, p. 10, No. 29; (b) WGM, III, p. 388; (c) WGM, III, p. 389; (d) WGM, III, p. 401.

98 (a) Gastoué, op. cit., p. 29; (b) WGM, III, p. 387

99. Dom Leclercq, in *Dictionnaire d'archéologie chrétienne*, article 'Alphabeth vocalique des gnostiques'.

100. Cf. WGM, I, p. 57. 'The highly developed type of musical punctuation may very well have its origin in the practice of Jewish precentors'; also G. Reese, op. cit., p. 63: 'The singing of the Alleluia was doubtless taken over from the Synagogue'; also K. Wachsmann, op. cit., p. 118: 'Ihre Bedeutung [of the ancient Jewish chants] hat nunmehr den Weg in die Literatur gefunden, die die belegte Gemeinsamkeit jüdischer und gregorianischer Weisen allenthalben anerkennt und ihrem Bestande einverleibt hat.'

101. *JM*, pp. 40, 42, 47.

102. This becomes even more obvious through the neume *tristropha* upon 'Israel', which always indicates a simplification of an originally melismatic texture to a more syllabic phrasing. Cf. WGM, II, pp. 123 ff.

103. Cf. WGM, III, pp. 366 ff.

104. Clement of Alexandria, *Paedagogus*, II, Chapter 4. For a full discussion of that significant passage, see E. Werner, 'Notes on the Attitude of the Early Church Fathers towards Hebrew Psalmody', in *Review of Religion* (May 1943), p. 349, where also numerous musical illustrations are quoted.

105 (a) After WGM, III, p. 239; (b) ibid.

106. Cf. my article on 'Leading Motifs in Synagogue and Plain Song', in *Proceedings of the American Musicological Society*, (Detroit 1946).

107. Cf. WGM, III, pp. 376 ff: 'The technique of wandering melismata is an ancient heritage of Synagogue psalmody'; ibid., p. 396. On the *hirmoi* and the related Syrian forms, see G. Reese, op. cit., pp. 66, 78 ff.

108. In Gerbert, *Scriptores de musica sacra* I, 20a: 'Nisi enim ab homine memoria teneantur, soni pereunt, quia scribi non possunt'.

109. The notation of the Cod. Ephraemi Syri (Nat. Libr., Paris, Greek div. Cod. resc. 9) is, according to recent examinations, considerably more recent than the text of the palimpsest, which originated in the fifth century. Cf. C. Høeg, *La Notation ekphonétique* (Copenhagen), pp. 107–8.

110. Cf. F. Praetorius, *Über die Herkunft der hebräischen Akzente*, and *Reply to Renée Gregory* (Berlin, 1901–2). See also E. Werner, 'Preliminary Notes for a Comparative Study of Catholic and Jewish Musical Punctuation', *HUGA* (1940), pp. 338 ff.

111. Cf. Cassiodorus, *De inst. divin. litterarum* (*PL*, LXX, 1105): . . . 'sicut apud Alexandriam multo tempore fuisse traditur institutum, nunc etiam in Nisibi civitate Syrorum ab Hebraeis sedulo fertur exponi, collatis expensis in urbe Romana professos doctores scholae potius acciperent Christianae. . . .' See also P. Kahle, *Masoreten des Westens*, p. 52.

112. Cf. Moberg, *Bar Hebraeus' Buch der Strahlen*, II, p. 108; also T. Weiss, *Zur ostsyrischen Laut-und Akzentlehre* (1935), pp. 29 ff. Also E. Wellesz, 'Die byzantinischen Lektionszeichen', *ZFM*, XI (1929), p. 527; and E. Werner, op. cit., p. 339 (*supra*, n. 110).

113. The Latin neumes borrowed a good deal from the primitive grammatical accents (which served as models for some of them) and the Byzantine and Hebrew accents. But the relationship is rather complex. While, e.g. the Latin *quilisma* equals the Byzantine *kylisma*, which in turn is identical with the Hebrew *shalshelet*, their functions are clearly different.

114. Cf. J. Strzygowsky's monumental work *Asiens Bildende Kunst*, pp. 715 f, also pp. 501 ff. See also the same author's 'Ravenna als Vorort aramäischer Kunst', *OC*, NF. V, pp. 83 ff.

115. Cf. W.-S., pp. 274 ff.

116. Plutarch, *Quaest. conviv.*, IV, 5-6. Also in Reinach, *Texts d'auteurs grec et romains relatif au Judaisme*, p. 144.

117. Cf. S. Mackenna, *Plotinus on the Nature of the Soul* (Fourth Ennead) (1924), p. 96. The metaphor of the string is borrowed from Philo, *De Somn.*, III, 212.

118. Against P. H. Láng, *Music in Western Civilization*, p. 59. The author includes Greece and even the oldest strata of plainsong in Western Civilization, but neglects entirely the oriental basis of the whole Mediterranean culture. Cf. T. Hermann, 'Die Schule von Nisibis vom 5.-7. Jahrhundert', *ZFNW*, XXV (1926), pp. 89-126.

119. See W-S, pp. 272 ff.

120. Cf. J. Parkes, *The Conflict of the Church and the Synagogue*, pp. 300 ff.

121. *PL*, CXXVIII, 74, 225; also Jerome, *Ep. 20 ad Damasum*.

122. Cf. J. Parkes, op. cit., pp. 164, 274 ff.

123. These, in turn, betray certain traces of Burgundian composers of the thirteenth to fourteenth centuries. On the other hand, the liturgy of the Church absorbed Jewish ideas well up to the tenth century.

124. Cf. A. Baumstark, 'Nichtevangelische syrische Perikopenordnungen des ersten Jahrtausends', *Liturgiegeschichtliche Forschungen*, III (Münster, 1921), Chapter III. See also the examples 9a, c, and 10a, b, *supra*, pp. 342-3.

125. Cf. H. G. Farmer, *Historical Facts for the Arabian Musical Influence* (London, 1930), p. 52. The recent findings of Iranian art would lead us to expect parallel discoveries in music. But these expectations have not been fulfilled as yet and are not likely to be realized. The reasons are manifold, and not only lack of musical notation. E. Wellesz, following Strzygowsky's ingenious lead, promised decisive musical discoveries through careful study of Manichaean-Soghdic manuscripts. Yet these manuscripts originated in a time when Byzantines, Armenians, Romans, and Jews had already well developed their respective ecphonetic notations. Beyond this nothing has been established to vindicate the great hopes which were set upon Iranian music.

126. Cf. H. G. Farmer, op. cit., p. 271, quoting Mirkhwand *Raudat al-Safa*, I, II, 357. The Persian text in *Histoire des sassanides* (Paris, 1843), p. 217.

127. E. Sachau, 'Die Chronik von Arbela', *Sitzungsberichte der Preussischen Akademie der Wissenschaften*, Hist. Phil. Klasse (1915), pp. 91 ff.

128. Ibid., p. 86. Cf. also Chabot, 'Schola Nisibena', *Journal asiatique*, VIII (1896), pp. 43 ff.

129. Cf. Dom R. H. Connolly and E. Bishop, 'The Liturgical Homilies of Narsai', in *Texts and Studies* (Cambridge, 1916), VIII, p. 117. See *supra*, Chapter IV, p. 116.

130. C. Sachs's statement, 'The Persians had been under strong Hellenistic influence until the dynasty of the Seleucids (226-641) brought a nationalist anti-Greek reaction' (*Rise of Music in the Ancient World*, p. 278), is correct, but not quite accurate. I suppose the author had the Sassanids in mind when he wrote 'Seleucids'. I suspect that the Iranian cult of the *chthonic* deities, which must be adored in silence, was the reason for the lack of music. Cf. F. Cumont, *Oriental Religions*, pp. 151 ff.

131. Note the resemblance of Ex. 10d and 10e on p. 343 (instances of cantillation).

132. Cf. P. Panoff, *Die altslavische Volks-und Kirchenmusik* (Potsdam, 1932—in Bücken's *Handbuch der Musikwissenschaft*), p. 14.

133. See *supra*, p. 341, also the examples 16, 17, 18, 22 in Panoff's work.

134. Cf. E. W. Brooks, *James of Edessa*, p. 6; the Hymns of Severus of Antioch, in *PO*, VI, (1911), and VII, (1911), pp. 597-802.

135. Cf. H. G. Farmer, op. cit., pp. 55, 60, 163-4, 307.

136. Cf. E. Werner, 'The Psalmodic Formula *Neannoe* and its Origin', *MQ* XXVIII (January 1942), pp. 93 ff.

137. Cf. O. J. Gombosi, 'Studien zur Tonartenlehre des frühen Mittelalters' in *Acta Musicologica*, X, XI, XII (1938-40) and C. Sachs, *The Rise of Music in the Ancient World* (New York and London, 1943), pp. 223-38.

CHAPTER TWO

The Origin of the Eight Modes of
Music (Octoechos)

R. Judah ben Ilai said: 'And how many strings does the Kinnor have?'
Seven, as it is said: 'Seven times a day do I praise Thee'. And for the
days of the Messiah eight, as it is said: 'To the Chief Musician upon
the eighth mode (sheminit)'.—(*Midrash Tehillim*, Ps. 81:9.)
Socrates: Then, if these and these modes are to be used only in our
songs and melodies, we shall not want multiplicity of notes or a pan-
harmonic scale.—Plato, *Republic*, Book III.
Die tiefsinnige Wahnvorstellung kam zuerst in der Person des Socrates
zur Welt, jener unerschütterliche Glaube, dass das Denken, an dem
Leitfaden der Causalität, bis in die tiefsten Abgründe des Seins reiche,
und dass das Denken das Sein nicht nur zu erkennen, sondern sogar zu
Korrigieren im Stande sei. Dieser erhabene metaphysische Wahn ist als
Instinkt der Wissenschaft beigegeben und fuehrt sie immer und immer
wieder zu ihren Grenzen, an denen sie in *Kunst* umschlagen muss: *auf
welche es eigentlich bei diesem Mechanismus abgesehen ist.*—Nietzsche,
Die Geburt der Tragödie aus dem Geist der Musik.

I

THE existence of modes in the music of all Oriental cultures is a well-
known fact. Their superimposition upon Occidental music through the
chants of the Roman Church was an event of far greater weight than is
generally recognized. Since this development took place under the
various mantles of music, theology, philosophy, and mathematics, apart
from the truly overwhelming consequences it has wrought upon the
history of music, it has left its traces throughout Western civilization in
manifold ways.

While the general principle of modality is an organic out-growth of
Oriental life,[1] it is the selection of and limitation to eight modes, which
have played so important a part in musical tradition, that confronts the
student with some fundamental problems. Not only do these eight
modes vary from country to country, from liturgy to liturgy, and from

age to age, but there is ample reason to doubt their actual existence as a phenomenon, outside of *a posteriori* constructions by medieval theorists. Recently some scholars have even reached the conclusion that in many cases the categorization of an individual tune under one of the eight general modes was an act of artificial and rigid systematization rather than one of simple classification.[2]

It is our conviction that the principle of eight modes is one of the oldest attempts of mankind to organize the chaotic and to select with discrimination. It will be the task of this chapter to explore the origin of the eight modes and to show how much or how little the idea of an eightfold modality has been in accordance with the actual practice of notated music.

Since the idea of modality has found many expressions in many languages, in the course of twenty-five centuries a great deal of confusion has resulted from the wide variance in the terms used for the word 'mode'. It will, therefore, be useful to examine briefly the terminology of the issue. This can be done here only in a summary way; when we study the individual sources, the terms involved will be discussed extensively.

Hebrew Terms:	*n'gina, niggun, ta'am, ne'ima, lahan* (Arab.)
Greek Terms:	*tonos* (?), *tropos* (?), *eidos* (?), *harmonia, nomos*
Latin Terms of the MA:	*tonus, modus, tropus, modulatio*
Byzantine Terms:	*echos, octoechos* (8 modes), *tropos*
Arabic Terms:	*nagham, ghina', anwa', maqam*
Syriac Terms:	*qala, 'ikhadia* (from Byzant. *octoechos*)

Since the so-called Church Tones, today a system of scales, have been as often confused with genuine modes as, vice versa, the ancient Greek and Byzantine modes with certain scales or 'species of octaves', it will be necessary to investigate first the possibility that there is a genuine connexion between octave scale and mode. Only when we shall have arrived at a clear distinction will it be possible to trace the various systems of modality. The tangle of the terminology concerning modes and modality is truly unbelievable. Each century and its writers added to, and increased, the confusion. Only in the last fifty years a group of scholars have, through their profound studies in this field, been able to clear up a good deal of the accumulated maze. There is no need here to discuss in detail the methods that they applied to the solution of the tangle: let it suffice to set down the main results of their efforts. The most important contributions to the better understanding of the terminological problem came from the following scholars: H. Riemann,[3] A. Gastoué,[4] Dom Jeannin,[5] P. Wagner,[6] C. Sachs,[7] O. Gombosi,[8] and E. Wellesz.[9] In the following paragraphs we cite briefly their main conclusions with reference to the respective terms:

Octave: A clear distinction should be made between the octave as an acoustical relation 1:2—between the fundamental tone and the first overtone, on the one hand, and the octave as designing the range of a diatonic scale, on the other. This distinction was sharply established by Riemann and this writer.[10]

Species of Octaves (Oktavengattung): The ancient Greeks developed a system of scales with subsequent divisions into transposed keys. Sachs has shown, in irrefutable manner, that the terms 'scale' and 'key' are by no means interchangeable. The scales, themselves, bore certain regional names such as Dorian, Phrygian, etc.[11] The *Oktavgattungen* never, originally, had the function of tonal categories in the sense of modalities.[12]

Tropus: In ancient Greek theory, this is a species of octaves but not *modus* or *harmonia*.[13] Sachs and Gombosi interpret it similarly.[14]

Modus: In Roman Church theory, the system of Church Tones was based upon certain psalmodic paradigms and later was mistakenly confused with species of octaves (*tropi*), etc. Gombosi has demonstrated that, up to the tenth century of our era, the Church Tones were in no way connected with the species of octaves.[15]

Echos, Octoechos: Today, this is the Byzantine system of eight Church Tones, but, originally, it was a liturgical designation of eight individual melodic patterns, each of which was used for one of eight Sundays.[16] The system is older than that of the Roman Church Tones. It represents best what is today understood as a musical mode.

Church Tone: This was originally a system of eight Psalm Tones, but it was later confused with the octave species. Today it is used in the meaning of the various species of octave-scales as employed and classified in the Gregorian chant.

Contrafact (Nomos?): This is a stylized melodic type, which, in the course of time, becomes adaptable to various texts. Thus, the slightly paraphrased tune of 'God Save the King' is, as it were, the *nomos* of 'My Country, 'tis of Thee', the latter tune being a mere contrafact of the former.

For the sake of brevity, we shall use here for the principle of eight-fold modality the term *Octoechos*, but without its specifically Byzantine connotation. The medieval theorists invariably derived the number eight of the *octoechos* from the number of notes within the range of a diatonic octave. In spite of all efforts of recent scholarship, the real origin of that enigmatic eightfold modality has not been explained as yet. The less so, since these eight modes are by no means identical in the various musical cultures. It will, therefore, be necessary to study first the question whether, notwithstanding all the misunderstandings of the old theorists, there was not originally a connexion between the eight notes of the octave and the eight modes of the *octoechos*.

II

The term *octave* designates today two entirely different things. (a) As stated previously, the acoustic relation between a fundamental tone and its first overtone, the mathematical ratio being 1:2. (b) The second meaning of the word octave applies to its being the eighth, or more correctly expressed, the seven-plus-one note of the diatonic scale. The Occident holds both functions identical, and it would be unreasonable to distinguish between them. Yet this identity was not always valid, as it is not valid everywhere even today. The two functions have a different history and a different origin. The theoretical conception of the octave 1:2 is generally ascribed to Pythagoras by Nicomachus,[17] Gaudentius,[18] Iamblichus,[19] Philolaos,[20] and all of their commentators. According to the legend, Pythagoras discovered the relation between music and number in a blacksmith's shop, where he noticed that a heavy hammer produced a lower note than a lighter one. This led him to invent the monochord, by which device he established the ratio of the octave and that of most of the other intervals. This intuition was glorified by most of the chroniclers of ancient music.

Yet, there exists another much older version of that famous discovery which reaches deep into the realm of mythology. Ancient Phrygian chroniclers tell us that the great Asian goddess Rhea Kybele, the Magna Mater or Bona Dea of the Romans, employed dwarfs (*daktyloi*) in her services, skilled masters of all crafts.[21] These gnomes discovered in the rhythm of their hammers and in the different notes of their anvils the essence of all music, namely—the mathematical basis of rhythm and note. For about twenty years we have had positive knowledge that Kybele, called Kumbaba, belonged to the ancient Hittite Pantheon. The goddess of fertility was adored long before the time of King Hattushiliš, the contemporary of King Rameses II of Egypt. Before that time, the thirteenth century B.C., the Hittites had built a mighty empire which reached from north-east Mesopotamia down to Egypt. They were a non-Semitic, probably Indo-European people, but used the Accadian cuneiform script of their neighbours.[22]

The obvious resemblance of the two legends proves that the Pythagorean conception of the relation between music and number is of ancient Asiatic origin. Heretofore it was considered to be a Mediterranean rather than an Asiatic legacy, although at least Porphyry must have known the ancient tradition, for he states that Pythagoras learned the secret of music from the *daktyloi*.[23] In passing, it may be noted that the legend of the musical gnomes might enable us to understand better certain rather strange pictures of Sumerian musicians, who looked very much like dwarfs.

The Hittites are memorable in musical history for another even more important reason: to my knowledge they were the first ones who, admittedly in obscure language, alluded to the existence of eight musical modes. My colleague Professor Julius Lewy, who gave me his kind assistance in interpreting certain cuneiform Hittite texts, has directed my particular attention to one of them: 'Know that if thou offerest hymns to the Gods with the help of little *Istar* [a musical instrument], it is best to do this eightfold [or in eight ways or hymns]'.[24] What does this enigmatic precept indicate? Either to chant one hymn eight times, or to offer eight hymns to please the gods. For the present we shall leave the question unanswered; we shall return to it later.

What do we know about the octave being the eighth note of the diatonic scale? The oldest literary source which clearly divides the octave into eight tones seems to be Euclid.[25] It can be safely assumed, however, that long before his time the division of the octave interval into eight notes was familiar to Greek musicians. It is again characteristic that Pythagoras is accredited with the addition of the eighth note to the former heptachord. This statement comes from so many sources that it merits brief consideration. Nicomachus tells us that Pythagoras added the eighth string to the lyre, which heretofore had had only seven.[26] Philolaos also refers to that great invention of the eighth tone,[27] and

Gaudentius remains in character and confirms the prior observations.[28] With the exception of Euclid, all these remarks are couched in intentionally obscure, almost mystical, language.

Let us remember here again that the *acoustic* octave was long in existence before it was identified with the eighth note of the scale. This fact emerges from the frequent references to older scales, such as Terpander's heptachord.[29] While praising the simplicity and economy of Terpander, Plutarch attempts to explain that Terpander, by the omission of one or two notes of the diatonic scale, obtained especially fine results.[30] This sounds very much as if one would say: 'I do not want to spend so much money; it is not that I do not have it, but, by saving it, I will be able to buy even better things'. Nor can we believe Plutarch's argumentation, since Nicomachus, quoting Philolaos, a much older witness than Plutarch, calls the old seven-note scale Terpandrian and pre-Pythagorean.[31] There is no doubt that the old heptachord scale has left traces in the music of Asia and Europe; it occurs, in a form practically identical with Plutarch's so-called *Tropos Spondeiakos*, a heptatonic unit, in Hebrew, Byzantine and Gregorian chant.[32] In passing it should be noted that the Greek term for octave, *dia pason*, does not say anything about the number of notes which go to make up the interval, and it is only so recent a source as Pseudo-Aristotle that elucidates the question, whereby reference is made again to the old seven-note scale.[33] Our first conclusion, then, must be that the mathematical ratio of the octave interval 1:2 is an ancient Asiatic invention which preceded Pythagoras by at least 900 years. The identification of the octave interval 1:2 with the eighth note of the diatonic scale seems to have taken place at the time of Pythagoras or not long before. Now the question arises: why did it have to be the number eight which designated the octave? In other words, why was the interval 1:2 divided into *eight* unequal steps? The historic importance of this problem is obvious, for out of this eightfold division our present diatonic scale was brought into being.

It has already been acknowledged by some scholars that purely acoustic reasons could not have caused this particular division; pentatonic, hexatonic, heptatonic divisions are also in evidence, not to mention the divisions into smaller fractions such as the chromatic scale, the Hindu, Chinese, and other Eastern systems. We must search for other than acoustic reasons.

To begin with, the number eight was considered by the Pythagoreans to be the perfect number for music.[34] But this bare fact explains nothing; for it might be argued that since Pythagoras made the acoustic octave the eighth note of the scale, it was but natural that his followers should have regarded the number eight as the ideal number in music. Therefore, we must look for essential corroboration in older sources. Throughout the ancient Near East the number eight holds the significance of the musical number *par excellence*. We remember now the enigmatic Hittite injunction, demanding hymns in the eightfold; moreover, in three of the four recently rediscovered Babylonian tablets with a cuneiform type of notation—the latest one I have not seen as yet—the columns are all arranged in seven lines plus one. For Professor Curt Sachs this constitutes a special triumph, since today it is generally accepted by Assyriologists that these tablets represent some kind of notation even though not exactly that note by note system which Professor Sachs originally proposed and later withdrew.

From here on we turn to the Hebrews; one of their psalms bears the superscription: *ba-neginot 'al hasheminit*[35] which is usually rendered 'on Neginot upon Sheminit', a translation which contributes nothing to our understanding of the text. The usual interpretation of *Sheminit* as meaning 'eighth' tends to produce titles like 'tunes in the octave', or 'upon an instrument with eight strings', like kithara or lyre; this sounds more acceptable since, in another passage, mention is made of 'kitharas upon the eighth',[36] whatever that means. Neither interpretation is very satisfactory to musicians. There is, however, an old rabbinic explanation of the passage in question, probably of the sixth century A.D., which we must not disregard. R. Saadya Gaon, quoting an older rabbinic authority in Arabic, writes:

This is a hymn of David, in which the regular singers of the Temple were ordered to praise God in the eighth *lahan* [the Arabic term for mode]. The expression *'al hashminit* demonstrates that the Levites used eight modes so that whenever one of their regular groups sang, it did so according to a single mode.[37]

Why the eighth section (more correctly 'mode') was the most important is explained in the subsequent paragraph of this study.

A similar remark comes from R. Petachyah (twelfth century), who reports that the Jews of Baghdad, in accordance with the term *'al hashminit*, used eight modes for the chanting of the Psalms.[38]

In these cases the number eight had nothing to do with the octave or the diatonic scale. This is evident from the fact that the Arabs and Jews employed a system of eight *rhythmic* modes besides the melodic ones; obviously the number eight was artificially imposed upon this rhythmic system, for there is no equivalent to the octave in rhythm.[39] But this is certainly not the only occasion where the Psalms stress the number eight in connexion with music.

Ps. 119, an alphabetic acrostic, provides eight verses for every letter; some of these eight-line stanzas were sung in the second Temple. If this fact already induces us to think of musical modes, the principle of modality is, in a religious manner, much more strongly evident in the ancient commentaries to Ps. 29. The text of that psalm contains the expression 'The voice of God' seven times. This was understood very clearly to be an allusion to the harmony of the spheres. Ibn Latif, a mystically inclined philosopher, writes thus:

> The science of music envisages eight melodic modes which differ from each other because of their expansion and contraction. . . . The eighth mode functions as a genus which comprehends the other seven modes. . . . The Psalmist has cryptically alluded to this by means of the number seven in the repetition of the term 'God's Voice' . . . while the phrase 'All say Glory' (Ps. 29:9) refers to the eighth mode which comprises all the others. I cannot explain any further. . . .[40]

This kind of mystic musical emphasis upon the number eight reached its peak in the first two centuries of the Christian era under the aegis of a powerful Gnostic movement which tried to combine all the prevailing ideas of Greek as well as oriental philosophy in one great synthesis. Indeed, the entire concept of Christianity may be viewed as such a universal synthesis. Of the many relevant passages, only two will be quoted, the first from the Apocryphal Acts of St John—Christ's hymn to his disciples.

> . . . I would be thought, being wholly thought. Amen.
> I would be washed, and I would wash. Amen.
> Grace (*charis*) danceth. I shall pipe; dance ye all. Amen.
> I would mourn; lament ye all. Amen.
> The number eight (*Ogdoas*) singeth praise with us. Amen.[41]

This piece originated at the end of the second century. In it the *Ogdoas* has attained divine significance; but what is its place in the Gnostic system? This is explained about two centuries later in one of the magic papyri, the so-called Eighth Book of Moses. There we read:

Stored up in it is the Omnipotent Name, which is the *Ogdoas*, God, who creates and administrates everything. . . . Only by oracle may the Great Name be invoked, the *Ogdoas*. . . . For without Him nothing can be accomplished; keep secret, O disciple, the eight symbolic vowels of that Great Name.[42]

To our surprise we encounter here the famous Gnostic vowels as an invocation of the *Ogdoas*; these vowels have already provided some interesting clues to the notation of early Christian music as it has been interpreted by Ruelle, Poirée, and Gastoué. These are seven or eight vowels representing either notes or modes. But even this unexpected supplement does not fully clarify the significance of the *Ogdoas* for music. The first definite clue comes from a strictly theological source. Tertullian, the West-Roman Church Father, writes in his polemic against certain Gnostic sects:

According to them, the Demiurge [creator], completes the seven heavens with his own throne above all. Hence he had the name of Sabbatum from the hebdomadal nature of his abode; his mother, Achamoth, has the title Ogdoasa after the precedent of the primeval Ogdoas.[43]

At first this sounds like a wildly syncretistic fantasy; yet it contains two very ancient conceptions: the seven heavens, above which the Almighty has his throne, and the calendaric term *Sabbatum*.

This dependence of this passage on Pythagorean musical cosmological ideas and the Semitic calendar is obvious; indeed, the Syrian Pythagorean, Nicomachus, writes in similar terms, substituting 'star' or 'planet' for 'heaven'.[44] Similar statements are common to most of the Pythagoreans. We are, however, confronted again with the most important question: why it was the number eight that assumed so predominant a place in the musical, theological, and cosmological ideas of Near Eastern Hellenism. The Arabs were the first ones to raise this question in blunt terms, but their answer is not fully satisfactory. It says:

Eight is the perfect number for music and astronomy; there are eight stations of the moon, five planets plus sun, moon and earth, eight modes of music corresponding to the eight moods of nature: hot-wet, cold-dry, cold-wet, and hot-dry.[45]

Since this source originated in the ninth century, it is burdened with the full load of Neo-Pythagoreanism which found many adepts in Arabic literature. We must go back many centuries if we hope to find pre-Pythagorean explanations. It is here, precisely, that the ancient calendar of the Near East provides the decisive clues. As has been pointed out before (Part I, pp. 74 ff), the most ancient calendar of the Near East was based upon the Pentecontade, a unit of seven weeks plus one day.[46] This calendar rested upon the conception of seven winds, each of which corresponds to a god. Over these seven gods there ruled a supreme deity, which in later centuries the Gnostics called the *Ogdoas*. This hermaphrodite divinity was the parent of *Sabbatum*, the demiurge. All such fantasies were syncretistic-mythological contaminations and personifications of the original concept of the Pentecontade. The calendaric symbolism survived in Judaism and Christianity after the Gnostic interpretation had faded away in the dusk of dying antiquity.

The *liturgical octoechos*, composed or redacted by Severus of Antioch at the end of the fifth century, was nothing but a hymn book for the eight Sundays of the seven weeks after Pentecost.[47] Baumstark and other prominent Syrian scholars have proved beyond any doubt that the *musical octoechos* was only an arrangement by which the hymns were sung according to a different mode on each of the eight Sundays of the Pentecontade. This development occurred at the end of the seventh century, the eight modes naturally corresponding to the eight Sundays of a Pentecontade. These were the modes of the musical *octoechos* of the Eastern and Western Churches, of the Armenians no less than of the Ethiopians and the Hebrews. It is not necessary here to repeat the history of the *octoechos*; Baumstark and Jeannin have explored the matter from the philological as well as from the musical point of view.[48] From all the sources the fact emerges that the *octoechos* is but another of the numerous indications that Liturgy, Calendar, and Music have stood in an inseparable and millennia-old relationship with each other. While the old rule prescribes that the eight Sundays should run the gamut of all the eight modes, no provision was made for the clear identification of the *finales* of the musical *octoechos* with the eight notes of the diatonic scale. Byzantine theory shows the consequences of that identification with the eight species of octaves since the famous Hagiopolites manuscript of the thirteenth century. At any rate, the Pentecontade Calendar solves the riddle of the eight modes.

It remains for us only to sketch the development in the theory of the Middle Ages during which the *disjecta membra*, viz. the acoustic octave, the eighth note of the scale, and the eight modes were interlaced. Many of the accomplishments of ancient culture were lost during the storms and migrations which accompanied the decline of the Roman Empire.

That which has survived was either misunderstood or distorted and was, in most cases, falsely provided with the halo of classical Greek scholarship. Thus we are not surprised to find that the conception of the octave as the eighth note was half forgotten. In the early West European theory, the hexachord, at least for the purposes of solmization, took occasionally the place of the diatonic eight-note scale.

Gombosi, in his 'Studies of Early Scale Theory' has correctly pointed out that 'until the tenth century the species of octaves were in no way connected with the modes of the Church'. He continues: 'It is not the range of the octave that defines the church mode, but its *finalis* and the relation of that *finalis* to the dominant tone of psalmody'.[49] Only with Guido is the octave, again and without ambiguity, thought of as the eighth note of the scale. In his *Micrologus* he calls that eighth note the octave.[50] He goes on to say: 'For there are seven different notes in music just as there are seven days in the week'.[51] This calendaric comparison is not astounding since the term *octava*, as eighth day of the week, was perfectly familiar to every member of the Roman clergy since the time of Augustine.[52] Even before Guido, the cosmological derivation of the number eight in music was not entirely forgotten. Aurelianus Reomensis links the number of the modes with astronomical and calendaric observations.[53] From Guido on, the identity of the acoustic octave with the eighth note of the scale is firmly re-established; likewise, the modes of the *octoechos* were arranged in a diatonic scale. In this scheme the eighth mode naturally presented the greatest difficulties.[54]

III

After the delimitation of the respective origins of octave and *octoechos*, we are now confronted with the task of tracing the vestiges of the conception of eight musical modes in the main traditions of the ancient East—of Judaism, Byzantium, Arabia and the early medieval civilization of Europe. Therefore we should not lose sight of the remarkable interdependence between calendar, ritual, and theological and musical conceptions that is so characteristic of ancient cultures.

Looking through the rich Babylonian-Accadian ritual, we find an interesting enumeration of eight hymn incipits. It is not quite clear whether each of these texts corresponded to a mode of its own. Thureau-Dangin cites in his *Rituels accadiens* the same eight beginnings of sacrificial hymns from three different sources.[55] Some of these incipits occur in other sources edited by various other scholars.[56] The order of these incantations, however, is not always the same. Yet, in two places, even the order of the hymns is identical (with one exception—*U-'u-a-ba mu-hul* for *U-li-li en-zu*). We are told that *U-'u-a* is an expression of laments, and that *Ni-tug-ki Nigi(n)-na* means 'O Prince, turn Thyself (to the city!)'[57] There we learn that Marduk, the chief god, is in full glory at the central sanctuary on the eighth day of his journey with the festival processions. Referring to the fact that frequently the same hymn texts occur in various sources and at various occasions, Langdon comments:

> The order of the Psalmists (*Kalu*) charged with the musical part of the Temple services, was not compelled to learn a long liturgical service for each day of the year, as I had supposed, but only the liturgies prescribed for certain days of each month, and these were not too many. The Psalmists of the Ashur cult were burdened with liturgies for only eight days of Adar, and some of these were repeated in other months.[58]

In the ritual calendar which Langdon published the number of eight days and of pentecontadic units also plays a significant part.[59]

From here there seems to be a direct line leading to the psalm superscription *'al hasheminit* in Ps. 6:1 and 12:1. The text itself does not clearly indicate the meaning of *sheminit*. The earliest commentaries upon the enigmatic term are the *Sifra*, the Targum and the *Midrash Tehillim*. The *Sifra* (*Shemini*) has a calendaric implication; so does *Midrash Tehillim* by an allegorical connexion of *sheminit* with the day of circumcision, the eighth day after the child's birth.[60] The Targum knows nothing, however, of allegorical or calendaric overtones and interprets *sheminit* simply as a lyre with eight strings.[61] Ibn Ezra, on the other hand, gives us an alternative explanation: the first one corresponds completely with the Targum's notion of a lyre with eight strings; the alternative comment, however, comes very close to the idea of eight distinct modes.

> With regard to the *sheminit* there are those who say (it is) an instrument having eight strings or a hymn (*piyyut*) having eight modes. Therefore it is written *bineginoth*, and this upon the eighth mode (*sheminit*).[62]

The idea of eight musical modes remained alien to the Ashkenazic commentators for many centuries. Quite different is the literary evidence in the Sephardic, especially in the Judaeo-Arabic realm. Saadya's statement, quoted above, evoked many corroborating utterances by

Sephardic commentators and philosophers up to the fifteenth century. It is interesting to observe how Saadya's terminology compares with Christian and Arabic expressions. He translates *Lamnatzeach* (Ps. 6:1) by an Arabic term which he equates with the cabbalistic Hebrew *vatikim*, a designation of the incessantly God-praising Levites.[63] In the Christian sphere, the analogue is the *akoimetai*, the ascetic monks or nuns of the Byzantine Church from the time of the fifth century.[64] As we know from musical history, they were the real champions of the *octoechos*. The earliest passage containing the term *octoechos*, in a musical sense, clearly demonstrates the connexion between *akoimetai*-ascetics and musical modes. The anecdote is somewhat abridged in the following.

A monk asked his abbot, Sylvanus, then at the Sinai monastery in Palestine [fourth century], how he could ever attain true penitence and contrition since he was unable to remain awake when singing the antiphons of the psalms every night. Sylvanus replied that the singing of antiphons itself constitutes an act of pride and haughtiness, for song hardens the heart and impedes true contrition. He advised the monk to cease singing altogether. The monk answered: 'But, my father, since the time when I became a monk, I always chanted the series of the canon, the hours and the hymns of the *octoechos*'. The stern old abbot reprimanded him by emphatically referring to the great masters—Abbot Paul, Anthony, Pambo, etc., who did not know any *troparia* [chanted verses or small hymns], who knew no antiphons, but conquered the devil—not by chanting hymns, but by prayer and hard fasting. And they shone like the stars in the world.[65]

The commentary given to this story in the *Plerophoriai* of Johanan Ruphos of Maiouma goes beyond the simple narrative. The abbot added that singing is a secular custom; important only is incessant waking and prayer for the monks.[66]

Saadya, however, equates the eight modes of *rhythm* to the basic modes of *melody*. The passage in his *Emunoth Vedeoth* has been analysed by Professor Farmer, and jointly by my good friend Dr I. Sonne and myself. Independently, we have all come to the same conclusion, namely, that the system of eight rhythmic modes represents an artificial imposition of the musical number eight upon rhythm. In melody, the notion of eight modes still might be justified through the principle of the octave with its eight notes, but there is no rhythmic equivalent of the octave. Moreover, we know that the Arabs admitted of ten or even more rhythmic modes. Thus it was only the urge for consistent and logical systematization on the part of Jewish and Arab scholars which evoked the postulation of eight rhythmic modes.[67] Saadya always uses the same term, *lahan*, for melodic mode, and for the rhythmic modes—*'iqa'at*—in both his psalm commentary and his *Emunoth Vedeoth*.

But the confusion began immediately after Saadya. Even in the Pseudo-Saadya commentary to the Song of Songs the author speaks of nine modes and uses four different terms indiscriminately—sometimes all four in one sentence.[68] In many of the commentaries on musical remarks, the idea of the eight modes is still retained, but often obscured, occasionally and intentionally couched in esoteric language. In the following, only a few of the most characteristic passages can be quoted in order to show the growing confusion.

Abraham ibn Ezra to Ps. 6:1: 'A hymn (*piyyut*) having eight modes'. This is still in accordance with Saadya's tradition.

Isaac ben Abraham ibn Latif to Ps. 29:[69]

> The Science of Music envisages eight modes of melodies which comprehend the other seven modes: and this is the meaning of *Lamnatzeach 'al hasheminit*. The Psalmist has alluded to this cryptically. . . .[70]

Here the esoteric intention is conspicuous. The terms employed are *min* and *qol* (string or mode, and tone). Mystical elaboration or, at least, intent of this passage is unmistakably evident.

Bachya ben Asher:

> The song which the Levites rendered at the sacrifices did also have eight modes (*lahanim*):

> (1) *lamnatzeach* (the unceasing) (2) *al haneginot* (melody upon strings?)
> (3) *al mahalat* (the melancholy?) (4) *al alamot* (high tones)
> (5) *hanehilot* (flutelike?) (6) *al shoshanim* (of the lilies)
> (7) *al hagitit* (mode of Gath?) (8) *'al hasheminit* (in the eighth [mode])[71]

To this somewhat artificial interpretation, Bachya's commentator, Samuel Tartas, adds: 'He wishes to say "eight types of melodies".'[72] This is, however, by no means equivalent to Saadya's explanation of Ps. 6:1 as stated by Schlesinger in his translation of Albo's *Ikkarim*.[73]

A later glossator of Bachya, R. Herz Treves, obviously does not feel quite at ease with the general Sephardic notion of the eight *lahanim*, and he, in his commentary, takes the attitude of *relata refero* without giving his own opinion. Thus he says: 'R. Joseph Castile wrote (eight) *lahanim* to the chief Musician; for it (*lahanim*) is used in the sense of "melodies",' thus hiding behind the authority of R. Joseph Gikatilia. I was unable, however, to locate the passage to which Treves alludes.[74]

The only Ashkenazic author who factually reports the use of eight modes by contemporary Jews is Petachyah of Regensburg, but the Jews who actually make use of the eight *lahanim* are the singers of the Baghdad Synagogue:

. . . (During the intermediate days) the *Mizmorim* [probably psalms] are rendered along with musical instruments, for which there is a tradition (of several melodies). For the *'Asor* they have ten melodies and for the *hasheminit* they use eight melodies. . . .[75]

Even this author, who merely reports, seems to confuse the instrument *'Asor*, to which he ascribes ten notes, with the mode *sheminit's* eight, entirely missing the point of the eightfold system of modality. He was obviously unfamiliar with the entire conception of a limited number of modes, for he added cautiously: 'and for each *Mizmor* there are several melodies'.[76]

The Arabic and Jewish philosophers endeavour even to define their technical terms, especially *lahan*. The least ambiguous is the one offered by the great Alfarabi.[77]

The term *lahan* designates a group of various notes (*nagham*) which are arranged in a definite arrangement. It also refers to a group which is composed in a definite composition, and with which (besides notes) are also connected letters out of which the words are composed, which—through general uses— bear a special meaning.[78]

It is fairly clear that Alfarabi has two different meanings of the term *lahan* in mind: first a musical significance and afterward a literary designation ('It also refers', etc.).

The term *'al hasheminit* was connected with the Arabic empire in a more playful way by Al-Harizi, and it is not even clear whether he meant the allusion seriously:

Beginning with the forty-seventh century [after the creation of the world] the Spanish Jews were inspired with good advice, strength, and clear expression. They began to train themselves in poetry. When the forty-eighth century entered, they awakened and began to use the mode called *sheminit*.[79]

With this passage we break off our survey of the discussion of the eight modes in Hebrew literature, omitting a large treasury of cabbalistic writings, since these abound in too allegorical interpretations and can, therefore, not be considered evidential source material.

In conclusion, we can say that the conception of eight modes occurs, not counting the enigmatic psalm superscriptions and some hints in Midrashic literature, exclusively with Sephardic-Arabic Jewish writers. The only two exceptions are found in Petachyah and Herz Treves, neither of whom understood fully the significance and function of the eight modes. Moreover, the style of the Sephardic writers displays, with few exceptions, an inclination to allegorize upon the number eight of the *lahanim*. While this allegorical tendency is indigenous to medieval rabbinic literature, we should bear in mind the fact that we nowhere encounter a concrete implementation, that is, a technical description, of the eight modes. Those passages in medieval literature that speak about the construction of musical melodies are by no means connected with the psalm verses or their modes, but discuss the musical problem from a secular and propedeutic aspect.[80]

IV

Outside of the Jewish realm, the conception of eight modes finds its main expression in the church literature of Syria, Byzantium, Rome, and occasionally in secular Arab writers. We shall, in the following, survey the field chronologically.

The oldest Christian term, and the most widely used—Octoechos—occurs, for the first time, in the *Plerophoriai* of Bishop Johannan Ruphos of Maiouma, a monastery in Southern Palestine. This work, from which we have quoted above, was written about 515.[81] The Abbot's contempt of ecclesiastical song, which stands in violent opposition to the report of Aetheria Silvia, his contemporary, is by no means typical of the prevailing situation at his time in Palestine. It reminds one strongly of the attitude of the fanatical ascetics of the Egyptian monasteries; actually the great abbots and saints which Sylvanus cites as exemplary were all Egyptian monks. One of the Abbot's replies refers to the songs of the angelic hosts: 'Nowhere do we hear that they [the hosts] sing psalms; but one chorus sings incessantly the Hallelujah, and the other the "Holy, Holy, Holy" '. Here the Abbot quotes a text from a *Kedusha* which seems to be the first source in which we encounter the juxtaposition of Isa. 6:3 and Ezek 3:12. This combination occurs first in the contemporary *Constitutiones Apostolorum*.[82]

The term *octoechos* has here a clearly musical meaning, but in the great hymnal of Severus of Antioch named *Octoechos* (early sixth century) very little, if any, musical significance can be discovered in the work and its name. The first editor of this monumental work, E. W. Brooks, stated in the Preface that few musical indications are evident in the manuscript, and even these stem from a later hand.[83] Of the more than forty manuscripts, only these, which date later than the eleventh century, contain a consistent arrangement of the hymns according to the eight modes.[84] We are indebted to A. Baumstark for having pointed out the evasive and multifarious nature of the term *octoechos* in its full scope. He also emphasized the exceedingly strong links which connect the *octoechos* with the arrangement of the liturgical calendar throughout the year.[85] Often he comes close to the core of the problem—the relationship between the *octoechos* and the system of eight Sundays within the Jacobite calendar.[86] Once he states:

On every eight successive Sundays, the eight modes (*echoi*) are used, and for each mode there is a special text . . . in the Office. The whole of these cyclically arranged texts constitutes the contents of the *octoechos* in its more limited sense. . . .[87]

And further:

One of the old Berlin Penquitta manuscripts knows, for the period after the feast of the Apostles (June 29) eight other *taxeis* of resurrection (i.e. Sundays), which are arranged according to the *echadias* (MS. Sachau 236). Even farther go certain manuscripts of Jerusalem and Damascus. . . . No less than four series of Sunday Offices are offered there . . . [sets of eight].[88]

Compared with this scholarly accomplishment, Jeannin's elaboration upon the *octoechos* (Ch. VII of his *Mélodies liturgiques syriennes*) cannot be considered a notable progress. Despite his profundity, the author lacks the ability of freeing himself from old and traditional views which obscure a clear vista. Thus, when Jeannin arrives at the critical point, viz. the question of whether or not the *octoechos* has any link with the ecclesiastical year, he completely misses the significance of the problem and turns, instead, to a discussion of the hypothetical relation of the (musical) *octoechos* with the modes of ancient Greece and the medieval Western Church. Here, too, he becomes a victim of traditional views; unable to deviate too strongly from orthodox French viewpoints, such as expressed fifty years ago by Gevaert and later by Dom Gaisser and Emmanuel, he contents himself with slight and insignificant modifications of the traditional theories, accomplishing nothing of real value in this historical chapter.[89] However, he does contribute a great deal of new and unexplored material in the purely musical chapters of his work.

Clearer appreciation of the various aspects of the problem is displayed in the studies of A. Auda, H. Besseler and especially of E. Wellesz, G. Reese and K. Wachsmann. A. Auda, while not completely disentangling himself from the conceptions of the French school, no longer insists upon the hypothetical dependence of the musical *octoechos* on the ancient Greek modes. Moreover, he linked the *octoechos* with the alchemistic-musical writings of Zosimos of Panopolis. While important spadework has been done before him in this respect by A. Gastoué and others, he noticed the connexion between the eight modes and certain magical conceptions of the syncretistic religions of the Near East during the fourth and fifth centuries.[90]

Quite different again is H. Besseler's approach. He completely detached the Syro-Byzantine *octoechos* from the 'rationally determined octave scales': 'They [modes of the *octoechos*] are fundamentally a series of typically melodic formulas. Hence, all tunes of the same modus are closely related to one another . . .'[91]

The first scholar to approach the problem of the *octoechos* from a liturgical as well as from a musical standpoint was E. Wellesz in his book *Aufgaben und Probleme auf dem Gebiete der byzantinischen und orientalischen Kirchenmusik* (Münster, 1923). His is the merit of having applied the principles of set melodic formulas, as demonstrated by Idelsohn's study 'Die Maqamen der arabischen Musik',[92] to all church music of the Near East. After more than twenty years of intensive study, he arrived at the following conclusion, radically departing from all traditional theories:

> We can only touch on the problem of modes, which is one of the most contradictory in the history of early medieval music. It may prove that the entire problem of ecclesiastical modes needs new treatment, in view of the results of the investigation of Byzantine music. For, in this domain, it becomes more and more evident that the essential reason for attributing a melody to a certain type does not consist in its belonging to a particular scale or mode, but in the occurrence of certain melodic formulas in the structure of a phrase. I dealt with the problem for the first time in an article on the structure of the chants of the Serbian *octoechos*, and I was able to show that the so-called 'ecclesiastical modes' are *post-factum* constructions of theorists.[93]

It is astounding, however, that this ingenious author did not fully realize the deep-seated calendaric origin of the *octoechos* after having written the following words in 1923:

The Syrian ecclesiastical year commences with the first Sunday of November and runs in cycles of eight Sundays, on which the chants of the *octoechos* are sung in their order of modal succession; this custom spread from Western Syria to the Byzantine Empire.[94]

In many respects Wellesz's views are supported and even amplified by G. Reese in his excellent *Music in the Middle Ages*. This scholar touches upon a number of interesting ramifications of the problem of the *octoechos*. Taking as his point of departure a passage by Bar Hebraeus,[95] Reese arrives at the following conclusion:

> The actual literary evidence affords no basis on which to claim that the original Syrian Oktoechos derived its form from Greek or any other scale theory, or, for that matter, from any purely musical consideration. The melodies were doubtless assigned their places in the Oktoechos according to such symbolical meanings as were attached to them and as ostensibly rendered them suitable for particular liturgical occasions. . . . To the mystical value of the melodic outlines is added an artistic one, but they are not necessarily, or even with likelihood, recognized as conforming to particular scales. . . . The Syrian echoi—which, roughly speaking, may be regarded as eight specially favoured *ris-qolé*—are like ancient Greek nomoi before the heyday of the theorists.[96]

Elsewhere, Reese directs attention to the probable influence of Hebrew music on Byzantine music which is testified to by the Greek legend ascribing the four 'authentic' modes of the *octoechos* to King David, and the plagal four to King Solomon.[97] This writer has since given concrete evidence to Reese's theory by demonstrating that the hitherto unintelligible paradigms of Byzantine psalm-tones, as *Neannoe, Nana, Nennoa*, etc., are all variations of the Hebrew musical term *nin'ua'*, used for a trill or a melisma.[98]

It was K. Wachsmann who came closest to the complete solution of the puzzle of the *octoechos*. He also quoted Bar Hebraeus on the symbolical meaning of the *octoechos*, but, like Reese, he entirely overlooks that Bar Hebraeus, in his statement, reflects only typical Arab conceptions. The critical passage states:

> The inventors of the *octoechos* constructed it upon four fundaments, following the number of physical qualities. As one cannot find a mode in pure condition without its entering combinations with another, so it happens also with the elements: whatever is warm is also wet, as air and the blood, or dry, as fire and the yellow bile. . . .

There follows a strictly Christological application of that *tetraktys*. One glance at Arab writers of the ninth to the twelfth centuries would have convinced both Reese and Wachsmann that Bar Hebraeus was literally copying the general consensus of opinions of Arab writers on music. We content ourselves by quoting only one passage from the ninth-century *Ikhvan es-Safa* (Brethren of Purity):

> The musicians restrict the number of the strings of their lute to four, no more nor less, in order that their work might resemble the things of sublunar nature in imitation of God's wisdom.
> The treble string is like the element of fire; its tone dry, being hot and violent.
> The second string is like the element of air; its tone corresponds to the humidity of air and to its softness.
> The third string is like the element of water; its tone suggests waterlike moisture and coolness.
> The bass string is like earth—dry, heavy and thick.[100]

This writer has shown that these conceptions were brought into European theory after European Scholasticism became familiar with Arabic philosophy. Aegidius Zamorensis, especially, took over the Arab theories in their entirety.[101] On the other hand, the Arabs knew the Syro-Byzantine *octoechos* as early as the ninth century. In a manuscript by Al Kindi (d. 874), quoted by H. G. Farmer, the author mentions the differences in the musical arts between the celebrated modes (*turaq*) of the Persians, the eight modes (*alhan thamaniyya*) of the Byzantine theorists (*astukhusiyya*) and the eight rhythmic modes (*sul*) of the Arabs to which we already referred above.[102]

In spite of his somewhat irrelevant starting point, Wachsmann analyses with great astuteness the critical questions of the *octoechos*, scrutinizing carefully the entire musical and literary evidence. He summarizes his conclusions in the following words: 'The legends of Syrians and Byzantines concerning the *octoechos* stress the ecclesiastical year and its importance'.[103] Emphasizing the allegorical-symbolistic background of the *octoechos*, Wachsmann states:

> Our evidence shows that the liturgical system upon which the *octoechos* rests displaces every other consideration. . . . One cannot help giving precedence to liturgic-symbolic conceptions rather than to musical facts concerning the basic idea of the *octoechos*. Elements of cult must have determined its form (*Gestalt*) in contradistinction to the theory of antiquity which gained its form by way of speculative contemplation and scientific observation.[104]

Of what nature, then, is the symbolism to which most of the recent scholars referred? It ought to be fairly obvious by now that the symbols for which we must search must belong to some syncretistic ideology, since at least one of their many aspects—the calendaric one—is of ancient Mesopotamian origin. On the other hand, the fact that early Christianity could so relatively easily absorb the symbolism, indicates that it was not altogether foreign to Greek ideas. This combination would point to certain features of Neo-Pythagoreanism, and—indeed—this finds us on the right track. From an entirely non-musical realm comes the statement that 'the ancient mysticism of the number eight, which plays such a part with the Christian Gnostics, is most probably borrowed from the philosophic system of the Pythagoreans'.[105]

V

The task of tracing the time when the majestic confluence of Greek and indigenous Near East ideologies took place is complicated by the conflicting and confusing reports which have come down to us. In view of the multifarious Gnostic notions, each of which had erected another system of cosmogony, the confusion must be considered a natural concomitant of the brooding and brewing syncretistic fermentation which altered and modified wantonly, to the point of corruption, the original constituent systems of Greek hermetic philosophy, biblical Judaism, incipient Judaeo-Christianity, and their combination—Pauline theology. Hence, our investigation will seemingly lead us far away from our subject proper, and only in the last stages of our disquisition shall we be able again to link the loose threads of theology and philosophy to our musical starting point.

It was within the scope of Pythagoreanism to expand the original *tetraktys* to two such systems, especially when they could quite naturally explain the phenomenon of the octave by two tetrachords which were considered as concrete manifestations of the cosmic *tetraktys*. Thus Nicomachus of Gerasa, a Syrian (middle of the second century), begins to symbolize, in typical Pythagorean manner, the facts of musical theory.[106] Only shortly before this, Plutarch pondered on the idea of the eight in the cosmos and its great mysteries without making any mention of music.[107] For the first time, the number eight, here already called *Ogdoas*, was identified with the creator and the essence of music in the apocryphal hymn of Jesus quoted in the second section of this chapter. The hymn probably originated in Egypt or in Southern Palestine in the middle of the second century. At about the same time we receive the first information about the theological nature of the *Ogdoas*. In his polemics against the Gnostic heresies of Basilides of Alexandria (*ca.* 120–40) and his fellow-countryman Valentinus, Irenaeus from Asia Minor (*ca.* 140–220) makes the Neo-Pythagorean origin of the *Ogdoas* quite clear.[108] He writes: '[and these] call the first and primeval Pythagorean *tetraktys* the root of all things . . . and that this founder is the *Ogdoas*, the root and quintessence (*hypostasin*) of all things'.

Irenaeus and Clement of Alexandria give as the members of the *Ogdoas* the following ideal persons:

Pater:	Father
Nous:	Mind
Logos:	Logos
Phronesis:	Prudence
Sophia:	Wisdom
Dynamis:	Power
Dikaiosyne:	Righteousness
Eirene:	Peace[109]

Elsewhere, Irenaeus relates the Gnostic theogony in which the mother of the entire universe is the *Ogdoas*; her derivations are called *Yaldabaot, Yao, Sabaot, Adoneus, Eloheus, Oreus* and *Astapheus*, all of which are corruptions of the Old Testament names of God.[110] Interwoven here is also the idea of the seven heavens, which is of ancient Oriental origin, along with the Neo-Platonic conception of the Demiurge who is not yet understood as the Anti-God.

They [the Valentinians] say that seven heavens were built, the highest of which (is inhabited) by the Demiurge. Therefore they call him the *Hebdomas*, but his mother—*Achamoth* or *Ogdoas*. [*Achamoth* from the Hebrew form *hochmoth* acc. to Prov. 9:1.] They have restored the number of the first-begotten and primary *Ogdoas* as the *Pleroma*.[111]

Similar Hebrew-Greek-Christian syncretisms are evident in Hippolytus's *Refutatio Omnium Haeresium*, especially when he speaks about the conception of the *Pleroma* and the *Ogdoas*. There he says:

Outside then, *Horos* or *Stauros* [crucifix] is the *Ogdoas* as it is called . . . and is that *Sophia* which is outside the *Pleroma*. . . . And the animal essence is . . . of a fiery nature and is also termed the super-celestial *topos* (space) and *Hebdomas*, or 'Ancient of Days'.

Underneath the *Ogdoas*, where *Sophia* is, but above matter—which is the

Creator (Demiurge), a day has been formed, and the 'Joint Fruit of the *Pleroma*'. If the soul has been fashioned in the image of those above, that is—the *Ogdoas*, it became immortal and repaired to the *Ogdoas*, which is, he [Valentinus] says, heavenly Jerusalem.[112]

All this sounds rather confused, not to say abstruse, and it would be hard to systematize these wild syncretistic fantasies. Even Tertullian's description of the Valentinian Gnosis does not shed much more light upon this maze, but it contains the calendaric term *Sabbatum* for the hebdomal nature of the Demiurge's abode, and the *Ogdoas*, the Demiurge's mother, is still identified with *Achamoth*.[113]

This report comes again from a North African, Tertullian, at the end of the second century. Egypt and Southern Palestine were also the homelands of the two heretics, Kolarbasos and his disciple, Marcus— probably contemporaries of Irenaeus. This Church Father informs us about two notions of Marcus which are of great importance to our subject and have hitherto been neglected. They are the seven or eight magic vowels and the combination of the four elements—earth, air, fire and water with the four qualities hot, dry, cold and wet. The idea of the seven magic vowels is coupled with the expressions of the seven heavens in Ps. 19:1. Children likewise use the vowels as a form of praise, following the Davidic prediction: 'Out of the mouth of babes and sucklings hast Thou found Thy might' (Ps. 8:3).[114] The eighth vowel contains the *Logos* itself and can, therefore, not be pronounced by mortals. If we compare these Gnostic doctrines with Ibn Latif's interpretation of Ps. 29, quoted above, a surprising resemblance will be apparent. The same holds true for the theory of the two *tetraktys* of the elements and qualities which we encountered in Arabic as well as in the Jewish philosophy of music.[115]

When surveying our sources, we cannot escape the conclusion that the ideas of the *Ogdoas*, the magic vowels, the *tetraktys* of the elements and qualities, indiscriminately mixed with more or less corrupt biblical conceptions, originated in Egypt and southern Palestine during the second and early third centuries. Pythagorean, Orphic and even Aristotelian features, as well as ideas of the ancient Near East, were dragged into these violent metaphysical dreams.

The speculations of this time were posited in two forms: the first one was destined for the theologians, philosophers, apologists, etc., in a highly intellectual language; the second was the popular edition, written

14

for the more or less practical purposes of magic art, liturgies of the new syncretistic religions, etc. Only a few fragments of the original philosophic sources have come down to us; the rest is reported to us by the very enemies of these speculations, viz. the Church Fathers, whom we cannot expect to be completely objective in their remarks. We possess, however, a relatively large amount of the popular versions of these writings—the so-called 'Magic Papyri'.[116] The best survey and interpretation of these documents was given in A. Dieterich's *Abraxas* (Leipzig, 1891).

In the 'Magic Papyri' the theoretical speculations of the metaphysicians are applied to practice, i.e. to magic art, or to the liturgies of the new syncretistic religions. And here, music, the 'magic art' *par excellence*, plays a predominant part. The magic vowels were understood as notes of a cosmic octave, as incantations of the *Ogdoas*, as the esoteric music of the illuminates, etc. Here we are confronted with a complete syndrome of calendaric, ritualistic, magic, philosophic, and musical traditions and notions.[117] The exact musical interpretation of these enigmatic vowel-incantations is still much disputed; there is no doubt, however, that a number of the 'Magic Papyri' contain symbols for music, especially vocalizes upon the magic vowels. As in all esoteric cults, so here, too, the initiate is warned not to divulge the secret of incantation: 'Only by oracle may the great name be invoked, the *Ogdoas*, God, who administrates everything in Creation. . . . Keep secret, O disciple, the eight (or nine) symbols'.[118] This magical book stems from Egypt—probably from the fourth century. Dieterich writes about its contents:

> These *hierai bibloi* drew their intellectual substance, of a religious and theological nature, from traditions as they were cultivated among the ritual Greek-Jewish-Egyptian communities on the Mareotis.[119]

This is not the place to elaborate further upon the origin and meaning of these speculations. Returning to our subject, we remember that by the end of the fourth century we encounter the term *octoechos* used in a monastery near Gaza, and spoken by Egyptian monks. It should be possible by now to trace the development and itinerary of the eight modes concept. There can be no doubt, in view of Hittite, Babylonian, and old Hebrew documents, that the idea of the eight modes originated in Mesopotamia, probably as a ritualistic and calendaric reflection of some cosmological ideas, as is, e.g. the principle of the Pentecontade season.

After the collapse of the great empires of the Hittites and the Babylonians, remnants of the basic idea were preserved as priestly tradition by the psalmists, but, possibly, they were forgotten during the Exile.

Meanwhile, elements of the doctrine of 'seven plus one' fundamental things had come to Greece, either by Pythagoras or, perhaps, even earlier. This great thinker and his followers elaborated on and enhanced the idea, transforming it into the doctrine of the Pythagorean *tetraktys* that was reflected in the macrocosmos of nature as well as in the microcosmos of human music (*musica humana*), here assuming the form of two joined tetrachords that were said to mirror the heavenly *Ogdoas*.

Some of these speculations were brought to Egypt, the bulwark of Hellenism in general, and of Pythagoreanism in particular. There they were expanded and corrupted under the double spell of Egyptian mythology and Judaeo-Christian canonic and apocryphal cosmogony.

The *Ogdoas* was identified with the supreme Deity by the Gnostics and considered the fountainhead of *musica mundana* by hellenized Christians. As such we encounter it in the apocryphal hymn of Jesus and his disciples whose dance around their master strongly suggests some cosmic symbolism, perhaps the Zodiac.

From Egypt, the new Pythagoreanism invaded Christianity, and a number of Gnostic heresies resulted from that hybrid union. In Palestine, the ancient Mesopotamian calendar of seven weeks plus one day was preserved by the Syrian and Nestorian Churches, and the conceptions of the *Ogdoas* and the eight modes were eagerly adjusted to the eight Sundays of the Pentecontade. It is characteristic that the ancient calendaric institutions were best preserved by the Northern and Eastern Churches of Syria where ancient Aramaean ideas might have been kept alive. From Syro-Palestine, the *octoechos*, together with other liturgical institutions, was brought to Byzantium and to the spiritual leaders of Western Christianity. All of these centres seem to have accepted the *octoechos* as a welcome systematization of the embarrassingly abundant features of calendar, hymnody and psalmody. Via Syria, the eight modes eventually were absorbed by Arabic and rabbinic musical theory, the latter renewing the ancient concept of the psalmists. At the same time, and together with Christianized Pythagoreanism, the ideas of the magic vowels and of the combined (twofold) *tetraktys* (four elements and four qualities) made definitive inroads in the thinking of the Near

East, and later on exerted a strong spell upon the Aramaean, Arabic, and Jewish thinking of the Middle Ages.

VI

The study of the ancient, widespread and involved structure of eight modes causes us to expect to find tangible musical evidence to corroborate the literary sources. What, then, is the concrete musical evidence concerning the eight modes? Since almost every nation, and certainly every Church, has established an *octoechos* of its own, it will be necessary to investigate each of the main traditions separately. Before doing so, one more question must be posed and answered. Was there ever one, and only one, *octoechos* of which all other later constructions are mere derivatives? This fundamental question cannot be answered and probably will always remain an unsolved problem. The reason for this is that the first notated sources that can be clearly deciphered originated with the Greeks, beginning in the fourth century B.C. At that time, and even long before then, certain oriental modes were in existence and were known to be very much at variance with the classic Greek ones. We know these facts from some of the Greek writers on music, e.g. Plutarch, who paid much attention to the story that Olympus, from Western Asia, had introduced, not without resistance from the side of the Greeks, certain new modes or styles among which Plutarch especially mentions the enharmonic scale.[120]

Close examination of Olympus's new style shows its kinship with the *Tropos Spondeiakos*, the mode referred to by Clement of Alexandria as the one in which the Jews of Alexandria chanted the psalms.[121] At any rate, Olympus, in the ninth century B.C., long before the era of Greek classic music, knew modes that were quite different from the then prevailing Greek style. A modern scholar sums up the situation most concisely: 'A West-Asian contributed an Asiatic scale to Greek music'.[122] Obviously, the idea of one general *octoechos* is not tenable after the ninth century, and it seems, in general, to be a rather fantastic notion.

Returning to the examination of musical evidence for the *octoechos*, we shall search for it in the chants of the Syrian, Byzantine, Roman Catholic and Jewish liturgical traditions.

Syrians. Due to the fact that the Syrians had lost the understanding of their own notation about 900, as testified by Bar Hebraeus,[123] we must take recourse to relatively recent sources. Parisot's and Dom Jeannin's studies on the music of the Syrian Churches provide a rich material, but there is no safeguard concerning the age or even the authenticity of the melodies reproduced in their books. With this reservation, the musical evidence, as produced in these two standard collections, presents the following picture.[124]

The Syrians knew of eight modes and rendered them regularly in their liturgy. It is, however, most difficult to identify the modes—with the exception of the first, second and third—with any degree of scientific exactitude. The first and second modes, in particular, seem to be identical with the *echoi* of the same order in Armenian, Byzantine and Gregorian chant.[125] Even the Arabs of the tenth century seem to have known at least the first mode.[126] Interpreting the evidence of three manuscripts, Dom Gaisser, a fine student of Christian oriental chant, suggests that the first mode is identical with the ancient Greek Dorian *harmonia*; this theory has been justly disputed by Jeannin. Dorian it is, not in the classical Greek sense, but in the terminology of the Western Church.

While the first three modes might have originally been common to all Churches of the Near East, it is obvious that, in the course of time, they diverged more and more from each other. Says Jeannin:

Inutile de dire que, s'il est difficile de prouver un bouleversement général postérieur de l'organisation modale pour les divers *octoechos*, il est, par contre, tout à fait raisonnable de supposer, en Orient surtout des perturbations mélodiques nombreuses pour les chants particuliers.[127]

According to Jeannin, the chant of the Syrians consisted of eight modes. Yet these modes, even if they were unequivocally established, which they are not, have so many variants, that the system of modes—restricted to eight—is for all practical purposes, no more than a fiction. While the Syrians have a theoretical *octoechos*, their chants are by no means limited to these eight modes, as a study of Parisot's and Jeannin's collections will clearly prove. In contradistinction to the systematization of the Gregorian chant, these authors have refrained from classifying every tune as belonging to a definite mode. Thus, in Syrian music, the *octoechos* exists, but it is by no means the only musical system in evidence.

Moreover, our two main authorities on Syrian music, Dom Parisot and Dom Jeannin, are at variance with regard to the question of the first mode. According to Parisot, it can hardly be considered subtonal, whereas the chief example of the first mode, as quoted by Jeannin, bears outstanding subtonal features.[128]

EXAMPLE 16

In general, only the first, third and fifth Gregorian modes are evident in Syrian music. Jeannin quotes examples of all the eight modes of the *octoechos*, but it is hard to see how he is able to distinguish between some of these modes, e.g. the third and the fifth Syrian modes, as they are extremely similar.

Still another difficulty confronts us here. Parisot, as well as Jeannin, cites a number of tunes which simply do not fit into any of the eight modes, e.g.[129]

EXAMPLE 17

Bo 'uto de mor Ya'qub

Summing up the musical evidence of today's Syrian music, it may be said that the scale skeleton of the first three modes occurs most frequently. Its melodic patterns are, however, vastly different from those used by the Roman Church for the very same three modes. In addition to these three scales, a great number of tunes are known in Syrian music that do not correspond to any of the canonized modes of the *octoechos*. In the last analysis it is impossible to give an accurate and concise definition of all the modes of the *octoechos*. Hence, it appears most doubtful if the theory of the *octoechos* has been actually implemented where the practice of music is concerned.

Byzantine Church. The Byzantine *echoi* are defined as eight distinct modes, but they are not necessarily based upon a scalar structure. Egon Wellesz, the greatest authority on the subject, states:

I . . . have found that . . . the mode (*echos*) is *not* absolutely connected with a certain *finalis*, but with the occurrence of a group of *maqams* which form the melody of each mode (*echos*). . . . The scales were gradually developed from the melodies by a process of grouping certain . . . formulas of which all melodies were built.[130]

While these melodic formulas were arranged in a system of eight modes, it is not easy to classify every Byzantine tune under one of the eight *echoi*. The scheme of the *echoi*, as reconstructed by modern scholars, is quoted here:[131]

Echos	Starting Note of the Interval-Sign of the Melody	Finalis
I	a (rarely D)	a or D
II	b-natural or G	E or b-natural
III	c or a	F or c
IV	d or G	G or d
Plagal I	D or G (rarely E)	D (rarely a)
Plagal II	E or G (rarely a)	E
Plagal III (Barys)	F or a	F (rarely b-flat)
Plagal IV	G, a or c	G (rarely c)

There are, in addition, several by-forms to the echoi (as we have indicated in discussing notation), so that this table is not all-embracing, although it includes the principle forms.[132]

Now let us analyse the end of a most famous and ancient Byzantine hymn.

EXAMPLE 18
End of Byzantine hymn 'Hote to stauro'[133]

Wellesz discusses its mode in the following way:

The melody is composed in the second mode (*echos B* . . .). As this mode begins, according to Medieval theory, one note above Mode I, we shall expect

the opening on E, but, in fact, the melodies start on G, A and B natural. . . .
The *finalis* of Mode II is either E or B natural; in the present case, the melody
ends on B and uses as other important centres of melodic structure G and D.
We have the impression, therefore, that the melody is written in a kind of G
major rather than in the second Byzantine mode, as E has no importance at all
in its development.[134]

Again we are confronted with certain discrepancies between the
theory and the practice of modal music. It may be pointed out that,
in the field of Byzantine music, too, there are tunes that do not fit into
the scheme of eight modes, tunes that exceed that limit considerably.
Wellesz and Tillyard's excellent publications on Byzantine music contain a considerable number of such instances.[135]

Surveying our results, we are bound to admit that the Byzantine
octoechos does exist in practice as well as in theory. Yet, even within the
octoechos, theory and practice do not often coincide.

The Roman Catholic Church. It is in the tradition of the Roman Church
where the theory and the practice of the eight modes were developed to
their highest stage. It would exceed by far the scope of this study were
we to examine the history and the authenticity of the Roman Church
Tones, but a few pertinent facts ought to be briefly remembered:

(1) The psalmodic modes are not uniform with respect to their final
notes; there are different *finales* for the same modes in the psalmody of
the *officium*, of the antiphons of the Mass, and of the responses of the
officium.[136]

(2) The psalmody of the Roman Church contains, in addition, the
regular Psalm Tones and a number of other psalmodic types, such as the
so-called *Tonus Peregrinus*, 'In Templo Domini', etc., which cannot be
subsumed within the framework of the *octoechos*.

(3) Now and then attempts were made to increase the eight modes to
twelve in order to bring the individual melodies into a clear and rigid
system, but all these attempts failed.[137]

The congruence, however, of scalar mode and melodic pattern is obvious in Gregorian chant. Practically every mode possesses certain
melodic formulas of its own, and while, occasionally, such formulas
also occur in other modes, these cases are rather the exception than the
rule.

Best developed of the modes are the first, third, fifth and seventh, the
so-called authentic tones. Their typical melodic patterns are:

EXAMPLE 19

The authentic Church Tones according to the *Commemoratio brevis.*
(Tenth century)[138]

Yet, were we to add up the various psalmodic formulas of the Church, we would probably reach no less than eighteen to twenty modes. It is, therefore, obvious that the number eight, with regard to musical modes, is again a theoretical construction, very much at variance with the actual number of melodic types within the basic psalmody.

The Tradition of the Synagogue. In sharp contrast to Syrian, Byzantine, and Roman theory and practice, Jewish musicians never seriously attempted to systematize their traditional tunes according to the eight modes. This fact seems to contradict the various statements by Jewish writers that the psalms were sung in the eight modes. It is quite possible that an ancient tradition regulated the psalmodic chant according to an eightfold framework of modes. Yet this system has not come down to us, and any attempt to reconstruct the eight *original* modes must be unsuccessful in view of the almost chaotic state of the present tradition.

While the Christian Churches tried, at least, to systematize their tunes, the Synagogue has never encouraged such an enterprise. It might even be argued that opinions were voiced that objected to any systematization of liturgical chant. Most articulate on that subject was Yehuda Halevi, who, in his *Kuzari*, claimed that only semi-improvisational music could really express the divine longings of the soul. He termed that type of song *Tartil*, in contradistinction to a more regulated type with clearer rhythmic contour which he called *Anshadia*.[139]

Two antagonistic attitudes can be clearly discerned in the development of Synagogue music: the Orthodox or Hasidic, granting the *hazan* every freedom of improvisation; the more progressive one, championed by men like Leon da Modena, Rossi, Sulzer and the entire liberal Synagogue, purporting to eliminate as far as possible any cantorial improvisation.

Notwithstanding all these difficulties, serious attempts were made by some Jewish scholars to reinstitute at least part of our musical tradition. Samuel Naumbourg[140] was the pioneer in the field; following him were men like Joseph Singer,[141] Pinchas Minkowsky,[142] Eduard Birnbaum[143] and A. Z. Idelsohn.[144] It was Idelsohn who, in his monumental *Thesaurus of Hebrew Oriental Melodies* (10 vols.), undertook a profound analysis of the whole question.

These endeavours remained not altogether fruitless. Certain basic modes were reconstructed and proved to be common to the various regional Jewish traditions. They are named after the chanted prayers which are considered to contain the archetypes of these modes. Thus we know of the *Magen Aboth* mode, corresponding to the first mode of Gregorian psalmody, of the *Ahaba Rabba* mode, having as its counterpart a comparatively recent Byzantine *echos*, and the *Adonai Malakh* mode which is the equivalent of the seventh Gregorian Tone. Aside from these prayer modes, many others are known to us, such as the Torah and Haftara cantillations, the various modes of the Song of Songs, modes of confession and penitence, etc. Were we to add up all of the most frequent modes of Jewish chant, the result would be a multiple of eight.

While the three basic prayer modes seem to be of ancient origin and correspond to some of the Syrian, Byzantine, and Gregorian patterns, the same cannot be said of many other modes. They have to be investigated one by one, as they do not submit to general principles. Thus we arrive at almost the same conclusions with reference to Jewish tradition as we reached in our discussion of the three Christian traditions mentioned above. However, one modification must be stated: before the nineteenth century not even an attempt had been made in Synagogue music to classify the individual tunes according to comprehensive modes. This late date lets all attempts at reconstruction appear rather problematical.

CONCLUSIONS

Our examination of the origin of the *octoechos* and the ancient modes of music results in the following conclusions:

1. The conception of an eightfold musical modality dates back, at least, to the beginning of the first millennium B.C. It originated in Mesopotamia.

2. It is possible that the division of the acoustic interval between a fundamental tone and its first overtone ($1:2$) into eight unequal steps owes its origin to the same ideas as the conception of eight modes.

3. The principle of the *octoechos* originated *not in musical but in cosmological and calendaric speculations*. While the principle of eight modes is common to the entire Near East and, through Christianity, conquered Europe, its concrete musical implementations vary greatly according to the indigenous traditions of musical folk-lore in the respective orbits.

4. While the existing ecclesiastical modes must be considered *post factum* constructions of the theorists, the conception of an eightfold modality was an *a priori* postulate of a religio-mythical nature to which theorists had to adjust the various systems of modes.

5. The musical evidence of the various ecclesiastical and secular traditions is of a twofold nature:

(a) Where a system of eight modes is actually demonstrable and evident, there occur also tunes that do not fit into the prefabricated system of eight modes. This is the case in the musical traditions of the Roman and of the Byzantine Church.

(b) Frequently the *octoechos* is merely the result of a recent reconstruction of the eight modes after the original framework had been forgotten or corrupted due to the lack of musical notation. Such is the case in the musical traditions of the Syrian, Coptic, and Armenian Churches and of the Synagogue. In these traditions, not even the *a priori octoechos* can be reconstructed with a reasonable degree of certainty, and many more modes would have to be set up in order to account for the various melodies outside the *octoechos*.

6. The modes of the *octoechos* were not originally based upon a scale or a system of scales; they were melodic patterns which, first through constant usage, and later by theoretical systems, were set into an invariant musical framework. Common to all modal systems, however, are the first (Dorian), third (Phrygian) and fifth (Lydian) modes of the Gregorian chant.

NOTES CHAPTER II

1. Cf. R. Lachmann, *Die Musik des Orients* (Breslau, 1929), pp. 9, 38, 60–63.

2. 'The so-called ecclesiastical modes are post-factum constructions of the theorists' (E. Wellesz, *Eastern Elements in Western Chant*, London, 1947, p. 31); in the same vein Gustave Reese, *Music of the Middle Ages*, pp. 74 ff.

3. Cf. Riemann-Einstein, *Musiklexikon*, article 'Griechische Musik'.

4. Amédée Gastoué, *Les Origines du chant romain*, p. 134.

5. Dom Jeannin, *Mélodies liturgiques syriennes*, I, pp. 98 ff.

6. WGM, III, pp. 107–8.

7. Curt Sachs, *The Rise of Music in the Ancient World*, pp. 66–69, 216 ff.

8. Otto Gombosi, 'Studien zur Tonartenlehre des frühen Mittelalters', *Acta Musicologica*, X, pp. 149–73.

9. Egon Wellesz, *Aufgaben und Probleme auf dem Gebiete der byzantinischen und orientalischen Kirchenmusik* (Münster, 1923), pp. 101 ff.

10. Hugo Riemann, *Handbuch der Musikgeschichte*, I, 2; also E. Werner, 'The Sources of Octave and Octoechos', *Acta Musicologica*, 1948.

11. Cf. Sachs, op. cit., pp. 216–18.

12. Cf. Gombosi, op. cit., pp. 149 ff.

13. Antoine Auda, *Les Modes et les tons de la musique* (Bruxelles, 1931).

14. Cf. Gombosi, op. cit., p. 149.

15. Ibid.

16. Cf. WGM, III, pp. 88 ff; also E. Wellesz, op. cit., p. 101, n. 9.

17. Nicomachus, Chapter 6, in von Jan., *Musici Scriptores Graeci* (Leipzig, 1895), p. 249.

18. Gaudentius, in von Jan., op. cit., p. 340.

19. Iamblichus, *De Vita Pythagorae*, ed. Kuester, 18, 81.

20. 'Philolaos', in A. Boeckh's *Philolaos des Pythagoräers Lehre* (Berlin, 1815), Fragm. 5.

21. In Gressmann, *Die orientalischen Religionen im hellenistisch-römischen Zeitalter*, p. 59; cf. also Stith Thompson, 'Dwarfs have Music', *Motif Index of Folk Literature*, III, p. 100; also Grimm, 'Däumlinge-Daktyloi', *Deutsche Mythologie*; also Strabo, lib. X, 'Studium musicum inde coeptum cum Idaei dactyli modulos crepitus et tinnitu aeris—in versisicuum ordinem transtulissent'.

22. Cf. E. Benveniste in *Mélanges syriens*, I, pp. 250 ff.

23. Porphyry, *De Vita Pythagorae*, Chapter 17 (English translation in K.S. Guthrie, *Pythagoras Source book* (1919), whose inferences I cannot fully endorse.

24. KBo IV–KUB XI.

25. Cf. Euclid, Sectio Canonis, in von Jan., op. cit., pp. 165 ff. Also I. Düring, *Ptolemaios und Porphyrios über die Musik* (Göteborg, 1934), p. 64.

26. Nicomachus, Chapters 5 and 7, in von Jan., op. cit., pp. 244, 249.

27. The Philolaos quotation in *Hagiopolites MS.*, ed. A. J. Vincent, *Notices et extraits* (Paris, 1847), p. 270.

28. Gaudentius, *Harmonike Eisagoge*, ed. Meibom, p. 14.

29. Ps.-Euclid, *Introductio Harmonica* (Cleonides), ed. Meibom, p. 19; also Ps.-Aristotle, *Problemata*, cap. 19, in von Jan., op. cit., p. 94, probl. 32.

30. Plutarch, *De Musica*, ed. Reinach-Weil, Chapter 11, pp. 74 f.

31. Nicomachus, Chapter 12, in von Jan., op. cit., pp. 263-4.

32. Cf. my study 'The Attitude of the Early Church Fathers to Hebrew Psalmody', *Review of Religion* (May, 1943), pp. 349 ff.

33. Ps.-Aristotle, *Problemata*, in von Jan., op. cit., p. 94, probl. 32.

34. *Theologoumena Arithmetica*, ed. Ast., p. 62, 17-22.

35. Ps. 6:1.

36. I Chron. 15:20.

37. *Saadias Psalmübersetzung*, ed. Galliner, p. 22; comprehensively treated in W.-S., *HUCA*, XVI (1941), pp. 295 ff.
To quote from M. Zulay's fine study 'A Plea for a "Corpus of Genizah Piyyutim" ', *Journal of Jewish Studies*, I (London, 1948), pp. 113-14:
'These characteristics of Saadyah's style are again clearly discernible in the following lines of the *Ofan*:

> Thou createdst the eighth heaven from
>   the ice of fire and water;
> Thou selectest from the eight choirs
>   the melody of the eighth.

can be understood only in the light of Saadyah's commentary on Ps. 6, in which he explains that there were eight melodies in use in the Temple, each of which was assigned to a separate section of the Levites. But he does not mention there that the eighth section was the most important, and I am unable to indicate a source for this assertion.'

38. Text and translation in *Literaturblatt des Orients*, IV, col. 541, n. 44.

39. W.-S., *HUCA*, XVI (1941), pp. 297 ff.

40. W.-S., *HUCA*, XVII (1943), p. 552.

41. *The Apocryphal New Testament*, ed. M. R. James (Oxford, 1924), p. 253.

42. *Papyrus Magicus Leyden W*; quoted from A. Dieterich, Abraxas, p. 194.

43. Tertullian, *Contra Valentinianos*, in *Ante-Nicene Fathers*, III, 514. Cf. *supra*, n. 37.

44. Nicomachus, in von Jan., op. cit., p. 241.

45. Cf. *Ikhvan es-Safa*, ed. Dieterici, pp. 128-31.

46. Hildegard and Julius Lewy, 'The Origin of the Week', *HUCA*, XVII (1943), pp. 41, 45, 47, 99-101.

47. A. Baumstark, *Festbrevier und Kirchenjahr der syrischen Jakobiten* (1910), pp. 26, 44.

48. Cf. Dom Jeannin, *Mélodies liturgiques syriennes* (Paris, 1924-28), pp. 85-94; also Baumstark, op. cit., p. 26 *et passim*; idem., *Geschichte der syrischen Literatur*, p. 190; also *The Octoechos of Severus of Antioch*, (*Patrologia Orientalis*, ed. Brooks, VI and VII).

49. Cf. Gombosi, op. cit., p. 155.

50. Guido Aretinus, *Micrologus*, Chapter V.

51. Ibid., Chapter VII, 'Nam sicut septem dies sunt in hebdomada, ita septem voces sunt in musica'.

52. Augustine, *Sermo de Tempore* CXI, 1. 'Hodie octavae dicuntur infantium. . . .'

53. Aurelianus Reomensis, in Gerbert, *Scriptores*, I, p. 40.

54. Gombosi, op. cit., pp. 168-9.

55. Cf. Thureau-Dangin, *Rituels accadiens*, pp. 20, 21, 35, 41.

56. Ibid., p. 21, n. 81 ff.

57. Ibid., p. 21, n. 82, after Reisner, *Babylonische Hymnen*, No. 48, rev. 28, and p. 147.

58. S. Langdon, 'Calendars of Liturgies and Prayers', *Amer. Journal of Sem. Languages*, XLII (1915-16), p. 112.

59. Ibid., p. 118.

60. *Midrash Tehillim*, ed. Buber p. 53.

61. Targum to Ps. 6:1.

62. Ibn Ezra to Ps. 6:1.
63. Cf. I. Margulies, *Saadias arabische Psalmübersetzung*, p. 8, n.1; also Ewald-Dukes; *Hebr. Schriftsteller*, I, p. 14.
64. Cf. Haneberg, *Saadias arab. Psalmkommentar* (Munich, 1841), p. 383. *Akoimetos* is a person who does not rest.
65. *Patrologia Orientalis*, VII, pp. 180 ff. A parallel in O. Wessely, 'Die Musik anschauung d. Abtes Pambo' in *Öster. Akad. d. Wissensch*, 1952, No. 4.
66. Ibid., p. 181.
67. Cf. W.-S., p. 297, and nn. 153, 144, 145.
68. Ewald-Dukes, op. cit., p. 106.
69. Cf. W.-S., *HUCA*, XVII (1943), p. 552.
70. Hebrew text in W.-S., *HUCA*, XVII (1943).
71. Bachya ben Asher, *Biur*, Parsha Shemini (Amsterdam, 1724), p. 150.
72. Cf. Steinschneider, *Catalogus librorum Hebr.*, I, p. 779, 12.
73. Cf. Schlesinger, *Albo's Ikkarim*, p. 661 (German Text and commentary).
74. Herz Treves, *Be'urim al Rabenu Bahya* (Thiengen and Heddenheim, 1546), *Parsha Shemini* (with reference to Ikkarim III, 10).
75. Text and German translation in *Literaturblatt des Orients*, IV, col. 541, n. 44.
76. Ibid., col. 541.
77. Simon Duran's definition, ibid, col. 540.
78. *Literaturblatt des Orients*, IV, col. 248.
79. Ibid., col. 341, English translation by Morris Berman.
80. Cf. W.-S., *HUCA*, XVI (1941), Chapters 1, 2, 3.
81. *Supra*, p. 385.
82. Cf. CAF, VII, cap. 35, 3–4, p. 430; see also *supra*, Chapter IX.
83. *Patrologia Orientalis*, VI, preface p. 1.
84. Cf. A. Baumstark, *Geschichte der syrischen Literatur*, p. 190, n. 3.
85. Cf. A. Baumstark, *Festbrevier und Kirchenjahr der syrischen Jakobiten*, p. 84.
86. Ibid., p. 269.
87. Ibid., p. 267.
88. Ibid., p. 268.
89. Jeannin, op. cit., pp. 93–94.
90. Cf. A. Auda, op. cit. (n. 13), pp. 151, 158, 161.
91. Cf. H. Besseler, *Die Musik des Mittelalters und der Renaissance* (Potsdam, 1931— in E. Bücken's *Handbuch der Musikwissenschaft*), p. 53.
92. Cf. A. Z. Idelsohn, 'Die Maqamen der arabischen Musik', *SIM*, XV, pp. 1 ff.
93. E. Wellesz, *Eastern Elements in Western Chant*, pp. 30 ff.
94. E. Wellesz, *Aufgaben und Probleme*, p. 101.
95. Gregory Bar Hebraeus, *Ethikon*, ed. Bedjan (in Syriac), pp. 69–72. (French translation in Jeannin, op. cit., p. 21.)
96. Cf. G. Reese, op. cit., pp. 74–75.
97. Ibid., p. 79.
98. Cf. E. Werner, 'The Psalmodic Formula *Neannoe* and its Origin', *MQ* XXVIII (January, 1942), pp. 93 ff. See also A. Auda, op. cit., pp. 162, 170.
99. Bar Hebraeus, *Ethikon*, ed. Bedjan, p. 69.
100. W.-S., *HUCA*, XVI, pp. 275 ff (quoted from *Ikhvan es-Safa*, ed. Dieterici, pp. 126–8). Also R. Lachmann, Al Kindi, *Über die Komposition der Melodien* (Gesellschaft zur Erforschung der Musik des Orients, Leipzig, 1931).
101. Cf. W.-S., *HUCA*, p. 276, n. 78.
102. Cf. H. G. Farmer, *A History of Arabian Music to the XIIIth Century* (London, 1929), p. 151.
103. K. Wachsmann, *Untersuchungen zum vorgregorianischen Gesang* (Regensburg, 1935), p. 95, and n. 69, in which he refers to observations of R. Lachmann on Hebrew liturgical music.
104. Ibid., pp. 99–100.
105. Cf. F. J. Doelger, 'Das Oktogon und die Symbolik der Achtzahl', in *Antike und Christentum* (Münster, 1934), pp. 153–87.

106. Nicomachus, in von Jan., op. cit., p. 282, line 10.
107. Plutarch, *Moralia*, ed. Bernardakis, II, 774b.
108. *PG*, VII, col. 448, 494.
109. Irenaeus, *Adversus haer.*, I, 1–4; Clement of Alexandria, *Stromata*, IV, 25. A. Hilgenfeld comments on this, in his extensive *Ketzergeschichte des Urchristentums*, p. 219: 'This conception might well be compared with Parsism, which places an *Ogdoas* of Ormuzd and the seven Amshapands on top of the realm of light.'
110. Irenaeus, *Adv. haer.* I, 30 ff.
111. Irenaeus, (*PG*, VII, 494).
112. Hippolytus, *Refutatio omnium haeresium*, in *Ante-Nicene Fathers*, V, book 6, Chapter 26, 27, pp. 87–89.
113. Tertullian, in *Ante-Nicene Fathers*, III, p. 514.
114. Irenaeus, op. cit., II, 13 ff.
115. See *supra*, pp. 381, 392, 393.
116. Best editions: Ch. Ruelle, 'Le Chant gnostico-magique', *Congrès internat. d'histoire de la musique* (Paris and Solesmes, 1900–02), pp. 15–27; C. Wessely, 'Neue Zauberpapyri', *Abhandlungen der K. Akademie der Wissenschaften, Philos.-Hist. Klasse* (Vienna, 1888).
117. Cf. J. Combarieu; *La Musique et la magie*, I, Chapter 3; also J. Wolf, *Handbuch der Notationskunde*, I, pp. 25 ff, and A. Gastoué, op. cit. (n. 4), pp. 24–31.
118. A. Dieterich, *Abraxas*, p. 194.
119. Ibid., p. 165.
120. Plutarch, *De Musica*, ed. Reinach-Weil, c. 11.
121. Clement of Alexandria, *Paedagogus* II, 4; also E. Werner, op. cit. (*supra* n. 32).
122. Cf. C. Sachs, *The Rise of Music in the Ancient World*, p. 209.
123. Bar Hebraeus, *Buch der Strahlen*, ed. A. Moberg, II, pp. 127 ff.
124. Cf. Dom Parisot, *Rapport sur une mission scientifique*, etc., Preface pp. 21–35. Also Dom Jeannin, *Mélodies liturgiques syriennes*, I, Chapters I–V.
125. Jeannin, op. cit., I, p. 98.
126. Cf. P. Collangette, 'Etude sur la musique arabe', *Journal asiatique*, July–August, 1906, Sér. X, Vol. 8.
127. Jeannin, op. cit., I, p. 106.
128. Ibid., II, p. 267; Dom Parisot, op. cit., p. 219.
129. Dom Parisot, op. cit., p. 217, No. 301.
130. Cf. E. Wellesz, in *Proceedings of the Musical Association* (1932), p. 21.
131. Cf. G. Reese, *Music of the Middle Ages*, p. 89, abstracted from Wellesz-Tillyard *Monumenta Musicae Byzantinae*, I.
132. Ibid.
133. Cf. E. Wellesz, *Eastern Elements in Western Chant*, p. 100.
134. Ibid., p. 104.
135. Wellesz-Tillyard, *Monum. Music. Byzant.*, III, Sticherarium.
136. WGM, III, pp. 110, 165, 194.
137. Ibid., p. 108.
138. Ibid., p. 89.
139. Yehuda Halevi, *Kuzari*, ed. Cassel, II, 72–73.
140. S. Naumbourg, *Recueil des chants religieuses des israelites* (Paris, 1871).
141. J. Singer, *Die Tonarten des traditionellen Synagogengesanges* (Vienna, 1888).
142. P. Minkowsky, *Die Entwickelung der synagogalen Liturgie* (Odessa, 1902).
143. E. Birnbaum, *Liturgische Übungen*, I (Berlin, 1902).
144. A. Z. Idelsohn, *Thesaurus of Hebrew-Oriental Melodies*, Vols. I, II, IV, V, VI, VIII, IX (Prefaces).

CHAPTER THREE

Ecphonetic Notation in Judaism and Christianity

AFTER the two chapters dealing with some aspects of the point-counter-point in the relations of Jewish and early Christian music, we must now deal with the problem of musical notation. Its more general aspects have been outlined in Part I, Chapters III and IV, and we are now able to present the more technical side of the question, namely: in which way do the early notated sources of Christianity reflect Judaistic elements? Musical paleography can at least in part answer the question.

The following study of primitive notation is limited to the elements common to the notation of Judaism and Christianity. Yet it must not be too limited in its approach and methodology. Since the ecphonetic accents (or the primitive neumes) had both a syntactic-rhetoric and a musical function, it will be useful to investigate the basic problem along the following three lines of (1) strict paleography, (2) philology, and (3) musical research. Only where the conclusions confirm each other may we assume sound and tenable reasoning.

THE ECPHONETIC NOTATION

As was demonstrated above (Part II, Chapter I), Christianity was in musical matters the heir to Greece and Judaea. So organic was this synthesis that the Greek method of notation, as first employed by the Christians in the famous Oxyrhynchos Hymn, was applied to music of more Hebrew than Greek character. Later, the new ecphonetic notation came into the foreground, and the ancient Greek system faded altogether from the sources of Christian music.[1] In contradistinction to the exact Greek system that defined every note, the new ecphonetic method contented itself with an approximate representation of the musical *phrase*; the note is no longer the musical unit.

Yet it would be a mistake to assume that we are now concerned with purely musical matters. Actually, the ecphonetic system purports the notation of music only as a secondary result; as a by-product, as it were. The first and most important aim of that notation was the fixing of a, syntactically well ordered rhetorical delivery of sacred texts, whereby the more conspicuous inflexions of the voice are carefully noted. Where is the origin of these ancient signs, the forerunners of our modern notation?

Former Studies on Hebrew Accents and Middle-Byzantine Neumes

O. Fleischer has indisputably demonstrated that the systems of accentuation of the Hindus, Armenians, Copts, Syrians, Jews, etc., may all be traced back to a common origin.[2] Whether this source is to be found in the prosodic accents of the ancient Greeks, or whether it can be traced back to a much earlier time, possibly to Babylonian culture, is an interesting but unsolved problem which, however, leads us far away from our subject proper.[3] May it suffice here to give a conjectural table of the development of musical notation after the initial phase of ecphonetic notations had passed.[4]

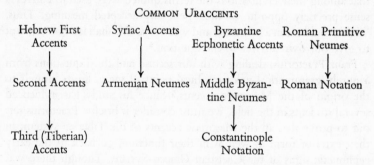

COMMON URACCENTS

Hebrew First Accents	Syriac Accents	Byzantine Ecphonetic Accents	Roman Primitive Neumes
↓	↓	↓	↓
Second Accents	Armenian Neumes	Middle Byzantine Neumes	Roman Notation
↓		↓	
Third (Tiberian) Accents		Constantinople Notation	

Here the three crucial questions of the entire topic arise. (1) To what extent were these notations genuinely intended to convey musical phrases? (2) Wherein lies the distinction between general grammatic-phonetic accents, punctuation and real signs of musical cadences? (3) How did these accents that served the purposes of music, grammar, mnemonics, and punctuation simultaneously, originate in the first place?

It is not easy to answer the first question. For the lines of demarcation between rhetoric inflexion and of genuine musical rendering are extremely flexible. That the *Neginot* or *Ta'amim* of Scripture were not primarily designed as musical signs is today generally believed, and the same seems to be true of the other ecphonetic accents. They assumed a semi-musical function soon after their first and most important object was achieved, that is, the exact syntactic punctuation of the text. Thereafter the grades of musical rendering, as practised by the various peoples and churches, diverged to a considerable degree. Some of them indicate a kind of mere oratorical delivery, whose pitch cannot be established precisely. Others attained genuine cantillation and subsequently developed their originally primitive ecphonetic accentuation into a truly musical notation.

The second question can be answered in a similar vein; as cantillation represents the highest point of rendering, elevated speech the lowest, with many intermediary steps betwixt and between, there are numerous shades and functions of notation. Eberhard Hommel attempted to handle this question in a rather universalistic manner, yet it cannot be said that he arrived anywhere at any concrete conclusion, with the exception of his debatable hypothesis concerning the terms 'high' and 'low' in the literature of the Western Oriental peoples. He maintains that among these civilizations the terms quoted were used to convey a sense precisely opposite to their generally accepted meaning. Thus, 'high' would mean a low tone, and vice versa. We shall later on attempt to give our own answer to the question.[5]

Franz Praetorius, dealing with our second and third questions from a purely grammatical-paleographical point of view, limits himself to the origin of the Masoretic accents.[6] Since his study has influenced several students in the field, we must consider it briefly. Praetorius sets out to prove that all the Masoretic accents of the Tiberian system, in their exterior form as well as in their function, go back to the early ecphonetic signs of the Christian Graeco-Syrians. Though there was undoubtedly a relationship of give and take, we can say absolutely nothing as to who took, who gave, or under what circumstances this exchange took place. Praetorius contents himself with showing the similarities of the two systems, and on this basis alone he claims that the Masoretes borrowed the ecphonetic system from Greek lectionaries. He offers no proof whatsoever for this contention.[7] In spite of the strong probability that the Jews actually did borrow some accents from the Greek ecphonetic system, Praetorius still falls down on the following points, the first of which is a matter of fact with which he could hardly have been familiar at the time of his work (1901).

(a) Praetorius knows nothing of the so-called Proto-Palestinian system of accentuation that consists almost exclusively of dots and is very unlike the Greek system, but resembles rather the Syriac system.[8] Praetorius's main thesis thus becomes unconvincing, since a connexion between the Proto-Palestinian and the Tiberian Masora has been adequately proven, indicating that not everything in the later (Tiberian) system had been borrowed from the Greeks.

(b) Praetorius is absolutely silent about one of the most important later ecphonetic signs, viz. the *Ison* or *Oligon*, which designates the tenor of a cantillation or psalmody. Why should the Masoretes not have adopted this all-important symbol? How essential it was, we may realize from Johannes Damascenus, (d. about 750), who wrote: 'The beginning, middle, end, and backbone of all the signs in psalmody is the *Ison*, indicated by the sign ⌒.'[9]

(c) Praetorius holds the opinion that the primary function of the accents was that of providing punctuation and of indicating special stress on certain syllables. He regards the use of the accents for guides to cantillation as a mere accessory function, stating (again without any proof) that the text was read only in a *leidlich schlichter Sprechvortrag* (rather plain recitation). We know today, however, that the use of accents to indicate the stress of individual syllables was a later development that did not exist in the Babylonian Hebrew system and certainly not in the Proto-Palestinian Masora.[10] Moreover, the oldest and most authentic tradition of Bible cantillation, that of the Yemenite Jews, is definitely of a musical character and under any circumstances far more than a *leidlich schlichter Sprechvortrag*. Finally, Praetorius fails to consider the possibility of a common ancient source[11] from which the early medieval Greek as well as the Masoretic and Syrian accentuations may have been derived. There are, in fact, hints that certain *Urakzente* were known centuries before the Greek ecphonetic system.[12] As for the chief subject, however, namely that of the kinship of Greek and Tiberian accentuation, Praetorius has taken an important step forward.

Mention has been made before of the 'Ur-accents'; toward their study Fleischer had done important spade-work, having succeeded in reconstructing the Byzantine neumes as far back as the tenth century. While his transcriptions have, during the last forty years, been surpassed by more exact studies, chiefly by E. Wellesz and H. J. W. Tillyard, they represented the first serious attempts. The signs of the manuscripts antedating the tenth century are much more enigmatic the farther back we go.

Here I shall attempt to apply a method of my own for the identification and the understanding of the interrelation of Hebrew accents. It will be based upon a three-fold comparison of accents, whereby first their exterior shapes, then their syntactical, and finally their musical significance will be studied.

It seems that the oldest Masoretic tradition was a complexity of signs taken both from the contemporaneous Syrian system and the ancient Hebrew practice of cheironomy.[13] The old Palestinian system, at any rate, was similar to the Syrian accentuation, consisting mainly of dots and simple strokes, while the Tiberian tradition displays much more kinship with early medieval Byzantine signs.

Since the neumes of the Roman Church stem ultimately from the same source as the Byzantine signs, it is logical to compare the Hebrew, medieval Greek, and early Roman accents or neumes. Unfortunately, we are not in a position to include the Syrian accents as well, since no oral, let alone written, tradition has come down indicating their musical or even rhetorical significance. Their accents have not been understood for centuries by the Syrians themselves.[14] Most probably, however, it was Syrian accents that played the decisive part in the whole process of borrowing, transforming and transmitting the various signs.[15]

The main question is how to identify the *Urakzente*. Since their names are manifold, changeable, and ambiguous, they offer no solid basis. We shall, therefore, first compare the exterior form of the accent together with its traditionally musical function; then the accent as syntactical-logical device.

Since the parallelism of the Hebrew poetry has been preserved in all translations, the half or full stops and their accentuation should be easily recognizable.[16] As will be seen later on, it was this principle of parallelism which has decisively influenced the musical structure of psalmody and cantillation in all languages, rites, and Churches.[17]

Thus we compare:[18]

EIGHTH AND NINTH CENTURIES

Sign in Greek Manuscripts	Ecphonetic Name	Latin Name	Hebrew Sign and Name (in Job, Prov., Psalms)
	Oxeia	Acutus (Virga)	Tifcha
	Apostrophos		'Atnah
	Bareia	Gravis	Legarmeh
	Hypocrisis	Quilisma descendens	Shalshelet or Darga
	Kathiste	Circumflexa	Zarqa
	Apeso exo	Clivis, Flexa	Zaqef qatan, or Ole veyored
	Syrmatike kai Teleia		Tifcha-Silluq
	Kentemata	Flexa	'Atnah

LATER DEVELOPMENT: ELEVENTH AND TWELFTH CENTURIES

Sign in Greek Manuscript	Byzantine Name	Name of Corresponding Latin Neume	Hebrew Sign and Name
	Oxeia	Virga	Tifcha or Yetib
	Ison or Oligon	Virga iacens	
	Kremaste ap'exo	Clivis	'Atnah
	Teleia	Punctus	Sof Pasuq

The most frequent combinations of accents at the close of sentences are:

I   ⌒ + = :| ˙ʃ

II   ⌣ + = :| ⌣

N.B. Greek to be read from left to right, Hebrew from right to left.

In later Latin sources, instead of the *circumflexa* (Hebr. *zarqa*), the *clinis* or *clivis* appears, that corresponds to the Byzantine *apeso hexo*, sometimes, as a comma-accent, the *podatus*. Later on, it will be possible to compare entire Greek ecphonetic passages with their Hebrew counterparts.

Investigating the neumes of the Codex Amiatinus, the oldest complete manuscript of the Vulgate, Fleischer reaches the following conclusions:[19]

> The sign of the comma-cadence is the *podatus* . . . , the sign of the semi-colon cadence is the *circumflex*, likewise placed on the last emphasized syllable of that part of the sentence. The *punctus*-cadence occurs only at the end of a full paragraph . . . [corresponding with the Hebrew *sof pasuq* at the end of a paragraph; the *silluq*, basically and for all purposes identical with the *sof pasuq*, closes the individual sentence].

An example of this primitive notation of the Latin *lectio* may convey an idea of this stage of transition to a more musically intended notation:[20]

Lectio Isaiae prophete
Propter Syon non tacebo et propter
Jerusalem non quiescam
donec egrediatur ut
splendor iustus eius
et salvator eius ut
lampas accendatur

According to this text, the *punctus circumflexa* or *flexa* corresponds to the *zakef*, indicating in the theory of neumes a step downward to the lower Third or Second. It represents the clear comma-cadence. The *climacus resupinus* is here obviously equivalent to 'atnah, which corresponds with our table. It likewise indicates a falling of the voice followed by a slight rise. The musical rendering of the Latin and Hebrew accents, likewise, shows distinct kinship. The Syrian, Italian, and Morroccan Torah cantillation uses a motif for the 'atnah, which we compare with the Roman *climacus resupinus*.

EXAMPLE 20[21]

a. Climacus resupinus   b. 'Atnah of Syrian Jews   c. 'Atnah of Italian Jews

The *punctus* **;** is to be equated with the *silluq* , since both of them always close a sentence. Its musical rendering is identical in the Torah cantillation of the Ashkenazic, Yemenite, and Syrian-Jewish Haftara cantillation with the rendering of the *punctus* in the Latin and the *apostrophos* in the Byzantine tradition.

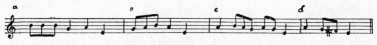

EXAMPLE 21[22]
a. Punctus versus (Tonus antiquus) (Transposed)
b. Ashkenazic cantillation
c. Yemenite cantillation
d. Syrian Haftara cantillation

Apart from the comma, semi-colon, and full stop accents and their musical representations, it was the similarity of the Hebrew *shalshelet* {, the ecphonetic *hypokrisis* {, the later Byzantine *kylisma* ⌇⌇, and the Latin *quilisma*, that struck the curiosity of the scholars, such as Fleischer, Thibaut, and Idelsohn. No clear conclusions were reached here, however. Originally, the accent seems to have indicated only a tremolo of the voice.[23] Later it was frequently misused as a pretext for embellishments and coloraturas. Thus the first transliterations of the Hebrew accents *after* Reuchlin's pioneer effort, by Sebastian Munster Ingelheimensis (Basel, 1529), a very valuable source, notates the *shalshelet* as follows:[24]

EXAMPLE 22

This goes beyond the original intention of the *shalshelet*, just as the practice of the *quilisma* exceeded its original function, as expressed by Aurelianus Reomensis, who calls it a 'rising tremolo'.[25]

In connexion with melismatic neumes, such as the last quoted one, the interesting question arises: did the Masoretes indicate in their accentuation the melismatic character of the Hallelujah? Were they even aware of it? The point is important, since apart from the basic accents and their neumes the analogies between Jewish and Christian musical paleography are rather scarce. It would be also very interesting to know whether the Hallelujah at the time of its great rise in Christian liturgy was considered equally essential by the bearers of Hebrew tradition.

As was pointed out at the end of Part I, Chapter IX, the Masoretic accentuation of the Hallelujah is remarkably consistent.

The *opening* Hallelujah always bears the *legarmeh* accent, with the exception of Ps. 146.[26] This is a strong disjunctive accent which sets the Hallelujah apart from the subsequent words.

The closing Hallelujah itself, bearing the *silluq* (full-stop sign), is regularly preceded by the *Great Rebia'*, the third strongest disjunctive accent. Hence, it may be inferred that this accentuation indicated a break in the chant, not unlike the neume of a *responsorium*, which shows where the soloist ends and the chorus begins, or vice versa.

Hebrew grammarians, such as Hayyug, Gikatilia, and their disciples have frequently stressed the existence of three kinds of accents for the 'poetical' books of Scripture (Job, Proverbs, and Psalms). In a few cases this distinction was stated in musical terms.[27]

The famous grammarian Ibn Bal'aam (eleventh century) divided the accents into sections that have a bearing on music; according to Ibn Bal'aam, the *Great Rebia'* stands for an extended melody in the higher tones of the scale. Since it precedes the final Hallelujah, it shows that the *closing* Hallelujah was rendered in a descending phrase. This precedence of a higher note or phrase before the closing Hallelujah is still evident in Gregorian and Jewish psalmody, as the following examples will show:[28]

EXAMPLE 23

The *initial* Hallelujah, usually bearing a *legarmeh* accent, is regularly followed by one or two conjunctive and one strong disjunctive accent, frequently the *'atnah* (half stop); the only exception to this rule is, as we saw above, Ps. 146. According to Ibn Bal'aam, the *pazer* accent of this Hallelujah indicates a sustained rising of the voice, and we may therefore propose the conjecture that the beginning of Ps. 146 had a musical rendering somewhat different from the other Hallelujah psalms.[29]

In order to check the results of our comparisons we shall now employ a completely different method. Thus far our method has been one in which we have taken accents whose *functions* were similar and then examined them as to their *musical* relationship. Now we shall proceed in precisely the reverse manner, that is to say, we shall examine analogous musical psalmodies as to their accentuation and neumation. For this purpose we have selected a few examples from the rich treasury of psalmodies which are common both to the Jewish and Christian tradition.

Alongside of a neumated version of the so-called *Tonus Peregrinus*, probably a most ancient psalmodic formula, with still fluctuating *tenor*, we place several similar tunes of the Sephardic-Oriental, of the Lithuanian and of the Ashkenazic Jews, comparing the accentuation of these various motifs.[30]

EXAMPLE 24

The results of our comparison are quite satisfactory. The half-close (*flexa*, used as a substitute sign for the *zakef* in the less symmetrical and more elaborate poetic style of the prophets; used in place of the *'atnah* in the Psalter) is in all cases rendered by a descent to the lower third of the *tonus currens*. The full close, neumated here by the *climacus* or *virga subbipunctis*, the extended form of *punctus*, is rendered in every instance by a descending progression to the lower fourth. Beyond the musical resemblance and the interrelation of the accents used, we note a striking correspondence of the respective accentuations of Ps. 114:1 and Ps. 29:1, both of which we have previously used as examples. This becomes evident from an examination of the Hebrew texts.

If, in Ps. 29, we disregard the superscription which was apparently not used in cantillation, we get completely identical schemes of accentuation.

Accentuation of Ps. 114:1.

B'tzeth Yisrael mimitzrayim | beth Ya'akov me'am loez.

Accentuation of Ps. 29:1.

Havu ladonai b'nay elim | havu ladonai kavod va'oz.

We are now able to equate with some certainty three accents of the Greek and Roman Churches with the corresponding Hebrew accents. However, it was only the strongest accents of division which we were able to examine and compare.[31] We may well ask whether our method would lend itself to an extension of the comparison to include the minor accents of the subdivisions. The answer must probably be given in the negative, for the following reason.

The Vulgate and Itala attempt, at least in the Psalter, to place the half-stop and full stop exactly on those words which correspond to the Hebrew words bearing 'atnah, 'oleh veyored (zakef), and silluq. A few examples will clarify this statement (. = silluq; : = 'atnah or 'oleh veyored).

Ps. 2:1.
    Quare fremuerunt gentes:et populi meditati sunt inania.
Ps. 5:2.
    Verba mea auribus percipe, domine,:intellige clamorem meam.
Ps. 6:4.
    Et anima mea turbata est valde:sed tu domine, usquequo?

These examples might be easily multiplied. Especially striking is the obvious carefulness with which the Latin translator has made the words which in his text occur at the half and full divisions correspond to those words in the Hebrew text which bear the accents 'atnah or silluq. Very interesting is the third example, where, contrary to usual Latin usage, the word *valde* (= very) is placed at the caesura, and the word *usquequo* is chosen for the close of the verse, it being accented on the last syllable to correspond with the Hebrew *ad-mathai*. This correspondence can be maintained, and even here with difficulty, only at the caesura and full stop. In the body of the sentence, however, the laws of Greek or Latin syntax, which are quite different from those of the Hebrew, prevail unhampered. Since the lection neumes were inseparably bound up with the relative positions of the words (a relationship which later became less rigid), these syntactic-logical signs, in the body of the sentence, tend to deviate more and more from the Hebrew pattern of accents. For this reason, even between the Greek and Roman neumes there exists a gulf which can be bridged only with greatest difficulty, and then only to a small extent.[32]

CODIFICATION OF MASORETIC ACCENTS

We know today that the final codification of the Bible text, as well as of its accents, is the result of efforts extending over centuries. Thus Kahle writes:

It ought to be stated here that the way of reciting Scripture was extremely flexible . . . . Furthermore, we must realize that the relative uniformity of the Tiberian MSS was but the result of Masoretic efforts that lasted for centuries.[33]

In Masoretic times, the basic traditions of cantillation with regard to the cadences of the main caesuras were for the most part still alive and the chief task of the theorists was that of eliminating the improvisations of the accents between the main caesuras.[34]

In order to call attention to a few details of this development we may mention the fact that the ancient Babylonian Masora knew nothing of connecting accents (*servi*). These were invented only in later Palestinian punctuation and were thence introduced into the Tiberian system. This correlates well with the fact that the Yemenite Jews, who are in possession of the oldest and most authentic tradition of cantillation, up to this very day do not chant any *servi*, but only *distinctivi* and, even among the *distinctivi*, they observe only the older and stronger accents.[35]

Accordingly, the final codification of the accents was a long and carefully prepared process. The passage of time was evidently well used to establish permanently and carefully the connexion of the old musical reading (*Urakzente*) with the new regulation of the cantillation by accents that are found between the main caesuras.

Thus, as far as the accentuation or neumation of the biblical texts for the public reading is concerned, the tendencies of Church and Synagogue run, in general, parallel to the final goal of strict regularity, unequivocally fixed and hostile to improvisation.[36] Yet, in all details, they diverge considerably according to the laws of the respective languages and scripts. (Semites from right to left, Indo-Europeans from left to right.)

After this more general exposition, we shall now investigate the extent to which the ancient Jewish tradition of cantillation has left its imprint in the documents of Christian ecphonetic notation. Having demonstrated the existence of common *Urakzente*, at least remnants of that evidence, common to the ancient Near East, should be found in the early ecphonetic documents.

But here the scholar suffers under a double handicap: the Jewish cantillation had not been transcribed into modern musical notation until 1518, when Reuchlin and Böschenstein set down the accents of the Torah cantillation;[37] on the other hand, none of the Christian lectionaries, if they are provided with notation at all, originated before the seventh century, and the task of deciphering and transcribing this semi-musical notation is most difficult.

There are not many Jewish auxiliary sources; one of them has already been discussed, namely Ibn Bal'aam's attempt to 'describe' the musical course of the various accents. Of slight assistance also are the so-called *zarqa*-tables of the High Middle Ages. They presented a systematical table of the accents and their most frequent combinations in the cantillation of the Pentateuch. Some contain timid attempts at musical description, as e.g., a manuscript in the Library of the Hebrew Union College, where at the end of a rabbinic commentary by R. David Kimchi there is added such a *zarqa*-table with some brief musical explanations. Similar instances of musical description are found in the writings of Moses of Provence, David ben Kalonymos, and others.[38]

In spite of the numerous attempts of philologists and theologians to establish the most authentic tradition of the scriptural accents, no conclusive results were achieved until the beginning of this century. In 1907 A. Gastoué ingeniously treated the musicological as well as the paleographical problems of the accents. In his *Origines du chant romain*, he investigated the melismatic formulas that embellish Ps. 118 in its Gregorian rendering during Easter week. He compared them with the accent-signs of the Hebrew text of the same psalm; and he found that certain Gregorian melismata of the Latin version correspond exactly with recurrent Hebrew accents. Since the verses of Ps. 118 constitute an integral part of all ancient Christian liturgies, it stands to reason that in the chant of their verses some Hebrew tradition has been retained, the more so since this *Hallel* psalm plays a similar role in the Jewish Easter ritual. It was the first positive result of Gastoué's studies to demonstrate the interdependence between the Latin punctuating melismata and some accents of the Hebrew text. Since he, however, had no access to ancient Hebrew manuscripts and did not know about the earlier ecphonetic systems of the first Palestinian Masora, he could not pursue effectively his promising comparisons.[39]

P. Wagner did not follow Gastoué's approach; whereas he pays much attention to Hebrew elements in the Gregorian tradition, he confines his observations concerning the common origin and the undeniable resemblance of ecphonetic accents and Hebrew *ta'amim* to a few critical remarks about Praetorius's findings.[40] He closes with the cautious observation: 'A certain relationship between ecphonetic and Hebrew accents cannot be denied'.[41]

The investigation was resumed by J. B. Thibaut, who, in 1913, for the first time seriously probed into the puzzling history of the Byzantine ecphonetic signs;[42] by E. Wellesz, who specialized in the old neumes of Byzantium which had grown directly out of the *ecphonesis*,[43] and, finally, by C. Høeg, who produced definite results and with whom the period of groping in the dark came to an end.[44] In the following, we shall refer to *his* conclusions only, since he had more manuscript material at his disposal than anybody heretofore, and since his attempts at deciphering them have definitely surpassed all of the other scholars.

Of the three problems that we faced earlier, the first one concerns the primary function of ecphonetic signs: were they only punctuating and rhetorical designs or had they a clearly musical significance? This question has been answered by Høeg once and for all. Studying carefully the lectionary Codex Sinaiticus Eight, he discovered that there and in similar manuscripts the ecphonetic signs were co-ordinated with genuinely musical notation; hence, lectionary (ecphonetic) notation did in many cases have a really musical purpose.[45] Høeg attempts an approximate transliteration into modern musical notation, which, however, remains somewhat vague. It is possible, though, to fathom the *general* course of early Byzantine cantillation, according to Høeg's findings.

The second question concerning the interrelation of the various ecphonetic systems is by no means answered positively by Høeg. He agrees that these systems must have had a common origin. But this fact, he adds, is only a part of the true situation.[46] He states his objection in a negative way:

It is impossible to assume that the Jewish-Syrian system was a creative factor in the origin of the Byzantine system. The chronological facts would not permit serious consideration of such a solution and the relationship of the Greek (Byzantine) neumes with the signs of ancient (classic) prosody would make it very improbable.[47]

He is, of course, fully aware of the resemblance of the Syriac accents to those of the Proto-Palestinian Masora, and of the more Byzantine bent of the Tiberian school. He might, therefore, be right in rejecting the theory of a direct relation between *all*, even the remotest members of the ecphonetic system. On the other hand, some kind of relationship, mainly through the Syriac accents, of Jewish and Byzantine neumes does exist beyond any doubt; the evidence is overwhelming.

Høeg's least conclusive answer concerns the problem of origin and age of ecphonetic notation. Here he ventures hardly beyond some cautiously couched conjectures, such as: 'There appears to exist a strong kinship between the Byzantine and Hebrew accentuation'. Høeg's comparisons, however, failed to demonstrate anything tangible since he was not familar enough with the Hebrew accentuation. Moreover, he had only two or three scriptural passages, of which the Hebrew tradition was available to him, passages that he could collate with ecphonetic Greek manuscripts.[48] None the less, Høeg is convinced that a systematic comparison would clearly demonstrate the intricate relationship between Byzantine and Hebrew accents. He does not doubt the apostolic age of *cantillation* itself; this was in his opinion the main Jewish contribution to Byzantine *ecphonesis*. The ecphonetic *notation* might have originated in the hellenized atmosphere of Syria during the first centuries of Christianity under Greek and Hebrew influence. No serious evidence, no comparisons between Greek and Hebrew manuscripts are even attempted. This is obviously the weakest point in Høeg's otherwise excellent study—caused by the complete lack of written sources before the sixth century.

We shall now offer a comparison between the literary aspects of Greek and Hebrew accents based upon manuscripts of identical portions in both languages. The Greek passages were cited by Høeg, the Hebrew ones are quoted after the recognized version of the Masoretic text. The punctuating marks are especially stressed here, since they constitute the main ecphonetic effort.

GEN. 2:20–23

Byzantine Lectionaries

Hebrew Text of Scripture
(Only the strongly disjunctive accents are indicated here.)

,Ekalezen Adam onomata,pasi tois

ktenesi kai pasi tois peteinois tou

ouranou kai pasi tois theriois tes ges+

To de Adam ouch eurethe boethos

homoios auto+Kai epebalen ho Theos

ecstasin epi ton Adam kai hypnosen

kai elabe mian ton pleuron autou kai

aneplerosen sarka anti autes+Kai oko-

domese Kyrios ho Theos ten pleuran

hen elaben apo tou Adam eis gynaika

kai egagen auten pros ton Adam kai

eipen Adam+touto nyn ostoun ek

ton oston mou kai sarx ek tes sarkos

mou+Aute klethesetai gyne hoti ek

tou andros autes elephthe haute+

Vayikra ha-Adam shemot l'chol

hab'hema ul - 'of ha-shamayim; ul'

chol hayath ha-sadeh; ul'Adam lo

matza ezer k'negdo: Vayapel Adonai

Elohim | tardema al ha-Adam vayi-

shan vayikach achath mitzalothav

vayissgor bassar tachthena: Vayiven

Adonai Elohim | eth ha-tzela asher-

lakach min-ha-Adam l'isha vay' vieha

el-ha-Adam: Vayomer ha-Adam zoth

hapaam 'etzem me'atzamai ubassar

mibsari l'zoth yikare isha ki me'ish

lukacha zoth:|

Generally, the beginning accent is repeated at the end of the phrase in Byzantine notation. Not so in Hebrew accentuation. None the less, the placing of the accents upon the words of the text shows a remarkable identity of spirit. A few examples will suffice: *shemot = onomata* (names); *ezer k'negdo:* = *homoios auto* (like unto him); *Vayapel = Kai epebalen* (and He made fall); *vayikach = kai elabe* (and He took); *vayissgor bassar = kai aneplerosen sarka* (and He closed up the flesh); *l'isha = eis gynaika* (into a woman); etc.

In a literal translation, these isolated phrases would appear somewhat like this (| mild separation; || strong disjunction; { end of sentence):

Adam gave names | to all cattle | and to the fowl of the heaven || and to every beast of the field || but for Adam there was not found a help | suitable to him {

And the Lord God caused a deep sleep | to fall upon Adam | and he slept || and He took | one of his ribs || and closed up the flesh | instead thereof {

And the Lord God formed the rib | which He had taken from Adam | into a woman || and brought her unto Adam {

And Adam said | this time | it is bone of my bones || and flesh of my flesh || this shall be called woman (*isha*) || because out of man (*ish*) | was this one taken {

The passages *touto nyn* = this time; *eis gynaika* = into a woman; are almost torn out of their context, and follow strictly the principles of Hebrew accentuation. There are many such instances and it is easily seen that at least the Greek punctuation followed closely the Hebrew literary tradition.

Yet, if we try to equate some of the Greek accents with their Hebrew counterparts, according to their function, the result is no longer homogeneous. For the three strongest Hebrew accents (ˌ̣ *sof pasuq*, end of sentence); ᴧ *'atnah*, half-stop; and ˸ *zakef katan*; strong disjunctive accent, almost a half-stop) correspond, in turn to the following Byzantine signs:

Hebrew ˌ̣ = Byz. + (end of sentence)

Hebrew ᴧ = Byz. + or ϟ ϟ

Hebrew ˸ = Byz. ÷ or ❱

426

It is understandable that the + (*stauros*) sign corresponds to three Hebrew accents since the Septuagint usually makes two Greek sentences out of one Hebrew. For the '*atnah*—where the Greek text does not have a full stop—one finds regularly the *apostrophos* (❧ ❧); but the same signs stand also for the *zakef katan* and, occasionally, for the *tifcha* (⌣). The laws of the Greek language did permit a division of the sentences along the main lines of the Hebrew syntax, but could not in every instance follow the Hebrew original. Especially the strictly dichotomic style of the Psalter could not always be used, at least in the narratives of the Old Testament.

ATTEMPTS AT MUSICAL RECONSTRUCTION

What is the musical aspect of the *ecphonesis*? With the help of Sinaiticus 8 and other old manuscripts, Høeg attempted successfully to reconstruct the musical character of the notation. Unfortunately, he offers only one Old Testament passage in this transcription: Gen. 1:1–4. In the following we shall compare Høeg's findings, especially his musical reconstructions of ecphonetic signs, with the way the Yemenite and Babylonian Jews interpret and sing the scriptural accents. These modes of cantillation will be annotated here, as follows:

pause or comma | half-stop || end of sentence $\}\}$[49]

15

EXAMPLE 25

a. Byzantine *ecphonesis*: Gen. 1:1-4
b. Yemenite tradition: Gen. 1:1-4
c. Babylonian tradition: Gen 1:1-3

At the first glimpse the similarity between the Greek and the Hebrew renderings and their musical pictures is by no means obvious. Yet on closer examination the graphic representation of a Yemenite cantillation has many features in common with the Byzantine tradition. However, it must be candidly admitted: the time is not yet ripe to investigate this question fully, since the ancient Hebrew manuscripts of the early Palestinian Masora are accessible only in minor fragments. Until a considerable corpus of such manuscripts is amassed and readily accessible to the scholar, it will not be possible to obtain more than general results.

Under these circumstances, the only way open to us to pursue our examination is a thorough study of the punctuating melismata, such as they appear most conspicuously in the ecphonetic accentuation, and thereafter in the neumes and traditions of the various lectionaries; for it is only the punctuating melismata, where both paleography and musical evidence coincide, that represent the musical rendering of the *Urakzente*. The next chapter will deal with this subject.

428

NOTES CHAPTER III

1. So completely did the Greek system of notation vanish, that Isidore of Seville (sixth to seventh century) was convinced that music 'can by no means be notated or written down'. This at a time when the new, Judaeo-Christian neumatic system was already strongly in evidence in the Near East as well as in Rome. About the Oxyrhynchos hymn in Greek notation, see above, Part II, Chapter I.

2. O. Fleischer, *Neumenstudien*, I, Chapters I, IV, V, VI.

3. It is improbable that the Babylonians would have used a well developed system of musical notation; however, some traces of primitive reading-symbols are recognizable. Cf. *Baron von Oppenheim-Festschrift* (1933) and the discussions thereafter between B. Landsberger and C. Sachs. Meanwhile, new positive evidence has been discovered near Baghdad; cf. *Iraq*, 1946-7.

4. Cf. also J. B. Thibaut, *Origine byzantine de la notation neumatique de l'Église latine* pp. 100-2.

5. Eberhard Hommel, *Untersuchungen zur hebräischen Lautlehre* (Leipzig, 1917), pp. 39 ff; C. Sachs, *The Rise of Music in the Ancient World*, pp. 69, 223.

6. F. Praetorius, *Über die Herkunft der hebräischen Akzente* (Berlin), and F. Praetorius, *Reply to Renée Gregory* (*Die Übernahme der frühmittelgriechischen Neumen durch die Juden*), (1902).

7. He feels absolutely assured as to the non-existence of *Ta'amim* before the eighth century 'by the great *argumentum e silentio* of the Talmud' (*Übernahme der frühmittelgriechischen Neumen*, p. 12). However, on this point he is definitely mistaken, for the Midrash does refer to the accents at least in the clear remarks of the Tractate *Soferim* (XII, 1, III, 10, and XIV, 9-10) and Exod. Rabba.

8. Cf. Kahle, *Masoreten des Westens*, p. 34, furthermore Bauer-Leander, *Historische Grammatik der hebräischen Sprache*, pp. 138 ff.

9. Johannes Damascenus (Gerbert, *De cantu et musica sacra*, II).

10. Cf. Kahle, *Masoreten des Ostens*, pp. 172 f.

11. Cf. Hommel, op. cit., pp. 27, 39, 80, and Kahle in Bauer-Leander, *Historische Grammatik der hebräischen Sprache*, p. 138 f., furthermore Bergsträsser-Gesenius, p. 161. For the cantillation of the Yemenites see Idelsohn, *Thesaurus*, I, Introduction.

12. Hommel, op. cit., p. 152 shows that the phonetic term *nitzab* occurs already in Ps. 39:6, and that it then turned into the grammatical (and musical) terminology. It would be, in our opinion, the first biblical proof for the Hebrew analogue of the Greek *ison*, for *derekh nitzab* is the name for the normal position of the voice (the pitch of the *tonus currens*).

13. WGM, II, p. 80. Thibaut, op. cit. Chapter II.

14. Idelsohn is mistaken in stating that Syriac lectionaries do not contain any accent-signs of ecphonetic nature. (In his *Phonographierte Gesänge der syrischen und yemenitischen Juden*, Kaiserliche Akademie der Wissenschaften, Wien, p. 33). See also J. Wolf, *Handbuch der Notationskunde*, I, pp. 63-65, and Thibaut, loc. cit.

15. WGM, II, p. 80.

16. Exact dates are given in Wickes, *A Treatise on the Accents of the Three So-called Poetical Books of the OT* (Oxford, 1881). See also P. Kahle in Bauer-Leander, *Historische Grammatik der hebräischen Sprache*, Sect. 9.

17. For details cf. WGM, III, Chapter 1, and the entire second volume; also P. Johner, *Neue Schule des gregorianischen Gesanges*, chapter 'Psalmody'.

18. Idelsohn has attempted to extend Hebrew analogies of accents to the terms of Middle Greek Prosody, including their sub-divisions into *tonoi*, *chronoi*, and *pneumata*, adapting terms of an obscure Byzantine Jew. This abortive attempt follows slavishly the account given by Reuchlin in his *De Accentibus Linguae Hebraicae*, III. See my study 'Two Obscure Sources,' etc., in *Historia Judaica*, XVI (1954), pp. 39 ff.

19. Fleischer, op. cit., II, p. 11.

20. A. Gastoué, (op. cit.) goes as far as to equate the accentuation of a Hebrew psalm with that of a Latin one (cf. p. 79). Our example in its Latin version is to be found in WGM, II, pp. 86 ff.

21. (a) *LU*, p. viii; (b) after *JM*, p. 44, No. 4; (c) after *JM*, p. 44, No. 7.

22. (a) *LU*, p. 126; (b) after A. Baer, *Baal Tefilla*, p. 35, line 2; (c) after IT, I, Nos. 21 and 24; (d) IT, II, p. 52, line 3.

23. See also Wickes, loc. cit., Elia Levita. *Sefer Tob Ta'am* IV. (Hebr.)

24. It is significant that even until the present day the *shalshelet* has remained the least distinct accent—on account of its tendency towards musical 'coloratura'. Besides, it is rather rare; in the Torah it is to be found only four times: Gen. 19:16; Gen. 24:12; Gen. 39:8; Lev. 8:23. In all of these cases it is combined with a *Vav conversivum*.

25. Cf. Aurelianus Reomensis, *Musica disciplina*, Chapter XIII, in Gerbert, *Scriptores*, I, 47.

26. Cf. Augustine, *Enarr. in Ps.* 105 (106): 'Et hoc afferunt, quod omnes halleluiatici Psalmi habent in fine Halleluia, non omnes in capite, unde quicumque psalmus non habet in fine Halleluia nec in capite volunt eum habere. Sed nos, quousque nobis aliquibus artis documentis id verum esse persuadent, multorum consuetudinem sequimur, qui ubicumque legunt Halleluia eidem Psalmo adtribuunt, in cuius capite (post numeri notam) hoc inveniunt.'

(Approximate translation: '. . . all alleluiatic psalms have the Alleluia in the end, but not all in the beginning; hence some do not add an Alleluia to the beginning of a psalm that does not (originally) end with an Alleluia. But we, as far as certain documents of literature have convinced us, follow the custom of numerous scholars, who add a closing Alleluia to every psalm, in whose heading . . . they find it.') Graetz disputes the existence of this practice; he also questions the correctness of the *MAS*.

27. Cf. Ewald-Dukes, *Beiträge zur Geschichte der ältesten Auslegung des Alten Testaments* (Stuttgart, 1844) III, p. 197.

28. Cf. E. Werner, 'Preliminary Notes for a Comparison', etc., *HUCA*, XV, pp. 356-7. For a more technical examination, cf. E. Werner, 'The Doxology in Synagogue and Church', *HUCA*, XIX (1946), pp. 329-31.

29. Ibid., pp. 362 ff.

30. Cf. my article in *Jüdische Rundschau* (1934), Nos. 27-28. A very interesting suggestion as to the *Tonus Peregrinus* is given in Gerbert's *De Cantu*, etc., I, 3, comparing it with the Hebrew term *shigayon* (Ps. 7:1).

Example 24a: Zürich Kantonsbibl., Cod. 55 (thirteenth century).

The musical material for Examples 24b–d is very old and reliable; its common motif, widely spread, may be found in many sources, e.g.: 24b MS Jekel Singer, H.U.C. Library, Birnbaum collection 4f6, 24c and 24d, besides Idelsohn (IT, II, p. 65; *JM*, p. 55) in Sulzer, *Shir Zion*, II, p. 179, Baer, *Baal Tefilla*, p. 314, No. 1357.

31. As stated by Hommel, Kahle, and Idelsohn unanimously, the Yemenites cantillate only the strong distinctive accents.

32. Cf. WGM, II, p. 113:

'Actually, the assumption that there was a connexion between the Roman neumes and another, contemporary or older, type of neumation, disposes of all the difficulties. Such neumes would antedate the notation of Byzantine hymns, and probably would not even be of Byzantine, but possibly of Syro-Greek origin. The supposition of that prototype of neumation would explain the divergency of Latin and Byzantine neumes, and would, on the other hand, take into account the indubitable dependence of Rome upon the Near East in most liturgical and musical matters.'

And quite in the same way (p. 111):

'Quite similar is the case of the Gregorian chants themselves. Time and again they focus the scholar's direction on the Near East, notwithstanding the fact that they were . . . composed or collected and redacted in Rome.'

33. Kahle, *Masoreten des Westens*, II, p. 45.

34. The same intention caused the monks and grammarians of both the Western and the Eastern Church to abandon the previous ecphonetic signs in favour of the more elaborated musical neumes.

35. Cf. IT, I, pp. 22 ff.

36. This antagonism between the principle of strict decision on the side of Rabbinism and the impulse of improvisation on the part of the *Paitanim* and *Hazanim* led to a fruitful

as well as to a subtle, though sometimes disagreeable conflict, which burst out in a tremendous explosion in the sphere of Hasidism. After all, there was eternal conflict between the rationalistic and mystical forces within Judaism.

37. Johannes Reuchlin & Böschenstein (Hagenau, 1518). *De Accentibus Linguae Hebraicae.* There, the tenor carries the accents of cantillation; Böschenstein's attempt at harmonizing is only explicable as the result of the author's belief that 'respectable' music must be polyphonic, in the fashion of the contemporary forms of the motet and the madrigal.

38. Cf. *JE*, article 'Cantillation', Vol. III, p. 548. Mr. F. L. Cohen, the musical oracle of that excellent encyclopedia, was neither original nor accurate in his observations. Better references in Idelsohn, *Jewish Music*, and Wickes, *The Accents of the Prose Books of the Old Testament* (Oxford, 1887). The most promising approaches will be discussed later.

39. Cf. A. Gastoué, op. cit., pp. 78–80.

40. See *supra*, p. 429, nn. 6–10.

41. WGM, II, p. 31.

42. Cf. Jean-Baptiste Thibaut, *Monuments de la notation ekphonétique et hagiopolite de l'Église grecque* (St Petersburg, 1913).

43. Egon Wellesz, *Byzantinische Musik* (Breslau, 1927); 'Studien zur Byzantinischen Musik', *ZFM*, XVI (1934), pp. 213 ff, 414 ff. *Aufgaben und Probleme auf dem Gebiete der byzantinischen und orientalischen Kirchenmusik* (Münster, 1923), pp. 69 ff.

44. Carsten Høeg, *La Notation ekphonétique* (Copenhagen, 1935).

45. Ibid., pp. 24–25, 20–21, 26–35; see also Rahlfs, 'Verzeichnis der griechischen Handschriften des Alten Testaments', in *Mitteilungen des Septuaginta-Unternehmens*, Vol. II (Berlin, 1914).

46. Like P. Kahle, Høeg considers the Nestorian Masora the common source of Byzantine, Syriac, and Hebrew accents.

47. Høeg, op. cit., pp. 145 ff.

48. Ibid, p. 96.

49. Ibid., pp. 32–33.

CHAPTER FOUR

The Formulas and Cadences of
Lesson and Oration

RELATION OF CHANT TO TEXT

I venture to say that the principle of the formula is the basic principle of musical composition in the Syro-Palestinian countries, and it spread from there with the expansion of early Christian music to the countries of the Byzantine Empire and to those of the Mediterranean Basin. The kernel of the melodies of both the Eastern and Western Churches derived from the melodies of the Synagogue. But their character was considerably modified by the genius of the language to which they were sung . . . .[1]

This far-reaching statement by E. Wellesz epitomizes most of the previous results of the work of P. Wagner, A. Z. Idelsohn, A. Gastoué, and myself.[2] While it is based upon decade-long research, it has not yet been fully implemented; especially the influence of the various languages upon cantillation and psalmody has never been carefully examined. And yet, it was a signal and consequential touch, by which language changed entire structures of music.

The element common to the items of this chapter's contents is their relation to language; in other words: the varying application of music to types of pitched recitation. The word predominates completely over the note. The note and syntactic accents are all-important and both half and full stops of the texts are minutely pointed musically.

Desirable as it may be, it is not within the scope of this book to trace the primeval origin of the cadence, or of the inflexions of ancient or primitive recitations or wailing-exclamations back to their physiological and psychological causes. This remains the task of comparative musicology and forms a link between anthropology, the natural sciences, and musical history.[3] We must, however, make one exception from this limitation. It concerns the first nuclei of autonomous musical expression, in as much as they are at least partly independent from primitive *Sprechgesang*: the punctuating melismata and ornaments.[4]

They are only partly independent; for there is ample proof at hand

432

that some of them originated in answer to phonetic-linguistic reasons. The two Hebrew grammarians, Saadya Gaon and Dunash ibn Librat, use the Arabic term *tafchim*, Hebrew *pi'ur*, which mean 'ornament', for the full (not apocopated) pronunciation of a word.[5] According to the rules of classic Hebrew grammar the note accent in a *pausal form* (half or full stop) recedes usually at least one syllable from its normal place. Such a pronunciation is termed *mil'el*: e.g. in English—'cómparable' but 'to compáre'.

The *pi'ur* melisma occurs frequently in connexion with the *mil'el* accentuation and is therefore a direct consequence of the dichotomous structure of Hebrew poetry. Dunash formulates the rule in these words: 'If the ecphonetic accent (*ta'am*) stands in the middle of a word (*mil'el*), then its musical phrase (*ne'ima*) is to be drawn out, stretched and modulated.'[6]

It should be borne in mind that in half or full stop (*pausa*) the *mil'el* position of the accent is habitual; thus, the grammatical rule amounts to a postulate of musical melismata for a half or closing cadence. I hope I shall be forgiven for dwelling on this matter so long; but actually the passage quoted before is one of the greatest import for the musical structure of Hebrew psalmody and cantillation, in as much as it demonstrates the intricate connexion between syntax, punctuation, ecphonetic accents, pronunciation, and punctuating melismata.

This last mentioned term, the punctuating melisma, is the musical concomitant and by-product of a syntactic close in classic Hebrew literature.

Thus, two main categories of ornaments have to be recognized, which are clearly distinct from one another. The phonetic-syntactic-punctuating melisma is dependent upon, and bound to, linguistic principles and the genius of the Hebrew language. The other, more or less autonomous, musical ornament is the first and foremost expression of 'absolute' music, as we find it in the melismatic, yet wordless, chants of the Latin *jubili* or the Hebrew *niggunim*.[7]

The musical embodiment and equivalent of the phonetic-syntactic accents, as they appear on half or full stops, are the punctuating melismata and the formulas that accompany their corresponding cadences in psalmody and cantillation. Their positions within the biblical sentences, and probably their musical significance also, have to be considered invariant for the last two thousand years at least, although their musical character was considerably modified by the genius of the language into which the Scripture was translated.

Surveying now our material according to the geographic areas, we shall compare the following cadence formulas or melismata as they appear in the Syrian, Armenian, Byzantine, Latin, and Jewish traditions. The existence of typical cadence formulas in Syrian chant was first demonstrated by Jeannin and Puyade.[8] The Armenian tradition had not yet been as thoroughly examined as it might be desired; none the less, two fine studies on Armenian chant and its cadences are in existence, written by K. Kevorkian and P. Aubry.[9] Concerning Byzantine chant we can safely rely on the results of the profound studies by Wellesz, Tillyard, C. Høeg, and J. B. Thibaut.[10] The research of Latin cadences is best represented by the volumes of *Paléographie musicale*, the studies and books by A. Gastoué, Dom Mocquereau, and P. Wagner.[11] As for Jewish material, the sources edited by A. Baer, A. Z. Idelsohn, and my own studies may give the necessary basis for further investigations.[12]

PUNCTUATING MELISMATA

Although the musical significance of the Syriac ecphonetic accents has been lost for at least seven centuries, the fact that both the grammar and its system of accentuation obey certain general rules of Semitic languages will enable us to analyse some of the Syriac cadence formulas in the light of the syntactic or tonic accents, to which they are applied. As indicated earlier in this chapter, recession of accent, combined with punctuating melismata takes place at half or full stops of a sentence. From this point of departure we shall now proceed to analyse the typical cadence formulas of the various traditions.

Punctuating Melismata in Lection and Psalmody

The Yemenite Jews, who most probably represent the oldest and least contaminated tradition, use the following cadencing melismata as the musical expression of the main disjunctive accents (*mafsiqim*).

434

EXAMPLE 26[13]

Special attention should be given to 26d and 26e because of their final cadences which go beneath the tonic (subtonal); similar formulas occur also in Christian psalmody, as we shall see presently. Examples 26e, 26f and 26g have another element in common: the two-fold *tenores*. This phenomenon warrants extensive discussion, since it is typical of many psalmodic forms.

Corresponding with the dichotomous structure of psalmody, the body of the verse is chanted upon a reciting note, the *tenor*, also called *tuba* or *tonus repercussionis*. (The term used in the older literature is usually *tuba*.)[14] In many psalm types there is one *tenor* only, common to the first and second half verse. Some of the archaic psalmodies, however, contain double *tenores*, a feature that frequently indicates oriental origin.

The punctuating melismata of the Babylonian Jews are given in Example 27.[15]

EXAMPLE 27

Subtonal melismata are apparent in Examples 27e and 27h. A double *tenor* occurs in Example 27b; this type is common to all Jewish centres and resembles the structure of the famous *Tonus Peregrinus* of the Roman Church, which we shall discuss later on. Examples 27c and 27f show distinct similarity with cadence formulas of the Syrian and Roman Churches.

The main cadences of Sephardic Jewry are given in Example 28.[16]

EXAMPLE 28

Since Sephardic Jewry comprises all Jews of Spain, Southern France, Southern Italy, the Balkan countries, as well as those of Turkey and Asia Minor, we are considering here only the tradition of the oldest group, the direct remnants of the refugees from the expulsion from Spain in 1492. These are the Jews of Gibraltar, Southern Italy, and the—formerly Turkish—Balkan countries.

The characteristic double *tenor* of the *Tonus Peregrinus* is again apparent in Example 28b; also, the cadence of the versicle in Roman psalmody is patterned like Example 28d. Subtonal phrases are evident in

Example 28c, which shows clearly the features of the Dorian or Hypo-dorian church mode, respectively.

Much less conservative and more influenced by the music of their environment are the punctuating melismata of the Ashkenazic Jews, of whose chants only the Western tradition is discussed here, since it is older and less contaminated by Byzantine and Slavonic elements than the East European tradition.

A further word on this matter might not be amiss. For Jewish and Christian scholars alike are prone to accept a tradition as genuine when it is frequently pronounced so, be it by authorities or by laymen. Here A. Z. Idelsohn, one of the pioneers of Jewish music history, cannot be fully absolved from fault or bias. Being himself of Eastern Jewish extraction, he never freed himself completely from an affection for Eastern Jewish tunes nor was he able to evaluate them with that detach-ment which behoves the critical scholar.

When the main immigration of the Jews into Eastern Europe started, coming from Germany between the fourteenth and sixteenth centuries, the German Jews encountered older Jewish settlements in the Crimea and in south-eastern Ukraine. These older settlers were refugees from the Tartar, Persian, or Byzantine empires, having escaped the persecu-tion of former centuries. The music of the Tartars, the later Byzantine Church and the Russian Church contains modes and tunes very much akin to those of the Eastern Jews. Through the invasion of the Turks on one hand, and through the westward migration of Eastern Jewry, fol-lowing the pogroms of 1648 to 1660, on the other, the various Eastern modes, contaminated and compound as they were, came into Central Europe. They became evident there about 1700, as can be seen in some of the oldest and crudest manuscripts of East European cantors.[17] There is every reason, therefore, to assume that many of these modes were originally alien to Jewish tradition, and were not adopted before the sixteenth century.

Example 29[18] gives the typical cadences of lesson and primitive psal-mody, traditional with the (Western) Ashkenazic Jews.

EXAMPLE 29

Noticeable are here the double *tenores* of Example 29d and the closing formulas of Example 29b (the prophetic lesson), which resemble certain Gregorian cadences, showing also subtonal elements. Examples 29c and 29a are clearly influenced by Germanic modes; the Tonic-Dominant relation, utterly alien to Oriental chant, is especially apparent in Example 29c. Idelsohn makes the correct observation that 'in the modes for Torah and the Psalms of the Ashkenazim there is a certain confusion—the tenor or the tonic were changed—the tradition was contaminated'.[19]

With regard to scale we have pointed out . . . the German influence in re-shaping it . . . . Likewise, German music affected the re-shaping of the tetra-chordal form of Lamentations . . . . The influence went much deeper; it touched the very marrow of Jewish song. As already mentioned, German elements penetrated into the Semitic-Oriental song of the Jews and, by amal-gamating with it, became an organic part of it.[20]

The fifth Psalm Tone of the Roman Church shows the following structure:[21]

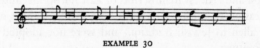

EXAMPLE 30

It is a pure Lydian with the *tenor* C.[22] Yet, its German version according to the practice of the eleventh and twelfth centuries was:[23]

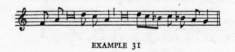

EXAMPLE 31

What has happened? The B flat has entered the mode, and the note G, and sometimes F, have been added to the end.

Let us compare with these two versions the two ways in which the German Jews have preserved the *Tefilla* mode:[24]

EXAMPLE 32

The first version has already the B flat, but still the *finalis* A; the second version adds the notes G and F, thus rendering it as a Mixolydian phrase with the *finalis* F. This development in Jewish psalmody took place simultaneously with the German change of the Roman psalmody, around the eleventh or twelfth century. Sometimes the results wrought by these changes are closely parallel.

EXAMPLE 33

Example 33a[25] gives the old Ashkenazic (German-Jewish) psalmody of Friday evening (Ps. 95:1). The very same text and a similar tune are contained in a German *Invitatoriale* of about 1640, a manuscript in the possession of the Library of the Hebrew Union College. Idelsohn already has drawn attention to the resemblance.[26] A complete identification of the fifth Psalm Tone with F major has taken place, possibly under the spell of German or Scandinavian folk-song.[27]

Even more complicated becomes the problem, if one compares the ancient Babylonian-Jewish mode of lesson, which apparently has been taken over by the Roman Church, with the Ashkenazic version of the same cantillation.[28]

EXAMPLE 34

What has taken place between 34a and 34c? Not only has the *tenor* shifted from E to F, but the clearly Phrygian or Hypophrygian character of the mode has changed toward an unmistakable F major with pentatonic elements. And yet even this F major shows ancient features in its second close (G–D), identical with the *punctus versus* of Examples 35 and the end of 36c.[29]

EXAMPLE 35

EXAMPLE 36

Apparently, Example 34a falls into the category of the fourth mode; cf. Example 34b, where the paradigm of that mode is quoted after Pseudo-Hucbald's *Commemoratio Brevis*.[30] Now, the fourth Tone has always been one of the problem-children of the Gregorian music theorists; P. Wagner observes that in that mode a shift of the *tenor* has taken place,[31] without being able to account for it. A. Auda shows clearly its subtonal features,[32] and A. Gastoué links it, rightly, as must be admitted, to the basic modes of the ancient Synagogue.

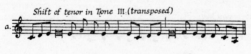

440

EXAMPLE 37

He calls it, however, 'Dorienne relâchée', attributing to it the follow-ing scheme:[33]

EXAMPLE 38

In a special study on Jewish and Gregorian Chant the same scholar elaborates on the fourth mode. A few of his fine and keen observations may find place here:

> One may see that the fourth tone is frequent among Jewish melodies. Yet it is mainly used with the *tenor* of the third (G), when the *finalis* is E, and with the *tenor* D, when the *finalis* is B. The chants of that mode, whose dominant is the fourth (A) are often sung like the plagal mode which correspond to it in the Oriental Churches, with a chromatic G sharp. Yet, in spite of the high age of this (chromatic) practice, one cannot ascertain if this chromaticism is original. At any rate, diatonic or chromatic, this type of ancient *Doristi* rendered in the 'échelle relâchée' conforms with the passage of Clement of Alexandria on the subject of the ancient Hebrew hymns which he had heard . . . .[34]

What does Gastoué here refer to?

As was shown in Part II, Chapter I, the antagonism of the Alexandrian fathers to excessive chromaticism was very outspoken.[35]

This attitude toward 'chromaticism' common to Plato and Aristotle was transposed into early Christianity; Judaism also displayed this attitude, though not so systematically, and not under the influence of Greek philosophy.[36] Fortunately, Clement describes the mode of the old Greek drinking song as having been almost identical with that of Jewish psalmody. Further on in the same section, this mode is designated as Dorian and *Spondaic*, which corresponds exactly to the rule that the song accompanying the libation must be kept in the *Tropos Spondeiakos*.[37]

The tonal framework of the *Tropos Spondeiakos* is actually a modification of the Dorian mode, a fact which is significantly hinted at by Plutarch himself.[38] The same explanation is given by Aristides Quintilianus in his *De Musica*.[39] Kathleen Schlesinger devotes several pages to an investigation of the *Tropos Spondeiakos* in her admirable work, *The Greek Aulos*. She arrives at the following conclusions:

> The *spondaic* song, an *auletic libation* hymn, is founded upon the *Dorian octave Harmonia* of seven notes, produced by *Determinant* 11. This mode is called by Plutarch the *Spondeiakos Tropos*; it is identical with the scale of the *Elgin aulos* (the straight one) in the Graeco-Roman department at the British Museum . . . . There are ample grounds for identifying the interval of ratio 11:10 with the Spondeiasmos, as rising interval on *Hypate Meson* in the *Dorian Harmonia*.[40]

Moreover, in confirmation of these statements, we actually possess an ancient Greek *aulos*, still playable, which Kathleen Schlesinger has proved to be tuned in the Dorian Spondaic mode.

Hence it becomes a basically important problem to rediscover that *Tropos Spondeiakos* which must have played so important a role in Jewish psalmody. The writer succeeded in tracing this most characteristic mode in Gregorian song, as well as in the traditional synagogal songs of the Yemenite, Moroccan, and Persian Jews, and even in certain important liturgical tunes of the Ashkenazic Jews. Similar traces are also found in the psalmody of the Syrian and Byzantine Churches.

bo - nae vo - lun - ta - tis Lau - da - mus te Be - ne - di - ci - mus te,

A - do - ra - mus te, Glo - ri - fi - ca mus te etc.

(3a) Sof pa - suq. (b) Ka - - doš - - -

(4a) Ye - ba - re - he - ha (b) Sof pa suq 'At - nah. Te - bir

Tar - ha; Kadma v'asla': Sof pa - suq.

(5) 'At - nah; Paš - ta; Se - gol - -, Te - bir; Ta - ha; Kad ma' ve - 'asla'; Dar -

- - ga' i Sof pa - suq.

(6) V' - ha - ko - ha - nim v' - ha - 'am ha - 'om - dim ba - 'a - za - ra etc.'af hu' 'haya mitzḥad

ven ve - 'o - mer la homtitharu

(7) Niš - mat qol hay t'var - eh etc. - - - etc. min ha - 'o

- lam 'ad ha - 'o - lam 'at - ta 'el.

(8) 'Elo he - nu še - Ca - ša - ma - yim še - ma' go - lenu etc. . . .

443

EXAMPLE 39

(1) The framework of the *Tropos Spondeiakos*.

       E . . . GAB(c) DE or E (F) GAB . . . DE

(2a) Gloria of Mass XIV.[41]
(2b) Gloria of Mass XV (*Dominator Deus*).[42]
(3a) *Sof Pasuq* of the Yemenite Torah cantillation.[43]
(3b) Torah cantillation of the Yemenite Jews.[44]
(4a & 4b) Motifs of the cantillation of the Moroccan and Central European (Ashkenazic) Jews.[45]
(5) Haftara cantillation of the Lithuanian Jews.[46]
(6) *Tefilla* psalmody of the Moroccan Jews.[47]
(7) *Nishmat* of the High Holydays of the Babylonian Jews.[48]
(8) *Tefilla* psalmody of the Yemenite Jews.[49]
(9) Psalmody of the Jacobite Church. *Teshbuhta*.[50]
(10) Syrian psalmody; *Unita*.[51]
(11) Medieval Byzantine Hymn of the eleventh–twelfth century. *Stichera Anastasima*.[52]

The Amen in 2a which represents a so-called *pneuma* (melismatic group) deserves special attention, for it contains *in nuce* the essence of most of the following examples. From the striking resemblance of these items to one another we see how widespread the use of this mode must have been. Since the Yemenite Jews never contacted the Roman Church, nor the Lithuanian or South German Jews the Jacobite or the Byzantine Church, our mode must have been used almost as common property.[53] Compare here the striking similarity of Nos. 2a, 6 and 7. All these facts seem to warrant our conclusion that the *Spondeiakos* originated in the early Hellenistic world of the Near East, under whose spell came both Judaism and the Churches.[54]

The texts of our examples convey throughout a laudatory and

majestic attitude. This fact corresponds again to the *ethos* of the *Tropos Spondeiakos*, which, proceeding in stately, spondaic rhythms, is described by all Greek authorities as dignified, quiet, and highly solemn. Thus, Dionysius of Halicarnassus praises its noble simplicity.[55] Iamblichus referring to the effective *ethos* of our mode, tells an interesting story of a mad flautist (*auletes*), in which Pythagoras is said to have soothed him by making him change his tune from the orgiastic Phrygian to the calming Dorian Spondeian mode.[56]

Clement, whose statement caused us to consider the *Tropos Spondeiakos*, desired that all chromatic and non-diatonic scales be banished from sacred music on account of their voluptuous character. This would leave only the Dorian and Phrygian scales. As the kithara, the instrument most frequently used for the accompaniment of psalms and one to which not even Clement had any objection,[57] was tuned in the Dorian scale, all indications point to that ideal conception of the noble and simple Doric style which Plato designates as *semnotes* and praises as the most appropriate for the education of the manly individual.[58] Let us not forget: the Platonic concept of music is not primarily one of aesthetics but of ethics and state philosophy. With Clement, who otherwise follows mostly the rigid Platonic ideology, the Church supersedes the state. It is well worth while to contemplate for a moment the chief functions of music within the cultures of antiquity; by the Greeks of the Aristotelian school music was considered a servant of the state, by the Jews an instrument of either holy ecstasy or unholy temptation, by the Church Fathers a handmaid of the Church. We have here a good illustration of how Judaism, Hellenism, and the Early Church fought their battles for the soul of man in the fields of religion, state, and music.

THE SO-CALLED CHROMATIC ORIENTAL SCALE

Returning to Gastoué's remark about frequent chromaticisms in mode IV, it will be useful to clear up the maze, which musicological investigations have not penetrated as yet. Idelsohn, for instance, does not press his examination of that problem after having stated that the augmented second is not an original or ancient element of Jewish Music.[59] On the other hand, in a study of the chant of Ukrainian Jews, he takes the mode with the augmented second (called *Ahaba Rabba*) very much for granted without probing into its historic or musical antecedents.[60] Dom H. Gaisser, more than twenty years before Idelsohn, considered the subject worthy of a special study; yet even he had to confess 'the complete absence of any historical indication which bears upon the introduction of that (chromatic) mode into Greek Orthodox music'.[61] While his main thesis, the identification of the 'chromatic oriental scale' with a poorly notated ancient Greek Lydian or Hypolydian scale, is not convincing, he has at least done important spade-work on this problem. Since in Jewish music that 'chromatic oriental scale' (called *Ahaba Rabba*—mode) plays a great part, its origin ought to be traced back as far as possible.

Where do we find the scale with the augmented second—for that is the main problem—where are modes with that interval frequent and native? The answer is: in Turkish, more recent Arabic, Hungarian, Tartar, late Byzantine, Spanish, Rumanian and Jewish music of Eastern Europe and of the Levant. The Yemenite Jews, the West Ashkenazic Jews, the Gregorian Chant, and the ancient Graeco-Slavonic chants do not employ it. This indicates that those regions which were left untouched by Turkish or Arabic influence have not absorbed the mode; those countries which know it, were without exception subject to Turkish or Moorish influence or invasion at one time or another. Still one contradiction remains: the East European Jews of Russia and Poland know and love this mode, while genuine old Slavonic music is left untouched by it. Yet even this contradictory observation can easily be explained: to the music of European Jewry, the mode came from south-east Russia. In the Crimea and the south-eastern Ukraine, the German Jewish immigrants mixed freely with the members of the older Jewish settlements which they encountered. Most of these older groups came from the Tartar or Byzantine empires. The Tartars, Persians, and Byzantines were under the rule of Turkish invaders from the early fourteenth century, and it is only natural that Tartar, Persian and late Byzantine tunes contain the 'Turkish' interval of the augmented second. Through the invasions of the Turks (never beyond Vienna) on one hand, and through the westward migration of Eastern Jewry on the other, the mode was finally carried over to Central Europe, but remained there always a strange intruder. The core of European Russia, where the official chant of the Orthodox Church was regulated had, however, never become subject to Turkish influence. This explains the seemingly contradictory fact that the Russian Jews know the mode, while it is alien to official Russian church music.

446

Idelsohn identifies the 'chromatic oriental' mode with the Arabic *maqamat Hedjaz* and *Hedjaz-Kar* and considers it a genuine folkish mode.[62] He attributes to it the accidentals:

and states its main and characteristic motif

EXAMPLE 40

in 'perpetual, monotonous recurrence'. The *'invitatorium'* of the *Muezzin* to attend worship in the Mosque *Allahu aqbar*, etc., is chanted in this manner.

But this mode, though identical with the Jewish *Ahaba Rabba*, does by no means parallel the 'chromatic oriental', as represented by Dom Gaisser. To quote only one of his illustrations:

EXAMPLE 41

The B has been reduced almost to B flat, while the G is elevated almost to G sharp. If we now, for simplification's sake, substitute B flat for B and G sharp for +G, we might approach the *Maqam Sabba*, whose characteristic feature is the diminished third (B flat —G sharp).[63]

Idelsohn quotes, among others, the following motif:[64]

EXAMPLE 42

The *finalis* of this mode is A, hence the similarity with Dom Gaisser's motif is no more than superficial. More interesting proves a comparison with the mode of Lamentations, as traditional with the Yemenite Jews:[65]

EXAMPLE 43

Here the *finalis* is F—again, the similarity with Gaisser's motif is not substantial enough to warrant a complete identification. While the chant of the modern Greek Orthodox Church is replete with 'chromatic oriental' passages, as a glance into Rebours's *Traité de psaltique* will prove, there is no direct evidence of this chromatic flavour in genuine Byzantine Chant. Indeed, the Byzantine manuscripts do not usually give any indication of chromatic mutations, although they were later added in performance, at least after the ascendancy of Arabic and Turkish taste.[66]

What, then, is the Turkish—or Persian—mode that corresponds to Gaisser's chromaticism, and might elucidate the origin of chromaticisms in Jewish and Oriental Christian chant?

Of all the *maqamat*, the mode *Sika* resembles most Gaisser's example. Parisot already points to the fact that tunes of that *maqam* can easily be misunderstood as our Major scale with an augmented fourth and a diminished sixth, somewhat like this:[67]

(*Finalis*)

EXAMPLE 44

Idelsohn, likewise, emphasized the inclination of the mode to end on the Third beneath the *finalis*, which creates the mixed *maqam Sika-Rast*; that mode is for all practical purposes identical with our Major scale.[68] Typical motifs of *Sika-Rast* are:[69]

EXAMPLE 45

Surveying now the various attempts at comparing Arabic modes with Gaisser's illustration, we must admit that the last quoted item, the *maqam Sika-Rast*, comes next to the Byzantine style. According to Idelsohn, the origin of this *maqam* dates back to the early Persian-Arab period; it was probably conceived as a transformation of the Phrygian Church

448

Tone.[70] This theory would well support Gastoué's remark that the chromatic shades entered the classic diatonic modes of the Church, coming from the Near East. Even in the Western orbit, these *dieses enharmonicae* remained in usage until the eleventh century.[71] Did not Guido of Arezzo still oppose these *dieses*, calling them 'softnesses' (*mollitudines*) and a deviation (*disgregatio*) from the true and correct style?[72]

The result of this brief investigation of the 'chromatic-oriental mode' shows that there is not one, but at least *three* chromatic modes analogous to certain Greek Orthodox, Syrian, and Eastern Jewish formulas. They all originated in the last third of the first millennium in the Arabic, later in the Turkish orbit; it will, therefore, be a safe conclusion to associate these modes with Arabic-Turkish influence. This influence was of no relevance up to the seventh century and could not have exerted itself during the formative age of either Christian or Jewish liturgical chant. It is an additional and regional flavour, which occasionally may spice a tune; but it is not an inherent part of liturgical chant. Nor is it, as Gaisser seems to suppose, a remnant of the chromatic or enharmonic genera of ancient Greek music. The musical evidence is too slender in this direction, too strong in the other, the Arabic-Turkish line.

THE CADENCES OF LESSON AND ORATION

Returning to our comparison of closing phrases or *pneumata*, as the Middle Ages called them, some of the most ancient Tones of the Gregorian Chant must be considered extensively, before we can reach conclusive results. The plain clauses of the versicle consist of the following phrases:[73]

EXAMPLE 46

Comparing Example 27g with Examples 26a and 46a, it is obvious that the formula is more or less common to the Syrian, Roman, and Jewish traditions. Even the German Jews knew it, possibly through the Gregorian Chant, as Example 29c (end), seems to indicate.

During the last days of Holy Week and for the Office of the Dead the versicle was read with the *finales* on the semitone (cf. Example 46b); Wagner considers it as of more recent origin than 46a and adds: 'In olden times this formula, too, was notated as *subtonal*', referring to a manuscript of the twelfth century. This is a modified version of Example 46b. I believe that Wagner's theory is not too well founded; for many instances speak for the assumption that both clauses of 46b represent old traditions of the Church. They always occur as regular punctuating cadences in the chant of the Syrian Churches.[74]

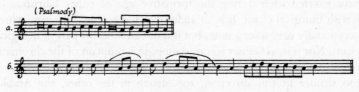

EXAMPLE 47

We find these cadences also in ancient strata of Jewish tradition, e.g. the last clause of Example 28c and Example 28d.

The same holds true of Example 46b, which parallels in Syrian tradition Example 48,[75]

EXAMPLE 48

and in the chant of the Babylonians, Example 27e. There it is the typical closing cadence of the Job cantillation, and clearly of very ancient origin. We shall encounter this characteristic formula again in the Gregorian and Jewish modes of Lamentations.

The developed ornament at the end of a versicle, called *pneuma* in the Middle Ages, is given as Example 46c; it is paralleled by Example 26g (end), the cadence of the *Tefilla* chant in Yemenite Jewry. Neither in Byzantine nor in Syrian tradition did I find a real counterpart of this ornament. Example 46d, which Wagner considers of ancient Semitic origin,[76] I found only in two instances outside the sphere of Christianity; both are of good and authentic tradition: East Babylonia and Morocco.[77]

EXAMPLE 49

Example 46e, finally, has many parallels in the chant of the Oriental Churches and in Judaism. There are obvious analogies with Example 50, quoted after Parisot, representing the Syrian Chant,

EXAMPLE 50

and Examples 27a and 27d of the Babylonian Jews, all punctuating melismata of scriptural cantillation.

Proceeding to the Gregorian Tones for the lesson, which represent a more fully developed stage of the versicle cadence, the parallel variants become more distinct. The Tones for the lesson are characterized by the divisions of a sentence into colon, comma, and punctus, which correspond roughly to the modern categories of main clause, subordinate clause, and end clause. Jerome, the author of the official Latin translation of the Bible, had made use of these divisions according to the concepts of older Greek and Hebrew grammarians, and thus the syntactic and musical divisions of the lesson (at least in Latin) seemed to originate with Jerome. This supposition has been accepted by Wagner.[78]

Actually, however, Jerome did nothing for which the rabbis and earliest translators of Scripture had not already set a carefully elaborated

451

pattern. The breakdown of the biblical sentences into smaller units followed a tradition which was considerably older than Christianity. Usually Jerome follows faithfully the rabbinic tradition, except where his ideal of good Latin was incompatible with it or where his translation was to stress the Christological aspect of the Old Testament.[79]

The cadences of the various lessons, as preserved in the Gregorian tradition, are given here as Examples 51 and 53.[80]

a. SIC FA-CIES FLEX-AM SIC VE-RO METRUM SIC AU-TEM PUNC-TUM

b. Punctus versus

c. Punctus elevatus

d. Punctus interrogativus

e. Punctus versus

f. Punctus interrogativus

EXAMPLE 51

Wagner stresses especially the fact that whenever indeclinable proper names (Greek or Hebrew) close a sentence, the accent of the last syllable does not move back to the penult. Thus, in lessons, where Hebrew names close a sentence, the last syllable is accentuated, as it should be. He adds:

For determining the age of these formulas of musical accent, the fact is of importance that the old High-German poetry of the Carolingian epoch has retained the foreign accent in the biblical proper names. This non-Germanic accentuation cannot have come into the German language from Hebrew or Greek directly, but only via the Latin pronunciation of these names. In Otfrid of Weissenburg's accentuation, as presented in his Gospel-Book, we read: Davíd, Laméch, Enóch, Noé, Barrabás, etc. This is an authentic proof of the pronunciation of biblical names, as they were spoken by the German clergy of the ninth century. The oldest manuscript of Cassiodorus, too, which originated about the time of Bede (d. 735) has the accents upon the last syllables of the Hebrew names.[81]

Whether or not we may assume direct Hebrew influence upon the correct accentuation of the proper names, the fact remains that Gregorian tradition has preserved it through the centuries. It also retained the typical Jewish 'closing accent', the *sof pasuq* in its music, as we see immediately when we compare Example 51a, b, with Example 27g or 29b. The characteristic descending fourth occurs also in Byzantine chant, as evidenced in Example 52a.[82]

EXAMPLE 52

The entire melody resembles the old tune of the Passover Night set to the text of the refrain song, 'It would have sufficed'. Above it was demonstrated (in Part I, Chapter VII) that the text was borrowed by the Byzantine and Roman theologians and was furnished with an anti-Jewish twist; in this new shape it has become the backbone of the *Improperia* of the last days of Holy Week. Now we see that along with the text, the melody, too, wandered from the Synagogue to the Church (cf. Example 51d).

Another punctuating melisma, the *punctus interrogativus*, which is used to mark a question in the text, occurs in Jewish tradition in the form of two main motifs of punctuation: cf. Example 27a, c. It is also familiar to Byzantine chant in the form of Example 52b.[83]

More interesting are the semitonal and subsemitonal versions of the epistolary lesson. The same formulas are used for the prophetic lesson of the Ember days, in whose liturgy we have frequently encountered archaic traces. These versions are given in Example 53a, b,

Lesson from the Epistle

453

EXAMPLE 53

and may be compared with the Oriental Jewish psalmody[84]

EXAMPLE 54

which occurs also in Syrian psalmody, as shown in Example 47b. The way Hebrew names are accentuated is given in Example 53c. It corresponds perfectly with the official Hebrew accentuation, as the *ta'amim* (Masoretic accents) indicate.

Finally, a word must be said about the so-called *tonus antiquus lectionis*. Its melismata run the following course:[85]

EXAMPLE 55

This is, for all practical purposes, identical with Example 51a and with the closing cadence of the Ashkenazic cantillation in Examples 29a and 29b, also with the Babylonian motif, Example 27g. Who gave, who took, is extremely difficult to decide in this instance. The earliest Gregorian manuscripts for the *tonus antiquus* date back to the eleventh or twelfth century. Perhaps the fact of the Babylonian Jews using this formula speaks for Jewish origin; but this is mere conjecture and can in no way be substantiated.

454

Between the formulas of the lesson and the Psalm Tones themselves fall certain types of plainly chanted prayers. In the Roman as well as in the Byzantine Church the highest forms of this category are the Lord's Prayer (*Pater Noster*) and the *Praefatio*, the latter at the beginning, the former at the end of Mass. The Byzantine Anaphora as well as the Latin *Praefatio* introduce the *Trisagion* and the *Sanctus*, respectively. They represent some of the oldest parts of the Eucharistic service and their synagogal counterparts are well known.

According to P. Wagner, the Mozarabic version of the Lord's Prayer is the oldest chanted prayer of the occidental Church. Its structure is given in Example 56a.[86]

EXAMPLE 56

Its parallel Example 56b, is the psalmody of the Persian Jews, and other similar versions may be found in the examples illustrating the *Tropos Spondeiakos* in this chapter; especially No. 7 (*Nishmat*) falls into this category. For it is basically the formula EGAB, with the *tenor* A and the *finalis* E (without an intermediate F), that is common to this tone as well as the Mozarabic *Pater Noster*.[87]

The *Praefatio* is, as its name indicates, a preface to the prayer of consecration and the *Sanctus*. It begins with a short, formal dialogue between priest and acolyte, and after the usual responses, the prayer itself begins with the words, 'Vere dignum et justum est' (It is meet and right) which is literally borrowed from the prayer-book of the Synagogue.

Of the various musical formulations, the oldest seems to be Example 57a which has a close parallel (Example 57b) in the High Holyday chant of the Babylonian Jews.[88]

EXAMPLE 57

It is interesting to note that this piece is sung, like the Roman *Praefatio*, in responsorial fashion. I was unable to find parallels in the chant of the Eastern Churches or in other traditions of Jewish centres.

It is not possible to compare simply Jewish and Christian practices concerning the chant of the lesson. Here the respective traditions are too incommensurate: while Judaism has established a minutely elaborated system of ecphonetic accents applied to every word, the Churches have limited themselves mostly to closing or pausal accents of verses. This was also a reason why we did not examine the Christian *modes* for lesson, oration, or chanted prayer, but only their *motifs*. In contrast to Jewish performance, the final melismata do not suffice to evaluate the phrases in terms of modality. The range of Christian lesson—apart from Nestorian practice—is small, never exceeding a fourth or, at most, a fifth; and only exceptionally does a third interrupt the otherwise step-wise and monotonous flow of the *tenor*.

NOTES CHAPTER IV

1. E. Wellesz, 'Words and Music in Byzantine Liturgy', MQ, 1947, pp. 306-7.

2. WGM III, pp. 236, 240, 367, 396, *et passim*; A. Gastoué, 'Chant juif et chant grégorien', *Revue du chant grégorien* (1930, fasc. 6, November to December and following through 1931); A. Z. Idelsohn, 'Parallelen zwischen Jüd. & Gregor. Melodien', ZFM (1922), pp. 515 ff; E. Werner, 'Preliminary Notes for a Comparative Study of Catholic and Jewish Musical Punctuation', HUCA, (1940); 'The Psalmodic Formula Neannoe and its Origin', MQ (January 1942); 'The Doxology in Synagogue and Church', HUCA (1946); 'The Origin of the Octoechos', Acta Musicologica (1949); W-S., HUCA (1941-43).

3. On the connexion between musical history and comparative musicology, see R. Lach's comprehensive study, 'Die vergleichende Musikwissenschaft, ihre Aufgaben und Probleme', *Akademie der Wissenschaften, Sitzungsberichte der Philol.-Hist. Klasse*, CC (Vienna, 1924).

4. On musical ornaments in general, see R. Lach's work, *Beiträge zur Entwicklungsgeschichte der Ornamentalen Melopoiie* (Vienna, 1931).

5. On this interesting question, see E. Hommel, *Untersuchungen zur Hebr. Lautlehre* (1917), pp. 92-93; the passages of Saadya and Ibn Librat in Bacher, 'Die Anfange Hebr. Gram.', ZDMG, XLIX (1895), 56-57, n. 383.

6. W. Bacher, op. cit., p. 383.

7. We omit here the many sorts of 'exegetic melismata', as they occur in Latin, Byzantine and Hebrew chant alike. E. Wellesz draws special attention to them in his *Eastern Elements in Western Chant*, pp. 71 ff.

8. Cf. Jeannin-Puyade, 'L'Octoechos syrien', OC, N.S. III (1913), pp. 278 ff.

9. Cf. Komitas Kevorkian, 'Das Interpunktionssystem der Armenier', SIM I, 1899, 1900, pp. 54 ff, a fine study on cantillation and primitive psalmody; also Pierre Aubry, *Le Rhythme tonique dans la poésie liturgique et dans le chant* (Paris, 1903), pp. 70 ff.

10. Also the following studies: cf. WAP; E. Wellesz: 'Das Alter der Melodien d. byz. Kirche', *Forschungen und Fortschritte* (1932), p. 431; 'Die byz. Lektionszeichen', ZFM (1929), pp. 514 ff; *Byzantinische Musik* (1927); Sticherarium Vindobonense, Facsim, ed. Wellesz, in MMB, I; Prophetologium, ed. C. Høeg and I. Zuntz, in MMB, IV; 'Words and Music in Byz. Liturgy', MQ (1947), pp. 306 ff.; Eastern Elements in Western Chant, MMB; Byzantine Hymnography (Oxford, 1949); H. J. W. Tillyard: Byz. Music and Hymnography (1923);

Signatures and Cadences of the Byz. Modes', *Annual of the British School at Athens*, XXVI (1923–25), pp. 78 ff; 'Byzantine Neumes; The Coislin Notation', *Byz. Zeitsch.*, XXXVII (1937), pp. 345 ff; J. B. Thibaut, *Monuments de la notation ekphonétique et hagiopolite de l'Église grecque* (1913); *Origine byzantine de la notation neumatique de l'Église latine* (1907); C. Høeg, *La Notation ekphonétique* (1935) *MMB*, Subsidia, Vol. I.

11. *La Paléographie musicale*, ed. by the Solesmes Benedictines, 16 vols. (1889–1931); A. Gastoué, *Les Origines du chant romain* (Paris, 1907); A. Mocquereau, *Le Nombre musical grégorien* (2 vols., 1908, 1927); P. Wagner, *Einführung in die gregorianischen Melodien* (3 vols., 1901–1921).

12. A. Z. Idelsohn, *Thesaurus of Hebr.-Orient. Melodies* (10 vols., 1913–1934).

13. IT, I, pp. 18–41; 156–8.

14. E. Hommel, op. cit., p. 69, n. 1, and O. Fleischer, *Neumenstudien*, I, 85 rightly stressed the identity of the name of the Hebrew ecphonetic accent *shofar* with the old Latin term *tuba*. Under these conditions we have to consider the usual explanation of the term *tuba*, as given in WGM, II, p. 89 and III, p. 26, with caution and even doubt. It is probably no more than one of the frequent 'popular etymologies'.

15. IT, II, pp. 6–21; 28–31; 33–78.

16. IT, IV, pp. 225; 226–30; 34–36; 197–8; 124; 130; IT, II, pp. 64–66.

17. Most of them are gathered in the E. Birnbaum collection, at the Library of the Hebrew Union College, Cincinnati. A thorough investigation of the relation between Eastern Jewish and Graeco-Slavonic music remains a pressing necessity. Too many loose assertions have been made concerning this type of music and it is high time to scrutinize the tradition, separating genuine from spurious elements.

18. IT, II, pp. 41, 44, 51, 52 ff.

19. IT, II, pp. 9 ff.

20. Idelsohn, *Jewish Music*, p. 133; also E. Werner, 'Preliminary Notes, . . .', *HUCA* (1940), pp. 360 ff.

21. *LU*, p. 115.

22. Cf. *LU*, p. 115.

23. Cf. WGM, III, p. 101.

24. Cf. IT, II, p. 75.

25. Cf. *JM* pp. 144–5.

26. Cf. *JM* pp. 145–6; WGM, III, pp. 140–1.

27. This is Dr. J. Schoenberg's (*Die traditionellen Gesänge des Israel. Gottesdienstes in Deutschland*, p. 29) and Idelsohn's (IT, VI, Chapter 3) conclusion. It would be convincing, had not the original mode of the prophetic lesson been preserved by the Ashkenazic Jews. How can it be explained that the tune of the prophetic lesson, which is read only once a week, has been left untouched by German influence, whereas the Torah cantillation, performed three times every week, was thoroughly assimilated to German modes? I am more reluctant to draw a definite conclusion in this case. First we would have to know whence came the alteration in the German version of the Roman Psalm Tones, before we could apply those reasons to Jewish psalmody. Until this spade-work has been done, everything suggested will not exceed the realm of mere conjecture and speculation. See also O. Fleischer, op. cit., I, p. 85; II, p. 42.

28. *JM* p. 40, No. 1; A. Auda, op. cit., p. 173; IT, II, p. 41. Cf. Table XII, 2a.

29. *LU*, p. 126; WGM, III, p. 38.

30. See A. Auda, *Les Modes et les tons de la musique* (Bruxelles, 1930), p. 173.

31. Cf. WGM, III, pp. 110 ff.

32. Auda, loc. cit.

33. A. Gastoué, *Les Origines du chant romain* (Paris, 1907), p. 154; also p. 145.

34. A. Gastoué, 'Chant juif et chant grégorien', *Revue du chant grégorien* (1931), p. 11. I myself had reached the very same conclusion, independent of Gastoué, in 'The Doxology in Synagogue and Church', *HUCA* (1946), pp. 332–5.

35. Clement of Alexandria, *Paedagogus*, II, Chapter 4.

36. Cf. E. Werner, 'Die Musikanschauungen des antiken Judentums', *Musica Hebraica*, II (1939), pp. 8–15, and Werner and Sonne, 'The Theory and Philosophy of Music in Judaeo-Arabic Literature', *HUCA*, XV and XVI (1941 and 1943).

37. Plutarch, *Moralia*, ed. Dübner (Paris, 1876–80). See also H. Riemann, *Handbuch der Musikgeschichte*, 2nd. ed., I, 1 (Leipzig, 1922) pp. 49 ff.

38. Plutarch, op. cit.

39. Cf. Aristides Quintilianus, *De Musica*, ed. Meibom (London, 1652), p. 28; also ed. Schäfke (Berlin, 1937), p. 204.

40. Cf. K. Schlesinger, *The Greek Aulos* (London, 1939), pp. 205–12.

41. *LU*, p. 53.

42. *LU*, p. 55.

43. IT, No. 44.

44. IT, II, p. 46.

45. IT, II, p. 52.

46. IT, II, p. 52.

47. IT, II, p. 73.

48. IT, II, No 58.

49. IT, I, No 86

50. Dom Parisot, *Rapport sur une mission*, etc., p. 238, No 344.

51. Ibid. No 335.

52. Tillyard, *Byzantine Music*, pp. 55 f.

53. Cf. E. Werner, 'Preliminary Notes for a Comparative Study of Catholic and Jewish Musical Punctuation', *HUCA*, XV (1940), pp. 345–9.

54. This wide propagation of the *Tropos Spondeiakos* may account for the often repeated view that the music of the ancient Synagogue and of the early Church was pentatonic to a considerable degree. It is true that the *Tropos Spondeiakos* bears a certain superficial similarity to pentatonic scales; it is also true that parts of both the Gregorian and the European-Jewish chant contain pentatonic elements. But all these elements are of much later origin. Neither the ancient Greek hymns, nor the famous hymnus of Oxyrhynchos of the third century A.D., nor the oldest strata of Gregorian, Ambrosian, Oriental-Jewish and Arabian chant show pentatonic tunes, unless the mode of the *Tropos Spondeiakos* is being mistaken for pentatonics, as was done by some scholars, particularly Yasser, in his *Medieval Quartal Harmony*.

55. Dionysius of Halicarnassus, *De compositione verborum*, 17; cf. also H. Abert, *Die Lehre vom Ethos in der griechischen Musik*, (Leipzig, 1899), pp. 133 ff.

56. Cf. K. Schlesinger, op. cit., p. 117.

57. The question of whether or not instrumental accompaniment of the psalmody be permissible, became the playground of all ascetic polemics and concepts in early, particularly Eastern, Christianity. The general view, held by the Eastern Fathers, was that God had permitted the Jews to use instruments for the accompaniment of their psalms as a kind of harmless, if sometimes childish, play. Adult Christianity would and should renounce, therefore, these undignified toys and should concentrate on purely vocal hymns and psalms. Clement's view in *Paedagogus*, II, 4.

58. Plutarch, op. cit., Chapter 17, adds to Plato's words the following commentary of his own: 'Thus, there is much noble simplicity in the Dorian mode—and he [Plato] valued it.'

59. Cf. *JM*, p. 87.

60. Cf. A. Z. Idelsohn, 'Melodien der ukrainischen Juden', *Acta Musicologica* (1932).

61. Dom Hugues Gaisser 'L'Origine et la vraie nature du mode dit "chromatique oriental",' *Documents, mémoirs et voeux du Congrès international d'histoire de la musique* (Paris, 1901), ed. by Jules Combarieu.

62. IT, IV, pp. 99 ff.

63. Gaisser, op. cit., p. 98.

64. IT, IV, p. 80, No 35.

65. IT, I, p. 87, No 63.

66. G. Reese, *Music of the Middle Ages*, p. 90.

67. Cf. Parisot, op. cit., p. 28.

68. IT, IV, p. 82 ff.

69. Ibid.

70. Ibid.

71. Cf. A. Gastoué, op. cit., p. 134.

72. Guido Aretinus in Gerbert, *Scriptores* . . ., *Tractatus correctorius*, Par. 'De Modorum formulis'. See also Gastoué, op. cit., p. 131.

73. WGM, III, pp. 32–35.

74. Cf. Parisot, op. cit., No 337; No 314.

75. Ibid., No 315.

76. WGM, III, p. 34.

77. IT, II, p. 47, No 4; II, p. 50, No 9.

78. WGM, III, p. 36.

79. He occasionally complained that the constant occupation with Hebrew texts spoiled his fluent Latin style (*Ep. XX ad Damasum*).

80. WGM, III, pp. 38–51.

81. Ibid., p. 39. The question whether Otfrid of Weissenburg was personally familiar with Hebrews and Arabs is raised by E. Hommel, *Untersuchungen zur Hebr. Lautlehre*, p. 132. In view of the considerable Jewish influence upon civilization in the Carolingian period, it is not impossible that the Gregorian tradition was actually based upon a direct and sound knowledge of Hebrew. Even if Bishop Agobard's violent letter against the Jews (addressed to Louis the Pious) exaggerated Jewish influence and power beyond all reason, a nucleus of truth is well attested; indeed, Christians attended Jewish services, and rested on the Sabbath. Cf. also Grätz, *Gesch. d. Juden*, (1909), vol. V., Chapter VIII, and the Hebrew source, *Shibbole Halleket*, ed. Buber (Wilna, 1887), f. 113.

82. Cf. E. Wellesz, *Eastern Elements in Western Chant*, pp. 46–47.

83. Ibid., pp. 113 ff.

84. IT, IV, No 320.

85. LU, p. 126.

86. WGM, III, p. 58. Wagner adds here a significant footnote: 'Occasionally such types of recitation are being connected with the Greek Tetrachords. In this case the (Greek) Dorian is represented as EFGA . . . I hold these speculations to be entirely mistaken. In our tune (*Pater Noster*) the Dorian Tetrachord is exceeded already in the first part; and the same objection is valid for other types of recitation. This practice of recitation has nothing in common with Greek music; it comes directly from the Jewish and Christian liturgies of the Near East. . . .'

87. IT, II, pp. 46–47; and p. 99, No 58. It is also the ancient formula of the priestly benediction. Cf. IT, II, No 64.

88. WGM III, p. 70; IT, II, p. 98, No 53.

16

CHAPTER FIVE

Plain Psalmody;
Its Formulas and Intervals

MODES OF PSALMODY

A DIRECT comparison between the Psalm Tones of the Churches with the Psalm Tones of the Synagogue is impossible, since the Synagogue had never fully implemented the theoretical postulate of eight distinct Tones. This has been demonstrated above in Chapter II. With all respect due to so great a thinker as Saadya Gaon, who speaks, like a Byzantine theorist, of psalms which were sung to a melody of their own, and others, to which one of the eight Tones was applied (Greek, *automelon* and *hirmos*), there is no evidence of a Jewish *octoechos* as implemented in practice.[1] Actually the traditional rendering of the psalms has been poorly preserved in Jewry except in the Yemenite and Babylonian centres. In particular the versions of the European centres have been considerably contaminated by the folk-songs of their Gentile environments. The true musical equivalent of the ecclesiastical Psalm Tones are the Jewish *Tefilla* modes, which display a more authentic state of preservation.

Another difficulty results from the various organizations of the Psalm Tones in the Churches, which frequently diverge from liturgy to liturgy, from region to region. It is impossible to speak of 'one uniform tradition of psalmody' common to all Christendom. This in spite of a theoretical system of eight modes, supposedly common to each and all Churches. Even the numerical arrangements of the Psalm Tones show divergences. Thus, the Armenian and the Gregorian scheme have the Tones arranged as follows:

Authentic		Plagal
1.	$\longrightarrow$	2.
3.		4.
5.		6.
7.		8.

The Byzantine, Syrian, and older Gregorian order shows the following system:[2]

Authentic	Plagal
1.	5.
2.	6.
3.	7.
4.	8.

Even more problematic is the task of identifying and classifying a Psalm Tone if it does not follow the 'regular' cadence of its scheme, as happens frequently in the oriental Christian chants. Thus, doubting the substance of any regular model scheme in the Syrian and Byzantine chants, Jeannin is ready to accept the shadow of modality in the most general terms.[3]

He stresses the flexibility of most oriental modes, emphasizing that they cannot without misrepresentation or violence be forced into a system with a regular *finalis* and *tenor*. Even where an individual *finalis* occurs, it must never be looked for as a recurrent feature.[4] A part of this difficulty in classifying tunes according to their mode lies, according to R. Lachmann, in the fact 'that the nuclear tune of the piece, i.e. its basic *maqam* or *rāg*, never is played, that it does not exist as a separate entity, but solely in the sense of a Platonic idea'.[5]

It will, therefore, not be possible to base the following comparisons upon the orthodox criteria of modality, namely *tenor*, *finalis*, and *confinalis*, as usual in Gregorian chant. Even for this corpus of sacred music the infallibility of its modal categorization is being doubted more and more by modern scholars, such as Wellesz, Reese, Jeannin, and others; of the numerous examples to illustrate this fact, we cite only three.

ALLELUIA *"Haec est virgo sapiens"* Tone IV

ALLELUIA *"Angelus Domini descendit"* Tone VIII

END

461

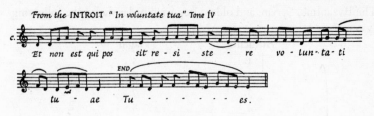

From the INTROIT "In voluntate tua" Tone IV

Et non est qui pos sit re - si - ste - re vo - lun - ta - ti

END.

tu - ae Tu - - - - es.

EXAMPLE 58

The Alleluia 'Haec est virgo sapiens' (Example 58a)[6] will be understood by every student of Arab music as an evident case of the *maqam Sika-Rast*; it is by no means what its superscription pretends to be, namely a Hypophrygian mode.

Similarly, another Alleluia 'Angelus Domini descendit' (Example 58b)[7] is classified as belonging to the eighth mode (Hypomixolydian). Actually, it ought to be understood as a typically oriental major mode with the *finalis* G.

Unexpectedly, the introit 'In voluntate tua' (Example 58c)[8] is classified as in the Hypophrygian (fourth) mode. Actually, the tune is based upon a pure D minor scale, or rather, upon the typical Hebrew *Magen Aboth* mode, with its ascending and descending fifths; it has two endings, one with the *finalis* D upon 'tuae', another upon the official *finalis* E ('tu es').

I am convinced that the application of strict Gregorian terminology and modal criteria to Jewish and oriental Christian chants would completely distort their fundamental character, and, what is worse, it would produce oblique parallels. Even so innocent a criterion as the relation of the range of a tune to its *finalis* has to be used with the utmost caution, for we are habitually inclined to identify subtonal features with a plagal mode; actually, the authentic or plagal character of the mode, (if these criteria have to be applied at all) depends more upon its respective cadences than upon whether the tune is situated above or below its *finalis*. While I cannot agree with Jeannin's thesis that the only genuine scales (not modes) of the Near East are those based upon C and D, their importance cannot be doubted. Yet this fact in no way does justice to the various modes, which may or may not be systematized in a C or D scale.[9] Indeed, there are numerous Psalm Tones or psalmodic chants that evade completely a subsumption under any established *scale*; nor will a musical Procrustean bed, into which they might be, and have been, forced, contribute anything constructive to their understanding.

Still another set of obstacles in the way of a systematic comparison between Jewish and Christian psalmody must be pointed out. It is not possible to apply to the analysis of Jewish musical tradition the same methods of discrimination as the great scholars of the Gregorian chant, foremost P. Wagner, have introduced.

Unlike the Oriental Churches and the Synagogue, the Roman Catholic tradition distinguishes well between various levels of Psalmody according to the criteria of their liturgical occasion.

The old Christian Churches have preserved a certain relation between the various liturgical occasions and their concomitant types of psalmody: the *psalmus in directum* is characteristic of the weekday office, while brilliant responsorial performances by soloist and choir are usually reserved for Sunday or Holyday Masses. Such a strict relationship does not exist in the Jewish liturgy. This is due to the absence in Judaism of the distinction between Eucharistic and non-Eucharistic services. Hence the liturgical occasion *per se* does not, in Judaism, predetermine its type of psalmody.

Not quite the same divergence exists with regard to the other distinguishing factor, the importance of the occasion. Indeed, there is quite a good deal of analogy between Church and Synagogue. From early times, a distinction was made between the liturgies of weekdays and Sabbaths, and again between the rituals of Sabbath and Holyday; the *shaharit* (morning) service held a lower rank than the *mussaph* (forenoon) service. Also, the *ma'ariv* service of Holydays, (evening service) from which the Christian vigil is derived, has a higher distinction than the *shaharit*, but a lower than the *mussaph*.[10]

Common to all liturgies, Christian and Jewish, is one general principle with respect to music: the greater the liturgical occasion, the more chant is applicable; and the solemnity of the chant is expressed and measured by the degree to which *ornate* tunes constitute an integral part of the musical service. The function of the ornament in liturgical music is not only that of a musical punctuation, as we understood it in Chapters III and IV, but also the solemnization of the liturgical moment or occasion. In this respect, and in this respect only, we may equate the Office with the Jewish weekday service, the Sunday Mass with the Sabbath, the feastday Mass with the *mussaph* of a Holyday.

For all these reasons, it is not possible for us to follow the admirable system by which P. Wagner analyses the psalmody, distinguishing between antiphonal psalmody of the Office and of the Mass, proceeding to the psalms of the *invitatorium*, thence to responsorial psalmody, again distinguishing between Office and Mass. There are only three possible counterparts of these degrees of organization and development in Jewish musical liturgy:

(1). The two types of ferial and of festive liturgy in Judaism, corresponding with the ferial and dominical Mass.

(2). The melismatic Antiphon and Gradual-Response, which parallel the ornately chanted prayers and recitatives of the Jewish Holydays.

(3). The distinction between Office and Mass, which is roughly analogous to the differentiation between *shaharit* and *mussaph* services on Sabbaths and Holydays respectively.

I am fully aware of the numerous objections which might be raised against these simplifying equations, from the liturgical as well as from the musical point of view.

STANDING FORMULAS OF PSALMODY IN THE VARIOUS TRADITIONS OF CHURCH AND SYNAGOGUE

P. Wagner derives many elements of plain psalmody from the lectionary practice; if this be a theory as far as Gregorian Chant is concerned, it is an indisputable fact in Judaism. For the practice of scriptural cantillation antedates all forms of psalmody extant. Though accepting the eight modes of psalmody, he observes that the 'tones of lesson and oration are independent of the modes'.[11] I do not think that such an artificial discrimination between the modes of psalmody and the 'Tones' of lesson or oration can legitimately be made. Did we not encounter psalmodic elements in the lesson? Even if such parallels were not immediately visible, there are sufficient analogies between some Gregorian lessons and typical modes of oriental Churches or the Synagogue to warrant a complete suspension of the principles which distinguish between modes of lesson, cantillation, etc., on one hand, and the established Psalm Tones, on the other. The time has become overripe to dispose of the old convenience of the theory of modal scales, which for decades has shackled modern scholarship. The convenience of the old theory consisted of its systematic applicability; now we possess finer and more exact tools, and can modify the old conceptions of modal scales in the chants of Christianity. What should replace them as regards methodology, and should be of lasting value and flexible applicability, are the conceptions of formula, melodic pattern, *maqam*, the well tested criteria of subtonality and subsemitonality, and, for immediately practical purposes, comparisons with the historic Psalm Tones. The modal scales were fictitious constructions at best, and now have become a serious impediment to unprejudiced scholarship.[12]

After this preamble, we shall proceed with the comparison of the various formulas of plain psalmody set out in the Tables at the end of the Chapter.

Table I presents the antiphonal Psalm Tones for Office and Mass of the Gregorian tradition according to the *Commemoratio Brevis* (ninth to tenth century), P. Wagner, and the *Liber Usualis*, ed. Vaticana. Where the occasion warranted it, special *finalis* and *differentiae* have been added. The *Tonus in directum* and *Tonus Peregrinus* precede the usual series of the eight Tones.

Table II gives examples of Jewish Psalmody, arranged in such a way that each Gregorian Psalm Tone is matched by one or more Jewish parallel. Added here are the Jewish counterparts of the *Tonus Peregrinus* and *Tonus in directum*.

Table III is the least controversial computation of Byzantine *echoi* and Psalm Tones, according to Wellesz and Tillyard.[13]

Table IV represents the Armenian Psalmody, as recorded by K. Kevorkian and P. Aubry.[14]

Table V finally endeavours to establish an approximation of the modal skeletons of Syrian Psalmody. I realized fully the inconclusiveness of that attempt, when I tried to systematize the various modes and *maqamat* of the Christian Syrians, using the material of D. Parisot, D. Jeannin, and A. Z. Idelsohn.[15] It was well-nigh futile to press these basically Arabic modes into the iron framework of the eight Psalm Tones.

The following analysis has to confine itself to typical formulas and cannot deal with each tune individually. The identity or similarity of the *basic* formulas is of paramount importance for the understanding of our task; in mathematical parlance, the equations of formulas and modes must be 'necessary and sufficient'.

The *Tonus in directum* or *directaneus* of Table I is quoted after the *Editio Vaticana*; its Jewish counterpart, for convenience' sake also marked *Tonus in directum*, is a basic formula of the Yemenite Jews. A. Gastoué has, in his fine study *Chant juif et chant grégorien* drawn attention to the Yemenite version.[16] In view of the great age of the Yemenite tradition, P. Wagner's assumption that the *Tonus directaneus* is of relatively recent origin, can hardly be maintained.[17]

The *Tonus Peregrinus* displays two distinctly oriental features: the double *tenor* and the closing formula. It has numerous parallels in Jewish chant. In the Gregorian tradition it is connected mainly with Ps. 114 'In exitu Israel'. The same tone is used for the very same psalm by the Lithuanian Jews during the Passover season (version a).[18] Version b is the Oriental Jewish chant of Ps. 137, 'On the waters of Babylon';[19] version c is the Yemenite chant of the Song of Songs, paralleling the second Gregorian version, which Wagner quotes from the Salisbury Antiphonale.[20] The first version resembles also the Jewish counterpart of the first Psalm Tone. Many similar structures will be found later on in the modes of Lamentations. Under these circumstances we are justified in the assumption that the *Tonus Peregrinus* is, as already suggested by P. Vivell, a direct remnant of ancient Jewish tradition.[21] This appears really to be an inevitable conclusion, since the mode occurs in almost all Jewish centres, and is used with the same text as in the Church, during the very same liturgical season, Eastertide.[22]

The first Psalm Tone itself occurs in Jewish tradition, but not nearly as frequently as some of its *differentiae*; these adjustments of the closing melisma according to the mode of the following piece, usually an antiphon, are identical with Examples 27b, 27g and 29a. The formula in Table I, Tone I, e, is practically identical with Examples 37c and d, one of which is Gregorian, the other Jewish. The latter constitutes the ancient chant of the eulogy in the weekday *Tefilla*. The corresponding Gregorian melisma is a closing formula of the second responsorial Psalm Tone.[23] This is but one of the many instances, where antiphonal and responsorial Psalm Tones do not conform. The last item under I of the Jewish parallels is the cantillation of the scriptural accents *Merkha-T'vir* for the Pentateuch.[24]

The second Psalm Tone is much more frequent; indeed, it belongs to the four or five basic modes of Jewish tradition all over the world. It is a genuine mode of the Sabbath Psalms of the Yemenite Jews, but is also familiar to the Western Jewish centres.[25] Gastoué draws attention to a parallel in the psalmody of Holy Saturday.[26]

The third Psalm Tone occurs only in the chants of Oriental Jewry; in Central and East Europe it is all but unknown. This fact led Gastoué to the erroneous notion that it is altogether lacking in Jewish tradition.[27] In the Near East, this mode is usually confused, or at least blended, with the *maqam Sika*, which may account for *finales* different from the Gregorian. On the other hand, the *finales* of Office and Mass psalmody are not identical either.[28] The Jewish example in Table II, Tone IIIb, is a quotation from the ancient mode of the priestly blessing, as chanted in Yemen, and should be compared with the older form of the Office psalmody and its *differentiae*.

More problematical is the fourth Psalm Tone. In the previous chapter certain 'irregularities' (a favourite word among music theorists) were encountered in connexion with that type. The Vatican edition offers no less than four different *finales*, and even the *tenores* are not clearly fixed. In the Jewish parallels, the *tenor* G prevails, in the Gregorian, the A. The two ancient melodies of the *Te Deum* and of the plain *Gloria in Excelsis* (XV) are based upon this mode.[29] This Psalm Tone is, for all practical purposes, identical with the *Tropos Spondeiakos*, discussed in the last chapter; in the *Gloria* the F is entirely avoided and it appears only in the subsequently added 'Amen', in order to demonstrate its belonging to the fourth Tone. This Tone is common among all Oriental Jews, but rather rare among the European centres. In the Synagogue, it represents the mode of praise and devotion: the *Nishmat* ('All living souls shall praise the Lord') and the *Shebahot* (praises) of the Oriental Jews are invariably sung in that mode. This fact confirms the great age of the *Te Deum* and of the *Gloria*, both from the textual and the musical angle.[30]

On Holy Saturday, some of the psalms display the ending which is the alternative Gregorian version of the fourth Tone.

EXAMPLE 59

It is very familiar to every Central European Jew who has heard the same formula as the obligatory Amen response during the High Holydays. Since this close does not occur in the Orient, we have to assume that the European Jews borrowed it from the Church.

The fourth Mode is also particularly susceptible to chromaticisms.

467

Under Turkish and Arabian influence the G was sharpened to G sharp, and in this form the mode has made vast inroads into the liturgical music of the Greek Orthodox Church, and East European and Levantine Jewry. For all practical purposes the mode with the G sharp is now identical with the chromatic oriental scale, discussed in the previous chapter.

The fifth Psalm Tone of the Gregorian tradition appears in at least three forms, the oldest of which is probably (c), the *invitatorium* of the Easter morning matins, the end of the Holy Saturday vigil. The very same psalm (95) is sung in the same mode at the corresponding liturgical occasion in the Synagogue, namely on Friday evening during the Passover season. In comparing Examples 33a and b with Table I, Tone V, a, b and c and its Jewish parallels in Table II, a and b, one may perhaps study the development of and the various influences that came to bear upon, the mode. It seems that Vb, with its *finalis* A and the Jewish parallels of the Tone V (Table II) version b, also ending upon A, represent the oldest versions. The same mode occurs also in the chant of the Syrian Jacobite Church.[31] European Jewry, no less than the Western Church, changed the *finalis* A, adding a melisma which ends in F, thus replacing the ancient oriental mode with a Western F major. This development was the more natural, as most traditions of the Tone indicate a B flat. From the Gregorian approach, P. Wagner considers the psalmody of the *invitatorium* an archaic stratum of plainchant. From the fact that certain 'scalar' modes are not fully developed in archaic psalmody, he concludes that the modes of the *invitatorium* were already in existence when the system of the *octoechos* became the norm and yardstick of ecclesiastical chant.[32] This would antedate the fourth century, and consequently the Council of Nicaea, thus leaving the doors open to synagogal influence.

The nucleus of the fifth Psalm Tone is contained in the opening melisma of the antiphon 'Alma Redemptoris Mater'; the identity of this formula with Jewish modes may perhaps explain a very strange fact: the oldest parody of Jewish music in Spain, a triplum motet upon a parody-*Kedusha* text, written about 1460, carries as *contra-tenor* the opening melisma of the Christian antiphon. If a Jewish composer had done this knowingly, he would have thereby signed his own death-warrant, since the Inquisition took an exceedingly stern attitude in similar cases. Probably, however, he merely quoted the melodic pattern familiar to every one of his fellow-countrymen.[33] Most recently, Dr Plamenac has proved the travesty-character of the piece, which nevertheless gives us an inkling of medieval Hispano-Jewish music.

The sixth Gregorian Psalm Tone approximates closely the first Tone, only the *finalis* is here F, there D. In precisely the same way it is treated in the Jewish tradition.[34] The *tenor* is usually A, the *finalis* F. As in Gregorian tradition, this mode is used for the chant of the Lamentations and the Book of Job (cf. Table I, Tone VI, b). These forms warrant a special examination to be presented later on in this chapter.

The seventh Psalm Tone is rather rare in Jewish tradition. Its formulas do occur, though, but its usual *finalis* is G, not B or A as in the Gregorian tradition, which, by the way, knows also G as *finalis*.[35] As long as strictly psalmodic formulas are compared, not many Jewish parallels will be found; yet, at the very moment when the term 'Mixolydian' is pronounced, all doors are opened for misunderstandings and confusion.

Peccatur extra muros et intra! Two such outstanding scholars as Amédée Gastoué and the late Professor Idelsohn fell at the same time into the same pitfall. Gastoué quoted the *Tefilla*-mode of the Ashkenazic Jews, given in Example 32, as an instance of the seventh Psalm Tone.[36] Why? Because the seventh Tone is usually called Mixolydian, and the *Tefilla*-mode is Mixolydian in character. But the seventh Psalm Tone cannot be identified with any particular scale, as the various *finales* indicate. Idelsohn, a little more cautious than Gastoué, contented himself with the observation, 'The modern Ashkenazic cantors designate as *Mixolydian* the mode originally called *Adonai Malakh* after the first text (Ps. 93)'.[37] It defeats the meaning of scale, if it contains three or even more variable notes.

The eighth Gregorian Psalm Tone with its characteristic *initium* G-A-C and the *finalis* G, is very popular in Jewish tradition. It is the mode of the Pentateuch and the daily praises among the Yemenite Jews (Table II, Tone VIII, a) the solemn mode for the Day of Atonement in the Sephardic tradition (b, c), the mode which permeates the feast of *Shabuot* (Pentecost) in Ashkenazic tradition. The main *piyyut* of that festival, *Akdamut*, is sung in an old chant, the framework of which is presented in Table II, Tone VIII, d.[38] Thus, all of the important Jewish centres know and use this mode for praise and thanksgiving. In Gregorian tradition the eighth Psalm Tone is said to express the very same *ethos*.[39]

The most frequent Gregorian Psalm Tones to occur in Jewish chant are the Second, the Fourth, and the Eighth. These very same Tones constitute some of the oldest chants of the Gregorian tradition.

Thus far, we have confined our comparisons to the Roman and Jewish traditions; before extending them to the realm of oriental Christianity, a word of caution will be appropriate.

In spite of wide divergencies within the Gregorian tradition, it has been, as a whole, excellently preserved. Thousands of manuscripts and printed sources enable the scholar to ascertain its continuity throughout the centuries. The same cannot be said of the traditions of the Armenian, Syrian, East Aramaean (Nestorian), and even Byzantine Churches. Of these, the last mentioned has been best explored, but even now it is not yet easy to evaluate completely the musical sources as to their respective authenticity. So many shifts have been made in the Byzantine notation, so many foreign civilizations have had their influence upon the chant, that these facts burden the student with the constant problem of distinguishing between genuine old Byzantine tradition and the Syrian, Turkish, and Slavonic importations. Even more difficult is a serious evaluation of the Armenian, Nestorian, and Syrian chant, the ancient notations of which have not been clearly deciphered, or do not exist as such (as in the Syrian Churches). In such cases a conjectural element is inevitable, but should be reduced to a necessary minimum.

Byzantine and Jewish Psalmody

Originally, Byzantine chant must have been abundant in psalmodic structures. Unfortunately, few traces of plain psalmody have remained in Byzantine manuscripts. These meagre remnants are heavily overlaid with later, much more complex, usually hymnodic strata. This state of music is closely paralleled by a similar situation in the liturgy and the liturgical arts of Byzantium. The scriptural dichotomy has been preserved, but is musically expressed only in the *stichoi* (verses) that are sandwiched between the more elaborate and hymn-like *Kontakia* and *troparia*; the latter may properly be compared with early types of Roman antiphons (see Table III).[40] The complete psalms that form an integral part of the morning services are usually recited in an ecphonetic chant that has either deteriorated excessively, or else has never reached a truly musical stage.

Closest to the idea of psalmody as we know it from Gregorian and

Jewish tradition come the *hirmologia* (collections of model-stanzas), some of which may have originated in Syria before they came to Byzantium in the fifth or sixth century.[41] Here the psalmodic dichotomy is frequently discernible, and a semblance of *tenores* is recognizable:[42]

EXAMPLE 60

Translation: Out of the night we rise early to praise thee, Christ,
The Son ruling with the Father, and Saviour of our souls,
Grant peace to the universe, O Benefactor.

This is the *hirmos* (model-melody) of the Odes of the *Kanon* of St John Monachos. The ideal *tenor* is here A, which occurs 21 times in the 57 notes of the melody; in the other *hirmoi* of the same collection the ratio between *tenor* and other notes is similar: 73:23; 63:20; 59:21; etc. All that is rigid in the strict Gregorian psalmody has here been dissolved into little ornaments or patterns, yet the original psalmodic skeleton still shines through these musical arabesques, somewhat like this:

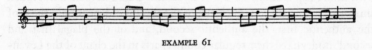

EXAMPLE 61

Corresponding to the three lines of the text, the tune has two divisions, instead of the more usual single.

If we search for the forces that disintegrated the strict psalmodic style, the word 'arabesque' tells the tale: medieval oriental Arab, then Turkish and Seldjuk elements have made heavy inroads into the ancient Byzantine tradition. The centuries that formed the gigantic and yet minute arabesque style of Islamic art, were also the formative periods of the later Byzantine music. The continuity of ancient psalmody was definitely broken by the group of the 'embellishers' (*maistores, melurges*), who superimposed their new, coloratura-like ornaments upon the more simple style of classic Byzantine chant.[43]

If manuscripts dating before the tenth century were extant to a considerable degree, they probably would show much more of plain psalmody than the musical documents of the three subsequent centuries, which constitute the main sources of the musicologist. E. Wellesz has shown in a series of fine studies why so little of earlier documents has come down to us; he links the bloody struggles of the iconoclastic revolt with the destruction of thousands of illuminated manuscripts, and this suggestion would indeed explain the deplorable dearth of earlier Byzantine sources.

Another misleading element of Byzantine chant is its chromaticism; some of these (dubious) chromatic passages show a clear resemblance to tunes of the East European Jews. Yet this similarity is not genuine; and we know the common element that brought forth these chromaticisms: the music of the Turks and Persians. When the Jews in Russia, after 1400, encountered this type of chant, they absorbed a good deal of it, just as the Byzantines did after 1300. Tillyard, one of the best authorities in this field, states:

Anyone who has listened to modern Greek church music must have been struck by the frequency of its chromatic passages; but in Middle Byzantine music we never find a whole hymn in the chromatic species, but only a short passage here and there. Further, the introduction of the chromatic sign seems usually, if not always, to be due to a later hand than the thirteenth century and may be regarded, in the main, as a fifteenth-century development.[44]

Within the psalmodic modes of Byzantine tradition there is not much similarity to ancient Jewish chant; of the typical cadences only those of the authentic first, the authentic second, and of the plagal first and second modes have their regular counterparts in the chant of the Levantine Jews, *and only there*.[45] Seen in fairly general terms, the relation between Jewish and Byzantine chant is much more distant than that between Jewish and Roman tradition. As we demonstrated in Chapters VI and VII of the first part, the situation is entirely different with regard to liturgical and theological literature.

One interesting exception from this general rule may be presented here: Tillyard quotes in his *Handbook of the Middle Byzantine Musical Notation* a hymn from the *Octoechos* with the following *incipit*:[46]

EXAMPLE 62

Translation: We praise the Saviour, made flesh and incarnate of the Virgin.

This tune shows a distinct resemblance to the old Moravian Passover-melody 'The next year in Jerusalem'.

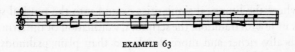

EXAMPLE 63

Yet, if the Byzantine tune was known in Russia, the probability is that the Jews learned the tune there, although it shows some traces of Synagogue Scripture cantillation. Thus, it is extremely difficult to form any judgement in cases like this, without being aware of at least three possible alternatives: (1) There is a common source for both melodies; (2) The Jews learned it from the chant of the Russian Orthodox Church; (3) The original Byzantine tune is a remnant of ancient Scripture cantillation.

Such alternatives should caution the student against any rash conclusions, especially when a melody has wandered over large geographical areas during the last thousand years.

Armenian Psalmody

In contrast to Byzantium, plain psalmody plays a considerable part in the liturgy of the Armenian Church. Here, evidently, simple psalmody remained on the level of an ecphonetically ordered cantillation amounting to little more than a slight intonation, while the Prophetic and New Testament lessons are clearly melodic, and abound with typical formulas.[47] Oral tradition, supported by a well developed system of ecphonetic notation and neumes, seems to have preserved reasonably well the cantillation of Scripture and a part of the psalmody. The hymns and the richly ornate psalmody of a later period are also notated in these neumes, but unfortunately we are unable to decipher them. Thus, where oral tradition is lost, as in the case of many hymns, we are confronted with closed doors. This is the more deplorable as the Armenians have a wonderful melodic genius: the beauty of their tunes matches fully the best Gregorian and Synagogue examples, and excels the Byzantine chant.

In the first part of this book we have pointed out the mysterious affinity of Armenian and Jewish liturgical forms and tried to trace it

473

back to the second century. While a study of the musical analogy to the liturgical situation is handicapped and heavily obscured by our inability to read the medieval Armenian neumes, there are at least three points where the liturgical similarities extend into the musical sphere.

(1) As in Jewish tradition, the scriptural cantillation of the Armenians is melodically richer and more developed than plain psalmody. It is the only Church of which this statement is valid. The closing cadences exhibit a distinct resemblance with some motifs of Hebrew cantillation, especially of the Yemenite Jews. We cite a few instances in Table IV: cf. No. 1 with No. 3,[48] No. 2 with No. 4.[49]

(2) Armenian psalmody, like Jewish, shows a strong preference for the interval of the fourth; this fact is emphasized by the (hypothetical) scalar mode of cantillation and psalmody, consisting of three conjunct Tetrachords:[50]

EXAMPLE 64

Similar scales pervade the cantillations of Oriental Jewry; especially the Caucasian Jews and also some of the East Mediterranean Jews build their psalmody and recitatives upon the very same scales (cf. Table IV, Nos. 5, 6).

(3) As in Judaism, the accent-motifs of scriptural cantillation form the oldest, continually recurring phrases and melismata of Armenian ornate psalmody and hymnody.[51] This constituent factor of elaborate chant is of great significance, since the Armenians are the only Christians who follow the principle that accents of cantillation form the basis of all psalmody. This fact will be more extensively discussed in the next chapter. As for plain psalmody, the Armenian chant approximates the synagogal tradition more in its general principles than in the individual features. Compare the interrelation of Table IV, No. 7 (Armenian) with 8a (Gregorian) and 8b (Yemenite Jewish).

West and East Syrian (Nestorian) Psalmody

Syrian psalmody is even more difficult to interpret with justice than the Armenian. Although the chant of the Syrian Churches has been explored more thoroughly than the Armenian, the usual criteria of

Psalmody seem to be inapplicable in this case. Several French scholars have clearly recognized this fact. This difficulty has been discussed most explicitly by Dom Jeannin in his extensive work on Syrian chant. The main impediment to a proper analysis rests with the following facts: (1) The psalmodic *tenores* change often and for no apparent reason; (2) There is no clearly established relation between *tenor* and *finalis*; and (3) Every mode may have three or even more *finales*.[52]

As a rule, the farther we go in an eastward direction from the Near East, the more anarchic and spontaneous becomes the music of the nations of Asia, until we reach the border of China, where an entirely different situation prevails; there again an ancient systematization has tamed the wildly growing musical jungle. We may deduce from this fact that the lessening degree of musical systematization parallels the decreasing influence of occidental forces or ideas. It has indeed been said of Indian music that it has a characteristic faculty of closing any tune on any note other than the tonic.[53]

In spite of all these difficulties, among which the lack of authentic sources is certainly not the least, we shall attempt to find some general principles applicable to, and valid of Syrian psalmody (see Table V).

A. Tonality

The main modes are a kind of Dorian (D-E-F-G-A-B(Bb)-C-D) and C major, or rather a variant of the *maqam Sika-Rast* that sounds like a major scale, but usually closes on the major third. The *finalis* may be in the first case D, G, or A, in the second case E, C, or G. An example of the first Psalm Tone follows:[54]

EXAMPLE 65

The obvious *tenor* is G, the *finalis* D; yet the same psalmody occurs also with the closing cadence upon either G or C. Otherwise, the structure is strictly syllabic, as in Jewish and Gregorian tradition.

However, this type of chant is not very frequent in the Syrian Churches; they show, as do also the Byzantines and Armenians, a strong predilection for hymnic forms, many of which fall into bar-like measures.

B. Performance

Psalmody is usually performed *choraliter*, if monks are celebrating the service, otherwise it is a solo chant with short responses by the congregation, not unlike the custom in small Jewish communities. The Syrian singers share with the Jewish *hazan* the love of heavily ornamented tunes in which they can exhibit their vocal gymnastics.

C. Foreign Influences

Even more than in Byzantine or Armenian chant, Turkish and Arab modes have asserted themselves in the Syrian Churches; especially the Turko-Arabian *maqamat Usul* and *Hedjaz* are widely popular in the chants of Syria, as a glance into Parisot's or Jeannin's books will prove.

Due to the lack of authenticity and the presence of so many beclouding or alien elements, the comparison of plain Syrian psalmody with Jewish tradition cannot be considered a fruitful or even promising enterprise, apart from a few modal similarities, due to the common Arabic influence. Cf. Table V, No. 1 with the following Oriental Jewish *finalis* tune:[55]

EXAMPLE 66

THE LAMENTATIONS AND COGNATE FORMS

In Part I of this book it was pointed out, after extensive examination of the historic sources, that the old Christian liturgy of the vigil before Easter Sunday combined the elements of the two greatest Jewish days of fasting, viz. *Yom Kippur* and the ninth day of Ab.[56] One of the integral parts of the liturgy of Holy Saturday is the Lamentations, common to almost all of the Catholic Churches. In Jewish liturgy, the Lamentations and the Book of Job were considered the proper lessons for fastdays; the latter is read at the season of the High Holydays, culminated by the Day of Atonement, the former constitutes an essential part of the liturgy of the ninth day of Ab, the memorial of the Temple's destruction. Among Oriental Jewry, these two scriptural cantillations are sung in modes that are interchangeable. Other special chants of these two fast-days are the

Selihot and *Qinot*, poetical centonizations of penitential passages, which are usually chanted in the modes of Job or Lamentations.

Long ago some liturgists had surmised Jewish elements in the Gregorian chant of the Lamentations. Their point of departure was usually the melismatic intonation of the Hebrew letters to designate the number of the verses (*Aleph, Beth, Ghimel,* etc.) that constitute an alphabetic acrostic and were, in their original Hebrew, included in the Roman tradition.[57] Yet for a long time these speculations did not amount to more than mere conjectures. Then, within the last forty years, new, and highly dramatic evidence came to light.

At the turn of the century O. Fleischer had published in his *Neumenstudien* Vol. I, a Naples version of the Latin Lamentations; fourteen years later Idelsohn, apparently unaware of the striking similarity, gave in his *Songs of the Yemenite Jews*[58] its Jewish counterpart, a *Selicha* chant. It was P. Wagner who established the complete identity of the two tunes (see Table VI). Nos. 4a and 4b display this congruence. Hence, Wagner concluded, 'this must be the oldest Latin version; . . . in this case a direct borrowing of synagogal chant by the Church has taken place'.[59]

Yet there are at least three main versions of the Lamentations extant in Gregorian tradition, of which the quoted one is only one. The most popular and authentic version is given in Table VI, No. 1.[60] Shortly after Wagner's discovery, Idelsohn demonstrated the identity of this chief Gregorian version with the Job cantillation of the Oriental Jews (Table VI, Nos. 2a and 2b).[61] One of the more extended melismata of this Gregorian tune recalls vividly the antiphon 'Alma redemptoris mater', whose Jewish counterpart has already been pointed out.[62]

Even the less known version found its way in a modified form into the authentic Vatican edition: namely as the chant for the *Oratio Jeremiae Prophetae*, sung on Holy Saturday.[63] We cite this tune and its Jewish parallels in Table VI, Nos. 3a and 4c. It is again the mode of the *Te Deum*, the *Sh'ma' Yisrael* and of the *Tropos Spondeiakos*, in short, one of the oldest, if not the oldest, ecclesiastical and Jewish mode.

Let us now, after these comparisons, stop for a moment in order to evaluate their relationship and interdependence.

The signal significance of the liturgies of Good Friday and Holy Saturday is so well understood that it needs no further emphasis. The outstanding features of the two chief Jewish fast-days had already been

477

transplanted to the end of the Holy Week at an early stage. This liturgical transposition comprised also their accompanying chants.

The cantillation of Job, a feature of the Oriental High Holyday season, has become the origin of the *main version* of the Gregorian Lamentations. The cadences and modes of the *Selihot* and of the Hebrew Lamentations, as chanted on the ninth day of Ab and during the High Holydays, have formed the basis of the other Gregorian versions. Even the Ashkenazic mode of the Pentateuch pericope for the High Holydays reflects again the Job cantillation.

What has happened here and when did it happen? What may musical research add to the findings of liturgists?

It will be useful to set down two additional factors, before essaying definite conclusions. (1) The Gregorian tradition has preserved the chant of the Hebrew initial letters in the Lamentations. The oldest complete Bible with ecphonetic accents, the Codex Amiatinus, does not only spell out the Hebrew letters, but provides each of them with a distinct neumated melisma. Hence, this chanting of Hebrew letters must date back to a time when they were still understood, and when bilingual chants were nothing extraordinary. No liturgical season uses so many bilingual chants as the end of Holy Week. There is good reason to assume that they originated in an early period of Christianity, as the 'Agios O Theos' or the 'Quando in cruce' that is identical with the Byzantine 'Hote to stauro' clearly show.[64] This practice was well established at the time of Aetheria Silvia; she reports the performance of bilingual, even of trilingual lessons during Holy Week.[65]

(2) The fact that the Central European Jews sing the Pentateuch pericopes of the High Holydays in a mode approximating the cantillation of Job and Lamentations of the Oriental Jews, indicates that this mode was well established when the various local traditions branched from the hitherto uniform Jewish ritual. We can only guess when this process of particularism began; probably during the time when the European and Near East communities could no longer maintain contact with the Jewish centres in Palestine and Babylonia. This obstruction of close intercommunication seems to have begun by the end of the fifth century, when the Pax Romana was almost universally broken, due to the rising power of Persia, the unrest of the Arabian tribes in the East, the 'migration of nations' (*Völkerwanderung*) and the invasion of the Huns in the West. Yet our mode must antedate this period.

For these reasons we cannot accept Idelsohn's thesis that it was Jerome who introduced the Jewish mode of Lamentations in the tradition of the Church. According to Idelsohn, he may 'have learned the mode from his Jewish teachers'.[66]

This conjecture is by no means convincing. For the Lamentations hold, in liturgics, the status of a lesson, not of a chant. Even today they are named *lectiones*.[67] The twelve lessons of the Easter vigil, however, were already well established at the time of Aetheria; and it is improbable that only Jerome should have set the order of the lessons. On the other hand, it is hardly possible to assume the introduction of a new Jewish chant for an already established and venerable portion of Christian worship as late as Jerome's time. Some of the recited (not chanted) lessons that follow the Lamentations of Good Friday belong to the oldest strata of Catholic tradition. Lesson VI and V, between which the famous *Tenebrae* is inserted, are full of violent anti-Jewish accusations.[68] This fact suggests that they were introduced into the liturgy after the Nicaean Council, but at such a time the Church would certainly not have consented to the conscious introduction of new *Jewish* elements. Too loud were the voices of the anti-Jewish hot-heads, such as Chrysostom and other Church Fathers, to permit such additional Jewish features as the tune of Lamentations.

It seems, therefore, an inevitable conclusion that both the text and chant of Lamentations were integral parts of the Christian liturgy *before* the Council of Nicaea; moreover, they must have been introduced at a time when Judaeo-Christianity was still a potent factor in the Church; otherwise the Hebrew initials would have made no sense. These arguments indicate the end of the second, or the beginning of the third century as the *terminus a quo.*

We shall probably not be in error if we credit that period with the institution of all the essential parts of the liturgy and chant of Good Friday, Holy Saturday, and the subsequent, all-important Easter vigil.

TYPICAL MOTIFS AND INTERVALS IN PLAIN PSALMODY

At the very outset we must clearly point out the very narrow limits which confine such a study. When surveying papers or lectures on subjects such as 'The Fourth (or Fifth, etc.) in Jewish (or Chinese, or Gregorian) Chant', one invariably reaches the judgement that they either smack of charlatanry or of over-simplification and *naïveté*. For it is impossible to set up anything which might serve as a criterion for the frequency of an interval in a given musical entity, unless one limits oneself to a definite form or a clearly circumscribed stratum of music. Nor does every form-type lend itself to such an investigation. The very suggestion of a study on the subject 'The Third in Beethoven's String-Quartets', could be dismissed *a priori* as an absurdity.

Yet the closely circumscribed and plain structure of psalmody or psalmodic chant displays in clearer contours and to better advantage the frequency of typical intervals. Since the punctuating melismata that usually accompany the half and full close of the verse consist chiefly of seconds, and the bulk of the verse is chanted upon one tone, the *tenor*, there remains only the *initium*, the *punctus*, and occasionally the *flexa* as the points where intervals greater than a second might occur. Therefore, we shall proceed under the proviso that this exposition be confined to short motifs and typical intervals of plain or moderately ornate psalmody (see Table VII).

The Gregorian *plain* psalmody shows a predilection for the following intervals:

A. Opening formulas (*Initia*). (1) Ascending second, followed by a third, resulting in a fourth (Tones II, IV and VIII). (2) One or two ascending thirds (Tone V). All others open with ascending seconds.

B. Closing formulas (*Puncti*). Descending third or fourth regularly in Tones I, II, III and IV and occasionally V, VII and VIII.

The Byzantine *plain* psalmody prefers:

A. For opening formulas: (1) Ascending seconds and thirds, or direct fourths. (2) Descending third.

B. For closing formulas: (1) Descending seconds, usually from the upper fourth. (2) Ascending seconds, often from the third below the *finalis*.

Jewish *plain* psalmody prefers:

A. For opening formulas: (1) Ascending seconds up to the fifth, or ascending seconds and thirds, resulting in a fourth; (2) Immediately ascending fourth; (3) Two ascending thirds, resulting in a fifth.

B. For closing formulas: (1) Descending second from the upper third or fourth of the *finalis*; (2) Descending third or fourth; (3) Ascending seconds or thirds rising usually from the third below the *finalis*.[69]

If we compare briefly the similarities and divergencies, it is obvious that the Gregorian tradition is closer to Jewish *melos* than the Byzantine formulas. We notice, further, the resemblance of the *initia* of the second, fourth and eighth Gregorian Psalm Tones to the intervals that usually open synagogal psalmody. Gregorian closing melismata are even more akin to Jewish chant; this is only natural, since the final melismata were very early indicated by ecphonetic accents, whereas the notation of initial words of a verse dates from a later period. This holds true both for primitive Roman and Jewish musical accentuation. In general, the fourth —without intermittent seconds—occurs more often in Jewish than in Gregorian psalmody, where it usually is dissolved in running seconds, or is the result of a second plus third.

TYPICAL MOTIFS AND INTERVALS IN ORNATE PSALMODY

Considerably different from these rough conclusions are the results, if moderately ornate psalmody is being included in the survey. It is not, of course, possible here to enter into a thorough investigation of that question from the purely Jewish angle; as for Gregorian Chant, most important spade-work has already been performed by the *Paléographie musicale*, P. Wagner, and C. von Gevaert.[70] Yet a brief and admittedly preliminary sketch of my findings in the question of typical intervals in more melismatic psalmody might not be altogether useless, and hence find a place here.

It has already been established by Gevaert that certain typical opening and closing phrases permeate the entire Gregorian Chant. Usually each of these typical phrases is connected with a specific mode, or even one of the eight artificial scales into which medieval theory forced most of plainchant, not altogether successfully.

Here we shall examine some of these typical recurrent openings, as they occur in Gregorian Chant, and compare them with similarly recurrent phrases of the Jewish tradition.

Phrases typical of the various Tones are shown in Table VII.

This sketchy tabulation yields the following results, always roughly simplified:

A. In general, the various modes are well characterized by their typical intervals. Yet certain ambiguities and duplicities do occur (cf. 1a with 6e). The *post factum* statement of Gregorian theorists that the sixth Tone is often treated like the first does not explain anything. For if it is practically identical with the first Tone, where is its *raison d'être*? Only to constitute a complete *octoechos*?

B. The ascending fifth and fourth are characteristic of the first and seventh modes. The ascending fourth, broken up in a second plus third, is typical of Tones II, VI and VIII. Two ascending thirds signify the *initium* of the fifth Tone; sometimes the preceding antiphon or gradual ignores this fact, but as soon as the psalm verse appears, the two thirds open it. One ascending and descending third occurs frequently in the fourth Tone, but again chromaticisms mar the purity of that modality (cf. 4b). This example, and 8a, c, evade entirely the orthodox systems of Tones and modes. Descending thirds occur in the second, fourth, fifth, and seventh modes. Descending fourths, frequently broken up into second plus third, are characteristic of the Tones I, II, V, VI and VIII.

C. The sixth and the seventh Tones show such an abundance of various *initia* and standing phrases, that their general category of modality is seriously impaired. 7c, for instance, can hardly be identified as belonging to the same mode as 7d. Nowhere in either c or d does a psalm verse occur, which by its Tone might clarify the characteristic features of the mode.

Jewish chant, on the other hand, shows predilection for the following interval phrases of opening and closing formulas:

A. The ascending fourth, sometimes (but not as often as in Gregorian tradition) broken up into second plus third. The Oriental Jews, especially the Yemenites, use a descending fourth frequently. The ascending third is frequent, but not as much as in Gregorian Chant. Ascending fifths are not rare; descending jumps to the lower fifth occur only in European Jewry under the influence of the Dominant-Tonic relation of the occidental harmonic system.

B. For closing formulas, all Jewish tradition shows decided preference for descending seconds or thirds. Only the archaic elements of the Torah and Haftara cantillation use the descending fourth for the final formula. This type of closing melisma occurs also in the archaic formulas of the Gregorian lesson.

C. Much more significant than in Gregorian Chant are the 'wandering melismata' which characterize whole portions of a feast day's musical liturgy. While such 'standing phrases' are by no means unknown to Gregorian Chant, as we shall see in the next chapter, they play a paramount part in the structure of Jewish chant.

In Roman plainchant, it is often the brief motifs, consisting of three or four intervals, which frequently recur and thus constitute a homogenizing factor in Gregorian psalmody; in the chants of the Synagogue, an intensive development from the small recurrent motifs to wandering melismata has taken place. These wandering melismata were filled with literary and ceremonial associations and eventually became veritable 'leitmotifs', integrating the various tunes, which were linked by such melismata into an organic corpus, full of meaning and significance to every Jew familiar with the tradition of the Synagogue.

Time and again we recognize the organizing and ordering genius of the Occident, the freer, more spontaneous, also more inspirational genius of the Orient. In Gregorian chant as in the music of European Jewry, Eastern and Western forces were blended to perfection; yet in plainchant there reigns systematization, in Jewish chant emotional expression.

EXAMPLES OF PLAIN PSALMODY IN SYNAGOGUE AND CHURCH

Plain psalmody in the Synagogue is primarily to be found in the weekday prayers, and parts of the Sabbath liturgy. As a general rule, the chants become more elaborate and more embellished the greater the liturgical occasion. Thus, on the High Holydays, plain psalmody plays but a small part in the traditional music. Even when a melody has originally had a simple psalmodic character, it is, on festivals, adorned with a melismatic array, and it takes close scrutiny to reduce such chants to their originally simple nucleus. Some of these plain psalmodies will be compared with plainchant tunes (see Table VIII).

The first two illustrations (Table VIII, Nos. 1a and 2) are plain psalmodies; No. 1 shows a certain kinship to the *Tropos Spondeiakos*, discussed in Chapters II and III. No. 2 compares the typical mode of the evening prayer of the Synagogue with compline of Saturday in the Church; the liturgical organization of compline is closely analogous to the evening service of the Synagogue, as we have seen before.

No. 3 is a typical mode of the *Invitatorium* in Church and Synagogue and has been discussed before.

Much more interesting are the comparisons given in Nos. 4 and 5. The Great Doxology of the *Kaddish* on Sabbath morning shows close resemblance to the *Praeconium Paschale*, the blessing of fire and light in the vigil of Easter Sunday. Since this custom dates back to the early centuries of the Church—Augustine knew it already[71]—it stands to reason that the chant is fairly old, an opinion confirmed by P. Wagner.[72] The Sabbath morning chants, likewise, belong to the oldest strata of Synagogue music, and some of the elements are common to the Yemenite, Sephardic and Ashkenazic rites. From the musical point of view the second half of the illustration is the more interesting one. While the first part is clearly supratonal, the second part tends to a subsemitonal type, sharply emphasized by some melodic jumps that are not too frequent in plainchant.

The most remarkable instance, both from the musical and liturgical angle, is No. 5. Here the opening words of the *Tefilla*, 'God of Abraham, God of Isaac, God of Jacob', are juxtaposed with the passage of the genealogy of Christ (Matt. I), 'and Abraham begot Isaac; and Isaac begot Jacob', chanted at Christmas. The highly solemn tune is almost the same in Church and Synagogue. Since the text of the *Tefilla* antedates the genealogy of the Gospel by at least 150 years, and the synagogal mode is known among the three main rites of Judaism, the priority of the Synagogue seems to be a natural conclusion. The only doubt might arise when one stops to think that the ecclesiastical mode of today appears not to be the oldest version. Yet A. Gastoué has drawn attention to this identity and does not hesitate to trace the Church's tradition to Jewish sources.[73] Nos. 6a and 6b finally juxtapose an ancient Jewish prayer chant with two typical antiphons 'Vado ad eum' and 'Diriget mansuetos'.

The last three numbers exceed the realm of plain psalmody; Easter and Christmas were the occasions in the Christian liturgy from which the chants of these illustrations are quoted. The parallel Jewish examples occur in the services of Sabbath morning and the Three Festivals. Since the liturgical significance of these services goes far beyond those of weekdays, the Psalm Tones in both Church and Synagogue are replaced here by ornate psalmody, in order to enhance the liturgical occasion. This type of psalmody is the best cultivated and most developed field of sacred music, yet also the most complex one. The next chapter will discuss this intricate subject.

NOTES CHAPTER V

1. See *supra*, pp. 403 ff; also S. Cohn, 'Saadyas Einleitung zum Psalmenkommentar', in *Magazin f. d. Wissenschaft d. Judentums* (1881), pp. 65 ff.
2. Cf. *MLS*, I, p. 77.
3. Ibid., I, p. 106.

4. Ibid., I, p. 105. 'Nous avons vu, en effet, que les formules syriennes ne finissent pas toutes sur la fondamentale, pas même sur la finale la plus ordinaire du mode.'

5. Cf. R. Lachmann, *Musik des Orients*, p. 59.

6. *LU*, p. 1050.

7. *LU*, p. 697.

8. *LU*, p. 896; cf. *MLS*, I, p. 102.

9. Cf. *MLS*, I, pp. 99–100. See also the article in *Publikationen der Internationalen Musik-gesellschaft*, II, fasc. 5, pp. 55 ff.

10. Cf. *M. Taanit*, I; also Maimonides, *Hilchot Tefilla*, c. VIII. One may also think of the Early Mass and the High Mass as analogies.

11. WGM, III, p. 88.

12. The conception of the modern scholar of the technique of composition during the First Millennium is best expressed by E. Wellesz, in his *Eastern Elements in Western Chant* (p. 88): 'Each melody consists of a number of formulae, which can also be found in other melodies of the same mode . . . . Each *echos* consists of a number of groups of melodies, built up on the same formulae . . . . The process of musical composition consisted in fitting together and slightly varying phrases, cadences and formulae which were already in existence . . . .'

A Jewish mystic of the Middle Ages, Abraham Abulafia, compared his system of planned and combined meditation (*Tseruf*) with the principle of musical composition: 'Know that the method of *Tseruf* can be compared to music; for the ear hears sounds from various combinations, in accordance with the character of the melody and the instrument . . . . This enjoyment can be produced only through the combination of sounds (motifs) . . . .'

Cf. Gershom Scholem, *Major Trends in Jewish Mysticism* (New York, 1946), p. 134.

13. H. J. W. Tillyard, *Handbook of the Middle Byzantine Musical Notation*, in *Monumenta Musicae Byzantinae*, Subsid. vol. I (1935); E. Wellesz, *Byzantinische Musik* (1927); idem, 'Byzantine Music', in *Proceed. of Mus. Ass.* (1932).

14. K. Kevorkian, 'Die armenische Kirchenmusik' in *SIM*, I; and P. Aubry, 'Le Système musical de l'Église arménienne', *Tribune de St Gervais* (Paris, 1901–3).

15. Parisot, op. cit.; Jeannin, op. cit.; A. Z. Idelsohn, 'Der Kirchengesang der Maroniten', *ZFMW* (1929–30).

16. A. Gastoué, op. cit., pp. 115–16.

17. WGM, I, p. 27 f. The rule of St Benedict, where reference is already made to that tone, originated in 530. It is not too bold an assumption to date the tradition back for two more centuries, that is, to the Nicaean Council, where the final separation was made between Judaism and Christianity. This decision forced, as we know, a number of Judaeo-Christians into the camp of the Gentile Church. These converts probably were the transmitters of old Jewish traditions.

18. Cf. Eric Werner, 'Preliminary Notes, . . .', *HUCA* (1940), p. 359.

19. IT, IV, No 172.

20. IT, I, No 18.

21. P. Vivell, in *Revue du chant grégorien*, XVIII, pp. 147 ff. Recently A. Gastoué has again brought new evidence to bear on the Jewish origin of the *Tonus Peregrinus*. See his *Chant juif et chant grégorien*, p. 114.

22. The version (a) of the *Tonus Peregrinus* is sung at Passover night; the *In Exitu* usually during the Easter season; and, to complete the picture, Gastoué's Gregorian example is 'Afferte Domino', which is sung at the vigil of Holy Saturday, the eve of the Christian Passa that is *Passover's counterpart*. How unbreakable sometimes is the chain of liturgical tradition!

23. WGM, III, p. 191.

24. The examples of Table II are quoted from Idelsohn, *Thesaurus of Hebrew Oriental Melodies*; the same author's *Jewish Music*; A. Gastoué's *Chant juif et chant grégorien* and my own publications. As for other parallels to I. Ps. T., see IT, IV, Nos 293, 287, *Jewish Music*, p. 82, No 2; p. 63.

25. Our instance is quoted from IT, II, No 41.

26. Gastoué, op. cit., p. 130.

27. Actually, he himself quotes an instance of it; op. cit., p. 114.

28. WGM, III, pp. 89, 141; *LU*, p. 111. Cf. IT, I, No 14.

29. *LU*, p. 55. Wagner reaches exactly the same conclusion: WGM, III, pp. 451 f, 226 ff; also *Paleogr. mus.*, VI, 316, where an even more primitive version is given.

30. The Jewish examples from IT, II, No 127 and No 58. See also IT, IV, No 214 and the Table of the *Tropos Spondeiakos* of the previous chapter.

31. The Gregorian examples are quoted from WGM, III, pp. 89, 179; *LU*, pp. 680 ff (*Dominica Resurrectionis*). The corresponding Jewish pieces in *JM*, p. 76; IT, II, p. 75 (Jacobite mode), where are also other parallels.

32. Cf. WGM, III, pp. 186 f.

33. Cf. my article 'The Oldest Sources of Jewish Music', *Proceedings of the American Academy for Jewish Research* (1947), where a photographic reproduction and a modern transliteration of that interesting MS. are given.

34. Cf. *JM*, p. 63, No 10.

35. WGM, III, pp. 142, 165. The Jewish examples in IT, II, p. 97, No. 49 ff.

36. Cf. A. Gastoué, op. cit., p. 132.

37. Cf. *JM*, p. 73.

38. Cf. IT, I, p. 60; IT, IV, Nos 184, 260; A Friedmann, *Chasonus*, v. *Akdomus*; also *JM*, p. 156.

39. Cf. P. D. Johner, *Schule des gregorianischen Gesanges*, p. 1; also Joh. Wolf 'Anonymi Cuiusdam Codex Brasiliensis', in *Vierteljahrsschrift für Musikwissenschaft*, IX (1893), pp. 409 ff.

40. Cf. E. Wellesz, 'Studien zur Byz. Musik', *ZFM*, XVI (1934), pp. 220 ff.

41. Ibid., p. 225.

42. Ibid., pp. 417–19.

43. RMA, pp. 82 ff; also Wellesz, 'Studien zur Byz. Musik', *ZFM*, XVI, p. 227, and A. Gastoué, 'La Musique byzantine', in Lavignac, *Encyclopédie de la musique*, Part I, p. 548.

44. Cf. H. J. W. Tillyard, *Handbook of the Middle Byzantine Musical Notation*, in *Monumenta Musicae Byzantinae*, Subsidia, vol. I, fasc. I, Copenhagen, 1935, p. 35; also E. Wellesz, *Byzantinische Musik* (Breslau, 1927), p. 92.

45. Tillyard, op. cit., pp. 32–34, where the typical cadences are given.

46. Ibid., p. 40.

47. The little exact material on Armenian music has been provided by three scholars: P. Aubry, 'Le Système musical de l'Église arménienne', in *Tribune de St. Gervais* (Paris, 1901–3); the same author's fine study *L'Accent tonique* (Paris, 1903); Komitas Kevorkian, by far the best Armenian musicologist, himself a *choregos* (director of music) at Etchmiadzin; unfortunately not much of his writings is available in occidental languages: *Musique arménienne populaire*, I, II (Paris, 1925–30). 'Die armenische Kirchenmusik', in *SIM*, I (1899–1900); and E. Wellesz, 'Die armenische Messe und ihre Musik, in *Jahrbuch d. Musikbibliothek Peters* (1920), pp. 1 ff, also the same author's *Aufgaben und Probleme auf dem Gebiete der byzant. und oriental. Kirchenmusik*, where the puzzle of Armenian chant and notation is discussed.

48. K. Kevorkian, 'Die armenische Kirchenmusik', *SIM*, I, pp. 58 ff.

49. IT, II, p. 85.

50. K. Kevorkian, loc. cit.

51. The same observation was made by Gastoué in his study on the liturgical music of the Eastern Churches, in Lavignac, *Encyclopédie*, I, p. 552.

52. This is the essence of Jeannin's chapter on the *octoechos*, esp. pp. 100–5.

53. M. Grosset in Lavignac, *Encyclopédie de la musique*, I, 'Inde', pp. 290 ff; 314–25 ff. See also C. Sachs, *The Rise of Music in the Ancient World*, pp. 172 ff.

54. Gastoué in Lavignac, *Encyclopédie*, I, p. 551, also Parisot, op. cit., Nos 281–300. A few interesting instances of modal inconsistencies in Gregorian Chant are cited in *MLS*, pp. 102 ff.

55. Jeannin, op. cit., p. 111.

56. See *supra*, Part I, Chapters III and IV.

57. Parisot in *Tribune de St. Gervais*, VIII, p. 351; in the same author's *Rapport sur une mission scientifique*, etc. (1899), p. 246. Cf. also S. Naumbourg, *Recueil du chant israelite*, preface, and O. Fleischer, *Neumenstudien*, II, p. 45.

58. IT, I, p. 88 No 67.

59. WGM, III, p. 240.
60. *LU*, p. 634.
61. IT, II, p. 70, No 2; ibid., No 187.
62. *Supra*, n. 33; also WGM, III, p. 242.
63. *LU*, p. 637, 'Alter Tonus ad libitum', and IT, I, combined Nos 79, 80.
64. For a thorough discussion of the bilingual elements in Western Liturgy, see E. Wellesz, *Eastern Elements in Western Chant*, Chapters I–V. Most recently (1955), Prof. L. Schrade has informed me of his discovery of a MS. of Latin Lamentations stemming from the seventh century, and containing some highly significant details in the shape of neumes and in the spelling of the Hebrew letters.
65. Cf. *Peregrinatio Aetheriae*, in P. Geyer, *Itinera Hierosolymitana*, in *CSEL* (Vienna, 1898), XXXIX, 99: 'Lectiones etiam, quaecumque in ecclesia leguntur, quia necesse est graece legi, semper stat, qui siriste [i.e. Syriac,] interpretatur propter populum, ut semper diceant. Sane quicumque hic latini sunt, id est, qui nec graece moverunt, ne contristentur, et ipsis exponitur eis . . . .' (All of the lessons of the church have to be read in Greek, and also to be translated into Syriac in order that the people may always understand them. Certainly, there are also Latin-speaking people, that is, such as do not understand Greek . . . and for them the lesson is interpreted . . . .)
66. IT, II, p. 16.
67. WGM, III, p. 235.
68. To inform the benevolent reader about the spirit of these lessons, I quote one literally from the *Liber Usualis* (Lectio VI on Good Friday, immediately after the Responsory, 'Tenebrae factae sunt'). 'Non dicant Judaei: Non occidimus Christum. Etenim propterea eum dederunt judici Pilato, ut quasi ipsi a morte ejus viderentur immunes. Nam cum dixisset eis Pilatus: vos eum occidite; responderunt: nobis non licet occidere quemquam. Iniquitatem facinoris sui in judicem hominem refundere volebant; sed numquid Deum judicem fallebant? Quod fecit Pilatus, in eo ipso quod fecit, aliquantum particeps fuit: sed in comparatione illorum, multo ipse innocentior . . . . Sed si reus, quia fecit vel invitus: illi *innocentes, qui coegerunt* ut faceret? Nullo modo. Sed ille dixit in eum sententiam, et jussit eum crucifigi, et quasi ipse occidit; *et vos, O Judaei, occidistis!*' (Italics mine) *LU*, p. 598. What do modern scholars say to this passage, or even the Holy See, which has so courageously proclaimed, 'Spiritually, we are all Semites'? The passage quoted originates with St Augustine, *Enarr. in Ps. 63* (PL, XXXVI, 762). I am indebted to Fr Mrozek of the Pontifical Institute of Oriental Studies, Rome, for this reference.
69. Cf. IT, II, pp. 29 ff.
70. Cf. Gevaert, *La Mélopée antique dans le chant de l'Église latine* (Ghent, 1895), Chapter V. Many of his theories have meanwhile been replaced by more solid conclusions; and his main thesis of the ancient Greek elements in Gregorian Chant has been entirely abandoned by musicologists. Yet his special study on the structure and certain typical features of the antiphon has retained its value and should be considered an outstanding contribution to the study of plainchant.
71. The main sources about this custom in L. Duchesne, *Christian Worship: its Origin and Evolution*, pp. 250–3.
72. WGM, III, pp. 251 ff, where even MSS. without lines are mentioned.
73. A. Gastoué, 'Chant juif et chant grégorien', in *Rev. du chant grégorien*, (Dec. 1930), p. 162.

TABLE 1

Roman Church

GV = *Graduale Vaticanum*
W = *P.Wagner, Gregorianische Melodien III*
LU = *Liber usualis*
G = *Gastoué, Les Origines du chant romain*

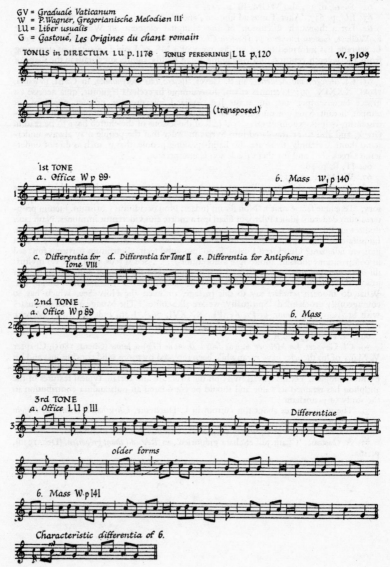

TONUS in DIRECTUM LU p.1178   TONUS PEREGRINUS LU p.120   W. p109

(transposed)

1st TONE
a. Office W p 89·   b. Mass W₁p 140

c. Differentia for   d. Differentia for Tone II   e. Differentia for Antiphons
Tone VIII

2nd TONE
a. Office W p 89   b. Mass

3rd TONE
a. Office LU p III   Differentiae

older forms

b. Mass W·p 141

Characteristic differentia of b.

TABLE 2
Jewish Parallels

IT = Idelsohn, Thesaurus of
    Hebrew Oriental Melodies
EW1= E.Werner, Preliminary
    notes (HUCA 1940)
EW2= E.Werner, Doxology in
    Church and Synagogue (HUCA 1946)

Synagogue

JM = Idelsohn, Jewish music in
    its historical development

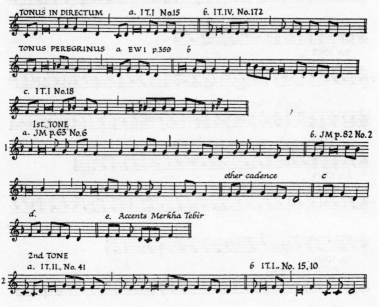

TONUS IN DIRECTUM   a. IT.I No.15   6. IT.IV. No.172

TONUS PEREGRINUS a. EW1 p.359   6

c. IT.I No.18

1st. TONE
a. JM p.63 No.6   6. JM p.82 No.2

other cadence   c

d.   e. Accents Merkha Tebir

2nd TONE
a. IT.II., No. 41   6 IT.I., No. 15,10

3rd TONE
a. IT. II No.50   6 IT.I., No.14

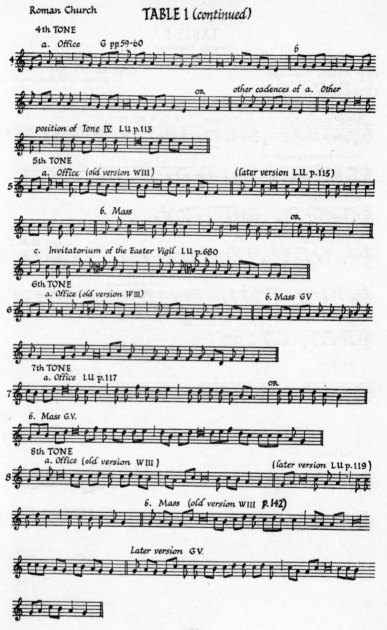

TABLE 2 (continued)

Synagogue

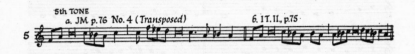

17

TABLE 3

Byzantine echoi

Byzantine formulas

From Wellesz, Eastern Elements in Western Chant

Characteristic passage from the Troparion, Kyrie, epi to pathos. p 47

Formulas of the hymn, Hote to stauro. (transposed) p 105

(middle line)   (upper line)

TABLE 4

Armenian Psalmody

KK = Komitas Kevorkian
in SIM vol. I
IT = Idelsohn, Thesaurus

Closing formula of prophetic lesson KK. p.61

Closing formulas of chanted prayer KK. p.61-2

Lamentations of Yemenite Jews (Transposed) IT I, No. 58-62

Prayer-mode for feast days of Babylonian Jews IT II, p.85 No. 8 (Transposed)

Armenian Psalmody KK p.56

Armenian lesson and chant KK p.61

etc.

Armenian chant of prayer

(After A. Apcar, Melodies of the Church of Armenia, Calcutta 1897, p. 25)

a Gregorian Alleluia LU. p.88

6 Yemenite Jewish Song of Songs IT I, No. 17

PLAIN PSALMODY

TABLE 5

Syrian Psalm Tones

P = Dom Parisot,
   Rapport scientifique

J = Dom Jeannin,
   Mélodies liturgiques syriennes

I. *Gregorian* = III *Syrian Tone*   P.149 or P.88

II. *Gregorian* = IV. *Syrian Tone.*   P. 76, 82, J.91   ("Ton Grecq")

III. *Gregorian* = V *Syrian Tone* P. 184 J.106

IV. *Gregorian* = VI. *Syrian Tone*   P.195   or P.183 J.113

V. *Gregorian* = VII *Syrian Tone* . P.201

VI. *Gregorian* = VIII *Syrian Tone* P.206

VII. *Gregorian* = I. *Syrian Tone* (*Maqam Sika - Rast, transposed to* G)
  a. P.36   6 P.29 J.110

VIII. *Gregorian* = II. *Syrian Tone* (*Transposed to* G)   P.19

TABLE 6

Lamentations and Cognate Forms

IT = Idelsohn Thesaurus
LU = Liber usualis
WGM = P. Wagner, Gregorianische
    Melodien III

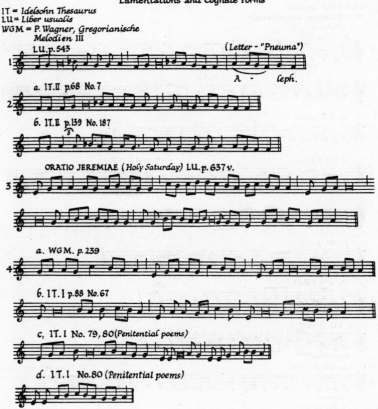

TABLE 7
Typical motifs and intervals

LU = Liber usualis
W = P. Wagner, Gregorianische
    Melodien III.

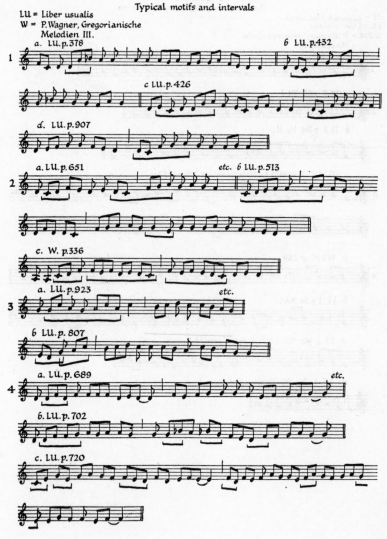

TABLE 7 (continued)

TABLE 8

Plain Psalmodies of Synagogue and Church

CI = F Consolo, Canticle d'Israel
JM = Idelsohn Jewish Music
BT = Baer, Baal Tefilla
LU = Liber usualis
W = Wagner, Gregorianische Melodien III

a. *Weekday morning Psalmody of the Synagogue* BT.I pp.14-24

b. *Gloria of Mass XIV* LU p.52

a. *Final clause of weekday evening Psalmody* BT.I p.49

b. *Compline of Saturday* LU.p.293

a. *Friday eve Psalmody of the Synagogue* (Invitatorium) Ps.95 JM. p.145 No 3

b. *Invitatorium of Easter Sunday* Ps.95 LU. p680

a. *Kaddish in Yotzer of Sabbath and Festival morning after* BT. II and CI

TABLE 8 (*continued*)

6. Praeconium paschale (*Blessing of fire on Holy Saturday*) W III. pp. 234-5

a. Psalmody of Tefilla on Festival mornings BT. III and CI

E - lo - he avra - ham ve - lo - he yitz - ha ve - lo - he ya - a - -
etc.
- - kob - -

b. Genealogy of Christ, after Matthew. (Lesson) W. III p. 254

Ab - ra - ham ge - nu - it Is - a - ac I - sa - ac autem -
ge - nu - it Ja - cob

a. Tefilla chant on Festivals JM p. 138, No. 2

b. Vado ad eum LU p. 722

c. Diriget mansuetos (Ps. - verse of Gradual "Dulcis et rectus") LU. p. 818. V.

CHAPTER SIX

Ornate Psalmody and Cognate Forms

UNLIKE plain psalmody, which is a form-type that obeys, in all its traditions, the two basic principles of dichotomy and the dominance of the word-accent, ornate psalmody consists of a multitude of different and variegated forms, which only under close examination can be reduced to a few archetypes. And when this *embarras de richesse* is subjected to the theorist's analysis, his categories show often an embarrassing similitude to a Procrustean bed, to whose dimensions everything is fitted, by hook or crook.

Under the term 'ornate psalmody' we understand all forms of sacred chant that (a) contain traces of genuine psalmody, however embellished and disguised, and (b) do not fall into the category of metric hymn melody. These boundaries are wide and comprise an enormous area. Nevertheless, it is a cultivated area, not a wild-growing jungle. The mechanical explanation: ornate psalmody equals Psalm Tone plus ornaments, will not suffice, unfortunately. Nor will the traditional term *concentus* do full justice. For the melismatic element has, wherever it enters, a tendency to change the underlying psalmodic basis; thus, the melismata are more than just an additional factor, they transform the entire melodic structure. Still, it is often possible to trace the patterns of certain typical and recurrent embellishments, which pervade many seemingly unrelated forms of ornate psalmody. These recurrent melodic clauses show a tendency to disengage themselves from the original and plain texture; they go, as it were, astray, and become 'wandering melismata' that appear in many different melodies; thus they constitute a characteristic component of ornate psalmody.

THE 'WANDERING MELISMA'

The chants of Synagogue and Church are replete with these little flowers of music which spring up here and there in many geographic and historic orbits. The concept of wandering melismata has two roots or prerequisites deeply embedded in ancient civilization: (a) the principle of crystallized melodic patterns (formulas), that later burgeoned into the system of modality: and (b) the associative function of such patterns, when they were applied to sacred texts. Let us not forget that almost all sacred music is word-bound. Whenever recurrent wandering melismata show an associative function, connected with certain texts, we are confronted with a phenomenon very much akin to the technique of the leitmotif. Thus it will be necessary, whenever the occasion demands it, to differentiate between leitmotif proper and its historical antecedent without associative function, the wandering and recurrent melisma.

The distinguishing element between leitmotif and wandering melisma is, of course, its extra-musical associative function. The first witness to testify for the leitmotif is R. Wagner. He writes:

A musical motif can exert a distinct, thought-stimulating impression only when the emotion as expressed in the motif itself is pronounced before our eyes . . . with reference to a distinct object as a distinct and well-conditioned sentiment . . . .[1]

Apologies are due for this kind of English, but the reader may be assured that the original German is in no way more elegant. Translated into simpler language, Wagner's statement could amount to a definition somewhat as the following:

A leitmotif is a melodic-rhythmic passage which by its recurrences or transformations serves extra-musical associations of visible, memorable things, emotions, or ideas.

This draws a line of demarcation between associative reminiscences on one hand, and the purely musical recurrences of tunes, as demanded by certain form conceptions, like the *ritornello*, the ternary form *ABA*, and the like.

The traditional music of the Synagogue is replete with wandering melismata, many of which became leitmotifs in the course of its historical development. It is easy to explain the causes of this phenomenon. Scripture, when read in public, must be chanted according to the Masoretic accents of punctuation and cantillation. The Prayers, on the other hand, are full of scriptural quotations, which had to be duly cantillated. In the course of time, some motifs of scriptural quotation, which recur daily or weekly in the prayers, were so firmly associated with both the biblical text and the prayers enveloping these passages, that they evoked in the minds of the listeners the ideas which the chanted verses expressed.

Later on, not even the biblical text was needed for the creation of these associations: the motifs of the cantillation alone would carry with them the spirit of the text. Some of these formulas were then taken out of their original context and used, whenever a memento of the respective biblical passage was deemed appropriate or desirable. This practice was consistently observed during the Middle Ages; and gradually all festivals, especially the High Holydays (which, due to their long ritual, used scriptural quotations abundantly) were surrounded by specific musical atmospheres of their own. When the motifs were thoroughly filled with associative meaning, they became leitmotifs; i.e., musical symbols of religious conceptions. This development was all but completed by the end of the fourteenth century in the European Synagogue. The Non-European Synagogue, while knowing leitmotifs, has never followed this principle so consistently nor so artistically. No clear association is as discernible as often as it is in the Ashkenazic ritual, and it may be said that the Synagogue-tradition outside Europe used the wandering melismata frequently without any associative function.

Of post-biblical texts, it was in the *Selihot* and *Qinot* (supplicatory and penitential) poems that wandering melismata with and without discernible association first appeared. Since the *Selihot* and their tunes form an integral part of the service of the High Holydays, it is but natural that their modes and typical ornaments are partly responsible for the musical atmosphere of these days. Musically they show a distinct resemblance to the *Tonus Peregrinus* of the Roman Church.

In accepting Wagner's criterion of the associative function of the leitmotif, the scholar is bound to search for antecedents for such conceptions. Every programmatic type of music presupposes a considerable level of sophistication. That this was not lacking as early as in the eighth century is demonstrated by the following rule of R. Yehudai Gaon (about 720).

If you chant a prayer for a *special* occasion, preceded and followed by the eulogies obligatory for such an occasion, take care that you chant the opening and concluding eulogy in the same mode, whereas the prayer in between ought to be sung in a mode different, but *not too* different, from that of the framing eulogies.[2]

This is not only the first realization of the ternary form *ABA*, but at the same time it indicates a consistent use of the leitmotif, inasmuch as it is associated with eulogies for special occasions. No wonder, then, that both the ecclesiastical seasons and ceremonies, as well as literary-scriptural allusions, provided numerous organic associations. In most cases the leitmotifs originated as melismata with a closing, punctuating, or purely ornamental function. Yet they detached themselves from their original context whenever the entire piece was over-saturated with ornaments.

One may propose the following law, applicable to all music stemming from folk-lore. Whenever a melismatic section of a piece expands beyond certain proportions, it tends toward emancipation from its original musical framework. It is at this stage that it frequently assumes the function of a leitmotif, to remind the listener of its original text and liturgical occasion.

Within the Synagogue a large crop of ornate psalmodic forms with leitmotif melismata emerged about the year 1000 in the Rhineland. Later, during the thirteenth and fourteenth centuries it burgeoned into the finest bloom of all Synagogue music known before the end of the nineteenth century. These tunes were early felt to form an organic unit, and were accordingly termed *Missinai* (from Mt. Sinai). They were held so sacred that nothing short of divine origin could do them full justice in the eyes of the medieval Jew.

Born out of the heroic self-sacrificing attitude of medieval Jewry, which often was tested to the bitter end of martyrdom, these tunes reflect, in every musical and textual phrase, the eschatological and mystical longings of a besieged and persecuted people.

While quite a number of these *Missinai* tunes show the influence of Burgundian art-music of the end of the fourteenth century, the borrowed elements are by no means easily discernible, for they were thoroughly assimilated to, and integrated into, the traditional style of European Synagogue music. This style was replete with wandering melismata, and constitutes the *locus classicus* of ornate psalmody in Judaism, developed to the highest level.

In Gregorian Chant, the forms in which over-extension of melismata constitutes the starting point for wandering melismata are the Gradual Response, the Tract and the *Jubilus*. There is no need to discuss the *Jubilus* here, since it merits special consideration as a 'wordless hymn', and will be discussed separately in this chapter.

Concerning the Gradual Response, P. Wagner has demonstrated in exemplary fashion that this form is full of recurrent, almost stereotyped, melismata; moreover, he has shown that 'the melodies of this type of Gradual are nothing but brilliant, melismatic paraphrases of a very ancient psalmodic formula'.[3] Connecting this fact with the phenomenon of punctuating melismata and typical formulas, as they occur in these forms, he poses the question:

Where does this procedure stem from, a procedure that is so antagonistic and strange to our Western ideas of musical composition? Is it an invention of Roman singers who put down and spread the songs of plainchant? Here only one answer is possible, the same that was given with reference to the melismata of the Tract: the technique of wandering melismata having a punctuating function is a legacy of synagogal psalmody.[4]

Applying this theory to plainchant, then, he tests his theory: 'If my theory is correct, then melismatically rendered Latin texts can easily be notated in the same manner as the corresponding Hebrew with its accents of cantillation.' And by this method he actually proved the correctness of his thesis.

In the following, the technique of wandering melismata will be demonstrated in some selected chants of the Roman Church and Synagogue. Wherever the associative function of the melismata is obvious, its leitmotif significance will be explained.

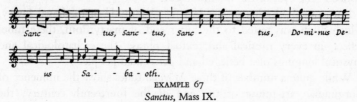

Sanc - - - tus, Sanc - tus, Sanc - - - tus, Do-mi-nus De-

us Sa - - ba - oth.

EXAMPLE 67
Sanctus, Mass IX.

It is obvious that this *Sanctus* and the *Agnus* from the same Mass are paraphrases of one melismatic nucleus; similarly the *Agnus* of Mass XVII is linked to its *Sanctus* (cf. p. 569). It is not evident, however, that an ideological association is intended here; it might well be an analogous elaboration upon a melismatic nucleus which is emphasized by the fact that each pair belongs to the same Mass.

A - le - nu le sha - be - ach la - a - don ha - kol.

EXAMPLE 68

A. *'Alenu* ('It is upon us').
B. *Korim* ('We bow down').
C. *Noflim al penehem* ('They prostrated themselves').

Clearly Example 67 (Church) and Example 68 (Synagogue) are almost literally identical tunes.[5] Whereas in the *Sanctus* the wandering melisma does not necessarily have the function of a leitmotif, in the Synagogue it obviously is charged with all the undercurrents of a Creed; indeed, the text of the *'Alenu* (A of Example 68) comes next to a Jewish *Credo*:

> It is our duty to praise the Lord of all things, to ascribe greatness to Him who formed the world in the beginning, since He hath not made us like the nations of other lands . . . nor assigned to us a lot as unto all their multitude . . . . For we bend the knee and offer worship and thanks before the supreme King of Kings, The Holy One, blessed be His Name.

The same doxological idea is borne out in B and C, *Korim* and *Noflim*:

> And they [the priests of the Temple] prostrated themselves [when the High-priest entered the Holy of Holies] and when the terrible, ineffable Name was pronounced by him.

This is a part of the ancient *'Aboda*, the description of the Day of Atonement in the Temple of Jerusalem. All of these prayers stem from about the same time, the third century A.D., and express in enthusiastic terms Israel's duty to humiliate himself before the Lord, while emphasizing His Oneness. Here the theological association which pervades these tunes is quite evident—the opening melisma is a characteristic leitmotif.

a. Bar - ku et A - do - nai

b. I - ste con - fes - sor Do - mi - ni co - len - tes.

EXAMPLE 69[6]

A. *Barku* ('Praise ye').
B. *Nishmat* ('The soul of every living soul').
C. *Baruch Adonai ham-vorach* ('Blessed be the Lord, to whom every praise is due').
D. *Mi chamoka* (Exod. 15).

The four texts of Example 69a constitute Doxologies or doxological prayers, and the common idea is quite transparent. Since these texts occur in the morning service of every Sabbath and Holyday, quite a number of traditional settings of these prayers are extant. Only the tunes of the High Holydays show mutual relationship, and here the element of seasonal motifs enters, that plays so important a part in Jewish liturgy. Actually, the characteristic leitmotif of these prayers pervades many prayers of the High Holydays; it is here that ideological and seasonal associations coincide. It is noteworthy that the *incipits* of these examples are identical with the Gregorian hymn 'Iste confessor', Example 69b; since the tune seems to be of rather recent origin, and is not common to the Sephardic or Yemenite tradition, we must conclude that the melody was borrowed from the Church during the High Middle Ages. Palestrina used the very same *incipit* as a Tenor of one of his most famous Masses, and it may be assumed that the tune was better known during the Middle Ages than it is at present.[7]

Tal prayer (for dew and rain)

EXAMPLE 70[8]

A. *Tal* (Prayer for dew).
B. *Kedusha* (Thrice-Holy).
C. *Hallel* (Ps. 113–18).

The melodies belong all to the category of *Missinai* tunes. This group of melodies, interconnected by many wandering melismata, will be discussed later on. The examples stem from the Passover service, for many Passover chants carry the characteristic motif of the prayer for dew and rain (*Tal*) that is recited twice every year. Even the *Hallel*, whose psalmody is much older, could not resist the intrusion of the *Tal* motif, whose function is strictly season-bound, and has no ideological connexion with the Thrice-Holy (*Kedusha*) or the psalms. The motif itself is probably of non-Jewish provenance, as I have shown elsewhere, and stems from Burgundian art-music, especially the music of Guillaume de Machault.[9] Yet so organically has it been interwoven with the much older elements of the *Kedusha* or the *Hallel* that it was thoroughly assimilated to traditional Jewish chant.

The question arises now as to where wandering melismata occur most frequently. Originally most of the wandering melismata of the Hebrew liturgy belonged to doxological responses. Significantly enough, most of the Gregorian leitmotifs or recurrent melismata occur also in the responsorial parts of the Gradual or in the *Jubilus*. There are, however, two important exceptions from that rule: the Tract and certain antiphons, which also show this structural ornament of recurrent melismata. We may infer that in all of these cases analogous forces were at work; at first autonomous principles of melopoeia, then the intention of creating literary or musical associations.

One might imagine that the melismata of one piece became too dominant, and subsequently split into numerous little melodies of their own; thus, they formed small melodic patterns, almost like modes, but, due to their original and lasting connexion with responsorial texts, never reached the stage where they would become completely autonomous and separate entities such as the modes. In other words, these melismata are—to use a drastic expression—half-baked modes. A pertinent observation has been made by R. Lach; he writes:

While in the formative stage of occidental Church music . . . ancient oriental Jewish *melopoeia* was vigorously flourishing, we realize that later there occurred a gradual freezing of these tunes within the Gregorian chant, a certain petrification of these melodic lines, that were once so fluid . . . .[10]

This writer is convinced that this was a well-planned development in order to regulate the exuberant music of the Near East; and only by performing that dry and thankless task of systematization was the genius of the Occident able to master and to absorb the great streams of Hebrew and Syrian melody. It was a creative accomplishment of the first magnitude to organize the irregular, to eliminate the superfluous, to select, and to assimilate the essential substance of the Near East's music. This task fell upon the authorities of the Roman and Greek Churches, and of these two bodies it was the Roman organization that preserved the ancient legacy much more faithfully than Byzantium.

One should not assume, however, that the leitmotif or the wandering melismata are the only devices of musical association. Frequently a mode or a structural type can just as well serve associative functions, sometimes even more impressively, as, for instance, the characteristic form-type of the paschal Alleluias. Nor should the fact be forgotten that most of these chants where typical intervals recur frequently lean towards leitmotif development. This holds equally true for those melodies that are linked to certain seasons, such as the Tract (Lent), Lamentations (Holy Week) and some Alleluias (Eastertide). They constitute merely special cases of the general principle of both Church and Synagogue, according to which certain texts, modes, and colours correspond to seasons, occasions, and ideas, all of which express their respective ethos. This conception was probably the basis of all subsequent 'synesthetic' experiments, especially those motivated by Romanticism.

In the last analysis, it is the belief in the ethos of modes and melodies that accounts for the systematical and well-integrated musical organization of all ancient liturgies, be they Jewish or Christian. Liturgical music is usually functional and reflective, seldom naive, and the student should be well aware of the distinction between spontaneous, enthusiastic music, generated by a momentary *religious* impulse, and the rigidly organized functional character of *liturgical* music. The transition from one stage to the other is usually a complex and involved process, beset with theological, musical, and technical problems.

The most important of these ornate forms, perhaps the most precious gem of Jewish and Christian musical beauties, is the Antiphon.

THE ANTIPHON

Hardly any other form-type in all sacred music is as 'problem-ridden' as the Antiphon. From the term 'Antiphon' itself to the details of its *melopoeia* and even to its performance nothing is unequivocal and uncontroversial. Some of its liturgical-philological problems were discussed in Part I; here we may confine ourselves to the musical aspects. Yet even they evince at every step the problematical nature of the form. Only a few of the essential questions connected with the Antiphon will be presented here, such as have a definite bearing upon the principal topic of this book.

Relation to Psalmody and Psalm-Tones

The musical and textual root of all Antiphons was undoubtedly a psalm quotation; thus far all authorities agree. When and why that originally close connexion was loosened has become a subject of speculation. Various conjectures have been ventured; the most convincing seems to be that the 'autonomy' of the chant was increasingly emphasized against, and finally prevailed over, the strict and rigidly psalmodic type of the scriptural chant. F. Gennrich, who suggests this development, also links this emancipation with the emergence of the 'autonomous' musical forms of the Sequence.[11]

This hypothesis is corroborated by two historical phenomena, the one in the sphere of the Church, the other in that of the Synagogue. The oldest Antiphons without scriptural quotation are the so-called Marianic Antiphons, which originated about 1050; that is exactly the time when the 'autonomous' musical forms, such as the Sequence, emerged in full bloom. Even these Antiphons did contain psalm verses originally, but abandoned them when the liturgy placed them at the end of the daily hours.[12] P. Wagner states with satisfaction that this 'chant without any psalmody has only in a few cases been incorporated in the organism of the divine worship'.[13]

While in Synagogue ritual the Antiphon plays a much smaller part than in the Church, a similar trend toward 'free composition', not shackled by textual and musical quotations from Scripture, becomes evident between the ninth and thirteenth centuries. There the main reason was the introduction of metrical poetry into the liturgy; as long as these *piyyutim* quoted, or alluded to, verses that normally would be rendered psalmodically, there was no danger of losing the ideological nucleus of the form; but when, as happened in Spain and later in France and Germany, poems of free religious spirit, great philosophical soliloquies of the religious thinkers, invaded the prayer-books of the time, the scriptural element became more and more incidental. These noble poems of the highest literary and religious quality were set to entirely new tunes, and here, as in the Church, the psalmodic style was abandoned. Yet, as in the Church, only very few of these poems have remained in the official liturgy; their untraditional nature both in text and music, and also their over-abstract language may have been the cause of their desuetude. Of the many thousands of *piyyutim* created during the Middle Ages, no more than threescore are still used in the prayer-books.

The Antiphon in Office and Mass

The interesting differentiation between the Antiphons of the Office and those of the Mass sheds a good deal of light upon the liturgical significance of the Antiphon in general. Here not only historic, but also musical evidence tends to show that in the Office, where the chant was not necessarily performed by professional singers, the framework into which the psalm verses were inserted was intentionally confined to a few relatively simple melodies. In the Office the verses of the antiphonally rendered psalm were always and without exception provided with the same simple formula. 'Many monks or clerics who would have been hard put to intone a new, unfamiliar antiphon melody were content to chant an old, familiar tune. . . . Hence, the number of tunes for Office Antiphons is very small in proportion to the number of texts to which they are sung.'[14]

If one keeps in mind the fact that the Mass Antiphons were sung by the *schola cantorum*, i.e. by professional singers, the Office Antiphons by secular priests or monks without special musical training, the analogy with Jewish practices appears obvious: on weekdays a lay cantor officiated in the Synagogue throughout the Middle Ages, on Sabbath and Holydays a professional singer with a semblance of a professional choir. Only in the nocturnal Office do soloists appear in the Church, otherwise the Offices are left to simple choral singing. This predominance of liturgical over musical considerations, typical of the Office, preserved the singing of *whole* psalms for many centuries. Yet Gregory the Great was so much of a traditionalist that, notwithstanding his usual severity, he preferred curtailing the singing of the whole Psalm in the Mass Gradual to abandoning it altogether, if by so doing, he could preserve the rich Jewish-Oriental psalmody of the soloist even in *one* verse.[15]

This remarkable distinction between the role of the Antiphon in Office and Mass hints also at the different *liturgical* functions of these chants. Obviously, some of the longer melismatic Antiphons of the Mass are to divert the audience's attention from some lengthy ceremonies around the altar. On the other hand, the Graduals have an intrinsic liturgical function, and this is true, to a slightly lesser degree, of most of the Office Antiphons, which are actually chanted prayers.[16]

In Judaism a similar situation prevails; wherever a special ceremony takes place, as on such occasions as Tabernacles, the solemn procession through the Synagogue, or the Preamble to the Priestly Blessing on the High Holydays, the accompanying chants are of a diversionary nature, and, therefore, do not belong to a very ancient stratum. Those richly embellished pieces that signify the highlights of the liturgy are well authenticated, and belong, with one exception (the eve of *Yom Kippur*) to the *Mussaph* part of the liturgy, which we above had compared with High Mass.

The musical characteristics of the Office Antiphon are, according to P. Wagner, syllabic composition, small range, stepwise movement, few jumps, and brevity; all prerequisites for a performance that was to be

easily attainable to the average cleric and even many laymen.[17] Moreover, the framework of the Antiphon preceding the psalm adjusted itself
musically to the Psalm Tone, as well as the latter to the following part of
the Antiphon. In so doing, a natural homogeneity was accomplished
which contributed greatly to the dignity of the Office. It may suffice
here to state that similar criteria regulate the weekday service, and the
Shaharit chants of Sabbaths and Festivals in the Synagogue.

The Form Structure of the Antiphon

In its original conception the form of the Antiphon was undoubtedly
a musical refrain that concluded the chant of every or almost every
psalm verse. To a certain extent this principle holds true even today for
some of the Office Antiphons. In the majority of cases, however, the
Antiphon is only intoned at the beginning and only a few psalm verses
are chanted between the first and second intonation of the antiphonal
framework. At the end, the whole Antiphon with closing doxology is
chanted.[18] The archaic structure originates, of course, in the refrain
psalms of the Old Testament.

The further development of the Antiphon brought with it a simpler
form for the Office, a more complex one for the Mass; yet each of them
preserves at least a trace of the refrain. Sometimes the chant of the refrain and that of the Psalm Tone are beautifully interwoven, so that one
may speak of a 'progressive repetition' whereby the leading textual or
musical idea is repeated on a higher level. We may cite here a lovely
example of such a type of textual repetition:

He shall call on me, and I will harken unto him:	(Antiphon)
Whoso dwelleth under the defence of the Most High:	(Ps. 91:1)
Shall abide under the shadow of the Almighty.	
He shall call on me, and I will harken unto him:	
I will deliver him and will bring him to honour:	
With length of days will I satisfy him.	(End of Antiphon Ps. 91, 15.)

This type suggests, of course, the ternary form *ABA*.

Similar conceptions can be found in the early prayers of the Synagogue and it might be reasonable to assume that both the textual and
musical principle of 'progressive repetition' is a legacy of the Synagogue.
This will later on be analysed from the musical point of view.

The last step in this development was the entire omission of the nuclear psalm verse, as we encounter it in the antiphons of the Communion, of the Processions, and those of the Virgin, the so-called Marianic Antiphons. None of them quotes a Psalm Tone any more, be it in plain or in ornate manner. One may properly call these forms paraphrases of embellished psalmody, since their connexion with the traditional chant of the psalms is only loose. All of these free forms originated well after the first millennium and fall, therefore, outside the scope of this book.

Had the Antiphonal Melos an Iranian Origin?

Considering the strong Old Testament element of most Antiphons, and the evidence of antiphonal performance in Jewish sources (Bible, Philo, Josephus), this form has been generally considered an indisputable Jewish legacy. This unanimity was broken when certain German scholars discovered the necessity of the world's salvation through true Aryan culture. Thus, even before certain German professors had the welcome excuse that 'they were all the time under duress', two musicologists of repute, H. Besseler and O. Ursprung, came to the conclusion that, properly investigated, the Antiphon is originally an Aryan form. (This before 1933!) Besseler writes:

> In the lines of these new compositions (fourth century) the new concept of tonal space comes to full expression . . . . Many factors seem to speak against a leading role of Syrianism. Mani and probably also Bardesanes were Iranians, and Ephraem came from strongly Persian infiltrated Eastern Mesopotamia, which even during his lifetime fell to the empire of the Sassanides, and was finally active in Byzantian Edessa at a 'School of the Persians'. Thus, one gains the impression that the foundations of Syrian choral style and, consequently, the fundaments of Gregorian chant were created less by the Semitic than by the Hellenistic-Iranian genius.[19]

Let us briefly consider Besseler's arguments. Although the meaning of 'new concept of tonal space' (*das neue Tonraumverhältnis*) is more than problematical in any language, we shall not take issue with this remark. That the Syrians and their musical culture were at the vanguard of musical development is, as Besseler realized, doubtful. In literature, at any rate, they held that initiative, as we know for certain today. (See Part I, Chapter VII.) He then quotes some of the leading spirits of the epoch, viz. Mani, Bardesanes, and Ephraem. Although not one tune or musical form is even ascribed to any of them, they are, for Besseler, convincing evidence. Actually more interesting is the fact that in the authentic literature of Manichaeism, of which few documents have come down to us, the hymns show traces of that very same 'progressive parallelism' that is so characteristic of Hebrew and Syriac poetry.[20] By the way, Mani came from Babylon, and his 'Iranian extraction' is highly controversial. Now, as to Bardesanes, one knows next to nothing about his origin; he wrote in Syriac, in some kind of metre. (See Part I, Chapter VII.) Whether or not Ephraem came from Jewish parentage, as some legends have it, is irrelevant; much more important is it that he wrote in Syriac exclusively and was instrumental in introducing the isosyllabic principle in Near Eastern and Byzantine hymn literature.[21]

Returning from genealogical-racial examinations to music, the chant of the Persian and Nestorian Church is notoriously poor. E. Bishop, in his fine study on the liturgical homilies of Narsai, writes:

He [Narsai] practically says nothing about either singers or the singing, which . . . was as yet more a popular than an artistic element of Christian worship . . . . It is only necessary to read the early chapters of the first formal Western treatise on liturgy, the *De officiis ecclesiasticis* of St Isidore, to see how great is the contrast. The note of church-song is continually struck, and singing in one form or another is dwelt on by him again and again. It is hard to believe that, if singing had been any prominent feature in the celebration of the East Syrian Mass of Narsai's day, that rhetorical writer would have passed over it in silence. It seems much more probable that both he and Isidore spoke naturally, and that each renders, the one by his reticence, the other by his abundance, the actual state of things around him.[22]

All documents of Persian Christianity show the same reticence about, not to say disinclination for, music; it is not entirely unknown that the Iranians, in general, were a non-musical people, and often had to import their musicians from the neighbouring peoples, chiefly Arab and Syrian. What remains of Besseler's arguments? After his 'historic' evidence has collapsed, his entire reasoning breaks down. It cannot be otherwise: to build a mountain of conjecture upon a grain of sand is easy, and occasionally profitable, especially at the time when the Aryan millennium chose the very same grains of sand as its building material.

Antiphonal Forms in the Synagogue

We have seen that form and rendering of the Antiphon run through various phases from (1) antiphonal rendering of a whole psalm, (2) ornate refrain framework with inserted plain psalmody, (3) ornate framework with an inserted paraphrase of a Psalm Tone, and (4) ornate framework without any psalm verse, or only with an alleluiatic close.

Only the Roman Church has developed all these structures, while the Eastern Churches did not go beyond the second phase.

Remarkably enough, one may discern a constant state of tension between forces of formal construction on one hand, and between the forces of spontaneous melodic improvisation, on the other. In the pattern of stylized folk-lore (to which category belong both the Gregorian and the Synagogue chant) it seems that either of those forces may gain only at the expense of the other. This precarious balance of power accounts for many facts, hitherto not fully explained. Two examples may illustrate this:

(a) When the quotation of the simple Psalm Tone was replaced by an elaborate and melismatic paraphrase, the refrain form had to be abandoned, and not even a strict ternary form could be maintained.

(b) Where the formal forces were strong enough to prevent the complete abandonment of the psalm verse, or an Alleluia was inserted in its stead, the compromise forced the curtailment of the *Jubilus*. Such examples occur frequently in the alleluiatic Antiphons of Eastertide.

In the Synagogue, a somewhat analogous state prevails. Of the four phases mentioned above, the Synagogue no longer uses the first one. It has been completely replaced by responsorial rendering, since the medieval Synagogue had only a solo singer and the lay congregation at its disposal. The second and third phases of the antiphonal form occur in the European Synagogue, although they do not often appear. The fourth phase is entirely unknown. Here, too, formal-constructive and melodic-expansive forces are in constant tension.

It might be interesting to quote a few texts that constitute synagogal Antiphons; though it should always be understood that antiphonal performance by two choirs never, in fact, takes place.

(1) *Agil v'esmach* (Morning service of *Simhat-Torah*).

Framework: I shall exult and rejoice on *Simhat-Torah*.

The Saviour will surely come on *Simhat-Torah*.

Quotation: The Torah is a Tree of life (Prov. 3 : 18) replete with
(Cantillated) life; for with thee is the fountain of life (Ps. 36 : 10).

Framework: Abraham rejoiced on *Simhat-Torah*.

The Saviour will surely come on *Simhat-Torah*.

(2) Morning service of weekdays; also in *Mussaph* service of New Year.

Framework: Ps. 22 : 29

Quotation: Obad. 1:21.
(Cantillated)
Conclusion: Zech. 14:9.

Here the progressive repetition is so impressive that I cannot resist the temptation to give it below *in extenso*:

Framework: For the Kingdom is the Lord's; and He is ruler over the Nations.

Quotation: And saviours shall come up on Mount Zion to
(Cantillated) judge the mount of Esau; and the Kingdom shall be the Lord's.

Conclusion: And the Lord shall be King over all the earth; on that day shall the Lord be One, and His Name be One.

The idea of the coming kingdom of God is so beautifully climaxed that the inserted cantillation from Obadiah, both literally and musically, forms a poignant contrast to the surrounding framework.

Antiphon Melodies in Synagogue and Church

While similarities between Gregorian and Jewish Chant are plentiful, their formal structure and concept of performance usually differ essentially. Thus, in the category of Antiphons, I have been unable to discover even one example where both institutions have set to music the same words in the same manner. This is not very astounding, as the form of the Antiphon has been neglected in the Synagogue for more than 900 years. Yet, notwithstanding the divergent form-conceptions of the illustrations, the tunes and the liturgical occasions for which they stand still show clear traces of interrelation.

EXAMPLE 71

Example 71a, 'Posuerunt super caput',[23] the last Antiphon of Lauds on Good Friday, is compared with Example 71b,[24] the old Ashkenazic version of Gen. 2:1–3, which on Friday evening is not cantillated according to the scriptural accents, but chanted in one of the most typical prayer modes of Judaism, the so-called *Magen Aboth* (Shield of the Fathers). Idelsohn has already demonstrated that this mode is identical with the old Arabian *Bayati* mode; here it may be added that this melodic type is well known to every student of plainchant.[25] Parallel passages to the 'Posuerunt' are the 'Canite Tuba',[26] 'Colligite primum',[27] 'Jacob autem genuit'[28] and others. Obviously we face here the phenomenon that a wandering melisma has begun to mould its own melodic patterns, almost creating a subdivision within the first (Dorian) mode. These various melodic formulas which constitute the vast treasury of Antiphons (more than 2000), have been investigated by Gevaert and others, who reduced the number of typical patterns to forty-seven, or, at most, fifty.[29]

EXAMPLE 72

Examples 72a and 72b juxtapose the famous Antiphon of Palm Sunday 'Pueri Hebraeorum',[30] chanted in the morning before Mass, and the analogous *Shaharit-Kaddish* of the Three Festivals, as sung by the Babylonian Jews.[31] Here the liturgical function of the two pieces is very similar, especially on Tabernacles; it is the last chanted piece before the beginning of the procession of the palm-leaves (Heb. *lulab*).[32]

EXAMPLE 73

Example 73a, an Introit of Ash Wednesday[33] is a 'Misereris' with a psalm quotation from Ps. 57:2. It is here compared with a *Seliha* (Supplication) of the Yemenite Jews.[34] Both from the musical and the liturgical point of view, the two examples stem from a common source, namely the cantillation of Job and Lamentations. The musical similarity with the Gregorian and Jewish Lamentations and Job is obvious (see Table VI, p. 495); and liturgically, there could not be a more fitting occasion than the penitential atmosphere of Ash Wednesday.

THE ORNATE RESPONSORIAL FORMS

In the Synagogue, the origin of the responsorial form goes back to the doxologies and the Hallelujah psalms (see Part I, Chapter IX). Basically, it was a solo performance of the cantor, who occasionally was joined by the congregation. It was not before the eighth or ninth century that in the Talmudic academies choristers assembled, and even this happened only on sporadic occasions. The Roman Church followed originally this practice, as we learn from Isidore of Seville; in his time, however, the choir had already taken over and alternated with the soloist.[35] Even the *Ordo Romanus* provides for a soloist, and the choir only repeated the intonation; the scriptural verse was chanted by the soloist, and then the choir repeated part or all of the beginning.[36] This rule applied especially to the oldest type of response, the Gradual. Yet Wagner assumes an original solo performance for *all* of the great responses.[37] He emphasizes the fact that all responsorial chant was originally connected with the scriptural lesson; and 'as in the Mass the responsorial psalm was the oldest chant, so it is certainly not by chance that this form of psalmody has its place of honour in that part of the Office which was the oldest in the history of liturgy, namely in the nocturnes'.[38]

If we accept Wagner's ideas as a working hypothesis, we should be able to test it: then we should find traces of textual connexion with the lesson in both synagogal and ecclesiastical responses as well as of ternary conception in these forms, due to the alternating practice. Finally, if the solo responses are the oldest musical types which the Church inherited from the Synagogue, the most likely place in which to search for these common roots is the Offices and Masses just before and during Easter week.

Remembering the transposition of lessons from the High Holydays to the Easter season, as outlined in Part I, Chapters III and IV, the first task must be to investigate the textual connexion of responses with the lesson. Remarkably enough, most responses draw their framework not from the Psalter, as do the Antiphons, but from the narrative or prophetic portions of the Old and New Testaments. This reminds us of the Haftara lesson, which consists precisely of portions of the narrative and prophetic books of the Old Testament.

These examples of the Easter liturgy will prove Wagner's hypothesis correct.

(1) *Palm-Sunday*

Lesson. Matt. 21 (Entrance of Jesus into Jerusalem).
Response: Ingrediente Domino in sanctam civitatem (When the Lord entered the Holy City).

(2) *Good Friday*

Lesson of the Passion.
Lamentations: Jerusalem, Jerusalem, convertere ad Dominum Deum tuum (Jerusalem, return ye to thy Lord God!).
Response: Vinea mea electa (Paraphrase of Isa. 5:2, with inserted quotation from that chapter).

(3) *Holy Saturday*

Prophetia IX, Exod. 12; Proph. IV, Exod. 14–15; Proph. VII, Ezek. 37; Proph. VIII, Isa. 4; Proph. XI, Deut. 31–32.
Tract: Exod. 15 (Miriam's Song of the Red Sea).
Tract: Isa. 5:1–4.
Tract: Deut. 32:1–4.[39]

Thus, the connexion of lesson and response is clearly established.

In the Synagogue we find as the Haftara of Passover, Ezek. 37 (Proph. VII) the Torah lesson during the week, Exod. 12–15 (Proph. IX and IV). Finally, another most important common element has to be mentioned: Ps. 116, 117 and 118, the last three of the Haftara, are distributed over the liturgy of the Church from Holy Saturday to the Friday of Easter week.

As for traces in the Synagogue of ternary forms connected with the lesson, the eulogies before and after the Haftara obviously provide exactly the framework for such a ternary form-type. What is more, it will be seen that a characteristic motif of the eulogies of the Haftara

corresponds with a typical wandering melisma of the Easter responses
and Tracts:

EXAMPLE 74[40]

Let us examine which words carry this characteristic melisma. In the
Hebrew, it is 'Zion, the house of Life', and at other occasions, the word
'Adonai (Our Lord). In the quotations from the Gregorian chant, the
words connected with this melisma are: (Example 74b) 'Sion'; (Example
74c) 'Israel'; (Example 74d) 'Domino'; (Example 74e) 'Cantemus
Domino'; (Example 74f) 'Domino'. Can this astounding identity be
mere coincidence? It is not probable since the melismatic motif occurs
also in the chant of Oriental Jewry. This factor, together with the literary
associations, the connexions with the lesson, and the predominance in
Eastertide tends to show that this motif is actually one of the very
oldest of Christian and Jewish solo chants, occurring solely in Responses
and Tracts.

Even in cases where the motif carries no directly theological words, it is always connected with words of leitmotif character in the respective tracts. In Example 75a[41] it carries the words 'malo', 'peccatoris', 'peccatori', 'peccatoris' 'eorum' (peccatorum); in Example 75b,[42] only 'oculi'; in this case, it is neither a final nor a punctuating melisma.

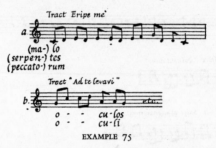

EXAMPLE 75

Another instance to support our theory is the fact that the verses of Ps. 118, distributed over Easter week, have certain recurrent half and full closes—and these closes correspond here with the Hebrew ecphonetic accents of the respective verses. They are:

EXAMPLE 76

Under these circumstances, we are justified in stating the following principle: the starting point of all responses and Tracts was the set of preceding and closing eulogies of the Haftara. They (together with the chant of the Haftara lesson) form a loose ternary structure, inasmuch as these eulogies have a common set of melodic motifs. If this is true, a good deal of the *Responsoriale*, or at least its oldest strata, reflects the musical atmosphere of the Haftara.[43] Indeed, the Haftara mode corresponds roughly with a mixture of Tones II and VIII, while the framing eulogies are chanted in a pure VIII (Hypomixolydian) mode. The favourite modes of the responses are, after P. Wagner, the modes I, VII, and VIII, and all Tracts belong either to mode II or mode VIII.

The Strata of the Responsorial Chant

There are various criteria by which the strata might be differentiated from each other. The first, liturgical-historical, principle teaches us to expect some of the oldest elements in Holy Week and Eastertide. This rule has, however, to be balanced by the fact that most of these responses are fully ornate. Another criterion of age is a relatively small range, a third one the simplicity of the psalmodic insertion. All of these demands are satisfied only by the so-called *Responsoria brevia*, whereas the large and ornate responses of Matins are termed *Responsoria prolixa*.

That part of plain psalmody into which the small responses fall has already been discussed: the large responses therefore remain our sole subject of examination. Here we shall fail to find even one *plain* psalm quotation; the question arises whether or not the melody of the inserted verse (the quotation), however embellished, reflects a simpler, older type. If this is so, the principle of psalmodic variation which plays so dominant a role in synagogal chant is clearly evident in Christian plainchant.

We are not confined this time to Gregorian chant, but shall also consider Armenian, Byzantine, and Syrian pieces, for it seems that there the principle of variation is more easily discernible than in Roman or Ambrosian Chant.

EXAMPLE 77

The Armenian variation is exhibited in Example 77. Example 77a represents the plain, Example 77b the heavily embellished, psalmody. The first example is the traditional tune, the second its ornate version from the Armenian *Sharakan*. The first was recorded by K. Kevorkian in Armenia, 1901, and represents doubtless the ancient tune; its words and melody are attributed to Moses of Chorene (seventh to eighth century).[44] The ornate form was, if not composed, then edited by Baba Hampartzum, the reformer of Armenian notation, during the eighteenth century.[45]

It so happens that the Armenian chant has its counterpart in Jewish tradition, as demonstrated in Example 77c. This tune is known to us from two sources, Isacco Abulafia of Southern Italy (about 1630) whose manuscript is in the possession of the Hebrew Union College Library; and it is also part of the Ashkenazic tradition and appears in Baer's standard work on Ashkenazic chant.

EXAMPLE 78

Examples 78a and 78b show the technique of variation and paraphrase in Byzantine chant; here it is not so much embellishment as psalmodic transformation that arrests our interest. The principle of progressive repetition is very much in evidence as may be seen in the passages B1, B2, C1, C2 and E. Transformation contains, in this case at least, also transposition; for the melisma D of Example 78b is obviously identical with A of Example 78a; in one case it is the beginning, in the other the second motif of the tune. In general, ornamentation plays a much smaller part here than in Armenian, Syrian, and Gregorian examples. The reason for this lies in the fact that both examples are drawn from the same *Kanon* of St John Monachos.[46] The conception of repetition and variation comes very much to the fore in these examples, and E. Wellesz's words about this matter are still valid:

> The European moulds a work of art in the shortest, most characteristic, most impressive cast, whereas the Oriental man repeats the representation or provides it with little variants, so that the perception becomes a sort of meditation.

This principle may have made inroads in poetry and music of Byzantine liturgy under the influence of the new ideas, unfolding under the new realm of Islam.[47]

This illustration antedates by at least three centuries the period of the 'embellishers', the *Maistores*.

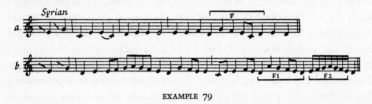

EXAMPLE 79

Examples 79a and 79b show a Syrian *Sogitha* and its ornate counterpart. The variation is here limited to moderate melodic ornamentation. Progressive repetition occurs only in the passages F1 and F2, which build up to a fine climax.[48]

EXAMPLE 80

The Synagogue is represented by a genuine *responsorium*; Example 80a quotes the verse refrain 'The Lord is King; the Lord hath reigned; the Lord will reign for ever and ever';[49] and Example 80b gives the solo paraphrase of the motto.[50] The original two measure motifs are expanded to four measure melismata. Progressive repetition is noticeable in the clauses G1, G2, G3 and H. Both textually and musically the chant reminds me somewhat of the famous *tricolon*, 'Christus vincit, Christus

523

regnat, Christus imperat', of Lauds. In the numerous versions of that piece, the 'Christus vincit' and 'Christus regnat' have the same melody, just as in the synagogal counterpart. They are also concluded by that characteristic motif of the falling fourth, as in the Synagogue. Most akin to the Jewish chant is the Worcester version, as presented in the valuable study by M. Bukofzer.[51] It is not easy, however, to form a historical conclusion in this case, since the Hebrew acclamation is not documented before the eighth century.[52] The Latin acclamation seems to originate in the same century, or a little later; at any rate, neither the historic nor the musical evidence justifies any definite conclusion. It is interesting that in both the papal Lauds (or the Litanies of the Saints) and in the Hebrew *piyyut*, the insertion serves as a response to be sung by the choir or the congregation.

EXAMPLE 81

The Gregorian chant shows the most excessive technique of embellishment and variation. P. Wagner first discovered and investigated the fact that in some cases ornate psalmody is nothing but a brilliant, melismatic paraphrase of a very ancient Psalm Tone. We quote in Examples 81a and 81b one of his comparative illustrations.[53] The very same psalm formula occurs in the tradition of the Yemenite Jews and is quoted in Example 81c.[54] The melismatic Psalm Tone 'Dextera Domini fecit virtutem' shows traces of progressive repetition, but even more the simple reiteration of the same clause or even interval, (I, K) which might be considered an indication of its antiquity.

Two remarks might summarize and interpret our findings. The

technique of variation, common to the chant of Church and Synagogue, is developed in three ways, which are closely akin to each other. The oldest practice seems to be the simple repetition of a motif or an interval, as is frequently the case with archaic Gregorian and, even more, Ambrosian melismatic chants. Another, on a higher artistic level, is the principle of *progressive* repetition, which easily develops into melodic sequences; this type is frequent in the chants, tropes, proses and sequences of the tenth to twelfth centuries; the most recent technique seems to be that of 'diminutive' embellishments and expansion of the basic tune; it is hardly older than the thirteenth or fourteenth century, and in Gregorian, Byzantine, Armenian, and Jewish chant this technique dominated the High Middle Ages. The principle of diminution was a powerful tool in the development of instrumental music, as the sources of the fourteenth and fifteenth centuries with their preambles and intermedia demonstrate. The vocal style of these two centuries depended for its melodic development almost exclusively on the technique of diminution, and the *Ars Nova* practically legalized this state of affairs.[55]

Variation has many aspects and knows thousands of various nuances and fashions. Of our five basic examples none is like the other; and it can correctly be said that each variation is a type most characteristic of its parental musical culture. Hence it should be possible to distinguish from the historical as well as from the ethnological point of view certain types of plainchant. While the Byzantine and the Armenian Churches and liturgies are closely akin, nobody can say that their way of varying a chant shows any similarity at all. In other words; it is rarely the theological affinity, *but always and exclusively historical or ethnological kinship that determines musical proximity*. In contradistinction to liturgical forms, determined chiefly by theological and poetic considerations, the music of the Eastern and also of the Western orbit was basically a stylized folklore, connected with all of its fibres to the mother country, its earth, its language, its mores. Liturgy and its forms often are international and never naïve; liturgical music is basically national and often naïve, while at the same time indifferent to intellectual concepts.

The Gradual Response and its Cognate Forms in Synagogue and Church

All Christian sources testify to the Apostolic age of the songs between and before the scriptural lesson. Those chants were termed by the

Latin Churches *Gradualia*, and especially Gradual Responses, when they constitute that part of the liturgy that is inseparably connected with the Mass. The origin of the term Gradual has been examined in Part I, Chapter VI, together with its liturgical significance. Here the musical evidence will be scrutinized.

We again face the problem that the first Jewish sources testifying to the singing of chants before and after the scriptural lessons do not ante-date the seventh century (Tractate *Soferim*). Thus we had to suspend final judgement concerning the origin of this custom, leaving the question open as to whether Synagogue or Church had initiated it.

Now we should be in the position to re-examine the question. Of the twelve psalm-verses that surrounded the lessons in the Synagogue of the ninth century, only Ps. 24 and Ps. 29 are mentioned as part of the ritual in older Talmudic liturature (between the second and the sixth century).[56] The other passages, mentioned first in *Soferim*, XIV,[57] are:

Ps. 24	Ps. 148:13–14
Ps. 99:5 and 9	Ps. 132:9–11
Ps. 34:4	Ps. 68:5
Ps. 19:8 and 9	Ps. 89:15
Ps. 29:1	Ps. 84:5
Ps. 18:31	Ps. 144:15

In what way and on what occasion do these psalms or psalm-verses occur in the Roman liturgy? The answer to this question might give us a cue as to the liturgical origin of the Gradual Response.

Ps. 24 is sung as a whole on Holy Saturday in the second nocturne before the lesson,[58] also on Tuesday at Prime,[59] and finally at the funeral of children.[60]

Ps. 99:5, 9 constitutes the Antiphon of Lauds on Friday.[61]

Ps. 34:4 is the Gradual of the twelfth Sunday after Pentecost. Also response on the Feast of the Name of Jesus.[62]

Ps. 19:9 is the offertory after the lesson on the third Sunday of Quadragesima, also at Prime on Tuesday, together with Ps. 24.[63]

Ps. 29:1 is the offertory of the *Missa Votiva* for the Propagation of Faith, between two lessons.[64]

Ps. 18:31 does not play a significant part in the Roman liturgy.

Ps. 148:13, 14, the Gradual of the Mass of the Angels, also appears in the Feast of the Name of Jesus, and at the funeral of children.[65]

Ps. 132:9, 10, 11 is the Introit and Gradual of the Mass of Pope and Confessor and also occurs at the Vespers of that feast.[66]

Ps. 68:5 is the Gradual of the third Sunday of Quadragesima, and the Communion of Ascension.[67]

Ps. 89 is sung as a whole in the third nocturn of Christmas.[68]

Ps. 144:15 occurs in the regular Vespers of Saturday.[69]

The result of this perfunctory search demonstrates that of the twelve psalm-verses connected with the lesson in the Synagogue, no less than eight appear in the very same position in the Roman liturgy. In spite of the fact that Ps. 24 is chanted on Holy Saturday, which must be considered the Jewish core of the Christian liturgy, and seems to indicate Jewish influence, the evidence is still not convincing either way. The next two steps must ascertain, whether (a) there exist common melodic elements between those eight psalm-verses, and (b) whether these same elements form a fairly ancient stratum of Jewish musical tradition. Such an examination ought to be conducted with the utmost caution, since the problem is difficult, for dearth of authentic sources, and its solution might easily prove to be of great consequence for the fundamental understanding of the interdependence between Church and Synagogue.

The result of the first investigation is clearly negative: there is no discernible common ground between the various Graduals. Occasional wandering melismata occur, common to two or three, but these must never be construed as evidence of common origin or even of like age.

As for the second examination—comparison with Jewish traditional chants—only two or three cases show genuine resemblance. They are:

(a) The Gradual of the third Sunday in Quadragesima, 'Exsurge Domine', compared with a *Tefilla* mode.[70]

EXAMPLE 82

527

(b) The offertory on the same Sunday, compared with a Babylonian prophetic lesson.[71]

EXAMPLE 83

(c) The Gradual of the twelfth Sunday after Pentecost, compared with a Synagogue chant of the Mediterranean tradition.[72]

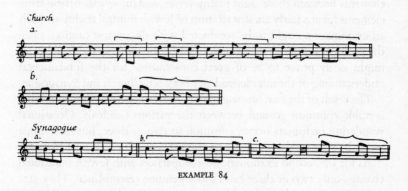

EXAMPLE 84

Here the analysis can be very brief. All of the characteristic motifs of the Gregorian examples are familiar to us by now: they are punctuating melismata and have their typical counterparts in Hebrew tradition. This, of course, proves nothing; and at this point we must close our examination, since nowhere did we reach any conclusive evidence, be it liturgical or musical. The paradox of the silence of the Jewish sources concerning just those parts of its service which already Apostolic Christianity claimed as its synagogal legacy remains an enigma. It has not been solved and constitutes a serious problem for future generations of scholars.[73]

There is, however, definite evidence of workings of progressive repetition and variation. Examples 82a and 82d display it, and even more obvious is their appearance in Examples 84a and 84b, where the descending fourth plays so significant a part in the sequence-like chain of motifs. In this respect, and in this alone, can we see the affinity with the chant of the Synagogue, as far as the Gradual Response is concerned.

Nowhere in Gregorian Chant do recurrent melismata play as great a part as in the Graduals. Often such a Gradual would, if exactly analysed, prove to be a mere series of such melismatic motifs, skilfully connected with each other. P. Wagner has undertaken the difficult task of a systematic analysis of these pieces. He ponders, at the end of his investigation, whether this technique of combining motifs can really create a work of art. Here is his answer:

If many precious stones are put together in a piece of jewellery, the ensemble will give the impression of an artistic accomplishment only if the stones are connected in a precious setting and an artistic arrangement. Are the melismata of the Graduals arranged in such a fashion? This question can emphatically be affirmed . . . .[74]

The same attitude is taken by Wellesz in the following words:

The process of musical composition consisted in fitting together and slightly varying phrases, cadences, and formulae which were already in existence . . . . Evidently we have to deal with a principle of musical composition which, starting from Asia, penetrated the whole Mediterranean civilization and spread out from there towards the north . . . .[75]

This technique of composition confronts the musicologist with another problem, already faced by Wagner:[76] the synagogal origin of this technique. We quoted his answer on p. 504.

In spite of this scholar's statements, our detailed investigation has not shown any conclusive results that might indicate a direct transition of Gradual melodies from the synagogal into the ecclesiastical realm. We shall reach more positive conclusions in those forms that were, as in the Synagogue of old, originally rendered in solo fashion, namely the Tract and the Alleluia.

Forms Originally Performed by Soloists
THE TRACT

This form is in many respects the most remarkable one in all Gregorian Chant. It is richly melismatic, yet comprises only a relatively small number of recurrent melismata, it is performed by a soloist, yet it stands in place of an Alleluia; it is limited to only two modes, II and VIII, whereas all other songs of the Church make use of all eight modes. After a thorough investigation, P. Wagner reached the conclusion that the Tract is a direct legacy from the ancient Synagogue:

> The punctuating melismata, typical of the Tract, are not of Latin origin . . . the preservation of numerous archaic elements causes us to say: the real source of the Tract can be nothing else but Jewish synagogal solo psalmody.[77]

Before we take any definite position, we shall examine briefly the historical and musical evidence. The Tract takes the place of an Alleluia during Lent and in seasons of fasting or mourning. Therefore it seems to be older than the Alleluia, which was introduced by Pope Damasus in the fourth century. As a matter of fact, it was considered a second psalm (after the Gradual).[78] Before the full Antiphonale made its way to Europe from the Eastern shores of the Mediterranean, and before choirs regularly sang the Alleluia, the solo performance of a psalm was usual and generally accepted. It was Ambrose who introduced the new, *choral* and *antiphonal* chant in the West, which gives us a *terminus post quem*. The Tract, as most solo forms, seems to antedate Ambrose, who died in 397.

The Tract is the only form type, except the non-scriptural hymn, that renders entire psalms or canticles *in florid, richly embellished fashion*, like a cantor in a Synagogue. At least five canticles are sung as Tracts: Exod. 15; Deut. 32; Isa. 5; Dan. 3 (the apocryphal canticle of the three men); and Luke 2:29 ff (the Canticle of Simeon); in addition, Ps. 91 is chanted in its entirety as a Tract, and the major parts of Ps. 42, Ps. 140, Ps. 117, Ps. 70 and others likewise. This fact itself hints at the archaic character of the form.

The uniqueness of the Tract is also evident from the musical aspect. Apart from its limitation to only two modes, its melismata are of an extremely rigid, ever-recurrent character; they appear like ornaments that were moulded in one master cast, and then applied by the architect (here the composer) lavishly on all significant parts of a building, as, e.g., a Corinthian Acanthus-motif would appear on all capitals of the columns. Even so are the melismata of the Tract displayed. In spite of the profound investigation of P. Wagner, and Riemann's special study,[79] which brought these facts into clear perspective, an important fact has been overlooked by all scholars. All Tracts, whether they belong to mode II or VIII, have two cadencing melismata in common. These melismata, in turn, are identical, apart from minor modifications, with the Hebrew half stop and full stop accents of the prophetic lesson (Haftara) in all centres. They constitute therefore ancient punctuating melismata of scriptural cantillation (*Urakzente*). These two melismata, as shown in three Tracts of mode II and three of mode VIII, run as follows:[80]

EXAMPLE 85

Obviously in each pair, A and C are fundamentally the same motif, whereby C may be considered a melismatic extension of the cell. If we transpose A a fifth higher, we obtain almost exactly C *without any addition of accidentals*. Motifs B and D also show close relationship with each other; if we transpose D a fourth lower and read it with B flat, we

531

reach approximately B. The motif A was encountered before, and then already it was linked with the Haftara chant and its accents (see above pp. 519 ff).[81]

It must be emphasized here that motifs A, B, C, and D occur *only as punctuating melismata*. The Hebrew counterpart of B and D is:[82]

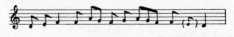

EXAMPLE 86

This represents the Yemenite, and approximates the Babylonian tradition, the two oldest and most authentic remains of scriptural cantillation.

Both motifs also form an important cadence type of the Prayer-modes of all Jewish centres, which generally were modelled after the accents of scriptural chant. Motifs A and C have been identified as of Hebrew origin before.

There is *one* Tract, one only, where this otherwise rigidly pursued system of punctuating melismata seems to be broken or at least confused: the prayer for a virgin martyr 'Veni sponsa Christi'.[83] A part of the text is not scriptural, which explains the lack of dichotomous verse structure—and consequently the confusion that reigns in the punctuating melismata. In the midst of the verse the motif (C) is applied without discernible reason, and before the end there appears motif (D). We give here the full text with the marks for the occurrence of the typical melismata (C) and (D).

(C)

Veni, sponsa Christi, accipe coronam, quam tibi *Dominus* praeparavit

(D)

in *aeternum*

Pro cujus amore sanguinem tuum fudisti

(C)

Dilexisti justitiam, et odisti *iniquitatem*

(C)

Propterea unxit te Deus, Deus *tuus* oleo laetitiae prae consortibus tuis.

(C)   (D)

Specie tua, et pulchritudine *tua* intende, prospere procede et *regna*.

(Come, thou bride of Christ, accept the crown that the Lord has prepared for thee for ever. For whose love thou hast shed thy blood. Thou lovest justice and hatest iniquity; therefore the Lord anointed thee, thy Lord, with the oil of gladness before thy fellows. By thy fairness and beauty, prosper, proceed and reign!)

The first verse, which is not of scriptural origin and has consequently no genuine half stop, must have created a difficult problem for the composer, who wanted to remain within the venerable tradition of scriptural melismata. Thus, he applied the full stop accent motif to 'aeternum'. The following two verses are scriptural and dichotomous, and the picture improves conspicuously: while the half stop is applied twice in one verse ('iniquitatem' and 'tuus') such cases do occur, if only rarely, in the Hebrew texts. In the last verse the position of (C) is problematical from the Hebrew point of view, but at least not impossible.

Since this Tract serves also at the commemoration of a virgin martyr, usually a nun, it cannot have originated before the organization of the *parthenoi* (nun groups), that is, not before the early fourth century. Probably no Judaeo-Christian cantor was at hand at so late a period, and so the Gentile Christian composer tried to imitate the old practice of the Old Testament *psalmistae*. That he did not fully succeed was not his fault, but due to the non-scriptural character of the first verse.

By now, our conclusion ought to be obvious and plausible: the Tracts are, next to some Psalm Tones and lesson Tones, the oldest and best preserved strata of Gregorian chant. They go back to the eulogies connected with the prophetic lesson of the Synagogue (Haftara), and to the oldest elements of the *Tefilla* chant.

When Jesus recited the Haftara from the book of Isaiah, as described in Luke 4:16–20, that reading or chanting was probably performed in the way a Tract is chanted today, only in a much simpler manner.

The Alleluia

The chant of the Alleluia, the second musical insertion between the lessons, is in all liturgical textbooks considered a direct legacy of the Synagogue. Since the Alleluia occurs in the Psalter and hence in the prayer books of the ancient Synagogue, the traditional view has a sound basis. But its predominant position before the Gospel lesson and the great musical-mystical significance ascribed to it in Christian literature are not easily explicable from the Jewish point of view. In the Synagogue the two passages that close with Hallelujah are chanted *after* the prophetic lesson. Also, the veritable alleluiatic psalms form here an intrinsic part of the daily morning service; yet this has hardly influenced the Mass, and it is in the Mass only that the melismatic character of the Alleluia unfolds itself in its full splendour. In the Synagogue the Alleluia plays a part only on Sabbaths and Festivals, while in the Church it is more frequently used, especially in the Eastern rites, where this praise is sung even at funerals.[84] The Roman Church has all but limited the Alleluia to Sundays, the great feasts, and to certain minor festivals; it excludes the Alleluia during Lent and from all major seasons of mourning. There is considerable controversy concerning the age of the Alleluia. Some scholars trace it, like the Tract, to Apostolic times; I cannot agree with their opinion. The best account is still that given by Gregory the Great, who attributes it to Jerome;[85] indeed, one of Jerome's Epistles to Pope Damasus openly advocates the introduction of the Alleluia for the time between Easter and Pentecost.[86] The first reference to the Alleluia in general seems to occur with Tertullian, who mentions that zealous Christians used to add that exclamation to their psalms.[87] Yet this was an incidental acclamation, not the great Alleluia chant of the Mass. Apparently Jerome was really the first one to introduce the melismatic Alleluia into the Roman Mass. Pope Gregory's remark that neither he nor Pope Damasus followed the Byzantine custom in giving the Alleluia a certain exalted stature is extremely important, since he immediately adds that the Alleluia is an importation from the Church of Jerusalem; and this is the consensus of the earlier Church Fathers.[88]

Under these circumstances we might assume that certain Jewish traits were preserved in the customs and ceremonies of the Jerusalem Church. The musical evidence, apart from minor details, does not bear out this seemingly natural assumption. Before analysing the Ambrosian and Gregorian Alleluias, the successors to Damasus' (366–384) importation, let us first state briefly the major differences in the performance of the Alleluia.

Synagogue	*Church*
Briefly sung, not much extended.	Extended into a long *Jubilus*.
Usually chanted as an integral part of the respective psalm.	Separated from the original context of the psalm.
In no way a special part of the liturgy.	Important part of the Mass.
Usually chanted in Roman mode I	Usually Chanted in Roman mode II and Roman mode VIII.

In contrast to the Tract, where we observed typical and recurrent melismata, the Alleluias do not contain melismatic punctuation. However, they make use of the contrafact technique, that is, a number of Alleluias with different psalm verses carry the same melody. While this practice is certainly very old (some of the headings of the psalms indicate it, e.g. 'According to the hind of the morning', Ps. 22), it is not necessarily Jewish. The Byzantines and Syrians knew this technique as *hirmos* and *riš-qolo*, respectively, and probably the principle of contrafacts dates back to the second millennium B.C. It is true that the liturgical usage of the Alleluia in the Early Church shows some affinity with the Synagogue, but the musical evidence is not promising.

P. Wagner distinguishes between three strata of alleluiatic chants; the oldest belongs, as does the Tract, to modes II or VIII.[89] This is one of the few facts that might suggest synagogal influence; we remember that these two modes—actually but one—dominate the Tract. Yet the inserted psalm verses of the Alleluias show little likeness to synagogal tunes. In no case was I able to find any real similarity between Ambrosian, Gregorian and Jewish Alleluias. The lack of any definite kinship between the Gregorian Alleluia and Jewish chant must be candidly admitted. Still, the historical and liturgical implications of the Alleluia point so strongly in the direction of the Synagogue, that one more attempt should be made in order to clarify the issue.

First, a sharp distinction must be established between the responsorial Alleluia, added to a Doxology or a psalm verse, especially during Eastertide and the independent Alleluia chant between or after the lessons. All Churches know this type of chant during or after the lesson, from the fifth century on.

Closest to the old Jewish practice comes the Nestorian ritual; it has the *Zumara* (chant, psalm) to the tune of 'Shepherd of Israel' (Ps. 80:2) before the Gospel; upon this contrafact tune one chanted an almost literal paraphrase of Ps. 68:33–36, and Ps. 29:11, also with an added Alleluia.[90] These very same psalm verses accompany the prophetic lessons on the Three Festivals of the Synagogue; in the Sephardic rite, even the lessons on weekdays.[91] Yet in all of these cases the Alleluias do not form an integral part of the scriptural verses; they are free additions[92]

Surprisingly enough, Aetheria Silvia, the chief witness of the Jerusalemite-Antiochene liturgy, nowhere refers to an Alleluia, not even during Easter week, of which she gives a glowing and wordy account.

The first reference to an independent Alleluia song, that is not added to a Doxology or any psalm verse, seems to occur in Jerome; in that passage he demands that even nursery songs be replaced by Alleluias.[93] Otherwise there is silence in the extensive literature of the Church: the *Constitutiones Apostolorum* do not even contain the term Alleluia; Chrysostom knows as the psalmodic Easter refrain only Ps. 118:24 ('This is the Day'[94]) and the account of the Syrian liturgy of the fifth century contains no Alleluia either.[95] It is only thereafter that the independent Alleluia appears in the writings of the Egyptian and Byzantine Fathers.[96] Indeed, the Alleluia chants of the Byzantine and Syrian Churches (of the ancient Egyptian Church nothing authentic has come down to us) display much more resemblance to Synagogue chants of Europe and Asia than the Gregorian *Jubili*. A few examples will demonstrate this fact.

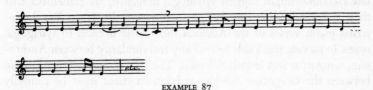

EXAMPLE 87

Example 87 represents the Alleluia before the Lesson in the Jacobite Church;[97] it consists of the Alleluia proper and a versicle, followed by the same tune that opened the piece.

EXAMPLE 88

Example 88 is the typical chant of the *Tefilla* and the eulogies of the Haftara, as customary among the Yemenite Jews;[98] they were never in contact with Northern Syria. This melody type belongs to the *Maqam Sika*, comparable to the Third (Phrygian) Church Tone.

EXAMPLE 89

Example 89 gives the East Syrian chant of the *Hullala*, i.e. an alleluiatic section of the psalms.[99]

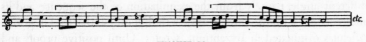

EXAMPLE 90

Example 90 is a Babylonian-Jewish chant, mainly for Passover.[100]

In contrast to the Roman (Gregorian) and Milanese (Ambrosian) traditions, Syrian chants and their derivates, the Byzantine Alleluias, are not particularly long, are not exceedingly abundant in little melismata, and can by no means be called extravagant. The same holds true of the Jewish illustrations. They all seem to be interrelated, which fact may be traced back to scriptural accent motifs and ancient prayer modes. Some of these motifs have also found their way into Gregorian Chant, especially the bracketed passages of Examples 89 and 90, which we encountered as typical melismata of the Tract. (See above, p. 531.)

Under these circumstances, we are bound to arrive at some rather unorthodox, though inevitable, conclusions. They may be summarized in the following statements:

(1) Liturgically, the Alleluia after a Doxology is a direct legacy of the Temple and the Synagogue.

(2) In contradistinction thereto, the Alleluia before or after the Gospel-reading is a Christian innovation and has no direct Jewish counterpart.

(3) The Byzantine and Syrian Alleluia chants display some resemblance to Jewish chant; not so the Gregorian melodies.

(4) The Alleluia, 'custom of the Oriental Church', was introduced into the Western Church by three Graecophiles: Pope Damasus, St Jerome, and St Ambrose, during the end of the fourth and the beginning of the fifth century. It probably originated in Syria (Antioch) and came to Byzantium; from there it made its way into the Roman Church.

The Gregorian Alleluia has, in the course of centuries, undergone a series of radical transformations, and must be considered an essentially *occidental* creation. This is supported by the disparity between the small Alleluia responses after a Doxology and the extended *Jubili* of the Mass. The alleluiatic responses are much more akin to Jewish style than the elaborate Alleluias of the Mass. This is due to the fact that the Alleluia after a Doxology is an ancient Jewish tradition, whereas the melismatic *Jubili* evolved outside the sphere of the Synagogue and its customs.

(5) The foregoing exposition receives strong support from an entirely

different angle, namely from the examination of the sequence and its antecedents. C. Blume, turning against the hypothesis that the Gregorian Alleluias originated in Byzantium, wrote: 'Until positive proofs and historic documents force us to explain some obscure items in the development of a purely occidental product as alien, Byzantine influence, one has to resist that . . . by now fashionable propensity.[101] This writer agrees in substance with F. Gennrich's assumption that most of the *Jubili* tunes developed on occidental, not oriental soil.[102] This notion fits well into the picture presented here.

The Music of Jewish and Christian Doxologies

In the following, some of the main features of the musical Doxologies, as we find them in Church and Synagogue, will be examined and compared. Just as the literary style of the ecclesiastical Doxology has changed from poetic spontaneity to impersonal solemnity, so its practice of execution has turned from semi-improvised melismatic style to simple and dignified psalmody. The development in the Synagogue shows another, but in some respects analogous, picture. There, the Temple Doxologies were relegated to a secondary position within the liturgy, and the four or five extended doxological prayers took their place. Musically, the once free-swinging melismata became gradually stereotyped, and, permeating as itinerant melodic formulas the whole of Jewish musical tradition, they constituted many of its various leading motifs. A similar development took place in the Church, and around the end of the first millenium this formative period of liturgical music approached its end in both Church and Synagogue. The subsequent epoch created most of the 'individual melodies' of which the preceding centuries had laid but the *modal* foundation. Before the end of the first millennium an intimate give-and-take relationship between Church and Synagogue is clearly evident in liturgy and music. This relationship came to an end, and after 1200 the situation grew decidedly one-sided.[103] In spite of all rabbinic decrees, the Church began to make inroads in the Jewish liturgy, and the Synagogue assumed more and more of a passive defensive attitude; hence, the music of the Church often found its way into the Synagogue.[104] We shall, therefore, limit the following examination to the Doxologies that are textually and musically indigenous of the old *Oriental Synagogue*—outside the Western Church orbit—and constitute, to the present day, an integral part of its liturgy.

THE SH'MA' AND BARUK SHEM K'VOD

Since the *Baruk shem* was recited as an audible response only on *Yom Kippur*, it assumed there the melody of the *Sh'ma'*. The following example[105] shows the Yemenite tradition of the High Holydays.

EXAMPLE 91

The typical melismata of the *Sh'ma'* occur in the preceding *Kaddish* and *Barku*. Thus they must be considered as leading motifs of the High Holydays, forming an integral and uniform part of all of the four doxological prayers; moreover, the *Kol Nidre*, preamble of *Yom Kippur*, employs the same motif. The illustration is to demonstrate the crystallization of recurrent patterns into a typical musical atmosphere permeating the service of an entire Holyday.

BARKU

This invitatory and its responsive Doxology contain a rich array of wandering ornaments which also occur, significantly, in other prayers of the High Holydays among the Babylonian Jews. There is an interesting parallel to this tune in the Roman Church, the modes of the 'Benedicite Te Dominum' and of the Solemn Orations; and it should not be overlooked that not only the tune but also the texts show some affinities. Moreover, the very same mode and the same melismata appear in the Yemenite *Barku* and *Sh'ma'*. All of these chants are connected with doxological passages, so that *Barku*, *Kaddish* and *Sh'ma'*, whenever they occur, are interconnected by wandering and final melismata. This example[106] shows the earlier stage before the wandering melismata had been finally crystallized into a definite pattern.

EXAMPLE 92

KEDUSHA

The melodies of the text and its corresponding Christian pieces, the *Hymnos epinikios* and the *Tersanctus* are of widely differing age. Some of them, such as the Yemenite *Kedusha*, might be very old; while the Gregorian tunes for the *Sanctus* do not antedate the eleventh or twelfth, and in some cases the fourteenth, century. The Byzantine example stems probably from the end of the first millenium. The Ashkenazic parallel to one of the Catholic *Sanctus*, the famous '*Alenu* (Adoration) of the High Holydays, is certainly the original from which the Church formed its chant. For not only do we possess an old description of the Hebrew melody sung in 1171 at Blois by Jews at the stake, while the Christians looked on admiringly,[107] but the motif typical of this tune occurs often in Jewish psalmody and is not limited to the European Jews. (See Examples 67 and 68.)

The following Byzantine example of the *Trisagion* and its Doxology displays a chromatic strain of the *octoechos*, which is identical with the Jewish mode *Ahaba Rabba* and the Arab *maqam Hedjaz*.[108] A direct influence from one sphere to the other is improbable; since that mode is common in the Near East, we need not assume real importation, the less so, since the Jewish example comes from West Germany of the eighteenth century.

EXAMPLE 93

Characteristic for its use of leitmotifs in connexion with the chain-like style of the Great *Kedusha* is the following example of the Yemenite Jews. (Cf. Part I, Chapter IX.) It is remarkable how consistently the wandering melismata connect the recurrent words with their respective musical phrases. The whole melodic framework is very similar to the formula of the Roman Lesser Doxology.[109]

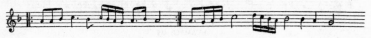

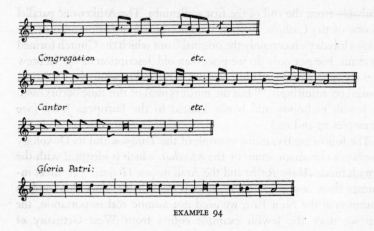

EXAMPLE 94

These chants must belong to the oldest strata of both Roman and Jewish tradition. Several reasons urge this conclusion. First, the range of the mode is small, indicating its antiquity. Secondly, its structure is strictly tetrachordal, another sign of its age. Thirdly, the mode is common to both the Yemenites and to the Roman Church, which never came into contact with one another. Finally, *the mode and its melismata* are identical with the priestly blessing of the Yemenites, which seems to accord well with the description of its Temple performance, as reported in Talmudic literature.[110] Yet the fact that the blessing is divided into three sentences, each one to be followed by the response 'Amen', contrary to the custom of the Temple, may indicate that the Yemenite tradition is younger, perhaps of the first or second century of our era.[111] The long drawn coloraturas remind us of the rabbinic controversy against excessively extended singing of the blessings.[112] We quote, in the following, the Yemenite tradition of the priestly blessing and the ancient tone of the Roman *Invitatorium* which, in turn, is a variant of the mode of the Doxology, quoted above.[113]

EXAMPLE 95

The identity is astonishing and, in this writer's opinion, almost self-explanatory. In addition, this is a classic example illustrating the occidental systematization of the once richly flowing melismata of the Orient.

THE ORNAMENTS OF MELISMATIC CHANTS

The flourishing melismatic style is characteristic of the entire music of the Orient. The singers of the Near East, in particular, were as inexhaustible when it came to inventing new forms of embellishments and ornaments as their listeners were insatiable in their demands for these coloratura-arabesques. Of all these embellishments the most functional are the final melismata which form a part of the cadence and are an integral part of every well-balanced melody, be it occidental or oriental. As we saw in Part II, Chapter IV, the Gregorian Chant has preserved a good many of these final melismata in their original settings, but they are also evident in Byzantine, Syrian and Jewish musical culture. Many of the embellishments of Jewish *hazanut* fall into the category of final melismata.

In a brief analysis of the main ornaments of synagogal and ecclesiastical chant we follow the guiding principles suggested by R. Lach's work on the development of ornamental melopoeia. The three archetypes of all musical ornaments are:

(1) The *periheletic* kind which plays around a specific note, dissolving one sustained note into an encircling ornament.

(2) The proceeding kind, originating from the *portamento* which replaces a straight run by a part of the scale in a series of ornaments all going in one direction.

(3) The punctuating kind which adorns and stresses all important caesuras of the melody or the text; to this type belong all final melismata.

The first type is the one most generally known; all trills, tremolos, mordants, etc., fall into this category. It is also the most primitive type of ornamentation, for it stems from the repetition of a single note, broken up into little circumvolutions. The chants of all Churches abound in this type; it is often combined with the second, scale-like type. This combination always indicates a step forward, from the spontaneous and unorganized chanting and howling of primitive civilizations in the direction of architectural and structural evolution.

The pure periheletic melisma is illustrated in the following examples:[114]

EXAMPLE 96

The combination of periheletic with scale-like melismata, a somewhat higher type, likewise occurs in all liturgical chants. Yet, in this instance the Gregorian and the Jewish tunes display progress toward finer organization and clearer structure than the chants of the Oriental Churches. A few illustrations may elucidate this point:[115]

EXAMPLE 97

The farther we go Eastward, the more infrequently do really well-developed and organic melismata of that type occur. Hence, Syrian chant is poorer in this respect than Byzantine melos, and the Nestorians have very little to show of firmly organized ornamentation. An exception to this rule is the Armenian chant; its ornaments are in every respect as well-developed and taut as those of Gregorian or Jewish culture.[116]

The third, or punctuating type of melismata has been abundantly referred to in the foregoing chapters. Again, Jewish, Gregorian, Byzantine, and Armenian accent-motifs show the clearest contours. (See Chapter IV above.)

Is it possible to define or distinguish the chants of the various Churches according to their typical melismata? This question cannot lightly be answered. It is true, there are melismatic passages, characteristic of the Gregorian, Jewish, Armenian and Byzantine tradition. But from recognizing this fact to identifying or defining the various traditions by their ornaments is a long way. For the task is complicated by the various strata that are embodied in liturgical style, reflecting various chronological phases of that style. In the Jewish sphere an additional obstacle occurs: one has to deal not only with the various historical strata of its chant, reaching from the beginning of the Christian era up to the eighteenth century, but also with the three main geographic traditions, viz. the Yemenite, the Sephardic, and the Ashkenazic rites. Still, there cannot be any doubt that there are melismatic passages which belong to, and are typical of, one and only one, style of ecclesiastical chant. We are inclined to trace all of these 'typical' melismata to ecphonetic accents and their cantillation.

Crystallization of such melismatic patterns probably preceded the modal organization of the entire tradition. In the Byzantine chant the *enechemata*, that is, the cue-words and closing formulas of the Psalm Tones, played a decisive part in the final codification of the modes, as has been realized during the last twenty years.[117]

The question of the extent to which those typical melismata have contributed to the final crystallization of the various systems of modality awaits further clarification. Its answer will solve many a problem of Gregorian and Jewish chant.[118] The composers of ornate chant did not take special cognizance of the poetic structure of their texts; if they noticed it at all, they were not impressed by any but the most glaring traits. This situation changed immediately when clearly recognizable pieces of numbered stresses or otherwise defined kinds of metre entered the liturgical repertoire. The radical departure from psalmodic style was the crucial factor in the development of the metrical hymn; the analysis of this new style will be the subject of our next chapter.

NOTES CHAPTER VI

1. R. Wagner, *Gesammelte Schriften & Dichtungen*, Volksausgabe, IV, p. 185.
2. Cf. *Acta Gaonica*, No. 215.
3. WGM, III, p. 374.
4. Ibid.
5. *LU*, p. 40; *JM*, p. 148, No 1.
6. After *JM*, p. 146, No 7; *LU*, p. 1005.
7. WGM, III, p. 470.

8. After *JM*, p. 138, No 2; p. 149, No 19; J. Schoenberg, op. cit., p. 83.

9. See *supra*, p. 457, n. 30.

10. Cf. R. Lach, op. cit., pp. 288–9, also pp. 140, 203, 266 ff *et passim*.

11. Cf. F. Gennrich, *Grundriss einer Formenlehre des mittelalterlichen Liedes* (Halle, 1932), pp. 36 ff.

12. WGM, I, pp. 157–8; also Bäumer, *Breviergeschichte*.

13. WGM, I, p. 159.

14. Ibid., pp. 209 ff.

15. Ibid., p. 211.

16. Ibid., p. 212.

17. WGM, III, pp. 305 ff.

18. In the Greek term *Troparion* (equals Refrain-piece), this ancient form conception has been preserved.

19. H. Besseler, *Die Musik des Mittelalters und der Renaissance* (Potsdam, 1931—in Bücken's *Handbuch der Musikwissenschaft*), p. 49.

20. Cf. A. V. Williams Jackson, *Researches in Manichaeism* (New York, 1932), pp. 132, 133, 151; see also Alfaric, *Les Écritures manichéennes*, II, pp. 125–6, and W. Bang, 'Manichaeische Hymnen', *Museon* (1925), pp. 1–55.

21. About the rhythm of Manichaean hymns, see A. V. W. Jackson, op. cit., p. 133, where the old Iranian metre (8 plus 8) appears, which is not of isosyllabic nature.

22. Cf. *The Liturgical Homilies of Narsai*, ed. by R. H. Connolly and E. Bishop (Cambridge, 1909), p. 117. In an interesting footnote Bishop refers to a passage of Gregory of Tours' *History* (lib. X, c. 26), where the Bishop of Tours relates that one Eusebius, a Syrian merchant, by means of money, was elected Bishop of Paris in 592; whereupon he immediately dismissed the hitherto famous *Schola Cantorum* of Paris. It seems, then, that the love of music in East Syria and ancient Iran was not too fervent, as Herodotus relates, *History*, II, I, 132. (Music was a contemptible art with the ancient Persians.)

23. *LU*, p. 611.

24. Baer, *Baal Tefilla*; A. Friedmann, *Chasonus*.

25. Cf. *JM*, pp. 50, 52, 53; A. Z. Idelsohn, 'The Magen Aboth Mode', *HUCA* (1939), pp. 559 ff, esp. Example VI.

26. *LU*, p. 324.

27. *LU*, p. 442.

28. *LU*, pp. 428, 1296.

29. Cf. F. A. Gevaert, op. cit., p. 125; also P. Ferretti, *Estetica Gregoriana* (1934), I, pp. 362–3.

30. *LU*, p. 519.

31. A. Friedmann, *Chasonus*; IT, III.

32. About Palm Sunday and its connexion with Tabernacles, especially in the Eastern Churches, see my study, 'The Hosanna in the Gospels', *JBL*, 1946, July issue. The palm branch is called a *Hoshano* in the Syrian Churches; the processions around the altar on Tabernacles with the *lulab* are likewise called *Hoshanot*, because of the refrain of the accompanying litanies, *Hoshana*, meaning 'Save Now!'

33. *LU*, p. 468.

34. IT, I, p. 88.

35. Isidore of Seville, *De Officiis Ecclesiasticis*, I, 9 (PL, LXXXIII, 744).

36. *Ordo Romanus*, I, 26, (PL, LXXVIII, 950).

37. WGM, III, p. 327.

38. WGM, I, p. 132.

39. We notice that on Holy Saturday the link with the lesson is provided not by a choral *responsorium*, but by a strictly solo *tractus*. Since this is exactly the way in which these texts were, and are, rendered in the Synagogue, and since the Easter vigil is certainly the oldest remnant of the primitive Christian liturgy, there can be no doubt but that the *tractus* type was the ancestor of most responsorial forms.

40. A. Friedmann, *Chasonus*, 82; *LU*, p. 500; *LU*, p. 507; *LU*, p. 674; *LU*, p. 660; *LU*, p. 1105.

41. *LU*, p. 614.

42. *LU*, pp. 493-4.

43. It is remarkable that the old medieval MSS of antiphons and responses list some groups of responses, to be chanted during the summer and early fall. They bear titles such as *De Historia Regum, De Job, De Esther, De Tobia, De Machabaeis, De Prophetis*, etc. Some of these books were used in the synagogue for the Haftara lesson. Cf. WGM, I, p. 140, where also the MSS are cited.

44. Cf. P. Aubry, op. cit., pp. 80-81.

45. Ibid, pp. 79-81; also K. Kevorkian, loc. cit.

46. E. Wellesz, 'Studien zur byzant. Musik', II, *ZFM* (1934), p. 418.

47. Ibid. I, pp. 225 ff.

48. Parisot, op. cit., Nos 120, 121, p. 100.

49. A. Friedmann, *Chasonus*.

50. IT, VI, p. 34.

51. M. Bukofzer, 'The Music of the Laudes', Appendix I to Ernst H. Kantorowicz, *Liturgical Acclamations and Mediaeval Ruler Worship* (University of California Publications, vol. 33, 1946), where also the entire bibliography is given.

52. The poem, in which the acclamation 'The Lord is King, the Lord hath reigned' is inserted as refrain and response, was written by Eliezer Kalir in the eighth century; the refrain occurs first in the treatise *Soferim* (middle of seventh century).

53. WGM, III, p. 374.

54. IT, I, No 80.

55. So anti-instrumental a musician as Adam of Fulda admonishes the composer of vocal music to study intensively the various forms of ornamentation and figuration that are best displayed by good instrumentalists. Cf. Riemann, *Handbuch der Musikgeschichte*, I, 2, pp. 44-45.

56. Ps. 24 mentioned in *Sab.* 30; cf. Abrahams, *Companion to the Prayer Book*, p. lxxxi. As to Ps. 29, cf. J. Miller, *Chillut Minhagim*, No. 49. See also A. Berliner, *Randbemerkungen zum Gebetbuch*, I, 25.

57. Most recent edition of this important tractate by J. Higger, (Philadelphia-New York).

58. *LU*, p. 638, v.

59. *Ant. Vat.*, 66.

60. *LU*, p. 1200.

61. *Ant. Vat.*, 142.

62. *LU*, p. 862: *Ant. Vat.*, 509.

63. *LU*, p. 494: *Ant. Vat.*, 66.

64. *LU*, p. 1126.

65. *LU*, p. 1103: *LU*, p. 414: *LU*, p. 1201.

66. *LU*, pp. 414-5: *Ant. Vat.*, 45.

67. *LU*, p. 492: *LU*, p. 745.

68. *LU*, p. 351.

69. *LU*, p. 286.

70. *LU*, pp. 492-3: Baer, *Baal Tefilla*; also IT, VI, 2

71. *LU*, p. 495: IT, II (Tones of Cantillation).

72. *LU*, p. 863: Italian tradition of Haftara-blessing. After Consolo, op. cit.

73. Recently, A. Baumstark (*Liturgie comparée*, p. 49) has offered the bold hypothesis that there was a variable Gradual in the ancient Synagogue; when Christianity took over the custom, using the various psalm-verses as Christological material, Judaism abandoned its own institution. Baumstark's hypothesis has been surprisingly verified: see *infra*, p. 549, n. 118.

74. WGM, III, p. 395. About the various forms of performance of the Gradual, see A. Fortescue, *The Mass*, pp. 267 ff.

75. Cf. E. Wellesz, *Eastern Elements in Western Chant*, p. 89; see also P. Ferretti, *Estetica Gregoriana*, pp. 114 ff; also A. Z. Idelsohn, 'Die Maqamen der Arabischen Musik', *SIM*, XV, pp. 1 ff; and G. Reese, *Music of the Middle Ages*, pp. 74, 86.

76. The same position is taken by Wellesz, op. cit., and Gastoué, *Chant juif et chant grégorien*, throughout.

77. WGM, III, pp. 366-7. In the same way, E. Wellesz, op. cit., p. 140.

78. Cf. Amalarius, *De Eccles. Offic.*, III, 12 (*PL*, CV, 1121); see also A. Fortescue, *The Mass*, p. 271.

79. H. Riemann, 'Der Strophische Bau der Tractus Melodien' *SIM*, IX (1907-8), pp. 183 ff. The study suffers from Riemann's untenable conception of Gregorian metric rhythm; the melodies in his redaction are so badly distorted that one has trouble in identifying them.

80. Mode II: *LU*, p. 1104; *LU*, p. 616; *LU*, p. 480. Mode VIII: *LU*, p. 1120; *LU*, p. 675; *LU*, p. 663.

81. The theory has been proposed that the Tract came to the Roman liturgy via Byzantium; E. Wellesz, in tracing the melismata back to the Synagogue, tries hard to prove the existence of the characteristic melismata in Byzantine chant. But his thesis is not convincing, since the Byzantine examples show only a superficial relation to the Roman cadences, and mainly because the Byzantine melismata have no punctuating function whatsoever, at least not in his examples. Cf. E. Wellesz, *Eastern Elements*, pp. 136-8. It is interesting to note the (subconscious) influence of the motifs (A) and (C) on Beethoven. The second theme of the first movement of his Fifth Symphony opens with just that motif, probably a reminiscence of the organist days of his youth.

82. *JM*, p. 52.

83. *LU*, p. 1045.

84. Cf. Duchesne, *Christian Worship*, pp. 114, 167 ff.

85. Gregory, *Ep. 12 ad Joh. Syracus.* (*PL*, LXXVII, 956).

86. Cf. *Decreta Damasi Papae* (*PL*, XIII, 659).

87. Cf. Tertullian, *De Oratione*, Chapter 27. See also Part I, Chapter VI. Such an example from North Africa is the Fayyum Fragment, given in *Monumenta Ecclesiae Liturgica*, ed. Cabrol & Leclercq, p. 156.

88. I cannot agree with Wellesz's interpretation of Gregory's Epistle; it seems that C. Blume and H. U. Bannister understood the critical passage better, especially if the words 'quae hic a Graecis fuerat tradita' are understood to mean that Greek popes or monks brought the Alleluia to Rome (Blume & Bannister, Introduction to vol. 53 of *Analecta Hymnica*, p. xxviii). Indeed, Damasus was a Greek; yet, as Gregory states, he knew the Alleluia from Jerusalem. Cf. J. Glibotic, 'De Cantu Alleluia in Patribus Saeculi VII antiquioribus', in *Ephemerides Liturgicae*, 1936.

89. WGM, III, p. 417.

90. BLEW, pp. 258-9.

91. ELB, p. 138; also Abrahams, *Companion to the Prayer Book*, p. lxxxi.

92. So e.g. in *Chronicon Paschale*, A.D. 624, p. 390 (*PG*, XCII, 1001); also St Maximus, *Mystagogia*, 23 ff. About the small Doxologies of the Psalter and their use in the Byzantine Church before the seventh century, see BLEW, p. 530, n. 2.

93. Cf. Jerome, *Ep. 107 ad Laetam de Institutione Filiae*, 4, 8, (*CSEL*, LV, 295): 'When she sees her grandfather, she should throw herself at his breast, hang from his neck and sing to the unwilling man an Alleluia.'

94. Cf. Chrysostom, *Expositio in Ps. 117*.

95. BLEW, pp. 481-4. The added Alleluia is rare in the Syrian liturgy. Much more usual are such endings as *barehui* (blessed) or *kadishat* (holyness) or *olmayo* (into eternity) than in the liturgy of the Synagogue.

96. Mainly Cyril of Alexandria, *De Adoratione in Spir.*, XII; also *In Malachiam*, I; Athanasius, *De Fuga*, 24 and St Maximus, *Mystagogia*, 11, 23, 24.

97. Cf. Parisot, op. cit., No 195.

98. IT, I, p. 35.

99. Parisot, op. cit., No 290.

100. R. Lachmann, *Cantillation of Oriental Jews*, (Jerusalem, 1937), p. 14.

101. Cf. Blume, *Analecta Hymnica* (1911), LIII, p. xxvi.

102. F. Gennrich, *Grundriss einer Formenlehre des mittelalterlichen Liedes*, p. 120.

103. The last gift of Judaism to the Church was probably the model of the famous sequence, 'Dies irae'. We have seen, however, in Part I, Chapter VII, that the hymn came to the Occident via Byzantium, where its model was a composition of the Syrian-born

Jewish convert Romanus. Thus, even the roots of the 'Dies irae' reach down to the fifth century.

104. Cf. *JM*, pp. 178 ff.

105. IT, I, pp. 98–100 and No 116.

106. IT, II, pp. 97–8; *LU*, p. 358; IT, I, Nos 10, 27; *LU*, p. 376.

107. Cf. *Emek ha-bakha* (ed. Leipzig, 1858), p. 8. The entire reference also in *JE*, art. 'Olenu', also *JM*, p. 157. F. L. Cohen, the musical 'expert' of the *JE* was unaware of the Gregorian counterpart of the '*Alenu*.

108. Cf. Rebours, *Traité de Psaltique*, pp. 154 ff. The Jewish example is the Hebrew Union College Library MS 9 f, 45, a *Kedusha* composition of Judah Stettenheim (end of eighteenth century).

109. The first example is a Yemenite *Kedusha*, IT, I, p. 92. The second is the Roman doxology, *Gloria Patri*, after WGM, III, pp. 141 ff.

110. *Tosefta Sota*, 40a; *Yoma*, 39b.

111. *M. Tamid*, VII, 2; *M. Sota*, VII, 6.

112. ELB, p. 70.

113. Example 95 is the Priestly Blessing after the Yemenite tradition, *JM*, p. 75, No 1 (transposed). Example 95b is the *Invitatorium* after WGM, III, p. 179.

114. Example 96a is a Byzantine *Kylisma* (roll), quoted after O. Fleischer, op. cit., III, p. 60.

Example 96b is the Yemenite Jewish accent, *Zaqef Katon*, according to IT, I, p. 156.

Example 96c occurs in the Offertory of the Saturday before Pentecost, 'Emitte Spiritum', *LU*, p. 757.

Example 96d is a quotation from a Jacobite chant according to Parisot, op. cit., No 297.

Example 96e is taken from an ancient Byzantine hymn, quoted after E. Wellesz. *Eastern Elements in Western Chant*, p. 99.

115. Example 97a from the Alleluia of the fifth Sunday after Easter, *LU*, p. 728.

Example 97b from the songs of Yemenite Jews, IT, I, p. 107.

Example 97c from Wellesz, op. cit., p. 99.

116. Cf. R. Lach, op. cit., Part II (Musical Tables, No III).

117. On the musical significance of the *enechemata* see E. Wellesz, *Trésor de musique byzantine*, I, (1934), p. 23; also H. J. W. Tillyard, *Handbook of the Middle Byzantine Musical Notation* (1935), p. 31. A good summary and complete bibliography of the question in G. Reese, op. cit., p. 87. That the names of the *enechemata* are derived from the Hebrew, I have shown in my study, 'The Psalmodic Formula *Neannoe* and its Origin', *MQ*, Jan., 1942.

118. After the book had gone to press, I learned that there is, after all, a positive indication of the lost synagogal background of the Gradual. The late Dr Jacob Mann has demonstrated beyond any possible doubt that the ancient Synagogue knew the changing *Psalm lesson* side by side with the lesson from the Law and the Prophets. This *proprium psalmorum* would constitute the Jewish basis for the Christian Gradual, which changes with the lesson and the ecclesiastical season. Cf. Jacob Mann, *The Bible as Read and Preached in the Old Synagogue* (Cincinnati, 1940). Cf. references to *Aggadath Bereshit*.

CHAPTER SEVEN

The Music of the Hymnic Forms

NOWHERE more than in truly inspired hymns is Santayana's word verified that poetry and religion spring from the same source. Music,
another gift of mankind, rounds off that great work of effort and aspiration: to attune human souls to the Divine.

And yet the devout worshipper, and the enthusiastic student of medieval culture approach the realm of the hymn with different sentiments.
They are not antagonistic to each other, for the element of reverence,
common to both, remains in their hearts, but otherwise their aims
diverge widely.

The liturgical significance of the hymns, though always taken into
consideration, cannot serve as our point of departure; for neither in
Christianity nor in Judaism are we certain that the hymn was originally
intended to serve primarily *liturgical* purposes. None the less, very few
items of any liturgy have eventually attained so universal a popularity
as the metrical hymns; perhaps only certain acclamations, such as Amen,
Alleluia, or Hosanna could compete with the enormous popular appeal
of the hymn.

THE SHARE OF THE NATIONS

Nowhere in the entire compass of liturgy does the *genius loci*, the
spirit of the language and of the people, play so great a part as in hymnology. The reasons are fairly obvious; the scriptural background is no
longer a *sine qua non*; ethical and artistic-aesthetic impulses rather than
rigid liturgical impositions determine the composition of a hymn. The
hymn form originated in the Near East, as we saw in Part I, Chapter
VII, as a perfect blending of the spirit of Hellenistic antiquity with the
apocalyptic ideas of Judaism. Yet, these originally free and spontaneous
outbursts of religious souls had soon to yield to certain artistic-literary
demands. While the Syrian and Byzantine hymnodists resorted to all
kinds of devices that satisfied the eye more than the ear (Acrostics,
Isosyllabism), the Latin genius demanded more tangible principles of

form. A new ethos is discernible in the Latin hymns, the powerful urge towards a new organization, in a way comparable to the old *Imperium Romanum,* but of a much more spiritual nature. Perhaps the new organization longed for, or expressed by, these Latin hymns, was Augustine's dream, the City of God.

Apart from these literary and spiritual differences between Eastern and Western hymns, a methodological difference demands serious consideration: the terminology. Whereas the Occidental Latin Church uses the term *hymnus* usually for a new poetic creation, at least since the fourth century, the Oriental and Greek Churches understand as a hymn a scriptural psalm, a *Troparion,* an *enyana,* a Doxology, the *Trisagion,* or anything the occasion might justify. They apply the term rather loosely.

Finally, the musical scholar will clearly distinguish between an Eastern and a Western hymn. The latter is almost invariably metrical, with numbered stress accents (beats) and a discernible musical periodicity; not so the Eastern hymnodies: the chants of a *Kontakion,* a *Kanon,* or a *Troparion* are not sufficiently different from a Psalm Tone or Antiphon as to enable us to establish clear distinctions between the hymnic and non-hymnic tunes, as we recognize them in the sharply drawn contours of a Roman hymn. All attempts of Byzantine and Syrian hymnologists to demonstrate the influence of metre without regular stress upon the chant have failed.

For these reasons we shall have to limit our comparisons mainly to Latin and Hebrew hymns; the latter ones had accepted the accentuating metrical system during the late eighth century and some of the early Hebrew hymn tunes may have been composed under the spell of this revolutionary innovation. Another limitation ought to be mentioned: since this book concerns itself with the development of the musical liturgy of the first millennium, we shall have to disregard the extremely interesting and creative period between 1150 and 1350. Some of the finest creations of Christian and Jewish liturgical music originated in that interval.

Introduction to Hebrew Hymnody

The two phases of Hebrew hymnody within our scope arose in (1) the Palestinian, Babylonian, Levantine, and (2) the North-African and Spanish orbits. The main types, according to topic, are:

(a) *Selihot* (supplications, penitential litanies)
   Hoshanot (litanies)
   Kerobas and *Yotzrot* (poetic insertion in the *Sh'ma'* and the *Tefilla*
   portions on festivals)

(b) Hymns in free praise of God
   Theological-dogmatic poems.

The first category is closely connected with midrashic-exegetic elements, and many hymns of that category, especially *Kerobas*, are actually based upon scriptural exegesis in midrashic form. The second category, though still linked to Scripture through thousands of overtones and allusions, is much freer in thought and expression. It comprises the greatest masterpieces of Hebrew poetry since the Psalms.

Of the many and various Arabic metres that were taken over and elaborated upon by the Jews, the most important are those which are of accentuating metre and have a time-value assigned to each syllable as well. Outstanding among them are the following five schemes:

(1) *Hazağ* metre ‿ — — ⏊   'The Lord of áll
                    — — ⏊   Who reigns supréme'

(2) *Rağaz* metre ‿ ⏊ ‿ ⏊   analogous to 2 Greek iambic
                  ‿ ⏊ ‿ ⏊   dimeters

(3) *Mutakarib* metre ‿ — ⏊   usually repeated four times

(4) *Ramal* metre { ⏊ ‿ — —   a trochaic-spondaic system
                  { ⏊ ‿ — —
                  { ⏊ ‿ ⏊

(5) *Kamil* metre ‿ ‿ ⏊ ‿ —   anapaestic-iambic structure[1]
                  ‿ ‿ ⏊ ‿ —

Contents, metre and style together create the specific atmosphere of the various hymnodies. We shall, in the following, observe the way in which these three main constituents have shaped early Hebrew hymns.

A *Seliha*, that has no accentual metre as yet, but counts only the number of words of a line ('Word-metre'), none the less shows a rhythmical, almost symmetrical structure. Usually its music is of considerably later origin than the text, a state of affairs which we shall encounter in numerous hymns of the Roman ritual.[2]

EXAMPLE 98

On the other hand, there are clearly metrical and rhymed hymn texts whose music shows no direct traces of metre or symmetry. To quote one example[3] whose metrical scheme is

EXAMPLE 99

The first principle is, therefore: a non-metrical text is frequently set to a metrical tune; conversely, a metrical text sometimes fails to display in its music any metrical or symmetrical features whatsoever. In general, examples of the first category are much more numerous than those of the second, especially in Occidental Jewry.

Where the number of syllables, words, and accents composing one metrical unit never changes, there are invariably clear metrical impulses discernible in the music. An interesting example is the old Babylonian-Jewish ditty, that serves as a mnemonic rule for the ritual of the Passover-meal. Its text is nothing but a rhythmically arranged schedule for the occasion, but its lines always consist of two words, each of two syllables, that rhyme:

		Significance	
Kadésh	urhátz	Eulogy of wine	washing (of hands)
Karpás	yahátz	Fruit of earth	break the *matza*
Magíd	rahátz	Tale of Exodus	wash hands before meal
Motzeé	matzá	Blessing of *matza*	
Marór	kórech	Bitter herbs	combination of herbs and *matza*
Shulhán	órech	Set table	(meal)
Tzafún	bórech	Last *matza*	saying grace
Hallél	nirtzá	Singing of *Hallel*	God-pleasing end.

Nobody will claim that such a text is inspired or inspiring, and yet, due to its strict metre and rhyme, it was (probably for mnemonic purposes) set to a sharply rhythmical tune that sounds exactly like a hymn:[4]

EXAMPLE 100

Formal analysis shows the following structure:

$$
\begin{array}{ccccc}
& a & b & & c & b \\
A & & & B & & \text{or AABB} \\
& a_1 & b_1 & & c & b
\end{array}
$$

This is a surprisingly symmetrical type that also occurs in German folk songs of the sixteenth or seventeenth century; and yet no direct contact of the Babylonian Jews with occidental groups can possibly be assumed.[5]

The second principle to be remembered is the fact that a metre, however strictly observed in poetry, lends itself to a variety of musical rhythms and formations. This shall be demonstrated presently: three compositions of the same hymn will be presented that differ exceedingly from each other.

The text is the tenth-century hymn '*Adon 'Olam* (text and translation in Part I, Chapter VII, p. 243) of which the metrical scheme is:

$$
\begin{array}{c}
\smile - - \perp \\
\smile - - \perp \\
\smile - - \perp \\
\smile - - \perp
\end{array}
$$

EXAMPLE 101[6]

Tunes (a) and (d) have nothing at all in common; yet it is the same hymn and the same metre; apart from the gradual loosening of the strict 4-4 of (a), a melismatic expansion has taken place all the way from (a) to (d); for (d) gives the same four measures (and the same tune) as (c), but (d) has only arrived at the end of the first line of the text (eight syllables) whereas (c) has all sixteen syllables in the same tune and (b) shows not even a trace of metrical accent. This exemplifies the third general principle of the development of Hebrew hymnody. There are two antagonistic forces that generally counterbalance each other: the free rhythm of the recitative and the accented beat. Up to the thirteenth century, the first tendency prevailed, later the second, at least in the Occident. Yet whenever the latter became too predominant—usually under the influence of occidental melos—the influx of Eastern cantors provided a counterweight, with their preference for either purely melismatic or recitative-like rendering of the hymn texts.

In the Western orbit the leading-motifs also permeated some of the hymns, especially those of the High Holydays; this is the rule whenever the hymn serves as a poetic insertion of the Sh'ma' or Tefilla. In such cases, the non-metrical tune of the nuclear prayer is applied to the metrical insertions. There are some characteristic exceptions to this rule; as e.g. the Tal (dew) Keroba, whose tune permeated the older preceding and following prayers. Usually, however, the original tune of the

555

19

basic prayer, or some of its leading melismata, shape the melody of the new hymn. One example may illustrate this principle: the nuclear prayer of the shofar ritual is the rabbinic eulogy, 'Praised be thou, Lord, our God, King of the Universe, who hath commanded us and ordered in His laws to hearken to the sound of the shofar'. Before this prayer a poetic paraphrase of Ps. 47:6 is inserted (*Adonai beqol shofar*). Naturally the psalmody of the ancient eulogy was a creative factor in the composition of the hymn. In the following we present the chant according to the tradition of the Babylonian Jews:[7]

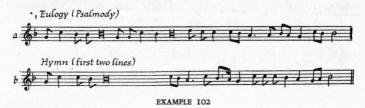

EXAMPLE 102

We shall see later on that this principle of musical as well as textual expansion of psalmodic nuclei in hymnic lines has a direct counterpart in the Roman tropes and sequences. It is by no means suggested that either form is a result of Jewish ideas or formal conceptions: nothing could be further from the truth. The reason for this remarkable analogy is simple: if two liturgical developments start from the very same point of origin, they will, in spite of all divergences, occasionally run parallel. Since hymns are—unlike Scripture—untranslated and indigenous products of linguistically differentiated regions, and since the inherent rhythms of those languages differ enormously from each other, as e.g. Latin from Hebrew, we cannot expect many musical analogies between the two cultures. On the other hand, the attitude of the Roman Church toward formal and liturgical structures was sometimes retrospective. Only in such cases might we succeed in unearthing analogies; yet they are no longer genuine or primary, but derivations of older, originally oriental elements.

The Spirit of Latin Hymnody

When surveying the enormous variety of Latin hymnody, from centonized psalms to most intricate tropes and proses, from spontaneous outbursts of ecstatic souls to dry didactic or polemic rhymes, one may reach the conclusion that this field is so variegated, as full of surprises and imponderable elements as life itself, and therefore evades any systematic clarification. Such could by no means be our task, since it would, as the great standard works prove, entail work on a monumental scale. All that can be offered here will be a few characteristic examples of Western hymns, without the implication that they represent the most valuable or even the most frequent types. These examples are shown here to give the reader an inkling of the variety of the spirit of certain liturgical aspects of this hymnody, since, after all, this study is mainly concerned with problems of musical liturgy.[8]

Systematic centonizations of psalms must have played a great part in the early Latin Church, since quite a few have come down to us.[9] They are, of course, non-metrical, and follow more or less literally the scriptural text.

Exegetic allegorical hymns are not rare; curiously enough, some of them follow the post-biblical Jewish line of exegesis. One of the most interesting hymns of that kind is St Bede's composition on God's work during the first six days of creation. In his hymn he likens the seven days of creation to seven aeons of the world; this concept occurs already in Philo[10] and in the Midrash. Of the Church Fathers, Augustine was familiar with this allegory, doubtless through Philo.[11]

Remnants of apparently Judaeo-Christian *midrashim* have also left their traces, as we see in a stanza from a hymn by Ambrose:

> Under the impact of Jesus's mystical baptism
> The waves of Jordan receded . . .[12]

This is obviously a Jewish-inspired Christian midrash that occurs also in the Byzantine liturgy; it is probably based upon Ps. 114:3: 'The sea beheld it, and fled; the Jordan was driven backward.'

Since Ps. 114 is part of the messianic *Hallel*, it was very familiar to every Judaeo-Christian.

The Greek monks seem to have been the intermediaries between Rabbinism and Latin hymn-poets, for most of these midrashic elements originated in Byzantium. Another example occurs in the sequence, ascribed to Hermann the Lame (Herimannus Contractus).

> King of Kings,
> Great Lion of Judah
> By virtue of the cross,

Thou death of sin,
Life of justice,
Granting the first of the tree of life . . .
Thou openest the garden of the paradise,
Thou offspring of obedience . . .

The term 'Lion of Judah' does not refer to Rev. 5:5 as the old commentary of this hymn indicates, but to Jacob's blessing in Gen. 49, since Jesus is acclaimed as the 'Son of David', who, in turn, comes from the tribe of Judah.[13]

Another paraphrase of a psalm, this time on a much higher level, is the (*Troparion*) hymn:

Let all of us sing
Now Alleluia.
In praises of the eternal King
Thy people exults in Alleluia, etc . . .[14]

Daniel in his *Thesaurus Hymnologicus* observes rightly that this hymn is a highly poetic paraphrase of Ps. 147–48: each stanza ends with an Alleluia.

There are also hymns whose structure and function resemble that of a *Kedusha-Keroba*; i.e., they serve as poetic insertions between the nuclear prayers of the Ordinary of the Mass. Such a piece is the hymn called *Trisagion*. It begins with the *Sanctus* of the Thrice-Holy, which is then interrupted by the following verse:

Sanctus . . .
All-powerful Father
By thy mercy
And love
Grant us
Deliverance
From enemies' ire,
And association
With Thy Saints.

It is continued by another *Sanctus*, interrupted by another verse, concluded by the third *Sanctus*, whereupon the Ordinary proceeds with the prescribed words 'Dominus Deus Sabaoth, pleni sunt coeli et terra gloria tua'.[15]

Very much akin to the *Keroba* type is the regular trope of a Mass, that is, the hymnic interruption and paraphrase of the Ordinary of the Mass.

Sometimes these tropes reach the very pinnacle of liturgical poetry and music. Many of them have been preserved, but have not played any part in actual services since the Council of Trent. Perhaps the finest collection of them is to be found in the Winchester Troper; which is interesting to us on account of some curious Hebraisms that occur therein; one example may suffice here:

> Adoneus Kyrrius, dominus kyrrion christleison Hel sother, saluator, messias, christus, unctus, rucha, pneuma.[16]

No less than four languages are mixed here:

Adoneus = Hebr. *Adonai* (Lord)
Kyrrius = Gr. *Kyrios* (Lord)
Christleison = Gr. *Christe eleison*
Hel = Hebr. *El* (God)
Sother = Gr. *Sother* (Saviour)
Messias = Hebr. *Meshiah* (The Anointed)
Rucha = Aramaic *Rucha* (Spirit)
Pneuma = Gr. (Spirit)

The polyglot character of this piece, however, is a far cry from the naïve Hebraisms of the New Testament and the Apostolic Fathers; this is obviously a learned composition of a doctor of theology.

The pastiche style that we encountered time and again in the Hebrew *piyyutim* is by no means alien to Latin hymnody, as the hymns on the fifteen *cantus graduum* (Ps. 120–34) clearly indicate. Such hymns are not mere centonizations or paraphrases of psalm verses, but genuine and original poems containing frequent allusions to certain verses of the 'Songs of Degrees'. This style comes very close to the *piyyut* of the ninth or tenth century. One stanza may indicate the technique of such hymns.

> I shall lift up mine eyes   (Ps. 121:1)
> To the primeval mountains . . .
> I was glad when   (Ps. 122:1)
> They said unto me
> Unto the house of the
> Lord let us go![17]

By now it will be apparent that the hymns of the Western Church are neither limited to 'functional' (that is, strictly liturgical) poetry, nor to individual and spontaneous creations of religious poets; nor even to 'practical' compilations for the study and memorization of the Psalter. There are hymns that were considered charms against drought, famine, the plague, personal misfortunes;[18] there were others of apologetic, dogmatic, and sometimes of an openly polemic nature. In other words, the field of Latin hymnody knows no bounds—it covers the whole thinking of a devout Christian, be he layman or priest, knight or peasant.

The liturgy, however, has discriminated very carefully among this motley output of medieval life, and has selected only a very small group of songs. They convey pure praise, either of the Divinity, or of His attributes (the Trinity), or of Sacraments, or of the Virgin, or of some Saints: a few litanies were permitted in the realm of hymns, but they constitute a negligible minority; for most of the litanies do not fall into the category of hymns. Thus the hymns which were admitted to strictly liturgical use follow a rather narrowly prescribed course, but in this path they accomplish monumentality.

Comparisons

A plain comparison of Gregorian and Jewish hymn tunes would, if attempted, necessarily lead to wrong perspectives; no melodic coincidence would be conclusive, unless the age of tunes and texts were known to us. Yet such cases are extremely rare. At any rate, genuine analogies can only be expected as long as the contact with the Orient or Byzantium was kept alive within the body of the Church. The weakening of these influences in the Western Church is palpable long before the actual Great Schism (1054).

Hence, we cannot expect any genuine parallels after the eighth century; it may rightly be considered a turning point in the history of both Christianity and Judaism. For the latter it was significant since it marked the beginning of the mass migration from Babylonia into Spain, Italy, and subsequently into the Rhineland. For Western Christianity the eighth century stands for the more or less general acceptance of the Church as the ultimate arbiter throughout the Occident, a development to be crowned by the establishment of the Holy Roman Empire under Charlemagne.

During this period the great *scholae cantorum* in Western Europe, especially in or near the Rhineland, emerged as the finest artistic centres of Catholic plainchant. Our oldest and best sources come from these centres.

Gregorian Chant is almost without exception based upon oratorical accent and evolved an oratorical type of *melos*. The law of tonic accent dominates most of its area, but the hymns, due to their strophic and metrical structure, cannot follow rigidly the law of accent. Only in those archaic hymns that originated between the time of Ambrose and the seventh or eighth century does the tonic accent sometimes prevail, and there beats and accents often coincide. In such cases where it is not possible to speak of a strict metre, a relationship might have existed between Church and Synagogue. The best and most famous example is the *Te Deum*; the Jewish background of its text has already been discussed above (Part I, Chapter VII). It will now be examined from the musical point of view.

Its rhythmical structure shows an inclination towards the old Oriental principle of homotony, whereby the number of tonic accents (or of words) in one line remains more or less constant. Thus:

Té Déum laudámus	We praise Thee, God
Té Dóminum confitémur	We extol Thee, Lord
Té aetérnum Pátrem	Thee, the eternal Father
Ómnis Térra venerátur	Reveres the whole earth
Pátrem imménsae majestátis	Father of tremendous majesty
Venerándum túum vérum	Thee and Thine true
Ét unícum Fílium . . . etc.	Oneborn Son we adore . . .

The Latin text shows three words (accents), this English translation four for every line. Ancient Hebrew hymns of the third and fourth century display a similar structure, as e.g.:

'Alénu leshabéach la'adón hakól	'Tis our duty to praise the Lord of all
Latéth geduláh leyotzér bereshíth,	To ascribe greatness to the world's
etc.	creator in the beginning, etc.[19]

The chant of the *Te Deum* reflects faithfully this poetic scheme as we shall see presently:[20]

Te Deum (first verses)

Te De-um lau-da-mus, Te Do-mi-num con-fi - te - mur,

(later verses)

Ve-ne- ran-dum tu-um ve-rum Tu Pa-tris sem-pi-ter-nus es Fi-li-us.

EXAMPLE 103

This hymnic psalmody shows a striking resemblance to an equally old hymn of Christianity, the *Gloria in excelsis*, which we here compare with its Hebrew counterpart. Its tune according to the week-day version (certainly the oldest one) runs in such phrases:[21]

EXAMPLE 104

Can it be mere coincidence that two of the oldest hymns of the Church have the same melodic pattern, the same motifs as the two oldest elements of synagogue-worship—the *Sh'ma'* and the scriptural cantillation? In this case, both Jewish illustrations stem from the most authentic tradition, the Yemenite ritual; but in almost all of the Jewish centres of the world one may hear similar phrases, modes, and cadences.

We had occasion to refer to all four examples before, but never together; now we can clearly see that all these melodies fall into *one* category: the *Tropos Spondeiakos*. This mode of the Hellenistic Jews in the Near East became extremely popular throughout Christendom; and thus we find similar motifs in Byzantine as well as in Nestorian chant.

None of these forms is metrical: the recitative-like rendering equally suited the prayers of Judaism and the hymns of the incipient Church.

Proceeding to strictly metrical hymns: almost two-thirds of them belong to the three modes I, II and VIII, in the same way as does the Tract; yet in contrast with that ancient melodic form, the hymn's first and second modes serve as approximations to the plain minor, while VIII comes actually very close to the major. It would, therefore, be in no respect permissible to draw any further conclusions on the selection of the modes for hymns.

Before the Occidental Jews began to borrow extensively from ecclesiastical songs (i.e. middle of the sixteenth century) there was very little similarity between Jewish and Gregorian hymn melodies of *metrical character*. Two rather atypical examples may illustrate this point:[22]

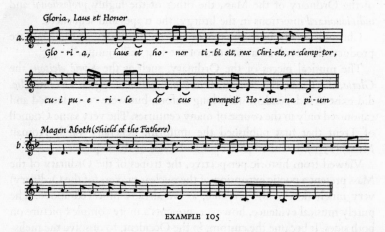

EXAMPLE 105

The Text of 'Gloria, laus et honor', written in Elegiac couplets, was composed by Theodulph, Bishop of Orleans (d. 821).[23] The assumption is that its melody, which follows the metre, is not older than 820. It still corresponds with elements of the ancient Jewish mode *Magen Aboth*, indeed, with its pattern prayer, which certainly antedated the sixth century.

There is some similarity, but much more divergence; none the less, the basic character of the common mode is still palpable in both of its representations. That the Jewish melody does not belong to the oldest strata is evident in the absence of punctuating melismata; and the same holds true, more or less, for the Gregorian hymn.

One may consider the period from 850 to 1000 the one most problematic for our investigation, since too little is known about the social life of Jews in the Christian community of the Western orbit. For no longer was Jewish substance transferred to Christianity through Church Fathers or Judaeo-Christians; whatever was absorbed by the Church came into its realm either through personal example, or as a second 'orientalizing' wave, after the first major one had already been transformed and reshaped in Byzantium. It is therefore most difficult and hazardous to express any founded opinions.

During those centuries two important forms of ecclesiastical chant craved for general recognition and commenced their formal codification. They are antagonistic manifestations, the one of the *popular* chant of the Ordinary of the Mass, the other of the highly *professional* and *individualized* insertions in the liturgy, the tropes and sequences.

Chronologically both the tropes and the Ordinary of the Mass are products that evolved at the end of the first millennium.[24]

The musical pieces of the Ordinary, such as the *Kyrie eleison*, the *Gloria*, the *Credo*, the *Sanctus, Benedictus, Hosanna, Agnus Dei*, and *Ite*, did exist as independent units long before, but were co-ordinated and canonized only in the course of many centuries. The very same Council of Trent that first published the uniform, generally valid, Roman Missal (1570), banished all tropes and most of the sequences.

Viewed from historic perspective, the tropes of the Ordinary of the Mass present a poetic expansion of the nuclear prayers (of the Ordinary) very much akin to the *piyyutim*, as we already observed above. The purely musical evidence, however, presents a more complex picture on both sides. It became the custom, in the Occident, to dissolve the melismatic elements of the original chants into syllabic diction by setting new, metrical-syllabic texts to the ancient, florid tunes. In some cases even the text of the lesson was interspersed with tropes; P. Wagner gives some interesting examples of that chaotic practice.[25] Usually the 'syllabization' of the melismatic tradition is interpreted as a sort of mnemonic aid for the singers, at a time when written music was not too easily obtainable. However, there might be another reason beneath this rationalizing idea that accounts for the dissolution of melismata into syllabic units. The secular folk-song of the Occident began to emerge at the end of the eleventh century; in general the Church was not too fond of it, since it rightly sensed a relapse into barbaric-pagan customs. The pieces of the Ordinary, on the other hand, were those most familiar to the native population. It is possible that the peoples of the West sensed the ancient chants of the Church as alien elements, especially the long extended melismatic songs; and the clergy compromised with that latent animosity by dissolving these melismatic chants in the (syllabic) tropes and sequences. This was especially useful at the great feasts of the Church, when popular interest and acclamation were most desirable. We learn accordingly that the tropes were sung particularly on high feasts and were designated 'festival lauds'.[26]

The Ordinary, with the exception of the *Credo*, was more pervaded by tropes than any other part of the liturgy. Apparently, nobody dared to tamper with that most sacred and dogmatic part of the Mass. Similar is the situation with the *Sh'ma'* in the Jewish liturgy; while few of the nuclear prayers were left free from *piyyutic* infiltrations, this most sacred watchword of Judaism was left untouched.

Of the Ordinary, the oldest pieces are the *Kyrie, Sanctus,* and *Credo.* The *Gloria* and the passage of the Ps. 118 (*Benedictus*) with the subsequent *Hosanna* have already been examined. In the following, some of these ancient chants will be compared with the Jewish legacy.

The Ordinary of the Mass

The rigidly stylized character of Gregorian, Byzantine, and Jewish chant is by now familiar to the reader. The phase of 'chainlike' composition of melodies faded gradually away after the thirteenth century. Even before that time the sequences and hymns of the Latin Church, no less than the *piyyutim* of the Synagogue had demanded and received individual tunes of their own, tunes that were no longer paraphrases of generally known patterns, but more or less original creations, befitting the new texts.

The musical comparisons that will be offered in the following pages do not any more contemplate branches of the same tree: the pieces might be likened to individual flowers of a garden, irrigated by the same river. Their colouring, their fragrance are different, yet they are still offshoots of the same earth.

THE KYRIE

Some of our examples exhibit a distinctly archaic *melopoeia*. This is always evident when the mode officially indicated in the Kyriale or Antiphonale does not tally with the actual course of the melody. A fine example of this disparity is the *Kyrie* of Mass XV (*Dominator Deus*) used for weekdays and minor feasts. It was observed here before that the chants of weekdays in general retained more of the genuine tradition than those of high feasts, simply by their daily repetition.

EXAMPLE 106

This illustration shows, according to the aaabbbaaa structure of the acclamation *Kyrie eleison* (three times), *Christe eleison* (three times), *Kyrie* (three times), the following musical structure:

a—b—a (*Kyrie*) c—d—c (*Christe*) e—b₁—f (*Kyrie*).

The melismatic close that underlines the *eleison*, the motif *m* in the example, permeates the whole composition, except b₁ and f, the last links of the otherwise cyclic piece. The Vatican edition considers it as belonging to the Fourth Tone; yet there is no cogent reason for this arbitrary categorization. Allowing for a transposition a fifth lower, where the *finalis* would be E, the chant has still a range of a full seventh, and the hexachord G–E is, of course, not fully identical with E–C. Moreover, the melodic line has both subtonal and supratonal traits. None the less, in its present form the composition betrays a fine sense of balance and form; even the extension of the last *Kyrie* uses motifs that have appeared before. We must, therefore, consider this piece an artistic redaction of an originally much simpler chant. Such an archetype might be Example 106b or 106c.[27] These chants know of no formal structure, since they follow strictly the scriptural text and are regulated by the accents. Yet their mode resembles that of the *Kyrie*.

Another resemblance, much more striking than the last one, was noticed and emphasized by Idelsohn.[28] He juxtaposed a *Kyrie* from the Roman *Processionarium* with another scriptural cantillation, and behold! the two chants appear like a simple cup put alongside a goblet shaped by an artist.[29]

EXAMPLE 107

This *Kyrie* has an unusual structure. Actually, it is a trope of a *Kyrie*, and its first part, which we quote, shows the following scheme:

$$a—b—b—c—b—c—b_1$$

Its artistry is by no means as highly developed as that of the foregoing example. Its range is likewise limited to a sixth, which in itself is an indication of considerable age. Its Jewish counterpart is again a scriptural cantillation of the Babylonian Jews. Since this group was never in contact with the Roman Church, we must assume, in this case, a common older source, probably the cantillation or its secularized contrafacts in Palestine during the first two Christian centuries.

The *Kyrie* of Mass X (*Alme Pater*) shows the highest level of musical craftsmanship[30].

EXAMPLE 108

Its formal scheme is of extraordinary symmetry and beauty. Its well-balanced structure shows the following scheme:

Cauda

A—B—A | A₁—A₂—A₁ | C—A₂—C̄—C—A₂ |

$$A—B—A \mid A_1—A_2—A_1 \mid C—A_2—\overset{\frown}{C—C}—A_2 \mid$$

The ninth and last acclamation, traditionally the longest, includes in this case all motifs, except Β; this *cauda* summarizes, as it were, the entire chant. In addition to this fine symmetry, two closing melismata (m and n in the illustration) pervade the piece. If we consider them, we obtain the structure:

$$Am—Bm—Am \mid A_1n—A_2m—A_1n \mid Cn—A_2m—CCn—A_2m$$

Such an accomplishment is, of course, the result of an old and well-cultivated tradition, as well as of sophisticated artistic maturity. Indeed, this is a relatively recent *Kyrie* and stems from the twelfth or thirteenth century.

Example 108b, a chant of the Oriental Sephardic Jews, shows only the opening motif as similar to 108a, and the closing melisma m. The parallel is a vague one, to be sure, since all of these motifs are typical formulas of the First mode. On the other hand, the *Kyrie* contains also the characteristic clause o, which we found typical of both the tract tunes and the eulogies of the Haftara (see p. 519). Thus, Example 108a contains two characteristic Hebrew punctuating melismata. It may safely be assumed that the melody of the *Kyrie* was formed in conscious imitation of other Gregorian tunes of older strata. The resemblance to the Jewish tune is, therefore, only indirect and secondary.

CREDO

This ancient profession of Christian faith has only a few tunes, and they are, as Wagner remarked, 'hewn out of granite'. They avoid melismata and are, in general, strictly syllabic. In the tune of *Credo* III we find a simplified reflection of two much older tunes of the Church; the chants of *Sanctus* IX and XVII and *Agnus* XVII. We give below the four ecclesiastical melodies as Example 109a and the parallel Hebrew chants as Example 109b.

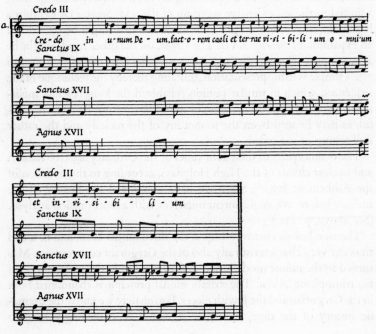

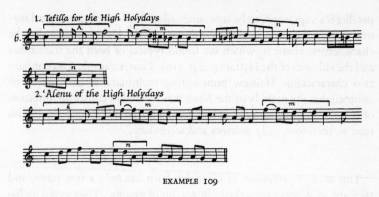

EXAMPLE 109

These four melodies spring apparently from one common source; in this writer's opinion, *Sanctus* XVII is the oldest of the four chants, since its *Benedictus* corresponds with an ancient Gradual formula, and since the third *Sanctus* proclamation is identical with the first one. Probably all three *Sanctus* exclamations were sung upon one and the same motif, according to ancient Jewish custom. *Agnus* XVII is clearly the same tune, adjusted to the less extensive wording of the text. *Sanctus* IX exhibits a highly developed, beautifully melismatic line that might be considered an expansion of *Sanctus* XVII. The *Credo*, on the other hand, might be an attempt to dissolve the impressive melodic lines of the two *Sanctus* into a simple syllabic presentation, imitating thereby the technique of the sequences, which in similar fashion syllabized the long Alleluia melismata. Yet the skill of the arranger of the *Credo* tune was far from masterful, as may be seen from the monotony of the melody and the rather dull setting of the words.

The counterparts to these four tunes of the Ordinary are two famous and nuclear chants of the High Holydays, according to the tradition of the Ashkenazic Jews.[31] Since we have mentioned the history of the melody before, we shall content ourselves with a short musical analysis. (See above, p. 541.)

The two Jewish chants rest upon the three motifs k, m, and n. k and m occur very characteristically also in the Gregorian counterparts. M is turned to the minor mode in the *Tefilla*, remains in the major mode in the triumphant *'Alenu*. The strictly modal principle is abandoned both in the Gregorian and the Jewish pieces. Fortunately we know the dramatic history of the tune, otherwise it would be exceedingly hard to determine on what side the chant originated. Since the pogrom in Blois, whence the tune came into the Church, took place during the First Crusade, we may consider this beautiful chant the Synagogue's last outright loan to the Church.

From then on, the Jews were more and more segregated from their neighbours, especially in Europe; and when the various pretexts for pogroms arose, such as the tales of 'Black Death', 'Poisoning of Wells', 'Ritual Murder' and similar convenient fables manufactured to arouse hatred, life for European Jewry became a veritable century-lasting, agonizing crucifixion. Small wonder that Jewry detested and hated everything connected with the Church, so that the *Book of the Pious*, during the fourteenth century, expressly forbade the teaching of Synagogue melodies to a Christian. Only during and after the Renaissance there prevailed especially in Italy a somewhat milder climate in the relations between Church and Synagogue: yet even this short glimpse of light vanished before the lasting darkness of the Ghetto. Let us here forget this period, shameful for Jew and Christian alike.

The complex and intricate interrelation of Church and Synagogue that symbolizes—unwittingly and unwillingly—the One World of Spirit, has in these pages been examined in detail. Lest we forget the greater lines of this historical development, we shall summarize our main conclusions and, in retrospect, view them with detached perspective.

NOTES CHAPTER VII

1. The schemes of the Arabic metres are quoted after Idelsohn, *Jewish Music*, pp. 114 ff. I was told, however, that these representations only approximate the actual system of Judaeo-Arabic prosody, which contains many shades and nuances.

2. *JM*, p. 121, No 4.

3. *JM*, p. 121, No 6.

4. IT, II, No 16.

5. The type AABA is often the basis of St Ambrose's hymns and of their melodies; we shall examine this hymn type later on. The very same structure is also evident in a number of Ephraem's *Madrashe*, and it is quite possible that at least the formal conception came from Syria.

6. *JM*, p. 117; IT, IV, No 56; Baer, *Baal Tefilla*, No 995; Friedmann, *Chasonus*, No 228.

7. IT, II, No 70; IT, II, No 68.

8. The monumental collection, *Analecta Hymnica*, ed. Dreves and Blume, contains by now more than 100 volumes. Everyone who seriously deals with problems of hymnody will have to resort to this work.

9. E. 9. in the Irish *Liber Hymnorum*, ed. J. H. Bernard (London, 1898), I, pp. 144 ff.

10. Cf. Philo, *De opificiis mundi*, I, 3; also *De Allegoriis Legum*, I, 2 *et passim;* and Midrash Genesis Rabba, VIII, 2 *et passim*.

11. The text of the hymn in F. J. Mone's still valuable *Lateinische Hymnen des Mittelalters*, I, pp. 1–3.

The comparison of the seven days with the aeons of the world occurs in Augustine, *Sermo 259 in Octava Paschae*. The idea of the *Ogdoad* as superior to the seventh day, as discussed in Part II, Chapter II, is expressed by Athanasius, commenting on the enigmatic heading of Ps. 6: *Al ha-sheminit*. This is an exact parallel with the Midrash, where the eighth mode is symbolic of the messianic and eternal aeon. (Athanasius, *In Ps. 6*; also *In Ps. 11*.) Also Hilary, *Praefatio in Psalmos*, c. 12–14. Jerome refers to the seven as to the Old Testament, to the eight as to the New Testament (*Advers. Lucif.* 22). A fine study on this topic is F. J. Doelger's, 'Die Acht-Zahl als christliches Symbol', in *Antike und Christentums*, IV, pp. 160–82.

12. The text in Mone's collection, p. 75, where also Greek parallels are given.

13. Text in Mone's collection, pp. 191 ff. The passages, 'Life of Justice', 'Tree of Life', etc., are scriptural.

14. Text in Mone, p. 88.

15. Text in Mone, pp. 304–5.

16. The text in *The Winchester Troper*, ed. W. H. Frere (London, 1894), p. 48. Similar Hebraisms in Mone, e.g. Notker's sequence: 'Alma chorus domini compangat nomina summi: Messias, Sother, Sabaoth, Adonai, Est, Emmanuhel, Unigenitus, Via, Vita, Manus, Homousios.'

One additional word about the frequent and puzzling Hebraisms in early Irish hymnody. They seem to have originated with Eastern, mainly Greek, monks and missionaries who visited Ireland between the sixth and tenth centuries. As is generally known, the continental monasteries of St Gallen and Reichenau were strongly influenced by Irish monks; the St Gallen monastery was for three or four centuries in constant and close connexion with Byzantium; is it too much to assume that its parental homes in Ireland learned their Greek and Hebrew words from the same source, namely from Greek monks? Cf. WGM, I, pp. 250–1 and 253–75; and *Analecta Hymnica*, LI, xiii ff. One of these Greek monks was the later Archbishop of Canterbury, whom Pope Vitalian sent to England and Ireland, Theodore from Tarsus in Cilicia. Cf. Duchesne, op. cit., pp. 99 ff. Also Riemann, *Handbuch der Musikgeschichte*, I, 2, p. 85, and Besseler, *Die Musik des Mittelalters und der Renaissance*, where he says (pp. 69–70): 'That the Irish clergy were familiar with the hymns of the Eastern Church, is demonstrated by their Latin hymns, whose stanzas, exactly like those of a Syriac *Sogitha* or of a Byzantine *Kontakion*, were connected with each other by alphabetic acrostics.' How deeply the Hebraic roots reach in some cases may be seen in the Irish-Latin preface to the *Gloria in Excelsis*. The pertinent passage reads: 'The angels sang the first verse of this hymn during the night of the nativity—they composed it at the Tower of Gabder [i.e. a mile east of Jerusalem], etc.' The 'Tower of Gabder' is actually the Tower of Eder, Gen. 35; 16 and Mic. 4:8. It is apparently through Jerome that this place was linked with the *Gloria in Excelsis*, since he referred to it first (*Epitaphium Paulae, Epist. 108 ad Eustochium*). See also the Irish *Liber Hymnorum*, II, p. 135. The problem is extensively discussed from the Jewish angle in Michael Sachs, *Beiträge zur Sprach-und Altertums-Forschung* (Berlin, 1852), I, p. 65; II, pp. 98 ff, where the midrashic sources are given; also W. F. Castle, *Syrian Pageant* (London, 1952), p. 90.

17. The text in Mone, p. 393. An exact parallel to this poetic abbreviation of fifteen psalms is in the Jewish Authorized P.B., pp. 28, 100. In those prayers a sort of paraphrase of the eighteen benedictions (*Tefilla*) takes place whereby each eulogy is reduced to one verse.

18. Hymns that were used as charms were especially popular in Irish Christianity. They found their most characteristic form in the so-called *Loricas* (breast-plate). A good introductory note on these hymns used as charms is given in Hastings, *Encyclop. of Religion and Ethics*, VII, 27 (Hymns, Irish-Christian).

19. For directing my attention to the fact that some of the earliest post-biblical poems are measured after the number of words that constitute a verse, I am indebted to Prof. G. Scholem of the Hebrew University in Jerusalem.

20. Our version of the *Te Deum* follows a MS. of the twelfth century; while the version accepted as authentic by the Vatican editions shows still more similarities to Jewish chants, it was our conviction that the older the source, the more genuine it is. Cf. WGM, III, p. 225.

21. *LU*, p. 55; IT, I, chapter 2.

22. The musical version of 'Gloria, laus et honor', after Riemann, op. cit., I, 2, p. 29, who offers it as the Solesmes version: of *Magen Aboth*, after Friedmann, *Chasonus*, No. 144.

23. *Analecta Hymnica*, L, pp. 160 ff.

24. P. Wagner sees an organic connexion between these 'late-comers' of the Roman liturgy; cf. WGM, I, pp. 60 ff; III, pp. 436 ff.

25. WGM, III, p. 513 and I, pp. 286 ff.

26. Cf. Gerbert, *De Cantu*, I, p. 341; also *Analecta Hymnica*, XLVII, p. 376; and *Graduale Sarisburiense*, Preface.

27. IT, II, p. 54; IT, II, p. 66.

28. IT, II, pp. 10 ff.

29. Ibid.; and IT, II, p. 33. Idelsohn quotes the *Kyrie* according to the edition of Frühwirth (Rome, 1894), p. 36. I doubt very much whether this edition is acceptable to modern Gregorian scholarship; unfortunately the edition quoted by Idelsohn was unavailable to me.

30. *LU*, p. 41; the Jewish example is from IT, IV.

31. Baer, op. cit., p. 275.

CHAPTER EIGHT

Results, Outlooks, Perspectives

A MIGHTY bridge of the spirit has spanned the vastness of the ocean and linked the Near East with the European continent since time immemorial. During the first millennium of Christianity an unending host of profound ideas has crossed it. Sciences, religious arts and all the elements of civilization went first to the West and have returned again.

LITURGY
Temple and Church

A direct Christian continuation of Temple worship was impossible. Considering the indifference of Primitive Christianity to rigidly organized worship, and its antagonistic feeling toward a 'professional' hierarchy, one may safely discount the notion of the Temple's survival in Christian liturgies. Only faint echoes of the Temple's tradition may be found in the ancient Armenian liturgy, particularly with regard to sacrificial institutions. On the other hand, the Jewish concept of prayer being a perfect substitution for sacrifices was accepted unanimously by all Churches. This principle was implemented immediately after the Fall of the Temple. The doxological prayers, so characteristic of the Temple, lost a good deal of their dominance in the succeeding Synagogue. Only superficial vestiges of these texts and their general form and atmosphere were retained in the Christian liturgy. In other words, an imaginary Temple was rebuilt in the minds of the Christian poets and theologians; a Temple that resounded with Doxologies, but this time the Doxologies had a rigid and inflexible Christian note of dogmatic character.

The Synagogue has preserved other traditions of the Temple than the Church, but they constitute neither the prominent nor the characteristic elements within the present liturgy.

The Common Ground

The most striking proof of the penetration of Jewish elements into Christian worship is given by the (translated) post-biblical Hebraisms that can be found abundantly in the liturgies of the *Constitutiones Apostolorum*, and in the ancient Armenian ritual. The bearers of these traditions were unquestionably Judaeo-Christians, or other heretical Jewish sects. Scriptural passages, simple eulogies, litanies, and other paraphrases of Scripture are also remnants of ancient Synagogue liturgies; but these elements underwent numerous and often radical transformations.

The lectionaries of both Synagogue and Church originated in the same formative period. Here, a peculiar relationship did exist, reflecting sometimes polemical, sometimes apologetic tendencies on both sides. The concept of the Jewish ecclesiastical year was, after various regional or sectarian transformations, borrowed by the Church and linked with its Christological system of pericopes. This continuation of the Jewish tradition with Christian adjustments created many and complex problems. Interestingly enough, the oldest, even pre-Jewish, element, the system of the Pentecontade, was maintained in all institutions, Jewish or Christian. It also exerted a fundamental influence upon the organization of liturgical chant.

Practices of prayer, such as fasts, vigils, processions, litanies, acclamations, etc., characteristic of the Synagogue, found their way into Christian worship, after due Christological re-interpretation. Some of them were altered so thoroughly that their function became the reverse of their Jewish prototypes, as for example the acclamation 'Hosanna'.

Notwithstanding such transformations, there are certain common traits permanently extant in Synagogue and Church, and they became lasting foundations of both liturgies. These are the static forces in the further development of the worship of both institutions.

Common Beginnings

Other concepts of Christian worship which had originated in the sphere of the Synagogue deviated radically from their Judaistic beginnings. These are the forms that constitute the distinguishing features of the individual Churches: the Roman *Proprium de Tempore*, the Byzantine *Kontakion* and *Kanon*, and the various Syrian hymn forms are such highly individualized and regionalized structures as characterize stylized folk-lore and high religious art. Just as the Hallelujah developed (whose concept is common, but whose performance is different in all liturgies), so these dynamic, ever expanding forms and expressions grew out of Jewish germinal cells.

The hymn and its various versions is the most interesting representative of this group. Non-scriptural in origin, it gradually absorbed post-biblical elements, many of which are midrashic in origin and character. The midrashic hymn type was once very popular in Byzantium, in old Ireland, and in the Jacobite Syrian liturgy. A classic example of the migration of such hymns is the pedigree of the sequence 'Dies Irae': its literary motifs occur in a hymn by the Byzantine Romanus (Romanus, a converted Syrian Jew, heard them as midrashic hymns in his youth). Up to this day, the synagogal liturgy contains the Hebrew counterpart of the Romanus hymn and of its Latin sequence.

It is necessary to appraise in this and analogous cases the specific regional, linguistic, and general ideological climate, in which such forms developed. Notwithstanding the basic doctrinal homogeneity of Christianity during its first six or seven centuries, the aesthetic and liturgical expressions of the doctrines varied extensively in individual liturgies. In these respects the ethnic divergencies apparently overshadowed the fundamental spiritual unity.

The Wider Horizon

So interwoven and in so many ways interrelated are the Jewish and Christian liturgies that the scholar must be on the lookout for wider implications. A case in point is the ancient Pentecontade. Its creative influence upon liturgy, calendar, and sacred music may be cited as an illustration of the numerous ancient patterns and archetypes that have moulded our liturgical ideas as well as their expressions. Actually an ancient Mesopotamian background is dimly visible in many of our liturgical forms. It will be the task of the student of comparative liturgy to trace back the constituent elements of Jewish and Christian worship to their common sources, be they Hittite, Egyptian, Babylonian, or even the remoter realms of the 'sea-faring tribes' of Asia Minor and old Sumeria. The discoveries of Ugarit should encourage such a research. Yet, it should not be forgotten that historic examination, such as the one suggested, calls for an investigation of forms rather than of abstract ideas. In short, it ought to be orientated more toward literature and art than toward comparative theology, notwithstanding the intimate and creative interdependence of these two fields of human aspiration. If it

were possible to trace these venerable creations as far as ancient India in
the East, and to Hellas and Etruria in the West (to name only the geographical limits), we might gain a view of the history of religion, liturgy
and their related arts that would by far exceed, in scope, space, and
time, all our previous, unfortunately sectarian, concepts.

MUSIC

Temple and Church

Apart from the Canticle, Response, and Refrain forms which Christian worship inherited from the Temple, most of Christian musical
substance, if at all Jewish in origin, came from the ancient Synagogue.
The fact that no notation (except the Greek) existed at the time of rising
Christianity is not of real relevance for our study. If we remember the
faithfulness with which some ancient melodies, common to Church
and Synagogue, were handed down from one generation to another
until their tentative notation, we must reach the conclusion that absence
of musical script cannot have been the decisive factor which would
account for the total loss of the Temple's exalted music. Yet the resentment of the Early Christians against hierarchy and ceremonial must
seriously be considered, and even more attention must be paid to the
reluctance of the Levites, a strictly professional guild, to divulge their
'trade secrets'. The talmudic literature is replete with passages indicating
their unwillingness to give away some of their esoteric expressions,
rituals, or texts, even to learned rabbis, simply because they did not by
birth belong to the priestly caste.

The Common Ground

As in the literary, so in the musical liturgy, the form conceptions of
dichotomous psalmody, of scriptural cantillation, and of extended
canticle chant, are basic and lasting elements of the Jewish heritage.
They remained a substratum common to all derivatives of Judaism and
Christianity. To the same stratum belongs the earliest and most primitive
concept of the eight modes, the *octoechos*. It originated in pre-
Christian (probably even in pre-Jewish) time in Mesopotamia, spread
throughout the entire Near East, and, after finding access to European
shores, came back to the Orient in a refined, hellenized transformation.
The *octoechos* displays its various types and variants chiefly in the closing

psalmodic formulas and melismata, which constitute an integral part of the common legacy. In comparison with these more general structures and musical archetypes, the identity of individual chants in Church and Synagogue, while frequently evident, is not of too great a relevance. Of greater interest and import, however, are entire form-types, as well as their constituent individual tunes, which are to be found in both liturgies. All forms of solo psalmody in Gregorian and Armenian chant belong to this archaic category, especially the Tract, whose melodic lines can be traced back to Jewish archetypes. The Gregorian Tract and its Armenian counterparts breathe the air of the early Judaeo-Christian Synagogue and must be fully understood in this perspective. The same observation holds true for some ornate versions of the Lamentations and cognate solo psalmodies.

Common Beginnings

The element that demonstrates best the divergent evolution of an originally common cell is the primitive notation of Judaism and Christianity. Many shades and nuances of human endeavour are represented here, from the forgotten accents of the Syrian Church to the modern *nota quadrata* of the Roman Church. The end results of the various evolutions of musical notation differ radically from each other. None the less, there existed originally a close kinship between all ecphonetic accents. The raw material of chanted texts was shaped and moulded in ways that best corresponded to the needs and standards of the respective languages or civilizations.

In a similar way there originated a multitude of melodic patterns to which the various notations were adjusted. These recurrent melismata, which, in the course of many centuries, formed entire melodic families, came originally from more or less common stock. Most of the ornate psalmody, rendered *choraliter*, falls into this category; e.g. the Antiphon, the Gradual, the older elements of the Roman *Proprium de Tempore* and the Byzantine *Tropologion*. Divergent and heterogeneous as these melody types may appear to us today, they were all born in the same cultural and spiritual climate, the Near East of the first three or four Christian centuries. The musical tradition of Judaism, on the other hand, was undoubtedly influenced by the melodies of its neighbours. Thus, a considerable part of Oriental Jewish chant owes its origin to the Jewish emulation of certain Christian creations. The synagogal hymn forms and their development up to the tenth century bear special witness to this 'give and take' relationship.

The pure melismatic forms, such as the *Jubili* of the Latin tradition, started, it is true, in the Jewish-Syrian sphere and have remained indigenous there; but their classic expansion and majestic development into the battle-songs of the Occidental *Ecclesia Militans* took place in Western Europe after the eighth century. Very few, if any, of the Western Alleluia chants can be traced back to synagogal or even Syro-Byzantine sources. Here again the West systematized and brought order to the endless, often improvised, flourishes, until these Oriental tunes became clearly organized structures that display a high degree of artistic taste.

The same organizing hand of the Occident is discernible in simpler chants of more archaic character, such as the *Te Deum*, the *Gloria*, and similar forms between psalmody and hymn. Since these pieces were not, as a rule, subject to improvisation, their final codification was less rigid and retained more of the ancient Hebraic *melos*. While fundamentally occidentalized, they have preserved the spirit of lofty monotony characteristic of the ancient Synagogue.

The Wider Horizon

Two main lines of approach will determine future research in the field of sacred music. They are antithetical, but must always complement each other in the interpretation of music and its development: the hermeneutic and the formalistic. How far back can either the magic-ritualistic or the expressive function of music be traced? How was a compromise then reached with the artistic ideas of form and style, which are discernible even in the early chants of Synagogue and Church? Undoubtedly improvisation with magic intent, the technique of primeval ritualistic music, is the older concept and practice. Where and when did the concept of forms, archetypes, and aesthetic values emerge and modify the older, more primitive performances? If it were possible to answer, however rudimentarily, these questions, we would gain much deeper insight into the history of religious music. For history of religious music must always be understood as a description of the unceasing conflict between the opposing forces of the magic-expressive trend on the one hand, and the artistic-rational on the the other.

Confluence and transformation! These words spell what we generally call the history of culture and ideas. Spontaneity and order, while fundamentally antagonistic, are the mutually indispensable forces that have imprinted their seal upon the entire relationship of Orient and Occident. These antithetical dynamics, so capable of synthesis on a higher level, are of signal importance in the realm of religious art. The spectrum of religious art has more than the customary seven colours. Its rainbow spans the whole earth. Its historical symbol throughout the ages is the Sacred Bridge.

Glossary

This list contains such basic terms as not extensively explained in the text.

(Arm. = Armenian; AS = Aramaic-Syriac;
G = Greek; H = Hebrew)

ABINU MALKENU (H, Our Father, our King), opening of various litanies and penitential prayers, some of which originated in pre-Christian times. Their present form is attributed to R. Akiba (d. 135).

'ABODA (H, service), originally the eulogy during the morning sacrifice in the Temple, also the usual name of the entire Temple service; in Rabbinic Judaism the nuclear part of the MUSSAPH service of the Day of Atonement, based upon sections of Mishna *Yoma* and Ecclus. 46 ff.

ADAR (H and AS), name of the twelfth month of the old agricultural, the sixth of the ritual calendar of Israel; it coincides approximately with March. In certain years a thirteenth month is intercalated, called *Veadar* or Second *Adar*.

'ALENU (H, It is our duty), one of the most celebrated prayers of Jewish worship, combining the elements of creed, adoration, and messianic faith. It was originally and regularly accompanied by prostration; today this ceremony is performed only during the A. of the High Holyday liturgy, while the prayer itself closes the daily worship. Its composition is attributed to Rab (third century), but the complete absence of any passage referring to the rebuilding of the Temple has led some scholars to assume its origin before the destruction of the Sanctuary (A.D. 70). During the Middle Ages the A., together with the *Sh'ma'*, became the prayer of the martyrs, due to its passionate monotheism and belief in Israel's sacred mission.

'AMIDA (H, stand, cf. G, STASIS), the eighteen, now nineteen eulogies that constitute the second most important prayer of daily worship. The first and last three eulogies remain unchanged throughout the year, whereas the central group varies on Sabbaths and Holydays. In its original version (cf. TEFILLA), it antedates Christianity.

'AMMEI-HA'ARETZ (H, people of that land), cf. Kings, 24:14; Ezra

9:1; derogatory term for that part of the Jewish population that was either disinterested in the study of the Law, or simply ignorant. The expression and the ideology that stand behind it played a decisive part in Primitive Christianity, since Jesus championed the cause of the A.H. The intellectual and pietistic snobbism as expressed in the (misunderstood) maxim 'No A.H. can be pious' has harmed Judaism in many respects.

ANAGNOSTES (G, reader, lector), in the Byzantine Church the appointed reader of Scripture. He belonged to the lower clergy and was ordained.

ANAPHORA (G, offering up, cf. H. KEROBA), the offering of the Eucharist. Properly the consecration and thanksgiving prayer accompanying the Eucharist, hence the central section of the Greek Mass ritual. In Churches with Semitic languages it is called *Kuddasha* (sanctification, cf. H. KADDISH, KEDUSHA).

'ATNAH (H, rest; AS, *etnachta*), the second strongest masoretic accent, comparable to semicolon or colon. In the Masoretic text of Scripture it marks regularly the end of each first half-verse.

BARKU (H, Praise ye), cf. Neh. 9:5, the call to worship in the daily liturgy. It must be responded by a short doxology. The B. is comparable to the Roman *Invitatorium*.

BARUKH SHEM K'VOD, etc. (H, Praised be His name, Whose glorious kingdom is forever and ever), usual doxology following the recitation of the *Sh'ma'*. While its text is non-scriptural, it served as the obligatory response to any *beraka* pronounced in the service of the Temple.

BA'UTHA (AS, petition, supplication), Syrian hymn type of petition or litany, usually in a metre of 7 or 12 syllables per line.

BEMA, BIMA (G, rostrum, speaker's tribune), is the elevated platform placed in the centre of many synagogues, from which Scripture is read, announcements are made, and certain prayers are chanted by the cantor. The term B. although used in the Septuagint Neh. 8:4, has been replaced in many Jewish places by the corrupted Arabic word *Almemor* (from *al-min-bar* 'the chair').

BERAKA (H, praise, genuflection, benediction; G, *eulogia*), formula of worship and devotion attributed to the sages in Ezra's time. The form of the B. has become the archetype of every blessing, public or private. The pious Jew was expected to recite 100 *berakot* every day.

'ENYANA (AS, argument, matter, response), a Syrian Jacobite song or hymn, usually a refrain-like insertion between verses of psalms or canticles.

GAON (H, 'the exalted one', excellency), official title of the head of either of the two Babylonian talmudic academies in Sura and Pumbeditha; occasionally substitute of the exilarch. (End of sixth to end of tenth century.)

GENIZA (H, hiding-place, treasure-chamber), is the name of a vault or a store room of medieval synagogues, where old and useless prayer books, ritualia, etc., were buried. (They were not allowed to be burned, as they contained the ineffable name of God.) Prof. Salomon Schechter discovered in 1896 the G. of Fostat near Cairo containing many thousands of Hebrew and Arabic manuscripts, most of which date from the eighth to the twelfth centuries and have shed entirely new light on Jewish liturgical poetry of the Middle Ages.

HABDALA (H, separation, distinction), the rabbinic law required that a formal separation be made between the Holy and the Profane, also between various grades of holiness, as, e.g. between Sabbath and work-day, or between Sabbath and feast-day. In particular, the H. stands for a special ceremony of great beauty and deep symbolism. It is regularly performed at the end of the Sabbath or of a holyday. Wine, spices, and the newly kindled light are blessed and the distinction between the Holy and the Profane is stressed.

HAFTARA (H and A, conclusion, dismissal), the prophetic lesson in the morning services of Sabbaths, feast-days, and fast days. Previous to the introduction of tye *Mussaph* section on Sabbath and Holyday the H. was the last item of the service, whence its name.

HALLEL (H, praise), the ancient rabbinical title given to Ps. 113–18, considered as one unit. The H. was and is one of the most characteristic rubrics of the festival liturgy. Cf. HULLALA.

HANUKKA (H, dedication), the feast of re-dedication of the Temple, also called feast of the Maccabees, beginning on 25 Kislev (approximately December) and lasting for eight days. Modern scholars have demonstrated the high age of this feast of lights in connexion with ancient solstice rites long before the time of the Maccabees.

HAZAN (H, overseer, official; G, *hazanites*), originally the overseer and caretaker of a synagogue; during the Gaonic age he assumed the functions of the reader from Scripture and of the precentor. The office of the H. increased in importance with the centuries. He had to be thoroughly familiar with the Hebrew language, with the laws of prayer, with the niceties of the ritual, had to possess a pleasant voice and the ability of rendering the service in an artistically satisfactory manner. Also, he had to be a man of great piety and humility, a rare combination indeed. The H. attained, for these reasons, and due to his place in public worship, an influence which often superseded even that of the rabbi. Hence the antagonism between rabbi and H., which lasted for many centuries. During the high Middle Ages the H. added to the liturgy often his own poems as well as his musical compositions.

HIRMOS, (G, train, tract), in Byzantine hymnody the model stanza whose metre and tune is followed throughout the entire hymn. Its function is completely identical with that of the Syrian riš-qolo.

HUDRA (AS, cycle, cf. H, MAHZOR), the complete Proper of the Nestorian Mass and Office for the ecclesiastical year; also the collection of hymns for the Proper.

HULLALA (AS, praise, cf. H, HALLEL), any of the twenty sections into which the Psalter is divided in many of the Eastern Churches. (See also KATHISMA, MARMITHA, MOTVA, and STASIS).

IMPROPERIA (Latin, reproaches), is the name of a set of texts which form a part of the Good Friday service in the Roman Church. The stanzas of the I. are interrupted by the *Trisagion*, chanted in Greek and Latin. The chief substance of the I. is a bitter and sorrowful remonstrance of Jesus with his people, whereby many anti-Jewish passages are put into his mouth.

JASHOU PSALMS (Arm., 'Psalms of dinner-time'), the psalms or psalm-verses chanted before the prophetic lesson in the Armenian Mass. Their chant belongs to the oldest strata of all Christian music.

KADDISH (AS, Holy), the great doxology of the Synagogue. The text is almost entirely Aramaic and composed of four paragraphs, linked by responses. The age of the K. reaches far back into pre-Christian times, as indicated by the similarity of its first three sentences with the so-called 'Lord's Prayer'.

KANON (G, rule), is the name of an archetype of Byzantine hymnody. It evolved out of a poetic elaboration of nine scriptural canticles or odes.

KATHISMA (G, session, seat), is one of the twenty divisions of the Psalter used in the Byzantine Church; it contains various psalms and inserted *Troparia*. The twenty *Kathismata* are divided, in turn, into sixty *staseis*, as sub-sections. This peculiar division is old and seems to derive from a sectarian Jewish practice. Cf. MARMITHA, MOTVA, STASIS.

KEDUSHA (H, sanctification), any extensive Thrice-Holy of syna-gogal liturgy, consisting of the third eulogy of the *'Amida*, with a minimum of three responses (Isa. 6:3; Ez. 3:12; Ps. 146:10), with various texts linking these responses. Of the various *Kedushot* one or two originated before the destruction of the Temple; some of them are replete with angelological references and seem to have originated in the circles of the Essenes or other mystical bodies.

KEROBA (H, approach, offering), Hebrew hymn form, usually a poetic insertion in the first three eulogies of the *'Amida*, and preceding the *Kedusha*.

KIDDUSH (H, hallowing), ceremony and prayer on the eve of Sabbath or Festivals, whereby two loaves of bread are blessed to-gether with a cup of wine. Originally this ancient ceremony was only performed at the home; as such it originated long before Christianity. Later on it became an integral part of the public worship. As to the *Kedusha* and to the *Kaddish*, mystical significance was attributed to the ceremonial act of the K., which in various ways passed into the ritual of Early Christianity.

KOHEN (H, priest), name and title of the Aaronides; this term has been frequently adjusted to the various languages of Jewish settle-ments: thus Kagan, Sacerdoti, and Katz are merely variants of the same hierarchical family name.

KONTAKION (G, liturgical scroll or rod of a scroll), an archetype of Byzantine hymnody, usually containing a series of equal stanzas preceded by a preamble. The strophes of the K. are chanted in the melody of its model-stanza, the *Hirmos*.

KUDDASHA (AS, hallowing), the Syrian, especially the Nestorian *Anaphora* of the Mass; also the Thrice-Holy.

LAHAN (H, and Arab. 'tune, modulation'), is the usual medieval designation of a model tune or contrafact melody by Jewish-Arabic music theorists. See also MAQAM and NE'IMA.

MA'AMADOT (H, bystanders, standing men) (1) The official laymen's representatives who were, during a year's course, delegated to watch the divine service in the Temple of Jerusalem. Each of the 24 districts of Palestine sent several M. for their turn of office to Jerusalem. There they were instructed by Levites. The delegating communities organized regular services during the term of their representatives. Thus all synagogues of the country had services in regular intervals. (2) Fast-day prayers of poetic nature, which were recited while standing; in some of them older *Selihot* were inserted.

MA'ARIV (H, evening), is the daily evening prayer; it was a voluntary service until the high Middle Ages, yet none the less generally considered a binding obligation.

MADRASHA (AS, homily, study), a special type of Syrian hymnody. In general, a M. is a homiletical or didactic, occasionally polemical poem of theological character, usually provided with a responsorial refrain. See 'UNITHA.

MAHZOR (H, cycle; cf. HUDRA), the corpus of festive prayers of Judaism, divided into the various festive seasons, and containing, besides all regular prayers, many poems and hymns. Due to the differing regional rites of Jewry, there are about ten types of M. extant, some of which are obsolete today. The most important M. represent the Ashkenazic, Sephardic, Levantine, and Yemenite ritual, respectively.

MAQAM (Arab, musician's rostrum), the classic Arabic designation of mode as a conglomeration of recurrent melodic patterns. The M. is not understood to be a scale; rather it is to be considered a system of more or less fixed phrases each of which represent an ethos of its own. The Egyptian equivalent of the M. is the *Naghma*, the Indian is called *raga*. See also LAHAN.

MARMITHA (AS, rising), the subdivision of the Nestorian *Hullala*, each of which contains two or three *Marmyāthe*; it is that part of the Hullala which is chanted in standing position, in contradistinction to the *Motva*.

MEMRA (AS, saying, sermon), a Syrian hymn type of homiletical nature, usually evolved out of the text of a sermon. In fact, a versified sermon.

MIDRASH (H, exegesis, scriptural exposition), the corpus of rabbinic exegeses of Scripture with moralizing, speculative, homiletical, and legendary tendency. The term M. stands for the whole treasury of many volumes of such biblical exegesis as well as for any individual part. It originated centuries before Christianity and has in the course of many centuries exerted powerful influence upon the theological and literary output of Judaism. Many *piyyutim* are based upon midrashic motifs, and such motifs have often crossed the theological barriers erected by both rabbis and Church fathers.

MINCHA (H, offering, gift), properly the late afternoon sacrifice of the Temple. Then the afternoon service of the Synagogue, already referred to as one of the three daily services in Dan. 6:10. Usually it precedes immediately the regular (*Ma'ariv*) evening service.

MISSINAI-TUNES (H, 'tunes from Mt. Sinai'), a corpus of festive tunes of the Ashkenazic rite, which originated in the Rhineland during the eleventh to fifteenth centuries. Of great melodic beauty, the M.T. are linked to one another by a set of wandering motifs, with associative functions, which, in consequence, approximate the conception of the *Leitmotiv*.

MOTVA (AS, session, seat), any of the twenty divisions of the Psalter used in the Nestorian Church, comparable to the Byzantine *Kathisma*.

MUSSAPH (H, addition), originally the additional sacrifice for Sabbath and Festivals in the Temple. In the Synagogue that part of the morning service which is added on Sabbath or holyday. It follows immediately upon the reading of Scripture and was firmly established only at the end of the talmudic period.

NE'IMA (H, sweetness, melody), the usual term of Hebrew authors for an individual or contrafact melody. See LAHAN.

N'GINA (H, melody), in particular the melodic line of scriptural cantillation according to the proper rendering of the masoretic accents. See TROP.

NIGGUN (H, tune, melody-type) (1) Designation of a melodic contrafact (see also LAHAN); (2) the 'wordless hymn' of the medieval mystics and of the Hasidim.

NISHMAT (H, soul, breath), the opening word of a celebrated prayer in the morning service of Sabbath and festival. ('The breath of every living being shall bless Thy name.') It ends with a glorification of God in musical terms and is therefore called 'Praise of Song'.

OCTOECHOS (G, eight tones; cf. Arab. *ikkhadia*) (1) A collection of hymn poems by Severus of Antioch, Jacob of Edessa, and John of

Damascus, destined for the eight Sundays of the pentecontade after Pentecost, ordered according to the eight modes of music; (2) the systems of eight modes of music, as envisaged by the medieval theorists; they differ considerably from one ecclesiastical tradition to another.

'OMER (H, sheaf; cf. Lev. 23:10–11), in the Synagogue the substitute for the actual waving of sheaves of grain, once practised in the Temple as a memento of the Manna; hence a liturgical formula pronounced during the pentecontade between Passover and *Shabuot* (Pentecost), during which every day of the seven weeks of O.-waving is ritually counted.

PAYTAN (H, poet from G *poietes*), the author of a *piyyut*.

PIYYUT (H, from G *poietes*), is the generic Hebrew term for any metrical, or rhymed liturgical hymn composition. As the Byzantine and other Eastern Churches know various archetypes of hymnody, so does the Synagogue. The term P. is the most general designation.

PI'UR (H, ornament), the poetic elongation of a word in a caesura or at the end of a verse (Pausa). The practice of elongation, often coupled with change of the normal word-accent, is the grammatical root of punctuating melismata in the Semitic languages. See also TAFCHIM.

PIZMON (H from G, *proasma* or *prosomoion*), a Hebrew refrain hymn, usually the main metrical poem inserted in a group of *Selihot*.

P'SUQE DE ZIMRA (H, verses of song), a group of psalms which constitute an integral part of the daily morning service; the P. D-Z. are the Jewish counterpart of the regular Lauds of the Church.

PURIM (H, lots), the feast of deliverance of the Persian Jews, as described in the Book of Esther.

QALA (AS, tone, melody), a short stanza of liturgical poetry in the Jacobite and Maronite Churches of Syria, usually inserted between psalm verses. The Q. have no model-stanza (*riš-qolo*) and most of them are chanted in tunes of their own, which are frequently improvised *ad hoc*.

QINA (H, dirge, lament), originally a lament for the dead; in the liturgy of the Synagogue a poem of mourning over the destruction of the Temple on the 9th of Ab. The 'Lamentations of Jeremiah' are also considered *Qinot*.

RIŠ-QOLO (AS, model-tune), a stock or model melody which serves many poems of similar metre; a contrafact. See LAHAN.

ROSH HASHANA (H, head of the year), the Jewish feast of New Year on the first of Tishri. In its ritual the shofar is sounded.

R'SHUT (H, permission), is the term for the preamble of an extensive *Piyyut*, usually a *Keroba*. It is the synagogal counterpart of the Byzantine *prosomoion* or *kukulion*. The R. is the precentor's prayer for God's gracious acceptance of his worship as the congregation's spokesman. As such it is comparable to the priestly prayers of preparation before the Mass in the Roman and Byzantine liturgies.

SEDER (H, order), the ritual Passover meal on the eve of the feast. It consists of eulogies over four cups of wine, bitter herbs, unleavened bread, over the meal proper, and is accompanied by midrashic texts, the *Hallel*, popular songs, and the saying of grace.

SELIHA (H, forgiveness), is the general term of penitential prayers and litanies, some of which antedate Christianity. Most S. use as refrain Exod. 34:6, 7. According to the Talmud (Tract. Rosh hashana 17 b) this refrain will attain God's mercy.

SHAHARIT (H, morningtide), the daily morning service, which may be public or private. To the faithful Jew it is the most important daily service which he is obliged to render. The mystics saw in its four parts a whole, composed according to the principle *a minori ad maius*: the first part corresponds to the earthly, sublunar world, the second to the world of the spheres, the third to that of the angels, and the fourth to the realm of God.

SHARAKAN (Arm., songster, cf. H *shir*), is the name of the old Armenian hymnal which contains all the songs and texts of Mass and Office.

SHIBA'TA (AS, seven, sevenfold), a Hebrew or Aramaic hymn consisting of seven parts or stanzas, inserted between eulogies of the 'Amida. The S. resembles, both in spirit and form, the Byzantine *Kanon*, which uses eight or nine scriptural canticles as framework.

SH'MA' (H, hear!), the nucleus and kernel of all Jewish liturgies, called the 'watchword of Israel', consisting of Deut. 6:4-9; (the *Sh'ma'* proper); Deut. 11:13-21; Num. 15:37-41.

SHURAYA (AS, beginning), in the Nestorian Church the antiphon preceding the Apostolic lesson.

SIFRA (AS, book), legalistic Midrash to Leviticus.

SIFRE (H, writings), Midrash to Numbers and Deuteronomy.

SILLUQ (H and AS, cessation), the Masoretic accent marking the end of a verse; as pure punctuation it is also called *Sof pasuq*.

SOGITHA (AS, subject, argument), the Syrian archetype of a hymn with responsorial and often dialogue-character, the forerunner and cell of the Byzantine *Kontakion*.

STASIS (G, stand), part of the Byzantine system of *Kathismata*; every *Kathisma* contains two or three *staseis*. See also MARMITHA, MOTVA.

TA'AM, pl. TA'AMIM (H, sense, taste, meaning, category), here usually employed in the sense of *ta'ame ha-miqra,'* the Masoretic accents of the biblical text. The primary function of the T. is the proper punctuation and accentuation of Scripture; the older tradition of scriptural cantillation was later connected with, and adjusted to, the T. Thus, the T. have come to be considered the ecphonetic notation of the Bible.

TAFCHIM (Arab, elongation, adornment), the Arab equivalent of the Hebrew PI'UR: the poetic elongation of a word in the pausal place of a sentence.

TAHANUN (H, supplication), is the name of that part of the Hebrew Prayer book which contains most of the supplicatory prayers for grace. According to rabbinic law, any T. prayer must be preceded by a prayer of praise or thanksgiving.

TAL (H, dew) the solemn, hymnic prayer for dew pronounced at the Passover service, when summer begins in the Holy Land. Its counterpart in the fall is the prayer for rain (*Geshem*), when the rain-period commences.

TANNA, pl. TANNAIM (A, teacher) a sage or doctor of Mishnaic literature of the time between Hillel and Judah Hanassi, roughly 75 B.C. to A.D. 200; the founding fathers of rabbinic theology.

TARGUM (AS, translation, interpretation), in particular the Aramaic translations and paraphrases of Scripture which were most popular among the Jews during the earlier Middle Ages. Some Church Fathers also were familiar with the *Targumim*.

TEFILLA (H, from *hithpallel* 'invoking God as judge'), now the common designation of the '*Amida* prayer and its insertions. Pl. *Tefillot*, the corpus of all Hebrew prayers.

TETRAGRAMMATON The customary term for the four Hebrew

letters which constitute the name of God; in older translations it is erroneously rendered as Jehovah.

TRISAGION A formula of exaltation of God in the Byzantine liturgy and its derivatives: it emphasizes the strength, the immortality, and the holy mercy of the Lord. The term *Trisagion* is often confused with the *Ter-Sanctus* (Thrice-Holy).

TROP (from G, *tropos*—turn, manner, mode) the popular Jewish term for the musical style and aspect of scriptural cantillation. The T. antedates the Masoretic accents of cantillation (the *ta'amin*) by many centuries.

TROPARION (G, derivative of *tropos*), the general name of short hymns or verses which form an integral part of the Byzantine Office; a T. is being inserted periodically after a number of psalm-verses. A group of *Troparia*, together with their psalm-verses constitute a *Kathisma*.

TROPOS SPONDEIAKOS (G, the Spondaic mode), a metrically distinct, scale-like mode of the Hellenistic centres in Egypt and the Near East. Whether the T.S. was ever indigenous in classic Greek music remains problematical, in spite of Plutarch's claim. The T.S. shows distinct resemblance to ancient Jewish and Christian Psalm Tones; this similarity was attested to already in the second century.

UNETHANE TOQEF (H, we will emphasize), beginning of a celebrated *piyyut* in the New Year's service; its eschatological vision of the Day of Judgement forms the basis of a Byzantine *Kontakion* and of the famous Latin sequence 'Dies irae, dies illa'.

'UNITHA (AS, response), the choral refrain of a hymn usually chanted by a soloist. The *madrashe* always make use of the U. for their refrain.

YOTZER (H, he who creates, creator), the cue word of a prayer in the daily and festive morning service. Its mystical and angelological elements were echoed in some prayers of the Early Church.

ZOHAR (H, splendour), title of a famous cabbalistic *midrash* of the Pentateuch. Some of its traits indicate very ancient tradition.

ZUMARA (AS, song), is the name of liturgical chant in the Nestorian worship; in particular the Alleluia before the lesson of the Gospel.

List of Scriptural References

592

LIST OF SCRIPTURAL REFERENCES

Luke (contd.)—

1:68–79	140
2:14	275
2:29	530
2:29 f	140
2:46	22, 307 n. 37
4:6	140
4:16	9, 53, 188
4:16–20	533
4:17	56
6:5	285
7:32	255 n. 9
24:51	229

John

3:8	93
14:23–31	92
2	10
2:1–11	92
2:15	4
3:1	4
3:11	22, 307 n. 37
5:12	22, 307 n. 37

Acts

6:9	45 n. 35
9:29	45 n. 35
10:3	4
10:34	92
10:42–48	92
10:46	168
11:19–27	203 n. 35
13:1–14	203 n. 35
13:15	9
16:25	319
19:6	168
21:40	45 n. 36
22:2	45 n. 36

Romans

1:25	271 n. 12
9:5	265
10:9–11	368 n. 27
11:1–2	323
11:36	271 n. 12; 299

I. Corinthians

5:19	165 n. 104
12:30	168

I. Corinthians (contd.)—

14:5	168
14:6	265
14:14–19	368 n. 27
14:15	306 n. 26
14:16	29, 45 n. 36
14:34	323, 345

II. Corinthians

11:31	299

Ephesians

1:21	307 n. 36
5:19	271 n. 12

Philippians

2:25	1
4:4	14 n. 14
4:6	310 n. 92
4:20	299

Colossians

3:16	165 n. 104; 255 n. 4
4:2	14 n. 14

I. Thessalonians

5:16	14 n. 14
5:17 f	310 n. 92

I. Timothy

1:17	299
2:1	310 n. 92
6:16	274

James

2:2	20

Jude

25:?	306 n. 23

Revelation

1:3	96 n. 25
1:4–6	266
1:6	265, 271 n. 12
3:14	266
5:5	558
5:8–13	318
5:8	369
5:14	271 n. 12; 265
7:10	271 n. 24
7:12	265, 271 n. 12
14:3	318
19:1–8	302, 303
19:4	265, 271 n. 12

General Index

(Names are printed in roman, foreign words, and incipits of chants in italics.
R. after a proper name indicates the title of Rabbi.)